YALE LANGUAGE SERIES

THE DAWN OF SLAVIC

An Introduction to Slavic Philology

Alexander M. Schenker

Yale University Press New Haven and London

Designed by James J. Johnson and set in Times Roman type by The Composing Room of Michigan, Grand Rapids, Michigan. Printed in the United States of America

Library of Congress Cataloging-in-Publication Data

Schenker, Alexander M.
The dawn of Slavic : an introduction to Slavic philology / Alexander M. Schenker.
p. cm. — (Yale language series)
Includes bibliographical references and index.
ISBN: 978-0-300-21240-2

1. Slavic philology—History.
2. Slavs—History. I. Title.
II. Series.
PG25.S34 1996
491.8'09—dc20 95-17853

A catalogue record for this book is available from the British Library.

The paper in this book meets the guidelines for permanence and durability of the Committee on Production Guidelines for Book Longevity of the Council on Library Resources.

to Krystyna

CONTENTS

MAPS

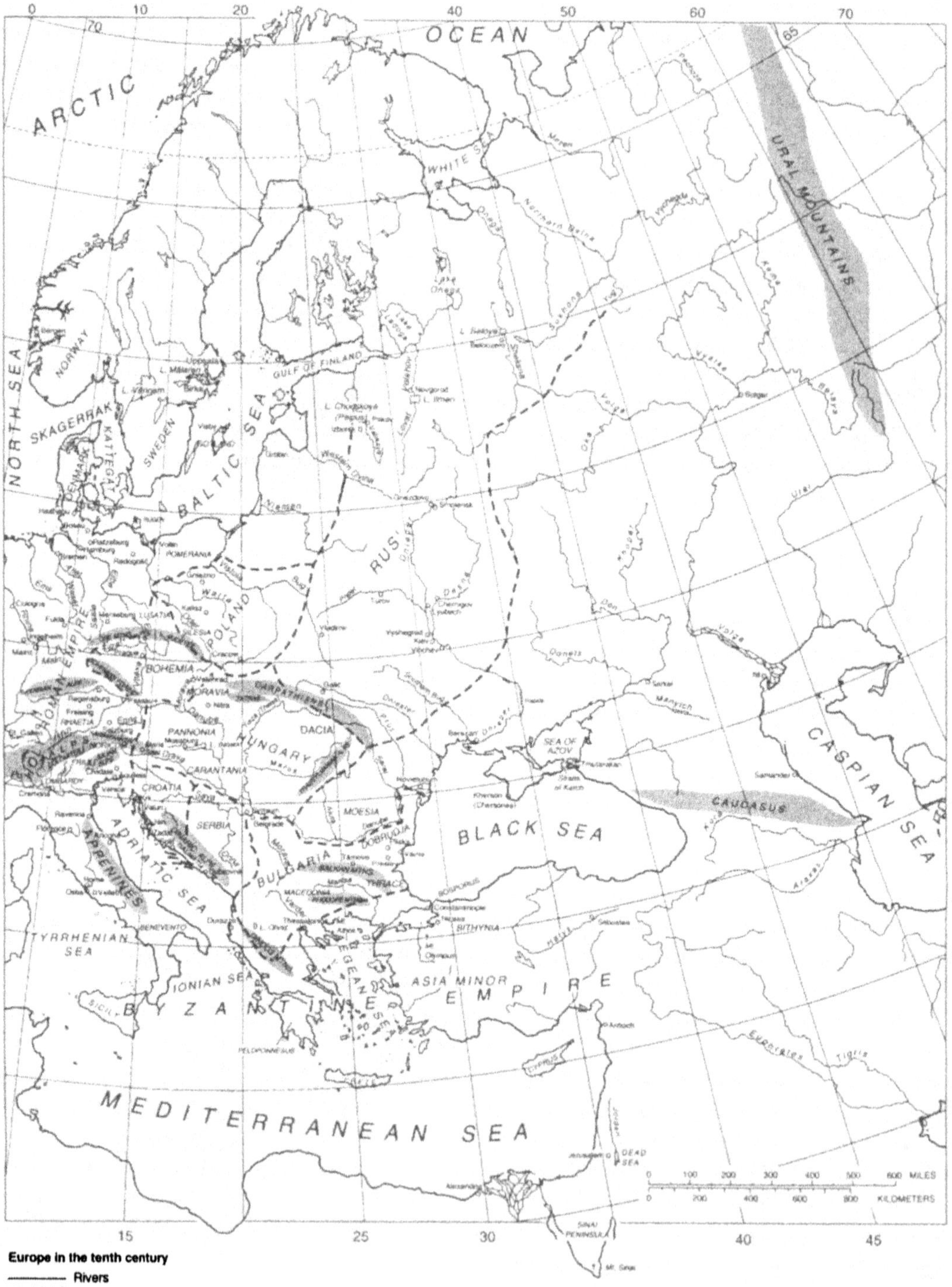

Europe in the tenth century

- Rivers
- Mountain ranges
- Approximate boundaries of Slavic states in the tenth century
- † Byzantine monasteries

PREFACE

Philology as a name of a discipline has gone out of fashion. Its two principal components, studies of language and texts, have become fully emancipated and have gone their independent ways as elements of linguistics and literary studies. There are good reasons for this separation. Traditional philology, whose sole concern was with the classical world, could not encompass the newly sanctioned fields of scholarly inquiry, the living languages, the modern literatures and folklore, which were brought out from obscurity by the Enlightenment. Yet, with an appropriately altered definition, philology remains a convenient cover term for the study of the earliest linguistic manifestations of any national culture. This is how it has been used with reference to Slavic antiquities, and this is how it will be used in the present book.

Slavic philology has generated an immense body of scholarly literature, most of it written in languages other than English and much of it couched in arcane, specialized terminology. My aim here is to mediate between that literature and the beginning student of the earliest period of Slavic culture. If my hopes for the book are fulfilled, it will serve not only as an introduction to a discipline notoriously wanting in handbooks, but also as a guide to further reading, an invitation to a deeper and broader study of subjects barely touched upon here.

To present such a broad discipline in one volume is an ambitious, even foolhardy, undertaking. Any attempt to distill so vast a corpus of knowledge confronts the author with a myriad of selection quandaries, a constant obligation to choose between the compass of the book and its size. Realizing that many of my choices may appear arbitrary, I hope nonetheless that among the book's faults the sins of omission are graver than the sins of commission. Some of the latter may be attributable to the introductory nature of the book, which mandates a preference for conservative solutions, for keeping close to the mainstream of the discipline, and for shunning the cross-currents of scholarly controversy.

My awareness of these difficulties may have delayed, but has not diminished, my resolve to place before the student an overview of a subject which for years has been the stuff of my research and teaching. It is, in fact, my classroom experience which has convinced me that the potential rewards of writing a book of this kind outweigh the inevitable risks entailed by such a project. High on the list of such perils are false expectations of readers, and it may therefore be appropriate to say a few words about what this book does and what it does not purport to be.

Chapter 1 is a historical sketch of Slavic settlement in Europe and the integration of the Slavs into medieval European cultural commonwealth. It is not meant, however, to be a history of early Slavdom. Its emphases are not on an orderly, narrative account but rather on the presentation of samples of primary sources in order to show the student where the historian of the early Slavs gets the pieces of the puzzle which he then tries to fit into a larger picture. To view the full canvas of early Slavic history the student will have to consult such works as Cross 1948, Dvornik 1956 or Obolensky 1971.

Chapter 2 is an account of the development of Slavic from its Indo-European beginnings to the breakup of Slavic linguistic unity. It does not, however, pretend to be a full-scale historical grammar. Nonetheless, the essential facts of Slavic linguistic history are presented and an emphasis is placed on the interdependence of the processes of linguistic change. To deepen their understanding of the problems of Proto-Slavic, students must turn to such fundamental works as Meillet 1934, Vaillant 1950–1977, or Shevelov 1965.

Chapter 3 contains an outline of the beginnings of Slavic writing. It includes sections on Slavic paleography and on the formation of (Old) Church Slavonic and its role as the first Slavic literary language and the only Slavic supranational medium. The chapter ends with a classification of the oldest Slavic texts. The chief concerns of that section, however, are philological rather than literary. The texts are there for their value as monuments of early Slavic writing and not for their aesthetic qualities. For the latter, the student is advised to turn to the works concerned with national literary histories.

It is my pleasant duty to acknowledge here the help and encouragement I received in the course of my work from friends, colleagues, and students. My greatest debt of gratitude goes to Michael S. Flier of Harvard University, who read the typescript of a draft of the book for Yale University Press and sent in detailed corrections and suggestions. He also prodded me to take up several matters which were not included in my original draft and have now found their way into the appendices.

The chapter on language incorporates many of the formulations used in my article titled "Proto-Slavonic," which appeared in 1993 in *The Slavonic Languages* (London: Routledge). To Bernard Comrie of the University of Southern California and Greville G. Corbett of the University of Surrey, the editors of the volume, goes my deep gratitude for the skill and care with which they oversaw the publication of my text. This is particularly so in the case of Professor Comrie, who offered detailed comments on the phonological part of my contribution. "Proto-Slavonic" benefited also from the attentive reading of Jay Jasanoff of Cornell University, who drew on his mastery of Indo-European to keep me from stumbling clumsily through that domain. Equally precious to me were the comments of Kazimierz Polański of the Jagiellonian University, who commented on the drafts of "Proto-Slavonic" and the language chapter with his characteristic erudition, reliability, generosity, and common sense. Borjana Velčeva of the University of Sofia discussed with me some of my linguistic formulations.

Several distinguished medievalists were good enough to offer me the benefit of their criticisms on the chapter on early writing. I am especially grateful to Riccardo Picchio, currently of the University of Naples, for reading the first draft of the chapter and for his valuable comments and suggestions for improvement. Aleksander Naumow of the Jagiellonian University shared with me his profound knowledge of Slavic medieval texts and Orthodox theology, offering critique and advice. Aksinia Džurova of the University of Sofia was a gracious host during my 1991 visit to the Ivan Dujčev Research Centre for Slavo-Byzantine Studies in Sofia, allowing me the free run of its rich library holdings and opportunities for direct contact with Bulgarian medievalists. Of these, the most helpful for me was the meeting with Stefan Kožuxarov of the Bulgarian Academy of Sciences, who read and commented upon the section dealing with the classification of early Slavic texts. I am also much obliged to Predrag Matejic for his interest in my undertaking and for putting at my disposal the holdings of the Hilandar Research Library of Ohio State University, which he directs with great skill and devotion.

My readiness to accept the challenge of writing a book of this nature is due in large measure to the stimulating philological and linguistic environment created by my departmental colleagues at Yale, first and foremost Riccardo Picchio and Edward Stankiewicz. The three of us collaborated on the Yale University Project on the Formation of Slavic National Languages and in many formal and informal settings talked over the very topics with which this book is concerned. Of my other colleagues at Yale whose generosity I should like to acknowledge, Robert G. Babcock of the Beinecke Library clarified for me the architectonics of the medieval codex and facilitated the photographing of the Beinecke Glagolitic Fragment, Victor Bers guided me through the intricacies of John Chrysostom's Greek syntax, Harvey Goldblatt helped me formulate some of the notions of textual criticism, and Peter Patrikis of the Consortium for Language Teaching and Learning provided me with an outsider's view as he commented on the clarity of the earliest draft of my project. I appreciate also Konstantin D. Hramov's readiness to offer me the benefit of his vast experience in matters pertaining to the Russian Orthodox church. Elizabeth Papazian amplified and corrected the bibliography, Nike Agman made apt editorial suggestions for the historical and phonological parts of the book, and Christopher Lemelin compiled the index. It was my good fortune that Richard Miller, the editor of my manuscript, is a Slavist at heart and by training. His knowledge of matters taken up in this book made the care and skill he lavished upon it all the more valuable and effective.

I thank Aksinia Džurova and Predrag Matejic for the transparencies they sent me, some of which are reproduced here by gracious permission of several research institutions: in Croatia the Academy of Arts and Sciences in Zagreb (*Baška stone, Hum graffito*); in Germany the Bavarian State Library in Munich (*Freising Fragments*); in Russia the Institute of the Russian Language of the Academy of Sciences in Moscow (*Birchbark gramota #109*), the Central State Archive of Ancient Documents in Moscow (*Sava's Book*), the National Library in St. Petersburg (*Codex Zographensis, Codex Suprasliensis, Ostromir's evangeliary*); in Ukraine the Research Library of the Academy of Sciences in Kiev (*Kiev missal*); in the United States the Beinecke Library at Yale University in New Haven (*Beinecke Glagolitic Fragment*); in the Vatican the Apostolic Library (*Codex Assemanianus*). The many fading reproductions of texts found in older publications received a new lease on life under the skillful hands of Sean Kernan of Stony Creek, Conn.

The research for the book was facilitated by an IREX travel grant to Bulgaria and a U.S. Department of Education Title VI travel grant to Poland as well as by research assistance from the A. Whitney Griswold Faculty Research Fund at Yale.

The book is dedicated to my wife as an infinitesimally small token of gratitude for her wisdom, forbearance, good cheer, and inner strength which helped me persevere in this undertaking.

The accomplishments of the many generations of scholars on whose labor and learning

I have leaned so heavily call to mind the parable with which John the Exarch acknowledged the literary debts of his *Hexaemeron*:

> If someone . . . wished to build an edifice . . . but lacked the means to do so, he would go to rich men and ask them for [help], one man for marble, another for bricks. And he would raise the walls and cover the floor with the marble that the rich men gave him. But if he wished to make the roof and had no roofing worthy of the walls and of the marble floor, he would plait twigs and put straw on top of them, and he would cross branches and thus make the door.

It is my hope that the twigs and branches which I have added to the marble and bricks brought in by those who were there before me will make the edifice of Slavic philology more accessible and more hospitable for those who wish to enter.

NOTE ON TRANSLITERATION AND ABBREVIATIONS

The transliteration is that used in the *Slavic and East European Journal*, except that (a) in the section providing samples of early Slavic writing (**4.4**) Glagolitic ⰟⰊ / ⰟⰉ / ⰠⰊ and Cyrillic ъı/ъі/ьı are transliterated (or retained) as digraphs (**3.4.d**) and the Cyrillic digraph оү is transliterated as *ou*; elsewhere these spellings are rendered as *y* and *u* respectively; (b) Slavic names are cited in their modern spelling, reflecting regional differences; e.g. Proto-Slavic *svęto-* appears in East Slavic names as *Svjato-* but in Moravian names as *Svato-*; (c) names of well-known persons are occasionally cited in their traditional spelling, e.g. *Svyatoslav* for *Svjatoslav.*

Greek names and specialized terms are given in their Latin form, e.g. *Methodius* for *Methodios, euchologium* for *euchologion.*

The alphabetical order of letters which do not occur in English is as follows (plus sign means 'followed by'): *c* + *č*; *d* + *d'* + *ʒ* + *ǯ*; *e* + *ę* + *ě*; *i* + *ь*; *l* + *l'* + *l̥* + *l̥'*; *n* + *n'*; *o* + *ǫ*; *r* + *r'* + *r̥* + *r̥'*; *s* + *s'* + *š*; *t* + *t'*; *u* + *ъ*; *z* + *ž*.

Abbreviations include (a) *names of languages*: Ba. = Bavarian, Bg. = Bulgarian, Br. = Belarussian, BSl. = Balto-Slavic, ChSl. = Church Slavonic, Cr. = Croatian, Cz. = Czech, Eng. = English, EPSl. = Early Proto-Slavic, ESl. = East Slavic, Goth. = Gothic, Gk. = Greek, It. = Italian, LPSl. = Late Proto-Slavic, Lat. = Latin, Lith. = Lithuanian, LSo. = Lower Sorbian, M = middle, Mac. = Macedonian, Mod. = modern, N = Norse, O = old, OCS = Old Church Slav(on)ic, OHG = Old High German, P = Proto- (as in PGmc. = Proto-Germanic, PIE = Proto-Indo-European, PSl. = Proto-Slavic), Plb. = Polabian, Po. = Polish, Ru. = Russian, S = Serbian, Skt. = Sanskrit, Slk. = Slovak, Sln. = Slovenian, Ukr. = Ukrainian, USo. = Upper Sorbian; (b) *phonetic terms*: B = back, C = consonant, F = front, N = nasal, R = liquid, V = vowel, # = word-initial; (c) *grammatical terms*: Acc. = accusative, Dat. = dative, Du. = dual, F = feminine, Gen. = genitive, Impv. = imperative, Instr. = instrumental, Loc. = locative, M = masculine, N = neuter, Nom. = nominative, Pl. = plural, Pple. = participle, Pr. = present, Rslt. = resultative, Sg. = singular, Voc. = vocative; (d) *names of alphabets*: Cyr. = Cyrillic, Glag. = Glagolitic; (e) *names of Old Church Slavonic monuments* as specified in **3.27.**

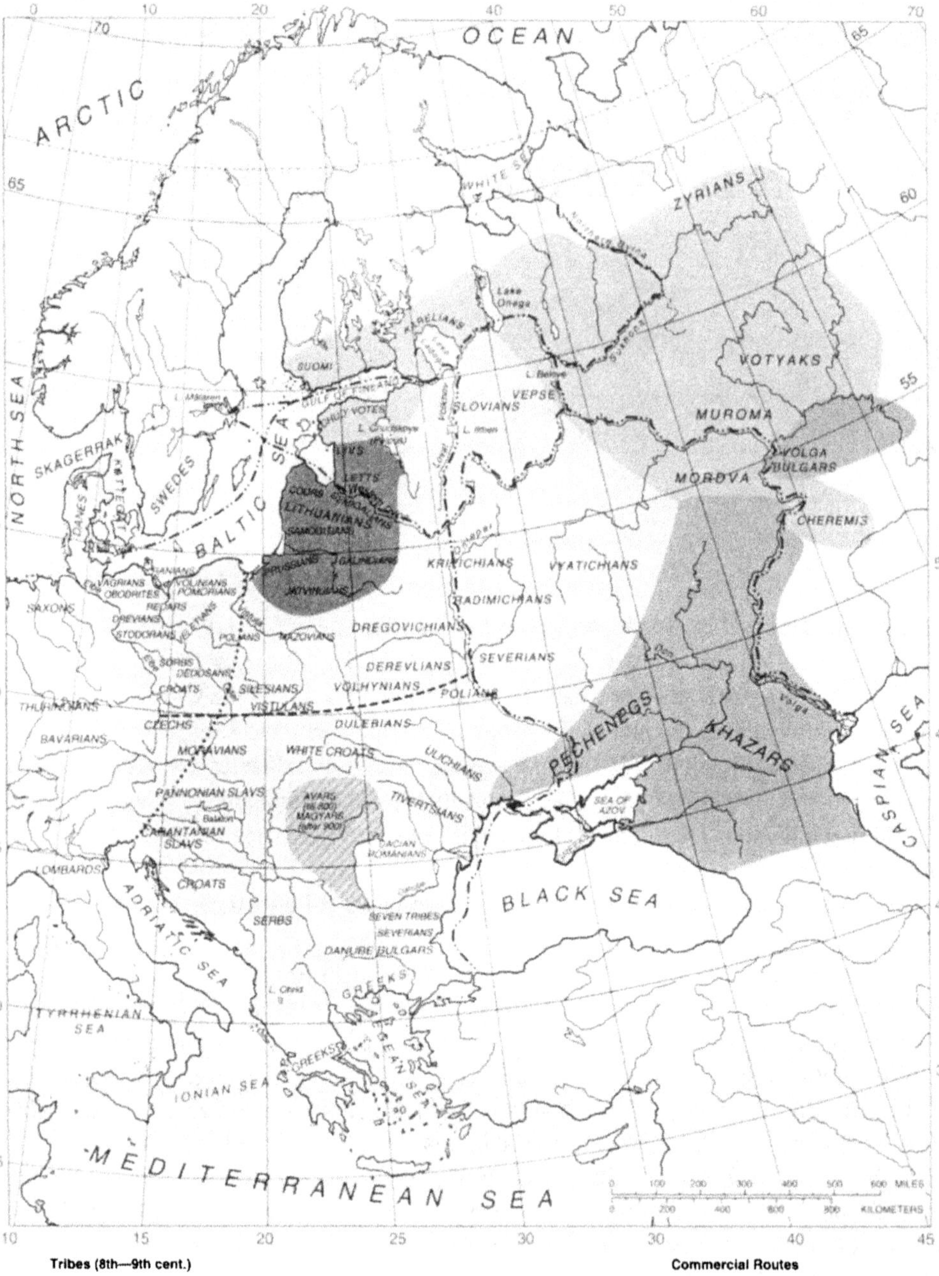

Tribes (8th—9th cent.)

Slavic-speaking
Finno-Ugric-speaking
Baltic-speaking
Turkic-speaking

Commercial Routes

Viking (Varangian) waterways with overland portages
Dnieper route (Baltic Sea—Black Sea)
Volga route (Baltic Sea—Caspian Sea)
"Amber" route (Adriatic Sea—Baltic Sea)
West-East route (Prague—Cracow—Kiev)

1. HISTORICAL SETTING

1.1. In search of roots. Human collectives have always strived to discover their origins. Held fast by linguistic, tribal, or religious bonds, societies are wont to test the strength of their union by examining its age and provenience. In this quest for a genealogy the Slavs find themselves in a less fortunate position than many other members of the Indo-European family of languages. Speakers of Greek and the Romance languages have the satisfaction of being heir to the glorious traditions of ancient Greece and Rome. The Celtic and Germanic peoples know much about their past from what was written about them by classical authors and from their own tales and legends. The Slavs, by contrast, did not enter the records of history until the sixth century A.D. Their early fates are veiled by the silence of their neighbors, the muteness of their own oral tradition, and the ambiguity of such nonverbal sources of information as archaeology, anthropology, or paleobotany.

Yet, the darkness of prehistory has not inhibited the Slavs in their search for roots. Scholars have fanned the few flickers of evidence hoping to illumine the past and reveal some heretofore hidden contours and shapes. How useful a search of this kind may be is best illustrated by the ingenious investigations of the Polish botanist Józef Rostafiński. Having noticed that Slavic lacked a native term for beech (*Fagus silvatica*) and for several other plants, Rostafiński assumed that there was a correlation between the easterly extension of the beech and the western limit of prehistoric Slavic settlements and concluded that the original homeland of the Slavs was located in the basin of the upper and middle Dnieper.[1]

Such insights, however, are few and far between. All too often the absence of concrete evidence and reliable source material gave scholars free rein to engage in fanciful speculation, unrestrained by considerations of fact and probability. As a result, theories have been proposed in which the line between ascertainable reality and more or less imaginative conjecture has been blurred or is altogether absent.

1.2. The autochthonous theory. One such theory would have the prehistoric Slavs dwell continuously upon the shores of the Vistula and Oder rivers and the Baltic Sea, a territory roughly coextensive with that of today's Poland, since the middle of the second millennium B.C. Championed mainly by Polish scholars and dubbed, therefore, the autochthonous theory, it was summarized by the Czech historian of early Slavdom Father Francis

1. In Trubačev's (1991) otherwise thorough discussion of the clues used in the determination of the Slavic homeland, the significance of plant names is surprisingly understated.

Dvornik: "The modern Polish school of archaeologists . . . came boldly forward with the theory that the primitive habitat of the Slavs should be located in the lands between the Elbe, Oder, Vistula and Bug rivers and that the so-called 'Lusatian culture' . . . was a product of the primitive Slavs" (Dvornik 1956:9).[2]

Could, however, the rich finds of the so-called Lusatian culture, which thrived from about 1300 to 400 B.C. in the basins of the Vistula, the Oder, and the upper Elbe, be shown to have been Slavic in origin? While harboring some doubts on that score, Dvornik finds the autochthonous hypothesis persuasive: "Most of the prehistoric maps show a vacuum in the lands where the Lusatian culture flourished. On several grounds it would seem reasonable to fill this vacuum with the Slavs" (Dvornik 1956:10). Reasoning *ex vacuo,* as one might call Dvornik's attempt to assign an area to the Slavs chiefly because no one else is claiming it, is used also when a name or a term comes down to us in the form of a label separated from its referent. A striking instance of such an approach is the persistent attempt to prove that the names of the Neuri and the Budini, two tribes which according to the Greek historian Herodotus (fifth century B.C.) lived somewhere on the territory of today's Ukraine or Belarus, are Slavic in origin. We know absolutely nothing of the ethnic affiliation of these tribes—their names have no clear etymology and could be associated with any branch of Indo-European—yet both or either of them have been considered Slavic (Łowmiański 1967: 367–369; Gołąb 1991:284–287) in an eager effort to establish some lineage for the historical Slavs who live in that area.[3]

In addition to claiming a connection between the Lusatian culture and the Slavs, the adherents of the autochthonous theory rest their case on several other assumptions. They include the claims that the ancient tribe of the Veneti, who lived along the Vistula and the Baltic, was linguistically Slavic and that Slavic etymologies can be postulated for the names of the river Vistula, which was well known in antiquity, and the town of Kalisz, which was mentioned by Ptolemy (ca. A.D. 100–178). Let us try to ascertain whether these assumptions can stand up to critical scrutiny.

1.3. Material culture and language. As far as the possibility of identifying the bearers of the Lusatian culture with the Slavs, one must remember that there is no necessary organic connection between material culture and language. Independent historical evidence for the purported connection between the Slavic language and the Lusatian culture is totally missing. Besides, the contrast between the finely shaped and ornamented ceramics of the Lusatian era and the unrefined burial jars of the demonstrably Slavic Prague-period pottery (sixth–seventh centuries) is so striking as to render such a connection implausible. Slavic artifacts are also cruder than those of the post-Lusatian cultures of the so-called Roman era, demonstrating the existence of a considerable cultural lag of the Slavs vis-à-vis their Central European predecessors (Godłowski 1979:13, 20–21).

2. Polish scholars subscribing to the autochthonous theory include the linguists Lehr-Spławiński (1946), Rudnicki (1959–1961), and Nalepa (1968); the historian Hensel (1980); the archaeologists Jażdżewski (1948–1949), Kostrzewski (1962), and Sulimirski (1956); and the anthropologist Czekanowski (1957). It should be noted that the autochthonists' views have not been favorably received by many scholars. To be noted in particular are a well-argued critique of the autochthonous theory by the Polish archaeologist Godłowski (1979) and an overview of the current state of research on the linguistic evidence for the location of the original homeland of the Slavs by Miodowicz (1984). The most recent survey of the problem, including a large bibliography, may be found in Birnbaum's 1993 review of Trubačev 1991, Popowska-Taborska 1991, Gołąb 1992, and Mańczak 1992.

3. It is equally difficult to prove that the Scythian Ploughmen, who were also mentioned by Herodotus, might have been Slavic (Gimbutas 1971:46–53).

1.4. Were the Veneti Slavic? From various ancient sources we know of three different tribes bearing the name of the Veneti or Venedi.[4] A large tribe of the Veneti, first mentioned by Herodotus, lived along the northern shores of the Adriatic Sea. A few surviving place names and brief inscriptions suggest that the Adriatic Veneti spoke an Italic dialect. The memory of the Italic Veneti survives in the names of the province Venetia and the city of Venice. There was also a Celtic tribe of the Veneti living in the Morbihan district of Brittany. According to Caesar, the Veneti of Brittany excelled "in the theory and practice of navigation."[5] Today several French place names, such as Vannes or Vendée, remind us of this tribe's existence. Finally, a tribe of the Veneti was mentioned by Pliny the Elder (A.D. 23–79) who located it along the Vistula. Tacitus (ca. A.D. 55–120) identified the Vistula Veneti as the eastern neighbors of Germania, while Ptolemy placed them along the southern shores of the Venedic Bay (*Ouenedikós kólpos*), that is, of the Baltic Sea. The Veneti are also mentioned twice on a Roman road map known as the *Tabula Peutingeriana* whose protograph may go back to the third or fourth century A.D.

Since the Vistula/Baltic Veneti left no written records, their linguistic affiliation can only be gleaned indirectly. Tacitus was alone among the ancient authors to tackle the problem of their ethnic origin. After hesitating whether to classify them as Germanic or Sarmatian, he finally decided in favor of the former on the basis of their cultural similarity with the Germanic peoples. Yet, in most investigations dealing with Slavic prehistory, the Baltic Veneti are not considered Germanic, as Tacitus would have it, or Illyrian, like their namesakes on the Adriatic, or Celtic, like the Morbihan Veneti. Rather, they are generally regarded as Slavic. To justify such an identification, which if correct would directly confirm the autochthonous theory, three circumstances are mentioned. It is noted, in the first place, that the Veneti of the first and second centuries A.D. and the historic Slavs of the sixth century inhabited the same area. Second, the name of the Veneti has survived in German as *Wenden* or *Winden*, where it designates the Slavs who live in the closest proximity of Germany. And, last, the sixth-century Gothic historian Jordanes (**1.10**) applied the terms *Veneti* and *Slavs* to the same ethnic community (Niederle 1923:32–33).

These arguments, however, are not decisive. There is no reason to doubt that by the sixth century the Slavs were on the Vistula (though it is quite unlikely that they had by then reached the Baltic). This does not mean, however, that they had to be there in the time of Tacitus. During the intervening four hundred years Europe underwent its most momentous transformations, as the fall of Rome and the Hunnic invasions started the ethnic whirligig known as the Great Migrations. To assume a lack of change during the period of such profound ethnic perturbations is to strain the laws of historical probability.

Nor can the German practice of designating their Slavic neighbors by the names *Wenden* or *Winden* help us in solving the question of the ethnic character of the Veneti. Transfers of names from one ethnic group to another have frequently occurred in history and signify no more than some kind of spatial and temporal contiguity between the two communities. The German usage may merely indicate that some non-Germanic Veneti lived in the area occupied later by the West Slavs and that the Germans transferred the name of the former to the latter. In an analogous way the Lithuanians transferred the name *Gudai* (Goths) to the East

4. The alternation of *t* and *d* is due to the so-called Grimm's Law in Germanic (**2.3**). In this book the term *Veneti* is used throughout, regardless of its spelling in the ancient sources.

5. Caesar, Gaius Julius (1933), *The Gallic War*, trans. H. J. Edwards, London: William Heinemann.

Slavs or the Germans referred to the Czechs as the Böhmer, which was the name of the Celtic tribe of the Boii who lived in Bohemia before the Czechs. There is no reason, however, to assume that the transfer of the name Veneti to the Slavs occurred much before the sixth century.

There is also no compelling evidence to justify the claim that Jordanes' identification of the Veneti with the Slavs reflects an ancient situation. The Slavicization of the Veneti is possible in the sixth century but most improbable in the first. To take an analogous example, the Franks in eighth-century France were already fully Romanized and could be identified with the native Gallo-Roman population. It would be absurd, however, to extend such an identification to the fifth-century Germanic Franks, who were then just embarking upon their conquest of Gaul.

Quite aside from these considerations, the very fact that the ancient sources locate the Veneti on the Baltic provides the most persuasive argument against their identification with the Slavs. The point is that Slavic vocabulary does not contain any indication that the early Slavs were exposed to the sea. Proto-Slavic had no maritime terminology whatsoever, be it in the domain of seafaring, sea fishing, boat building, or sea trade.[6] Especially striking is the absence of a Proto-Slavic word for amber, the most important item of export from the shores of the Baltic to the Mediterranean. In view of this, the very fact that Ptolemy refers to the Baltic as the Venedic Bay appears to rule out a possible identification of the Veneti of his times with the Slavs.

It is interesting to recall in this connection a story that many scholars, from Šafařík (1862:133–138) on, have adduced in support of the identification of the Veneti with the Slavs.[7] The story originated with Cornelius Nepos, the Roman historian of the first century B.C., and was repeated after him by Pomponius Mela and Pliny the Elder: "Cornelius Nepos . . . reports the testimony of Q. Metellus Celer who . . . said that when he was a proconsul in Gaul, the king of the Boti presented him with several Indians [*Indos*] and that when he inquired whence they had arrived in this land, he found out that a violent storm snatched them away from the Indian sea [*ex Indicis aequoribus*] and that, after traversing [the expanse] that lay in between, they were thrown out on the shores of Germany."[8]

Could one claim that the Indi of this account were Slavs? In suggesting that this indeed could have been the case, Šafařík had to accept a number of hypotheses: that Nepos' story was not fictitious; that a sea voyage from India (or some other place referred to as India) to Western Europe was not feasible in or before the first century B.C.; that *Indi* and *Indicus* are to be read as *Vindi* and *Vindicus*; that the Indi (now identified as the Vindi) were in fact the Venedi < Veneti; that the Indi (now identified as the Veneti) arrived on the shores of Germany from the Baltic rather than from some other sea, like the Adriatic; that the watery expanse [*aequora*] which the luckless sailors had to traverse was merely the Kattegat and the Skagerrak; that the Indi (= Vindi = Veneti) were Slavs; and that the Slavs were capable of making long sea voyages in or before the first century B.C. The degree of probability of most of these assumptions is fairly low, and Šafařík was duly cautious in advancing his hypothe-

6. Proto-Slavic *morje* 'sea' originally meant a marsh (incidentally, from the same Indo-European root) and dialectally still means a lake. Similarly, Proto-Slavic *ostrovъ*, composed as it is of *o-* 'around' and *str-* 'flow', suggests a river island rather than a sea island (Meillet 1927:8).

7. Gil'ferding (1868), Pogodin (1901), Niederle (1925), and many autochthonists of the modern period.

8. Mela, Pomponius (1880), *Chorographia*, text established by Karl Frick, books 1–3, Leipzig: B. G. Teubner, book 3, 5.45.

sis ("we surmise that should our interpretation of this matter be correct, it would throw more light on [Slavic] antiquities," 133). Šafařík's followers, however, show no hesitation in considering his surmise a proven fact.[9]

Another piece of evidence countering the claim that the Veneti of the times preceding the Great Migrations were Slavic is furnished by Henry of Livonia (Henricus de Lettis), who in his Latin chronicle, dating from the very beginning of the thirteenth century, described a clearly non-Slavic tribe of the Vindi (German *Winden*, English *Wends*) which lived in Courland and Livonia (on the territory of today's Latvia). The tribe's memory lives on in the name of the river Windau (Latvian *Venta*), with the town of Windau (Latvian *Ventspils*) at its mouth, and in Wenden, the old name of the town of Cēsis (East Slavic *Kesь*) in Livonia. The location of this tribe coupled with recently discovered archaeological evidence (Ochmański 1982) suggest that the Vindi of Courland and Livonia may well be the descendants of the Baltic Veneti.

1.5. Evidence of place and river names. The autochthonists assume that the names of several Central European rivers and of the town of Kalisz in Poland (Ptolemy's *Kalisía*) have demonstrably Slavic etymologies. The highly conjectural nature of these etymologies, however, seriously undermines their value as underpinnings of any attempt to establish the habitat of the early Slavs. While an etymology of a common noun can be tested on the semantic level, most proper names do not lend themselves to such verification. This is the case of the Vistula (Polish *Wisła*), the only river of the area known by the same name or its variants (*Vistla, Visculus, Viscla, Visula*) to both the ancients and the moderns. Neither the Vistula nor Kalisz, however, has a transparent Slavic or Indo-European etymology. These names could be Slavic, Germanic, Celtic, or even pre-Indo-European (Schenker 1987).

1.6. Classical sources. The advocates of the Slavic presence in Central Europe before the Great Migrations must also account for the fact that the writers of the classical world, and in particular the Romans, never mentioned their purported neighbors. The Romans, who reached the Danube before the birth of Christ and who could be found soon afterward on the banks of the Elbe, appear to have been totally unaware of the Slavs settled allegedly just beyond these rivers, despite the fact that the so-called amber route, a well-traveled track leading from the Mediterranean to the Baltic, had to pass through the presumably Slavic lands. The tens of thousands of Roman coins found along that route testify to Rome's lively commercial interest in the lands lying between its borders and the Baltic. And why is it that the Slavs, who in the second half of the first millennium A.D. became the object of a brisk slave trade throughout the basin of the Mediterranean, were not known in that capacity before?[10]

These questions would not arise if scholars did not ascribe the silence of the classical sources to a mere accident. Dvornik deplores "the scarcity of information about the Slavs in the works of the old classical writers" but insists that "it helps to explain why the civilized people of the West were so little interested in the historical and cultural evolution of the Slavs. . . . Matters would have been quite different if the Romans had come into direct contact with the Slavs, as they did with the Celts and the Germans. This would not have been impossible," Dvornik concludes, "for twice the Romans came very near to the territory in-

9. See Schenker 1987:359–360.

10. Eventually lending their ethnic name to the Mediterranean designation of the slave: Greek *sklábos*, Latin *sclavus*, Arabic *saqlab*. Note that the initial consonant cluster *sl* did not occur in the classical languages and was regularly replaced by the cluster *skl*.

habited by the Slavs" (Dvornik 1956:14). One wonders about the value of history written in the conditional mood. The fact that something did not happen is of course significant, but a historian's duty is to explain rather than bemoan it. The lack of contacts between the Romans and the Slavs could not have been accidental. It can be explained simply by the fact that the Slavs, unlike the Celts and the Germans, had not arrived on the frontiers of the classical world until after the Great Migrations.

1.7. *Médos* and *strava*. In 448 the Byzantine historian Priscus of Pania traveled through Hunnic Pannonia as a member of an embassy sent by Emperor Theodosius II to the court of Attila. The local population, identified by Priscus as Scythian,[11] treated the Greek travelers to two local drinks, *médos*, described as a substitute for wine, and *kámon* (or *kámos*), made of barley and offered to the servants (Priscus of Pania, 300). The term *médos* could be the Slavic *medъ* 'mead', adapted to Greek by the addition of the nominative singular ending *-os*. However, reflexes of PIE *mĕdh-ŭ-* 'honey, mead' occur in many Indo-European languages (e.g. Lithuanian *medùs* and Latvian *medus*), and the possibility that *médos* was borrowed from some non-Slavic Indo-European language like Baltic, Illyrian or Thracian cannot be ruled out. The fact that *kámon* is definitely not Slavic makes such a possibility all the more likely (Filin 1962:62). Even if one assumed that the source language was Slavic, one would still be left with the unanswerable question whether the loan was made in the fifth century in Pannonia or at an earlier time and in another place.

The term *strava* 'wake' was mentioned by Jordanes in his description of Attila's funeral in 453.[12] The meaning of the term is inferred from Jordanes' claim that it referred to a huge feast held at Attila's graveside. Since *strava* occurs also in modern North Slavic languages meaning 'food' (in West Slavic 'living expense'), it has been suggested that the Hunnic term referred to the food served at the wake and that it was borrowed from Slavic (Brückner 1927:518, Dvornik 1956:30). However, if for no other reason, this conjecture fails on linguistic grounds, for modern Slavic *strava* comes from Proto-Slavic *i̯ĭz-trāu̯ā* (root *trāu̯-* 'digest, use up'), and it is absolutely unthinkable for Proto-Slavic *ĭ* not to have been perceived as a full vowel in the fifth or sixth century (**2.38** and **2.40**).

1.8. The Danubian and mid-Dnieper theories. It is generally agreed that the search for the Slavic ancestral home can be limited to the region bordered by the Dnieper, the Danube, the Oder, and the Baltic—by and large, the area of current Slavic settlement, excepting the lands known to have been colonized in historical times. Despite this limitation, however, there is no agreement on the more exact location of the Slavic homeland within that region. The paucity and ambiguity of available data coupled with the expanse of the territory in question have allowed for a wide range of opinion and have engendered an intense debate, colored occasionally by a nationalistic bias. The autochthonous hypothesis appears to fall into the latter category. Where, then, was the original homeland of the Slavs?

In an early passage from the East Slavic *Primary Chronicle* (**3.50.3**), immediately after the description of the fates of the three sons of Noah, the Slavs are described as situated on the lower Danube: "Over a long period the Slavs settled beside the Danube, where the Hungarian and Bulgarian lands now lie. From among these Slavs, parties scattered through-

11. This anachronistic identification is merely a reflection of the Greek habit of referring to all non-Turkic peoples living across the Danube as Scythians.

12. Jordanes may have taken his account of the funeral from a lost fragment of Priscus.

out the country and were known by appropriate names, according to the places where they settled. Thus some came and settled by the river Morava, and were named Moravians, while others were called Czechs" (*Primary Chronicle*, 52–53). It has sometimes been claimed that this passage, which includes a long list of Slavic tribes, all of which are said to have come from the Danubian region, is the first expression of the so-called Danubian (Pannonian) theory of the Slavic homeland. Further reading indicates, however, that the chronicle speaks of the situation in the sixth and seventh centuries rather than of prehistory. Such datable events as the arrival of the Bulgarians on the lower Danube in the mid-seventh century or the reign of Emperor Heraclius (610–641) make this quite clear: "Now while the Slavs dwelt along the Danube, as we have said, there came from among the Scythians, that is from the Khazars, a people called Bulgars who settled on the Danube and oppressed the Slavs. Afterward came the White Ugrians, who inherited the Slavic country. These Ugrians appeared under the Emperor Heraclius, warring on Chosroes, King of Persia" (*Primary Chronicle*, 55).[13]

The Danubian theory finds few modern adherents. One of them is the Russian linguist Oleg N. Trubačev (1982 and 1991), whose views, based mainly on place and river names of the Danubian region, have engendered a lively polemic between him and his critics (Godłowski 1985, Udolph 1988).

Many scholars assign to the prehistoric Slavs the basin of the middle Dnieper, roughly the territory of today's north-central and western Ukraine and southeastern Belarus. Among the most convincing advocates of this theory are the linguists Rozwadowski (1913), Vasmer (1926), and Filin (1962); the botanist Rostafiński (1908); and the ethnologist Moszyński (1957). The mid-Dnieper theory is supported by comparative linguistic data which allow scholars to infer the time and place of social and cultural contacts among languages. According to these data, Proto-Slavic had close ties not only with Baltic but also with Germanic in the domain of household terminology and with Iranian in the domain of worship (**2.47**). There is evidence to show that the Balts used to inhabit the area between the Baltic Sea and the upper Dnieper and that the lands north of the Black Sea were first occupied by the Iranian Scythians and Sarmatians (the second half of the first millennium B.C.) and later by the Germanic Ostrogoths (the beginning of the first millenium A.D.). It would thus be reasonable to assume that the prehistoric Slavs lived in the basin of the middle Dnieper, an area contiguous to the lands occupied by Baltic, Germanic, and Iranian tribes.[14]

To sum up, neither the autochthonous nor the Danubian theory is supported by any direct evidence. No tribal or geographic name mentioned in ancient sources can be interpreted as definitely Slavic; no archaeological remains going back to the Roman period bear any systematic resemblance to the demonstrably Slavic artifacts dating from after the fifth century; no first- or second-century accounts of central and south-central European lands contain any reference to the Slavs (in contrast to the clearly identified Celtic, Germanic, and even Baltic tribes); no unmistakably Slavic words were cited in early Greek or Latin sources; no Slavic names were recorded during the Great Migrations (Menges 1953:18–19). Whatever scant ev-

13. The reference to the Khazars as Scythians represents a typical transfer of names from one ethnic group to another. Similarly, the Avars were called Huns and the Magyars were referred to as Avars or Turks. The identity of the White Ugrians is uncertain; they were probably a branch of the Bulgars.

14. The Slavic ancestral home has also been placed in other locations, including the marshes of the Pripet basin (Hirt 1907), the fertile lands of Volhynia (Gołąb 1983 and 1992), the foothills of the Carpathian mountains (Udolph 1979), and various combinations of all the aforementioned theories (Niederle 1925, Tret'jakov 1953).

idence we do possess points to the mid-Dnieper basin as the area where the Slavs lived before their sixth-century invasion of Central Europe and the Balkan Peninsula.

1.9. The Indo-European homeland. Just as Slavic linguistic unity presupposes the existence of a common primordial territory, so the Indo-European community of languages implies that the speakers of Proto-Indo-European once inhabited a specific area, their original homeland. Unfortunately, the enormous time remove makes it next to impossible to ascertain with any degree of certainty the location of that homeland. The most likely scenario would place the Proto-Indo-European speech community on the plains north of the Black and Caspian seas. Not only is this area located approximately midway between the Atlantic and Chinese Turkestan, that is, between the historic abodes of the westernmost (Italo-Celtic) and easternmost (Tocharian) branches of Indo-European; it is also the most probable ancestral home of the Slavs, who, as can be historically ascertained, were the last of the Indo-European language groups to strike out from their prehistoric quarters.

The territorial disintegration of the Indo-European linguistic unity was most certainly a gradual process during which successive waves of Indo-European speakers moved away from their primordial homes to settle in those areas of the Eurasian continent where they are found in historical times. The beginning of this process, which may have occurred more than five thousand years ago, is buried deep in prehistory. In the last four thousand years or so, however, various Indo-European language families have revealed themselves to us either through their own written records or in the writings of others.

It should not be surprising that the earliest documentation of the existence of individual Indo-European languages comes from the so-called Fertile Crescent, the lands strung along the most important sea routes of the Ancient World, from the Indian Ocean and the Persian Gulf to the Black Sea and the Mediterranean. The oldest among them are the records of the Hittites (ca. eighteenth century B.C.), followed by Mycenean Greek—Linear B (ca. fourteenth century B.C.) and the Vedic Sanskrit hymns (between 1500 and 1000 B.C., transcribed from oral tradition around 500 B.C.). The oldest Avestan liturgical texts come from the days of Zoroaster (eighth–seventh centuries B.C.), which is also the approximate time of the composition of Homer's *Iliad* and *Odyssey*. The oldest Latin inscription is from about 600 B.C.

Other Indo-European languages, whose speakers roamed the areas north of the Eurasian sunbelt, entered the arena of history at a relatively late time. The tales of their wanderings, wars, and beliefs have come down to us not in their own literary monuments but as reflected in the records of the established centers of ancient civilizations. Such was the case of the Celtic and Germanic tribes that were mentioned in various Greek and Roman sources long before the appearance of texts in their own languages: the oldest Germanic runic inscriptions come from as late as the third century A.D. Celtic monuments are even younger—the first connected Old Irish texts date from the fifth century A.D. The Slavs were the last Indo-Europeans to emerge from the obscurity of their ancestral home. The first Slavic texts were not recorded till the middle of the ninth century,[15] and the first indubitable reference to the Slavs' appearance on the frontiers of the civilized world comes from the sixth century A.D.

15. One must remember, however, that the lateness of Slavic texts does not diminish their value as linguistic documents. When languages are studied for the purposes of linguistic comparison rather than as vehicles of civilized intercourse, all the data, regardless of their age, are equal in importance. An Ancient Greek form can be fruitfully compared to a Slavic one, even though their recorded appearances might be separated by more than two thousand years.

1.10. The Great Migrations. Jordanes' testimony. The arrival of the Slavs in central and southern Europe came on the heels of the Great Migrations, a series of mass tribal dislocations of the fourth and fifth centuries which utterly changed the ethnic and linguistic situation of the Eurasian continent. Although the Slavs must have been affected by this apparently universal impulse to shift tribal abodes, their peregrinations before the sixth century escaped the historian's detection.[16]

The migratory turbulence of the fifth century had hardly come to a standstill when the Slavs did make their appearance in the annals of history. Following the dynamics of the Great Migrations, the Slavs began moving westward and in the first decades of the sixth century reached the banks of the Danube. It was Jordanes who in his history of the Goths (*De origine actibusque Getarum*, ca. 550) made the first explicit reference to the Slavs as a large group of "consanguineous" tribes, the Veneti, the Antes, and the Sclaveni:

> Near the left ridge [of the Carpathian Mountains], which inclines toward the north, and beginning at the source of the Vistula, the populous race of the Venethi dwell, occupying a great expanse of land. Though their names are now dispersed amid various clans and places, yet they are chiefly called Sclaveni and Antes. The abode of the Sclaveni extends from the city of Noviodunum and the lake called Mursianus[17] to the Danaster [Dnestr], and northward as far as the Vistula. They have swamps and forests for their cities. The Antes, who are the bravest of these peoples dwelling in the curve of the sea of Pontus [Black Sea], spread from the Danaster to the Danaper [Dnieper] rivers that are many days' journey apart. (Jordanes, 59–60)

It is clear that the term *Sclaveni* designated the Slavs. The name *Veneti*, as suggested above, must have been transferred to the Slavs from a tribe with an uncertain linguistic identity which inhabited the basin of the Vistula before the arrival of the Slavs. Similarly, the name *Antes*, which may be etymologically related to the name *Veneti*, did not initially refer to the Slavs. Its original bearers, possibly an Iranian tribe, either became Slavicized or, as in the case of the Veneti, came to be identified with the Slavs by neighboring peoples. The geographic distribution of the three Slavic tribes mentioned by Jordanes may prefigure the dialectal division of Slavic, with the Veneti corresponding to the West Slavs, the Antes to the East Slavs and the Sclaveni to the South Slavs.

Even though, at the time of Jordanes' writing,[18] the Slavs had not yet crossed the Danube, the future course of events can be anticipated from Jordanes' anxious observation that the Slavs "are raging everywhere."

1.11. The Avars. The Slavs were not alone in appearing on the northern borders of the Byzantine Empire. In the historical sources of the period their name is almost invariably

16. The fact that during the Hunnic onslaught and the Great Migrations no Slavic names were recorded prompted Karl Menges (1953:18) to wonder why "in the historical account of all these important events, of these many names of tribes, tribal conglomerates and nationalities, there is not a single one that can be ascertained as Slavic,—a paradoxical fact." However, the paradox is there only if we assume that the Slavs participated fully in the Great Migrations, an assumption which, as I have tried to show, is not warranted. It must be remembered in this connection that the oft-quoted testimonies from before the sixth century A.D., unsupported as they are by firm linguistic and onomastic evidence, do not have any demonstrable value as source material for the history of the Slavs.

17. Novietunum ('New Town' in Celtic) was located at the mouth of the Danube; the Mursian lake may refer to the delta of the Danube.

18. Or slightly earlier, at the time of Cassiodorus (ca. 490–575), master of offices of Theodoric, the Ostrogothic ruler of Italy. Cassiodorus was the author of a twelve-volume history of the Goths summarized by Jordanes but subsequently lost.

linked with that of the Avars, a large Turkic tribe from eastern Central Asia. In the beginning of the sixth century the Avars set out on a westward trek, passing through the Caucasus and the Pontic steppes and reaching, by the mid-sixth century, the lower course of the Danube. During the next one hundred years the Avars represented a major political and military force in the Danubian region and ventured even to attack Gaul in 562 and 566. This is how the chronicler of the Franks, Gregory of Tours (538–594), described the second of the encounters between the Merovingian king of Austrasia Sigibert I (r. 561–575) and the Avars:

> The Huns[19] once more attempted to invade Gaul, and Sigibert led his army against them, having with him a great host of valiant men. But when they were about to engage, the Huns, who were versed in magic arts, caused fantastic shapes to appear before the Franks, and thus had great advantage over them. The army of Sigibert fled; he himself was surrounded, and would have been kept a prisoner had he not . . . overcome by his art in giving those whom he failed to conquer by his power in battle. For he gave their king rich presents, and entered into a treaty with him, so that while he lived no war took place between them. . . . On his part the king of the Huns gave many gifts to Sigibert. He was called Gagan [kagan], a name common to all the kings of this people. (Gregory of Tours, 138–139)

In 626 the Avars besieged Constantinople but were defeated by the Byzantines and had to retreat to Pannonia, which for the next century and a half became their main base of operations. At the turn of the eighth and ninth centuries, the Franks under Charlemagne and his son Pepin attacked and utterly destroyed the Avar kaganate. The initial power and the abrupt fall of the Avar state were a source of wonderment to the compiler of the East Slavic *Primary Chronicle*:

> The Avars, who attacked Heraclius the Emperor [r. 610–641], nearly capturing him, also lived at this time. They made war upon the Slavs, and harassed the Dulebians, who were themselves Slavs. They even did violence to the Dulebian women. When an Avar made a journey, he did not cause either a horse or a steer to be harnessed, but gave command instead that three or four or five women should be yoked to his cart and be made to draw him. Even thus they harassed the Dulebians. The Avars were large of stature and proud of spirit, and God destroyed them. They all perished, and not one Avar survived. There is to this day a proverb in Rus' which runs, "They perished like the Avars." Neither race nor heir of them remains. (*Primary Chronicle*, 55–56)

The enormity of the defeat of the Avars at the hands of the Franks is confirmed by Einhard, the contemporary biographer of Charlemagne:

> The war which came next was the most important which Charlemagne ever fought, except the one against the Saxons: I mean the struggle with the Avars or Huns. He waged it with more vigor than any of the others and with much greater preparation. He himself led only one expedition into Pannonia, the province which the Huns occupied at that period. Everything else he entrusted to his son Pepin, to the governors of his provinces and to his counts and legates. The war was prosecuted with great vigor by these men and it came to an end in its eighth year.[20] Just how many battles were fought and how much blood was shed is shown by the fact that Pannonia is now completely uninhabited and that the site of the Khan's palace is now so

19. The term *Huns* was used by western chroniclers as a catchall for Turkic-speaking invaders from Asia.
20. Actually, Charlemagne's campaigns against the Avars began in 791 and ended in 803.

deserted that no evidence remains that anyone ever lived there. All the Hun nobility died in this war, all their glory departed. All their wealth and their treasures assembled over so many years were dispersed. The memory of man cannot recall any war against the Franks by which they were so enriched and their material possessions so increased. (Einhard, 67)

The awe which the Slavs felt for the Avars and their gratification over the Avar downfall are confirmed by two Slavic loan words. In the languages spoken in the area of the Avar domination the word for 'giant' is formed from the root *obъr-* 'Avar': Sln. *óbər*, Cz. *obr*, Slk. *obor*, OPo. *obrzym*, ModPo. *olbrzym*. Also, the Frankish victories in Pannonia impressed the Slavs so much that Charlemagne's Germanic name *Karl* was borrowed into Slavic with the meaning 'king'. Though originally adopted by central Slavic dialects only, this word eventually spread throughout Slavic: Sln. *králj*, Cz. *král*, Slk. *kráľ*, Po. *król*, Ru. *koról'*, etc.

The testimony of the *Primary Chronicle* as well as the semantic development of the root *obr-* 'Avar' would suggest that during a good part of their association with the Slavs, the Avars were the dominating force. Yet, there are also indications that at various times different Slavic tribes entered into military alliances with the Avars not as their subjects but as free confederates.[21]

1.12. Constantinople and Christianity. The Slavs arrived at the frontiers of the civilized world at a time when the political center of gravity had shifted from the western to the eastern part of the Mediterranean. Rome, the ancient capital of the empire, laid low by successive waves of barbarian invasions, had to cede its preeminent position to Constantinople, a relative newcomer on the map of Europe. The very geographical position of the New Rome, as Constantinople was often called, represented the eastward outlook of the empire. The city was established by Constantine the Great (r. 306–337) on the site of Byzantium, a small Greek colony on the Bosphorus. Across the straits, less than a mile away, lay Asia Minor and, beyond it, the sources of new spiritual currents which, to a world rocked by barbarian invasions, offered a message of peace and a promise of better things to come.

Christianity, with its mystical eschatology of hope and redemption, proved more inspirational than other Oriental religions—Mithraism, Zoroastrianism, or Manicheanism. It spread across the world from Palestine and a mere fifty years after the reign of Constantine was proclaimed by Emperor Theodosius (r. 379–395) the official religion of the empire. Thus, one could view the founding of Constantinople as the West's symbolic gesture welcoming the new universal church. For more than four hundred years, the emperor reigning in Constantinople was the ultimate Christian monarch and the sole defender of Christianity throughout the world.

Although the political and economic fortunes of Rome declined to such a degree that it had to yield its status as the western capital of the empire, first to Milan and then to Ravenna, its religious prestige remained largely unshaken. Not only was it one of the original apostolic churches, but its bishop, or pope (from Greek *páppas* 'father'), inherited the dignity of St. Peter, who, as the keeper of the keys to the kingdom of heaven, held the pastoral authority over all Christians.

The special prominence of the church of Rome contrasts sharply with the virtual equality reigning among the eastern apostolic churches or patriarchates, the ancient ones in Anti-

21. The first to describe the relations between the Avars and the Slavs was the Byzantine historian Menander (second half of the sixth century).

och and Alexandria and the more recent ones in Jerusalem and Constantinople, whose very number inhibited supremacist tendencies. It is true that the flourishing of Constantinople lent its patriarch particular prestige and earned him the title of the ecumenical [universal] patriarch.[22] In practice, however, the authority of the patriarch of Constantinople did not extend beyond the borders of his patriarchate. His powers were further circumscribed by the peculiarly Byzantine blurring of distinctions between secular and ecclesiastic authority, a tendency often referred to as caesaropapism.

An example of the virtual identification of state and church is provided by the First Council of Christian Churches held in 325 in Nicaea. Despite its doctrinal preoccupations, not only was the council convoked and directed by Constantine but the emperor became the chief executor of the council's decisions. An ecclesiastic counterpart of this situation occurred in 626, during the siege of Constantinople by the joined Avar and Slav forces. With Emperor Heraclius away fighting the Persians, it was Patriarch Sergius who stepped into the breech and led the Greeks to victory.

The view that the interests of the state are concordant with the interests of the church had important consequences for the Slavs, for it made possible the establishment of a number of national churches with vernacular liturgies and eventually led to the creation of a Slavic liturgical language. Constantinople acquiesced willingly to such linguistic liberalism, while Rome, bent on the retention of doctrinal control over all of Christianity, favored the exclusive use of Hebrew, Greek, or Latin as the only languages whose dignity was commensurate with the exalted purpose of divine liturgy.

1.13. Europe after the Great Migrations. As the barbarians thundered across Europe, Constantinople, tucked in the extreme eastern corner of the Balkans and protected on three sides by the sea and on the fourth by mighty fortifications, though severely tested, was able to stand its ground and repel the attackers. It was not so elsewhere. When in the seventh century the ethnic maelstrom caused by the Great Migrations subsided,[23] the face of Europe presented an entirely new aspect.

Western Europe was almost totally overrun by Germanic peoples. Spain was in the hands of the Visigoths; France and western Germany were held by the Franks, Burgundians, Saxons, Allemani, and Bavarians; in Italy the Ostrogoths were succeeded by the Lombards; England was occupied by the Angles and Saxons; Scandinavia remained in the hands of various north Germanic tribes. Even the northern shores of Africa were under the sway of the Germanic Vandals. In view of these demographic realities, it should not surprise us that Germanic tribes were among the earliest converts to Christianity spreading from Constantinople and Rome and that, in the end, it was a Germanic tribe, the Franks, that inherited the political mantle of Rome in Western Europe.[24]

22. The adoption of this title in the sixth century by the patriarch of Constantinople, John the Faster (582–595), was understood by Rome as a challenge to its traditional primacy and brought on protests by Pope Gregory I (Magoulias 1970:89–90).

23. The Bulgars and the Magyars were still to arrive in Central Europe, the former at the end of the seventh and the latter at the end of the ninth century.

24. It must be remembered, however, that culturally and above all linguistically many Germanic tribes yielded to those whom they had subjugated. The old Roman provinces imposed their tongues on the Germanic invaders, giving rise to such Romance languages as Spanish, Portuguese, French, and Italian. Remaining on the linguistic map of Western Europe were several Celtic languages—Galician in northwestern Spain, Breton in Brittany, and Irish, Welsh, and Scottish in the British isles.

1.14. Christianization of the Goths and other Germanic tribes. Arianism. As a matter of fact, the Gospel of Christ reached some Germanic tribes long before the end of their migratory trek. Spreading along the northern frontier of the Roman empire, they exposed themselves early to the cultural currents emanating from the Mediterranean centers of civilization. The Visigoths, who at one time were settled in Moesia, north of the lower Danube, were the first Germanic tribe to embrace Christianity. They were converted through the missionary efforts of Bishop Ulfila (ca. 311–383), who translated the Bible into Gothic and transcribed it with the aid of a special alphabet of his own creation.[25]

Ulfila received his ordination at the time when the church in the eastern part of the empire was dominated by the heresy of Arianism.[26] Formulated by the presbyter Arius in Alexandria, Arianism disputed the dogma of consubstantiality, which pronounced God the Father and Christ to be of the same substance or essence. According to Arius, Christ, though endowed with all the attributes of divinity, was subordinate rather than coordinate in His relation to the Father. Since Christ had a beginning, Arius argued, He could not be considered to be fully identical or consubstantial with the eternal and infinite godhead and had to be relegated to the order of created beings. The First Council of Nicaea was convened to resolve these questions and ruled by an overwhelming majority against Arianism. The famous Nicene Creed or *credo,* formulated at the council, proclaimed Christ "begotten, not made, of one substance [in Greek *homooúsion,* from *homós* 'same' and *ousía* 'substance, essence'] with the Father." Despite the Nicene Creed, Arianism spread widely in the empire and far beyond its borders.[27]

Following their bishop, the Visigoths adopted Christianity in its Arian guise and, through missionary activity, helped spread the doctrine of Arianism among other Germanic tribes—the Vandals, Suevi, Burgundians, Lombards, Heruls, and Ostrogoths.

1.15. Christianization of the Celts and Anglo-Saxons. Of the Celtic tribes, the first to be baptized were the Irish. Their missionary leader was Bishop Patrick (ca. 385–460), whose Christianizing efforts earned him the title of Ireland's apostle and patron saint. Irish monasticism, which flourished in the sixth and seventh centuries, is famous for its extensive missionary activity. It was the Irish missionaries who were responsible for the Christianization of Scotland (St. Columba, 521–597) and who, together with their newly converted Scottish brethren, set out on missions throughout Europe, including Slavic Moravia and Carantania (Carinthia).

The Anglo-Saxons were brought into the Christian fold at the end of the sixth century through the efforts of Pope Gregory the Great (590–604) and his emissary Augustine, prior of the Benedictine monastery in Rome. King Ethelbert of Kent became the first Christian

25. The oldest extant manuscript is the *Codex Argenteus* in Uppsala, Sweden.

26. The term *heresy* (from Greek *haíresis* 'choice') was applied to teachings questioning some of the most fundamental tenets of apostolic Christianity, especially the dogma of the divinity of Christ and the interpretation of the mysteries, such as the Trinity and the Incarnation. In combatting heresies, the church gradually developed its *canon* (from Greek *kanon* 'straight rod, rule'), a set of established texts whose authority may not be questioned. The texts that were not incorporated in the canon were relegated to the rank of the *apocrypha* (from Greek *apókryphos* 'hidden, obscure'). Heresies were designated as such by the Councils of the Christian Churches, convened from time to time to discuss doctrinal issues.

27. Arianism in its ancient form disappeared toward the end of the seventh century. In name, however, if not entirely in doctrine, it arose again in sixteenth- and seventeenth-century Poland, where various anti-trinitarian movements (Socinians, Polish Brethren) came to be known as Arian.

ruler in England (597), and his capital in Canterbury has remained by tradition the episcopal see of the English church.

1.16. The Franks. In the long succession of barbarian conquerors of Gaul, the Franks came last and acted differently from their predecessors. Unlike the Turkic Huns, the Iranian Alans, and the Germanic Visigoths, Sueves, Vandals, and Burgundians, the Franks were colonizers rather than despoilers. Starting in the fifth century from the basin of the lower Rhine and establishing farmsteads along their way, they spread gradually in the southwestern direction and by mid-seventh century held most of Gaul. In the eighth century the Frankish state stretched from the Pyrenees in the west to Pomerania, Brandenburg, Bohemia, Moravia, Pannonia, and Croatia in the east. In the south, where their domains included the island of Corsica, most of Italy, and northern Dalmatia, the Franks came into direct contact with Byzantium.

Unlike their Germanic kinsmen, the Franks spurned Arianism and adopted Christianity (ca. 500) in its church-approved or canonical form.[28] The Frankish adherence to the canon had far-reaching political consequences. The Frankish state earned the status of a Christian realm, and its rulers were recognized by the church of Rome as Christian monarchs. Such recognition, in turn, entailed the necessary subordination of the Frankish rulers to the legitimizing authority of Rome and led to a new understanding of the royal prerogatives. The powers of the king were now seen as stemming from secular as well as ecclesiastic sources. This doctrine of dual derivation of royal authority made it possible to justify and sanction personal and even dynastic changes on the Frankish throne. Thus, upon the weakening of the Merovingians, the first Frankish royal dynasty, their successor, Pepin the Short (r. 751–768), had to seek the pope's consent to his enthronement. As a symbol of his submission to ecclesiastic authority, Pepin's coronation ceremony included the holy unction administered to him by Bishop Boniface, the most prominent and respected churchman of the Franks.[29]

1.17. Charlemagne and the papacy. With Rome's stamp of approval, the Frankish rulers obtained the legitimacy that heretofore had belonged solely to the Byzantine emperors. It should not surprise us, therefore, that they were soon reaching for the emperor's dignity as well. Such a claim was made by Pepin's eldest son, Charles (b. 742, r. 768–814), known in English by his Old French name as Charlemagne and in Latin as Carolus Magnus (hence the Carolingian dynasty). On Christmas Day of the year 800, Pope Leo III crowned Charlemagne "emperor of the Romans." In assuming the imperial title, Charlemagne challenged the Byzantine emperor's authority to act as the ultimate arbiter of Christian affairs. In fact, since his coronation coincided with the weakness of the papacy and a power crisis in Constantinople, where the empress Irene deposed her minor son Constantine VI, Charlemagne could now aspire to a leading role in church matters. Such was the burden of the celebrated letter which Alcuin, Charlemagne's closest adviser, addressed to his master in 799:

> There have hitherto been three persons of greatest eminence in the world, namely the Pope, who rules the see of St. Peter, the chief of apostles, as his successor—and you have kindly in-

28. The term *canonical* is used here in preference to the more traditional terms *orthodox* or *catholic* which, because of their modern confessional connotation, may be misleading.

29. St. Boniface (c. 673–754) was born Winfrid (Wynfrith) in Wessex. An extremely energetic church leader, he organized the Frankish church and set up the four Bavarian bishoprics of Regensburg, Freising, Salzburg, and Passau, which were to play a crucial role in the Christianization of Slavic Pannonia, Moravia, and Bohemia. In his letters and poems there are several harsh references to the western Slavs, with whom the Franks came into contact.

formed me of what has happened to him; the second is the Emperor, who holds sway over the second Rome [Byzantium]—and common report has now made known how wickedly the governor of such an empire has been deposed, not by strangers but by his own people in his own city; the third is the throne on which our Lord Jesus Christ has placed you to rule over our Christian people, with greater power, clearer insight, and more exalted royalty than the aforementioned dignitaries. On you alone the whole safety of the churches of Christ depends. You punish wrong-doers, guide the straying, console the sorrowing, and advance the good. (Alcuin, 111)

The strength of the Byzantines prevented Charlemagne from defying Constantinople's prestige in the East. In the West, however, Charlemagne's claim to sole imperial authority was not to be denied. The papacy, shorn of political power by Constantinople, found in Charlemagne a natural ally in the struggle to retain the leadership of the Christian world. Buttressed by the might of the Frankish state, it could now match its own authority against that of the Byzantines. What followed was an accentuation of the differences between the two ecclesiastic powers and a polarization of their ideological positions. A parting of ways became inevitable. The Great Schism which was to split Europe asunder in 1054 was a logical conclusion to a process symbolized by the festivities in the church of St. Peter in Rome on that fateful Christmas Day of the year 800.[30]

The Slavs spreading south into the Balkans and west into Germany came face to face with the two imperial adversaries. Their lands provided the main arena in which the rivalry between the Orthodoxy of Byzantium and the Catholicism of Rome and of the Frankish state was contested and in which it left the deepest scars.

1.18. The Slavs in the Balkans. Procopius' testimony. Jordanes' apprehensive remarks (**1.10**) were fully justified. His contemporary, the great Byzantine historian Procopius (died ca. 562), had many opportunities to observe the Slavs at close range. As adviser of Belisarius, the able military leader of Emperor Justinian, Procopius in his various writings (*De bellis, Historia arcana, De aedificiis*) vividly described the Slavs' crossing of the Danube and their destructive raids into Illiricum as they pushed toward the heartland of Byzantium. His account of the Slavs' habits and beliefs deserves to be quoted at length:

For these nations, the Sclaveni and the Antae, are not ruled by one man, but they have lived from of old under a democracy, and consequently everything which involves their welfare, whether for good or for ill, is referred to the people. It is also true that in all other, practically speaking, these two barbarian peoples have had from ancient times the same institutions and customs. For they believe that one god, the maker of the lightning, is alone lord of all things, and they sacrifice to him cattle and all other victims. . . . They reverence, however, both rivers

30. Doctrinal estrangement of East from West has, to be sure, a much longer history. It centered around three religious controversies, all of which originated in the eastern part of the empire: the Monophysite heresy ("Christ has a single nature"), which was tolerated by the emperors Zeno (474–491) and Justinian (527–565); the Monothelite heresy ("Christ has two natures but a single will"), which the emperors Heraclius I (610–641) and Constans II (641–668) viewed as an admissible compromise; and iconoclasm, which was the law under most of the Isaurian emperors in the eighth and ninth centuries. (For the *filioque* controversy, which heated up in the ninth century, see **1.39**.) Political tensions were of a more recent vintage. They may be said to have begun in the seventh and eighth centuries when Constantinople, beset by domestic strife and taxing wars, could no longer impose its authority in the West. Taking advantage of the weakness of imperial authority, the Papal See asserted its political independence by expanding its secular responsibilities and relying for military protection on the growing might of the Frankish state.

and nymphs and some other spirits, and they sacrifice to all these also, and they make their divinations in connection with these sacrifices. They live in pitiful hovels which they set up far apart from one another, but, as a general thing, every man is constantly changing his place of abode. When they enter battle, the majority of them go against their enemy on foot, carrying little shields and javelins in their hands, but they never wear corselets. Indeed, some of them do not wear even a shirt or a cloak, but gathering their trews up as far as to their private parts they enter into battle with their opponents. And both the two peoples have also the same language, an utterly barbarous tongue. Nay further, they do not differ at all from one another in appearance. For they are all exceptionally tall and stalwart men, while their bodies and hair are neither very fair or blond, nor indeed do they incline entirely to the dark type, but they are all slightly ruddy in color. And they live a hard life, giving no heed to bodily comforts, . . . they are continually and at all times covered with filth; however, they are in no respect base or evildoers, but they preserve the Hunnic character in all its simplicity. (Procopius, 269–273)

1.19. John of Ephesus' testimony. Toward the end of the sixth century, the Slavs pillaged the length and width of the Balkan peninsula, unimpeded by the Byzantines, who were busy fighting the Persians in Armenia and Mesopotamia. John of Ephesus, a Syrian historian and a leader of the Monophysite heretics, described in his *Ecclesiastical History* the extent of Slavic penetration of the Balkans and in particular their settlement and acculturation in Thrace, Macedonia, and Greece:

That same year [581] . . . was famous also for the invasion of an accursed people, called Slavonians, who overran the whole of Greece, and the country of the Thessalonians, and all Thrace, and captured the cities, and took numerous forts, and devastated and burnt, and reduced the people to slavery, and made themselves masters of the whole country, and settled in it by main force, and dwelt in it as though it had been their own without fear. . . . They still [584] encamp and dwell there, and live in peace in the Roman [Byzantine] territories, free from anxiety and fear, and lead captive and slay and burn: and they have grown rich in gold and silver, and herds of horses, and arms, and have learnt to fight better than the Romans, though at first they were but rude savages, who did not venture to shew themselves outside the woods and the coverts of the trees; and as for arms, they did not even know what they were, with the exception of two or three javelins or darts. (John of Ephesus, 432–433)

1.20. Emperor Maurice's *Strategikon*. The gravity of the problem presented by the invasion of the Slavs can be seen from a contemporary Byzantine war manual, *Strategikon*, attributed by most manuscripts to Emperor Maurice (r. 582–602). The author of the manual, faithful to the doctrine "know thine enemy," provided an exhaustive and apparently impartial description of the Slavs. Here is an extensive excerpt from it:

The nations of the Slavs and the Antes live in the same way and have the same customs. They are both independent, absolutely refusing to be enslaved or governed, least of all in their own land. They are populous and hardy, bearing readily heat, cold, rain, nakedness, and scarcity of provisions. They are kind and hospitable to the travelers in their country and conduct them safely from one place to another, wherever they wish. If the stranger should suffer some harm because of his host's negligence, the one who first commended him will wage war against that host, regarding vengeance for the stranger as a religious duty. They do not keep those who are in captivity among them in perpetual slavery, as do other nations. But they set a definite pe-

> riod of time for them and then give them the choice either, if they so desire, to return to their own homes with a small recompense or to remain there as free men and friends. They possess an abundance of all sorts of livestock and produce, which they store in heaps. . . . Their women are more sensitive than any others in the world. When, for example, their husband dies, many look upon it as their own death and freely smother themselves, not wanting to continue their lives as widows. They live among nearly impenetrable forests, rivers, lakes, and marshes, and have made the exits from their settlements branch out in many directions because of the dangers they might face. They bury their most valuable possessions in secret places, keeping nothing unnecessary in sight. They live like bandits and love to carry out attacks against their enemies in densely wooded, narrow, and steep places. They make effective use of ambushes, sudden attacks, and raids, devising many different methods by night and by day. Their experience in crossing rivers surpasses that of all other men, and they are extremely good at spending a lot of time in the water. Often enough, when they are in their own country and are caught by surprise and in a tight spot, they dive to the bottom of a body of water. There they take long, hollow reeds they have prepared for such a situation and hold them in their mouths, the reeds extending to the surface of the water. Lying on their backs on the bottom they breathe through them and hold out for many hours without anyone suspecting where they are. . . . They are armed with short javelins, two to each man. Some also have nice-looking but unwieldy shields. In addition, they use wooden bows with short arrows smeared with a poisonous drug which is very effective. . . . Owing to their lack of government and their ill feeling toward one another, they are not acquainted with an order of battle. They are also not prepared to fight a battle standing in close order, or to present themselves on open and level ground. If they do get up enough courage when the time comes to attack, they shout all together and move forward a short distance. If their opponents begin to give way at the noise, they attack violently; if not, they themselves turn around, not being anxious to experience the strength of the enemy at close range. They then run for the woods, where they have a great advantage because of their skill in fighting in such cramped quarters. Often too when they are carrying booty they will abandon it in a feigned panic and run for the woods. When their assailants disperse after the plunder, they calmly come back and cause them injury. . . . They are completely faithless and have no regard for treaties, which they agree to more out of fear than by gifts. When a difference of opinion prevails among them, either they come to no agreement at all or when some of them do come to an agreement, the others quickly go against what was decided. They are always at odds with each other, and nobody is willing to yield to another. (Maurice, 120–122)

1.21. Theophylact Simocatta's *History*. A curious case of three Slavic pacifist musicians is reported by the historian Theophylact Simocatta, who was the imperial secretary under Heraclius (r. 610–640). In this capacity he had knowledge of Avar and Slavic matters and mentioned them in his eight-volume *Historiae*. The incident described below happened in 595. Its protagonists were most probably Pomeranian Slavs who chose not to help the Avar kagan in his war against Byzantium:

> Three men, Sclavenes by race, who were not wearing any iron or military equipment, were captured by the emperor's bodyguards. Lyres were their baggage, and they were not carrying anything else at all. And so the emperor enquired what was their nation, where was their allotted abode, and the cause of their presence in the Roman lands. They replied that they were

Sclavenes by nation and that they lived at the boundary of the western ocean [probably the Baltic]; the Chagan [kagan] had dispatched ambassadors to their parts to levy a military force and had lavished many gifts on their nation's rulers; and so they accepted the gifts but refused him the alliance, asserting that the length of the journey daunted them, while they sent back to the Chagan for the purpose of making a defence these same men who had been captured; they had completed the journey in fifteen months; but the Chagan had forgotten the law of ambassadors and had decreed a ban on their return; since they had heard that the Roman nation was much the most famous . . . for wealth and clemency, they had exploited the opportunity and retired to Thrace; they carried lyres since it was not their practice to gird weapons on their bodies, because their country was ignorant of iron and thereby provided them with a peaceful and troublefree life; they made music on lyres because they did not know how to sound forth on trumpets. (Theophylact Simocatta, 160)

1.22. The siege of Constantinople in 626. The *Paschal Chronicle*. The beginning of the seventh century saw the Slavs occupy and plunder Salona, the largest city on the Dalmatian littoral.[31] The Latin-speaking population of the region managed to retain control over a narrow strip of the coast, including the cities of Iader (Zadar), Traugurium (Trogir), Spalatum (Split), Ragusa (Dubrovnik) and Dyrrachium (Durazzo). But the most daring foray of the barbarian forces against Byzantium came in 626, when Constantinople found itself under a simultaneous attack by the combined Avar and Slav forces from the north and a Persian army encamped across the Bosphorus. The city was saved by the Byzantine fleet, which prevented the linkup of the besiegers. The Slav *monoxyla*, or canoes made of hollowed-out tree trunks, were no match for the well-equipped imperial navy. The carnage that followed the Slav attempt to reach the Persians was described in the so-called *Paschal Chronicle* (*Paskhalion* or *Chronicon Paschale*), compiled soon after the debacle:

On that Sunday [August 3, 626] the accursed kagan went to Khalai [today's Bebek] and put in the sea the *monoxyla* which were to cross to the other side [of the Bosphorus] and bring him the Persians in accordance with their promise. When this became known our naval vessels accompanied by light boats set out on the same day to Khalai, despite an unfavorable wind, in order to prevent the *monoxyla* from reaching the other shore. . . . Neither on Sunday night nor at daybreak on Monday did their boats manage to deceive our watches and cross over to the Persians. All the Slavs who came in the *monoxyla* were thrown into the sea or were slaughtered by our people. (*Paschal Chronicle*, 1013–1014)

The Byzantine victory at the walls of Constantinople freed the capital from immediate danger but could not stave off the Slav conquest of the Balkans. By the mid-seventh century most of the peninsula down to the Peloponnesus was dotted with Slav settlements, known to the Byzantines as the *Sclaviniae*. Only some coastal cities such as Ragusa, Thessalonica, Athens, or Patras escaped the Slav occupation. Isidor, the archbishop of Seville (ca. 560–636), recorded in his *Chronica* that in the sixteenth year of the reign of Heraclius "the Slavs took Greece away" from the Byzantines.[32]

31. Pope Gregory the Great (590–604) mentioned the presence of the Slavs in Dalmatia and Istria and expressed anxiety about their proximity to Italy.

32. The siege of 626 was mentioned also by the Byzantine poet George of Pisidia (first half of the seventh century) in his poems *Bellum avaricum* and *Heraclias* and by Nicephorus (c. 750–829) in his *Concise History*.

1.23. The Croats and Serbs. The testimony of Constantine Porphyrogenitus. To help contain the Avar and Slav pressure upon Illiricum, Heraclius enlisted the help of two pagan tribes, the Croats dwelling in White Croatia north of the Carpathians and the Serbs settled in White Serbia north of the Sudeten mountains along the middle course of the Elbe. Here is how Emperor Constantine Porphyrogenitus (r. 944–959) described these events in his historical treatise known as *De administrando imperio*:[33]

> The Croats [*Khrōbátoi*] who now live in the region of Dalmatia are descended from the unbaptized Croats, also called 'white', who live beyond Turkey [Pannonia, where the Turkic Huns and Avars dwelled] and next to Francia [the realm of the Franks], and have for Slav neighbors the unbaptized Serbs [*Sérbloi*]. . . . These same Croats arrived to claim the protection of the emperor of the Romans Heraclius before the Serbs claimed the protection of the same emperor Heraclius, at that time when the Avars had fought and expelled from those parts [northwestern Illiricum] the Romani.[34] . . . And so, by command of the emperor Heraclius these same Croats defeated and expelled the Avars from those parts, and by mandate of Heraclius, the emperor, they settled down in that same country of the Avars, where they now dwell. (Constantine Porphyrogenitus, 147–149)

> The Serbs are descended from the unbaptized Serbs, also called 'white', who live beyond Turkey in a place called by them Boïki [probably modern Bohemia, whose name derives from the Celtic tribe of the Boii] . . . When two brothers succeeded their father in the rule of Serbia, one of them, taking one half of the folk, claimed the protection of Heraclius [who] received him and gave him a place in the province of Thessalonica to settle in, namely Serbia, which from that time has acquired this denomination. . . . Now, after some time these same Serbs decided to depart to their own homes, and the emperor sent them off. But when they had crossed the river Danube, they changed their minds and sent a request to the emperor Heraclius through the military governor then holding Belgrade, that he would grant them other land to settle in. And since what is now Serbia [and some lands in Bosnia, Hercegovina, and southern Dalmatia] were under the dominion of the emperor . . . , therefore the emperor settled these same Serbs in these countries. (Constantine Porphyrogenitus, 153–155)

The stem *xr̥vāt-* used in the ethnic designation of the Croats, though widespread throughout Slavic territory, appears to be Iranian in origin. The etymology of *sr̥b-*, from which the tribal name of the Serbs is derived, has not been determined with certainty. It lives on to this day in the name *Serbja* 'Sorbs', who constitute a small Slavic enclave in eastern Germany (**1.7**).

1.24. The Bulgars. Theophanes the Confessor's testimony. Slavicization was also the lot of the Bulgars, a Turkic tribe which in the mid-seventh century began to migrate from the Kuban region of southern Russia, first to the delta of the Danube and then south of the

33. The reliability of Constantine's account of the settlement of the Croats and Serbs in the Balkans has had its supporters and detractors (see Jenkins et al., eds. 1962:95–101).

34. The terms *Romans* and *Romani* are meant to render the Byzantine Greek distinction between *Rhōmâioi* 'Greek-speaking Byzantines' and *Rhōmânoi* 'Latinized inhabitants of Dalmatia'. This translation, however, may be confusing, for the term *Romans* has habitually been used to designate the Latin-speaking citizens of Rome. It might be advisable, therefore, to follow the native usage and translate *Rhōmâioi* as 'Romaei' and *Rhōmânoi* as 'Romani' or 'Romans'. The term *Romaei* would accord with the usage in other languages (Russian *roméi*, Italian *Romei*) without detracting from the Byzantine insistence on the empire's Roman heritage and identity.

Danube, to Dobruja, where they settled amid the local Slavic population.[35] Theophanes the Confessor (ca. 752–818), venerated among the Orthodox for his determined stand against the iconoclasts, described the Bulgarian conquest of Dobruja and the events leading up to it in his *Chronographia* under the year 6171 (679/680):[36]

> Also, the Bulgarian people attacked Thrace at this time. . . . The ancient Great Bulgaria stretches from the Sea of Azov along the Kouphis river [probably the Bay of Taganrog]. . . . The Kotrigurs, who are related to the Bulgars, also live there. During the period when Constantine [IV, r. 668–685] was in the west, Krobatos, the lord of Bulgaria and the Kotrigurs, died. He left behind five sons. . . . A little while after his death these five sons separated from one another, along with the folk subject to each of them. [There follows an account of the fates of the two oldest and two youngest brothers.]
>
> Now, the third brother, called Asparukh, crossed the Dnieper and the Dniester and reached the Oglos . . . rivers [probably the delta of the Danube] . . . , settling between them and the Danube. He thought the location secure and invincible from all sides, for it was marshy ahead and surrounded by rivers in other directions. It provided his people, who had been weakened by their division, relief from their enemies. . . . The Emperor Constantine was galled to learn that a foul, unclean tribe was living between the Danube and the Oglos, and that it had sallied forth to ravage the land near the Danube . . . He ordered all the thematic armies[37] to cross over into Thrace, equipped an expeditionary force, and moved against the Bulgars by land and sea, attempting to dislodge them by force. [There follows an account of the war against the Bulgars ending with the Byzantines fleeing in panic.]
>
> When the Bulgars saw this, they did pursue, putting many [Byzantines] to the sword and wounding others. They chased them to the Danube, crossed it, and came to Varna near Odyssos and its hinterland. They saw that it was securely located: from behind because of the river Danube and from the front and sides because of the mountain passes and the Black Sea. When the Bulgars became the masters of the seven tribes of Sclavini in the vicinity, they resettled the Sebereis [probably the tribe of the Severi] . . . to the east, and the remainder of the seven tribes to the south and west up to the land of the Avars. Since the Bulgars were pagan at that time, they bore themselves arrogantly and began to assail and take cities and villages under the control of the Roman Empire [Byzantium]. The emperor had to make peace with them because of this, and agreed to pay them an annual tribute. . . . Folk far and near were amazed to hear that the emperor, who had subjected everyone to himself, had been beaten by this newly arrived loathsome tribe. (Theophanes the Confessor, 55–57)

The Byzantines, weakened by wars against Sassanid Persia and by continuous Avar and Slav incursions, had to resign themselves to losing a sizable chunk of their territory. In 681 they recognized the existence of the new state and signed a peace treaty with its leader, Ka-

35. A branch of the Bulgars settled near the confluence of the Volga and Kama rivers. This location made them an important link on the eastern trade route, which in the ninth and tenth centuries connected the Baltic and Caspian seas.

36. Another famous iconodule who described the Bulgarian invasion of Dobruja was Nicephorus, the future patriarch of Constantinople (806–815).

37. In the seventh century the Byzantine empire was organized into districts called themes, each with its own capital, administration, and army. The strategus of a theme was at the same time its governor and military leader. The theme of Thrace was one of the earliest to be set up in order to defend the northern approaches to Constantinople against the Bulgars. An administrative subdivision of the theme was the drungus (Gk. *droûggos*), governed and commanded by a drungary. The father of Constantine and Methodius (**1.31**) was a drungary, presumably in the theme of Macedonia.

gan Asparuch. The establishment of a powerful state on the northern border of the empire altered radically the balance of power in Europe and for a time weakened Byzantium's political influence among the Slavs. Linguistically, however, it turned out to be a boon to the Slavic population in the Balkans. From a culturally inferior group threatened with imminent Hellenization (the actual lot of the Slavs in Epirus, Thessaly, and the Peloponnesus), the Slavs became a linguistically dominant force among the Bulgarian newcomers. Within a few generations, the Bulgars began to lose their Turkic linguistic identity, and from the ninth century on Bulgaria may be considered a Slavic state. This development had incalculable consequences for Slavic vernacular culture during its formative years in the second half of the ninth century. At that time Bulgaria was the only Slavic state powerful enough to resist both the Byzantines and the Carolingians. It thus became the natural breeding ground for Slavic letters.

1.25. Christianity among the Balkan Slavs. The acceptance of Christianity by the Slavs is usually connected with the arrival of the Byzantine mission of Constantine and Methodius in Moravia in 863. Yet the Slavs must have become exposed to Christianity as soon as they overran the Balkan peninsula and came into contact with the local Christian population. As a matter of fact, according to Constantine Porphyrogenitus, Heraclius made an attempt to Christianize the Slavic-speaking Croats and Serbs as soon as he brought them in to help the Byzantines in their fight against the Avars (Constantine Porphyrogenitus, 149 and 155).[38]

Since Illiricum, the western part of the Balkan peninsula, was till 732 ecclesiastically subject to the Roman patriarchate, it is not surprising that the early missionary activity of the Byzantines among the Balkan Slavs should be matched by similar efforts emanating from the West. In the seventh and eighth centuries these efforts must have been spearheaded by the Latin towns on the Adriatic such as Nona (Nin), where the first Croatian bishopric was to be founded in 850, Jader (Zadar), and Spalatum (Split), with its long Christian tradition. The main thrust of Western missionary work among the Slavs, however, was naturally enough directed not at the Balkans but rather at Central Europe, where the Slavs reached the eastern confines of the Germanic possessions along the line connecting the mouth of the Elbe with the Adriatic. It is therefore the Central European Slavs that will now command our attention.

1.26. Samo's Slavic state in Central Europe. Fredegar's testimony. It is likely that the western Slavs crossed the Oder and the Elbe in connection with the Avar attacks on Gaul in 562 and 566, at the time of the invasion of the Balkans by the southern Slavs. The chroniclers, however, do not confirm such an early Slavic presence in Central Europe.

Our first source of information on the subject is an anonymous Merovingian chronicle attributed to Fredegar.[39] It reports military encounters between the Franks and the Slavs in the region of Thuringia, from the first half of the seventh century on. It tells, in particular, of the creation of a Slavic state under the leadership of a renegade Frankish merchant named Samo,[40] who led an uprising of several Central European Slavic tribes against the Avars. After helping the Slavs gain a victory, Samo stayed on to rule the tribal confederation. Here is an excerpt from Fredegar's account of the Samo episode:

38. See Dvornik 1964:88–91, 100, on this and other early Christian missions among the Croats and Serbs.

39. The original part of the chronicle provides the history of the Franks from 584 till 642 and was composed in the mid-seventh century in Burgundy. It was later continued and brought up to 768, the year of Pepin the Short's death.

40. The name appears to be Celtic, which would indicate that Samo was a Gallo-Roman. Such an origin could account for Samo's vindictive sentiments against the Franks.

> In the fortieth year of Chlotar's reign [Clotaire II, r. 584–629], a certain Frank named Samo . . . joined with other merchants in order to go and do business with those Slavs who are known as Wends. The Slavs had already started to rise against the Avars, called Huns,[41] and against their ruler, the kagan. . . . Every year the Huns wintered with the Slavs, sleeping with their wives and daughters, and in addition the Slavs paid tribute and endured many other burdens. The sons born to the Huns by the Slavs' wives and daughters eventually found this shameful oppression intolerable; and so . . . they refused to obey their lords and started to rise in rebellion. When they took the field against the Huns, Samo, the merchant, . . . went with them and his bravery won their admiration: an astonishing number of Huns were put to the sword by the Wends. Recognizing his usefulness, the Wends made Samo their king; and he ruled them well for thirty-five years. Several times they fought under his leadership against the Huns and his prudence and courage always brought the Wends victory. Samo had twelve Wendish wives, who bore him twenty-two sons and fifteen daughters. (Fredegar, 39–40)

Fredegar tells also of Samo's military exploits against the Franks. In 630 Dagobert I (r. 628–638), the last great Merovingian ruler, demanded that Samo pay reparations for the many Frankish merchants robbed and killed by the Slavs. When Samo haughtily refused to comply, Dagobert

> ordered the raising of a force throughout his kingdom of Austrasia to proceed against Samo and the Wends. Three corps set out against the Wends. [There follows an account of the victories of the Lombards and the Alemanni.] Dagobert's Austrasians, on the other hand, invested the stronghold of Wogastisburg [probably in Bohemia] . . . and were crushed in a three-day battle. And so they made for home, leaving all their tents and equipment behind them in their flight. After this the Wends made many a plundering sortie into Thuringia and the neighboring districts of the kingdom of the Franks. Furthermore Dervan, the duke of the Sorbs, a people of Slav origin long subject to the Franks, placed himself and his people under the rule of Samo. (Fredegar, 57)

Samo's Slavic confederation did not survive its founder (he led it from 624 till 659). In fact, its abrupt disappearance from the records of history makes it difficult to determine its precise location. The scanty evidence available points to parts of Lusatia, Bohemia, Moravia, and Carantania.

1.27. The Alpine Slavs. Paul the Deacon's testimony. If Fredegar's chronicle is our main source of knowledge on the early history of the Slavs living north of the Danube, the earliest information on the Slavs in the Alpine region between the Danube and the Adriatic—that is, in the East March (modern Austria), Carantania (Carinthia and Styria), and the Friulian March (Istria and eastern Venetia)—is provided by the Lombard historian Paul the Deacon (ca. 720–ca. 790), one of the most learned men of his time. Paul's six-volume *Historia Langobardorum* recounts the history of the Lombards from their legendary beginnings in Scandinavia to their settlement in Italy. It tells, among other episodes, of the maritime expedition that the Slavs mounted in 642 against Benevento, a Lombard duchy in southern Italy. Benevento was ruled at that time by Aio and his affined brothers, Radoald and Grimoald, both of whom were born and raised in Friuli (Forum Iulii). In Paul's words,

41. Contemporaneous sources consistently referred to the Avars as Huns.

> the Slavs came with a great number of ships and set up their camp not far from the city of Sipontum (Siponto). They made hidden pit-falls around their camp and when Aio came upon them in the absence of Radoald and Grimoald and attempted to conquer them, his horse fell into one of these pit-falls, the Slavs rushed upon him and he was killed with a number of others. When this was announced to Radoald, he came quickly and talked familiarly with these Slavs in their own language. (Paul the Deacon, 199)

This incident shows the extent of the Slavicization of the Friulian March in the seventh century. Radoald, a scion of an aristocratic Friulian Lombard family, must have learned Slavic from the local population during his childhood and adolescence in Friuli.[42]

Although Samo's confederation was short-lived, the Alpine region of Carantania, which was its southernmost member, did enjoy a brief period of political independence. However, wedged between the Avars to the east, the Bavarians to the northwest, and the Lombards to the southwest, Carantania could not hope to preserve its freedom. Under Duke Boruta (r. ca. 743–748), the Carantanians (ancestors of today's Slovenes) had to plead for Bavarian help against the marauding Avars. In exchange they submitted to Bavarian and, ultimately, Frankish sovereignty.[43]

1.28. The Carantanian mission. The testimony of the *Conversio Bagoariorum et Carantanorum*. Carantania's political dependence upon the Bavarians brought about increased missionary efforts among the local Slavs. These efforts may have begun as early as the year 600, when the work of the Irish missions in nearby Bavaria could have spilled into Carantania. Definitely documented is the work of the Irish monk Virgil, who in 746/747 was appointed bishop of Salzburg. His evangelizing endeavors in Carantania earned him the designation as the apostle of the Slovenes. It was under his guidance that Boruta's son Gorazd (Cacatius) and his nephew Hotimir (r. ca. 751–769) adopted Christianity and helped to spread it among the Carantanian Slavs.

The victories of Charlemagne and his son Pepin over the Avars in Pannonia (791–803) and the subsequent southeasterly expansion of the Carolingian empire offered new opportunities for Christian missions in Carantania. The missionary work proceeded from two centers, the old patriarchate of Aquileia in the south and Salzburg in the north. Salzburg,which in 798 was promoted to the rank of archbishopric, instituted a training program for missionaries aimed specifically at the conversion of the Slavs. It is probable that the Slavic prayers in the so-called *Freising Fragments* (**3.41.5**) are an example of a vernacular text prepared for use in such missionary schools. The intensity of the missionary efforts in Carantania led to disagreements between the metropolitan sees in Aquileia and Salzburg about the limits of their diocesan domains. The controversy was settled at the synod convened in 796 "on the banks of the Danube," at which the river Drava was designated as the boundary between the rival churches. This division was ratified by Charlemagne during his visit to Salzburg in 803 and again in 811 in Aachen.

The vigor with which Salzburg engaged in missionary work in Carantania led to a num-

42. Paul recounts an interesting story about his family's debt of gratitude to the Slavs. It appears that one of his direct ancestors, while escaping from Avar captivity, became lost in the woods. Faint with fatigue, he appealed to a Slav woman for help. She nursed him back to health, supplied him with provisions, and directed him back to Italy.

43. Yet Carantania managed to retain a measure of political autonomy within the Frankish empire. It was symbolized by the use of a Slavic formula during the local ceremony of the installation of the German dukes, a custom that survived into the fifteenth century; see Kuhar 1962:51–66.

ber of pagan revolts. These are mentioned in one of the most interesting documents of the period, the so-called *Conversio Bagoariorum et Carantanorum* (*Conversion of the Bavarians and Carantanians*), commissioned in 870 by Archbishop Adalwin of Salzburg (859–873) in order to emphasize the role played by his diocese in the evangelization of the Carantanian Slavs. Here is how the *Conversio* presents the missionary activities emanating from Salzburg during the rule of the Carantanian dukes Hotimir and Waltunc[44] and the pagan reactions to them:

> After some time the above-mentioned duke of the Carantanians [Hotimir] asked bishop Virgil to visit his people in order to fortify them in their faith. He [Virgil] could not do this in any way and, to instruct those people, he sent in his place his bishop, named Modestus, along with his priests, Watto, Reginbertus, Cozharius and Latinus, as well as the deacon Ekihardus with other clerics. He gave Modestus the right to consecrate churches and to ordain priests in accordance with the canonical law, and he enjoined him from taking anything upon himself which would go against the decrees of the holy fathers. After they came to Carantania, they consecrated there the church of St. Mary and another one in the town of Liburnia and one *ad Undrimas* as well as in many other places.[45] Modestus remained there to the end of his life [ca. 765]. When he died, duke Hotimir again asked bishop Virgil to come to him if possible. The latter declined because a mutiny, which we call *carmula*,[46] had begun. However, he decided to send there the priest, Latinus. Soon afterward, there was another uprising and the priest Latinus departed. After the *carmula* was settled, bishop Virgil sent there the priest Madalhohus and, after him, the priest Warmannus. After the death of Hotimir, another uprising began and for several years there was no priest there, until their [Carantanian] duke Waltunc sent again to bishop Virgil and asked him to send priests. (*Conversio*, 42, 44)

Pagan resistance notwithstanding, one may assume that by the end of the eighth century a considerable portion of Carantania was Christianized and ecclesiastically subject to the metropolitan see in Salzburg.

1.29. The Aquileian mission. The *Gospel of Cividale*. Since Charlemagne's 811 decision, the missionary thrust from the patriarchate of Aquileia was supposed to be directed at the Slavic settlements south of the Drava. Nonetheless, as we learn from Chapter V of the vita of Methodius (**1.34**), the radius of the "Italian," that is, Aquileian or Lombard evangelizing efforts in the first half of the ninth century was still long enough to reach into Moravia. It is clear, however, that the missionary zeal of the Aquileian patriarchs was much weaker than that emanating from Salzburg. Patriarch Paulinus II (777–802), prodded by his English friend Alcuin, did engage in some missionary activity, but he did so on a much more limited scale than his Salzburg counterparts, the archbishops Virgil (746/747–784) and Arno (785–821). Paulinus' successors, the patriarchs Ursus (803–811) and Maxentius (811–842), continued the evangelization of the Slavs, but little is known of its extent.

44. The name Waltunc probably contains the root **vold-* 'rule' which is frequent in Slavic first names; cf. Russian Church Slavonic *Vladímir* and its native hypocoristic modification *Volódja* with *polnoglasie* (**2.35.c**).

45. None of the three churches mentioned in the *Conversio* has survived. The identity of the first two, however, can be established. Of these, St. Mary's church near Karnburg (Krnski Grad) is called Gospa Sveta (The Holy Lady) in Slovenian and Maria Saal in German. It was the first Slavic church to be consecrated, and it became the base of the Carantanian mission.

46. This Popular Latin term was probably borrowed from OBa. *karmala*. It spread also into Slavic, witness OCS *kramola* 'uprising' and OESl. *koromóla* 'intrigue' (Vasmer/Trubačev 1967:365–366).

Aquileia, however, offers an oblique source for the history of the Christian penetration into the Slavic lands. It is provided by the so-called *Gospel of Cividale* (*Codex Aquileiensis*), a sixth-century Latin evangeliary originally kept in one of the Aquileian monasteries. This gospel was believed to be much older than it actually was and to be endowed therefore with miraculous powers. Hence, many distinguished visitors or benefactors of the monastery either signed personally or had their names entered on the margins of the manuscript. Among these signatures there are more than 350 Slavic names, including such celebrities as the dukes Kocel and Pribina of Pannonia, Rostislav and Svatopluk of Moravia, Braslav and Trpimir of Croatia, and Tsar Boris/Michael of Bulgaria.

1.30. Moravia and Pannonia in the ninth century. The Carolingian expeditions against the Avars led to a total destruction of the Avar state and to a dispersal of its population, creating a political vacuum in the basin of the middle Danube. The eastern part of this region up to the river Tisza (Theiss) was annexed by the expanding Bulgarian kaganate, the western sections of Pannonia passed under the Frankish jurisdiction as part of the East Mark within the Frankish system of marks or militarized frontier regions, and Bohemia became a Frankish vassal state. The only Slavic tribes that, for a while at least, succeeded in staying clear of either the Bulgarian or Frankish domination were settled north of the Danube, along the river Morava. Their state, which has come to be known as Moravia, enjoyed periods of political independence throughout the ninth century. Under its skillful rulers, Mojmir I (d. 846), Rostislav (r. 846–870), and Svatopluk (r. 871–894), Moravia extended its possessions in all directions. In 833, Duke Mojmir captured the Pannonian territories of his eastern neighbor, Duke Pribina of Nitra (modern Slovakia), and expelled him beyond the Danube to central Pannonia (modern Hungary). There were also Moravian thrusts into southern Poland, Bohemia, and parts of Silesia and Lusatia. Moravia's status as a Central European power is reflected in the name Greater Moravia, given to it by Constantine Porphyrogenitus. Nonetheless, the country remained within the political and ecclesiastic orbit of the Frankish state, and the Moravian ruling elite became Christian at the hands of the Bavarian clergy.

Pannonia was also of interest to Byzantium, which alone among the powers of the area could claim the formerly Avar lands on the Danube as its historical patrimony. The politically complex situation of Pannonia was aggravated by its ill-defined ecclesiastic status. The other Slavic lands on the southeastern periphery of the Frankish empire had more or less well forged links with either the patriarchate of Aquileia or any of the four Bavarian dioceses established by Boniface in 739, Carantania with Salzburg and Freising, Bohemia with Regensburg, and Moravia with Passau. Pannonia, however, before the Great Migrations was within the ecclesiastic jurisdiction of Constantinople. Technically speaking, the Frankish missionaries operating there were treading on Byzantine turf. Thus, in the first half of the ninth century Pannonia, though formally Frankish, could still be considered an unorganized territory. Its political fate was not to be permanently resolved till the beginning of the tenth century, when it was seized by the invading Magyars.

Moravia's political and religious dependence on the Franks prompted Duke Rostislav to seek the establishment of an autonomous Moravian church under the direct jurisdiction of Rome rather than as part of the Bavarian ecclesiastic hierarchy. With this end in mind, Rostislav sent out a call for Slavic-speaking missionaries who could translate and preach the Gospel in Slavic in order to neutralize and eventually preempt the work of the German clergy.[47] Rostislav's initiative brought about what has turned out to be the most momentous event in the cultural history of the Slavs, the arrival in Pannonia and Moravia in the fall of 863 of a Christian mission led by two Slavic-speaking Greek churchmen, the brothers Constantine and Methodius. Constantine, who headed the mission despite being ten years younger than Methodius, is also known as Cyril (hence the term *Cyrillo-Methodian*), a name he assumed when he took the monastic vows shortly before his death.

1.31. The Cyrillo-Methodian sources. The role and legacy of Constantine and Methodius in the development of Slavic letters, whether reflected in their own actions in connection with the mission to Moravia or in the activities of their disciples and followers in other Slavic countries, have come to be known as the Cyrillo-Methodian tradition. Our knowledge of the beginnings of that tradition comes from a variety of sources.

The *vitae* or hagiographies (**3.46**) deal directly with the lives and accomplishments of the brothers and their associates and provide the bulk of our knowledge about them. Especially informative are their so-called extensive or full vitae (*prostranьnaja žitija*), also known as the *Pannonian Legends* and referred to usually in Latin as *Vita Constantini* and *Vita Methodii*. The former exists in more than fifty copies, none, unfortunately, earlier than the fifteenth century, while the latter has come down to us in fifteen copies, the oldest of which is in the *Uspenskij sbornik* of the late twelfth or thirteenth century. (English translations are available in Kantor 1983 and Dujčev 1985.)

Deriving from the extensive vitae are the abbreviated vitae found in liturgical synaxaria or prologues (*prologi*), as they are known in the East Slavic tradition (hence, *proložьnaja žitija* or prologue vitae).[48] Some of them bring otherwise unknown details from the biographies of the brothers. Thus, a thirteenth-century South Slavic prologue vita of Constantine and Methodius (the so-called *Serbian Legend*) identifies Methodius' burial place as "the left side of the wall behind the altar of the Mother of God in the Moravian cathedral," presumably in the Moravian capital of Velehrad. Other prologue vitae mention Kanaon (Kaon, Kain, Nain) as the Slavic location of the brothers' activity.

Confirming the information provided by the much more detailed *Vita Constantini* is the Latin vita of Constantine, *Vita cum translatione s. Clementis,* also known as the *Italian Legend.* It was written most probably by the bishop of Velletri, Gauderich, who is otherwise known for his participation in the ceremony of the ordination of the Slavic disciples brought by Constantine and Methodius to Rome. The *Italian Legend* provides a summary of the life of Constantine and a fairly detailed account of the story of the finding of St. Clement's relics and their translation to Rome. The usual view is that the *Italian Legend* derives from the *Vita Constantini*; the relation between the two texts, however, is a matter of some scholarly contention (Devos and Meyvaert 1955). It is possible that its author obtained his data either directly from Constantine during the latter's visit to Rome or indirectly from the papal secretary (*bibliothecarius*) Anastasius, who was Constantine's friend and admirer. It is known, at any rate, that Anastasius translated Constantine's *Discourse on the Discovery and Translation of the Relics of St. Clement* (also called the *Kherson Legend* or *Brevis Historia*) into Latin

47. Despite the traditional view according to which Rostislav's appeal was sent specifically to the Byzantine emperor Michael III, there is no reason to doubt the claim of Pope Hadrian II that it was originally addressed to the Holy See as well (**1.36**).

48. The Slavic term *prologъ* was derived metonymically from Gk. *prólogos* 'preface'.

and mentioned it in his correspondence with Gauderich. The *Discourse* survives in a late Slavic translation (Vašica 1948). An outgrowth of the *Italian Legend* is the so-called *Moravian Legend* compiled in Bohemia in the twelfth century.

A monument bearing directly on the careers of Constantine and Methodius and on the Bulgarian chapter of their mission is the so-called *Bulgarian Legend* or the vita of Clement of Ohrid, composed in Greek in the beginning of the twelfth century by the archbishop of Ohrid, Theophylact. Especially interesting is Theophylact's account of the defeat and dispersal of the Moravian mission following the death of Methodius.[49] A Church Slavonic translation of the *Bulgarian Legend* has survived in several variants, the oldest of which is in a fourteenth/fifteenth-century codex kept in the State Public Library in Moscow.

Another monument dealing with the dissolution of the Moravian mission, its transplantation to Bulgaria, and Moravia's devastation (seen as a fulfillment of Methodius' prophecy) is the prologue vita of Naum, one of the disciples of Constantine and Methodius. It has survived in three Slavic and two Greek versions.[50]

Interesting, though historically unreliable, is a Bulgarian text of the fifteenth/sixteenth centuries called the *Dormition of Cyril the Philosopher.* It also derives from the extensive vita of Constantine but adds to it unverifiable Bulgarian episodes. Completely legendary is a late Bulgarian "autobiography" of Constantine, known as the *Thessalonican Legend.*

Important persons and events in the history of the church are commemorated in liturgical offices (*službby*), which bring together different texts pertinent to the particular occasion. Some of the surviving variants of the offices for Constantine and Methodius go back to the twelfth century. Unfortunately, the poeticized form of the offices makes it difficult to evaluate the reliability of new information contained in them. Such a problem is posed, for instance, by a line in the office for Methodius (April 6) from the *Dragan Menaeum* (**3.41.5**) which maintains that before entering the monastery Methodius had been married: "Having left your family, your country, your wife and your children, . . . you chose to live in the wilderness with the holy fathers" (Lavrov 1930, 123).

Artistically related to the offices are commemorative sermons or eulogies (*poxvaly* or *poxvalьnaja slovesa*). One such sermon, dedicated to Constantine and Methodius, has been attributed by many investigators to Clement of Ohrid. Two variants of the sermon have survived, the oldest in the *Uspenskij sbornik* of the twelfth/thirteenth centuries. Its highly ornate prose may be seen from the following account of the ability and prowess with which the brothers stood up for Christianity during their encounter with the Khazars:

> Among the Saracens and the Khazars [Constantine and Methodius] were invincible. For just as David once destroyed the pride of the alien and laid him low with three stones symbolizing the Trinity, and cutting off his head with his sword earned the praise of the multitudes among the sons of Israel, so now these fathers who were servants and ministers of the trihypostatic Divinity, finding themselves in the assembly of the Saracens and Jews, destroyed Islamic aberrations and Jewish iniquity with their own books and in their own language, cutting them down like weeds with a spiritual sword and burning them down with spiritual Grace. And they sowed the Divine Word like wheat on the field of their hearts and delighted all with

49. An excerpt of the description of the altercation between the Slavic monks and Frankish clerics is given in **1.36.**

50. The fifteenth-century copy from the monastery of St. Zographos on Mt. Athos and the sixteenth-century copy from the National Library in Belgrade are available in Lavrov 1930 and in an English translation in Dujčev 1985.

words flowing like honey. They openly preached the Divine Trinity which is without beginning, and taught that the Father, the Son, and the Holy Spirit shine equally in one essence. And thus they caught them like fish with a net of words and baptized up to two hundred among the Khazar nobles, not counting women or children. (Lavrov 1930, 84)

Historical writings are of course useful as sources of information (**3.50**). A brief history of the Moravian mission is included in the East Slavic *Primary Chronicle* under the year 898. It provides a laudatory summary of the missionary work of Constantine and Methodius, comparing it to the apostolic activity of St. Paul. The concise entries on the brothers in the chronographs also invoke St. Paul's precedent.[51]

Among ancillary sources, the most important is the treatise *On the Letters* by the monk Khrabr, which extols the role of the brothers in the creation of the Slavic alphabet (**3.49**). In the preface to the *Theology* John the Exarch credits the work of Constantine and Methodius with being the inspiration of his own translation. The two earliest Slavic poetic compositions, the *Preface to the Gospel* and the *Alphabet Prayer*, testify to the reverence in which the newly invented Slavic letters were held (**3.47**). Three Latin communications of Anastasius provide a moving testimony of his admiration for Constantine's achievements. A letter from the papal *bibliothecarius* may, in fact, have provided Bishop Gauderich of Velletri with some of the material for the *Italian Legend* (see above).

Records of diplomatic exchanges contemporary with Constantine and Methodius capture the immediacy and the flavor of the historical drama as it unfolds, providing us with a view unobstructed by later, more or less legendary accretions. Especially important is the papal correspondence with the main personages of the period. The 869 letter from Pope Hadrian II to the dukes Rostislav, Svatopluk, and Kocel introducing Methodius as the new bishop of Pannonia and Moravia exists in a Church Slavonic translation in the *Vita Methodii*. Of the ten letters written in 873 by Hadrian's successor, John VIII, five protest the imprisonment of Methodius in Swabia (to Adalvin, the archbishop of Salzburg; Paul of Ancona, the papal legate to Germany and Pannonia; Hermanrich, the bishop of Passau; Anno, the bishop of Freising; and King Carlomann). Two letters of John VIII addressed to Duke Svatopluk of Moravia deal with Methodius' third trip to Rome in 880. The second of these letters (incipit *Industriae tuae*) confirms the pope's sanction of the use of Slavic for services, biblical readings, and sermons. In the letter of 881 John VIII addresses Methodius himself in order to reassure him that he has the pope's full support. Two 885 letters from Pope Stephen V (VI) have also been preserved, forbidding the use of Slavic in the divine service but allowing it in sermons. (Selections from papal correspondence are given in **1.36.**)

In the *Conversio Bagoariorum et Carantanorum* of 871 Archbishop Adalwin of Salzburg attempts to show the historical rights of his metropolis in Carantania [and Pannonia]. Large portions of this memorandum are quoted in **1.28** and **1.37.**

1.32. Early careers of Constantine and Methodius. Constantine and Methodius were born in Thessalonica (Slavic *Solunь*) into the family of a well-to-do Byzantine drungary (see n. 37). Constantine, born in 826, was the youngest of the seven children in the family. Methodius was about ten years his senior. The countryside around Thessalonica was at that time

51. A short account of the mission is included in the chronicle of the "Slavic kingdom" composed in the twelfth [?] century by an anonymous priest from Duklja and preserved in a seventeenth-century Latin version as the *Presbyteri Diocleatis regnum Sclavorum*.

predominantly Slavic, and it is fair to assume that the brothers grew up bilingual, with a quasi-native knowledge of the local Macedonian dialect of Slavic.

From his youngest years, Constantine showed an exceptional aptitude and passion for learning, a trait which, later in life, was to earn him the epithet of Philosopher. His education, begun in Thessalonica, continued in Constantinople under the tutelage of two of the most outstanding scholars of the time, Leo the Mathematician and Photius, the future ecumenical patriarch (858–867 and 878–886). Constantine's extraordinary intellectual achievements were recognized and appreciated in the capital; they earned him the personal protection of the highest government official, Theoctistus the Logothete, who eventually offered him the position of librarian to the patriarch in the cathedral of St. Sophia. Constantine, however, preferred a career of scholarship and, around the year 850, accepted a chair of philosophy at the University of Constantinople.

Methodius' early career is less well documented. We know that he embarked initially upon government service, accepting an appointment as archon of a Slavic archontate (*knęženije* in the Church Slavonic of *Uspenskij sbornik*). The location of this Slavic district is a matter of conjecture. Perhaps it was in Methodius' native region of Thessalonica, as Dvornik (1970:58) surmises, perhaps in some other region of the Byzantine empire, in one of the many Slavic provinces left over from the Slavic conquest of the Balkans two hundred years before. At any rate, it would seem logical that Methodius' knowledge of Slavic was at least partly responsible for his selection. Methodius spent some twelve years in his post, but about 855, tired of the administrative career, he decided to don the monastic garb:

> He saw much disorderly tumult in this life and exchanged the desire of earthly darkness for heavenly thoughts. He did not wish to trouble his noble soul with transient matters. And finding the right moment, he gave up the governorship. And having gone to Olympus where holy fathers live, he had himself tonsured and clothed in black habit. And he humbly submitted to and fulfilled all the monastic rules and applied himself to the Scriptures. (*Vita Methodii* 3)

In or about 856, probably as a consequence of political upheavals in the capital, Constantine relinquished his teaching post in Constantinople and joined Methodius in the monastery on Mt. Olympus, in Bithynia just across the Bosporus. However, the two brothers were not destined to dwell long in the tranquility of monastic life. Within three years of Constantine's arrival at Mt. Olympus, they had to embark on an arduous foreign mission which took them across the Black Sea and overland to the shores of the Caspian. That was the mission to the Khazars, which is described at length in the *Vita Constantini*.[52]

1.33. The mission to the Khazars. It appears that the Khazars, a Turkic people inhabiting the plains between the lower Volga and the Don, were at that time uncertain which of the three great Western religions to adopt, Judaism, Christianity, or Islam (Dunlop 1967). This dilemma prompted the kagan of the Khazars to ask for learned Byzantine envoys who would be able to explicate the Christian doctrine to his people and help them out of their quandary.[53] Whereupon Emperor Michael III called upon Constantine to head the embassy to the Kha-

52. After the completion of the mission to the Khazars, Methodius returned to Mt. Olympus to assume the hegumenship of the Polychron Monastery.

53. Initial hesitation concerning which faith to adopt was a stock theme in accounts of Christian proselytizing efforts. Compare the tale of a similar difficulty experienced more than one hundred years later by the Kievan Slavs, as reported in the *Primary Chronicle*.

zars "to preach and answer for the Holy Trinity . . . for no one else is capable of doing this properly" (*Vita Constantini* 8). When Constantine agreed to undertake the mission, Methodius volunteered to accompany his younger brother.

The Byzantine embassy reached the Crimea in 860 and spent the winter in the Greek colony of Kherson (Khersones) on the southwest shore of the peninsula. During his short stay there, Constantine is said to have displayed uncommon linguistic gifts. Preparing himself for the forthcoming meeting with the Khazars, he learned Hebrew, translated a Hebrew grammar, and taught himself to understand Samaritan scriptures. He also learned a language whose identity, unfortunately, cannot be established with certainty but which is variously understood to be Semitic, Slavic, or Germanic (**3.5**).

Constantine's most important achievement during his stay in Kherson was the recovery of the holy relics of St. Clement, the third bishop of Rome (88–97?), who was believed to have died a martyr's death in the Crimea. Although this belief appears to be apocryphal,[54] a part of the relics accompanied the brothers on their future mission to Moravia and was eventually deposited by them in the basilica of St. Clement in Rome, the church in which Constantine (by then, Cyril) was to be buried in 869.[55]

The *Vita Constantini* tells us that Constantine and Methodius traveled to Khazaria by way of the Sea of Azov and the Caspian Gates of the Caucasian Mountains. It is silent, however, on the precise location of the meeting with the Khazar elders and their kagan. Most authorities assume that the meeting took place in the summer residence of the kagan in Samander, near today's Derbent, on the western shore of the Caspian Sea (Dvornik 1970:67–68).

On the other hand, the debates that took place at a series of meetings are described at considerable length and in great detail. Constantine was called upon to defend and justify Christianity against the arguments proffered mainly by the local Jews. The deliberations covered such doctrinal matters as the dogma of the Holy Trinity, the Immaculate Conception, circumcision, Jesus as the Messiah, the worship of images, and the dietary laws. The *Vita Constantini* expatiates on Constantine's theological learning and debating skills, which allowed him to defeat his Jewish and Moslem opponents. In the words of one of the participants of the disputations, "With God's help this guest has cast the entire pride of the Jews on the ground, while [the pride of the Saracens] has he cast to the other side of the river like filth" (*Vita Constantini* 11). Constantine departed from Khazaria accompanied by two hundred Greek captives freed upon his request by the grateful kagan. He also carried a letter from the Khazar kagan to the Byzantine emperor: "Lord, you have sent us a man who in word and deeds has shown us that the Christian faith is holy. Having convinced ourselves that it is the true faith, we have urged all to be baptized voluntarily in the hope that we too will attain it. We are all friends of your Empire and are ready to serve you wherever you require it" (*Vita Constantini* 11).[56]

1.34. The background of the Moravian mission. Rostislav's diplomatic appeal for Slavic-speaking missionaries arrived in Constantinople around 860. It was carefully worded so as not to offend the sensibilities of the Bavarian clergy. It cited the presence in Moravia

54. There may have been some local martyred saint called Clement whom popular tradition confused with the pope (Dvornik 1970:66–67).

55. According to the *Primary Chronicle*, the Kievan duke Vladimir transferred the other part of the relics from Kherson to Kiev on the occasion of the baptism of Rus' in 988.

56. The kagan's assurances notwithstanding, the Khazars adopted Judaism as their state religion.

of missionaries from many lands, including Byzantium, and the resulting confusion: "We have prospered through God's grace, and many Christian teachers have come to us from among the Italians, Greeks, and Germans, teaching us in various ways. But we Slavs are simple people [*prosta čędь*], and have none to instruct us in the truth and explicate it. Therefore, Good Lord, send such a man who would teach us the whole truth" (*Vita Methodii* 5). It also contained a request for missionaries willing to teach the Gospel in the vernacular rather than in Latin, a practice that was common in the Eastern churches (Armenian, Coptic, and Syriac) but totally unprecedented in the West: "Though our people have rejected paganism and observe Christian law, we do not have a teacher who would explain to us in our language the true Christian faith so that other countries which look to us might emulate us" (*Vita Constantini* 14).

The invitation was addressed to the youthful emperor Michael III (r. 842–867), but the decision to act on it was certainly not his alone. The actual rulers of Byzantium at that time were the emperor's uncle Bardas Caesar and the patriarch of Constantinople, Photius. It was most probably the latter who selected his former pupil to head the mission to Moravia.[57] Constantine's accomplishments in Khazaria and his well-known linguistic skills made him an obvious choice. It was soon to be vindicated: "And, following his old habit, the Philosopher went and gave himself up to prayer together with his other disciples. And God, who hearkens to the prayers of his servants, soon appeared to him. And he immediately devised the letters and began to write the words of the Gospel: 'In the beginning was the Word, and the Word was with God, and the Word was God,' and so on" (*Vita Constantini* 14).

The selection of the beginning of the Gospel of St. John for Constantine's first translation into Slavic is, of course, not accidental. On the one hand, it points up the linguistic and inspirational nature of Constantine's efforts. On the other, it probably reflects the order of Constantine's translating enterprise, for the first item on the mission's agenda was to provide the Moravians "with all the Scriptures which were considered necessary for church service" (*Italian Legend* 7).[58] One such liturgical book is the evangeliary or Sunday Gospel, in which Gospel texts are arranged for reading on Sundays and church holidays (**3.41.1**). The fact is that Byzantine evangeliaries always begin with the first words of John.[59]

Though the language of the first translations prepared by Constantine and Methodius must have reflected the peculiarities of the dialect of their native Thessalonica, it is safe to assume that in the brothers' lifetime the linguistic differences among the various Slavic provinces were negligible. In the mid-ninth century one may still talk of the various dialects of Proto-Slavic rather than of different Slavic languages. It is therefore perfectly natural to expect the Slavic translations executed by the brothers to be readily intelligible in Moravia.

Having prepared the necessary liturgical texts, the mission departed for Moravia with gifts, the purported relics of St. Clement, and an introductory letter to Duke Rostislav in which the emperor set forth the doctrinal justification for the newly invented Slavic alphabet and for the place of Slavic in divine service:

57. *Vita Constantini* 14 is careful to note the collective nature of the decision attributed to the emperor: "together with his uncle, Bardas" and "together with his counsellors."

58. The fact that not all the Scriptures were translated initially is confirmed in *Vita Methodii* 15, where we are told of Methodius' work on additional translations following those which he and Constantine had completed earlier.

59. So begins the *Codex Assemanianus*, the oldest Slavic evangeliary.

> *God, who will have all men to come unto the knowledge of the truth* [1 Tim. 2:4] and to aspire to greater dignity, having seen your faith and your diligence, has accomplished it now, revealing letters for your language in our time (this was never accomplished before, except in the years of old), so that you too may be counted among the great nations which praise God in their own language. And, therefore, we have sent you the one to whom God revealed them, a righteous and pious man, very learned and a philosopher. And now, accept this gift which is greater and dearer than all the gold, and silver, and precious stones, and fleeting riches. And strive zealously together with him to strengthen this word and to seek God with all your heart. And do not reject universal salvation but urge all men not to tarry but to take the true path. So that you too, having brought them by your deed to divine understanding, will receive for it your reward, in this age and in the coming one, for all the souls wishing to believe in Christ our God, now and evermore, bequeathing your memory to future generations like the great emperor Constantine. (*Vita Constantini* 14)

The Moravian mission generated intense missionary efforts and complex diplomatic maneuvers which for a quarter of a century thrust the Slavs into the very midst of European politics. Its history falls into two periods, the first associated with the name of Constantine, the second with that of Methodius.

1.35. The Constantinian period. Constantine and Methodius arrived in Moravia in 862/863, bearing with them a set of liturgical books which they had translated into Slavic and transcribed in the new Slavic alphabet devised by Constantine. It is clear, however, from the account in the *Vita Constantini* that their reception was less than cordial and that the work of the mission proceeded with difficulty. Franko-Bavarian clergy defended their prerogatives vigorously and attacked the brothers for transgressing against the custom, hallowed in the Western church, of glorifying God in three languages only, Hebrew, Greek, and Latin. Constantine tried to stand his ground, but to no avail. After forty months of work the brothers left Moravia, their departure hastened by the hostile attitude of the German clergy, the deeply rooted paganism of the native population, and an indecisive posture of Rostislav, who had been weakened by a recent (864) defeat at the hands of the Franks and Bulgarians. The ostensible purpose of their trip was the ordination of their Moravian disciples.[60]

The brothers' first stop was Mosaburg (local Slavic *Blatogradъ*), the capital of Pannonia on Lake Balaton. The mission's reception there appears to have been much warmer than in the neighboring Moravia. The Pannonian duke Kocel, son of Duke Pribina, welcomed the brothers with honors and "taking a great liking to the Slavic letters, learned them himself and supplied some fifty students to study them" (*Vita Constantini* 15). As a result of Kocel's support, the brothers were able to accomplish more during their seven-month stay with friendly Kocel than during their much longer stay in largely hostile Moravia.

Stopping in Venice, the brothers engaged in a disputation on the propriety of using Slavic in divine worship. Advancing the by now familiar arguments, the church leaders gathered there fell upon Constantine "like ravens upon a falcon," insisting that Hebrew, Greek, and Latin were the only languages in which "it was appropriate to praise God in the Scriptures." Constantine's lengthy condemnation of the "trilingual" or "Pilatian" heresy[61] takes up most of chapter 16 of the *Vita Constantini*. His rebuttal, leaning frequently on the authority of the

60. Neither Constantine nor Methodius had the requisite episcopal rank to perform the ordination.

61. Referring to Pilate's order to use Greek, Latin, and Hebrew for the inscription on the cross of the Lord's Passion (Luke 23:38).

Bible, ends with the words of the apostle Paul: "And that every tongue should confess that Jesus Christ is Lord, to the glory of God the Father" (Phil. 2:11).

From Venice the brothers proceeded to Rome, summoned there by Pope Nicholas I to answer charges preferred against them by the Bavarian clergy. By the time they arrived, however, Nicholas had died (November 13, 867) and it was his successor, Hadrian II, who received them. There is little doubt that this happenstance worked in the brothers' favor. Nicholas' animus against the ecumenical patriarch Photius, who had called for the pope's ouster, colored his policy toward Byzantium. The reception of Constantine and Methodius, who were Photius' protégés, would have surely been affected by it. By contrast, Hadrian II, whose investiture coincided with the downfall of Photius, followed a much more conciliatory line in his dealings with Constantinople, and the welcome he extended to the Greek visitors was most gracious.

The initial stage of the brothers' stay in Rome was taken up with the deposition of the relics of St. Clement and the ordination of the Slavic disciples of Constantine and Methodius performed by the bishops Formosus and Gauderich.[62] The pope, mindful of the potential value of the Slavic mission in his attempt to preserve and extend Rome's influence in Central Europe, surrounded the brothers with hospitality. He accepted and blessed a set of Slavic scriptures and had them deposited in the Church of St. Mary of the Manger while permitting Slavic services to be celebrated in a number of Roman churches. Also, the papal *bibliothecarius* Anastasius gave ample proof of his personal friendship for the brothers. He translated Constantine's *Discourse on the Discovery and Translation of the Relics of St. Clement* (**1.31**) into Latin and, in his correspondence, expressed great admiration for Constantine as a scholar and writer. In a letter to Gauderich written in 875 Anastasius professed his own inadequacy to the task of translating Constantine:

> Two of his [Constantine's] works, namely the aforementioned *Brief History* [the *Discourse*] and one declamatory sermon [a eulogy to St. Clement] translated by us in language which is coarse and which lags far behind the splendor of his eloquence, I commit to your paternal kindness . . . so that you would polish them with the grinding stone of your judgment. However, I did not translate one scroll of a hymn which that same philosopher composed to the glory of God and of the blessed Clement because a Latin translation would have produced now fewer, now more syllables and would not have rendered fittingly and resonantly the harmony of the hymn. (Anastasius to Gauderich, 65–66)

In Rome Constantine took the monastic vows and assumed the name of Cyril. Constantine/Cyril died in Rome on February 14, 869, at the age of forty-two. On his deathbed he pleaded with his older brother: "We have been harnessed together plowing the same furrow. Now, ending my days, I have fallen in the field. Although you have a great love for the mountain [the monastery on Mt. Olympus], do not for the sake of the mountain abandon your teaching, for it offers a surer way to salvation" (*Vita Methodii* 7).

Constantine was buried in the Church of St. Clement in Rome. However, as we find out from the *Italian Legend*, this was not the resting place that Methodius originally had envisioned for his brother:

62. Formosus, bishop of Porto (Ostia) and future pope, had just returned from a mission to Bulgaria where he must have had some exposure to Slavic. Nonetheless, according to *Vita Methodii* 6, he too "was afflicted with the [Pilatian or trilingual] disease." Gauderich, bishop of Velletri, whose cathedral church was dedicated to St. Clement, had an understandable interest in the brothers and the relics brought by them to Rome (Dvornik 1970:140).

The Holy Father decreed that all the clerics, both Greek and Roman, should come to [Constantine-Cyril's] funeral with psalms and songs, with candles and incense, and should render him the last service equal to that of the Pope.

Then his aforementioned brother Methodius approached the Holy Father and falling to his knees said: "I think it proper and necessary to tell your Holiness . . . that when we were leaving our home for the task which with divine help we have performed, our mother entreated us tearfully that, if one of us should pass away before our return, the surviving brother should bring the defunct brother back to his monastery in order to bury him there in a worthy and proper manner. May then your Holiness allow my wretched self to fulfil this duty, lest it seem that I go against maternal supplications and appeals." The Pope did not like this, but he found it rather difficult to oppose such a request and wish. Having carefully placed the dead body in a marble casket and having sealed it with his own seal, he gave [Methodius] the permission to depart after seven days. Then the Roman clergy gathered and, after taking counsel with the bishops and cardinals, as well as city nobility, they began saying: "O, venerable Father and Lord, it seems to us very inappropriate that you should allow for any reason to move to another land such a magnificent man through whose merit our city and church recovered such a precious treasure and whom, because of his great piety, God has deigned to bring here from such far-away and foreign lands and take him from here to His kingdom. But, if you permit, may he be buried here because it is altogether appropriate that a man of such glory and fame should have an honored place of burial in this most famous city." This counsel pleased the Pope and he decreed that [Constantine-Cyril] be laid to rest in the basilica of St. Peter, of course, in his own sepulchre.

Methodius, realizing that his plan had failed, asked again: "I beseech you, my lords, since you are not of the mind to grant me my request, let him be laid to rest in the church of St. Clement whose body he recovered with much difficulty and zeal and brought here." The most Holy Prince granted this request, and in the presence of a great many clergymen and people, thanking God with hymns and panegyrics, with inordinate joy and much reverence, they placed him in the specially prepared sepulchre in the basilica of St. Clement to the right of [St. Clement's] altar, in the marble casket in which he had been placed by the aforementioned Pope. (*Italian Legend* 63–64)

1.36. The Methodian period. Obeying Constantine's admonition, Methodius resolved to go back to missionary activity. This time, however, he was returning to the field with the full backing of the pope, who was alarmed by the East Frankish push into Moravia and the growing ambitions of the Bavarian church, which threatened to become the major force in ecclesiastic matters in Central Europe. The new Slavic church offered excellent opportunities in this tug-of-war. To strengthen Methodius' hand, Hadrian II decided to invoke an administrative precedent dating back to the era before the Hunnic and Avar invasions. In those days Pannonia, as part of Illiricum, was under the ecclesiastic jurisdiction of Rome and was governed by a bishop whose episcopal see was in Sirmium on the Sava. Now, Hadrian raised Sirmium to the rank of an archbishopric and consecrated Methodius as its first incumbent, with authority over all of Pannonia and, possibly, Moravia as well. [63] By this act the pope challenged the authority of the Bavarian church over these lands, especially of the dioceses of Salzburg and Passau.

63. As the pope said in his answer to Kocel's request for Methodius: "I send him not only to you alone but to all the Slavic lands" (*Vita Methodii* 8).

A few months after Constantine/Cyril's death, Methodius visited Pannonia briefly and in 870 returned there for good to fulfil his new episcopal duties. He bore with him an introductory letter (*Gloria in excelsis*) from Hadrian to the dukes Rostislav, Svatopluk, and Kocel which referred to Rome's ecclesiastic rights in Central Europe. The pope justified his current sponsorship of Methodius by recalling that the original request for a Slavic mission for Moravia was addressed not just to Constantinople but also to the Holy See. He also invoked the authority of the Bible to defend the use of Slavic in liturgy:

> You have asked for a teacher not only from this Apostolic See but also from the pious emperor Michael. And he sent you the blessed philosopher Constantine together with his brother, which we then could not do. And they [Constantine and Methodius], having learned that your countries belong to the Apostolic See, did not act in any way against the canon and came to us bearing the relics of St. Clement. And we, deriving threefold joy therefrom, considered the matter and decided to send to your lands our son Methodius, a man perfect of mind and true of faith, having ordained him and his disciples, to teach you as you have requested and to explain fully the Scriptures in your language according to all the rules of the Church, with the Holy Mass, that is, the liturgy, and the baptism, as Constantine the Philosopher had begun through the grace of God and the prayers of St. Clement. And also, if anyone else can preach correctly and truly, let this be deemed holy and be blessed by God, by us, and by the entire ecumenical and apostolic church so that you would readily learn God's commandments. But observe this one custom—during the mass read the *Apostol* and the Gospels, first in Latin and then in Slavic, so that the word of the Scriptures may be fulfilled: *O praise the Lord, all ye nations* [Ps. 117:1], and elsewhere: *All will proclaim in different tongues the greatness of God, as the holy Spirit gave them utterance* [Acts 2:4, 11], and if anyone of the teachers gathered among you, *having itching ears* and *turning away from the truth to error* [2 Tim. 4:3–4] will presume to corrupt you abusing the books in your tongue, let him be cut off . . . from the church till he mends his ways. (*Vita Methodii* 8)[64]

The Bavarian clergy did not take kindly to what they considered an arrogant tresspass and an unwarranted abridgment of their prerogatives in Central Europe. They saw that what began innocently enough as a small-scale Byzantine venture was now being turned into a powerful instrument of papal diplomacy and an excuse to reduce their ecclesiastic dominion. Pannonia was of special importance to them, for that is where most of their missionary activity took place and where they felt they could justify their presence. It was for the purpose of such a legitimization that the treatise *Conversio Bagoariorum et Carantanorum* (**1.28**) was produced. Reacting with vehemence to Methodius' arrival at Kocel's court, the *Conversio* recalled that the Bavarian rights in Pannonia could be traced back to Charlemagne, who, after the expulsion of the Avars, assigned the episcopal authority there "to the rector of the Salzburg church, namely to archbishop Arno and his successors, to hold and administer in perpetuity" (10). This situation, the document continued, did not change when the post-Avar lands were settled by the Slavs and Bavarians. In fact, the *Conversio* listed an uninterrupted succession of Bavarian priests in order to support the validity of the current Bavarian claims in Pannonia. The Bavarians also registered their dismay over the activities of Methodius:

64. A similar but briefer version of this letter may be found in the eulogy (*slovo poxvalьno*) for Cyril and Methodius by Clement of Ohrid.

> [After Dominicus, Swarnagel, and Altfrid, Archbishop Liupram] installed there Rihpald as the archpriest. The latter stayed there a long time, fulfilling his duties with competence as charged by his archbishop until, after the recent invention of Slavic letters, a certain Greek, Methodius by name, has with deceitful sophistry, slighted the Latin language, the Roman teaching and the authoritative Latin writings and in some sense discredited the mass, the Gospel and the church service for all the people who used to celebrate them in Latin. [Rihpald] could not bear this and returned to Salzburg. (*Conversio* 12)

Fortified by such claims, Bavarian clergy intensified their attacks on Methodius and the debate took on disturbingly bellicose tones. Methodius, secure in his knowledge that the pope was behind him, did not shrink from a gory metaphor. He warned his Bavarian foes not to covet the old boundaries "lest you spill your brains wishing to smash an iron mountain with your heads" (*Vita Methodii* 9). The Bavarians, however, had the might of the East Frankish army on their side. A successful military campaign against Moravia in 870 led by Carloman, governor of the Bavarian East Mark and son of Louis the German, king of Bavaria, resulted in the replacement of Duke Rostislav by his pro-Bavarian nephew Svatopluk. Rostislav was delivered to Louis the German, who had him blinded and imprisoned. Methodius himself was seized, summarily judged, and imprisoned for almost three years in a monastery in Swabia.

1.37. The testimony of papal correspondence. Alarmed by this turn of events, the newly elected pope, John VIII (r. 872–882), sent protests to the secular as well as ecclesiastic authorities in the area, Louis the German, Carloman, Archbishop Adalwin of Salzburg, and bishops Hermanrich of Passau and Anno of Freising. The pope's letters, borne to their addressees by the papal legate Bishop Paul of Ancona, denied the implications of the *Conversio* and expressed indignation over the actions of the Bavarian bishops. Preserved in the archives of the Holy See, these letters are the most reliable source of information on the history of the Moravian mission.

In the letter to Louis the German, John VIII tried to substantiate Rome's view that Pannonia had been and still remained under the jurisdiction of the Apostolic See:

> If divine justice resides, as is proper, with your Excellency, your wisdom will be able to comprehend from many different and clear indications that the Pannonian diocese has long been considered among the privileges of the Apostolic See. This is shown by synodal proceedings and demonstrated by written histories. However, because of the hostilities and animosities, the Apostolic See has not for a long time sent there a bishop, which has created doubts among the ignorant people. . . . Let no one seek succor in the passage of years[65] for the estate of the holy Roman church, which we serve according to the Divine Will and which is borne by the firm rocks of Peter's steadfastness, is not delimited by any time and is not decided by any royal partition. (Papal correspondence, 67)

Similar points were made in the letter instructing Bishop Paul of Ancona what to tell the Bavarians: "Not only in Italy and in other western provinces but in the territory of all of Illiricum, the Apostolic See has habitually and for a long time administered consecrations, ordinations, and dispositions, as proved by some registers and synodal records as well as by numerous charters of local churches."

65. This is a reference to the claim made in *Conversio* that for seventy-five years (that is, since Charlemagne's victory over the Avars) Pannonia had been under the jurisdiction of the archbishopric of Salzburg.

The passage of time, John VIII continued, should not affect the legal status of dioceses. He illustrated this contention with biblical precedents: the freeing of the Jews after 430 years of Egyptian bondage and the coming of Christ to redeem mankind after thousands of years of infernal torments. He then instructed Paul how to argue the case of Methodius:

> Tell them then: "I have been appointed to restore the [episcopal] see to him who during three years has suffered violence and not to pass judgment over the [status of] the diocese." And truly, in accordance with the promulgated decrees, it is appropriate that [Methodius] first be given back the [office of] bishop and then be brought into [legal] negotiations. . . . And should Adalwin and Hermanrich wish to begin the trial of our bishop Methodius, tell them: "Without a synodal decree you have condemned a bishop sent by the Apostolic See, you have kept him in prison, slapped him on the face, denied him the sacred ministry, and for three years kept him from his [episcopal] see, even though during these three years he appealed to the Apostolic See through very many envoys and letters. You have not deemed it appropriate to come to court, which you have always tried to evade. And now you intend to seek a judicial ruling without the Apostolic See, even though I have been sent to forbid you the practice of divine service as long as you prevent this venerable man from engaging in holy ministry and until he himself may, without reservations or questions, serve in the bishopric which has been entrusted to him. (Papal correspondence, 68)

The pope also mentioned the case of Methodius in his letter to Carloman: "Since the Pannonian bishopric has been reestablished and returned to us, our aforementioned brother Methodius, who was ordained by the Apostolic See, should be allowed to perform freely his episcopal duties in accordance with the ancient custom" (Papal correspondence, 67).

The brunt of the pope's displeasure, however, was reserved for his communications to the Bavarian bishops. Here is what John VIII had to say to Hermanrich of Passau:

> To bemoan your depravity we believe, like the prophet Jeremiah, a well of tears will not suffice. Would the cruelty of any layman, not to say a bishop, indeed of any tyrant, exceed your temerity? Would [it] go beyond your bestial ferocity when you imprisoned our brother and fellow bishop Methodius, tortured him for a long time in open air in sharpest cold and frightful rains, removed him from the affairs of the church which were entrusted to him, and went so far in your frenzy that you would have struck him with a horsewhip during a session of the council of bishops had you not been prevented by others? Is this, I ask, [fitting] for a bishop whose dignity, if exceeded, leads to greater misdeeds? A bishop attacking a bishop who had been consecrated by the Apostolic See and appointed its legate! We do not wish to try you now for what you have done so that we would not be forced to decide precipitously what is appropriate but, in accordance with the will of the almighty God and of the blessed princes of the apostles Peter and Paul, and by our own mediocre authority, we temporarily deprive you of [the right to participate in] the communion of Christ's mysteries and of your fellow priests; and if you do not arrive in Rome with the present venerable bishop Paul or with our most saintly brother Methodius to be heard together with him, just punishment will not fail [to follow] because such and so great was the presumptuousness committed; nor will the weight of the authority of the Apostolic See be lacking when the enormity of so grave a depravity is proved. (Papal correspondence, 69)

The tone of the letter to Bishop Anno was similarly indignant:

> Your audacity and your presumptuousness exceeds not only the clouds but the very heavens. You have usurped the office of the Apostolic See and you have appropriated the patriarch's right to judge an archbishop. What is graver, you have treated your brother Methodius, the archbishop of Pannonia sent as a legate of the Apostolic See to the pagans, in a tyrannical rather than legal manner and you have not deemed it appropriate to obtain the consent of the priests who are with you for [the deed which] you have perpetrated solely as an affront to the Apostolic See. Moreover, when he was asking, in accordance with the holy canons, to be surrendered to the judgment of the Holy See, you have not permitted it at all, but, together with your followers and associates, have issued a quasi-sentence and, preventing him from performing the divine service, have confined him in jail. In addition, although you proclaim yourself a man of St. Peter [i.e., of the Holy See], in so far as you attend to his patrimony in Germany, you have not only failed the duty of the faithful to report the imprisonment and persecution of this brother and fellow bishop and, what is more, our envoy to whom we owe an even greater solicitude, but when you were in Rome and were interrogated about him by our people, you denied mendaciously that you knew him, even though you yourself were the inciter, you yourself were the instigator, indeed you yourself were the agent of the afflictions caused him by your people. If the health of this venerable bishop does not improve to the point that he himself, with God's help, will be able to consign to oblivion all his injury, come to Rome without delay to give an account. Otherwise, after the month of September you may not receive communion as long as you exhibit stubborness in your disobedience towards us. (Papal correspondence, 70)

In spite of papal interventions, Pannonia succumbed to Frankish pressure and accepted the ecclesiastic jurisdiction of Salzburg. Yet the work of the Slavic mission in Central Europe was not over. Released from prison, Methodius was able to return to Moravia in 874 to resume his pastoral duties there. Although Svatopluk had to accept East Frankish political suzerainty, he managed to retain a large dose of cultural independence. A tightly controlled Slavic diocese in Moravia,[66] replacing the pope's unsuccessful attempt to resurrect the diocese in Sirmium, afforded him, at least for a time, a welcome alternative to the irksome intrusions of Bavarian clergymen. The Slavic mission was allowed to continue its work, even though the Moravian church was not as free in its linguistic practices as the eastern churches, where the whole service, including the administration of the holy sacraments and the sacred mysteries, was in the vernacular. In fact, Methodius' insistence on celebrating the mass in Slavic met with a rebuke of John VIII, who in a letter of 14 June 879 (*Predicationis tuae*) summoned Methodius to Rome to answer charges preferred against him by the Bavarians. At the same time the pope leaned upon the authority of the apostle Paul (invoked also by Constantine in Venice) in granting Methodius the permission to continue preaching in Slavic:

> We hear also that you chant the mass in the barbarian, that is, Slavic tongue although, in a letter transmitted to you by Bishop Paul of Ancona, we have enjoined you from celebrating the rites of the sacred mass in that language rather than in Latin or Greek, as it is chanted in the church of God which extends throughout the world and reaches all the peoples. You may, however, preach and give sermons in the vernacular because the Psalmist calls on all the peoples to praise the Lord and the Apostle says: "that every tongue should confess that Jesus is Lord to the glory of God the Father." (Papal correspondence, 72)

66. Methodius' Moravian archbishopric might have been located in Velehrad or Staré Město.

Upon his arrival in Rome a year later, Methodius succeeded in convincing John VIII that all his pastoral practices conformed to the teachings of the church as defined by the six ecumenical councils and obtained a ratification of his appointment as archbishop of Pannonia. The papal bull *Industriae tuae* addressed to Svatopluk demonstrates the pope's confidence in Methodius and his favorable attitude to the use of Slavic in church service:

> We direct that presbyters, deacons, and other clerics of whatever rank, whether Slavs or any other people, who are within the borders of your province, submit to and obey in everything our aforementioned brother, your archbishop, so that they would do nothing at all without his knowledge. And if those who are obstinate and disobedient are guilty of some impropriety or schism and do not mend their ways after the first and second admonition, we direct with our authority that they be banished from the church and from your borders as sowers of weeds in accordance with the legal authority which we gave him and sent to you. Finally, we duly praise the Slavic letters invented by one Constantine the Philosopher to render the lauds due to God and direct that the glorifications and deeds of Christ our Lord be recounted in that language. . . . And it does not go counter to sound faith or teaching to sing the mass in that Slavic language or to read the holy Gospel as well as lections from the Old and New Testament, well translated and explicated, or to chant all the offices of the hours, for he who created the three principal languages, to wit Hebrew, Greek and Latin, created also all the other [languages] for his praise and glory. We direct, however, that, for the sake of greater reverence, in all the churches of your land, the Gospel be read in Latin and then in a Slavic translation into the hearing of people who do not understand Latin. (Papal correspondence, 73)

Stephen V (VI)[67], though generally less favorably inclined to Slavic worship than his predecessors, confirmed John VIII's permission to preach in Slavic but was staunch in his interdiction of the use of Slavic in the divine liturgy. In September 885, five months after Methodius' death, the new pope sent the following instructions to Duke Svatopluk (*Quia te zelo*):

> The divine offices, the sacred mysteries and the rites of the mass, which Methodius dared to celebrate in the language of the Slavs, . . . let no one from now on presume to do; we forbid [it] with divine and apostolic authority under the punishment of excommunication, except that for the edification of simple and unlearned people we permit and encourage that the explication of the Gospel and of the Epistles be made by those who are learned in that language and we advise that this be done as frequently as possible. (Papal correspondence, 77)

Later that year Pope Stephen confirmed the interdiction to celebrate "the mass and the most sacred offices" in Slavic in his memorandum (*Commonitorium*) addressed to his legate Dominic and the priests John and Stephen as they embarked on the papal embassy to Moravia. In that same document the pope referred to Methodius' deathbed wish, reported in the vitae of Methodius and Clement, that his Slavic disciple Gorazd should succeed him as the archbishop of Moravia. The pope sided with Wiching, the suffragan bishop of Nitra, who bitterly opposed this nomination (**1.39**): "With our apostolic authority interdict him whom Methodius presumed to appoint as his successor in violation of the rules of all the holy fathers; he may not assume his post until he appears personally before us and expounds his views in oral testimony" (Papal correspondence, 75).

67. Since Stephen II (752) was not consecrated, the numbering of later popes named Stephen depends on his inclusion or noninclusion in the papal roster.

As one can see from this correspondence, the Moravian mission had the delicate task of navigating the narrow straits between the openly hostile attitude of the Bavarian clergy and the generally supportive though not altogether consistent attitude of the Holy See.[68] It is a tribute to Methodius' determination that despite these difficulties and diversions the mission managed to make the last decade of his life its most productive period.

1.38. Was the Moravian mission Byzantine or Roman? It is remarkable that from the time of their arrival in Moravia until their deaths Constantine and Methodius had their eyes turned toward Rome rather than Byzantium. It was to Rome that the brothers traveled (Methodius three times, against one undocumented trip to Constantinople); Constantine died in Rome and, against his mother's express wish, was buried there. Whatever correspondence with or about the brothers has survived is from or to Rome. It was the popes Hadrian II and John VIII who defended the work of the mission against the attacks of the Bavarian clergy. Hadrian, in fact, enrolled Methodius into the ranks of Roman church hierarchy by appointing him bishop of Pannonia and Moravia and went so far as to claim that Rostislav's original request for Slavic missionaries was addressed not only to Constantinople but also to the Holy See. At the same time contemporary Byzantine sources are totally silent about the brothers' activities. Why, then, is the Moravian mission traditionally described as a Byzantine undertaking?[69]

We know, of course, that the mission's protagonists were two Byzantine churchmen sent by a Byzantine emperor. These circumstances may provide a superficial label but should not be invested with far-reaching ideological connotations. The presumption that the term *Byzantine* captures the essence of the mission is misleading and to some degree anachronistic. All available evidence suggests that during the period of its activity the mission, whatever its genesis, fit into the mechanism of Roman rather than Byzantine diplomacy. It is only from the vantage point of later developments, above all the schism between the East and the West and the legacy of the mission in the lands dominated by Byzantium such as Bulgaria and Rus', that the mission's work may be viewed as Byzantine in the wider and deeper sense of the term.[70]

Rome's emergence as the main sponsor of the Moravian mission was due to a for-

68. The three popes, Hadrian II, John VIII and Stephen V (VI), all allowed the use of Slavic in sermons and biblical exegeses. There are, however, differences in their attitudes toward the conduct of the Holy Mass. Hadrian allowed the use of Slavic in all of the divine service including the liturgy and the baptism but specified that the Gospels and the *Apostol* be read first in Latin and then in Slavic (*Gloria in excelsis* of 870). John called for the Gospel to be read first in Latin and then in a Slavic translation but allowed Slavic in the mass (*Industriae tuae* of 880). As it appears, however, from John's 879 letter to Methodius (*Predicationis tuae*), this did not include the mysteries (*sacra missarum sollemnia*). This is also the position of Stephen, who in his instruction to Svatopluk (*Quia te zelo* of 885) and in the *Commonitorium* (885–886) forbade the use of Slavic in the divine offices, the sacred mysteries, and the rites of the mass. The diplomatic tangle enmeshing the mission was surely even more complex than the papal correspondence would indicate and may have involved complications on the Byzantine side. The existence of such complications is implied by the claim made in *Vita Methodii* 13 that Methodius' trip to Rome in 880 was followed by one to Constantinople in 881–882 to answer some unspecified charges of the emperor Basil I. The absence of any Byzantine confirmation of this report is puzzling. A number of scholars, however, among them Dvornik (1970:170–174) and Obolensky (1974:195), believe that the trip actually took place.

69. As in "The Byzantine Mission in Moravia," the title of chapter 4 in Dvornik 1970.

70. While Ševčenko (1988/1989:13) is no doubt right in noting the Byzantine character of the vitae of Constantine and Methodius, one must remember that these are conventional Byzantine hagiographies whose composition was not contemporaneous with the events described and whose political agendas were not necessarily coincident with the original goals of the Moravian mission.

tuitous concatenation of circumstances in the 860s and 870s. The defeat of the Avars created a power vacuum filled by a loose confederation of Slavic states from Moravia in the north, through Pannonia and Carantania, to Illiricum in the south. With Byzantium weakened by internal strife and Bulgaria not yet the power it was soon to become, the Bavarians and the Holy See emerged as the leading competitors for the domination of these lands. Kocel's independent stand, demonstrated by his wholehearted support of the Moravian mission, offered the pope a welcome opening. By reestablishing the bishopric in Sirmium, which at that time belonged to Kocel's Pannonian state, and making it submit directly to papal authority, Hadrian hoped to gain an important foothold in central Europe and eventually reclaim Illiricum, which figured prominently in the *Ostpolitik* of his predecessor, Nicholas. Methodius' loyalty to Rome made him an ideal candidate for the Sirmian diocese. To justify his selection to the clearly displeased Bavarian church hierarchy, the pope borrowed the arguments used by Constantine in Venice and affirmed the doctrinal correctness of the use of Slavic in liturgy.[71] He also presented Methodius as one who was uniquely qualified to further the goals of Christianity among all of the Slavs in Central Europe. This objective was clearly stated in the preamble to the Pope's letter *Gloria in excelsis*: "Not only to you [Kocel] but to all those Slavic lands do I now send him [Methodius] forth to be the teacher on behalf of God and St. Peter" (*Vita Methodii* 8).

1.39. The Moravian debacle. At first the diplomatic initiatives of Hadrian II and John VIII were successful, for Louis the German, preoccupied by various domestic problems, could not take a firm stand on behalf of the Bavarian bishops. Time, however, was not on the side of the mission. The pressure of the Bavarian ecclesiastic establishment was growing, and the Slavic missionaries had to assume a defensive posture, shielded temporarily by Methodius' prestige in Rome. His death in 885 marked the beginning of the end of the mission. Especially persistent in his hostility to the continued use of Slavic liturgy was Wiching, the Bavarian suffragan bishop of Nitra, which was the center of the Latin rite in Moravia. Wiching led an all-out assault upon the Slavic mission and, with the aid of the newly elected pope Stephen, interdicted the assumption of pastoral duties by Gorazd, whom Methodius had designated as his successor. The ostensible reason for Wiching's campaign was the controversy about the wording of the Nicene Creed. In the Orthodox church the Creed was (and still is) recited in its original form: "I believe . . . in the Holy Spirit, the Lord, the Giver of Life, who proceeds from the Father." Sometime in the sixth century this formula was extended in the West by the phrase "and from the Son" (Latin *filioque*, hence the name of the controversy). This addition became of doctrinal importance when it came to be viewed as a revision of Trinitarian theology, and the East and the West began to trade accusations of heresy.[72] The issue of the *filioque* was the subject of a debate between Methodius' disciples, led by Gorazd and Clement, and the representatives of the Frankish clergy. It ended in a free-for-all vividly described by the admittedly partial Greek archbishop of Ohrid Theophylact, who in the beginning of the twelfth century composed a vita of Clement:

> Wiching's disciples . . . raised a terrible racket and began turning everything upside down and all but started a fight with the Orthodox, imagining the strength of their arms to be the ally of

71. Adalvin, the archbishop of Salzburg, gave vent to his resentment in the memorandum *De conversione Bagoariorum et Carantanorum* of 871.

72. The issue of the *filioque* was cited as the formal cause of the Great Schism which was to divide the Eastern and Western churches in 1054; for a brief review of the history of the controversy, see Ware 1984:58–70.

their feeble tongues. At length they hastened and had recourse to their last resort, that vile Svatopluk, and began slandering the Orthodox of plotting against him and preparing to rise against his rule if they failed to agree with the prince in doctrine, because counterthought is counteraction. He summoned the disciples of Cyril and Methodius and told them, 'Why is there this dissention among you and why are you daily bickering among each other like enemies? Are you not all brethren? Are you not all Christians? Why do you not agree among each other and seek unity? (Theophylact of Ohrid, 105)

This eminently sound advice was not followed, and Svatopluk resolved the issue summarily by siding with the Bavarians and giving them power over the dissenters. Theophylact described the consequences of this ruling:

What speech can describe the evils that followed, once corruption was given power? This was indeed like a forest fire fanned up by the wind. The Franks tried to force the disciples of Methodius into joining the false teaching, while the Orthodox stood by the faith of the fathers. The Franks were prepared to do anything, the Orthodox to bear anything. The Franks inhumanely tortured some, plundered the homes of others, adding rapacity to their falsehood. Old men, over David's age, were dragged naked through thorny scrub. (Theophylact of Ohrid, 108)

The leading figures of the mission were imprisoned, tried, and expelled from Moravia, while some two hundred younger priests and deacons were sold by the Bavarians to Jewish slave merchants.[73]

1.40. The legacy of the mission in Bulgaria. Such was the end of more than two decades of Constantine's and Methodius' missionary efforts in Moravia. The brothers' teachings, however, did not come to naught. Three of their disciples, Clement, Naum, and Angelarius, succeeded in building a raft and floating down the Danube to Belgrade, which at that time was a Bulgarian frontier town. They eventually reached Pliska, the first capital of Bulgaria, where they were cordially received by the Bulgarian khan Boris (r. 852–889), who needed experienced Slavic missionaries to complete the Christianization of the country, begun by his own conversion in 865.[74] Clement was appointed to a teaching post in Kutmičevica in southwestern Macedonia and later became bishop of Velica near Ohrid in western Macedonia. During his tenure there Clement devoted himself to the training of Slavic clerics and bookmen. He himself composed homilies and translated many texts, trying to make them accessible and comprehensible to the populace. In the words of Theophylact, "Clement gave Bulgarians everything which concerns the Church and with which the memory of God and the saints is celebrated, and through which the souls are moved" (Theophylact of Ohrid, 118). Naum began the Bulgarian phase of his teaching activity in the vicinity of Preslav, the new capital of Bulgaria, whence he was moved to a post on Lake Ohrid. There he was connected with the construction of the Archangel Michael Monastery (known today as Sveti Naum), where he died and was buried in 910. Clement and Naum were joined in Bulgaria by another disciple of Methodius, Constantine of Preslav. Together they were responsible for inaugurating a period of great literary productivity in Bulgaria which has come to be known as the "golden age" of Bulgarian culture. It began with the Christianization of the country un-

73. It is possible that Constantine of Preslav (**3.35**) was among these young clerics.

74. In baptism Boris adopted the Christian name Michael in honor of the reigning emperor Michael III; hence he is often referred to as Boris/Michael.

der Boris/Michael but came to its greatest flowering during the rule of his well-educated son Tsar Symeon (r. 893–927), who was asked by his father to give up scholarly pursuits in a Byzantine monastic retreat and to assume the Bulgarian throne rendered vacant by the deposition of his older brother, Vladimir. Liudprand of Cremona (920–972), the Lombard churchman, historian, and diplomat of Emperor Otto I (r. 936–973), provides in *Antapodosis* 3.29 an outsider's view of Symeon's education in Constantinople and of his royal ambitions:

> King Symeon was . . . half a Greek, and in his boyhood was taught at Byzantium the rhetoric of Demosthenes and the logic of Aristotle. Later on, people say, he abandoned his literary studies and assumed the dress of a monk. But he soon left the calm retreat of a monastery for the storms of this world, and beguiled by desire of kingship preferred to follow in the footsteps of the apostate Julian rather than in those of Saint Peter. . . . He had two sons, one called Bojan, the other Peter, this latter being still alive and now ruling over the Bulgarians. (Liudprand, 123)

It was under Symeon that Bulgaria reached the apogee of its power in the Balkans, extending its dominion from the Black Sea to the Adriatic and from the Dniester to a line just north of Thessalonica.

While Clement, Naum, and Constantine of Preslav were direct disciples of Constantine and Methodius, their continuators on the Bulgarian literary scene, John the Exarch (**3.36**), the monk Khrabr, and the presbyter Cosmas (**3.49**), were trained in the new centers of learning in Bulgaria and in Constantinople. It is they, therefore, who inaugurated the cultural movement that has been the hallmark of Slavic Orthodoxy and has come to be known as the Cyrillo-Methodian tradition. Symeon himself is credited with the compilation of *Izbornik of 1073*, a miscellany known also as *Izbornik of Svyatoslav* or *Izbornik of Symeon* (**3.45**), and of one of the redactions of *Zlatostrui*, a collection of homilies of John Chrysostom (**3.44**).

1.41. From Moravia to Bohemia. With Moravia defeated in the beginning of the tenth century by a Magyar-Frankish coalition, it was Bohemia that became the principal Slavic state in the area, even though it too had to recognize the suzerainty of the Franks. Bohemia, however, was able to retain administrative autonomy and control over its internal affairs. Our main source of information on the origins of Bohemian statehood is the Latin *Chronica Boemorum* by Cosmas of Prague, composed in the first half of the twelfth century. The chronicle records the history of Bohemia from its legendary beginnings under Přemysl through the end of the eleventh century. Of special interest is the chronicle's account of the Christianization of the country under Duke Bořivoj of the Přemyslid dynasty, which was to reign in Bohemia till the beginning of the fourteenth century. According to the chronicle, Bořivoj's baptism occurred under the patronage of the Moravian church. Whatever its factual value, this story may be taken as evidence of the continued existence of vestiges of the Cyrillo-Methodian tradition in Latinized Bohemia. One example of the vitality of that tradition is the curious phenomenon of the Benedictine monastery of Sázava in southern Bohemia, where Slavic worship and contacts with East Slavic monastic centers were maintained throughout the eleventh century.[75] Cosmas, however, perhaps in deference to the prevailing attitudes of

75. There is a problem with Cosmas' claim that Bořivoj was baptized by Methodius himself in the year 894 since Methodius died in 885 and the Moravian mission was scattered soon afterward. The activities of the Moravian mission in Bohemia were preceded by Christianizing efforts of the Bavarian church; witness the baptism of fourteen Bohemian nobles recorded by the *Annals of Fulda* under the year 845.

his day, was diplomatically reticent about the Moravian connection of Bořivoj and his successors:

> How by God's grace, which always leads and follows everywhere, Duke Bořivoj received the sacrament of baptism, or in what way the piety of the Catholic [Christian] faith spread in these parts, day after day, through the work of his successors, or where and how many churches were built by which devout Christian duke, that we prefer to pass over in silence rather than to weary the readers, since we have already read what is written down by others: partly in the Charter of the Moravian Church, partly in the Epilogue to the history of that land and of Bohemia, partly in the vita and martyrology of our holiest patron and martyr Wenceslas. (Cosmas of Prague, 142)[76]

Of the non-Slavic sources dealing with Moravia and Bohemia, the earliest is an anonymous geographic register of West Slavic tribes (*Descriptio civitatum et regionum ad septentrionalem plagam Danubii*), known in modern scholarly literature as the *Bavarian Geographer.* It consists of two parts, the older of which was written down sometime in the first half of the ninth century. The immediate impulse for its compilation was provided by the contacts of the Carolingian empire and, after its division, the East Frankish kingdom with the many Slavic tribes dwelling north of the Danube. Among the tribes listed by the Bavarian Geographer were the Moravians (*Marharii, Merehani*) and the Bohemians (*Becheimare, Betheimare*), as well as a number of West Slavic tribes (**1.42, 1.43, 1.44**).

It may seem surprising at first glance that a confirmation of the information provided by the Bavarian Geographer should be couched in Old English. But such is the case. A list of north European tribes compiled by the learned king of England Alfred the Great (r. 871–899) is appended to his translation of the most popular world history of the time, *A History concerning the Pagans* (*Historia adversum paganos*) by the fifth-century Spanish scholar Paul Orosius. The West Slavic lands and peoples mentioned in King Alfred's list include Moravia (*Maroara*), Bohemia and the Bohemians (*Behemas, Baeme*), the [Lusatian] Sorbs (*Surpe*) and [White] Croats (*Horigti, Horoti, Horithi*), and the Vistula land (*Wisle lond*), that is, southern Poland. One has to remember that in the early Middle Ages England was more closely linked to the continent than at any time in its later history. The ancient bond to Rome, kept alive with the help of countless artifacts and structures left behind by the Roman legionnaires, was renewed when Christianity completed its gradual conquest of England in the second half of the seventh century. The ties to northern Europe were kept by linguistic and cultural connections between the Angles and the Saxons of the isles and their continental cousins. There was also the need to deal with the constant danger posed by the Norsemen, who raided the isles from their bases in Norway, Denmark, or Normandy. All these considerations made the knowledge of European geography a matter of great strategic and political importance for the English.

76. "Charter of the Moravian Church" refers probably to John VIII's bull *Industriae tuae* of 880 concerning the use of Slavic in liturgy. The Epilogue of Moravia and Bohemia has not survived under this name. St. Wenceslas (East Slavic *Vjačeslav*, Czech *Václav* < *Vęt'eslavъ*) was the grandson of Bořivoj and brother of Boleslav, by whom he was treacherously murdered in 929 (according to Cosmas) or perhaps several years later. Wenceslas and his grandmother Ludmila, also murdered by her daughter-in-law Drahomira, became the first Slavic martyrs and saints, and their cult spread throughout Christendom. Wenceslas' vita exists in Latin and in Church Slavonic, and a canon honoring him is preserved in an eleventh-century Novgorod menaeum (**3.41**). Compare also the traditional Christmas carol "Good King Wenceslas."

Carolingian chronicles concerned themselves mainly with the diplomatic and military encounters between the Franks and the Slavs. There are a number of references to the Slavs dwelling north of the Danube in the writings of Charlemagne's biographer, Einhard. While describing the territorial gains of the Frankish state under Charlemagne, Einhard had this to say about the emperor's *Drang nach Osten*: "Finally [Charlemagne] tamed and forced to pay tribute all the wild and barbarous nations which inhabit Germany between the rivers Rhine and Vistula, the Atlantic Ocean [the Baltic Sea] and the Danube, peoples who are almost identical in their language, although they differ greatly in habit and customs. Among these last the most notable are the Weletabi [Veletians], the Sorabians [Sorbs], the Abodrites [Obodrites] and the Bohemians, against all of whom he waged war" (Einhard, 69–70).

Other Frankish chronicles that provide valuable information on the Slavs with whom the Franks came into contact are the *Annals of St. Bertin* (*Annales Bertiniani*), so known because of the monastery of St. Bertin in Flanders where their oldest manuscript was discovered, and the *Annals of Fulda* (*Annales Fuldenses*), compiled in the Benedictine abbey of Fulda in Hessen in central Germany. Here, for instance, is how the *Annals of Fulda* describe the Frankish expedition of 869 against Moravia and Bohemia.[77]

> The Slavs known as the Bohemians made frequent raids across the Bavarian border, setting fire to some villages [*villae*] and carrying women captive. . . . In August king Louis [the German] gathered his troops and divided the army into three parts. The first he sent under his namesake [son, Louis the Younger] with the Thuringians and Saxons to crush the presumption of the Sorbs. He ordered the Bavarians to assist Carloman, who wished to fight against Zwentibald [Svatopluk], the nephew of Rastiz [Rostislav]. He himself kept the Franks and the Alemans with him in order to fight against Rastiz. When it was already time to set out he fell ill, and was compelled to leave the leadership of the army to Charles his youngest son and commend the outcome to God. Charles, when he came with the army with which he had been entrusted to Rastiz's huge fortifications, quite unlike any built in olden times, with God's help burned with fire all the walled fortifications of the region, seized and carried off the treasures which had been hidden in the woods or buried in the fields, and killed or put to flight all who came against him. Carloman also laid waste the territory of Zwentibald, Rastiz's nephew, with fire and war. When the whole region had been laid waste the brothers Charles and Carloman came together and congratulated each other on the victories bestowed by heaven. Meanwhile Louis their brother came against the Sorbs, and after he had killed a few forced the rest to turn and run. Many of them were killed, and the Bohemians, whom the Sorbs had brought to fight for pay, were partly killed, partly forced to return to their homes with dishonor, and the remainder surrendered. (*Annals of Fulda*, 58, 60)[78]

By contrast, Moslem and Jewish descriptions of the Slavs show far more interest in geographic, cultural, and commercial matters. Such emphases are evident in the work of Ibrāhīm Ibn Jaʿqūb, a Jew from Tortosa in Spain, who lived in the middle of the tenth cen-

77. The outcome of the expedition, which happened to coincide with the visit of Constantine and Methodius to Rome, may have been responsible for the pope's favorable attitude toward the work of the Moravian mission.

78. A comparison of this exultant account of the campaign against the Sorbs with another contemporary description of the same event provides an instructive illustration of the caution with which primary sources have to be used: "Louis, son of Louis king of Germany, waged war along with the Saxons against the Wends [Sorbs] who live near the Saxons. With great slaughter of men on both sides, he somehow managed to win, and got home successfully" (*Annals of St. Bertin*, 163).

tury. His account of a trip through the Slavic lands has been preserved in the writings of al-Bakrī, an eleventh-century Arabic geographer also from Spain:

> And the city of Prague is made of stone and lime. In merchandise it is the richest of the land. The Rus [Vikings] and the Slavs come there with merchandise from the city of Cracow. And the Moslems, Jews, and Turks [Magyars] come to them from the land of the Turks [Hungary] also with goods and commercial cargo and take out slaves, tin, and various furs. Their lands are the best of the lands of the peoples of the North and are best supplied with livestock. For one denarius they sell as much wheat as a man needs for a month, and for one denarius they sell as much barley as one horse needs for forty nights, and for one denarius they sell ten hens. In the city of Prague they make saddles, bridles, and shields of inferior quality which are used in their lands. In the land of Bohemia they make light cloth of very delicate fabric in the manner of a net which is not good for anything. In any season its price is ten pieces of cloth for one denarius and with them they buy and sell. And they keep them in stock. And they represent for them property and the value of things, they buy for them wheat, flour, horses, gold, silver, and all kinds of things. It is their characteristic that the inhabitants of Bohemia are dark-skinned and black-haired and that blond coloring is rare among them. (Ibn Jaʿqūb, 413–414)

1.42. The northwestern Slavs. The testimony of Frankish and Saxon chronicles. It is reasonable to assume that, just as was the case in the Balkans, the Slavic push into Central Europe was closely connected with the war activities of the Avars, such as the raids of 562 and 566 described by Gregory of Tours, the chronicler of the Merovingian Franks (**1.11**). It was about the time of these attacks that the Slavs made their appearance in Central Europe, reaching by the beginning of the seventh century the Baltic, the rivers Elbe and Saale, and the Bohemian Forest. Along this line the Slavs' westward progress was stopped by the Germanic Saxons, Thuringians, and Bavarians. The rise of the mighty Carolingian empire and, after its dissolution, of the strong East Frankish kingdom reversed the dynamics of power in Central Europe. Faced with the steady eastward drive of their Germanic neighbors, the Slavs had to abandon their original offensive posture and assume the role of defenders. The social organisms of the northwestern Slavs, however, were not sufficiently well developed to be able to offer resistance to Germanic colonization and gradual germanization.

The first records of Frankish campaigns against the northwestern Slavs come from Carolingian chronicles. This is how the *Royal Frankish Annals* (*Annales regni Francorum*) under the year 789 describe Charlemagne's raid into northwestern Slavia:[79]

> There exists in Germany, settled on the ocean coast, a certain people of the Slavs which is called in its own tongue Weletabi [Veletians] but in the Frankish Wiltzi. Always hostile to the Franks, the Wiltzi nourished constant hatred towards their neighbors who were either subject to the Franks or bound to them by treaty and were ever oppressing and harassing them by war. The king decided that their insolence was to be tolerated no longer and resolved to attack them. Collecting a vast army together, he crossed the Rhine at Cologne, marched through Sax-

79. This excerpt combines the account given by the *annals* (italicized) with its revised version (both cited after the *Royal Frankish Annals* 1987). The Veletabi or Viltzi were a confederation of Slavic tribes, also known as the Veleti or Ljutici; their ruler was Dragovit. The "ocean coast" refers to the Baltic. The Slavic tribes of the Sorbs and Obodrites (also known as the Abodrites) were allied with Charlemagne. The name Witzan is probably that of the Obodrite chieftain Vilčan (r. 789–795). The Latin term *civitas* was left untranslated in the English of the *Royal Frankish Annals* 1987; here it is rendered as 'town'.

ony and reached the Elbe. He set up camp on its bank and threw two bridges across the river, one of which he fortified with a rampart at each end and secured by assigning a garrison. *From there he advanced further and by the Lord's bounty laid the above-said Slavs under his dominion. Franks and Saxons were with him on the said campaign, while Frisians, along with certain Franks, came by ship on the river Havel to join him. The Slavs called Sorbs were with him too, as were the Abodrites [Obodrites], whose prince was Witzan.* Entering the country of the Wiltzi he ordered everything laid waste with fire and sword. But the Wiltzi, although a warlike people and confident because of their great numbers, were not able to hold out for long against the onslaught of the royal army; and consequently as soon as the town of Dragowit was reached . . . he immediately came out of the town to the king with all his men, gave the hostages he was commanded to furnish and promised on oath that he would maintain fidelity to the king and the Franks. (*Royal Frankish Annals* 87, 122–123)

Of the many Slavic tribes living between the Oder and the Elbe, only the Sorbs of Upper and Lower Lusatia managed to preserve their Slavic linguistic identity to the present. In addition, a small body of Polabian texts, collected in the beginning of the eighteenth century, testifies to a comparatively recent Slavic presence south of Hamburg (**2.7**). Other than that, the memory of the extent of ancient Slavic settlement on the territory of Germany is preserved in hundreds of Slavic place names in Mecklenburg and Brandenburg (Jeżowa 1961–1962).

Since archaeological evidence on the northwestern Slavs is sparse, most of our knowledge of their history and culture is due to the rich tradition of Saxon chronicle writing. Thietmar (975–1018), bishop of Merseburg, a Saxon frontier town founded as an outpost against the Slavs on the Saale River, provided in his chronicle (*Thietmari Merseburgensis episcopi chronicon*) much information on the Slavs living among the Germans or along their borders. Later sources are even more instructive. Adam of Bremen (d. 1076) is particularly valuable on the Baltic and Polabian Slavs in his history of the archbishopric of Hamburg (*Gesta Hammaburgensis ecclesiae pontificum*). Specifically Slavic is the large *Chronicle of the Slavs* compiled in the middle of the twelfth century by Helmold, a parish priest in Bosau,[80] a village in Wagrien between Kiel and Lübeck (*Helmoldi presbyteri chronica Slavorum*). Here is what Adam of Bremen has to say about the Slavic lands, especially those in the northwest:

> Slavia is a very large province of Germany . . . ten times larger than our Saxony, especially if you count as part of Slavia Bohemia and the expanses across the Oder, the Poles, because they differ neither in appearance nor in language. Although this region is very rich in arms, men, and crops, it is shut in on all sides by fast barriers of wooded mountains and rivers. . . . There are many Slavic peoples, of whom the first, beginning in the west are the Wagiri [Vagrians] . . . Their city is Oldenburg by the sea. Then come the Abodrites [Obodrites] . . . and their city is Mecklenburg. In our direction, too, are the Polabingi [Polabians] whose city is Ratzeburg [Ratibor]. Beyond them live the Linguones [Glinians] and Warnavi. Farther on dwell the Chizzini [Xyžans] and Circipani [Črezpěnians], whom the Peene river separates from the Tholenzi [Tolęžans] and from the Retharii [Redars] and their city of Demmin [Dymin]. . . . There are also other Slavic peoples, who live between the Elbe and the Oder, such as the Heveldi [Havelians] who are seated by the Havel river, and the Doxani [Došans], Leubuzi

80. Slavic Bozov < *bъz- 'lilac'.

[Liubušans], Wilini [Volinians], and Stoderani [Stodorans], besides many others. (Adam of Bremen, 64–66)

Helmold supplements Adam of Bremen by specifying that the Xyžans, Črezpěnians, Tolężans, and Redars formed a military confederation known as the Veletians or Ljutici. Another military federation appears to have existed under the leadership of the Obodrites. The administrative practices of the Veletians/Ljutici were described by Thietmar:

All these tribes, called jointly the Ljutici, are not ruled by a single master. They discuss their problems in a joint council and decide matters by general consensus. If some citizen of the land objects to the decisions which have been taken, they beat him with clubs and if he openly resists outside the council, he is either deprived of his property by fire or confiscation or is obliged to pay a sum of money according to his station. Though treacherous and fickle, they demand of others loyalty and complete faithfulness. They validate a peace treaty with a handshake and the offering of a tuft of hair along with a blade of grass.[81] However, they are easily induced by money to violate it. (Thietmar IV, 25)

Encounters between the Franks and the northwestern Slavs were mentioned in other chronicles as well, including the Carolingian *Annals of Einhard*, dating from the beginning of the ninth century, and their East Frankish sequels, the *Annals of St. Bertin* and the *Annals of Fulda*. Of the Saxon chronicles, much interesting information is provided by Widukind, who lived in the second half of the tenth century. He was a learned monk from the Benedictine abbey in Corvey in southern Saxony and author of the *History of the Saxons* (*Widukindi res gestae Saxonicae*). There is also some attention devoted to the northwestern Slavs by an anonymous twelfth-century Saxon chronicler who goes by the name of the annalist Saxo.

1.43. Religious beliefs of the northwestern Slavs as reported by Thietmar and Helmold. Both Thietmar and Helmold provide a wealth of information on the history and civilization of the northwestern Slavs. Of special interest are their accounts of local religious customs. Here is how Thietmar describes the cult practiced in Radogošč, the principal town of the Veletian confederation:

There is in the land of the Redars a certain town in the shape of the triangle with three gates therein, called Riedegost, which is surrounded on all sides by a large virgin forest. Its two gates are open to all the incomers; the third one, facing east, is the smallest; it opens up to a footpath leading to a nearby lake of a terrifying appearance. There is in that town only one temple ingeniously constructed of wood [and] supported by a foundation of horns of various wild animals. On the outside its walls are decorated by various images of gods and goddesses, marvelously sculpted, as one can see upon examination. Inside, dressed in terrifying helmets and cuirasses, stand statues of gods, each with an engraved name, the first of whom bears the name of Zuarasic [Svarožic], who is honored and revered above the others by all the people. Their banners are not moved from there at all unless they are needed for a campaign and then [they are borne] by foot soldiers. . . . There are as many temples and as many images of demons venerated by the infidels as there are regions in this land, among which the abovementioned town has the supremacy. When they hasten to go to war, they greet it, and when they return from it successfully, they honor it with proper gifts and they inquire diligently . . .

81. As symbols of personal and communal guarantees.

> which propitiating sacrifice the priests should offer to gods. They placate [the gods'] mute anger with human and cattle blood offerings. (Thietmar VI, 24–25)

Thietmar's testimony is amplified by Helmold:

> In those days [beginning of the twelfth century] a variety of idolatrous cults and superstitious aberrations grew strong again throughout all Slavia. Besides the [holy] groves and the household gods in which the country and towns abound, the first and foremost deities are Prove, the god of the land of Oldenburg, Siva, the goddess of the Polabi[ans], and Redigast, the god of the land of the Abodrites. To these gods are dedicated priests, sacrificial libations, and a variety of religious rites. When the priest declares, according to the decisions of the lot, what solemnities are to be celebrated in honor of the gods, the men, women and children come together and offer to their deities sacrifices of oxen and sheep, often, also of Christians with whose blood they say their gods are delighted. After the victim is felled, the priest drinks of its blood in order to render himself more potent in the receiving of oracles. For it is the opinion of many that demons are very easily conjured with blood. After the sacrifices have been consummated according to custom, the populace turns to feasting and entertainment. The Slavs, too, have a strange delusion. At their feasts and carousals they pass about a bowl over which they utter words . . . in the name of the gods, of the good one, as well as of the bad one, professing that all propitious fortune is arranged by the good god, adverse, by the bad god. Hence, also, in their language they call the bad god Diabol or Zcerneboch, that is, the black god. Among the multiform divinities of the Slavs, however, Zuantevit, the god of the land of the Rugiani [Ranians], stands out as the most distinguished: he is so much more effective in his oracular responses that out of regard for him they think of the others as demigods. On this account they are also accustomed every year to select by lot a Christian whom they sacrifice in his special honor. To his shrine are sent fixed sums from all the provinces of the Slavs toward defraying the cost of sacrifices. The people are, moreover, actuated by an extraordinary regard for the service of the fane, for they neither lightly indulge in oaths nor suffer the vicinity of the temple to be desecrated even in the face of an enemy. (Helmold, 158–159)

These passages are often referred to in the continuing debate on the religious beliefs of the Slavs. Most scholars agree that, in accordance with Procopius' testimony (**1.18**), the Slavs had one supreme deity—Svarog, the god of the sky, mentioned in the Slavic translation of the Byzantine *Chronicle of John Malalas* (**3.5.1**) and in the East Slavic Hypatian codex of the *Primary Chronicle*. It appears that Svarog could also go by the name of Perun ('thunder') who, according to some East Slavic sources, was the supreme deity of Kievan Rus'. This is the function assigned to Perun by the *Primary Chronicle* in the account of the treaties between Rus' and Byzantium in the years 912, 945, and 971 and in the reports of Vladimir's pagan rule in Kiev under the year 980 and of his baptism in 988.

Synoptic treatments of the subject of Slavic pagan religious beliefs have come from four Polish scholars: the historians Henryk Łowmiański (1979) and Aleksander Gieysztor (1982) and the linguists Stanisław Urbańczyk (1991) and Leszek Moszyński (1992). Although the social and functional emphases of Łowmiański and Gieysztor are complemented by the linguistic interests of Urbańczyk and Moszyński, the ambiguity of the available sources, representing strictly local traditions, and the difficulty inherent in the etymological interpretation of proper names have led these and other scholars to imaginative but largely unprovable constructs. Thus, in Moszyński's view, the names of the deities mentioned by Thietmar and

Helmold should be understood as instances of a religious tabu whereby Helmold's Prove and Redigast are cryptonyms for Svarog, with Prove being the metathesized form of the Celtic sun god Borvo and Redigast being the place name *Radogošč* < *Radogost-j-ь* described by Thietmar.[82] Thietmar's Zuarasic, in Moszyński's interpretation is also a cryptonym for Svarog, from which it is derived: *Svarožic* < *Svarog-it-j-ь*.

Other terms that occur in the quoted passages are easier to interpret: Siva may be read as Živa, the goddess of life; the opposition of a good and a bad god is probably an echo of Manichaean Christian beliefs; Diabol (< *diabъlъ*) is a borrowing from Church Latin *diabolus* 'devil'; Zcerneboch is a transcription of *čr̥'nobogъ* 'black god'; Zuantevit, the four-faced chief deity on the island of Rügen, is *Svętovitъ*, a compound of the roots *svęt-* 'holy' and *vit-* 'dwell', the latter occurring in a number of native Slavic names, such as *Vitoslavъ*, *Vitomirъ*, *Vitomyslъ*, *Jarovitъ*, and *Dorgovitъ*. The medieval chronicler's identification of *Svętovitъ* with St. Vitus, patron saint of the abbey of Corvey, was probably connected with the saint's missionary interest in the neighboring Slavs.

As can be seen from these excerpts, the northwestern Slavs held fast to their tribal customs and pagan beliefs, and the missionary efforts of the Saxon clergy, though admittedly feebler than those emanating from Bavaria, encountered strong resistance and suffered occasional setbacks. An interesting instance of these difficulties is to be found in Thietmar's account of the life of his predecessor in Merseburg, Bishop Boso, who was especially keen on converting the Slavs to Christianity: "To facilitate the instruction of those entrusted to his care [Boso] wrote texts in Slavic and asked [the Slavs] to sing the Kyrie eleison explaining to them its benefit. These witless people twisted it mockingly into the perverse *ukrivolsa* which means in our language 'an alder tree is in the bush', saying: 'This is what Boso has told us,' although he said it differently" (Thietmar II, 37).[83]

1.44. Poland. Primitive tribal democracy of the kind described above by Thietmar was not compatible with statehood. In order to function as viable members of a medieval polity, states had to possess permanent social structures. First of all, a state had to be identified with a definite geographical space, a stretch of land whose physical features could imprint themselves on the collective psyche. Such a rooting in a particular territory could not be brought about except by centralized political power which could define the territory's limits and organize their defense. This demanded, in turn, the development of a social hierarchy in which a ruler and a class of nobles shared the burdens of power and were able to interact with their social counterparts in other states. The definition of spheres of authority and the stabilization of administrative practices called for the adoption of definite legal procedures for whose formulation a supratribal literary language was needed. Cadres of learned, or at least literate, people had to be developed in order to use this language in the course of performing the necessary administrative functions. Hence the need for Christianity with its monastic tradition of learning, with its schools where Latin or Church Slavonic were taught, with its ability to replace tribal particularism with its own universalist message.

To initiate a social revolution of these dimensions, strong leadership and permanent po-

82. More persuasive is Urbańczyk's (1991:188) surmise that Svarog's cryptonym is the personal name Radogost rather than its derivative, the place name Radogošč.

83. *Ukrivolsa* is an attempt to render Slavic *v kři volša* which contains the locative case of *keř* 'bush' and the nominative *olьša* 'alder'. The noun *keř* is a reflex of **kъrjь* which arose from **kъrъ* 'bush' by analogy to the collective **kъr-ьje* 'shrubbery'. The noun *olьša* is the West Slavic reflex of **ălĭxā* by the third palatalization of velars (**2.31**) with a prothetic *v* (**2.21**).

litical institutions had to emerge. These were clearly lacking among the northwestern Slavs. In Bulgaria and in Rus' they were provided by non-Slavic elements, while in the other Slavic states they arose as soon as native conditions became propitious. In Moravia it was the political vacuum left after the defeat of the Avars and the emergence of a strong local leader in the person of Rostislav that supplied the impulse for the development of statehood. The downfall of Moravia opened the way for Bohemia to become the foremost state of the area, a goal achieved under the leadership of the tribe of the Pražans and its rulers from the house of Přemysl. In Poland favorable conditions for statehood did not arrive until the second half of the tenth century. With Germany weakened by civil wars, unsuccessful military engagements in west Francia and southern Italy, and an open rebellion of the northwestern Slavs, Duke Mieszko (ca. 930–992)[84] of the tribe of the Polans in the area known today as Great Poland extended his realm in every direction, reaching the Baltic in the north, the Bug in the east, and the Carpathians in the south, and annexing Silesia in the west.

Of the tribes mentioned by the Bavarian Geographer, only those known from other sources can be identified and their location approximated. The following must have been part of Mieszko's state: Gopleans (Glopeani) in Great Poland on Lake Gopło, Vistulans (Vuislane) along the upper Vistula, and Silesians (Sleenzane), Dědošans (Dadosesani), Opolans (Opolini), and Golensites (Golensizi) along the Oder. The most intriguing is the identity and location of the Lendites (Lenditi). This ethnic appellation, which does not appear in Polish sources, seems to be derived from the root **lęd-* 'untilled land'. Judging by the use of tribal names containing this root in non-Polish sources, Lendites may refer to the Poles, cf. Lithuanian *lénkas,* Hungarian *lengyel,* East Slavic *ljaxъ* < **lęxъ,*[85] all meaning 'Pole'. Also containing this root are Slavic tribal terms *lenzanênoi* and *lenzenínois* found in chapters 9 and 37, respectively, of Constantine Porphyrogenitus' *De administrando imperio* (**1.23**). The former refers to a tribe settled in the basin of the Dnieper, while the latter appears to be located somewhere on the southwestern border of Rus'. It is impossible to ascertain whether the **lęd-* formations of the Bavarian Geographer and those of Constantine Porphyrogenitus referred to the same Polish tribe.[86] If they did, the only possible location for such a tribe would be between the Bug and the upper reaches of the Pripet.

The earliest local source on Polish history is a chronicle compiled in the beginning of the twelfth century by a Benedictine monk who came to Poland from the West, most probably from France, but whose identity is unknown. His chronicle gives an account of the earliest

84. The lively discussion on the question of the origin of the Polish duke's name has not produced a generally accepted solution. In all likelihood it is a hypocoristic truncation of some Slavic name beginning with the syllables *me, mě* or *mь* and extended by the suffix *-x-ьk-* (cf. Russian *Míša, Míška* for *Mixaíl* 'Michael', *Páša, Páška* for *Pável* 'Paul'). Possible candidates for such a derivation are the roots *met-* 'throw' (cf. Po. *Miecisław*), *meč-* 'sword' (cf. Po. *Mieczysław*), *med-* 'honey' alone or in the compound *medvědь* 'bear', *měx-* 'sack'. Complicating matters further is an eleventh-century Latin document from the papal chancery in Rome in which Mieszko is referred to as *Dagome* (or *Dagone*) *iudex* 'judge Dagome'. This could be a compound of the name Dago (as in the Germanic name Dagobert), which Mieszko may have received at his baptism in 966, and the initial syllable of his Slavic name.

85. With the East Slavic change *ę* > *'a* and emotive replacement of root-final consonant by *-x-* (cf. Polish *brach* for *brat* 'brother' and the Ukrainian adjective *ljac'kyj* 'Polish' < **lędьskъjь*). It is from a Latinized form of **lęxъ* that the Polish chronicler Wincenty Kadłubek (ca. 1150–1223) coined the name *Lechite* as a synonym of *Pole.* This artificial term has been put to use in Slavic linguistics as the designation of the West Slavic languages whose reflexes of Proto-Slavic nasal vowels retain their nasal resonance. These languages include Polish and Kashubian as well as the extinct northwestern Slavic languages of which Polabian is the best known.

86. One and the same name may refer to different ethnic entities; compare the cases of the West Slavic (Gniezno) and East Slavic (Kiev) Polans or of the Veneti mentioned in **1.4.**

Polish history from the legendary beginnings of the Piast dynasty, through the rule of Mieszko and his son Bolesław the Brave (992–1025), leading up to the times of King Bolesław III Wrymouth (1102–1138). Known as the *Chronicle of Anonymous Gallus,* it is, like its contemporary Czech chronicle of Cosmas, couched in highly literate, versified Latin. In the introduction to Book I the chronicler sets Poland in its larger Slavic context, concluding his description with a glowing vision of Slavdom:

> Poland is in the northern part of Slavdom. In the east its neighbor is Rus', in the south Hungary, in the southwest Moravia and Bohemia, in the west Denmark and Saxony. From the side of the North Sea [the Baltic] . . . it has three very savage neighboring peoples of barbarian pagans, namely Selentia, Pomerania, and Prussia.[87] . . . The land of the Slavs, which in the north is divided into or consists of such different countries, stretches from the Sarmatians . . . to Denmark and Saxony; from Thrace through Hungary . . . and further on through Carantania it reaches Bavaria. Finally in the south, along the Mediterranean Sea beginning from Epirus through Dalmatia, Croatia, and Istria, it reaches the shore of the Adriatic Sea where Venice and Aquileia are situated and borders there with Italy. . . . Although this land is heavily wooded, it abounds in gold and silver, bread and meat, fish and honey. It is to be preferred over other [lands] because, even though it is surrounded by so many of the above-mentioned Christian and pagan peoples and was attacked by them many times jointly or singly, it has never been completely subjugated. A land where the air is healthy, the fields are fertile, the forests are flowing with honey, the waters are full of fish, the warriors are pugnacious, the peasants are hard-working, the horses are tough, the oxen are ready to till the land, the cows have plenty of milk, the sheep have plenty of wool. (Anonymous Gallus, 9–10)

Ibrāhīm Ibn Jaʿqūb (**1.41**) speaks equally highly of the natural riches of Poland but adds a note of practicality to his account of Mieszko's reign:

> As for the land of M.š.ka [Mieszko], it is the most spacious of the [Slavs'] lands and it has an abundance of food, meat, honey, and arable land. His taxes are set according to the weight of merchandise and they go for the pay of his men. Every month every one of them receives a fixed sum. He has three thousand armored men divided into units and every hundred of them is equal to ten hundred others. And he gives these men their clothes, horses, armor, and everything they need. If to one of them a child is born, he orders that it be paid a [soldier's] pay from the moment it was born, whether the child is of male or female sex. When the child grows up, then, if it is a man, he will marry him off and will pay a dowry for him to the [bride's] father. If it is a girl, then he will give her in marriage and will pay a dowry for her to the [groom's] father. . . . If some man has two or three daughters, then this is the cause of his wealth. If he has two sons, then this is the cause of his poverty. (Ibn Jaʿqūb, 415)

In 966, in a virtual imitation of Rostislav's preemptive invitation of Slavic missionaries to Moravia, Mieszko summoned missionaries from Bohemia and was baptized by them together with his countrymen. This led to the establishment of the Polish archbishopric of Gniezno and allowed the Polish church to answer directly to Rome rather than to the archbishopric of Magdeburg. Mieszko's baptism, however, championed according to tradition by

87. Selentia occurs only in Anonymous Gallus, and its domain is unknown. Had the chronicler not localized it by the Baltic, one could surmise that it refers to the region east of the Saal which was conquered by Bolesław the Brave and which in his days was still inhabited by the Slavs. Prussia was inhabited by the Baltic-speaking Prussians.

his wife Dobrava, daughter of Boleslav I of Bohemia, was not met with uniform enthusiasm by the Polans, even though the beginning of Thietmar's account of the event would seem to suggest the opposite: "[Mieszko], upon incessant pleadings of his beloved wife, spewed out the poison of paganism into which he was born and cleansed the stigma of the original sin in holy baptism, and immediately the previously infirm members of the populace followed their chief and beloved ruler and, clad in nuptial garments, were counted among the children of Christ" (Thietmar IV, 56). Yet in the very next sentence Thietmar tells us that "Jordan, the first bishop [of the Poles], labored hard among them before this industrious man, through word and deed, induced them to cultivate the Lord's vineyard."

The original reluctance of the native population to accept Christianity was widespread. According to a passage found in the *Vita Methodii*, some eighty years before Mieszko's baptism Methodius warned the southern Polish tribe of the Vistulans not to resist Christianization: "A very powerful pagan prince settled on the Vistula offended the Christians and did evil. Having sent [messengers] to him, [Methodius] said: 'My son, it would be well for you to accept baptism of your own will in your own land, rather than be baptized forcibly as a prisoner in a foreign land. You will remember me.' And so it happened" (*Vita Methodii* 11). This passage is often cited as one of the indications that Slavic liturgy introduced to Moravia by Constantine and Methodius was for a time used also in southern Poland. Some scholars go so far as to surmise that in the last quarter of the tenth century Cracow may have been the seat of a Slavic eparchy.[88]

1.45. The eastern Slavs. According to the *Primary Chronicle*, the eastern Slavic tribes were settled in the basins of the middle and upper Dnieper, the upper Western Dvina, the upper Volga, and the Lovat-Ilmen-Volkhov-Ladoga waterway. Of the dozen or so tribes mentioned by the chronicle, the dominant ones were the Polians on the Dnieper around Kiev, the Slovians on Lake Ilmen around Novgorod, and the Krivichians at the head waters of the Volga, the Dvina, and the Dnieper with Smolensk as their main town. Foreign travelers were struck by the harshness of their climate and curious bathing habits. In the words of Ibn Jaʿqūb:

> The lands of the Slavs are the coldest of all the lands. The greatest cold is when there is full moon at night and the days are cloudless. Then frost increases and ice increases. The ground hardens like stone, all liquids freeze, wells and puddles are covered with a hard layer so that they become like stone. And when people breathe out, there forms on their beards a coat of ice as if it were glass. . . . They have no baths but they use log cabins in which gaps [between logs] are stuffed with something that appears on their trees and looks like seaweed—they call it *m.x.* [Proto-Slavic *mъxъ* 'moss']. . . . In one corner they put up a stone stove and above it they open up a hole to let the smoke from the stove escape. When the stove is good and hot, they close up the opening and close the door of the hut. Inside are vessels with water and they pour out of them water onto the hot stove and steam comes from it. Each of them has in his hand a tuft of grass with which they make air circulate and draw it to themselves. Then their pores open up and the unneeded substances from their bodies come out. (Ibn Jaʿqūb, 418–419)[89]

88. A discussion and a bibliographic survey of this problem may be found in Łowmiański 1970:493–515.

89. This description of Slavic bathing habits is remarkably similar to the practices one still encounters in Russian provincial bathhouses (*banjas*), where bathers use bunches of fresh twigs (Ru. *veniki*) to sprinkle cold water over themselves in order to cool off. This habit has always puzzled foreigners; witness the account attributed to the apostle Andrew and cited, undoubtedly for its anecdotal value, in the *Primary Chronicle*. According to this apocryphal story, this is what Andrew saw as he was returning to Rome from a trip to the vicinity of Novgorod: "They warm [the bathhouses] to ex-

The challenges encountered by the eastern Slavs were less formidable than those facing the Slavic inhabitants of the Balkans and Central Europe. With the western Slavs preoccupied by the problem of containing German expansion eastward, the western periphery of the eastern Slavs was relatively secure. Their northern neighbors were the comparatively weak and peaceful Baltic and Finnish tribes. In the east, along the Volga, there lived the Turkic Bulgars and Khazars, who appeared to be more interested in profit from trade with the Islamic world than in making war on their Slavic neighbors. The southern border presented the greatest danger. It ran alongside the steppe corridor which stretched from the Caspian Sea to the mouth of the Danube and was the favorite route of migrant tribes heading toward the Greek colonies spread along the northern shore of the Black Sea and beyond them to the Balkans and Western Europe. Before the Great Migrations the southern regions were inhabited successively by the Iranian Scythians and Sarmatians and the Germanic Goths. The contacts of these peoples with the prehistoric Slavs living in this area left a lasting imprint on the proto-Slavic lexicon (**2.55**). During the Great Migrations and their aftermath the corridor's wide expanse of grasslands served as the roadway to Europe for the Turkic Huns, Avars, Bulgars, and Pechenegs, and the Altaic Magyars. These nomadic tribes left little lexical sediment on Slavic, but they may have influenced the development of Slavic phonology (Galton 1994).

Although the Pechenegs, who occupied the steppe corridor in the tenth and eleventh centuries, did conduct raids on the southernmost towns of Rus', the threat they presented to the emerging state was not one of direct military confrontation. More vexing was the fact that the Pechenegs were in a position to interdict or, at the very least, seriously hamper Europe's trade with Byzantium and the Near East. Sitting astride the lower Dnieper, which was the principal commercial route to the countries along and beyond the Black Sea, the Pechenegs posed a constant menace to river traffic. Especially vulnerable were the points of portage at the several Dnieper cataracts, where heavily laden boats had to be dragged overland through the territory controlled by the Pechenegs. With the eastern Mediterranean cut off by the Arab pirates, the availability of the Baltic-Dnieper–Black Sea alternative waterway was of vital concern to all of Northern Europe and, above all, to Europe's most active "international" traders, the Scandinavian Vikings or Norsemen.

1.46. The Norsemen in Eastern Europe. Trade, no doubt, was at the root of the Norsemen's lasting involvement in the political life of the eastern Slavs. Eager to maintain their commercial links with Eastern Europe and the lands beyond it, they explored and adapted to their use a vast network of trading routes which took full advantage of the rich system of eastern European waterways. One such route, which allowed the Norsemen to circle Europe on the way to and from Byzantium, is described in the *Primary Chronicle*:

> A trade-route connected the Varangians[90] with the Greeks. Starting from Greece, this route proceeds along the Dnieper, above which a portage leads to the Lovat'. By following the

treme heat, then undress, and after anointing themselves with an acid liquid, they take young branches and lash their bodies. They actually lash themselves so violently that they barely escape alive. Then they drench themselves with cold water, and thus are revived" (*Primary Chronicle* 54).

90. Local sources identify the Norsemen with whom the East Slavs came into contact as the Varangians. This term is probably derived from Old Norse **varing-* 'ally' (Vasmer/Trubačev 1964:276), and its choice may be due to the purely commercial interests of the Norsemen involved in the East European venture (compare Slavic *gostь* 'guest' and 'merchant'). In this respect, the ways of the Varangians differed significantly from the combative mentality of their West European Viking cousins.

Lovat', the great lake Il'men' is reached. The river Volkhov flows out of this lake and enters the great lake Nevo [Ladoga]. The mouth of this lake [the Neva] opens into the Varangian Sea [Baltic]. Over this sea goes the route to Rome, and on from Rome overseas to Tsar'grad [Constantinople]. The Pontus [Black Sea], into which flows the river Dnieper, may be reached from that point. (*Primary Chronicle,* 53)

More details on the Novgorod-Kiev-Constantinople portion of this route are provided by Constantine Porphyrogenitus:

The *monoxyla* [dugouts] which come down from outer Russia [Rus'] to Constantinople are from Novgorod, . . . and others from the city of Smolensk and from Lyubech and Chernigov and from Vyshegrad. All these come down the river Dnieper, and are collected together at the city of Kiev. . . . Their Slav tributaries . . . cut the *monoxyla* on their mountains in time of winter, and when they have prepared them, as spring approaches, and the ice melts, they bring them on to the neighboring lakes. And since these debouch into the river Dnieper, they enter thence on to this same river, and come down to Kiev, and draw [the *monoxyla*] along to be finished and sell them to the Russians [Rus']. The Russians buy these bottoms only, furnishing them with oars and rowlocks and other tackle from their old *monoxyla,* which they dismantle. . . . And in the month of June they move off down the river Dnieper and come to Vitichev, which is a tributary city of the Russians, and there they gather during two or three days; and when all the *monoxyla* are collected together, then they set out, and come down the said Dnieper river.

After overcoming the dangers of the Dnieper cataracts and the Pecheneg attacks, the travelers reached the island of St. Aitherios, today's Berezan', at the mouth of the Dnieper:

Arrived at this island, they rest themselves there for two or three days. And they re-equip their *monoxyla* with such tackle as is needed, sails and masts and rudders, which they bring with them.[91] . . . They come thence to the Dniester river, and having got safely there they rest again. But when the weather is propitious, they put to sea and come to the river called Aspros [probably lake Alibei], and after resting there too in like manner, they again set out and come to the Selinas, to the so called branch of the Danube river. And until they are past the river Selinas, the Pechenegs keep pace with them. And if it happens that the sea casts a *monoxylon* on shore, they all put in to land, in order to present a united opposition to the Pechenegs. But after the Selinas they fear nobody, but entering the territory of Bulgaria, they come to the mouth of the Danube. From the Danube they proceed to the Konopas, . . . Constantia, . . . Varna, and . . . the river Ditzina, all of which are Bulgarian territory. From the Ditzina they reach the district of Mesembria, and there at last their voyage, fraught with such travail and terror, such difficulty and danger, is at an end. (Constantine Porphyrogenitus, 60–63)

The *Primary Chronicle* also traces the Varangian route to the Middle East:

The Dnieper itself rises in the upland forest [the Valdai Hills], and flows southward. The [Western] Dvina has its source in this same forest, but flows northward and empties into the Varangian Sea. The Volga rises in this same forest but flows to the east, and discharges through

91. It is there, presumably, that boat outfitters made the *monoxyla* seaworthy by adding planks to the shipboards. The *monoxyla* with raised shipboards (known in Rus' as *nabojnye* from *nabiti* 'to nail on') were used in the Avaro-Slav attack on Constantinople in 626.

seventy mouths into the Caspian Sea. It is possible by this route to the eastward to reach the [Volga] Bulgars and the Caspians [Khazars], and thus attain the region of Shem [the Arabic lands] (*Primary Chronicle*, 53).

There are echoes of the actual exploitation of this route in the East Slavic epic folk songs, the bylinas, of the Novgorod cycle, particularly in those recounting the adventures of the happy-go-lucky Vasilij Buslaevič and the rich merchant Sadko. Vasilij's pilgrimage to Jerusalem is presented as a voyage by riverways only, beginning on Lake Ilmen and continuing via the Volga and the Caspian Sea to the Jordan. The bylina of Sadko describes the frequent trips of his flotilla of thirty boats from the Volkhov into Lake Ladoga and then by the Neva onto the "blue sea" [the Baltic]. There his boats turn around and make for the "Golden Horde," where Sadko sells his Novgorod merchandise at a fine profit. His boats, laden with barrels of gold, silver, and pearls, turn around again and take their precious cargo back to the "blue sea."

Foreigners also showed an interest in the commercial routes of Rus'. This is what Ibn Hurdāḏbeh, a ninth-century Persian scholar and civil servant stationed in Baghdad, had to say about them in his *Book of Routes and Kingdoms*:

> The route of the Rus' merchants: They are a tribe from among the Saqāliba. They bring beaver and black fox pelts as well as swords from the farthest limits of Saqlabīja to the Byzantine [Black] Sea, where the Byzantine ruler imposes a tithe on them. If they wish, they proceed on the Volga [*Tīn* or *Tīl*?],[92] the river [*Nahr*] of the Saqāliba,[93] . . . arrive on the Caspian Sea, and come ashore wherever they wish. . . . Sometimes they transport their wares on camelback from the Caspian to Baghdad. (Ibn Hurdāḏbeh, 77)

Smooth functioning of the Norsemen's commercial enterprise required the protection of their trading routes, whether they be in Eastern Europe or anywhere else around the world. To this end, the Norsemen developed an elaborate support system for their overseas operations. It consisted of a network of market towns established near particularly important locations along the trading routes. These settlements or vics, as they are often called, functioned as trading posts for the passing merchants and as military outposts guarding especially dangerous sections of the trading routes. Novgorod, Beloozero, and Izborsk, mentioned in the *Primary Chronicle* in its romanticized account of the "calling of the Varangians," were probably such vics:

> The [Slavic] tributaries of the Varangians drove them back beyond the sea and, refusing them further tribute, set out to govern themselves. There was no law among them, but tribe rose

92. Although the spelling of the river name is corrupt, the context suggests that its reconstruction as *Itīl*, the name of the Volga in early Turkic, yields a likelier reading than *Tanais*, that is, the Don (Lewicki 1956:133–137).

93. The terms *Saqāliba* and *Saqlabīya* are usually thought to designate the Slavs and Slavdom. Hence, the Arabic phrase *Nahr as-Saqāliba* has been rendered as 'the river of the Slavs'. Pritsak (1981:25) contests this interpretation, attributing it to the "patriotic historians of Eastern Europe," and claims that *Saqāliba* actually meant 'slaves' and that *Nahr as-Saqāliba* should be understood as 'the Highway of the Slaves'. This interpretation, however, clashes with Ibn Hurdāḏbeh's use of the terms *Saqāliba* and *Saqlabīya* as ethnic designations; witness his description of the Rādānīya Jewish traders as speakers of "Arabic, Persian, Greek, Frankish, Andalusian [Iberian Romance] and *Saqlabīya*" (Lewicki 1956:74–75). Ibn Faḍlān's (**1.47.e**) use of the term *Saqāliba* with reference to the Volga Bulgars is an example of the frequently observed transfer of names from one ethnic community to another (Kmietowicz et al., eds., 1985:118–119, cf. **1.4**). It is hard to imagine that Ibn Faḍlān's designation of the ruler of the Bulgars as the *malik as-Saqāliba* 'king of the *Saqāliba*' could be interpreted as the 'king of the slaves'.

against tribe. Discord thus ensued among them, and they began to war one against another. They said to themselves, 'Let us seek a prince who may rule over us and judge us according to the Law.' They accordingly went overseas to the Varangian Russes: these particular Varangians were known as Russes [Rus'], just as some are called Swedes, and others Normans, English, and Gotlanders, for they were thus named. The Chuds, the Slavs [Slovians], the Krivichians, and the Ves' [Vepse] then said to the people of Rus', 'Our land is great and rich, but there is no order in it. Come to rule and reign over us.' They thus selected three brothers with their kinsfolk, who took with them all the Russes and migrated. The oldest, Rurik, located himself in Novgorod; the second, Sineus, at Beloozero; and the third, Truvor, in Izborsk. On account of these Varangians, the district of Novgorod became known as the land of Rus'. (*Primary Chronicle*, 59–60)[94]

Kiev, with its strategic location at the crossroads of the commercial routes to Byzantium and the Khazars, became the next possession of the Varangians. Under its first Varangian rulers, the noblemen Askold and Dir and their successors Oleg and Rurik's son Igor, Kiev became the capital of Kievan Rus' and the metropolis of the eastern Slavs. Its leading role was rarely challenged by the independent-minded citizenry of Novgorod.

The importance of Kiev as the capital and trading center of Rus' was noted by the Persian geographer al-Istarkhī writing in the first half of the tenth century:

The Russians are of three kinds. The king of those nearest to Bulghār lives in a city called Kuyābah [Kiev]. It is larger than Bulghār. Another kind, farther off than these, is called Slāwīyah [probably the Sloveni of Novgorod], and there is a kind called Arthānīyah, whose king lives in Artha [Scandinavia?]. The people come to trade in Kiev. It is not recorded that any stranger has ever entered Artha, for they kill all strangers who set foot in their land. They descend by water to trade and say nothing of their affairs and merchandise. They let none accompany them or enter their land. From Artha are brought black sable-skins and lead. (al-Istarkhī, 99)

1.47. The terms *Rus'* and *Russian*. The problem of the origin of the term *Rus'* has divided scholarship into two camps, the "Normanists," who accept the general drift of the explanation given by the *Primary Chronicle*, and the "anti-Normanists," who do not.[95] According to the Normanists, the East Slavic *Rus'* is a borrowing either directly from Scandinavian, where we find such terms as the Old Icelandic *roþs-menn, roþs-karlar* 'oarsmen, seamen' and the Swedish *Ros-lagen* (the coastal area of Uppland, across the Baltic from the Gulf of Finland) or, what is likelier, from Finnish, where *Ruotsi* (< West Finnic *Rōtsi*) is the name of Sweden and *Ruotsalainen* denotes a Swede.[96] In this explanation, the people

94. Of the towns mentioned by Constantine Porphyrogenitus, Smolensk must have been an especially important vic, if we are to judge it by the very large necropolis in nearby Gnezdovo (Schenker 1989). The vics in the Baltic Sea included Birka and Gotland in Sweden, Grobin in Latvia, and Wollin and Haithabu in northeast Germany. The Volga route was protected by the vics in Staraja Ladoga (Aldeigjuborg) and Bulgar.

95. Anti-Normanist positions represent various agendas and theories, including the scholarship of the Eurasian view which, by and large, was also the official Soviet point of view. For extensive summaries of the controversy, see Mošin 1930 and Łowmiański 1957; shorter accounts may be found in the introduction to Samuel H. Cross and Olgerd P. Sherbowitz-Wetzor's edition of the *Primary Chronicle* (1953:39–50) and in Pritsak 1981:3–6. The latter book contributes to the debate on the origin of Rus' by offering revisionist interpretations of some of the known sources and adducing a number of Scandinavian and Oriental sources that had not been considered previously. The highly speculative inferences drawn therefrom offer an intricate but fragile network of constructs. Their examination is beyond the scope of the present survey.

96. Literally, 'a Swedish man'; similar terms exist in Estonian and other Finnic languages of the area.

who in Slavic were called *Rus'*, in Greek *Rhôs*, and in Arabic *Rūs* were Norsemen involved in trade with the Orient and Byzantium. The Rus'-Byzantine treaty of 912, cited by the *Primary Chronicle*, offers a striking confirmation of the identification of the Rus' with Norsemen since all the Rus' emissaries mentioned in the treaty bear Scandinavian names: "We of the Rus' nation: Karl, Ingjald, Farulf, Vermund, Hrollaf, Gunnar, Harold, Karni, Frithleif, Hroarr, Angantyr, Throand, Leithulf, Fast, and Steinvith, are sent by Oleg, Great Prince of Rus' . . . unto you, Leo, and Alexander and Constantine, . . . Emperors of the Greeks, for the maintenance and proclamation of the long-standing amity which joins Greeks and Russes" (*Primary Chronicle*, 63–64).

Although the primary connection of the Rus' was with the eastern Slavs, to whom they eventually lent their name, ancient sources mention them in other contexts as well. The following passages from non-Slavic sources are often quoted in support of the Normanist view:

(a) The Carolingian *Annals of St. Bertin* (830–882) tell of a diplomatic incident which occurred in 839 when a Byzantine embassy from the emperor Theophilus (r. 829–842) arrived in Ingelheim on the Rhine at the court of Emperor Louis the Pious (r. 814–840):

> [Theophilus] sent with them some men who called themselves, that is the people to which they belonged, Rhos; according to them, their king, called kagan, sent them to [Theophilus] in friendship. [Theophilus] asked in [his] letter that the emperor graciously give them permission and help to return to their country through his empire because the roads by which they had travelled to Constantinople fell into the hands of barbarian and exceedingly wild tribes and he would not wish to expose them to great danger. Having diligently investigated the reasons for their arrival, the emperor established that they belonged to the people of the Sueoni [Swedes]. (*Annals of St. Bertin*, 44)

Louis the Pious, concerned about the Viking raids on the coastal towns in the North Sea, suspected that the visiting Rhos could be spies. He detained them pending further investigation but promised Theophilus to have them repatriated or sent back to Constantinople if they turn out to be honorable people.

(b) Liudprand of Cremona (**1.40**) identified the Rus' seamen who assaulted Constantinople in 941 under the command of Prince Igor as Norsemen (Nordmanni):[97]

> There is a certain northern people whom the Greeks call Rusii from the color of their skins,[98] while we from the position of their country call them *Nordmanni*. In the German language *nord* means 'north' and *man* means 'human being', so that *Nordmanni* is the equivalent to 'men of the north'. These people had a king named Inger [Igor], who got together a fleet of a thousand ships or more, and sailed for Constantinople. (Liudprand, 185)

The Byzantines, Liudprand continues, though taken unawares by the attack of the Rusii, hastily recommissioned fifteen mothballed ships and, having equipped them with the redoubtable "Greek fire" or flame throwers, routed the invaders.[99]

(c) Constantine Porphyrogenitus in his description of the Dnieper cataracts distinguished clearly between their Rus' (Greek *Rhōsistí*) names, which were Scandinavian, and their

97. This attack on Constantinople was preceded by the expeditions of Askold and Dir in 860 and of Oleg in 907.

98. Liudprand's folk etymology is based on Greek *rhoúsios* 'dark red' or Latin *russus* 'red'.

99. A similar account of the battle is found in the East Slavic *Primary Chronicle*.

Slavic (Greek *Sklabēnistí*) counterparts. Four of these pairs are listed below (Constantine Porphyrogenitus, 58–61):[100]

1. Rus' Ulvorsi (< *hólmfors* 'island cataract')
   Slavic Ostrobouniprákh (< LPSl. *ostrovьnѣ̂jь porgъ* 'island cataract')
2. Rus' Aeiphór (< *aifors* 'ever-raging')
   Slavic Neasḗt (< *nejasytь* 'pelican' < LPSl. *ne-ję-sytь* 'unsatiable')
3. Rus' Barouphóros (< *varufors* 'rocky cataract')
   Slavic Boulnēprákh (< LPSl. *vl̥nьnѣ̂jь porgъ* 'billowing cataract')
4. Rus' Leánti (< *leandi* 'seething')
   Slavic Beroútzē (< LPSl. *vьrǫčѣ̂jь* 'boiling')

(d) Ibn Rustah (also Ibn Rosteh), a Persian writing in Arabic in the beginning of the tenth century, contrasted the Slavs and the Russes in his encyclopedic compilation entitled *A Book of Precious Valuables.* After giving a fairly detailed description of the localization and customs of the Slavs, in which he characterized them as forest-dwelling collectors of honey, raisers of pigs, and growers of millet, Ibn Rustah passes on to the Russes:

> As for Russes, they inhabit an island surrounded by a lake. The island is three days' journey large, covered with woods and woody swamps. It is so unhealthy and humid that when a man puts his foot on the ground, the ground shakes because of the soaked earth.[101] . . . They organize attacks upon the Slavs. They arrive in boats, approach, seize them into captivity, and take them to the Khazars and the [Volga] Bulgars and sell them to these people. They do not have tilled fields, but eat only what they bring from the land of the Slavs. . . . They do not own any land, or villages, or cultivated fields. Their only occupation is trade in pelts of sables, squirrels, and other fur animals which they sell to those who want to buy them. . . . They have numerous towns[102] and live well. . . . They are tall, stately, and courageous. However, they do not show this courage on land but conduct their assaults and campaigns solely on board ships. (Ibn Rustah, 39–43)

(e) Ibn Faḍlān was a member of a diplomatic mission to the Volga Bulgars dispatched in 921–922 by al-Muktadir, the caliph of Bagdad. The object of the mission was to forge an alliance against the Khazars, whose control of the lands north of the Caspian Sea posed a threat to the continued exploitation of the Volga as the principal waterway in the conduct of East-West trade. Ibn Faḍlān's *Risāla* ('writing'), that is, his description of the appearance and customs of the Rus' merchants whom he met in Bulgar, complements the observations of Ibn Rustah:

> I have seen the Rūs as they came on their merchant journeys and encamped by the Atil [Volga]. I have never seen more perfect physical specimens, tall as date palms, blond and ruddy; they

100. Reconstructions of the names of the cataracts, cited by Constantine, have been the subject of a long scholarly debate. Its history (and bibliography) may be found in Falk 1951; see also Shevelov 1955. It is interesting that Constantine cited Slavic **porgъ* 'threshold, cataract' in its South Slavic form as *prakh* (showing the Byzantine Greek spirantization of *g*), rather than in the East Slavic form with *polnoglasie*.

101. It is not known what locality Ibn Rustah had in mind. It could have been in a Scandinavian country (e.g. Birka on lake Malären in Sweden or the island of Gotland in the Baltic) or in Rus' (e.g. Novgorod, whose Norse name *Hólmgardr* means 'island town').

102. This is probably a reference to the vics (discussed above). Their profusion in Rus' is evident from the name *Gardaríki* 'country of (fortified) towns' with which the Scandinavians designated Rus' (compare Castile in Spain and Castelli Romani in Italy).

> wear neither *qurtaqs* [tunics][103] nor caftans, but the men wear a garment which covers one side of the body and leaves a hand free. Each man has an axe, a sword, and a knife, and keeps each by him at all times. Their swords are broad and grooved, of Frankish sort. . . . When they have come from their land and anchored on, or tied up at the shore of, the Atil, which is a great river, they build big houses of wood on the shore, each holding ten to twenty persons more or less. Each man has a couch on which he sits. With them are pretty slave girls destined for sale to merchants. (Ibn Faḍlān, 95–96)

Ibn Faḍlān's account ends with the celebrated description of a funeral in which a Rus' man, in a typically Viking fashion, is cremated together with his ship and his possessions, including a slave girl.[104]

Such testimonies could be multiplied.[105] They leave little doubt that the Rus' of early Slavic history were Norsemen (Varangians or Vikings) who, having settled among the eastern Slavs, became totally Slavicized. Originally the terms *Rus'* and *Russian* referred specifically to the Norsemen, but from the eleventh century on, they came to denote Slavic-speaking Christian inhabitants of Eastern Europe without any regard to their ethnic origin, be it Slavic, Scandinavian, Finnic, Baltic, or Khazar. Eventually the term *Rus'* acquired a geographic connotation and came to name the land, further specified as Novgorodian Rus', Kievan Rus', Moscovite Rus', and so on. Different historical destinies of the northeastern and southwestern portions of Rus' have resulted in the linguistic and political division of the area into the three modern states, Russia, Ukraine, and Belarus.[106]

103. Adapted into Russian and Polish as *kúrtka* 'jacket'.

104. In an abridgment of the *Risāla* composed by Amīn Rāzi, a sixteenth-century Persian geographer, the capital of the Rūs is said to be called *Kyawh*, that is, Kiev (Smyser 1965:102).

105. One could add here the accounts of the Arab al-Masʿudi, the Jew Ibrāhīm Ibn Jaʿqūb, the Greek Photius, and other Oriental and Byzantine writers (Tixomirov 1940:19–40).

106. With Russia, Ukraine, and Belarus having a shared past, it has been a common Russian and Western practice to refer to the medieval variety of their languages as "Old Russian," there being no specialized adjectives to correspond to the distinction between Rus' and Russia. This usage, however, has been found offensive and potentially confusing because of the concurrent use of the terms "Old Ukrainian" and "Old Belarussian." To remedy the situation some American scholars have used the adjective *Rus'ian* as a pendant to *Rus'*. This coinage, however, has not gained wide acceptance, and in this volume the term *East Slavic* is used to denote the pre-Petrine variety of Russian, Ukrainian, and Belarussian.

2. LANGUAGE

2.1. The historical comparative method and the concept of the proto-language. When learning a new language, we tend to stress the differences that separate it from other languages we know, especially our native language. This focus on the new and the unfamiliar may prevent us from realizing that languages exhibit many similarities in all areas of their structure, be it in phonology, grammar, or lexicon. Sometimes these similarities are random and may be due to sheer fortuity or linguistic borrowing. Ancient Greek *hólos* 'whole' or *rhaínō* 'I sprinkle' are at first sight similar in sound and meaning to English *whole* and *rain,* but further investigation shows that this similarity is not systemic and that it must be attributed to purely accidental causes. Ancient Greek *skholḗ* 'leisure, school' and Latin *posita* 'placed' (in its Italian *posta* or French *poste* forms) appear in dozens of languages around the globe, testifying to no more than the popularity of the Western educational system and the ubiquitousness of mail services.

In some instances, however, the similarities among languages are so regular as to rule out the possibility of a fortuitous development.[107] When such systematic similarities are discovered, they are best interpreted as a result of shared linguistic history. They imply that the languages in question go back to a common source, a "parent" language, from which they diverged at some point in the past and from then on followed their own, independent paths of development. Languages that show such similarities are said to be related, and the method by which their relatedness is established is called the *historical comparative method.*

A small sample of semantically similar English and German words (Table 1) should suffice to convince us that the correspondences between these two languages are so regular as to justify the positing of a parent language or a proto-language from which both English and German have descended. Other modern languages that appear to be derived from this same proto-language are those of Scandinavia and the Low Countries. All of them are conventionally called Germanic, and their common ancestor is referred to as Proto-Germanic.

107. The similarities referred to here do not include traits common to all the languages of the world, such as their analyzability in formal and semantic terms or the fact that they all possess features of structure (phonemes, morphemes, words, etc., and rules governing their arrangement). Nor do they refer to the so-called deep structure used in the transformational-generative model of language analysis and shown to be common to all languages. What concerns us here are surface phenomena, that is, observable facts and falsifiable interpretations of the place and rank of these facts in the structure of individual languages.

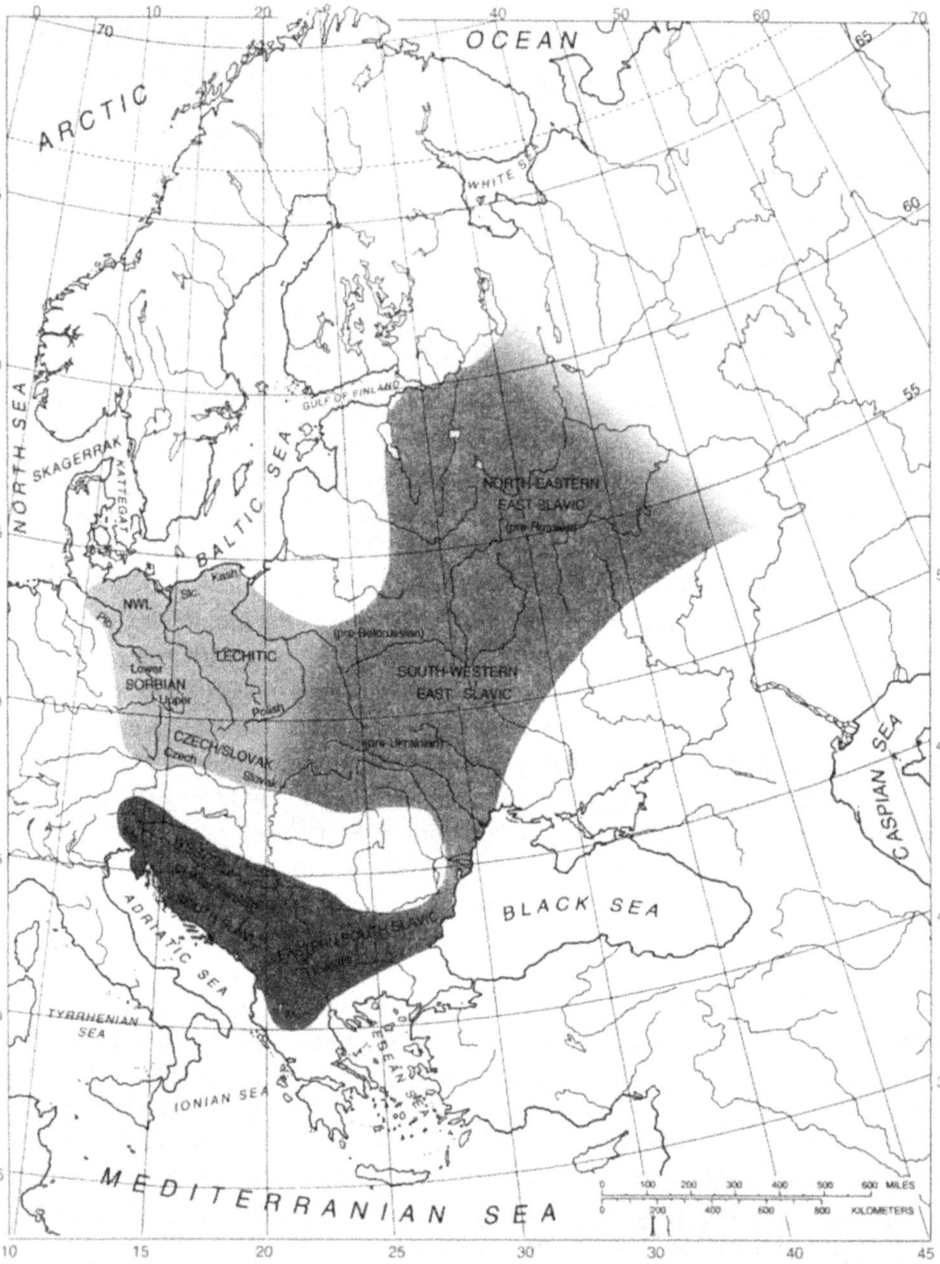

Schematic distribution of Slavic dialects in the tenth century

- South Slavic
- West Slavic
- East Slavic

Kash.	Kashubian
Mac.	Macedonian
NWL	North/West Lechitic
Plb.	Polabian
Slc.	Slovincian
Sln.	Slovenian

Table 1: Selected English and German lexical correspondences

English	German
father and mother	Vater und Mutter
heart and liver	Herz und Leber
bread and water	Brot und Wasser
two or three	zwei oder drei
eat and drink	essen und trinken
white and red	weiss und rot
cold blood	kalte Blut

2.2. Linguistic reconstruction and phonetic laws. Most proto-languages are not attested and have to be reconstructed on the basis of a meticulous comparison of the sounds and forms of the related languages. The examples given in Table 1 show that the English sound *t* corresponds to German *c* [*ts*] (spelled *z*), as in *two* vs. *zwei,* or to *s*, as in *eat* vs. *essen.* What Proto-Germanic sound are they derived from? By merely juxtaposing the English and German examples we would not be able to answer this question with any degree of certainty. If, however, we were to consider the totality of sound correspondences among all the known Germanic languages, we would be able to reconstruct the Proto-Germanic sound as *t* and assume that its modern reflexes are *t* in English and *c* and *s* in German.[108] And on the basis of additional correspondences between English and German (Table 2) one can formulate a rule, or phonetic law, whereby Modern German reflexes of Proto-Germanic *t* are *c* in word-initial position but *s* after vowels.

Table 2: Examples of English *t* corresponding to German *c* and *s*

English	German
ten	zehn
to	zu
tin	Zinn
toll	Zoll
kettle	Kessel
better	besser
foot	Fuss
out	aus

Such a phonetic law may be rewritten using traditional linguistic symbols in which the brackets delimit the participating factors of the process: the hatchmark means 'pause' (here the initial position), *V* stands for any vowel, the underline indicates the locus of the process, and the arrowhead, depending on its direction, means 'going to' or 'coming from':

108. It is a common practice in historical linguistics to provide reconstructed (i.e. unattested) forms with an asterisk. However, since this survey deals almost exclusively with reconstructions, asterisks will not be used except to avoid ambiguity and to mark "unreal" forms, that is, forms which could have occurred but did not. Otherwise, language labels will be relied upon to differentiate between attested and reconstructed forms.

[# ______] Proto-Germanic *t* > German *c*
[*V* ______] Proto-Germanic *t* > German *s*

The phonetic law as cited here is a condensed and simplified representation of the actual process of sound change. Sounds or phonemes are bundles of acoustic or articulatory features that characterize the sounds of a given language and are therefore called *distinctive.*[109] Shared distinctive features are responsible for similarities among sounds, while differences in the bundles of distinctive features reflect formal differences among sounds. Formal differences that are endowed with a meaning-differentiating function are defined as phonemic oppositions. These oppositions may be expressed in terms of the presence or absence of a distinctive feature, symbolized by a plus or minus sign. Enclosing distinctive features in brackets, we may rewrite the consonants in the example above as repertories of distinctive features for which they are specified. As it turns out, the consonants *t* and *c* share all but one distinctive feature specification. Both are [+ consonantal], [− vocalic], [− continuant], [+ front], [− labial], [+ coronal], [− nasal], [− voiced], but *t* is [− strident], while *c* is [+ strident]. We may say, therefore, that sound change is actually change in the specification of repertories of distinctive features. Since the specification of the feature of [stridency] opposes the bundle of distinctive features that make up the consonant *t* to the bundle of distinctive features that make up the consonant *c*, the change *t* > *c* is a change in the specification of [stridency], with the [− strident] *t* becoming the [+ strident] *c*. The change *t* > *s* implies a change in the specification of the distinctive features of [stridency] and [continuance], with the [− strident] and [− continuant] *t* becoming the [+ strident] and [+ continuant] *s*.

The distinctive-feature analysis makes it possible to account for the remarkable parallelisms observed in sound change. Thus, the Middle English great vowel shift, a series of changes which affected the English vowel system in the fifteenth century, was brought about by vowel raising or a change in the specification of the feature of [height] ([tenseness], in acoustic terms). This change in feature specification resulted in the parallel treatment of the long stressed vowels *ē* and *ō*, which were raised to *ī* and *ū* respectively: *beete* [bētə] > *beet* [bīt], *boote* [bōtə] > *boot* [būt]. Similarly, the distinctive-feature analysis allows us to formulate with greater economy and explanatory power the changes in Proto-Germanic encompassed by Grimm's Law (**2.3**). In spite of these advantages, the formalization of the distinctive-feature analysis is unwieldy and will not be used in the present survey. Also, because of the unfamiliarity of the acoustic analysis, references to sound systems and sound changes will be couched in articulatory terms.[110]

Occasionally the proto-language is attested. An instance of such a linguistic development is provided by the history of the Romance languages, which are descended from Latin (**2.4**)—not the classical Latin studied in school but the popular Latin (also called Vulgar Latin) spread by Roman legionnaires, administrators, merchants, and clergymen throughout the Roman empire. Popular Latin, however, was a colloquial idiom, and as such it is not well documented. Therefore, linguistic reconstruction retains its utility in establishing Proto-Romance,

109. The notion of the distinctive feature being the smallest unit of sound structure was introduced by Jan Baudouin de Courtenay. However, the formalization of the distinctive-feature analysis and its application to the synchronic and diachronic levels is due to the works of Roman Jakobson and Morris Halle. On the diachronic level, the distinctive-feature analysis breaks away from the older neogrammarian and descriptivist model embodied in Bloomfield's (1933:351) pithy formulation "Phonemes change."

110. For a consistent application of the distinctive-feature analysis to the phonology of Proto-Slavic, see Velcheva (1988).

even though reconstructed and attested forms frequently agree. Thus, the reconstructed proto-form of French *mer*, Spanish *mar*, and Italian *mare* happens to coincide with classical Latin *mare* 'sea'.

2.3. Indo-European languages and Proto-Indo-European. In fact, Proto-Germanic and Proto-Romance have also been found to be related. In order to explain this relationship it is necessary, just as in the case of English and German, to posit a proto-language, a parent language of Proto-Germanic and Proto-Romance. As it turns out, the relationship uniting Proto-Germanic and Proto-Romance includes many other languages and language families scattered throughout Asia and Europe, from the Indian Ocean to the Atlantic. For this reason these languages are called Indo-European, and their ancient ancestor is known as Proto-Indo-European (PIE). Needless to say, all the forms of Proto-Indo-European have to be reconstructed.

With the aid of Proto-Indo-European reconstructions we can account for such regular correspondences as those between the English initial continuants *f th h* as in *father three horn* and the Latin initial voiceless stops *p t k* as in *pater trēs cornū*. Upon further investigation we discover that related words in other Indo-European languages also begin with *p t k*, for instance, Greek *patḗr treîs kéras*. We feel justified, therefore, in setting up a Proto-Indo-European series of voiceless stops *p t k* and in deriving from it the Germanic continuants.

It turns out that in order to account for the development of Proto-Germanic consonants, we have to posit a series of interdependent sound changes:

PIE	p	t	k	>	PROTO-GERMANIC	f (ph)	þ (th)	h
	(b)	d	g			(p)	t	k
	bh	dh	gh			b	d	g

In terms of the distinctive-feature analysis this statement may be reformulated as follows:

PIE [− voiced]	>	Proto-Germanic [+ aspirated]
[+ voiced]		[− voiced]
[+ aspirated]		[− aspirated]

These sound changes have resulted in such correspondences as English *t k* vs. Latin *d g* and English *b d g* vs. Latin *f f h* (< PIE *bh dh gh*), e.g. *two* vs. *duo*, *kin* vs. *genus*, *brother* vs. *frāter*, *door* vs. *foris*, and *guest* vs. *hostis* 'stranger'.[111] The phonetic law formulated on the basis of these correspondences was discovered in 1818 by the Danish philologist Rasmus Rask. However, it is often referred to as Grimm's Law, after the German Indo-Europeanist Jacob Grimm, who incorporated it into his comparative grammar of Germanic (1822). It is also known as the First Germanic Sound Shift (**4.1.1**).

111. The posited PIE *b* has very few reliable examples. It may be illustrated by the correspondence between English *deep* and Russian *dno* 'bottom' from Proto-Slavic *dъbno* (cf. **2.8**).

2.4. Survey of the Indo-European languages. Slavic languages are also Indo-European and as such are related to Germanic and Romance. In order to understand the nature of this relationship it is necessary to take a brief look at all the branches of the Indo-European linguistic family before passing on to specifically Slavic matters. The survey that follows provides a basic classification of the Indo-European languages including information on the relevance of some of the non-Slavic Indo-European languages for the Slavic world. It proceeds from Asia to Europe and concludes with a presentation of the Slavic linguistic family.

Indic includes many languages of the Indian peninsula. Those with the largest number of speakers are Hindi, the official language of India; Bengali, spoken in Bangladesh and northeastern India; Marathi, used in central and western India; Gujarati, Panjabi, and Urdu in the western regions and Pakistan; Sinhalese in Sri Lanka. The oldest known Indic language is Vedic Sanskrit, used in the religious hymns called the Vedas. The Vedas were not written down until about 500 B.C., but it is generally assumed that they were composed between 1500 and 1000 B.C. Classical Sanskrit was the literary language of India and in particular of Hinduism, where it occupied a position comparable to that of Latin in the Roman Catholic church. Its structure was described by a number of ancient grammarians, the most famous of whom was Pāṇini in the fourth century B.C. The old vernacular languages that existed side by side with Sanskrit are known as Prakrits. One of the Prakrits was Pali, the native language of Buddha and hence the sacred language of Buddhism. Romany, the language of the Gypsies, is a northwestern Indic dialect with many Slavic and other non-Indic loan words assimilated by the Gypsies during their wanderings throughout the Eurasian continent.

Iranian is represented by Pashto (Pushtu) in Afghanistan; Tajik, the official language of Tajikistan; Farsi, the language of modern Iran; Kurdish in the region where Iran, Iraq and Turkey meet; Zaza in the eastern part of central Turkey; and Ossetian in the central Caucasus. The oldest preserved forms of Iranian are Avestan, the liturgical language of Zoroastrianism, dating from the seventh century B.C., and Old Persian cuneiform inscriptions from the Achaemenid period of Persian history (ca. 550–335 B.C.). From the seventh century B.C. Iranian-speaking tribes such as the Scythians and after them the Sarmatians ranged as far west as the Caspian and Black Sea steppes. There they must have come into close contact with the Slavs, as indicated by the Iranian borrowings in Slavic, especially in the domain of religion (**2.66**). The degree of kinship between Indic and Iranian appears so close as to suggest a common Indo-Iranian stage in their development from Proto-Indo-European.

Tocharian texts came to light at the beginning of the twentieth century in Chinese Turkestan in northern Xinjiang (Sinkiang). Unexpectedly, this easternmost Indo-European language bears more resemblance to Italic and Celtic than to the geographically closer languages of the Indo-Iranian family. Tocharian documents date from the sixth–eighth centuries A.D.

Anatolian languages, spoken in Asia Minor, include *Hittite*, which boasts the oldest Indo-European written records. The earliest Hittite cuneiform tablets, unearthed in Asia Minor at the end of the nineteenth century, date from the eighteenth century B.C. Of special interest is the fact that the long vowels of other Indo-European languages correspond to the Hittite combinations of a short vowel followed by a laryngeal. It is thus possible to assume that laryngeals existed in PIE and that their disappearance led to the lengthening of the adjacent vowel. This discovery provided a striking confirmation of the correctness of the methods of linguistic reconstruction, for the existence of laryngeals in PIE had been posited by the Swiss linguist Ferdinand de Saussure before the Hittite tablets were brought to light (**2.10**).

Armenian is the official language of Armenia, in Transcaucasia. It is also spoken by Armenians living in the northeastern corner of Turkey (ancient Armenia) and by the large Armenian diaspora around the world. The earliest Armenian records date from the fifth century A.D.

Greek is known to us from inscriptions and texts reflecting many dialects, the most important among them being Aeolic, Doric, and Ionic. Homeric Greek and Attic, the dialect of Athens and the idiom of the golden age of Greek literature, were both Ionic dialects. The oldest Greek written records, in the so-called Mycenean Linear B, go back to about the fourteenth century B.C. The conquests of Alexander the Great spread Greek over vast territories and led to the rise of *koiné*, a unified Greek idiom based on Attic. It was from *koiné* that the Scriptures were first translated into Slavic (**3.31**). The prestige of the Byzantine culture among the Orthodox Christians was responsible for the powerful influence that Greek exercised upon the language of the newly converted Slavs, especially in the domains of vocabulary and syntax (**2.66**).

Albanian is spoken in Albania and in the Kosovo-Metohija autonomous region of Yugoslavia. It is perhaps related to the Indo-European dialects of the Illyrian or Thracian tribes which inhabited the Balkans in antiquity.

Italic is the name given to a group of languages which were spoken on the Appenine Peninsula and whose most important members were Latin, Oscan, Umbrian, and Venetic. Latin, the language of Latium and Rome, emerged victorious in the rivalry with its neighbors and spread eventually to all the corners of the vast Pax Romana. As we have seen (**2.2**), the language used by the conquering Roman legions was not the codified Latin of the classical period but its spoken, popular variant, from which the modern *Romance* languages are descended. In the West these include Italian, Spanish, Portuguese, and French, which all became official languages in their respective states. In addition one could mention Catalán, the official language of Catalonia, with its center in Barcelona; Sardinian on the island of Sardinia; Provencal in southern France; and the Rhaeto-Romance dialects in the southwestern part of Switzerland. In the east, Romanian is the state language of Romania and Moldova. Medieval Latin, as the liturgical language of the Catholic church, was a major linguistic influence on the languages of the Slavs submitting to the ecclesiastic authority of Rome.

Celtic used to be spoken over vast areas of Western and Central Europe and in Asia Minor. Bohemia owes its name to its early Celtic inhabitants, the Boii; the Galatians in central Anatolia, to whom St. Paul addressed one of his epistles, were Celts; the British Isles, Cisalpine and Transalpine Gaul (that is, northern Italy and modern France), and Galicia in northwestern Spain were all inhabited by Celtic tribes. Today Celtic survives in a few linguistic enclaves in Ireland, Scotland, Wales, and Brittany.

Germanic is usually divided into three branches: the northern or Scandinavian branch, including Swedish, Danish, Norwegian, and Icelandic; the western branch with English and Frisian as one subgroup and German and Dutch (including Flemish) as the other; and the eastern branch, represented by Gothic, the language of the oldest Germanic literary monument, the fourth-century translation of the Bible by Wulfila, the Arian bishop of Moesia on the northern shores of the lower Danube. As late as the first half of the eighteenth century a dialect of Gothic was spoken in the Crimea by the descendants of the East Goths (Ostrogoths). Early Slavs were for a period under the cultural and political influence of the Goths, as attested by a number of Gothic loan words in Proto-Slavic (**2.66**). In the ninth century the eastern Slavs were exposed to the Scandinavian dialect of the Varangian (Viking) merchants and retainers who used the east Slavic waterways and colonized the lands along them. The linguistic traces of that encounter are not numerous, for the Varangians who settled in Rus' were Slavicized within a generation or two. The name of the country, however, as well as the names of its first rulers, is of Scandinavian origin (**1.45**).

Baltic languages appear to be so closely related to Slavic as to prompt many scholars to assume a period of Balto-Slavic linguistic community following the breakdown of Indo-European. Others ascribe the similarities between Baltic and Slavic to dialect mixing due to many centuries of geographic proximity and cultural contacts (for a brief discussion of the Balto-Slavic controversy, see **2.6**). Lithuanian and Latvian are the state languages of Lithuania and Latvia. Old Prussian, spoken along the southern shores of the Baltic between the estuaries of the Niemen and Vistula, died out in the seventeenth century.

Slavic consists of fourteen living speech communities, most of which are accorded the status of autonomous languages. Distinctions between a dialect and a language, however, are difficult to make on purely linguistic grounds, and decisions on the status of a speech community are often politically motivated. Hence there can be no unanimity on this issue in all instances, notably that of Kashubian as separate from Polish or of Serbian and Croatian as two languages rather than one (**2.7**). Also Slavic are Polabian, which died out in the eighteenth century, and Old Church Slavonic, which was a living idiom in the days of Constantine and Methodius (**1.31–1.36** and **3.23–3.30**) but which has since functioned mainly as the ecclesiastic language of the Orthodox church under the name of Church Slavonic. The Slavic languages are classified into three basic branches, South, West, and East, and are subdivided further to reflect formal differentiation within these branches. In Table 3 the extinct languages are placed in square brackets.

Table 3: Classification of the Slavic languages

<table>
<tr><td rowspan="6">Proto-Slavic</td><td rowspan="2">South</td><td>Eastern</td><td>[Old Church Slavonic]
Bulgarian
Macedonian</td></tr>
<tr><td>Western</td><td>Serbian
Croatian
Slovenian</td></tr>
<tr><td rowspan="3">West</td><td>Czech/Slovak</td><td>Czech
Slovak</td></tr>
<tr><td>Sorbian</td><td>Upper Sorbian
Lower Sorbian</td></tr>
<tr><td>Lechitic</td><td>Polish
Kashubian
[Polabian]</td></tr>
<tr><td colspan="2">East</td><td>Russian
Ukrainian
Belarussian</td></tr>
</table>

The classification of the Slavic languages given in Table 3 is not to be understood rigidly, and many linguistic features transcend the boundaries of the three branches posited above. In particular, it is often convenient to group the East and West branches into North Slavic and the East and South branches into East/South Slavic. However, the inherent dynamism of the traditional tripartite classification does not reduce its usefulness as a working approximation of the actual degree of affinity among the Slavic languages. Table 4 illustrates the closeness of Slavic as a linguistic family by juxtaposing the shapes of several related words in the sixteen Slavic languages.[112]

Table 4: Juxtaposition of related words in the Slavic languages

	‘sister’	‘neighbor’	‘dog’	‘tongue’	‘head’	‘short’
Old Church Slavonic	sestra	sǫsědъ	pьsъ	ęzykъ	glava	kratъkъ
Bulgarian	sestrá	săséd	păs	ezík	glavá	krátăk
Macedonian	sestra	sosed	pas	ezik	glava	kratak
Serbian	sèstra	súsed	pȁs	jèzik	gláva	krátak
Croatian	sèstra	súsjed	pȁs	jèzik	gláva	krátak
Slovenian	séstra	sósed	pàs	jézik	glâva	krátək
Czech	sestra	soused	pes	jazyk	hláva	krátký
Slovak	sestra	súsed	pes	jazyk	hláva	krátky
Upper Sorbian	sotra	susod	pos	jazyk	hłowa	krótki
Lower Sorbian	sotša	sused	pjas	jezyk	glowa	krotki
Polish	siostra	sąsiad	pies	język	głowa	krótki
Kashubian	sostra	sǫsåd	p’es	jązëk	głowa	kròtk’i
Polabian	sestră	sǫśodă	p’ås	jǫzěk	glåvă	kort’ě
Russian	sestrá	soséd	pës	jazýk	golová	korótkij
Ukrainian	sestrá	susíd	pes	jazýk	holová	korótkyj
Belarussian	sestrá	suséd	pes	jazýk	halavá	karótki

2.5. Periodization of Proto-Slavic. It may be assumed that the classification of the Slavic languages into three branches reflects the earliest dialect divisions within Proto-Slavic. It is not possible, however, to tell with certainty when exactly the cohesiveness of Proto-Slavic ceased to exist. At the time of the Moravian mission (863), and for perhaps two or three generations beyond it, one may still speak of Slavic linguistic unity. At that time, the dialect differentiation of Proto-Slavic did not pose serious obstacles to mutual comprehension. Soon, however, the process of independent state formation, taking place over an exceedingly large territory, deepened dialect cleavages. The Magyar invasion from the east, the German push from the west, and the religious rift between Byzantium and Rome could not but hasten the disintegration of Proto-Slavic. Thus, from about the year 1000 we may be justified in speaking of the histories, or rather prehistories, of individual Slavic languages or language branches.

It is useful to subdivide the period, perhaps four millennia long, separating the disintegration of the Indo-European linguistic unity and the formation of individual Slavic languages or language groups. While there is no agreement on the criteria for such a subdivision and hence on the number of Proto-Slavic subperiods, the least arbitrary formula appears

112. For the explanation of diacritic symbols, see n. 133.

to be one based on the differences in the extent of linguistic change. Thus, the period encompassing the beginning of dialect differentiation within Slavic is called *Late Proto-Slavic*, the period during which changes affected all of Slavic and only Slavic is termed *Early Proto-Slavic*, and the period characterized by changes affecting Slavic and Baltic is called *Balto-Slavic*. Analogously, it is convenient to subdivide Proto-Indo-European into dialectally diversified Late Proto-Indo-European and dialectally uniform Early Proto-Indo-European.[113]

2.6. The problem of Balto-Slavic. The similarities between Baltic and Slavic have long been noted. In phonology one could mention the common treatment of the Proto-Indo-European vocalic sonants (**2.9**) and the development of phonemic pitch (**2.2.9**); in morphology, the tendency of consonantal-stem nouns to acquire *-ĭ-* stem endings (**2.48.1n6**), the rise of the category of definiteness in the adjective (**2.49.1**), the development of a two-stem conjugational system (**2.50**), the extension of the participial suffixes *-nt-* and *-ŭs-* by the suffix *-i̯-* (**2.58**); in syntax, the use of the instrumental in the predicate and of the genitive as object of negated verbs (**2.64**). There are also many coincidences in Baltic and Slavic lexicon.

The existence of Balto-Slavic as an intermediate node in the development of Baltic and Slavic from Proto-Indo-European was first proposed by the German neogrammarian August Schleicher in 1861 (**4.1.1**). His theory was elaborated on by Karl Brugmann and supported by Jan Rozwadowski, Aleksander Brückner, Reinhold Trautmann, Jerzy Kuryłowicz, Nicolaas van Wijk, André Vaillant, and many other Indo-Europeanists. All of them attributed the Balto-Slavic linguistic similarities to a period of shared history and postulated the existence of Balto-Slavic as an autonomous, post-Proto-Indo-European linguistic entity.

Others, like Jan Baudouin de Courtenay, Antoine Meillet, Alfred Senn, Christian Stang, and Ernst Fraenkel, though representing a wide range of views, expressed reservations about a wholesale acceptance of the Balto-Slavic theory. They argued that the features common to Baltic and Slavic are, insofar as they are not inherited from Proto-Indo-European, a product of separate, though parallel, development, enhanced by territorial contiguity of the two speech communities and by their social and linguistic interaction.

This disagreement appears to be largely terminological in nature, and the two points of view need not be seen as contradictory. Since Baltic and Slavic were at the tail end of the process of the disintegration of the Indo-European speech community, what is termed Balto-Slavic is in fact the very latest stage of one of the Late Proto-Indo-European dialects. Once separated from each other, Baltic and Slavic (or at least some of their dialects) continued to exist side by side and underwent a period of parallel developments and of outright linguistic borrowing.

2.7. Survey of the Slavic languages. There are today close to 250 million speakers of Slavic in the world. Most of them live in their national states. Upper and Lower Sorbian, however, are fully within the borders of Germany, while Kashubian is spoken in the territory of

113. Some scholars use the term *Common Slavic* and apply it either to all of Proto-Slavic (using it, in fact, in lieu of Proto-Slavic) or to the last phase of Slavic linguistic unity approximating Late Proto-Slavic of this survey. Such, for instance, is the practice of Lunt (1984/1985:420), for whom the seam between Proto-Slavic and Common Slavic coincides with the establishment of $*u_2$. In opting for the term *Proto-Slavic* to designate the whole period between Balto-Slavic and the formation of individual Slavic languages, I was moved by a wish to fall in step with the established usage in Germanic and Romance linguistics as well as in Slavic historical linguistics as practiced in the Slavic countries. For a discussion of the use of the terms *Proto-Slavic* and *Common Slavic*, see Birnbaum (1975) and Andersen (1985); for the term *Common Slavic* applied to the earliest period of *written* Slavic, see **3.24**.

Poland. In addition, many emigrants from the Slavic countries live in their own linguistic enclaves in countries across the globe, chiefly the United States, Canada, Australia, Germany, and Israel.[114]

Old Church Slavonic and *Church Slavonic* are terms devised in the nineteenth century to describe two stages of the oldest Slavic literary language. Old Church Slavonic (also Old Church Slavic, Old Slav[on]ic, or Old Bulgarian) was first reduced to writing in the middle of the ninth century. Its well-defined and fairly limited corpus consists of Slavic texts translated chiefly from Greek and possibly Latin in connection with the Byzantine mission to Moravia and Pannonia led by the brothers Constantine and Methodius (**1.34–1.39**). The work on the translations began while the brothers were still in Constantinople and continued in Pannonia and Moravia during the second half of the ninth century, resuming in the tenth and eleventh centuries in Bulgaria.[115] Most of the texts belonging to the Old Church Slavonic canon come from the latter period (**3.27**).

Church Slavonic was the successor to Old Church Slavonic in its function as a Slavic supranational linguistic medium. As it spread to Rus', Serbia, Dalmatia, Bohemia, and Romania, it absorbed local linguistic features producing various regional recensions of Church Slavonic. At the same time, its use was broadened from strictly the ecclesiastic to other aspects of literary production (**3.28–3.30**).[116]

Bulgarian is the national language of Bulgaria with its approximately eight million inhabitants. Until the middle of the nineteenth century, when the codification of modern Bulgarian began, the function of the literary language of the country was fulfilled by Old Church Slavonic and Church Slavonic of Bulgarian recension, with an ever-increasing admixture of vernacular elements. Since the Bulgarian usage is to refer to Old Church Slavonic as Old Bulgarian, the Bulgarian scholars have adopted the term *middle* to correspond to the term *old* as it is used habitually in the histories of other Slavic languages.

Macedonian is the most recently codified Slavic language—its first scholarly grammar was written by the American scholar Horace G. Lunt in 1952.[117] There are about one and a half million speakers of Macedonian, living mostly in Macedonia, formerly one of the constituent republics of the Yugoslav federation, but also in adjacent countries, notably Greece. Macedonia figured prominently at the dawn of Slavic writing, for the brothers Constantine and Methodius hailed from the city of Thessalonica in Byzantine Macedonia, and their fluency in the local Slavic idiom destined them for missionary activity among the Slavs. Also, most of the surviving Glagolitic Old Church Slavonic texts may be attributed to the activity of the scriptorial center established by Tsar Symeon in Ohrid in Macedonia (then, western Bulgaria).

Croatian and *Serbian* are western and eastern forms of the most widely used language of the southern Slavs. Prior to the dissolution of Yugoslavia, it was known as Serbo-Croatian or Croato-Serbian. There are approximately sixteen million speakers of Croatian and Serbian residing in Croatia, Bosnia and Hercegovina, Serbia (including the multiethnic autonomous region of Vojvodina), Montenegro, and Priština-Kosovo (with a largely Albanian population).

114. For details on the structure of individual Slavic languages, see Comrie/Corbett 1993; for their external history, see Schenker/Stankiewicz 1980.

115. This includes Macedonia, which belonged to the First Bulgarian Empire.

116. See also Picchio 1980 and Huntley 1993.

117. The appropriateness of the qualification of Macedonian as an autonomous Slavic language has been questioned by some, chiefly Bulgarian, scholars.

The legacy of the church schism of 1054, which divided Slavdom into two cultural entitities defined chiefly by their allegiance to the Eastern or Western forms of Christianity,[118] and the deep cleavage caused by the partition of the Balkans between Ottoman Turkey and Austria-Hungary have strained relations among the Orthodox Serbs, Catholic Croats, and Moslem Bosnians and have caused them to deny the validity of a unitary view of their language. The fact that Serbian uses the Cyrillic alphabet and Croatian the Roman one has lent the claim of their dissociation an aura of visual verisimilitude.

The Croatian and Serbian speech communities include a number of dialects. The chief ones among them are defined by the form of the pronoun 'what' (*što* in the eastern and central regions, *ča* in the westernmost part of the Croatian littoral, and *kaj* along the Croatian border with Slovenia) and by the reflexes of the Proto-Slavic vowel *ě* (*e* in eastern Serbia, *i* along the Dalmatian coast, and *(i)je* in central and southern regions). Hence the division into štokavian, čakavian, kajkavian, ekavian, ikavian, and (i)jekavian dialects. Croatian and Serbian were standardized in the first half of the nineteenth century, chiefly through the efforts of the Hercegovinian Vuk Karadžić and the Croat Ljudevit Gaj. They settled on štokavian as the norm of the standard language but allowed for a choice between the ekavian (Belgrade) and (i)jekavian (Zagreb) standards.

Slovenian is the language of about two million Slovenes living mostly in Slovenia, but also in the adjacent regions of Austria and Italy. In the early Middle Ages Slovenia was part of Carantania, which along with Pannonia and Moravia formed a chain of Slavic states lining the southeastern border of the Frankish state. Geographically closest to the centers of Western civilization, Carantania earlier than other Slavic regions became accessible to its penetration. It was included in Samo's confederation of Slavic states (**1.26**) and was proselytized by Irish missionaries even before the arrival of missions from nearby Aquileia and Salzburg. The *Freising Fragments*, showing some Slovenian linguistic features, date from the end of the tenth century and are thus the earliest Slavic text written in Roman letters. However, it was not until the Reformation and the work of such sixteenth-century writers and scholars as Primož Trubar, Juri Dalmatin, Adam Bohorič, and Hieronymus Megiser that Slovenian began to function as a language of literary communication.

Czech is used by about twelve million inhabitants of the Czech lands, which since the dissolution of Czechoslovakia form the Czech Republic. Of its two provinces, Bohemia and Moravia, the former traces its roots to the principality of Bohemia of the tenth century, the latter to Greater Moravia of the ninth century. Early contacts with Byzantium and the Frankish empire exposed the Czech lands to Eastern and Western cultural influences and allowed for an initial coexistence of Slavic and Latin literary production. The earliest Old Church Slavonic literary monuments were composed between the ninth and eleventh centuries, the period encompassing the work of the Moravian mission of Constantine and Methodius and the scriptorial activity of the Bohemian Sázava Monastery. Texts in Czech proper, based on the dialect of Prague, started appearing in the thirteenth century. A scholarly adaptation of the Latin alphabet to the Czech sound system was the work of the religious reformer Jan Hus (1370–1415). In its modern form, Czech was codified at the turn of the eighteenth century by the philologist Josef Dobrovský.

Slovak is spoken by about four and a half million inhabitants of Slovakia, the easternmost of the two political heirs of the dissolved Czechoslovakia. There are also about one million

118. Termed *Slavia Orthodoxa* and *Slavia Romana* by Picchio (1972:7–13).

speakers of Slovak in the regions adjacent to Slovakia (chiefly Hungary and Ukraine) and in the Western Hemisphere (chiefly the United States). Early loss of political independence delayed the formation of the Slovak literary language, which did not come into its own until the end of the eighteenth century, when the Enlightenment heightened the consciousness of national identity. The codification of the standard language on the basis of central Slovak dialects was the work of L'udovít Štúr in the middle of the nineteenth century.

Upper and *Lower Sorbian* (also known as Upper and Lower Lusatian) are the two modern Slavic languages with the smallest number of speakers. They are used by about fifty thousand people in a bilingual setting, with German as the principal language. Promoted by the government of East Germany, these two languages face an uncertain future in reunited Germany. The Sorbian speech area is a small region of eastern Saxony between the Neisse and the upper course of the Spree. It is known as Upper Lusatia (Ober-Lausitz), with a center in Budyšin (Bautzen), and Lower Lusatia (Nieder-Lausitz), with a center in Chóśebuz (Cottbus).

Polish is spoken by about thirty-five million inhabitants of Poland and an additional ten million Poles living outside its borders, chiefly in the English-speaking countries. Connected Polish texts did not appear before the fourteenth century, although sporadic records of Polish place and personal names were made earlier. Since that time, Polish has gone through a gradual and continuous development, culminating in the standard language used today. It combines features of several dialect areas—Great Polish, where Poland's statehood began in the tenth century; Little Polish, around Cracow, the capital of Poland till the beginning of the seventeenth century; Mazovian, around Warsaw, Poland's present capital; Silesian, which was the gateway for Czech and German influences during the Middle Ages and the Renaissance; and the dialects of the eastern borderlands, with their rich literature of the Baroque and Romantic periods.

Kashubian is used by fewer than one hundred thousand inhabitants of a narrow strip of land, sixty or seventy miles long, stretching southward from the Baltic shore between the delta of the Vistula in the east and the former Polish-German border in the west. Thus, the Kashubian speech area is by and large coextensive with the notorious "Polish corridor" of pre–World War II politics. The question whether Kashubian is an autonomous Lechitic language or a dialect of Polish has not been, and probably cannot be, definitively settled. A dispassionate resolution of this issue has not been helped by the fact that practically all speakers of Kashubian know standard Polish and that linguistic similarities or divergences between Kashubian and Polish have been used as political arguments in Polish-German territorial disputes. In accepting the linguistic autonomy of Kashubian, I follow the narrow definition of a literary language adopted by Topolińska (1980:183 and 194), that is, of a language with its own spelling standard and its own belles lettres. Slovincian, the westernmost dialect of Kashubian and an important source of Slavic accentual data, died out in the beginning of the twentieth century.

Polabian, one of the western Lechitic languages, was still spoken in the beginning of the eighteenth century in several villages located on the Lüneburg lowlands (*Lüneburger Heide*) west of the river Elbe (Slavic *Laba*). The name *Polabian* was devised to reflect this location. Also used are the tribal name *Dravenian* and the German appellation *Wendisch* ('Venetic', **1.4**), which is applied generically to various Slavic linguistic enclaves in the German speech area. Other western Lechitic languages, which used to be spoken across northern Germany, died out without being recorded. Polabian, by contrast, survived long enough to benefit from scientific curiosity generated by the Enlightenment. The few extant Polabian glossaries and short texts were compiled and recorded in the late seventeenth and early eighteenth centuries by amateur ethnologists and lexicographers who wished to learn something about the customs of the Polabians and to preserve a trace of their dying idiom.

Russian is spoken natively or quasi-natively by close to a hundred and fifty million Russians living in Russia (officially known as the Russian Federal Republic) and beyond its borders on the territory of the Commonwealth of Independent States and in many Russian emigré communities around the world. In the pre-Petrine period, the language of literary texts was Church Slavonic in its East Slavic recension, which together with the language of subliterary documents is commonly referred to as Old Russian. This term, however, may be viewed as anachronistic, for at that time East Slavic had not yet diverged into Russian, Ukrainian, and Belarussian. It seems more appropriate, therefore, to use the general and neutral term *East Slavic* and indicate its dialectal varieties.[119] Before the reforms initiated by the Russian scholar Mikhail Lomonosov (1711–1765), some areas of social contacts were served by Church Slavonic, while others made use of the East Slavic vernacular, a linguistic situation which some scholars view as diglossia. Standard Russian, as we know it today, received its definitive shape in the works of the writers of the second half of the eighteenth and the beginning of the nineteenth century, especially Nikolaj Karamzin and Aleksandr Pushkin.

Ukrainian is used by about forty million speakers in Ukraine (out of some fifty-five million inhabitants) and by an additional four to five million residing outside its borders, chiefly in Russia, Belarus, Poland, the United States, and Canada. The emergence of Ukrainian as a separate East Slavic language was furthered by the political division of the East Slavic lands between Moscovy and the Polish-Lithuanian Commonwealth. Its maturation as an autonomous vehicle of cultural intercourse may be dated from the beginning of the nineteenth century and the advent of Romanticism. The standard language which was adopted at that time was based primarily on the dialects of the southeast, with a considerable admixture of Galician elements. In contradistinction to standard Russian, Ukrainian is relatively free of Church Slavonicisms.

Belarussian, the youngest standard East Slavic language, claims fewer than seven million speakers out of the ten million inhabitants of Belarus. Another million live in Belarussian linguistic enclaves in Russia, Poland, Lithuania, the United States, and Canada. Belarussian was the chancery language of the Great Duchy of Lithuania during the years of its union with Poland. This period resulted in an extensive polonization of the Belarussian lexical stock. Since the partitions of Poland, Belarussian fell under the sway of Russian. Though Belarussian was used by some writers in the second half of the nineteenth century, its standardization and codification began in the twentieth century when it achieved the status of the official language of Belarus.

119. Until the most recent reintroduction into Russian of the term *rossijskij* to refer specifically to Russia and complement the more general term *russkij,* Russian did not have adjectival means to discriminate between matters pertaining to Russia and those pertaining to Rus'. This situation, which exists also in English, has led to a surfeit of terms referring to medieval East Slavic. Depending on the local political situation the terms *Old Russian, Old Ukrainian,* and *Old Belarussian* have been applied to essentially the same body of texts. Thus, the *Paterik* of the Kievan Caves Monastery is included in *A History of Russian Literature* (Lixačev, ed., 1989) as well as in *The Harvard Library of Early Ukrainian Literature* (Heppel 1989) (**1.47**).

2.8. Problems in phonological reconstruction. The reconstructed system of Proto-Indo-European phonemes[120] is so remote from our own linguistic experience and so hard to verify that it is still a subject of scholarly debate. Among the most controversial issues are the role of the laryngeals and of the vowel ə (schwa) in the formation of the Proto-Indo-European vowel system and the number and nature of phonemically relevant features in the system of the Late Proto-Indo-European stops. The various approaches to these problems have shown that a consensus on the need to posit the existence of an opposition is not always matched by agreement on the opposition's formal content. In other words, it has turned out to be easier to determine the reality of a phonemic distinction than to pinpoint the phonetic nature of this distinction.

As an example of the problems in reconstruction let us examine briefly the controversy concerning the nature of Proto-Indo-European stops. In the view of the neogrammarian school of historical linguistics, active around 1870 and centered at the universities of Leipzig and Jena, Proto-Indo-European distinguished two oppositions in the manner of articulation: voiced versus voiceless and aspirated versus unaspirated; and a triple opposition in the place of articulation: labial versus dental versus velar. The velars were further subdivided into palatal (palatovelars), plain, and labial (labiovelars). These oppositions produced a system of twenty stop phonemes, as shown in Table 5.

Table 5: Neogrammarian reconstruction of PIE stops

		Labial	Dental	Velar		
				Palatal	Plain	Labial
Voiceless	Unaspirated	p	t	k'	k	k^w
	Aspirated	ph	th	k'h	kh	k^wh
Voiced	Unaspirated	b	d	g'	g	g^w
	Aspirated	bh	dh	g'h	gh	g^wh

This system was soon found to include subphonemic and dialectal features. In particular, the voiceless aspirates turned out to be distinctive in Indo-Iranian only, where they could be explained as a secondary development. Consequently, voiceless aspirates were eliminated from the inventory of stops, resulting in what has become the generally accepted triadic arrangement of Proto-Indo-European stops (*p, b, bh; t, d, dh,* etc.). In the new system, however, the voiced aspirates have no voiceless counterpart, and this imbalance was pronounced typologically anomalous (Prokosch 1938:39–41; Jakobson 1957:20; Martinet 1970:115). In its stead a differently defined set of triads was proposed, one in which glottalized stops were opposed to nonglottalized stops, the latter differentiating between voiced and unvoiced varieties (Hopper 1973:150–156; Gamkrelidze and Ivanov 1973:150–156 and 1984:5–80). As a result, the neogrammarian series

120. A phoneme is defined as a class of sounds whose distribution is complementary (that is, noncontrastive). The sounds that belong to the same phoneme are known as its positional variants (allophones). Thus the alveolar [l'] and velar [l] in the initial and final position of English *little* do not introduce a semantic contrast and are therefore considered positional variants of the English phoneme /l/. On the other hand, the contrast between Russian palatalized [l'] and nonpalatalized [l], shown by such minimal pairs as *kl'ast'* 'to curse' and *klast'* 'to put' or *jel'* 'fir' and *jel* 'he ate', qualifies them as independent phonemes /l'/ and /l/.

VOICED	UNASPIRATED ASPIRATED	d dh
VOICELESS		t

was replaced by the "glottalic" theory series

GLOTTALIZED		t'
NONGLOTTALIZED	VOICED VOICELESS	d t

Since the reason for this reformulation is the admittedly atypical occurrence of marked voiced aspirates without matching unmarked voiceless phonemes, one may ask whether the Proto-Indo-European aspirated stops have to be specified as voiced. In fact, the testimony of Greek and, to some degree, Latin points to their voicelessness. Thus, to the voiced root consonant in Sanskrit *dadhāmi* 'I put' and Old Church Slavonic *děti* 'to put' corresponds a voiceless consonant in Greek *títhēmi* 'I put' and Latin *fēci* 'I did'. One could, therefore, posit a contrast between unaspirated voiceless *t* and voiced *d*, on the one hand, and an aspirated stop, transcribed as *Th*, which is neutral as to the voiced versus voiceless opposition:

UNASPIRATED	VOICELESS VOICED	t d
ASPIRATED		Th

In such languages as Iranian, Albanian, Celtic, Baltic, and Slavic, which lost the feature of aspiration, one could imagine a process whereby the two marked stops (voiced *d* and aspirated *Th*) fell together, yielding a contrast between voiceless *t* and voiced *d*. In languages that retained the triadic contrast, the aspirated stops either could be interpreted as voiceless (Greek *th*, Latin *f*) or they could participate in sweeping sound shifts such as the one in Germanic encompassed by Grimm's Law or the Armenian consonant shift. As for Sanskrit, which exhibited a fourfold distinction (*t, th, d, dh*, etc.), one could assume that the new *th* (resulting from the sequence of *t* and a laryngeal) caused *Th* to be reinterpreted as voiced *dh*.

Whatever the intrinsic value of such speculative solutions, it is clear that they all present mutually convertible systems of phonemic oppositions. Therefore, the adoption in the present survey of the traditional triad of the voiceless *t* opposed to voiced *d* and *dh* should be viewed as a decision in favor of expediency rather than as a matter of principle.

Nor is the reconstruction of the development of the Proto-Slavic sound system entirely free of alternative solutions and scholarly controversies. They concern above all the questions of the interdependence and relative chronology of linguistic processes. Since an exhaustive examination of these controversies is outside the scope of the present survey, the solutions presented below reflect what are perceived to be generally accepted views.

2.9. Late Proto-Indo-European phonemic system. With these caveats in mind, we will assume that the Late Proto-Indo-European consonant system included the spirant *s*, three unaspirated unvoiced stops, *p t k*, three unaspirated voiced stops, *b d g*, and three aspirated stops which were neutral as to the feature of voicing and which in this presentation will be transcribed in the traditional way as *bh dh gh*. The three plain velar stops *k g gh*, contrasted with palatalized *k' g' g'h* and labialized k^w g^w g^wh.[121]

The vocalic system consisted of five short and five long vowels, *ĭ̄ ŭ̄ ĕ̄ ŏ̄ ă̄*. In addition, four sonants (or sonorants), *m n r l*, were consonantal (nonsyllabic) when preceded or followed by a vowel but vocalic (syllabic) in a nonvocalic environment. In their vocalic function these sonants were short or long. The mid and low vowels entered into tautosyllabic combinations with high vowels and sonants. In such combinations or diphthongs the high vowels *i u* became the semivowels *i̯ u̯*, that is, they acquired a nonsyllabic or consonantal function.

Since the environment points unambiguously to the phonetic value of *m n r l* and *i u*, the need to distinguish graphically between syllabic and nonsyllabic functions arises only when these sounds are quoted in isolation. It is, however, a common practice to assign to them special symbols even when their phonetic value is fully predictable. Syllabic sonants are indicated by a subscript circle: *m̥ n̥ r̥ l̥*. As for nonsyllabic *i u*, the American linguistic writings favor the transcription with *y w*, while the habitual Slavic practice, which is adopted in this survey, is to transcribe them with *i̯ u̯* in Proto-Indo-European and Balto-Slavic and with *j v* in Late Proto-Slavic.

Thus, Late Proto-Indo-European had the potential for thirty-six short and long diphthongs:

ĕ̄i̯ ĕ̄u̯ ĕ̄m ĕ̄n ĕ̄r ĕ̄l
ŏ̄i̯ ŏ̄u̯ ŏ̄m ŏ̄n ŏ̄r ŏ̄l
ă̄i̯ ă̄u̯ ă̄m ă̄n ă̄r ă̄l

In addition, during the Balto-Slavic period, the Proto-Indo-European syllabic sonants *m̥̄̆ n̥̄̆ r̥̄̆ l̥̄̆* developed epenthetic high vowels *ĭ̄* or *ŭ̄*[122] providing a potential for another sixteen diphthongs:

ĭ̄m ĭ̄n ĭ̄r ĭ̄l ŭ̄m ŭ̄n ŭ̄r ŭ̄l

2.10. Laryngeals. The multivocalic system presented above was a feature of Late Proto-Indo-European. Early Proto-Indo-European, by contrast, is thought to have had a much smaller inventory of vowels. The transformation of the older minimal vocalic system was due to a set of laryngeal phonemes, customarily transcribed as H_1 H_2 H_3. Since the role of the laryngeals in the development of Proto-Slavic was limited, only a cursory survey of the main aspects of the so-called laryngeal theory need be presented here.

121. The reconstruction of three kinds of Proto-Indo-European velar stops is also a matter of some controversy since no Indo-European language distinguishes all three of them. What we find instead is one reflex for *k* and *k'* in the centum languages and one reflex for *k* and k^w in the satem languages (see **2.12**). For this reason, some scholars have suggested that only two series need be posited for Proto-Indo-European, without agreeing, however, on the nature of the opposition (*k'*/*k* vs. k^w for Meillet 1937 and Lehmann 1952 but k^w/*k* vs. *k'* for Kuryłowicz 1956).

122. The distribution of the *ĭ̄* and *ŭ̄* variants in Balto-Slavic has not been conclusively explained. According to some it is regulated by the basic quality of the root vowel, according to others by the quality of the consonant environment of the sonants. For a discussion of these attempts bolstered by an exhaustive survey of evidence, see Shevelov 1965:86–90.

The neogrammarian model of the Proto-Indo-European sound system contained a short vowel whose phonetic value was thought to approximate that of the English *a* in *sofa* or the reduced vowel of Hebrew. This vowel, transcribed as *ə*, is traditionally referred to as the schwa which is the German rendition of its name in Hebrew. The schwa was posited for Indo-European in order to account for the correspondence of *ĭ* in Indo-Iranian and *ă* in other Indo-European languages. Thus, the words for 'standing' and 'father' appear in Sanskrit as *sthitá-* and *pitar* but in Greek as *statós* and *patḗr* and in Latin as *status* and *pater.* As a rule, the *schwa* alternated with long vowels, as in Sanskrit *sthitá-* 'having stood' (< PIE *stə-*) versus *ásthāt* 'he arose' (< PIE *stā-*); Greek *phásis* 'utterance' (< PIE *bhə-*) versus *phāmí* 'I say' (< PIE *bhā-*) and *phōnḗ* 'voice' (< PIE *bhō-*); Latin *factus* 'made' (< PIE *dhə-*) versus *fēcī* 'I did' (< PIE *dhē-*).

In 1879, the Swiss linguist Ferdinand de Saussure asserted that these alternations could be more economically accounted for if one posited the existence of a sonant-like sound which in a nonsyllabic position (that is, next to a vowel) caused the lengthening of the adjacent vowel and in a syllabic position (that is, in a nonvocalic environment) functioned as the schwa. When it was determined that the phonetic value of this sound approximated that of a laryngeal consonant, the letter *H* was adopted as its phonetic symbol and Saussure's hypothesis came to be known as the laryngeal theory.[123]

The laryngeal theory went further. Noting that *e* was the most frequent Proto-Indo-European vowel, Saussure suggested that the vowels *a* and *o* were instances of the coloring of *e* by the neighboring laryngeals. This required the positing of at least three laryngeals, the neutral H_1, the *a*-colored H_2, and the *o*-colored H_3. The Late Proto-Indo-European mid and low vowels[124] could now be rewritten in the following manner:

$$\breve{e} = H_1e \qquad \bar{e} = eH_1$$
$$\breve{a} = H_2e \qquad \bar{a} = eH_2$$
$$\breve{o} = H_3e \qquad \bar{o} = eH_3$$

Saussure's laryngeal theory was devised as a purely theoretical construct and as such it did not initially gain many adherents. In 1927, however, the laryngeal theory received striking factual confirmation when the Polish linguist Jerzy Kuryłowicz established a correspondence between the posited Proto-Indo-European laryngeals and the *h* (*hh*) of newly deciphered Hittite. Nonetheless, some aspects of the laryngeal theory remain controversial, especially the question of the number and phonetic nature of the laryngeal phonemes. The laryngeals are not needed in the reconstruction of the Proto-Slavic sound system. Their importance for Slavic lies in the role that Late Proto-Indo-European vowel length played in the development of the Proto-Slavic rising intonation (**2.11, 2.29**).

2.11. Proto-Indo-European ablaut. Comparative evidence suggests the existence of a Proto-Indo-European system of grammaticalized vowel alternations, best known by the German term *ablaut* (the terms *apophony* and *vowel gradation* are also used). It represents a system of morphophonemic relationships whereby the unmarked vowel *e* enters into a number of marked qualitative and quantitative alternations, depending on the grammatical

123. The determination of the phonetic value of the laryngeal was first made by the Danish linguist Hermann Møller, who based his conjecture on his knowledge of similar consonants in Semito-Hamitic languages.

124. The high vowels *i* and *u* were considered syllabic variants of the nonsyllabic *i̯* and *u̯*.

function of the form. In the qualitative ablaut, the vowel *e* (*e*-grade) alternated with the vowel *o* (*o*-grade). The *e*-grade characterized nonderived verbal roots, while the *o*-grade was typical of derived nominal roots. In the quantitative ablaut, a short vowel (normal grade) alternated with a long vowel (long grade) or the absence of a vowel (zero grade). The zero grade of diphthongs consisted in the loss of the vowel and the transfer of its syllabic function to the semivowel, sonant, or laryngeal, leading to their vocalization: *i̯ u̯ m n r l H* > *i u m̥ n̥ r̥ l̥ ə*.

The basic *e* ~ *o* ablaut is represented in Slavic by many roots, for example OCS *vezǫ* 'I transport' ~ *vozъ* 'cart', *grebǫ* 'I dig' ~ *grobъ* 'grave', *vedǫ* 'I lead' ~ *voždь* 'leader', *rekǫ* 'I say' ~ *rokъ* 'fixed time', etc. The *e* ~ *o* ~ *Ø* ablaut may be exemplified by roots containing semivowels or sonants. In the Old Church Slavonic examples below, the Proto-Indo-European diphthongs are no longer perceivable as such because of their monophthongization (**2.26, 2.34, 2.35**):

e-GRADE	o-GRADE	ZERO GRADE
-cvisti (*i* < *ĕi̯*) 'to bloom'	cvětъ (*ě* < *ŏi̯*) 'flower'	-cvьtǫ (*ь* < *ĭ*) 'I bloom'
bl'usti (*'u* < *ĕu̯*) 'to watch'	buditi (*u* < *ŏu̯*) 'to awaken'	bъděti (*ъ* < *ŭ*) 'to be awake'
-čęti (*ę* < *ĕn*) 'to begin'	konьcь (*on* < *ŏn*) 'end'	-čьnǫ (*ьn* < *n̥*) 'I begin'
berǫ (*er* < *ĕr*) 'I take'	sъborъ (*or* < *ŏr*) 'synod'	bьrati (*ьr* < *r̥*) 'to take'

These alternations suggest that in the Proto-Indo-European ablaut system, the vowel *e* was basic, *a* was marginal, *o* arose as an ablaut variant of *e*, and *i* and *u* were ablaut variants of diphthongs.[125]

The zero grade of diphthongs extended by a laryngeal yielded long vocalic sonants: *m̥̄ n̥̄ r̥̄ l̥̄*. Their Slavic reflexes developed a rising intonation which shows up as the fixed stress of Russian and the short falling intonation (̏) of Serbian/Croatian (**2.29**):[126]

LPIE	RUSSIAN	SERBIAN/CROATIAN	
n̥̄men-	ímja	ȉme	'name'
gʷr̥̄dl-	górlo	gȑlo	'throat'
pl̥̄n-	pólnyj	pȕn	'full'

2.12. Loss of aspiration. The dissolution of the Proto-Indo-European linguistic unity was attended by several sound changes that affected clusters of language families. First among them was the merger of the aspirated stops with the unaspirated voiced stops that occurred in Balto-Slavic, Iranian, Albanian, and Celtic. In Latin and other Indo-European languages the aspirated and unaspirated voiced stops remained distinct:[127]

125. English strong verbs offer many examples of ablaut, e.g. *sit, sat, set* from PIE *sĕd-* 'sit'; cf. also *seat, soot, nest*, all derived from the same root.

126. There are no reliable Slavic examples of *m̥̄*.

127. PIE *bh dh gh* yielded Latin *f f h* respectively.

LPIE	BALTO-SLAVIC	OCS	LATIN
bh b	b	berǫ 'I take' bolje 'more'	ferō 'I carry' dē-bilis 'weak'
dh d	d	dymъ 'smoke' dati 'to give'	fūmus 'smoke' dāre 'to give'
gh g	g	gostь 'stranger' ǫgъlъ 'corner'	hostis 'enemy' angulus 'corner'

2.13. Treatment of velar stops. An early dialect isogloss separated the south-central area of Indo-European from its periphery. The languages belonging to the former have come to be known as *satem* (Slavic, Baltic, Indic, Iranian, Armenian, and Albanian), while those belonging to the latter are referred to as *centum* (Tocharian, Anatolian, Greek, Italic, Celtic, and Germanic).[128] In the centum languages the palatalized velar stops merged with the plain ones, while the labialized velar stops remained distinct. In the satem languages, by contrast, it was the labialized velars that merged with plain velars, while the palatalized velars underwent *spirantization* whereby *k'* > *š* and *g'* > *ž* with further developments. Thus, satem *š ž* were retained in Lithuanian, but not in the other Baltic languages. In Slavic they changed into hissing *s z*, while in Sanskrit they developed into *ś* and *j* [ʒ́].

LPIE	B SL.	LATIN[129]	LITHUANIAN	OCS	LATIN
kʷ k	k	ku̯ k	kàs 'who' kraũjas 'blood'	kъto 'who' krъvь 'blood' (Acc. Sg.)	quod 'what' cruor 'blood'
k'	š	k	dẽšimt 'ten'	desętь 'ten'	decem 'ten'
gʷ	g	v g	gývas 'living' jùngas 'yoke'	živъ 'alive' (< gī) [j]ьgo 'yoke'	vīvus 'alive' iugum 'yoke'
g'	ž	g	žinaũ 'I know'	znajǫ 'I know'	co-gnoscō 'I know'
gʷh gh	g	f h	gariù 'I burn' gar̃das 'enclosure'	gorěti 'to burn' gradъ 'town'	formus 'hot' hortus 'garden'
g'h	ž	h	žiemà 'winter'	zima 'winter'	hiems 'winter'

2.14. Retroflexion of *s*. In Balto-Slavic and Indo-Iranian, that is, in the eastern group of the Indo-European languages, *s* became *ś* when preceded by *i/i̯*, *u/u̯*, *r*, or *k* and followed by a vowel or a sonant. This change, known as the retroflexion of *s*, had further developments which drove the first wedge into Balto-Slavic linguistic unity. In Indo-Iranian and Lithuanian *ś* changed to *š* in all positions; in Latvian and Old Prussian it reverted to *s*; in Slavic it yielded *š* before front vowels and sonants but *x* elsewhere (Andersen 1968):

128. The terms *satem* and *centum* (pronounced *kentum*) are the Avestan and Latin reflexes of PIE *k'm̥tom* 'hundred'.

129. This list of Latin reflexes of Proto-Indo-European aspirated velars and PIE *gʷ* is not exhaustive but will suffice for our purposes.

PIE	OCS	
nŏk'-ĕi̯-sĭ	nosiši	'you carry' (Present)
ōu̯s-ī	uši	'ears'
pĕr-sĭd-l-ā	prěšьla	'passed' (Rslt. Pple. F)
rēk-s-n̥t (> rēk-s-ĭnt)	rěšę	'they said' (Aorist)
ŏrbh-ŏ-i̯-sŭ	raběxъ	'servants' (Loc. Pl.)
ōu̯s-ŏ-s	uxo	'ear'
pĕr-sŏd-ī-tēi̯	prěxoditi	'to pass'
rēk-s-ŏ-m	rěxъ	'I said' (Aorist)

Notes: (1) The retroflexion of *s* did not involve *s* issued from the spirantization of *k'*. This suggests that retroflexion occurred before *š ž* had changed to *s z* in the satem languages (**2.13**)—an example of relative dating of linguistic change.

(2) Before the introduction of *š* from other sources, *š* and *x* were in complementary distribution.

(3) The Slavic results of the retroflexion of *s* may have arisen through a different sequence of changes: (a) *s* > *ś* > *x* before all vowels and sonants, (b) *x* > *š* before front vowels by the first palatalization of velars (Shevelov 1965:127–128 and **2.22**).

2.15. Merger of *ō̆* and *ā̆*. With the consonantal changes disc ussed above, the period of Balto-Slavic unity may be said to have ended. Among the vowels, the dividing line between Balto-Slavic and Early Proto-Slavic is provided by the merger of LPIE *ō̆* and *ā̆*. Short *ŏ* and *ă* became *ă* still in Balto-Slavic, while long *ō* and *ā* became *ā* in Slavic but remained distinct in Baltic. Similar changes occurred in other Indo-European languages: in Germanic the vowels *ŏ ă* > *a* and *ō ā* > *o* and in Indo-Iranian *ē̆ ō̆ ā̆* > *ā̆*.

PIE	Latin	Lithuanian	OCS
ŏu̯ĭ-	ovis 'sheep'	avìs 'sheep'	ovьca 'sheep'
sălĭ-	sāl, sălis 'salt'	saldùs 'sweet'	solь 'salt'
dō-	dōnō 'I present'	dúoti 'to give'	dati 'to give'
māter-	māter 'mother'	mótė 'wife'	mati 'mother'

Since Balto-Slavic *ă* eventually yielded Slavic *ŏ* (**2.34a**), questions arise about the quality of *ā̆* in Early Proto-Slavic. Some Slavists, anticipating future phonetic developments, transcribe it as *ă̊*, *ō̆ā̆*, or *ₒā̆*. Such symbols may reflect a phonetic reality (labialization and closed pronunciation of the short variant), but in a phonemic analysis they appear needlessly cumbersome and will not be used in the present survey. Besides, the adoption of *ā̆* as the symbol for the low-back vowel is supported by the facts of Baltic, where PIE *ă* remains as *ă*, by the fact that quantity was a distinctive feature in the Slavic vocalic system (yielding the equation *ă* is to *ā* as *ĕ* is to *ē*), and by loans from and into Slavic (Vaillant 1950:107).

There is also a question about the phonetic value of *ē̆*, whose position in the new vowel inventory of eight phonemes changed from mid-front to low-front and turned it into the front counterpart of *ā̆*. This change found its expression in the development of *ē* into *ā* in some environments in Proto-Slavic (**2.27**) as well as in several Slavic languages. To symbolize the new quality of *ě̆*, some scholars transcribe it as *æ̆* or *eă̯*. Here too, however, the simpler symbol *ě̆* seems preferable.

2.16. Phonemic inventory of Early Proto-Slavic. Thus, for the beginning of the Early Proto-Slavic stage, one may assume a balanced system of four short and four long vowels, in which the "mid" feature was no longer distinctive (with a corresponding reduction among the diphthongs):

	FRONT	BACK
HIGH	ī̆	ū̆
LOW	ē̆	ā̆

The consonants included six stops: labial *p b*, dental *t d*, and velar *k g;* two dental spirants: *s z;* the palatovelar spirants *š x*, which were in complementary distribution (**2.14**); and four sonants, *m n r l*. The semivowels *i̯* and *u̯* were in complementary distribution with the vowels *i* and *u* respectively, functioning as their nonsyllabic allophones.

2.17. Constraints on syllabic structure. Throughout its long history the Proto-Slavic sound system was affected by two fundamental tendencies in the structure of the syllable. The tendency toward *intrasyllabic harmony* manifested itself in the agreement between some consonantal and vocalic distinctive features within the same syllable. In accordance with this tendency, the vocalic feature *front* was correlated with the consonantal feature *palatal*, and the vocalic feature *back* was correlated with the consonantal feature *nonpalatal*. This resulted in various consonant-to-vowel and vowel-to-consonant accommodations, such as the palatalization of consonants before front vowels (**2.22, 2.31**), yodization (**2.23**), and the fronting of back vowels after palatal consonants and after *i̯* (**2.25**).

The tendency toward *rising sonority* was a tendency toward an intrasyllabic arrangement of phonemes proceeding from lower to higher sonority (the phonemes with the lowest sonority are voiceless spirants; those with the highest are low vowels). The most signal consequences of this tendency were the rise of prothetic semivowels (**2.21**) and the specification that all syllables must end in a vowel. The latter restriction, known as the *law of open syllables*, led to the loss of word-final consonants (**2.18**), changes in syllable-initial consonant clusters (**2.19**), and the elimination of diphthongs (**2.26, 2.34, 2.35**).

2.18. Elimination of word-final consonants. The tendency toward rising sonority led to the loss of all inherited word-final consonants (*s t d*):

BSl.	sūnŭs	OCS	synъ 'son'	cf.	Skt.	sūnus 'son'
	pādĕs		pade 'you fell'			ábharas 'you carried'
	pādĕt		pade 'he fell'			ábharat 'he carried'
	u̯ĭlkād		vlьka 'wolf' (Gen. Sg.)			vr̥kād 'wolf' (Abl. Sg.)

2.19. Resolution of syllable-initial clusters. Impermissible syllable-initial consonant clusters, which arose as a consequence of the law of open syllables, were simplified or modified:

BSl. pŏ-*ktŏs*	OCS potъ 'sweat'	cf.	OCS	pekǫ 'I bake'
dā-*dmĭ*	damь 'I will give'			dadętъ 'they will give'
sŭ-*pnŏs*	sъnъ 'sleep'			sъpati 'to sleep'
grē-*btē̯i*	greti 'to bury'			grebetъ 'he buries'
mā-*zslŏ*	maslo 'oil'			mazati 'to spread'
ŏ-*bu̯ī*-dē-tē̯i	obiděti 'to offend'			viděti 'to see'
nŏ-*ktĭs*	noštь 'night' (**2.36**)		Lat.	nox, noctis 'night'
ptrŭ-i̯ŏs	ChSl. stryi 'paternal uncle'			pater 'father'

Impermissible consonant clusters in borrowings into Old Church Slavonic were resolved through the insertion of a vowel, e.g. OCS *psalъmъ* 'psalm' (from Greek *psalmós*).

2.20. Shifting of morphemic boundaries. If the juxtaposition of a morpheme-final and a morpheme-initial sequence did not create an impermissible consonant cluster, the final consonant of a prefix or a preposition was transferred to the following morpheme. Such a transfer could cause a shift in morphemic boundaries. Thus, OCS *vъ-nušiti* 'to hear out' and *kъ njemu* 'to him' continued the etymological *vъn-ušiti* and *kъn [j]emu.*

2.21. Rise of prothetic semivowels. The tendency for rising sonority favored prothesis in syllable-initial vowels. Before *ū* there developed a prothetic u̯, while before front vowels and (in most dialects) before *ā*, a prothetic i̯ arose: *ŭz-* > *u̯ŭz-* > OCS *vъz-* 'up', *ūdrā* > *u̯ūdrā* > OESl. *vydra* 'otter', *ĭdōm* > *i̯idǫ* > OCS *idǫ* [*jьdǫ*] 'I go', *ĕsmĭ* > *i̯ĕsmĭ* > OCS [*j*]*esmь* 'I am', *āgn-* > (*j*)*agn-* > OCS *agnьcь* and *jagnьcь* 'lamb'. Short *ă* remained without prothesis: *ătĭkŏs* > OCS *otьcь.*

The tendency to develop prothetic semivowels remained active in Late Proto-Slavic, where it affected front vowels resulting from the monophthongization of diphthongs (**2.26**) as well as in some post-Proto-Slavic dialect areas.[130]

2.22. First palatalization of velars. The principle of intrasyllabic harmony led to the palatalization or affrication of Balto-Slavic velars before front vowels, whereby *k* > *č* (*sk* > *šč*) and g > ǯ > *ž* (*zg* > *žǯ*). Since this change was the first of two palatalizations in which front vowels acted upon the *preceding* velar consonants, it is referred to as the first regressive palatalization of velars (**2.31, 2.32**):

Voc.			Nom. Sg.		
BSl. u̯ĭlk-ĕ	OCS vlьče	cf.	BSl. u̯ĭlk-ŏ-s	OCS vlьkъ	'wolf'
băg-ĕ	bože		băg-ŏ-s	bogъ	'god'

The new palatal consonants *č* and *ž* were in complementary distribution with *k* and *g* respectively, paralleling the status of *š* and *x* (**2.14**):

Voc.			Nom. Sg.		
BSl. dŏu̯s'-ĕ	OCS duše	cf.	BSl. dŏu̯s'-ŏ-s	OCS duxъ	'spirit'

130. Prothesis remained an active process in the history of individual Slavic languages, witness the development of prothetic *u̯* before *o* in Polabian and dialectally in Polish and Czech or of prothetic *h* in Belarussian and Lower Sorbian.

Note: In eastern South Slavic and Czech/Slovak the clusters *šč* and *žǯ* were changed by dissimilation to *št* and *žd,* while in Russian they became *šš'* (spelled *šč*) and *žž'* (spelled *zž, žž,* or *žd*):

BSl.	skĕn- 'pup'	ChSl.	štenę	OESl.	ščenja
	măzg- 'marrow'	OCS	moždanъ (< măzg-ēn-)	Ru.	mozžečók

2.23. Yodization. Sequences of a consonant or sonant followed by the front semivowel *i̯* yielded palatal sounds. This change has come to be known as yodization (*yod* is the Hebrew name of the front semivowel).

(a) The yodization of *velar stops* produced the same results as the first palatalization of velars (**2.22**), *k* > *č,* g > ǯ > *ž* (also *sk* > *šč, zg* > *žǯ*), and may be considered part of the same phonetic process:

BSl.	plāk-i̯-ō-m	OCS	plačǫ 'I cry'	cf.	OCS	plakati 'to cry'
	lŭg-i̯-ō-m		lъžǫ 'I lie'			lъgati 'to lie'
	i̯īsk-i̯-ō-m		ištǫ 'I seek'			iskati 'to seek'
	brūzg-i̯-ō-m	Ru.	brýzžu 'I splash'		Ru.	brýzgat' 'to splash'

Note: Forms like OCS *duša* (< PIE *dhŏu̯s-i̯-ā*) 'soul', *dušǫ* (< PIE *dhŏu̯s-i̯-ō-m*) 'I blow' are usually considered instances of the yodization of the velar *x* (cf. OCS *duxъ* 'breath', *duxati* 'to blow') and are listed together with examples of the yodization of *k* and g. However, the derivation of *duša, dušǫ* does not require an assumption of the intervening stage *dŏu̯x-i̯-ā, dŏu̯x-i̯-ō-m* (cf. **2.14, 2.23b**).

(b) *Hissing sibilants* yielded hushing ones, *s* > *š* and *z* > *ž:*

BSl.	dŏu̯s-i̯-ō-m (s < s)	OCS	dušǫ 'I blow'	cf.	duxati 'to blow'
	pĕi̯s-i̯-ō-m (s < k')		pišǫ 'I write'		pьsati 'to write'
	māz-i̯-ō-m (z < g')		mažǫ 'I smear'		mazati 'to smear'

As a result of the yodization of *k g s z,* Early Proto-Slavic *č ž š* ceased to function as positional variants of *k g x* and became independent phonemes; cf. such minimal pairs as

lŏu̯kā 'garlic' (Gen. Sg.)		lŏu̯čā 'ray' (Gen. Sg.)
nŏgā 'leg' (Nom. Sg.)	vs.	nŏžā 'knife' (Gen. Sg.)
dŏu̯xā 'spirit' (Gen. Sg.)		dŏu̯šā 'soul' (Nom. Sg.)

(c) *Labials* developed an epenthetic *l*, i.e. *Pi̯* > *Pli̯* (transcribed as *Pl'* in Proto-Slavic but as *Plj* in Old Church Slavonic, cf. **2.23e**):

BSl.	sŭp-i̯-ō-m	OCS	sъpljǫ 'I sleep'	cf.	sъpati 'to sleep'
	gūb-i̯-ō-m		gybljǫ 'I perish'		gybati 'to perish'
	zĕm-i̯-ā		zemlja 'earth'		zemьnъ 'earthly'

Note: For similarly motivated changes compare the pronunciation [px'es] or [pśes] appearing in northeastern dialects of Polish for standard Polish *pies* [pjes] 'dog' or the French *š* (< pš < pi̯) as in *sachant* 'knowing' from Latin *sapiente*.

Epenthetic *l* does not normally appear in Bulgarian/Macedonian and West Slavic at morpheme boundaries, that is, in noninitial syllables. This anomaly is due, it seems, to the fact that *i̯* was a morphological marker without a constant phonemic identity and that, as such, it was susceptible to be lost through analogical leveling. Hence OCS *krъmja* (also *krъmlja*) 'food' (< *kr̥m-i̯-ā*) on the model of *krъmiti* 'to feed', Bulgarian *kupja* (< *kŏu̯p-i̯-ōm*) 'I will buy' on the model of *kupi* 'he will buy', Polish *robię* 'I do' (< *ŏrb-i̯-ōm*) on the model of *robić* 'to do' (Vaillant 1950:67–70).

The yodization of *u̯* was probably a Late Proto-Slavic change. It contributed to the consonantizatiion of the back semivowel: OCS *loviti, lovljǫ* 'hunt' (**2.43**).

(d) The *dental stops t d* produced different reflexes in different dialect areas. Their discussion, therefore, belongs properly to the Late Proto-Slavic period. To avoid this chronological disjunction and to preserve typological symmetry, some scholars assume *ti̯ di̯* > *t' d'* in Early Proto-Slavic with further developments in Late Proto-Slavic. This solution is adopted in the present survey, even though there is nothing in the structure of Slavic to militate against the continued existence of *ti̯ di̯* sequences until their ultimate replacement by palatal consonants (**2.36**).

Note: The clusters *st* and *zd* developed like *sk* and *zg* respectively (see **2.23a** and the note in **2.22**):

BSl.	pŏu̯st-i̯-ō-m	OCS	puštǫ	Ru.	puščú [pušš'ú]	I will let
	dŭzd-i̯-		dъždь		dožd', doždjá [doš', dažž'á]	rain

(e) Analogously, the *sonants n r l* are said to have yielded monophonemic reflexes, the palatal *n' r' l'*, even though the biphonemic sequences *ni̯ ri̯ li̯* would be permissible in Proto-Slavic. In Old Church Slavonic, however, these sequences are commonly rendered as *nj rj lj*, cf. OCS *vonja* 'smell', *volja* 'will', *zorja* 'dawn', derived from PSl. *u̯ăn'ā u̯ăl'ā zăr'ā*.

2.24. Proto-Slavic consonant system. Thus, except for the results of the second and third palatalizations of velars (**2.31**), which added the palatal *c* and *ʒ* and, dialectally, *s'*, from the end of early Proto-Slavic down to the end of Late Proto-Slavic the following consonant system may be posited:

	Labial		Dental		Palatal		Velar	
	Voiceless	Voiced	Voiceless	Voiced	Voiceless	Voiced	Voiceless	Voiced
Stop	p	b	t	d	t'	d'	k	g
Spirant			s	z	š	ž	x	
Affricate					č			
Nasal	m		n		n'			
Liquid			r l		r' l'			

The labial and palatal semivowels *u̯* and *i̯* were in complementary distribution with the vowels *u* and *i* respectively. The palatal consonants and sonants and the semivowel *i̯ (j)* are conveniently grouped as "soft," in opposition to the nonpalatal "hard" sounds.

2.25. Fronting of back vowels after soft consonants. In a process that operated throughout the Proto-Slavic period, back vowels were fronted after soft consonants. When not counteracted by analogy this change created "hard" versus "soft" vowel alternations, whereby *ā* was replaced by *ē* and *ū* by *ī*. The fronting of back vowels may be exemplified by Old Church Slavonic pairs: *nes-omъ* 'carried' vs. *zna*[j]-*emъ* 'known', *lьv-ovъ* 'leonine' vs. *zmi*[j]-*evъ* 'serpentine', *myti* (< *mū-*) 'to wash' vs. *šiti* (< *si̯ū-*) 'to sew', and so on (for Late Proto-Slavic changes in vowel quality, see **2.40**). It is also responsible for the alternating hard and soft endings in the inflection of such stems as OCS *sel-* 'village' vs. *polj-* 'field' (**2.48.1**):

Nom. Sg.	sel-o (< -ă)	polj-e (< -ĕ)
Gen. Sg.	sel-a (< -ā)	polj-ě (< -ē)
Loc. Sg.	sel-ě (< -ăi̯)	polj-i (< -ĕi̯, see **2.26**)
Instr. Sg.	sel-омь (< -ămĭ)	polj-емь (< -ĕmĭ)
Gen. Pl.	sel-ъ (< -ŭ)	polj-ь (< -ĭ)
Instr. Pl.	sel-y (< -ū)	polj-i (< -ī)

Except for *i̯ū* < *ēu̯* (**2.26**), this change was operative throughout the Proto-Slavic period; compare such Old Church Slavonic loans as [j]*erъdanъ* (< Greek *Iordános*) 'the Jordan', *židovinъ* (< Balkan-Romance *ǯūd-*) 'Jew'.

2.26. Monophthongization of diphthongs in *i̯* and *u̯*. Complying with the law of open syllables, the closed-syllable diphthongs were replaced by long vowels. Chronologically first was the monophthongization of the diphthongs in *i̯* and *u̯*. It resulted in the following changes: *ĕi̯* > *ī*, *ăi̯* > *ē*, *ĕu̯* > *i̯ū* (which was not liable to vowel fronting, see **2.25**), *ău̯* > *ū*. The resolution of the diphthongs in nasal and liquid sonants was dialectally differentiated and belongs, therefore, to the Late Proto-Slavic period. The new vowels resulting from the monophthongization of the diphthongs in *i̯* and *u̯* are often marked with subscript $_2$ to distinguish them from the older vowels which are unmarked or marked with subscript $_1$:

EPSL.	OCS		GREEK
běrē$_2$tě (ē < ăi̯)	berěte 'take!'	cf.	phéroite 'bring'
stī$_2$gnōm (ī < ĕi̯)	stignǫ 'I'll reach'		steíkhō 'I walk'
lū$_2$čĭ (ū < ău̯)	lučь 'light'		loûsson 'white wood'
bi̯ū$_2$dōm (i̯ū < ĕu̯)	bljudǫ 'I keep'		peúthomai 'I ask'

The instances of *ī*$_2$ occurring for the expected *ē*$_2$ (Nom. Pl. of the masculine-*ŏ*-stems, 2 Sg. Impv.) are probably analogical to the umlauted forms (Shevelov 1965:287–288; cf. also **248.1n7, 2.51.4**). Some scholars, however, formulate phonological rules to account for this development.

It is often suggested that before reaching the shapes posited in the process of the monophthongization, all or some of the diphthongs underwent a metathesis (Vaillant 1950:115,

121; Jakobson 1963:158; Shevelov 1965:285–286; Stankiewicz 1973:181–182; Lunt 1985: 260). Although the assumption of the sequence *ĕi̯* > *i̯ĕ* > *ī*$_2$ would help explain why *ī*$_2$ did not always participate in the so-called third (progressive) palatalization of velars (**2.31, 2.32**), there are several considerations that militate against the likelihood of the existence of such an intermediate stage:

(1) A metathesis would have satisfied the law of open syllables and would have rendered any further changes superfluous. Thus, if we assume that *ău̯* or *ĕi̯* developed into EPSl. *u̯ă* and *i̯ĕ* we must explain why the latter monophthongized to *ū*$_2$ and *ī*$_2$ while *u̯ă* and *i̯ĕ* from other sources yielded LPSl. *vo* and *je*. In other words, one would have to account for the difference in treatment between the presumed **u̯ăm-* (from BSl. *ău̯m-*), yielding LPSl. *um-* 'mind', and *u̯ădā*, yielding LPSl. *voda* 'water', or between the presumed **i̯ĕ-* (from BSl. *ĕi̯-*), yielding LPSl. *i-* 'go' (as in *iti* 'to go'), and *i̯ĕz-i̯-*, yielding LPSl. *ježь* 'hedgehog'.

(2) Had older *ăi̯* metathesized, the resulting sequence **i̯ă* would be expected, by the rules of vowel fronting (**2.25**), to become *i̯ĕ*, which should then monophthongize to *ī*$_2$ (as in the posited sequence *ĕi̯* > *i̯ĕ* > *ī*$_2$). Yet, except for analogical developments mentioned above, the reflex of *ăi̯* was *ē*$_2$.

(3) The metathesized sequences **i̯ă* and **i̯ĕ* would be expected to participate in the process of yodization (**2.23**) and, instead, of *cěna* (< *kăi̯nā*) 'value', *rěka* (< *răi̯kā*) 'river' should have yielded **čěna*, **r'ěka*. Similarly, had the stage **pi̯sātie*[131] 'to write' existed (Lunt 1985:165), it would not have yielded *pĭsātī* (OCS *pьsati*) but rather **pĭsāt'ě* (OCS **pьsašte*).

(4) No metathesis could have been involved in the change of *ĕu̯* to *i̯ū*$_2$.

(5) Indo-European languages offer many examples of monophthongization of diphthongs which do not require the assumption of prior metathesis, e.g. Sanskrit *edha-* (< PIE *ăi̯dh-ŏ-*) 'firewood', *veda* (< PIE *u̯ŏi̯dă*) 'I know', *ojas* (< PIE *ău̯g'-*) 'strength', *rocate* (< PIE *lĕu̯kĕtăi̯*) 'it shines'; Latin *lūcus* (< PIE *lŏu̯k-ŏ-*) 'clearing', *ūnus* (< PIE *ŏi̯n-ŏ-*) 'one'; French *laît* [lɛ] 'milk', *août* [u] 'August'.

(6) The Slavic treatment of the Proto-Indo-European diphthongs is said to have paralleled the developments in Baltic where a metathesis of the diphthongs *ĕi̯ ăi̯* > *i̯e* and *ău̯* > *uo* has been observed (Vaillant 1950:115 and 121). The metathesized reflexes of these diphthongs do not occur, however, in all the Baltic languages and modern dialects (Arumaa 1964:82–84, 92), suggesting that the Baltic change was late and independent of Slavic.

(7) The change of the word-initial *ai̯* to *i̯ā*, as in PSl. *i̯āzu̯ā* 'sore' (cf. Lith. *aížа* 'cleft') is not necessarily due to metathesis as claimed by Shevelov (1965:286). The change of word-initial *ē* [i̯ē] to *i̯ā* is part of the general Slavic backing of *ē* to *ā* after soft consonants (**2.27**) and, as such, it affects not only *ē*$_2$ but also *ē*$_1$, cf. OCS *jasti* 'to eat' (< PIE *ēd-tēi̯*).

(8) Foreign loan words in Slavic need not indicate, as is sometimes maintained, that metathesis functioned as an intermediate stage to monophthongization. Thus, the Slavic rendering of close *ō* [$_u$ō] as *ū*$_2$ in such examples as PSl. *bukъ* 'beech' (< Gmc. **bōka*) or PSl. *plugъ* 'plough' (< Gmc. **plōga*) and East Slavic *Rusь* (< West Finnic **rōtsi*) does not require the positing of the intermediate Slavic state *u̯ō*. It may merely suggest that in the native perception labialized non-Slavic labialized [$_u$ō] was phonetically closer to Slavic *ū*$_2$ rather than to *ā*. Similarly, lexical loans from Slavic into such non-Slavic languages as

131. Corresponding to **pĭsātēi̯* of this exposition.

Finnish or Lithuanian are, by and large, less reliable as sources of phonetic information than internal evidence.[132]

2.27. Backing of *ē* after soft consonants. In a departure from the tendency for intrasyllabic harmony, the long *ē* became *ā* after soft consonants. This change is best presented in three stages:

	'to shout'	'to hear'	'to hold'	'to stand'		'to see'
I	krīkētēi̯	slūšētēi̯	dĭr̥gētēi̯	stăi̯ētēi̯	cf.	u̯ĕi̯dētēi̯
II	krīčētēi̯	slūšētēi̯	dĭržētēi̯	stăi̯ētēi̯		u̯ĕi̯dētēi̯
III	krīčātēi̯	slūšātēi̯	dĭržātēi̯	stăi̯ātēi̯		u̯ĕi̯dētēi̯

Slavic languages show the final stage of this change, except for the Old Church Slavonic texts of Macedonian provenience which, faithful to the tendency for intra-syllabic harmony, retained Stage II:

ORu.	kričati	slyšati	dьržati	stojati	cf.	viděti
OCS (Mac.)	kričěti	slyšěti	drъžěti	sto[j]ěti		viděti

After prothetic *i̯* root-initial *ē* was sometimes retained by analogy to the sequences in which a prefix prevented the development of prothesis. Thus, next to PSl. *i̯ād-* 'eat' (< *ēd-*) there are instances of *i̯ēd-* under the influence of such forms as *sŭn-ēd-* 'eat up'. Hence the contrast between Old Russian analogical [*j*]*ěsti* 'to eat' (cf. *sъněsti*) and Old Church Slavonic regular *jasti*.

2.28. Rise of *ȳ*. Early Proto-Slavic back vowels were redundantly and hence weakly labialized (pronounced with lip rounding). The introduction of the fully labialized $\bar{u}_2$, however, endowed labialization with a phonemic status and contributed to a complete delabialization of $\bar{u}_1$ to *ȳ*, yielding such contrasts as OCS *tu* 'here' (< *tŏu̯*) vs. *ty* 'thou' (< *tū*).

2.29. Phonemic pitch and the new vowel system. The monophthongization of diphthongs led to the development of phonemic distinctions in pitch (intonation). Before the monophthongization, long vowels and long diphthongs were rising in pitch, while short vowels and short diphthongs were nonrising (falling). These differences in pitch were automatic, hence phonemically nondistinctive. When after the monophthongization Proto-Slavic obtained nonrising long vowels from originally short diphthongs or two contracting short vowels (**2.41d**) the formerly redundant distinctions in pitch became phonemic. Consequently, long *ī ē ȳ ū ā* could be either rising or nonrising, while short *ĭ ŭ ĕ ă* were inherently nonrising, contrasting with the corresponding long nonrising vowels. It is customary to transcribe the Proto-Slavic rising intonation with an acute accent (´) and the nonrising intonation with a circumflex (ˆ) and hence to refer to them as the "acute" and "circumflex" intonations.[133]

The new vocalic system consisted of five long acute vowels, five long circumflex vowels, and four short vowels. The vowels *ȳ* and *ā*, though typically acute, could be circumflex

132. For a contrary view, see Kiparsky (1979:79–82).

133. The acute accent mark, used as a vowel diacritic, has different values in different Slavic languages. It denotes (1) the Proto-Slavic acute, (2) Serbian/Croatian and Slovenian long rising pitch, (3) Czech and Slovak vowel length, (4) place of stress in East Slavic and Bulgarian, (5) Polish phonemic /u/ derived from Old Polish *ō*, (6) Sorbian tense [ô].

when they were not inherited from Balto-Slavic long vowels but resulted from Late Proto-Slavic developments such as contraction of circumflex vowels (**2.41**).

	ACUTE			CIRCUMFLEX				
	FRONT	BACK		FRONT	BACK		FRONT	BACK
		UNROUND.	ROUNDED		UNROUND.	ROUNDED		
HIGH	ī́	ȳ́	ū́	ī̂	ȳ̂	ū̂	ĭ	ŭ
LOW	ḗ	ā́		ē̂	ā̂		ĕ	ă

2.30. From Early to Late Proto-Slavic. The introduction of phonemic pitch distinctions marks the end of the uniform Early Proto-Slavic period. During the succeeding Late Proto-Slavic period, linguistic developments were dialect-specific, leading up to the eventual disintegration of Proto-Slavic. While it is virtually impossible to establish an absolute chronology of changes in Early Proto-Slavic, the task of dating particular Late Proto-Slavic changes is somewhat easier. One may surmise that they began when the territorial integrity of Slavic was breaking up in the sixth century as the Slavs started their push into the Balkans and Central Europe. It is even possible to assign certain changes to the beginning or the end of Late Proto-Slavic by assuming that greater dialectal variation implies a more recent event.

2.31. Second (regressive) and third (progressive) palatalizations of velars. Two other palatalizations of velars (cf. **2.22**) and the reflexes of the *tl* and *dl* clusters are responsible for a major isogloss separating West Slavic from South/East Slavic. While the velar stops palatalized by the second and third palatalizations of velars developed identically throughout the Slavic territory, *k* > *c* and *g* > *ʒ* (simplified to *z'* in most Slavic languages), the velar spirant *x* yielded *š* in West Slavic but *s'* in South/East Slavic. The second palatalization was caused by the new front vowel $\bar{e}_2$ or its variant $\bar{\imath}_2$ (both deriving from *ăi̯*) acting on the *preceding* velar. The third palatalization was caused by $\bar{\breve{\imath}}_1$ with or without an intervening nasal (N) acting on the *following* velar. The few Old Church Slavonic examples of *k* > *c* after *ĭr* appear to be analogical (Shevelov 1965:341). Because of its characteristic left-to-right action the third palatalization has often been called the *progressive* palatalization in contrast to the first and second palatalizations, which because of their right-to-left action have been labeled *regressive*.

SECOND (REGRESSIVE) PALATALIZATION

EPSL.
kăi̯nā 'price' găi̯l- 'very' xăi̯d- 'grey'

LPSL.	
EAST/SOUTH	WEST
cē$_2$nā ʒē$_2$lă	
s'ē$_2$d-	šē$_2$d-

OCS	OLD CZECH
cěna ʒělo sědъ	ciena zielo šiedý

The third palatalization seems to have started as a phonological development before *ā*. Soon, however, it became grammaticalized, and its occurrence came to depend on various nonphonological factors, chiefly morphological analogy.

THIRD (PROGRESSIVE) PALATALIZATION

EPSL.
ău̯ĭkā 'sheep' lěi̯kă 'face' kŭnĭng- 'ruler' u̯ĭx- 'all'

LPSL.	
EAST/SOUTH	WEST
ău̯icā līcě kŭnĭnʒ-	
u̯ĭs'-	u̯ĭš-

OCS	OLD CZECH
ovьca lice kъnęʒь vьsь	ovcie líce kniez veš

Additional dialect differentiation was provided by the behavior of the affricate *ʒ* and of the sequences *sk ku̯ gu̯*: *ʒ* was simplified to *z'* throughout the Slavic territory except in the oldest Old Church Slavonic texts and in Lechitic; *sk* yielded *sc* in South/East Slavic but *šč* in West Slavic, e.g. EPSl. *u̯ăi̯ĭsk-āi̯* 'army' (Loc. Sg.) yielded South/East Slavic *u̯ăi̯ĭsc-ē*$_2$ (OCS *voiscě* [vojьscě]) but West Slavic *u̯ăi̯ĭšč-ē*$_2$ (OCz. *vojščě*); *ku̯ gu̯* underwent the second palatalization in South Slavic and parts of East Slavic, but not in West Slavic, e.g. EPSl. *ku̯ăi̯t-* 'flower' and *gu̯ăi̯zd-ā* 'star' yielded South/East Slavic *cu̯ē*$_2$*t-* and *ʒu̯ē*$_2$*zd-ā* (Ru. *cvet zvezdá*, S/Cr. *cvȉjet zvijèzda*) but West Slavic *ku̯ē*$_2$*t-* and *gu̯ē*$_2$*zd-ā* (Cz. *květ hvězda*, Po. *kwiat gwiazda*).

2.32. The relative chronology of the palatalizations of velars. The traditional numbering of the three palatalizations of velars (**2.22** and **2.31**) reflects the order postulated by Jan Baudouin de Courtenay (1894), the first linguist to formulate the conditions of the third palatalization. The last placement of the third palatalization has not, however, been accepted by all scholars. Some have claimed that the so-called third palatalization was actually the second one to occur, others that it was one of the most ancient sound changes of Slavic. Thus, in order not to prejudge the issue, the third palatalization is best called the progressive or Baudouin de Courtenay palatalization.

The chronological order placing the second palatalization after the first one is beyond dispute. It is based on the fact that the conditioning factor of the second palatalization was the vowel $\bar{e}_2$ (in some environments also $\bar{\imath}_2$), whose frontness was brought about by the monophthongization of the Balto-Slavic diphthong *ăi̯* (**2.26**). The velars that underwent the second palatalization remained unchanged during the operation of the first palatalization caused by the PIE front vowels ē̆$_1$ and ī̆$_1$. Also significant in determining the relative age of these two palatalizations is the fact that, while the first palatalization had uniform results throughout Slavic, the second palatalization of *ku̯ gu̯ x* produced West Slavic *ku̯ gu̯ š* but East/South Slavic *cu̯ ʒu̯ s'*, pointing to the first dialect split within Proto-Slavic.

The assumption that the progressive palatalization followed the second one is more difficult to corroborate. There are two considerations that indicate the temporal proximity of the second and progressive palatalizations. One is the identity of their reflexes, the other the fact that the progressive palatalization did not occur after the Balto-Slavic diphthong *ăi̯* (e.g. *răi̯kā* 'river' > *rē*$_2$*kā* rather than **rē*$_2$*cā*).[134] This would suggest that the progressive palatalization

134. The progressive palatalization may also be inhibited by the diphthong *ēi̯*. However, the nonpalatalized masculine suffix *-nikъ* (< *-něi̯k-*), which is the most commonly cited example, may be due to the grammaticalized character of the progressive palatalization (cf. the palatalized feminine suffix *-nica*). More difficult to explain are such roots as *lix-* 'excessive' (< *lěi̯s-*).

occurred after the monophthongization of diphthongs which, as we saw above, was the principal conditioning factor of the second palatalization.

The partisans of the third-before-second order of palatalizations (Trubeckoj, Lehr-Spławiński, Mareš, and their followers) pointed to the fact that EPSl. *ătĭk-ăį* 'father' (Loc. Sg.) yielded OCS *otьci* rather than **otьcě*. In order for this derivation to be regular, one would have to assume that the progressive palatalization of $k > c$ was followed by the changes *ăį* > *ěį* > *ī* in accordance with the rule fronting back vowels after soft consonants (**2.25**) and the monophthongization of the diphthongs in *į* (**2.26**), the latter rule being the conditioning factor of the second palatalization. A more likely explanation of the paradigm of OCS *otьcь* 'father' is that its forms (except for the vocative *otьče*) are analogical to the paradigms of the -*į*-*ŏ*- stems, such as *mǫžь* 'man' (**2.25** and **2.48.1**). On the other hand, the paradigm of OCS *vьsь* 'all', which is isolated and hence less likely to yield to analogy, includes forms in which *s'* is followed by *ě* < $\bar{e}_2$ < *ăį*, e.g. OCS *vьsěxъ* (Loc. Pl.) < EPSl. *u̯ĭx-ăįxŭ*. Had the progressive palatalization operated before the monophthongization of diphthongs, it would have caused *x* > *s'* followed by vowel fronting, *ăį* > *ěį* > *ī*, as it did in the case of *vьsь* < *u̯ĭxŭ*-. The absence of vowel fronting in *vьsěxъ* suggests that this form is due to the second palatalization, which occurred after the monophthongization process had been completed.

Since vowel fronting preceded the monophthongization of diphthongs,[135] the absence of the reflexes of the progressive palatalization after *ĭ* derived from fronted *ŭ* has provided another argument in favor of the third-before-second chronology. It is, however, impossible to know whether OCS *igo* [*jьgo*] 'yoke' < PIE *įŭgŏ*- (cf. Lat. *iugum* 'yoke'), which is most frequently cited in support of this argument,[136] offers a true diagnostic test or whether it is merely one of the numerous instances of irregularity of the progressive palatalization, exemplified by such Russian doublets as *l'ga* 'ease' (dialectal) and *(ne)l'zja* '(not) permitted' (both from EPSl. *lĭgā*, cf. *lëgkij* 'light') or *zga*[137] and *stezjá* 'path' (both from EPSl. *stĭgā*).

Finally, there is the view that the progressive palatalization preceded the other two palatalizations. This hypothesis, championed by such scholars as Robert Channon (1972), Boryana Velcheva (1980), and Horace G. Lunt (1981), was suggested by the phonology of Old Church Slavonic formulated in terms of ordered rules. Endowed with historical relevance, these rules lead to the following ordering: (1) progressive palatalization of velars whereby *k* > *k'* and *g* > *g'*, (2) first regressive palatalization of velars whereby *k*/*k'* > *č* and *g*/*g'* > *ǯ* before the original front vowels and *į*, (3) fronting of back vowels after soft consonants, (4) monophthongization of diphthongs in *į*, and (5) second regressive palatalization of velars whereby *k*/*k'* > *c*, *g*/*g'* > *ʒ*, and *x* > *š*/*s'* before front vowels issued from the monophthongization of diphthongs in *į*.

For all its unquestionable logic, the third-before-first hypothesis exacts a high price for its adoption. First of all, one wonders about the nature of the difference between *k'*/*g'* followed by front vowels (hence participating in the first regressive palatalization) and *k'*/*g'* followed by back vowels (hence not participating in the first regressive palatalization). Is it realistic, one may ask, to posit a phonetic difference between the palatalized velars in the

135. Shevelov (1965:268) argues that the fronting of *ŭ* followed the third palatalization.

136. Examples with the suffix -*ĭk*- < -*ŭk*- are not conclusive because of the likelihood of analogical levelings; cf. such alternate forms as *įăį*-*ĭk*-*ă* and *įăį*-*ĭc*-*ĕ* 'egg'.

137. Only in the expression *ni zgí ne vídno* 'you can't see a thing'.

vocative *ătĭk'ĕ (OCS *otьče*) and genitive *ătĭk'ā (OCS *otьca*) 'father'. It is also puzzling that a change which is so sensitive to its conditioning factors should not have been inhibited by the presence of the nasal sonant in the diphthong *ĭN*, which could not have become monophthongized at such an early date (**2.34**). Linked with this is the problem of the late Germanic borrowings that offer clear examples of the progressive palatalization, e.g. OCS *pěnęʒь* 'coin' (< OHG *pfenning*). There is also the evidence of Slavic place names as rendered in non-Slavic languages, e.g. *Gardíki* in Greece derived from the nonpalatalized PSl. *Gărdĭkŭ* rather than the palatalized *Gărdĭcĭ* (cf. *Hradec* in Bohemia, *Graz* in Austria, *Grojec* in Poland, *Gorodéc* in Russia, with different permutations of the diphthong *CărC*, **2.35**). It is also clear that if the progressive palatalization predated the first regressive palatalization, then it cannot include the dialectally differentiated *x* > *s'*/*š* change. Therefore, the oft-cited Proto-Indo-European pronoun *u̯ĭs-ŏ-s* 'all' which yields EPSl. *u̯ĭx-* and eventually such forms as OCS *vьsь* and OCz. *veš* must be excluded from the ranks of its examples. In general, the question of dialectal divergence in the progressive palatalization and dialectal uniformity in the first regressive palatalization puts a strain on the third-before-first hypothesis. Finally, there is the need to reconcile the early dating of the progressive palatalization with the fact that it did not occur after the diphthong *ă̄i̯*. The monophthongization of diphthongs cannot be adduced to explain this anomaly, for it must have followed the progressive palatalization if the latter is projected into such a distant past. One possible recourse is to assume that in Slavic (but not in Baltic!) *ă̄i̯* went through the stage **ae* before eventually monophthongizing to $\bar{e}_2$ (Lunt 1985:156). Accordingly, the derivation of the word for 'river' would include the stages *răi̯kā* > **raekā* > *r*$\bar{e}_2$*kā*. This solution, aside from its ad hoc nature, calls into question the claim that the progressive palatalization was typologically and chronologically close to the retroflexion of *s* (Velcheva 1988:33) since i̯ in the diphthong *ă̄i̯* was one of the conditioning factors of that change (**2.14**).

2.33. Clusters *tl* and *dl*. The clusters *tl dl* were permitted in West Slavic only. Elsewhere they were assimilated to *ll* and simplified to *l* or, dialectally, replaced by *kl gl*. The latter change was characteristic of the Baltic languages and existed in the Slavic areas adjacent to them, the Pskov and Novgorod dialects of East Slavic and the Kashubian and Mazovian dialects of West Slavic. Today, except for a few vestigial forms, the *kl gl* clusters have yielded to the reflexes in the standard languages:

EPSl.	South/East	West
mētlā 'swept' (Rslt. Pple. F)	Ru. melá S/Cr. mèla	Cz. metla Po. miotła
sādlă 'fat'	Ru. sálo S/Cr. sȁlo	Cz. sádlo Po. sadło

2.34. Monophthongization of diphthongs in nasal sonants. The monophthongization of diphthongs (**2.26**) also affected diphthongs in nasal sonants (*N*), resulting in the creation of two nasal vowels, front *ę* derived from *ĕ̄N* and back *ǫ* derived from *ă̄N*. As for the diphthongs *ĭN* and *ŭN*, it appears that those derived from Proto-Indo-European vocalic sonants *n̥̆ m̥̆* were denasalized, while those resulting from later borrowings yielded *į* and *ų*, which eventually fell together with *ę* and *ǫ* respectively. Nasal vowels were retained in Lechitic and some Bulgarian and Slovenian dialects and denasalized elsewhere. In either case their reflexes differ so widely as to suggest that their phonetic value in Late Proto-Slavic was not uniform (**2.40.c**).

There is no unanimity of views on the phonemic status of Late Proto-Slavic nasal vowels. Ever since Trubeckoj's studies on the reflexes of the nasal vowels in Lechitic (1925) and Czech (1928) there have been attempts to interpret the nasal vowels as biphonemic sequences of an oral vowel (symbolized by *V*) followed by a generic nasal sonant (symbolized by *N*).[138] The proponents of this analysis (Birnbaum 1963, Shevelov 1965, Stieber 1979, Velcheva 1988) base it on the fact that after the monophthongization of diphthongs and before the elimination of the weak jers (**2.38**) tautosyllabic *VN* sequences were not permitted in Slavic. Invoking the principle of distributional complementarity, they conclude that the nasal vowels should not be considered phonemically independent because they do not contrast with biphonemic sequences *VN*.

This argument, however, fails to do justice to the phonetic structure of Late Proto-Slavic, for it is impossible to assume the existence of tautosyllabic *VN* sequences without denying the reality of the monophthongization of the *ĕ̄N ă̄N* diphthongs and without questioning thereby the validity of the most fundamental principle of Late Proto-Slavic syllabic structure, the so-called law of open syllables (**2.17** and **2.18**). On the other hand, the acceptance of the monophthongization of diphthongs as a fact of Proto-Slavic implies the automatic elimination of all tautosyllabic *VN* sequences with the concomitant neutralization of the contrast between *mC* and *nC*. The reasoning, which precludes any possibility of identifying ę and ǫ with the disallowed sequences *ĕ̄NC* and *ŏ̄NC*, is analogous to that which prevents us from analyzing the vowel $\bar{u}_2$, derived through the monophthongization of *ă̄u̯* (**2.26**), as a sequence of the vowels *a* and *u*. Such an interpretation would do violence to a phonemic system in which tautosyllabic sequences of two vowels were not permitted.

2.35. Resolution of diphthongs in liquid sonants. Early Proto-Slavic inherited from Balto-Slavic two types of diphthongs in the liquid sonants *r* and *l* (*R*), differentiated by the height of their vocalic nuclei: the high-vowel diphthongs *ĭ̄R* and *ŭ̄R*, derived from Proto-Indo-European vocalic liquids, and the low-vowel diphthongs *ĕ̄R* and *ă̄R*, the latter continuing PIE *ŏ̄R*/*ă̄R*. These diphthongs occurred word-initially (#VRC) or word-internally (*CVRC*).[139] In either position the law of open syllables demanded their elimination. There was little dialectal differentiation in the resolution of the #VRC diphthongs, testifying to the antiquity of this change. More variegated, and therefore more recent, was the resolution of the *CVRC* diphthongs. There is, in fact, evidence to suggest that this change was still operative in the ninth century. Its results subdivide the Slavic territory into four dialect areas: Area I (South Slavic and Czech/Slovak), Area II (East Slavic), Area III (Polish and Sorbian), and Area IV (Kashubian and Polabian).[140]

(a) The *#ă̄RC* sequences (the only examples of the #VRC formula) were resolved by metathesis, that is, reversal of positions of the vowel and sonant. In North Slavic, however, the distinction between long and short vowels was preserved, while in South Slavic (and cen-

138. Trubeckoj went so far as to claim that the nasal sonant was the velar *ŋ*.

139. Vowels are shown here in their Early Proto-Slavic form and consonant(s) are designated with the capital *C*. Most treatments of Slavic historical phonology, however, show vowels in their Late Proto-Slavic form and use the capital *T* to symbolize consonant(s). Thus, the traditional *oRT, TьRT, TъRT, TeRT, ToRT* formulas correspond to *ă̄RC, Cĭ̄RC, Cŭ̄RC, Cĕ̄RC, Că̄RC* of this survey.

140. This subdivision differs but little from Jakobson's (1952), whose two areas (I and II) have been compressed into one (I).

tral Slovak dialects) the short diphthongs were lengthened and merged with the long ones, transferring the difference in vowel quantity to that of pitch. As expected, Early Proto-Slavic long diphthongs gave acute vowels, while short diphthongs yielded circumflex vowels (**2.21**).

EPSl.	Russian	Polish	Czech	OCS	S/Cr.
ăru̯ĭn- 'even'	róvnyj	równy	rovný	ravьnъ	rávan
ălkŭt- 'elbow'	lókot'	łokieć	loket	lakъtь	lâkat
ārdlă 'plough'	rálo	radło	rádlo	ralo	rȁlo
ālkăm- 'greedy'	lákomyj	łakomy	lakomý	lakomъ	lȃkom

(b) The *CĭRC CŭRC* sequences developed in two stages. In the Early Proto-Slavic stage, common to all the Slavic languages, the vowel was lost and the vocalic function was transferred to the sonant which, depending on the quality of the vowel, was either soft, *r̥' l̥'* (< *CĭRC*), or hard, *r̥ l̥* (< *CŭRC*). Vocalic length was replaced by the acute.

In Late Proto-Slavic, vocalic sonants remained syllabic in Area I. In other areas, the sonant was preceded by a homorganic vowel, leading to the sequences of the *CVRC* type. Such a contravention of the law of open syllables suggests that the development of the vocalic sonants outside Area I belongs to the histories of the individual Slavic languages. The vocalic sonant *r̥'* merged with *r̥* in Area I but remained distinctive in the other areas; *l̥'* retained its distinctiveness in Polish, Sorbian, and partly Czech, merging elsewhere with *l̥*.

EPSl.	OESl.	Russian	Polish	Czech	S/Cr.
sr̥'p- 'sickle'	sьrpъ	serp	sierp	srp	sȓp
tr̥g- 'market'	tъrgъ	torg	targ	trh	tȓg
vl̥'k- 'wolf'	vъlkъ	volk	wilk	vlk	vûk
sl̥n-ĭk-ă 'sun'	sъlnьce	sólnce	słońce	slunce	sûnce
gr̥̄dlă 'throat'	gъrlo	górlo	gardło	hrdlo	gȑlo
pl̥̄'n- 'full'	pъln-	pólnyj	pełny	plný	pȕn

(c) The resolution of the *CĕRC CăRC* sequences was one of the last changes of Late Proto-Slavic. The *CĕlC* sequences fell together with *CălC* in Areas II and IV. In Area I the liquid diphthongs were resolved through metathesis, with the short diphthongs lengthened. The Late Proto-Slavic pitch distinctions were continued in Serbian/Croatian and Slovenian but reinterpreted as place of stress in Bulgarian and Macedonian and as quantity in Czech and Slovak. However, while in Czech acute length is preserved and circumflex length is lost, in Slovak both the acute and circumflex yield short vowels.

In other areas, the short and long diphthongs were resolved by the introduction of an epenthetic vowel creating disyllabic sequences of the CV_1RV_2C type. In Area II, V_1 was the vowel of the original diphthong and V_2 was an epenthetic short high vowel, homorganic with V_1, whose later development betrayed its similarity to the later front or back jers in the "strong" position (**2.38**). The resultant disyllable is known under its Russian name as *polnoglasie* (or, less frequently, *pleophony*). Late Proto-Slavic pitch distinctions were replaced by distinctions in place of stress. The *polnoglasie* sequences derived from the acute diphthongs stressed V_2, while those going back to the circumflex diphthongs did not.

In Areas III and IV, except Polabian, V_1 was an epenthetic short high vowel, while V_2 continued the vowel of the original diphthong. The epenthetic vowels were treated as "weak" jers (**2.38**) and were lost. Their existence may be postulated on the basis of evidence from Polish and Lower Sorbian.[141] As noted by Rozwadowski (1923:162–165), in Old Polish prepositional phrases of the type *we proch* 'into dust' or *ze błota* 'out of mud', the vocalized jer in the preposition implies the occurrence of a weak jer in the following syllable **vъ pъroxъ* (< **vъ porxъ*), **zъ bъlota* (< **jьz bolta* with an analogical change in the preposition). In Lower Sorbian the original clusters *pr tr kr* yielded *pš tš kš;* e.g. *pšosty* 'straight', *tšawa* 'grass', *kšaj* 'country'. However, when these clusters arose from liquid diphthongs, they remained unchanged; e.g. *proch* 'dust', *strowy* 'healthy', *krotki* 'short'. One may infer from this difference in treatment that in the second instance the stop and the *r* were separated by a jer-like vowel which inhibited the change.

Late Proto-Slavic pitch distinctions were replaced in Area III by distinctions in vowel quantity. In this area, however, only Upper Sorbian has preserved reflexes of quantity distinctions resulting from the acute/circumflex opposition.

The Polabian forms are difficult to interpret because of the paucity and unreliability of the written records. The *CĕrC* sequences seem to have developed similarly to those in Area III; *CărC* fell together with *Cr̥C*, and *CălC* yielded *ClŭC*.

EPSL.	RUSSIAN	POLISH	CZECH	U SORBIAN	S/CR.	BULGARIAN
bĕrg- 'bank'	béreg	brzeg	břeh	brjoh	brêg	breg-ъ́t
bērzā 'birch'	berëza	brzoza	bříza	brěza	brȅza	bréza
bărnā 'harrow'	boroná	brona	brana	bróna	brána	braná
u̯ārnā 'crow'	voróna	wrona	vrána	wróna	vrȁna	vrána
gĕlb- 'trough'	žólob	żłób	žleb	žłob	žlijeb	žljab-ъ́t
pēlu̯ā 'chaff'	polóva	plewa	pléva	pluwa	plȅva	pljáva
găld- 'hunger'	gólod	głód	hlad	hłód	glâd	glad-ъ́t
bāltă 'marsh'	bolóto	błoto	bláto	błóto	blȁto	bláto

In Late Proto-Slavic reconstructions, the diphthongs in liquid sonants (*R*) will be cited in their *VRC* form, e.g. *berg-* 'shore'.

2.36. Development of *t' d'*. The reflexes of Late Proto-Slavic *t'* and *d'* which issued from Early Proto-Slavic *ti̯* and *di̯* (**2.23.d**) were also characterized by dialectal fragmentation testifying to the lateness of this change. They fell into five groups: (1) *št žd* in Old Church Slavonic and Bulgarian; (2) *k' g'* in standard Macedonian; (3) *ć ǯ* (spelled *đ* or *dj*) in Croatian and Serbian; (4) *č ǯ* in Slovenian and East Slavic, with *ǯ* > *j* in Slovenian and *ǯ* > *ž* in Russian and, partly, in Ukrainian and Belorussian; (5) *c ʒ* in West Slavic, with *ʒ* > *z* in Czech and Sorbian.

Palatal *t'* had two sources, *ti̯* and *kt* (from *kt* and *gt* with devoicing of *g*) followed by a front vowel. The latter sequence presupposes the palatalization of *kt* to *k't'* and the simplification of *k't'* to *t'* through the resolution of syllable-initial clusters (**2.19**).

141. For a differing view, see Shevelov (1965:412–414).

EPSl.	OCS	Mac.	S/Cr.	Ru.	Po.
su̯ē$_2$t'ā (< su̯ăi̯t-i̯-ā) 'candle'	svěšta	svek'a	svéća	svečá	świeca
năt'ĭ (< năkt-ĭ-s) 'night'	noštь	nok'	nôć	noč'	noc
măt'ēi̯ (< măg-tēi̯) 'to be able'	mošti	mok'	mòći	moč'	móc
mĕd'ā (< mĕd-i̯-ā) 'boundary'	mežda	meg'a	mèđa	mežá	miedza

2.37. Word stress. A comparison of the phonological systems of individual Slavic languages suggests that, except for a small number of enclitics, Proto-Slavic possessed phonologically distinctive word stress. Although this proposition is generally agreed upon, the task of reconstructing the accentual system of Proto-Slavic and of tracing its evolution has been one of the most difficult and contentious areas of research in Slavic historical phonology. Is Slavic word stress derived from Proto-Indo-European? If not, is it a Balto-Slavic or purely Slavic phenomenon? To what extent is it subject to tensions between phonological principles and morphological patterning? What is the relation between the place of stress and Proto-Slavic pitch distinctions?

The last question was addressed at the end of the nineteenth century by two Indo-Europeanists, the Swiss Ferdinand de Saussure, who established a strict correlation between word stress and the acute pitch in Lithuanian, and the Russian Filipp F. Fortunatov, who independently of Saussure observed a similar phenomenon in Proto-Slavic, giving rise to what has been referred to in Slavic accentology as the law of Saussure/Fortunatov. This law, despite its great explicatory power, has not been universally accepted. Among scholars who admit its validity for Proto-Slavic one should mention the Slavists Jan Rozwadowski, Tadeusz Lehr-Spławiński, Leonid Bulaxovs'kyj, André Vaillant, George Y. Shevelov, and Edward Stankiewicz. The ranks of the opposing camp include scholars with Baltic and Balto-Slavic research interests, such as Jerzy Kuryłowicz, Christian S. Stang, Vladimir A. Dybo, Vladislav M. Illič-Svityč, Frederik H. H. Kortlandt, and Paul Garde.

It is the former view that is espoused in this presentation: word stress is considered an autonomous Slavic development conditioned by the law of Saussure/Fortunatov and serving a blend of phonological and morphological functions.[142]

(a) In words whose roots contained an acute vowel, word stress coincided with the acute and, unless overridden by morphological patterns, was *fixed* on the root (with the ictus on V_2 of the *polnoglasie* sequences). This can be seen in Russian word families derived from such roots as *u̯ē$_l$r-* 'believe' or *bē$_l$rz-* 'birch ': *véra* 'faith', *véry* (Gen. Sg.), *vérnyj* 'faithful', *uvérennyj* 'confident', *vérju* 'I believe', *Véročka* 'Verochka', *berëzka* 'birch', *berëzy* (Gen. Sg.), *berëzu* (Acc. Sg.), *berëzina* 'birchwood', *berëzka* 'small birch', *beréznik* 'birch grove', *berëzovyj* 'birchen'.

(b) In words whose roots did not contain an acute vowel, word stress was *mobile*. If no acute vowel followed the root, the onset of stress was recessive (Kuryłowicz 1958$_1$:52), that is, it fell on the first syllable of the phonological word. When an acute vowel followed the root, the stress was, in accordance with the law of Saussure/Fortunatov, on the acute vowel.

142. This is the view adopted and developed in the accentological writings of Edward Stankiewicz. Its concise formulation along with a critique of the revisionist theories may be found in Stankiewicz 1993:3–38. For surveys of recent developments in Slavic accentology, see Birnbaum 1979:116–124, 247–248; Birnbaum/Merrill 1983:12–21. Specifically on the law of Saussure/Fortunatov, see Bulaxovs'kyj 1980:221–225, 532–534, Kuryłowicz 1952:243, passim; Shevelov 1965:55–80.

Mobile stress may be exemplified by such Early Proto-Slavic roots as *běrg-* 'shore', *u̯ělk-* 'drag', *găd-* 'propitious time', *năkt-* 'night' whose Russian reflexes include *béreg* 'shore', *bérega* (Gen. Sg.), *beregá* (Nom. Pl.), *ná bereg* 'to the shore', *náberežnaja* 'embankment', *na beregú* 'on the shore'; *vólok* 'portage', *návoločka* 'pillowcase', *volokú* 'I drag', *óblako* 'cloud', *oblaká* (Nom. Pl.); *gód* 'year', *godá* (Nom. Pl.), *ná god* 'for a year', *gód ót godu* 'year in, year out', *v godú* 'in a year'; *nóč'* 'night, *ná noč'* 'for the night', *zá noč'* 'in one night', *vsénoščnaja* 'vespers', *v nočí* 'at night'.[143]

(c) The accentual patterns of the Slavic languages (chiefly East and South Slavic) demand the reconstruction of the *oxytonic* or word-final stress, whose Late Proto-Slavic motivation appears to be wholly morphological and lexical.[144] It characterized nouns derived from non-acute bases and may be exemplified by such Modern Russian forms as *molodéc* 'brave fellow', *molodcá* (Gen. Sg.) from the root *măld-* 'young' (cf. Russian mobile stress in *molodá, mólodo, mólody*) or *černéc* 'monk', *černecá* from the root *čr̥'n-* 'black' (cf. Russian end-stressed *černá, černó, černý*). Oxytonic stress was also common in nominal borrowings, e.g. *kot* 'cat', *kotá* (Gen. Sg.) from Gmc. *katts, koról'* 'king', *koroljá* (Gen. Sg.) from Old High German *Karl;* in root verbs with a short root vowel, e.g. Russian *nesú, nesëš', neslá, neslí, nestí* 'carry'; and in the present tense of the athematic verbs, e.g. Ukrainian 2 Sg. *dasý,* 1 Pl. *damó,* 2 Pl. *dasté* of *dáty* 'give' (**2.50**).

To take an example of a minimal accentual triad cited by Kuryłowicz (1952:280) and Jakobson (1963:160–161), the Russian forms derived from EPSl. *u̯arn-* 'black' have three different accentual implementations: *voróna* (< *u̯ārnā*) 'crow' has the fixed stress (cf. Gen. Sg. *voróny*); Gen. Sg. *vórona* (< *u̯arnā*) of *vóron* 'raven' has the mobile stress (cf. *žávoronok* 'lark'); and the genitive singular of the nominal (short) adjective *voroná* (< *u̯ărnā́*) 'black' has the oxytonic stress (cf. the pronominal form *voronój*).

2.38. Strong and weak positions of short high vowels (jers). In word-final position the short high vowels *ĭ* and *ŭ* (also referred to as the jers in anticipation of the name given to their reflexes ь and ъ in Old Church Slavonic) were further reduced in length, giving rise to their ultrashort or weak variants, which tended toward elision. The occurrence of these variants was regulated by an alternating pattern of weak and strong positions counting from the end of the phonological word. The jers were weak in word-final position, strong before a weak jer, and weak before a strong jer or any other vowel. This Slavic rhythmic law was formulated in 1889 by the Czech scholar A. Havlík and is known by his name. It is reminiscent of the distribution of the French *e muet* in such sequences as *Je l' donne* 'I am giving it', *Je t' le donne* 'I am giving it to you', *Je n' le donne pas* 'I am not giving it', *Je n' te l' donne pas* 'I am not giving it to you'. Since the distribution of strong and weak jers was automatic, there is no need for special symbols to distinguish between them. When the difference has to be emphasized, strong *ĭ ŭ* (ь ъ) will be shown in boldface: Nom. Sg. *d**ĭ**nĭ* (*d**ь**nь*) 'day', *s**ŭ**nŭ* (*s**ъ**nъ*) 'sleep'; Instr. Sg. *dĭn**ĭ**mĭ* (*dьn**ь**mь*), *sŭn**ŭ**mĭ* (*sъn**ъ**mь*). This shortening process culminated in the elimination of the weak jers, thus closing the era of open syllables and at the same time ending the Proto-Slavic period.

143. Words characterized by mobile stress are considered "stressless" by Jakobson (1963:161).

144. The morphological function of oxytonic stress is presented with particular insistence in the writings of Kuryłowicz (1952:277, 1958_1:43–44) who goes so far as to suggest that every Late Proto-Slavic oxytonic noun was a more or less transparent derivative (1952:358); cf. also Stankiewicz 1988:388.

2.39. Rise of the neoacute. The weakening of jers led to a shift of word stress from the weak jers to the preceding syllable. It is in the nature of things that the syllable which precedes a stressed syllable "rises" toward it. Therefore, the shift of stress to the pretonic syllable created a rising (acute) pitch. This new rising pitch was observed by many Slavists from the end of the nineteenth century,[145] but its first succinct interpretation was given by the Polish linguist Jan Rozwadowski (1915), who also christened it the *neoacute* and symbolized it with a superscript tilde (˜). Like the old acute, which was associated with long vowels (**2.29**), the neoacute tended to be accompanied by vowel length, either preserved or, in some instances, newly created. In fact, vowel length concomitant with the neoacute may be found in all the Slavic languages that show reflexes of Proto-Slavic quantity distinctions. The neoacute became one of the favorite devices of Slavic word derivation, especially with the suffix *-i̯-*.[146]

With the appearance of the neoacute the old binary opposition of pitch (acute vs. nonacute) was disturbed because in the initial syllable of disyllabic words a ternary opposition became possible: the acute (*párg-* 'doorsill') and the neoacute (*kãrl-i̯-* 'king') contrasting with the circumflex (*gȃrd-* 'town'). The binary relationship was restored when the old acute ceased to function as a phonemically distinct entity (Kuryłowicz 1952:259–260). Although this development affected all of Slavic, the varied modes of its implementation mark off four dialect areas (Jakobson 1963:164–173), suggesting a very late Proto-Slavic development.

(a) In Serbian/Croatian and Slovenian the acute/circumflex opposition was reinterpreted as a distinction of quantity, with the acute yielding a short fall (S/Cr. ̏, Sln. ̀) and the circumflex a long fall (̂). The long neoacute remained as a long rise (´). In the Čakavian dialect of Croatia, the three nouns listed above appear as *prȁg králj grȃd* and in Slovenian as *pràg králj grȃd.*

(b) In Czech and Upper Sorbian the acute fell together with the neoacute generating vowel length, which contrasted with vowel shortness under the circumflex: Czech *práh král* vs. *hrad.*

(c) In Slovak, Polish, and Lower Sorbian, the acute fell together with the circumflex, yielding vowel shortness, which contrasted with vowel length generated by the neoacute: Slovak *prah hrad* vs. *král.*

(d) In Bulgarian and East Slavic, where the original situation must have resembled that of Czech and Upper Sorbian, quantity distinctions were eventually lost. Instead, vowel length under the acute and neoacute, contrasting with the brevity under the circumflex, was reinterpreted in Bulgarian as an opposition between a stressed and an unstressed vowel and in the East Slavic *polnoglasie* sequences (**2.35.c**) as an opposition between a stressed and an unstressed V_2 (**2.37.b**); e.g. Bulgarian *prág-ъt králj-at* vs. *grad-ъ́t,*[147] Russian *poróg koról'* vs. *górod* or *prígorod* 'suburb'.

In addition, in Russian the vowel *ă* under the neoacute developed a prothetic back semivowel which, in the word-initial position, produced the sequence *vo,* e.g. *vósem'* 'eight', *vótčina* 'patrimony', *vóblyj* 'round' and word-internally yielded a strongly labialized vowel marked in Russian dialectology with a circumflex (the *kamora* of old East Slavic texts), e.g. *kôža* 'leather', *stôl* 'table', *nôsit* 'he carries' (Leka of the Ryazan district), genitives plural *nôg sôv* of *nogá* 'leg' *sová* 'owl' (Nikol'sk of the Vologda district).

145. A brief survey of these works may be found in Lehr-Spławiński 1918.

146. For a survey of the morphological functions of the neoacute, see Shevelov 1965:535–563.

147. Bulgarian *-ъt/-at* are postpositive definite articles.

2.40. Rise of qualitative distinctions in the vowel system. As shown in the preceding section, the introduction of the neoacute resulted in the shortening of some Early Proto-Slavic long vowels: the acute long vowels in Serbian/Croatian and Slovenian, the circumflex long vowels in Czech, Upper Sorbian, East Slavic, and Bulgarian, and both the acute and circumflex long vowels in Slovak, Polish, and Lower Sorbian. This shortening led in turn to the phonemicization of previously nondistinctive differences in vowel quality which characterized Early Proto-Slavic long and short vowels (Kuryłowicz 1952:260–261, Jakobson 1963, Stankiewicz 1966). The new qualitative distinctions involved the following changes:

(a) Early Proto-Slavic *short vowels* were more central (mid-high and mid-low) than their long counterparts. The shortening of some of the old long vowels rendered these differences in quality distinctive so that old short high vowels *ĭ* and *ŭ* yielded *ь* and *ъ* (the so-called front and back jers),[148] and the old short low vowels *ĕ* and *ă* yielded *e* and *o*. In other words, the old long/short opposition of *ī*/*ĭ* [ĭə], $\bar{u}_2$/*ŭ* [ŭə] and *ā*/*ă* [ăo] was now replaced by a new long/short opposition (*ī*/*ĭ*, *ū*/*ŭ*, *ā*/*ă*), while the allophonic coloring of the old short vowels received a fully phonemic identity: *ĭ* [ĭə] > *ь*, *ŭ* [ŭə] > *ъ*, *ă* [ăo] > *o*.

(b) Of the Early Proto-Slavic *long vowels*, the back vowels *ȳ* (< $\bar{u}_1$), $\bar{u}_2$, and *ā* remained as *y*, *u*, and *a*. The front vowels $\bar{i}_1$ and $\bar{i}_2$ fell together in *i*, while $\bar{e}_1$ and $\bar{e}_2$ merged in *ě* (the so-called *jat'* of Old Church Slavonic), a low front vowel. The testimony of many modern Slavic languages and of the oldest Old Church Slavonic texts suggests that the phonetic value of *ě* was that of the fronted *a* [æ]. Its position in the system, however, was unstable, and depending on other developments it was either pushed higher, as in East Slavic after the denasalization of nasal vowels, or back, as in Lechitic and Bulgarian after the phonemicization of consonant palatalizations (Stankiewicz 1973:183). Because of its dual origin (*ě* < $\bar{e}_1$ < *ē* and *ě* < $\bar{e}_2$ < *ăi*), *ě* exhibits different morphophonemic properties: *ě* < $\bar{e}_2$ alternates with *i* < $\bar{i}_2$ < *ēi̯*, while *ě* < $\bar{e}_1$ does not (**2.25** and **2.26**); also, *ě* < $\bar{e}_1$ and *ě* < $\bar{e}_2$ have different impacts on preceding velars (**2.22** and **2.31**). Since these differences prove important in Proto-Slavic morphology, it is convenient to retain the distinction between $\bar{e}_1$ and $\bar{e}_2$ as $ě_1$ and $ě_2$.

(c) The two *nasal vowels* were opposed to each other as front versus back. Since these features were sufficient to secure their distinctiveness, the nasal vowels displayed considerable latitude in the selection of the nondistinctive features of vocalic height and quantity. The South Slavic standard languages agreed on the reflex of the front nasal as *ę* (< *ę̆*), but disagreed on the back nasal: Serbian/Croatian *ų*, Bulgarian *ъ̨*, OCS and Slovenian *ǫ*, Macedonian *ą*.[149] The North Slavic languages favored a diagonal opposition between a low front nasal *ę̆* [æ̨] (< *ę̄*) and a high back nasal *ų*. Thus, the traditional transcription of Late Proto-Slavic nasals as *ę* and *ǫ* is an emblematic rather than a phonetic representation. The following are the reflexes of EPSl. *mĕnsă* 'meat' and *rănkā* 'hand' in several Slavic languages:

OCS	Bg.	S/Cr.	Sln.	Slk.	Cz.	U So.	Po.	Plb.	Ru.
męso	mesó	mêso	mesô	mäso	maso	mjaso	mięso	mąsi[150]	mjáso
rǫka	rъ̨ká	rúka	róka	ruka	ruka	ruka	ręka	rǫkă	ruká

148. With strong and weak variants (**2.38**).
149. These reflexes characterize the standard languages; the dialects display an even greater diversification.
150. Plb. *mąsi* continues Proto-Slavic collective *męsьje* 'meat'.

2.41. Rise of new quantity oppositions. The introduction of the neoacute and, dialectally, the loss of the intervocalic *i̯* led to a reshuffling of Late Proto-Slavic quantity oppositions. Some long vowels (going back to Early Proto-Slavic long vowels and monophthongized diphthongs) were shortened, while others were preserved. In addition, new lengths arose due to compensatory lengthening and vowel contraction.

(a) The transfer of the implementation of the rising pitch from the old acute to the neoacute retained the basic terms of Slavic pitch opposition (rising vs. nonrising).[151] Their distribution, however, had changed. With the neoacute being the result of a right-to-left shift, the word-final syllable lost its potential to bear the rising intonation, that is, its "intonability," as Kuryłowicz (1952:259) puts it, leading to the *shortening of long vowels in word-final position.* This development, affecting all of Slavic, is discernible in the languages that have or had ways of indicating phonemic length, such as Serbian/Croatian, Slovenian, Czech, Slovak, and Polish. Thus, PSl. *sěstrā* (Nom. Sg.), *sěstrȳ* (Gen. Sg.), *sěstrǭ* (Acc. Sg.) 'sister' yielded Cz. *sestra, sestry, sestru,* contrasting with *ostrá* (Nom. Sg. F.), *ostrý* (Nom. Sg. M.), *ostrú* (Acc. Sg. F.) 'sharp', whose length is due to vowel contractions (**2.41d**).

(b) In a development that was typologically linked with the rise of the neoacute, *long vowels were preserved in pretonic syllables in disyllabic words:*

LPSl.	Čakavian	Štokavian	Czech	Old Polish[152]
trau̯á 'grass'	trāvȁ	tráva	tráva	trāwa (dialectal *tråwa*)
mǫká 'flour'	mūkȁ	múka	mouka	møka (modern *mąka*)
barzdá 'furrow'	brāzdȁ	brázda	brázda	brōzda (modern *bruzda*)
su̯ět'á 'candle'	svīćȁ	svéća	svíce	świēca (dialectal *świca*)
tręstí 'to shake'	trēstȉ	trésti	třásti	trzøść (modern *trząść*)

(c) The reduction and loss of the weak jers led to *compensatory lengthening* of the short vowels in syllables immediately preceding the weak jers. Although this was a late change, whose extent differed from one dialect area to another, it clearly began in the Late Proto-Slavic period. Details of its realization, however, belong properly to the histories of the individual languages.

The clearest examples of compensatory lengthening are found in the central group of the North Slavic languages. Thus, in Upper Sorbian every *e* and *o* was lengthened before a weak jer. In Polish and Kashubian, the lengthening affected vowels before sonants and voiced consonants but not before voiceless consonants. Compensatory lengthening, though more limited in scope, occurred in Czech, Slovenian, Serbian/Croatian, and, to an even lesser extent, in Slovak and Belarussian.[153]

151. In Kuryłowicz's formulation, "nothing changed in the system of intonations; what changed . . . were the *representatives* of the *rising* intonation" (1952:260).

152. Štokavian and Czech vowel lengths are indicated by the acute stress mark; Czech *ou* arose from long *ū*; the long oral vowels of Old Polish were raised: *ā* to *å*, *ō* to *u* (spelled *ó*), *ē* to *i* and the long nasal *ą* (spelled *ø*) was raised to *ǫ* (spelled *ą*).

153. The lenghthening of *o e* in closed syllables in Ukrainian has not found a generally accepted explanation (Shevelov 1965: 447). The vocalization of the jers in the strong position, a fact of the histories of individual Slavic languages, may be considered a special case of compensatory lengthening. For a comprehensive view of compensatory lengthening in Slavic, see Timberlake 1983_1 and 1983_2.

(d) Toward the end of Late Proto-Slavic there developed a tendency for eliding the intervocalic *i̯* and for contracting the two vowels in hiatus, resulting in the creation of new vocalic lengths. The most important consequence of *vowel contraction* was the reintroduction of long vowels in word-final position.

Vowel contractions were more pervasive in South and West Slavic than in East Slavic, with Czech/Slovak and Russian at the two poles of the opposing tendencies. The following examples show the extent and sources of the contracted *ā* in several Slavic languages:

LPSL.	CZECH	OLD POLISH	S/CR.	RUSSIAN	
ai̯a	nová	nowā	nȍvā	nóvaja	'new' (Nom. Sg. F.)
ai̯e	zná	znā	znâ	zná[j]et	'he knows'
oi̯a	pás	pās	pâs	pójas	'belt'
ěi̯a	smáti se	śmiāć się	smȉjati se	smeját'sja	'to laugh'
ii̯a	přítel (< á)	przyjaciel	prȉjatelj	prijátel'	'friend'

Vowel contractions, not unlike the neoacute, acquired a morphological function by marking specific grammatical categories, such as the pronominal declension of the adjective, the present tense of the *-a-j-* class verbs, the instrumental singular of the *-ā-* and *-ĭ-* stem nouns.

2.42. Tense jers. The sequences *ьi̯V* and *ъi̯V* fell together with the sequences *ii̯V* and *yi̯V* in what is known as tense jers (transcribed *ь̂ ъ̂*). In Old Church Slavonic, tense jers were written either as *i* and *y* or as *ь* and *ъ*. In other Slavic languages, tense jers behaved like regular jers, contracting to *i* and *y* in the strong position (*ь̂i̯ь > i, ъ̂i̯ь > y*) and being lost in the weak position. Since Russian did not have contractions across *i̯* (**2.41.d**), its treatment of strong tense jers coincided with that of other jers.

LPSL.	OCS	CZECH	S/CR.	RUSSIAN	
prost-ъ̂-i̯-ь	prostyi/prostъi	prostý	prȍstī	prostój	'plain'
pit-ь̂i̯-e	pitie/pitьe	pití	píće	pit'ë	'drinking'

2.43. Phonemic status of *i̯* (*j*) and *u̯* (*v*). In Proto-Indo-European and Early Proto-Slavic, the semivowels *i̯* and *u̯* were pre- or postvocalic variants of the vowels *i* and *u*. When the monophthongization of diphthongs limited the semivowels to the prevocalic position, *i̯* and *u̯* began to acquire the consonantal status since they now occupied the position of consonants in the *CV* syllabic formula. Morphological patterning also pointed to the consonantization of *i̯* and *u̯* because such forms as *moi̯-ь, moi̯-a, moi̯-e* 'my' or *nou̯-ъ, noŭ-a, nou̯-o* 'new' did not differ in structure from *naš-ь, naš-a, naš-e* 'our' or *star-ь, star-a, star-o* 'old'.

The first indication of the changed status of *u̯* was when it joined in with the regular labial consonants in the process of yodization changes (**2.23.c**), producing such forms as OCS *gotovljǫ* (< *gotou̯-i̯-ǫ*) 'I prepare' or Old ESl. *lovlja* (< *lou̯-i̯-a*) 'hunting'. The new syllable-initial *u̯l'V* had to conform with the Slavic tendency for rising syllabic sonority, enhancing thereby the consonantal status of *i̯*. Similarly, in South and West Slavic, in the syllable-initial *u̯RV* created through the resolution of liquid diphthongs (**2.35.c**), *u̯* must have acquired the value of a consonant in order to fall in line with the regular *CRV* pattern of Slavic, e.g. PSl. *u̯ărnā* 'crow' > S/Cr. *vrȁna*, Cz. *vrána*, Po. *wrona;* PSl. *u̯ăls-* 'hair' > S/Cr. *vlâs*, Cz. *vlas*, Po. *włos*.

One may assume that in some areas, the reduction and loss of the weak jers was the ultimate cause of the change of the sonantic bilabial *u̯* into a consonantal labiodental. Thus, in the Bulgarian recension of Church Slavonic, the infinitives *uspěti* (< *u-spěti*) 'to succeed' and *uběgnǫti* (< *u-běgnǫti*) 'to escape' contrasted with *vspěti* (< *vъz-pěti*) 'to praise' and *vběgnǫti* (< *vъ-běgnǫti*) 'to run in'. In other areas, however, *u̯* remained bilabial and in nonvocalic environments merged with the vowel *u*. Such was the case in the older periods of Serbian/Croatian, Slovenian, Czech, and Belorussian and is still the case in Upper and Lower Sorbian, Ukrainian, and southern Russian dialects.

While we find strong evidence for the phonemic independence of *u̯* in Late Proto-Slavic, the phonemic status of *i̯* is in some doubt, even though it does pattern like a consonantal phoneme. In spite of this ambiguity, it is customary to treat both *i̯* and *u̯* as Late Proto-Slavic consonantal phonemes and to transcribe them as *j* and *v*. This practice will be adopted in the rest of this exposition.

2.44. Phonemes of Late Proto-Slavic and their distribution. We may assume that around the time of its dissolution Late Proto-Slavic possessed seven short and seven long non-jer oral vowels, two short and two long nasal vowels, two jers, twenty-six consonants, and the glide *j* (**2.43**). Among the consonants, the hushing *š ž č* are classified as alveolar, contrasting with the palatal *s' z'* and the dental *c:*

VOWELS

	Non-Jer Oral			Jers		Nasal	
	Front	Back		Front	Back	Front	Back
		Unrounded	Rounded				
High	ī̆	ȳ̆	ū̆				
Mid	ē̆	ō̆		ь	ъ	ę̄̆	ǭ̆
Low	ē̆	ā̆					

CONSONANTS

	Labial	Dental	Alveolar	Palatal	Velar
Stop	p b	t d		t' d'	k g
Spirant	v	s z	š ž	s' z'	x
Affricate		c ʒ	č		
Nasal	m	n		n'	
Liquid		r l		r' l'	
Glide				j	

Note: The consonants *t'* and *d'* developed differently in five dialect areas (**2.36**), *ʒ* and *z'* were dialect variants, and *s'* occurred in East and South Slavic only (**2.31**).

In accordance with the rules governing the structure of syllables (**2.17**), Proto-Slavic consonants were subject to a number of constraints. The distributional limitations of *CV* sequences allow us to distinguish four consonant classes: (1) labial and dental nonaffricate consonants, which occurred before all vowels; (2) velar consonants, which occurred before back vowels only; (3) dental affricate consonants, which occurred before the vowels *u, a, ǫ,* and all front vowels; and (4) palatal and alveolar consonants, which occurred before the vowels *u, a, ǫ,* and the front vowels except *ě*. For morphological statements it is convenient to oppose classes 1 and 2 to classes 3 and 4. The former will be called *hard,* the latter *soft.*

Aside from the results of the palatalizations of velars and yodization, *CC* clusters were limited to the sequences of (1) any stop + liquid; (2) dental or velar stop + *v;* (3) velar stop + *n;* (4) dental spirant + stop, subject to the requirement of uniform voicing within clusters; (5) dental spirant + nasal, *l,* or *v;* and (6) *x* + liquid or *v,* yielding the following *CC* sequences:

	p	t	k	b	d	g	m	n	r	l	v
p									pr	pl	
b									br	bl	
t									tr	tl	tv
d									dr	dl	dv
k								kn	kr	kl	kv
g								gn	gr	gl	gv
s	sp	st	sk				sm	sn		sl	sv
z				zb	zd	zg	zm	zn		zl	zv
x									xr	xl	xv

Notes: (a) The first palatalization of *sk* and *zg* produced the clusters *šč* and *žǯ* (**2.22**).

(b) By the second and progressive palatalizations, *sk* and *zg* yielded *sc* and *zʒ* throughout Slavic, while *ku̯* and *gu̯* yielded *cv* and *ʒv* in South Slavic and parts of East Slavic (**2.31**). In East Slavic, *xu̯* > *s'v;* cf. Old ESl. *vьlsvi* (Nom. Pl.) of *vьlxvъ* 'soothsayer'.

(c) The clusters *tl* and *dl* occurred in West Slavic only (**2.33**).

(d) Yodized clusters (**2.23**) of the type [stop + *R*] or [stop + *n*] yielded [stop + *R'*] and [stop + *n'*]. Yodized labials developed an epenthetic *l: pl' bl' vl' ml'*. Yodized clusters beginning with a spirant gave the following sequences:

sk > šč	st > št'	sn > šn'	sl > šl'	su̯ > šv
zg > žǯ	zd > žd'	zn > žn'		

(e) CCC clusters were limited to the sequences [spirant + stop + liquid] or [spirant + stop + *v*] with uniform voicing within clusters; yodized *str zdr* gave *štr' ždr'*.

spr	str (štr')	stv	skr	skl	skv
zbr	zdr (ždr')	zdv	agr	zgl	zgv

2.45. Nouns versus verbs. Words that are morphemically unanalyzable are called *simple;* those that are analyzable into two or more discrete morphemes, the etymological root accompanied by derivational or inflectional morphemes, are called *complex.* Except for some conjunctions and particles, Proto-Slavic words were complex. Of these, adverbs showed no inflectional morphemes, that is, they were uninflected, while other complex words were inflected. Inflected words belonged to two large classes which expressed different grammatical meanings or categories: *nouns* (or nominals), including substantives, pronouns, adjectives, and numerals; and *verbs*. Accordingly, Proto-Slavic distinguished between nominal and verbal inflections.

Nouns and verbs consisted of stems and desinences. Desinences included an obligatory inflectional ending which marked such inflectional categories as case, number, gender, person, infinitive, and supine. Verbs and adjectives could also have a pre-final desinential suffix which marked the inflectional categories of aspect, tense, and mood (e.g. *-ěa-*, the imperfect formant). Some inflectional categories were expressed with the help of an otherwise independent word (e.g. Acc. Sg. *sę* in the reflexive or an auxiliary verb in compound tenses or the conditional).

Stems consisted of roots, either alone or accompanied by one or more affixes which, depending on whether they preceded or followed the root, are called prefixes or suffixes. Affixes showed varying blends of lexical and grammatical meaning. Some could be exclusively or predominantly lexical, such as the negative prefix (e.g. OCS *ne-plody* 'barren woman', *ne-vidimъ* 'invisible'), the prefixes in many inperfective verbs (e.g. OCS *vъ-kušati* 'taste', *pri-běgati* 'take refuge'), and diminutive or agentive suffixes (e.g. OCS *dъšt-ic-a* 'small board', *uči-telj-ь* 'teacher'). Others could be exclusively or predominantly grammatical, such as the suffixes switching one part of speech to another (e.g. the suffix *-ьn-*, which formed adjectives from nouns). Proto-Slavic did not use infixation as a grammatical device. In a handful of forms, however, it retained traces of the Proto-Indo-European present-tense infix *-n-*. Thus, the Old Church Slavonic verbs *sěsti sędetъ* 'sit down', *lešti lęžetъ* 'lie down' show an alternation between the noninfixed infinitive stems *sēd- lěg-* and the infixed present-tense stems *sē-n-d- lě-n-g-*.

2.46. Grammatical categories. Number and gender were the only grammatical categories that were common to both nouns and verbs. Characteristically nominal was the grammatical category of case, while gradation and specificity were typically adjectival. Other grammatical categories were verb-specific.

All nouns were obligatorily marked for *case*. Late Proto-Indo-European had a seven-case system: nominative, accusative, genitive, dative, instrumental, locative, and ablative. The vocative was a case-like form of address used with personal substantives and having a distinct form in the singular only. Balto-Slavic merged the genitive and ablative,[154] creating a new six-case system in which the genitive represented the two syncretized cases. Case syncretism was also important in the dual number, which distinguished only three cases: the nominative/accusative, genitive/locative, and dative/instrumental, and in the formation of Proto-Slavic subgenders. Dative and instrumental endings contained the phoneme *m*, an Indo-European dialect feature connecting Balto-Slavic and Germanic and opposing them to the other Indo-European languages where the reflexes of *bh* are found.

Number characterized the nouns (including the participles and verbal substantives but excluding the nongendered pronouns and cardinal numerals 'five' and higher) and the finite forms of the verb. Of the three Proto-Indo-European numbers—singular, dual, and plural—the dual has shown itself to be least stable. It was still a regular category in Old Church Slavonic, and its vestiges are found in all the Slavic languages, but as a grammatical category it has survived only in Slovenian and the two Sorbian languages.

154. The ablative had a very limited currency in Proto-Indo-European, appearing as a distinct case in the singular of only one stem type.

Like most early Indo-European languages, Proto-Slavic distinguished three *genders:* masculine (M), feminine (F), and neuter (N). Showing morphological gender were the adjectives (including verbal adjectives, or participles), the gendered pronouns, the numerals from 'one' to 'four', and the compound verbal categories. Showing syntactic (or inherent) gender were the substantives. In addition, masculine substantives inflected according to the *-ŏ-/-i̯-ŏ-* inflectional pattern (**2.47**) developed a distinction between the personal and nonpersonal *subgenders.* The former was expressed by the syncretism of the accusative and genitive cases, the latter by an absence of such a syncretism. This distinction was later extended to oppose the animate and inanimate subgenders.

Proto-Slavic qualitative adjectives continued the Proto-Indo-European distinctions of *gradation* with positive, comparative, and superlative degrees. In addition, Proto-Slavic nonpossessive adjectives developed the distinction of *specificity,* whereby definite (also known as pronominal or compound) adjectives were opposed to indefinite adjectives.

Among verbs, Proto-Indo-European distinguished two diatheses, the active (or nonmiddle) and middle, the latter marked as a category that placed special emphasis on the grammatical subject, leading to the neutralization of the opposition between the agent and the patient (compare the English active *Mother washed the baby* or *Mother opened the door* with the middle *Mother washed* or *The door opened*). The active/middle opposition was expressed by special sets of inflectional endings. Proto-Slavic lost these formal distinctions but retained the semantic opposition between the active and the middle, expressing it with a newly developed contrast between two *genera,* the nonreflexive and reflexive, the latter formally distinguished by the particle *sę* (originally the accusative of the reflexive personal pronoun). The marked reflexive, like the middle, stressed the presence or absence of the grammatical subject.[155] Proto-Slavic added also a new *voice* opposition in which the active contrasted with the passive, the latter marked as the category specifying the patient of an action. The active/passive opposition was formally expressed only in the participle. Genus, by contrast, was an obligatory category of the verb (**2.62**).

Of the four verbal *moods* reconstructed for Proto-Indo-European (indicative, subjunctive, optative, and imperative), Proto-Slavic retained the indicative and the optative, the latter reinterpreted as the imperative. The subjunctive (or conjunctive), known from Vedic Sanskrit, Greek, Latin, and Celtic, expressed probability or expectation and was therefore frequently reinterpreted as the future tense. In Proto-Slavic it was replaced by the conditional, in which the resultative (or perfect) participle combined with a form of the auxiliary verb 'to be' to produce an analytical grammatical construction. The optative, which occurred in Sanskrit, Greek, Latin, and Germanic, expressed desire or potentiality. In Proto-Slavic it replaced the original Proto-Indo-European imperative.[156]

The oldest system of Proto-Indo-European verbal *tenses*—present, aorist, and perfect—appears to have had less to do with temporal relations than with the manner of performance or other characteristics of an action. The present referred to an action that at the moment of speech was not completed. The aorist viewed the action statically, as completed and therefore past. The perfect dwelled on situational dynamics and stressed the result of an action by linking the past and the moment of speech. The future was originally expressed through the modalities of the subjunctive or optative. Specific future-tense formations seem to be Late Proto-Indo-European dialectal innovations. So were the imperfect, which emphasized non-

155. Absence of grammatical subject characterized impersonal constructions.

156. The Slavic verb 'to be' may be said to have optative forms in the conditional (**2.51.6**).

completion of a past action, and the pluperfect, which referred to an action that preceded the narrated event. Proto-Slavic developed its own analytical perfect tenses, in which (like the conditional) the resultative participle of the verb was accompanied by an auxiliary form of the verb 'to be'. The perfect tense used the present of the auxiliary, while the pluperfect used the imperfect or the imperfective aorist of the auxiliary. A Proto-Slavic innovation was the imperfective future expressed by the infinitive accompanied by present-tense forms of one of the auxiliary verbs: 'to be', 'to have', 'to want', or 'to begin'.

The contrast between completion and noncompletion of action, inherent in the preterit tenses of Proto-Indo-European, developed into a fully articulated grammatical opposition of two *aspects:* the perfective, specifying a completed action, and the unmarked imperfective. Some imperfective verbs (chiefly the verbs of motion) distinguished also between two *subaspects,* the nondetermined, indicating a discontinuous (iterative) action, and the unmarked determined (**2.51**). The development of aspectual distinctions led in turn to the rise of an intricate interplay between aspects and tenses. Since the perfective expressed a completed action, the perfective present tended to assume the function of the future, leaving the imperfective present as the sole indicator of contemporaneity with the speech event.[157] Consequently, Proto-Slavic present-tense forms, referring either to the present or the future, may be viewed as nonpast and are often so termed. Among the preterit tenses, the imperfective aspect appears to have preempted the function of the imperfect, leading to its gradual disappearance or reinterpretation in individual Slavic languages.

The three *persons* of the Proto-Indo-European verb remained in Proto-Slavic. Verbal forms inflected for person (tenses and moods) are called *finite.*

Along with the finite verbal forms, Proto-Slavic had nonfinite forms. Of these, the *infinitive* and the *supine* were frozen case forms of Proto-Indo-European deverbal nouns, the *participles* were verbal adjectives, and *verbal substantives* were derived from the forms containing the past passive participial suffixes.

2.47. Nominal stems. Suffixes that assigned a stem to a particular inflectional pattern are called *thematic.* Most thematic suffixes of Proto-Indo-European lost their identity in Proto-Slavic—for example, the thematic vowels of the Proto-Indo-European nominal inflection, which in Proto-Slavic blended in with the inflectional endings. Their original morphemic independence is evident from such forms as OCS Inst. Sg. *grad-omь* 'town', *synъmь* 'son', *pǫt-ьmь* 'road', whose endings were derived from the sequence of the Proto-Indo-European thematic vowels *-ŏ-*, *-ŭ-*, *-ĭ-* and the inflectional ending *-mĭ.* Proto-Indo-European nominal stems containing a thematic vowel are called *vocalic (thematic);* those without a thematic vowel are called *consonantal (athematic).* This classification is retained here even though, from a strictly descriptive point of view, it is no longer applicable in Proto-Slavic. In addition, depending on the presence or absence of a noun-forming suffix (other than the thematic vowel), Proto-Slavic nominal stems may be classified as suffixed and unsuffixed. Most of the unsuffixed stems were derived from verbs and for that reason are referred to by Vaillant (1974) as "noms postverbaux."[158] The unsuffixed stems that are not so derived may be called *primary* (or unmotivated).

157. The development of this interrelationship between aspect and tense was a gradual process which affected individual languages in varying degrees. It was most complete in North Slavic, although even there we find early examples of perfective presents used to denote timeless states. This is still so in South Slavic; cf. Bg. *dójdat ta sédnat* 'they come and sit down (habitually)'.

158. Vaillant borrowed this term from the study of noun derivation in Latin by the French linguist Michel Bréal

Primary consonantal nominal stems were either lost in Proto-Slavic or transferred to a vocalic class, with or without a derivational suffix, e.g. *dēnt-s* 'tooth' (cf. Latin *dēns, dentis*) was lost and replaced by *g'ŏmbh-ŏ-s* 'stake' (cf. OCS *zǫbъ* 'tooth'), *k'r̥d-* 'heart' (cf. Latin *cor, cordis*) was replaced by *k'r̥d-ĭk-ŏ-m* (cf. OCS *srьdьce* 'heart'), *(s)nŏi̯gʷh-s* 'snow' (cf. Latin *nix, nivis*) was replaced by *(s)nŏi̯gʷh-ŏ-s* (cf. OCS *sněgъ* 'snow'), *mūs-s* 'mouse' (cf. Latin *mūs*) was replaced by *mūs-ĭ-s* (cf. OCS *myšь* 'mouse').

Proto-Slavic vocalic stems included *-ĭ-* (F and M), *-ŭ-* (M), *-ŏ-* (M and N), and *-ā-* (F and M) stems. Stems in which the thematic vowels *-ŏ-* and *-ā-* were preceded by the derivational suffix *-i̯-* are referred to as the *-i̯-ŏ-* and *-i̯-ā-* stems. As expected, back vowels after *i̯* were fronted (**2.25**). The *-i̯-ī-* stems (F and M) were a subclass of the *-i̯-ā-* stems, differing from them in the nominative singular only. Among the substantives all the vocalic stems were represented, but only the *-ŏ-/-i̯-ŏ-*, *-ā-/-i̯-ā-*, and *-ĭ-* (F) stems were fully productive. The indefinite adjectives belonged to the *-ŏ-/-i̯-ŏ-* (M and N) and *-ā-/-i̯-ā-* (F) classes. The Late Proto-Slavic numerals *jedin-* 'one' (Sg. and Pl. only) and *dъv-* 'two' (Du. only) belonged to the *-ŏ-* and *-ā-* classes, while *tr-ь-* 'three' (Pl. only), *pęt-ь-* 'five' (Sg. only), and higher belonged to the *-ĭ-* class.

Of the derived consonantal stems, Proto-Slavic retained stems in the suffixes *-mōn-/-mĕn-* (M), *-ōs-/-ĕs-* (N), *-tēr-/-tĕr-*, and *-ū-/-ŭu̯-* (F), which showed nominative singular versus non-nominative singular ablaut variants, and stems in *-(m)ēn-/-(m)ĕn-* (M and N) and *-ēnt-/-ĕnt-* (N), where the nominative singular length developed probably within Slavic (Meillet 1934:426). In addition, endings of the consonantal type occurred with the plural (second) stems of the masculine personal substantives in *-tĕl-i̯-/-tĕl-*, *-ār-i̯-/-ār-*, *(-i̯-ān)-īn-/(-i̯-ān)-*, the numeral *četyr-* 'four' (plural inflection only), and some forms of the numeral *desęt-* 'ten', as well as with the nominative singular of all genders and the nominative plural masculine of the present active and past active participles (**2.51.6**).

In the following survey Proto-Slavic nominal stems are arranged by their Proto-Indo-European stem types within which the most important derivational types are listed and exemplified. The suffixes of the vocalic stems are listed in their Late Proto-Slavic form and are arranged alphabetically by their (final) consonant, not counting the yod, which is transcribed as *i̯*. Included in the survey are some single-consonant Proto-Indo-European suffixes which in Slavic blended in with the root and thereby lost their morphemic status. Thus, the suffixes *-t-* of the *-ĭ-* stems (e.g. *čьstь* 'honor' < *kĭt-t-ĭ-s*) or *-m-* of the *-ŏ-* stems (e.g. *dymъ* 'smoke' < *dhū-m-ŏ-s*) were no longer perceivable as such in Late Proto-Slavic. Unless otherwise indicated, examples are given in their Late Proto-Slavic form.

2.47.1. Consonantal stems were heteroclite, that is, their paradigms used two stems (separated in the lists below with a slash). Stems in *-tĕl-i̯-/-tĕl-*, *-ār-i̯-/-ār-*, and *(-i̯-ān-)īn-/(-i̯-ān-)* formed masculine personal substantives in which the vocalic singular stem with the suffixes *-i̯-* or *-īn-* was opposed to the consonantal plural stem without those suffixes. Other consonantal stems opposed the nominative singular stem (also accusative singular in neuter substantives) to the stem of the rest of the paradigm.

Consonantal stems may be divided into productive stems in *-ēnt-/-ĕnt-*, *-ū-/-ŭu̯-*, *-tĕl-i̯-/-tĕl-*, *-ār-i̯-/-ār-*, and *(-i̯-ān)-īn-/(-i̯-ān)-* and unproductive ones in *-ēn-/-ĕn-*,

---

(1832–1915) and applied it to the Slavic masculine *-ŏ-* stems and feminine *-ā-* stems. For a description of Proto-Slavic nominal derivation, briefer than Vaillant's comprehensive treatment, see the opening sections of the first three volumes of Sławski 1974–.

-mōn-/-mĕn-, *-mēn-/-mĕn-*, *-ŏs-/-ĕs-*, and *-tēr-/-tĕr-*. They will be listed in that order in bold print, with the Early Proto-Slavic form of the suffix followed by its Late Proto-Slavic form in parentheses.

***-ēnt-/-ĕnt-* (*-ę/-ęt-*)** formed neuter substantives denoting younglings:

(j)agnę, -ęte 'lamb' (cf. Lat. *āgnus* 'lamb')
kozьlę, -ęte 'kid' (cf. OCS *kozьlъ* 'goat')
otročę, -ęte 'small child' (cf. OCS *otrokъ* 'child')
porsę, -ęte 'piglet' (cf. Lith. *par̃šas* 'piglet')
telę, -ęte 'calf' (cf. Latvian *teļš* 'calf')

***-ū-/-ŭu̯-* (*-y/-ъv-*)** was found with several feminine substantives inherited from Proto-Indo-European:

bry, -ъve 'brow' (cf. Lith. *bruvìs* 'brow')
kry, -ъve 'blood' (cf. Lith. *kraũjas* 'blood')
l'uby, -ъve 'love' (cf. Goth. *liufs* 'dear')
neplody, -ъve 'barren woman' (cf. OCS *plodъ* 'fruit')
svekry, -ъve 'mother-in-law' (cf. Lat. *socrūs* 'mother-in-law')

The suffix *-ū-/-ŭu̯-* also occurred with a number of Late Proto-Slavic borrowings from Germanic:

bordy, -ъve 'battle axe' (cf. OHG *barta* 'battle axe' < PGmc. *bardō*)
buky, -ъve 'letter' (cf. Goth. *bōka* 'letter' < PGmc. *bōkō*)
cr̥'ky, -ъve 'church' (cf. OHG *chirihha* 'church' < PGmc. *kirikō*)
koty, -ъve 'anchor' (cf. Low German *katt* 'small anchor')
smoky, -ъve 'fig tree' (cf. Goth. *smakka* 'fig')

***-tĕl-i̯-/-tĕl-* (*-tel'-/-tel-*)** was one of the most productive suffixes forming deverbal agentive masculine substantives:

dělatel'ь/dělatele 'maker' (cf. OCS *dělati* 'to make')
pravitel'ь/pravitele 'ruler' (cf. OCS *praviti* 'to rule')
prijatel'ь/prijatele 'friend' (cf. OCS *prijati* 'to be loving')
sъ-zьdatel'ь/sъ-zьdatele 'creator' (cf. OCS *sъ-zьdati* 'to create')
žitel'ь/žitele 'inhabitant' (cf. OCS *žiti* 'to live')

***-ār-i̯-/-ār-* (*-ar'-/-ar-*)** formed masculine substantives denoting occupations or professions:

gr̥nьčar'ь/gr̥nčare 'potter' (cf. Ru. *gornéc* < *gr̥nьcь* 'pot')
kl'učar'ь/kl'učare 'keeper of the keys' (cf. OCS *kl'učь* 'key')
rybar'ь/rybare 'fisherman' (cf. OCS *ryba* 'fish')
voldar'ь/voldare 'master' (cf. OCS *vladǫ* < *voldǫ* 'I rule')
vortar'ь/vortare 'gate-keeper' (cf. OCS *vrata* < *vorta* 'gate')

In addition to native Slavic formations, *-ar'-/-ar-* was common among lexical loans from Germanic, which suggests that the suffix itself may have been borrowed from Germanic:

bukar'ь/bukare 'bookman' (cf. *buky* 'letter', Goth. *bōkareis* 'bookman')
cěsar'ь/cěsare 'emperor' (cf. Goth. *kaisar* 'emperor')
lěkar'ь/lěkare 'physician' (cf. Goth. *lēkeis* 'physician')
mytar'ь/mytare 'publican' (cf. OCS *myto* 'tax', Goth. *mōtareis* 'publican')
vinar'ь/vinare 'vintner' (cf. Goth. *wein* 'wine')

-i̯-ān-īn-/-i̯-ān- **(*-i̯-an-in-/-i̯-an-*** or ***-ěn-in-/-ěn-*)** formed masculine substantives designating inhabitants of particular localities. Its singular variant included the singulative suffix *-in-* which goes back to PIE *-īn-* or *-ěi̯n-*:

gord'aninъ/gord'ane 'town dweller' (cf. OCS *gradъ* < *gordъ* 'town')
dvor'aninъ/dvor'ane 'courtier' (cf. OCS *dvorъ* 'court')
měst'aninъ/měst'ane 'local dweller' (cf. OCS *město* 'place')
Riml'aninъ/Riml'ane 'Roman' (cf. OCS *Rimъ* 'Rome')
Slověninъ/Slověne 'Slav' (derived from *slov-* of uncertain meaning)

Stems in the singulative suffix *-in-* could also be paired with stems of collective substantives which were then reinterpreted as plurals:

bol'arinъ/bol'are 'boyar' (cf. Turkic *bajar* 'lord')
gospodinъ/gospoda 'lord' (cf. OCS *gospodь* 'lord')
l'udinъ/l'udьje 'commoner' (cf. OCS *l'udъ* 'people')
Obrinъ/Obre 'Avar' (cf. Cz. *Obr* 'Avar')
poganinъ/pogane 'pagan' (cf. OCS *poganъ* 'pagan')

-ēn-/-ěn- **(*-ę/-en-*)** and ***-mōn-/-měn-*** **(*-my*[159]*/-men-*)** occurred in a small number of masculine substantives that tended to migrate to the *-i̯-ŏ-* or *-ĭ-* stem masculines:

grebę, -ene (also *grebenь*) 'comb' (cf. OCS *grebǫ* 'I dig')
jelę, -ene (also *jelenь*) 'deer' (cf. Lith. *élnis* 'deer')
korę, -ene (also *korenь*) 'root' (cf. Cz. *keř* < *kъr-i̯-* 'bush')
pr̥'stę, -ene (also *pr̥'stenь*) 'ring' (cf. OCS *prьstъ* < *pr̥'stъ* 'finger')
stepę, -ene (also *stepenь*) 'step' (cf. Ru. *stopá* 'foot')

jęčьmy, -ene (also *jęčьmenь*) 'barley'
kamy, -ene (also *kamenь*) 'stone'
kremy, -ene (also *kremenь*) 'flint'
polmy, -ene (also *polmenь*) 'flame'
remy, -ene (also *remenь*) 'strap'

-mēn-/-měn- **(*-mę/-men-*)** formed neuter substantives:

bermę, -ene 'burden' (< *bēr-měn-*, cf. OCS *berǫ* 'I take')
imę, -ene 'name' (< *n̥-měn-*, cf. Lat. *nōmen* 'name')
plemę, -ene 'tribe' (< plěd-měn-, cf. OCS *plodъ* 'fruit')
sěmę,-ene 'seed' (< *sē-měn-*, cf. Lat. *sēmen* 'seed')
znamę, -ene 'sign' (< *g'nō-měn-*, cf. Lat. *co-gnōmen* 'name')

-ŏs-/-ěs- **(*-o/-es-*)** occurred with a few neuter substantives:

čudo, -ese 'marvel' (cf. Gk. *kŷdos* 'glory')
dervo, -ese 'tree' (cf. Lith. *dervá* 'pine tree')
kolo, -ese 'wheel' (cf. Gk. *pólos* 'pivot')
nebo, -ese 'sky' (cf. Gk. *néphos* 'cloud')
slovo, -ese 'word' (cf. Skt. *śravas* 'fame')

-tēr-/-těr- **(*-ti*[160]*/-ter-*)** survived in only two feminine substantives:

dъt'i, -ere 'daughter' (cf. Lith. *duktė, -ers* 'daughter')
mati, -ere 'mother' (cf. Lat. *māter* 'mother')

159. For the development of *-my* < *-mōn-s*, see **2.48.1 *note* 3a.**
160. The Nom. Sg. *-tēr-* was replaced by LPS1. *-ti-* by analogy with the *-i̯-ī-* stems.

2.47.2. The vocalic **-ŭ- stems** included a small number of primary masculine substantives:

domъ 'house' (cf. Lat. *domus* 'house')
medъ 'honey' (cf. Lith. *medùs* 'honey')
synъ 'son' (cf. Lith. *sūnùs* 'son')
volъ 'ox' (cf. Ru. *valját'* 'to castrate')
vr̥'xъ 'top' (cf. Lith. *viršùs* 'top')

Proto-Indo-European -*ŭ*- stem adjectives were extended in Slavic by the suffix -*ъk*- and assigned to the -*ŏ*-/-*ā* stems:

bliz-ъk- 'near' (cf. Lat. *flīgere* 'strike')
lьg-ъk- 'light' (cf. Ru. *nel'zjá* 'it is not permitted')
męk-ъk- 'soft' (cf. OCS *mǫka* 'flour')
niz-ъk- 'low' (cf. Mod. Ru. *v nizú* 'below')
sold-ъk- 'sweet' (cf. Lith. *saldùs* 'sweet')

2.47.3. The vocalic **-ĭ- stems** were found typically among the feminine substantives, but they also included a few adjectives and masculine substantives. Although only the feminine substantives were productive, the -*ĭ*- stem declension accommodated both feminine and masculine borrowings into Late Proto-Slavic; e.g. OCS feminine *Elisavetь* 'Elisabeth' (from Greek *Elisábet*) and masculine *korabь* 'boat' (from Greek *karábion*). It also became the favorite receptacle for the ambulant consonantal stems of all genders (**2.47.1**).

Unsuffixed -ĭ- stems included feminine, mostly abstract nouns derived from verbs, adjectives, and participles:

bolь 'pain' (cf. OCS *bolěti* 'be painful')
rěčь 'word' (cf. OCS *rekǫ* 'I say')
rězь 'sharp pain' (cf. OCS *rězati* 'to cut')
sъn-ědь 'food' (cf. OCS *sъněsti* 'to eat')
vęzь 'link' (cf. OCS *vęzati* 'to tie')

bělь 'whiteness' (cf. OCS *běl-* 'white')
glušь 'backwoods' (cf. OCS *glux-* 'deaf')
gnilь 'rot' (cf. Ru. *gni-l-* 'rotten')
novь 'virgin land' (cf. OCS *nov-* 'new')
studenь 'cold' (cf. OCS *stud-en-* 'cold')

Some primary feminine and masculine substantives also belonged to this class. Among the feminines were:

dvьrь 'door' (cf. Lat. *foris* 'door')
kostь 'bone' (cf. Lat. *costa* 'rib')
myšь 'mouse' (cf. Lat. *mūs* 'mouse')
osь 'axis' (cf. Lith. *ašìs* 'axis')
solь 'salt' (cf. Lat. *sāl, salis* 'salt')

Primary masculine substantives were mostly animate. Being unproductive, they tended to follow the declensional pattern of the productive -*i̯*-*ŏ*- stems:

golǫbь 'pigeon' (cf. Ru. *golubój* 'blue')
gostь 'merchant' (cf. Lat. *hostis* 'stranger, enemy', Eng. *guest*)
tьstь 'father-in-law' (cf. Gk. *tétta* 'daddy')
zętь 'bridegroom' (cf. Lith. *žéntas* 'son-in-law')
zvěrь 'wild beast' (cf. Lith. *žvėrìs* 'beast')

-ěl-ь, -sn-ь, -zn-ь formed a limited number of deverbal feminine substantives:

gybělь 'destruction' (cf. OCS *gybnǫti* 'to perish')
kǫpělь 'bath' (cf. Ru. *kupát'* 'to bathe')
obitělь 'hermitage' (cf. OCS *obitati* 'to dwell')
pečalь 'sorrow' (cf. Ru. *pekú* 'I bake')
svirělь 'pipe' (cf. OCS *svirati* 'to pipe')

basnь 'tale' (cf. Ru. *bájat'* 'to speak')
pěsnь 'song' (cf. OCS *pěti* 'to sing')
vasnь 'quarrel' (cf. OCS *vaditi* 'to spread dissension')

bojaznь 'fear' (cf. OCS *bojati sę* 'to fear')
bolěznь 'pain' (cf. OCS *boléti* 'to be unwell')
kъznь 'cunning' (cf. OCS *kovati* 'to forge')
prijaznь 'friendship' (cf. OCS *prijati* 'to favor')
žiznь 'life' (cf. OCS *žiti* 'to live')

-t- occurred with concrete feminine substantives; it was an Indo-European suffix, not perceived as an independent morpheme in Slavic:

čьstь 'honor' (cf. OCS *čьtǫ* 'I count')
mastь 'ointment' (cf. OCS *mazati* 'to spread')
mot'ь 'power' (< EPSl. *măg-t-ĭ*, cf. OCS *mogǫ* 'I can')
sъ-mr̥'tь 'death' (cf. OCS *mьrǫ* 'I die')
věstь 'news' (cf. OCS *věděti* 'to know')

-ost-ь was and has remained productive in the formation of deadjectival abstract feminine substantives:

jarostь 'anger' (cf. OCS *jar-* 'strong')
mǫdrostь 'wisdom' (cf. OCS *mǫdr-* 'wise')
starostь 'old age' (cf. OCS *star-* 'old')
sytostь 'satiety' (cf. OCS *syt-* 'satiated')
junostь 'youth' (cf. OCS *jun-* 'young')

-ež-ь formed masculine abstract deverbal substantives which tended to switch their gender to feminine:

grabežь 'robbery' (cf. OCS *grabiti* 'to rob')
kradežь 'theft' (cf. OCS *kradǫ* 'I steal')
l'ubežь 'love' (cf. OCS *l'ubiti* 'to love')
mętežь 'mutiny' (cf. OCS *mętǫ* 'I confuse')
platežь 'payment' (cf. OCS *platiti* 'to pay')

Uninflected -ĭ- stems survived in three Old Church Slavonic adjectives. The general tendency, however, was to transfer them to the *-ŏ-/-ā-* stems through suffixation:

svobodь and *svobod-ьn-* 'free'
tajь and *taj-ьn-* 'secret'
udobь and *udob-ьn-* 'easy'

gor-ь-k- 'bitter' (cf. OCS *gorěti* 'to burn')
tęž-ь-k- 'heavy' (cf. Ru. *tjažëlyj* 'heavy')
glǫb-ok- 'deep' (cf. Ru. *glub'* 'depth')
šir-ok- 'wide' (cf. Ru. *šir'* 'width')
vys-ok- 'tall' (cf. Ru. *vys'* 'height')

2.47.4. The most common and most productive class of Slavic vocalic nouns were the **-ŏ-/-ā- stems** (here treated jointly). The *-ŏ-* stems included masculine and neuter nouns, while the *-ā-* stems were typically feminine but also included a small group of masculine personal substantives. Except for the latter group, the gender of a substantive may be inferred from the endings of the nominative singular, and these are therefore included in the lists of substantives: *-ъ/-ь* for masculine, *-o/-e* for neuter, and *-a* for feminine (but the adjectives are listed by the stem). Most of the *-ŏ-/-ā-* stems contained a pre-thematic suffix. Of these, the most common suffixes are listed below and are grouped by their last consonant in its Balto-Slavic shape. A few examples of the unsuffixed *-ŏ-/-ā* stems are given first. The suffixed stems containing the derivational suffix *-i̯-* are known as the *-i̯-ŏ-/-i̯-ā-* stems (*-i̯-ĭ-* stems are a subclass of the *-i̯-ā-* stems).

(a) **Unsuffixed -ŏ-/-ā- stems** were typically substantival. The masculine *-ŏ-* stems were frequently formed from prefixed verbs, e.g. *do-borъ* 'addition', *jьz-borъ* 'choice', *orz-borъ* 'analysis', *pri-borъ* 'implement', *sъ-borъ* 'gathering', *za-borъ* 'seizure' (cf. *do-bьrati* 'to add', etc.), and were frequently marked by the *o*-grade of the root vowel (*o* < *ŏ*, *a* < *ō*, $ě_2$ < *ŏi̯*, u_2 < *ŏu̯*, *ǫ* < *ŏN*), alternating with the *e*-grade or zero grade of the base verb:

grobъ 'grave' (cf. OCS *grebǫ* 'I dig')
morъ 'pestilence' (cf. OCS *mrěti* < *merti* 'to die')
rokъ 'fixed time' (cf. OCS *rekǫ* 'I say')
světъ 'light' (cf. OCS *svьtěti* 'to shine')
tokъ 'current' (cf. OCS *tekǫ* 'I flow')

Unsuffixed *-ā-* stems included a number of feminine substantives and several masculine personal substantives:

doba 'time' (cf. OCS *dobr-* 'good')
kora 'bark' (cf. Lith. *kérti* 'to peel')
měna 'change' (cf. Lith. *maĩnas* 'change')
soxa 'forked bough, primitive plough' (cf. Lith. *šakà* 'branch')
vьdova 'widow' (cf. Skt. *vidhā́vā* 'widow')

sluga 'servant' (cf. Lith. dial. *slaugà* 'service')
voje-voda 'military leader' (cf. OCS *vedǫ* 'I lead')

(b) **Suffixes containing *b*** were limited to two feminine formations.
-ьb-a formed denominal and deverbal abstract substantives:

borьba 'fight' (cf. OCS *brati* < *borti* 'to fight')
družьba 'company' (cf. OCS *drugъ* 'companion')
rězьba 'incision' (cf. OCS *rězati* 'to cut')
službba 'service' (cf. OCS *sluga* 'servant')
tatьba 'theft' (cf. OCS *tatь* 'thief')

-ob-a formed denominal abstract substantives:

ǫtroba 'innards' (cf. OCS *ǫtrь* 'inside')
xudoba 'poverty' (cf. OCS *xud-* 'poor')
xvoroba 'sickness' (cf. Ru. *xvór-* 'sick')
zъloba 'evil' (cf. OCS *zъl-* 'bad')
žaloba 'plaint' (cf. Ru. *žal'* 'pity')

(c) **Suffixes containing *d*** were limited to the suffix ***-ьd-a,*** which formed a few abstract denominal substantives:

krivьda 'injustice' (cf. Ru. *kriv-* 'crooked')
pravьda 'truth' (cf. OCS *prav-* 'right')
storžьda 'watch' (cf. OCS *stražь* < *storžь* 'guard')
voržьda 'enmity' (cf. OCS *vragъ* < *vorgъ* 'enemy')

(d) **Suffixes containing *g*** were rare. Their chief representative among the *-ŏ-/-ā-* stems was ***-ęʒ-ь*** (from *-ing* by the progressive palatalization), which occurred in several borrowings from Germanic.[161]

koldęʒь 'well' (cf. Gmc. **kaldingaz* 'well')
kъnęʒь 'prince' (cf. OHG *kuning* 'prince')
pěnęʒь 'coin' (cf. OHG *pfenning* 'coin')
retęʒь 'chain' (cf. Gmc. **rekingaz* 'chain')
vitęʒь 'hero' (cf. ON *víkingr* 'Viking')[162]

(e) **Suffixes containing *-i̯-*** followed either a consonant or a jer. In the former case the sequence *Ci̯* produced reflexes in accordance with the rules of yodization (**2.23**); in the latter case the jer became tense and showed the appropriate alternations (*-ь̂i̯-* with *-ii̯-*, **2.42**).

-i̯- was a productive suffix forming desubstantival possessive adjectives:

jelen'- 'deer-' (cf. OCS *elenь* 'deer')
kъnęž- 'princely' (cf. OCS *kъnęʒь* < OHG *kuning*'prince')
osьl'- 'donkey-' (cf. OCS *osьlъ* 'donkey')
otьč- 'paternal' (cf. OCS *otьcь* < PIE *ătĭk-* 'father')
velьbǫd'- 'camel-' (cf. OCS *velьbǫdъ* 'camel')

-i̯-a formed denominal feminine substantives:

duša 'soul' (cf. OCS *duxъ* 'spirit')
koža 'goatskin' (cf. OCS *koza* 'goat')
suša 'dryness' (cf. OCS *sux-* 'dry')
svět'a 'light(er), candle' (cf. OCS *světъ* 'light')
večer'a 'evening meal' (cf. OCS *večerъ* 'evening')

and deverbal feminine substantives:

grobl'a 'dike' (cf. OCS *grebǫ* 'I dig')
lъža 'lie' (cf. OCS *lъgati* 'to lie')
nǫd'a 'need' (cf. OCS *nǫditi* 'to compel')
sad'a 'soot' (cf. OCS *saditi* 'to set')
zor'a 'dawn' (cf. OCS *zьrěti* 'to see')

It occurred also in several masculine personal compounds:

dr̥'vo-děl'a 'carpenter' (cf. OCS *dělati* 'to do')
prědъ-teča 'precursor' (cf. OCS *tekǫ* 'I flow')
velь-moža 'potentate' (cf. OCS *mogǫ* 'I can')

161. Among the *-ĭ-* stems the suffix *-ežь* was derived from *-ěg-ĭ-* (**2.47.3**).
162. It is assumed that in both *retęʒь* and *vitęʒь* Slavic *t* < *c* by dissimilation (Vaillant 1974:503).

-i̯-e formed neuter substantives:

gor'e 'sorrow' (cf. OCS *gorěti* 'to burn')
lože 'bed' (cf. OCS *let'i* < PIE *lĕg-tēi̯* 'to lie down')
mor'e 'lake, sea' (cf. OCS *morьsk-* 'maritime')
pol'e 'field' (cf. OCS *polьsk-* 'field-')
vět'e 'council' (cf. OCS *větъ* 'resolution')

-i̯-ь formed masculine substantives. In deverbal formations the root vowel was often in *o*-grade; in other derivatives the underlying form is frequently difficult to establish on solely Slavic grounds:

nožь 'knife' (cf. OCS *vъnьznǫti* 'to pierce')
plačь 'crying' (cf. OCS *plakati* 'to cry')
storžь 'guard' (cf. OCS *strěgǫ* < *stergǫ* 'I guard')
vod'ь 'leader' (cf. OCS *vedǫ* 'I lead')
vъpl'ь 'scream' (cf. OCS *vъpiti* 'to scream')

dъzd'ь 'rain' (< PIE *dŭs-di̯ŭs* 'bad day')
kl'učь 'key' (cf. Ru. *kl'uká* 'hook')
korl'ь 'king' (< *Karl*, Frankish name of Charlemagne)
kon'ь 'horse' (< *kŏb-n-i̯-*, cf. OCS *kobyla* 'mare')
mečь 'sword' (< Gmc. **mēkeis* 'sword')

-ȋi̯-a was productive in desubstantival collectives:

bratrȋja 'brotherhood' (cf. OCS *bratrъ* 'brother')
kъnęžȋja 'princes' (cf. OCS *kъnęʒь* 'prince')
svatȋja 'matchmakers' (cf. *svatъ* 'matchmaker')

-ȋi̯-e was a productive suffix in verbal substantives (**2.60**):

bytȋje 'being' (cf. OCS *byti* 'to be')
dviženȋje 'movement' (cf. OCS *dvignǫti* 'to move')
pitȋje 'drinking' (cf. OCS *piti* 'to drink')
znanȋje 'knowledge' (cf. OCS *znati* 'to know')
želanȋje 'desire' (cf. OCS *želati* 'to wish')

It also formed neuter substantives from prepositional phrases (especially those denoting land features):

bezdъnȋje 'abyss' (cf. *bezъ dъna* 'without bottom')
podobȋje 'similarity' (cf. *po době* 'according to nature')
podъgorȋje 'foothills' (cf. *podъ gorǫ* 'by the hill')
primorȋje 'littoral' (cf. *pri mor'i* 'by the sea')
zarěčȋje 'land across the river' (cf. *za rěkǫ* 'across the river')

It was also common in denominal collectives and deadjectival abstracts:

listȋje 'foliage' (cf. OCS *listъ* 'leaf')
perȋje 'feathers' (cf. Ru. *peró* 'feather')
sъnȋje 'dreams' (cf. OCS *sъnъ* 'dream')
trupȋje 'corpses' (cf. OCS *trupъ* 'dead body')
ustȋje 'delta' (cf. OCS *usta* 'mouth')

bělȋje 'white objects' (cf. OCS *běl-* 'white')
sъdorvȋje 'health' (cf. OCS *sъdrav-* < *sъdorv-* 'healthy')
veličȋje 'grandeur' (cf. OCS *velik-* 'big')
veselȋje 'joy' (cf. OCS *vesel-* 'gay')
zelȋje 'vegetables' (cf. OCS *zelen-* 'green')

-ь̂i̯-i (a subclass of ***-ь̂i̯-a***) was a suffix of several masculine personal and feminine substantives:

balь̂ji 'medicine man' (cf. OCS *balьstvo* 'medicine')
sǫdь̂ji 'judge' (cf. OCS *sǫdъ* 'judgment')
větь̂ji 'speaker' (cf. OCS *větъ* 'resolution')

ml̥nь̂ji 'lightning' (< *ml̥nī* 'lightning')
korbь̂ji 'basket' (cf. Ru. *kórob* < *korbъ* 'basket')
oldь̂ji 'boat' (< *ŏldī*, cf. Cz. *lod'* 'boat')
olnь̂ji 'doe' (< *ōlnī*, cf. OCS *elenь* 'deer')
svinь̂ji 'pig' (cf. OCS *svin-* 'swinish')

-ь̂i̯-ь was used to form a limited number of masculine substantives:

inь̂jь 'frost' (cf. Lith. *ýnis*)
rebrь̂jь 'ladder' (cf. OCS *rebro* 'rib')
solvь̂jь 'nightingale' (< *solv-* 'grayish', cf. Po. *słowik* 'nightingale')
vorbь̂jь 'sparrow' (cf. Blg. *vrabec* < *vorbьcь* 'sparrow')
zmь̂jь 'dragon' (< *zm-/zem-* 'earth', cf. OCS *zemьn-* 'earth-')

(f) **Suffixes containing *k*** included its palatalized reflexes, *c* and *č*.

-ic-a was a productive suffix forming denominal feminine substantives. Its variant was the suffix *-ьnic-a*, which was abstracted from derivatives based on the adjectives in *-ьn-*. The substantives in which *-ic-a* functioned as a suffix designating female beings were frequently paired with corresponding masculine substantives. In such derivatives the suffix *-ic-a* extended masculine stems or replaced suffixes designating male beings:

lьvica 'lioness' (cf. OCS *lьvъ* 'lion')
proročica 'prophetess' (cf. OCS *prorokъ* 'prophet')
voldyčica 'lady' (cf. OCS *vladyka* < *voldyka* 'master')
vl̥'čica 'she-wolf' (cf. OCS *vlьkъ* < *vl̥'kъ* 'wolf')
vortarica 'female doorkeeper' (cf. OCS *vratar'ь* < *vortar'ь* 'doorkeeper')

čr̥'nica 'nun' (cf. OCS *črьnьcь* < *čr̥'nьcь* 'monk')
starica 'old woman' (cf. OCS *starьcь* 'old man')
samica 'female' (cf. Ru. *samék* < *samьcь* 'male')
telica 'female calf' (cf. OCS *telьcь* 'calf')
junica 'young cow' (cf. OCS *junьcь* 'young bull')

blǫdьnica 'fornicatrix' (cf. OCS *blǫdьnikъ* 'fornicator')
grěšьnica 'female sinner' (cf. OCS *grěšьnikъ* 'sinner')
mǫčenica 'female martyr' (cf. OCS *mǫčenikъ* 'martyr')
pǫtьnica 'female traveler' (cf. OCS *pǫtьnikъ* 'traveler')
učenica 'female disciple' (cf. OCS *učenikъ* 'disciple')

-ic-a also designated female beings in unpaired substantives derived from underlying feminine nouns, frequently endowing them with an expressive value:

babica 'grandmother' (cf. Ru. *bába* 'old woman')
děvica 'girl, virgin' (cf. OCS *děva* 'girl, virgin')
korvica 'cow' (cf. Ru. *koróva* < *korva* 'cow')
rybica 'fish' (cf. OCS *ryba* 'fish')
vьdovica 'widow' (cf. OCS *vьdova* 'widow')

Inanimate substantives in ***-ic-a*** were derived from nouns, adjectives, and numerals:

lěstvica 'ladder' (derived from *lěsty, -ъve* 'step')
ǫdica 'fishing hook' (cf. Ru. *udá* 'fishing rod')
pьšenica 'wheat' (cf. Ru. *pšenó* 'millet')
rǫkavica 'glove' (cf. Ru. *rukáv* 'sleeve')
stolica 'capital' (cf. OCS *stolъ* 'seat')

desnica 'right hand' (cf. OCS *desn-* 'right')
gorьnica 'room' (cf. Ru. *gorn-* 'upper')
gostinica 'inn' (cf. Ru. *gostin-* 'guest-')
tьmьnica 'prison' (cf. OCS *tьmьn-* 'dark')
žitьnica 'granary' (cf. OCS *žitьn-* 'corn-)

dъvojica 'twosome' (cf. OCS *dъvoj-* 'two-')
edinica 'one' (cf. OCS *edin-* 'one')
pętьnica 'Friday' (cf. OCS *pętь* 'five')
sedmica 'set of seven, week' (cf. OCS *sedmь* 'seven')
trojica 'triad' (cf. OCS *troj-* 'three-')

-ьc-a was productive in the formation of masculine deverbal agentive substantives; it alternated occasionally with *-ьc-ь*:

jadьca 'eater' (cf. OCS *jadь* 'food')
grabьca 'robber' (cf. OCS *grabiti* 'to rob')
grebьca (also *grebьcь*) 'oarsman' (cf. OCS *grebǫ* 'I dig')
sěčьca (also *sěčьcь*) 'fighter' (cf. OCS *sěkǫ* 'I chop')
ubѣjьca 'killer' (cf. OCS *u-bѣjǫ* 'I will kill')

It was unproductive in the formation of feminine diminutives:

dvьrьca 'small door' (cf. OCS *dvьrь* 'door')
myšьca 'muscle, arm' (cf. OCS *myšь* 'mouse' and Latin *mūsculus* 'little mouse')
ovьca 'sheep' (cf. OCS *ovьnъ* 'ram')

-ьc-e formed neuter diminutives:

čędьce 'baby' (cf. OCS *čędo* 'child')
jajьce 'egg' (cf. Po. *jaje* 'egg')
městьce 'place' (cf. OCS *město* 'place')
sl̥nьce 'sun' (cf. Ru. *solnopëk* 'full sunlight')
sr̥'dьce 'heart' (cf. OCS *milosrьd-* 'compassionate')

-ьc-ь was a productive suffix forming masculine substantives. It designated male beings in deverbal and deadjectival formations:

borьcь 'fighter' (cf. OCS *bor'ǫ* 'I fight')
čьtьcь 'reader' (cf. OCS *čьtǫ* 'I read')
lovьcь 'hunter' (cf. OCS *loviti* 'to catch')
tvorьcь 'creator' (cf. OCS *tvoriti* 'to create')
žьrьcь 'priest' (cf. OCS *žьrǫ* 'I sacrifice')

čr̥'nьcь 'monk' (cf. OCS *črьn-* < *čr̥'n-* 'black')
mǫdrьcь 'wise man' (cf. OCS *mǫdr-* 'wise')
mr̥'tvьcь 'dead man' (cf. OCS *mrьtv-* < *mr̥'tv-* 'dead')
prišьlьcь 'newcomer' (cf. Ru. *príšl-* 'newly arrived')
slěpьcь 'blind man' (cf. OCS *slěp-* 'blind')

Animate denominal derivatives in **-ьc-ь** were frequently expressive:

jagnьcь 'lamb' (cf. OCS *jagnę* 'lamb')
bratrьcь 'nephew' (cf. OCS *bratrъ* 'brother')
otьcь 'father' (cf. OESl. *otьn-* 'paternal')
starьcь 'elder' (cf. OCS *star-* 'old')
žerbьcь 'foal' (cf. OCS *žrěbę* < *žerbę* 'foal')

Inanimate substantives in -*ьc-ь* were denominal, occasionally with the value of a diminutive:

gordьcь 'small town' (cf. OCS *gradъ* < *gordъ* 'town')
konьcь 'limit' (cf. OCS *iskoni* 'from the beginning')
palьcь 'finger' (< *palъ* 'finger', cf. Ru. *bespál-* 'fingerless')
stolьcь 'throne' (cf. OCS *stolъ* 'seat')
věnьcь 'crown' (cf. Po. *wianek* < *věnъkъ* 'wreath')

-č-ь was a formant of deverbal substantives. In its form **-a-č-ь** (extended from the infinitives in *-ati*) it also functioned as a denominal suffix. The productivity of this suffix in modern Slavic languages and its infrequency in Old Church Slavonic suggests that in Proto-Slavic it had an expressive or pejorative value (Vaillant 1974:321–322).

bičь 'whip' (cf. OCS *biti* 'to strike')
jьgračь 'player' (cf. OCS *igrati* 'to play')
kovačь 'smith' (cf. OCS *kovati* 'to forge')
oračь 'ploughman' (cf. OCS *orati* 'to plough')
tъkačь 'weaver' (cf. OCS *tъkati* 'to weave')

bogačь 'rich man' (cf. OCS *bogat-* 'rich')
bordačь 'bearded man' (cf. OCS *brada* < *borda* 'beard')
golvačь 'big-headed man' (cf. OCS *glava* < *golva* 'head')
kolačь 'round cake' (cf. OCS *kolo* 'wheel')
silačь 'strong man' (cf. OCS *sila* 'strength')

-išč-e (< *īsk-i̯-ŏ*) formed place names from substantives and adjectives:

grobišče 'grave site' (cf. OCS *grobъ* 'grave')
sъkrovišče 'treasury' (cf. OCS *sъkrovъ* 'hiding place')
sъnьmišče 'meeting place' (cf. OCS *sъnьmъ* 'gathering')
tržišče 'marketplace' (cf. OCS *trъgъ* 'market')
žilišče 'abode' (cf. Ru. *žil-* 'habitable')

In West Slavic the suffix *īsk-ŏ* is more frequent than *īsk-i̯-ŏ:*

Cz. *hnojisko* (also *hnojiště*) 'dung heap' (cf. OCS *gnoi* [gnojь] 'dung')
Cz. *ohnisko* 'focus', Po. *ognisko* 'campfire' (cf. OCS *ognь* 'fire')

-k-ъ formed deverbal substantives:

borkъ 'marriage' (< *bьr-/ber-/bor-* 'take', cf. OCS *bьrati* 'to take')
tukъ 'fat' (< *tŏu̯-/tū-* 'grow fat', cf. Po. *tyć, tyję* 'grow fat')
znakъ 'sign' (< *zna-* 'know', cf. OCS *znati* 'to know')
zolkъ 'grass' (< *zel-/zol-* 'green', cf. OCS *zelen-* 'green', *zlakъ* 'grass')
zorkъ 'sight' (< *zьr-/zor-* 'see', cf. OCS *zьrěti* 'see')

-kъ was common in forms containing onomatopoeic roots:

bykъ 'ox' (< BSl. *bū-* 'moo', cf. Eng. *boo*)
rykъ 'roar' (< BSl. *rū-* 'roar', cf. OESl. *rjuti, revu* 'roar')
sykъ 'hiss' (< BSl. *sū-* 'hiss')

stǫkъ 'noise' (cf. Ru. *stonъ* 'moan')
zvǫkъ 'sound' (cf. *zvonъ* 'tone')

-kъ was also used in transferring consonantal stems to vocalic ones:

kamykъ 'stone' (cf. OCS *kamy* < PIE *kām-ōn-s* 'stone')
językъ 'tongue' (based on **języ* < *n̥g'ū-s* 'tongue', cf. Lat. *lingua* 'tongue')

-ik-ъ was a productive suffix of the diminutives; its expressive value makes it difficult to ascertain its antiquity:

Ru. *dómik* 'small house' (cf. OCS *domъ* 'house')
Ru. *dóždik* 'light rain' (cf. OCS *dъždь* 'rain')
Ru. *kljúčik* 'small key' (cf. OCS *kl'učь* 'key')
Po. *konik* 'small horse' (cf. OCS *kon'ь* 'horse')
Po. *stolik* 'stool' (cf. OCS *stolъ* 'seat')

-ik-ъ was a suffix denoting persons or objects endowed with the quality expressed by the underlying adjectives in *-ьn-* and past passive participles in *-en-*. The productivity of the formation with *-ьn-* gave rise to a new compound suffix *-ьn-ik-* (see below):

dl̥žьnikъ 'debtor' (< *dl̥žьn-* 'owing', cf. Ru. *dolžník* 'debtor')
grěšьnikъ 'sinner' (< *grěšьn-* 'sinful', cf. Ru. *gréšnik* 'sinner')
kъn'ižьnikъ 'bookman' (< *kъn'ižьn-* 'book-', cf. Ru. *knížnik* 'bookman')
sьrebrьnikъ 'silver coin' (< *sьrebrьn-* 'silver', cf. Ru. *srébrenik* 'silver coin')
stornьnikъ 'foreigner' (< *stornьn-* 'foreign', cf. Ru. *stránnik* 'wanderer')

mǫčenikъ 'martyr' (< *mǫčen-*, cf. OCS *mǫčiti* 'to torment')
svęt'enikъ 'priest' (< *svęt'en-*, cf. OCS *svętiti* 'to consecrate')
učenikъ 'disciple' (< *učen-*, cf. OCS *učiti* 'to teach')
vъzl'ubl'enikъ 'beloved' (< *vъzl'ubl'en-*, cf. OCS *vъzljubiti* 'to love')

-ьn-ik-ъ was abstracted from adjectival derivatives in *-ьn-* (see above):

istočьnikъ 'source' (cf. Ru. *istók* 'source')
naměstьnikъ 'deputy' (from *na městě* 'in place of')
ǫzьnikъ 'captive' (cf. OCS *ǫza* 'fetters')
ponedělьnikъ 'Monday' (from *po neděl'i* 'after Sunday')
věstьnikъ 'announcer' (cf. OCS *věstь* 'tidings')

-ьsk- was a productive formant of desubstantival adjectives:

čьlověčьsk- 'human' (< *čьlověkъ* 'human being')
mirьsk- 'worldly' (< *mirъ* 'world')
orbьsk- 'slavish' (< cf. OCS *rabъ, orbъ* 'slave')
rajьsk- 'paradisiac' (< *rajь* 'paradise')
zemьsk- 'earthly' (< *zem-* 'earth', cf. OCS *zemьn-* 'earth')

-ъk-a/-ьk-a formed feminine substantives and denoted similarity with the underlying word, frequently endowing it with an expressive value, which accounts for the rareness of this suffix in Old Church Slavonic. The front-jer variant occurred after soft consonants (**2.24**):

bajьka 'fable' (cf. Ru. *bájat'* 'to speak')
klětъka 'cage' (cf. OCS *klětь* 'cell')
měrъka 'measuring cup' (cf. OCS *měra* 'measure')
pętъka 'number five' (cf. OCS *pęt-* 'fifth')
rǫčьka 'handle' (cf. OCS *rǫka* 'hand')

This suffix (along with *-ic-a*) designated also female beings and in this function was often derived from and paired with corresponding masculine stems:

bl̥garъka/bl̥garinъ 'Bulgarian'
družьka/drugъ 'friend'
sǫsědъka/sǫsědъ 'neighbor'
voržьka/voržь 'magician'
vъnučьka/vъnukъ 'grandchild'

-ъk-o/-ьk-o and ***-ъk-ъ/-ьk-ъ*** formed neuter and masculine substantives expressing similarity with the underlying substantive including its diminutivization. The front-jer variant occurred after soft consonants:

dervъko 'small tree' (cf. OCS *drěvo* < *dervo* 'tree')
jajьko 'egg' (cf. Po. *jaje* 'egg')
kolъko 'circle' (cf. OCS *kolo* 'wheel')
očьko 'eye(let)' (cf. OCS *oko* 'eye')
ušьko 'ear' (cf. OCS *uxo* 'ear')

krǫžьkъ 'round object' (cf. OCS *krǫgъ* 'circle')
listъkъ 'leaf' (cf. OCS *listъ* 'leaf')
pьsъkъ 'dog' (cf. OCS *pьsъ* 'dog')
volsъkъ 'hair' (cf. OCS *vlasъ* < *volsъ* 'hair')
zǫbъkъ 'tooth' (cf. OCS *zǫbъ* 'tooth')

These suffixes also served to substantivize adjectives:

bělъko 'albumen' (cf. OCS *běl-* 'white')
pętъkъ 'Friday' (cf. OCS *pęt-* 'fifth')
vъtorъkъ 'Tuesday' (cf. OCS *vъtor-* 'second')
žl̥'tъko 'yolk' (cf. Ru. *žëlt-* 'yellow')

(g) **Suffixes containing *l*** were deverbal.

-l- was the suffix of resultative participles employed in the formation of compound verbal categories (**2.57**); they were frequently adjectivized:

běgl- 'fugitive' (cf. OCS *běgǫ* 'I run')
byl- 'past' (cf. OCS *byti* 'to be')
gnil- 'rotten' (cf. OCS *gniti* 'to rot')
vędl- 'wilted' (cf. Po. *więdnąć* 'to wilt', Ru. *vjal-* 'wilted')
zьrěl- 'mature' (cf. OCS *sъzьrěti* 'to ripen')

-dl-o and ***-sl-o-*** formed deverbal substantives denoting instruments of actions (mainly implements and materials):

mydlo 'soap' (cf. OCS *myti* 'to wash')
čr̥'nidlo 'ink' (cf. Ru. *černít'* 'to blacken')
ordlo 'plough' (cf. OCS *orati* 'to plough')
pravidlo 'rule' (cf. OCS *praviti* 'to direct')
šidlo 'awl' (cf. OCS *šiti* 'to sew')

čislo 'number' (< *čit-sl-o*, cf. OCS *čьtǫ* 'I count')
jaslo 'creche' (< *jad-sl-o*, cf. OCS *jasti* < PIE *ēdtēi̯* 'to eat')
maslo 'butter' (< *maz-sl-o*, cf. OCS *mazati* 'to spread')
pręslo 'loom' (< *pręd-sl-o*, cf. OCS *prędǫ* 'I weave')
veslo 'oar' (< *vez-sl-o*, cf. OCS *vezǫ* 'I transport')

(h) **Suffixes containing *n*.**

-in- formed possessive adjectives from substantives of the *-ā-/-i̯-ā-* and *-ĭ-* stems and from feminine consonantal stems:

materin- 'mother's' (cf. OCS *mati, -ere* 'mother')
vьdovin- 'widow's' (cf. OCS *vьdova* 'widow')
vojevodin- 'commander's' (cf. OCS *voevoda* 'commander')
zmь̂jin- 'viper's' (cf. OCS *zmija* 'viper')
zvěrin- 'beast's' (cf. OCS *zvěrь* 'wild beast')

-in-a formed deadjectival abstract or generalizing substantives:

cělina 'virgin land' (cf. OCS *cěl-* 'whole')
glǫbina 'depth' (cf. OCS *glǫb-ok-* 'deep')
orstlina 'plant' (cf. Ru. *rósl-* < *orstl-* 'grown')
orvьnina 'plain' (cf. OCS *ravьn-* < *orvьn-* 'even')
tišina 'stillness' (cf. Ru. *tíx-* 'still')

In desubstantival derivatives *-in-a* expressed possession (and, by extension, origin):

dědina 'inheritance' (cf. OCS *dědъ* 'ancestor')
otьčina 'fatherland' (cf. OCS *otьcь* 'father')
ovьčina 'sheepskin' (cf. OCS *ovьca* 'sheep')
pajǫčina 'spider web' (cf. Po. *pająk* 'spider')
rodina 'family, clan' (cf. OCS *rodъ* 'birth')

-in-a also particularized underlying mass substantives or cardinal numerals (cf. the singulative masculine suffix *-in-*, **2.47.1**):

desętina 'tithe' (cf. OCS *desętь* 'ten')
godina 'hour' (cf. OCS *godъ* 'appropriate time')
pěsъčina 'grain of sand' (cf. OCS *pěsъkъ* 'sand')
sněžina 'snow flake' (cf. OCS *sněgъ* 'snow')
solmina 'blade of straw' (cf. Ru. *solóma* < *solma* 'straw')

-ьn- was the favorite suffix of denominal adjectives:

bolьn- 'sick' (cf. OCS *bolь* 'patient')
čьstьn- 'honorable' (cf. OCS *čьstь* 'honor')
gněvьn- 'angry' (cf. OCS *gněvъ* 'anger')
rǫčьn- 'manual' (cf. OCS *rǫka* 'hand')
věčьn- 'eternal' (cf. OCS *věkъ* 'age')

-yn'-i formed feminine derivatives from masculine personal substantives and from adjectives:

bogyn'i 'goddess' (cf. OCS *bogъ* 'god')
gospodyn'i 'lady' (cf. OCS *gospodь* 'lord')
kъnęgyn'i 'princess' (cf. OCS *kъnęʒь* 'prince')
orbyn'i 'female slave' (cf. OCS *rabъ* < *orbъ* 'slave')
sǫsědyn'i 'female neighbor' (cf. OCS *sǫsědъ* 'neighbor')

bolgyn'i 'goodness' (cf. OCS *blag-* < *bolg-* 'good')
gr̥dyn'i 'pride' (cf. OCS *grъd-* < *gr̥d-* 'proud')
mękyn'i chaff' (cf. OCS *męk-ъk-* 'soft')
pustyn'i 'desert' (cf. OCS *pust-* 'empty')
svętyn'i 'holy place' (cf. OCS *svęt-* 'holy')

(i) **Suffixes containing *r*** were limited to **-*r*-**, which occurred in a handful of adjectives and substantives:

bъdr- 'awake' (cf. OCS *bъděti* 'be awake')
dobr- 'favorable' (cf. OCS *doba* 'appropriate time')
iskr- 'near' (cf. Lat. *sequor* 'I follow' < PIE *-sěk^{w}-/sk^{w}-* 'follow')
mokr- 'wet' (cf. Ru. *móknut'* 'to get wet')
pьstr- 'dappled' (cf. OCS *pьsati* 'to write')

měra 'measure' (cf. Lat. *mētior* 'I measure < PIE *mē-* 'measure')
vydra 'otter' (cf. OCS *voda* 'water')
rebro 'rib' (cf. OE *ribb(i)* < 'rib')
darъ 'gift' (cf. OCS *dati* 'to give')
pirъ 'feast' (cf. OCS *piti* 'to drink')

(j) **Suffixes containing *s*,** including its reflexes *š* and *x*.

PIE **-*s*-** appeared in a few nouns in which it was no longer perceived as a suffix (cf. also the *-ŏs-/-ĕs-* stems, **2.47.1**):

běsъ 'demon' (< *bŏi̯-s-*, cf. OCS *bojati sę* 'to be afraid')
golsъ 'voice' (cf. OCS *glagolati* < *golgolati* 'to speak')
kolsъ 'blade of grass' (cf. OCS *klati* 'to stab', Ru. *kólos* 'blade of wheat')
rus- '(brownish) red' (< *rŏu̯dh-s-*, cf. OCS *ruda* 'ore, mine')
volsъ 'hair' (cf. OESl. *vólodь* 'hair')

The suffix **-*x*-** (from PIE *-s-*, **2.14,** spelled *-ch-* in West Slavic) became productive in individual Slavic languages as an expressive suffix with truncated personal nouns, especially masculine:

Po. *brach* 'brother' (< Po. *brat*)
Ru. *Ljax* 'Lach, Pole' (< **lęxъ*, cf. Cz. *lado* < *lędo* 'virgin land, field')
Po. *Stach* 'Stanislaus' (< Po. *Stanisław*)
Po. *swach* 'matchmaker' (< Po. *swat* 'matchmaker')
Cz. *hoch* 'boy' (< Cz. *hol-* 'barefaced')

In Proto-Slavic it occurred in a handful of masculine nouns:

grěxъ 'sin' (cf. OCS *grěti* 'to warm')
lix- 'extra' (cf. Gk. *leípō* 'I leave')
maxъ 'waving' (cf. OCS *pomajati* 'to wave')
směxъ 'laughter' (cf. Ru. *smeját'sja* 'to laugh')
spěxъ 'haste' (cf. OCS *spěti* 'prosper')

-*ux-a* and **-*ux-ъ*** were the most productive of several expressive suffixes with *x:*

čr̥'nuxa 'black object' '(cf. OCS *črъn-* < *čr̥'n-* 'black')
goruxa 'mustard' (cf. OCS *gor'ьk-* 'bitter')
kožuxъ 'sheepskin' (cf. OCS *koža* 'skin')
pastuxъ 'shepherd' (cf. OCS *pastyr'ь* 'shepherd')
staruxa 'old woman' (cf. OCS *star-* 'old')

(k) **Suffixes containing *t*,** including *t-i̯-* > *t'*.

-*t*- occurred in a few substantives of all genders:

bersta 'birch bark' (cf. Ru. *berëza* < *berza* 'birch')
cěsta 'clearing' (< *kŏi̯d-*; cf. *čist-* < *kěi̯d-* 'clear')

dolto 'chisel' (< *dălb-t-*; cf. Ru. *dolbít'* < *dl̥biti* 'to hollow')
potъ 'sweat' (< *păk-t-*; cf. OCS *pekǫ* 'I bake')
sito 'sieve' (< *sēi̯-t-*; cf. OCS *sěti* < *sōi̯-tēi̯* 'to sow')

-ot-a formed abstract, chiefly deadjectival, substantives:

čistota 'cleanliness' (cf. OCS *čist-* 'clear')
dobrota 'goodness' (cf. OCS *dobr-* 'good')
pravota 'uprightness' (cf. OCS *prav-* 'right')
sirota 'orphan, orphanness' (cf. OCS *sir-* 'orphaned')
slěpota 'blindness' (cf. OCS *slěp-* 'blind')

There were also some denominal formations:

orbota 'work' (cf. OCS *rabъ* < *orbъ* 'slave')
sormota 'shame' (cf. OCS *sramъ* < *sormъ* 'shame')

-it'-ь denoted provenience, usually family descent and, by extension, young beings. Added to the possessive suffix *-ov-* it had the value of the patronymic:

dědit'ь 'descendant' (cf. OCS *dědъ* 'ancestor')
korl'evit'ь 'son of a king' (cf. Ru. *koról'* < *korl'ь* 'king')
kъnęžit'b 'son of a prince' (cf. OCS *kъnęʒь* 'prince')
popovit'ь 'son of a priest' (cf. OCS *popъ* 'priest')
rodit'ь 'relative' (cf. *rodъ* 'birth')

dětit'ь 'small child' (cf. OCS *děti* 'children')
kozьlit'ь 'kid' (cf. OCS *kozьlъ* 'buck')
lьvit'ь 'lion cub' (cf. OCS *lьvъ* 'lion')
otročit'ь 'small boy' (cf. OCS *otrokъ* 'boy')

(1) **Suffixes containing *v*.**

-av- and ***-iv-*** were suffixes of denominal descriptive adjectives; the suffix ***-(ь)l-iv-*** was abstracted from formations based on an underlying resultative participle:

krъvav- 'bloody' (cf. OESl. *kry, krъve* 'blood')
lǫkav- 'deceitful' (cf. OCS *lǫka* 'deceit')
sědinav- 'graying' (cf. OCS *sědina* 'gray hair')

čьstiv- 'honest' (cf. OCS *čьstь* 'honor')
lěniv- 'lazy' (cf. OCS *lěn-* 'lazy')
lьstiv- 'deceiving' (cf. OCS *lьstь* 'deceipt')
pravьdiv- 'just' (cf. OCS *pravьda* 'truth')

gněvьliv- 'irascible' (cf. OCS *gněvъ* 'anger')
ml̥'čaliv- 'taciturn' (cf. OCS *mlьčati* < *ml̥'č-* 'to be silent')
tr̥'pěliv- 'patient' (cf. OCS *trьpěti* < *tr̥'p-* 'suffer')
zavistьliv- 'envious' (cf. OCS *zavistь* 'envy')

-ov- formed possessive adjectives from masculine substantives other than those belonging to the *-ā-/-i̯-ā-* stems; cf. *-in-* (**2.47.4h**):

(j)avorov- 'pertaining to a plane tree' (cf. OCS *avorъ* 'plane tree')
popov- 'priest's' (cf. OCS *popъ* 'priest')
sъpasov- 'savior's' (cf. OCS *sъpasъ* 'savior')
synov- 'son's' (cf. OCS *synъ* 'son')
vračev- 'medicine man's' (cf. OCS *vračь* 'medicine man')

dǫbov- 'oak-' (cf. OCS *dǫbъ* 'oak')
gromov- 'thunder-' (cf. OCS *gromъ* 'thunder')
lьvov- 'lion's' (cf. OCS *lьvъ* 'lion')
tr̥gov- 'market-' (cf. OCS *trъgъ* < *tr̥gъ* 'market')
volov- 'ox-' (cf. OCS *volъ* 'ox')

-ьstv-o formed abstract, chiefly denominal substantives. In South Slavic and in Czech/Slovak this suffix was often extended by the formant *-ьi̯*-to form ***-ьstv-ȇi̯-e:***

bogatьstvo (*bogatьstvȇje*) 'riches' (cf. OCS *bogat-* 'rich')
božьstvo (*božьstvȇje*) 'divinity' (cf. OCS *bogъ* 'god')
dějьstvo (*dějьstvȇje*) 'action' (OCS *dějǫ* 'I act')
mъnožьstvo (*mъnožьstvȇje*) 'multitude' (cf. OCS *mъnog-* 'many')
otьčьstvo (*otьčьstvȇje*) 'patrimony' (cf. OCS *otьcь* 'father')

2.48. Declensions. According to their stem, gender, and phonetic developments at the juncture of stem and inflectional ending, Proto-Indo-European and Proto-Slavic nouns may be assigned to several inflectional classes or declensions. The shape of inflectional endings allows us to group these declensions into two larger subtypes, a *substantival* one for the substantives and the cardinal numerals from 3 to 10, and a *pronominal* one for the pronouns and the cardinal numerals 1 and 2. The inflection of Proto-Indo-European adjectives did not differ from that of the substantives. In Proto-Slavic, however, only the indefinite adjectives declined like substantives, while the newly created definite adjectives followed the pronominal inflection.

2.48.1. Substantival declensions. Substantival declensions distinguished one consonantal and four vocalic declensions: *-ŭ-*, *-ĭ-*, *-ŏ-/-i̯-ŏ-*, and *-ā-/-i̯-ā-/-i̯-ī-* (see Table 6). While the Proto-Indo-European endings of the *-i̯-ŏ-* and *-i̯-ā-* stems did not differ from those of the *-ŏ-* and *-ā-* stems, in Proto-Slavic, due to the fronting of back vowels (**2.25**), there arose a distinction between the hard (*-ŏ-* and *-ā-*) and soft (*-i̯-ŏ-* and *-i̯-ā-*) stem endings, which manifested itself in the alternations *-ъ* ~ *-ь; -o* ~ *-e;* $-ě_2$ ~ $-i_2$; *-y* ~ *-i;* $-y_2$ ~ $-ě_3$/*-ę-* (see **2.48.1** *note 3a*).

Late Proto-Slavic substantival endings that developed from the Proto-Indo-European system are listed in Table 7 (only the hard stem endings are included).

Notes: (1) The loss of final consonants (**2.18**) and the monophthongization of diphthongs in i̯ and u̯ (**2.26**) caused the Proto-Indo-European thematic vowels and endings to blend into Proto-Slavic monomorphemic endings; e.g. PIE 'son' *sūn-ŭ-s* (Nom. Sg.), *sūn-ŏu̯-s* (Gen. Sg.), *sūn-ŏu̯-ĕi̯* (Dat. Sg.) > PSl. *syn-ъ, syn-u, syn-ovi.*

(2) Differences in the shape of the thematic vowel are due to Proto-Indo-European ablaut variations, e.g. *-ŏ-s, -ā-Ø* (Nom. Sg.) versus *-ĕ-Ø, -ă-Ø* (Voc.); *-ŭ-s, -ĭ-s* (Nom. Sg.) versus *-ŏu̯-s, -ĕi̯-s* (Gen. Sg.). In the Nom./Acc. Sg. of the consonantal stems, the Proto-Indo-European stem suffixes were reinterpreted as Late Proto-Slavic inflectional endings (listed in parentheses).

(3) Some Proto-Slavic endings that cannot be derived from the postulated Proto-Indo-European forms by the application of general phonetic laws may be explained by developments restricted to particular inflectional endings:

(a) In *-Vn(t)s, n* was lost and the preceding vowel, if short, underwent compensatory lengthening. The low back vowels were, as a rule, raised to *ū;* e.g. *kām-ōn-s* 'stone' (Nom. Sg.) > *kām-ū* > *kamy*. Similarly, in the accusative plural *sūn-ŭ-ns* 'son' > *sūn-ū* > *syn-y,*

Table 6: Substantival endings of Proto-Indo-European

		CONSONANTAL	-ŭ-	-ĭ-	-ŏ-	-ā-
	VOC.	-Ø	-ŏu̯-Ø	-ĕi̯-Ø	-ĕ-Ø	-ă-Ø
SINGULAR	NOM.	-s, -Ø	-ŭ-s	-ĭ-s	-ŏ-s	-ā-Ø
	ACC.	-m̥	-ŭ-m	-ĭ-m	-ŏ-m	-ā-m
	GEN./ABL.	-ĕs	-ŏu̯-s	-ĕi̯-s	-ŏ-ăd > -ād	-ās
	LOC.	-ĭ	-ŏu̯-Ø	-ĕi̯-Ø	-ŏ-i̯	-ā-i̯
	DAT.	-ĕi̯	-ŏu̯-ĕi̯	-ĕi̯-ĕi̯	-ŏ-ĕi̯ > -ōi̯	-ā-ĕi̯ > -āi̯
	INST.	-mĭ	-ŭ-mĭ	-ĭ-mĭ	-ŏ-mĭ	-ā-m
DUAL	NOM./ACC.	-ī, -ē	-ŭ-ĕ > -ū	-ĭ-ĕ > -ī	-ŏ-ĕ > -ō	-ā-i̯
	GEN/LOC.	-ŏu̯s	-ŏu̯-ŏu̯s	-ĕi̯-ŏu̯s	-ŏ-ŏu̯s > -ōu̯s	-ā-ŏu̯s > -āu̯s
	DAT./INST.	-mō	-ŭ-mō	-ĭ-mō	-ŏ-mō	-ā-mō
PLURAL	NOM.	-ĕs	-ŏu̯-ĕs	-ĕi̯-ĕs	-ŏ-es > -ōs, -ŏi̯	-ā-ĕs > -ās
	ACC.	-n̥s	-ŭ-ns	-ĭ-ns	-ŏ-ns	-ā-ns
	GEN.	-ŏm/-ōm	-ŏu̯-ŏm	-ĕi̯-ŏm	-ŏ-ŏm > -ōm	-ā-ŏm > -ām
	LOC.	-sŭ	-ŭ-sŭ	-ĭ-sŭ	-ŏi̯-sŭ	-ā-sŭ
	DAT.	-mŭs	-ŭ-mŭs	-ĭ-mŭs	-ŏ-mŭs	-ā-mŭs
	INST.	-mīs	-ŭ-mīs	-ĭ-mīs	-ŏ-ōi̯s > -ōi̯s	-ā-mīs

kŏst-ĭ-ns ‘bone’ > *kŏst-ī* > *kost-i*, *ŏrbh-ŏ-ns* ‘slave’ > *ŏrb-ū* > *orb-y*, *g^{w}ĕn-ā-ns* ‘woman’ > *gĕn-ū* > *žen-y*. In the sequence *Cn̥s*, *n̥* was lengthened, yielding *i*; e.g. *kām-en-n̥s* ‘stone’ (Acc. Pl.) > *kameni*. In the *-i̯-ŏ-* and *-i̯-ā-* stems the sequences *-ĕ-ns*, *-ē-ns* (< *-i̯-ŏ-ns* and *-i̯-ā-ns*, by **2.25**) yielded the expected *-ē* in North Slavic (referred to as *-ě$_3$*), while in South Slavic *n* was retained, yielding *-ę*; e.g. *măng-i̯-ŏ-ns* ‘man’, *kŏz-i̯-ā-ns* ‘goatskin’ (Acc. Pl.)

Table 7: Substantival endings of Late Proto-Slavic

		CONSONANTAL	-ŭ-	-ĭ-	-ŏ-	-ā-
	VOC.	= NOM.	-u	-i	-e/-u	-o
SINGULAR	NOM.	(-y, -o, -i, -ę)	-ъ	-ь	M -ъ/N -o	-a
	ACC.	-ь (-o, -ę)	-ъ	-ь	M -ъ/N -o	-ǫ
	GEN.	-e	-u	-i	-a	-y$_2$
	LOC.	-e	-u	-i	-ě$_2$	-ě$_2$
	DAT.	-i	-ovi	-i	-u	-ě$_2$
	INST.	MN -ьmь/F -ě̂jǫ	-ъmь	M -ьmь/F -ě̂jǫ	-omь/ъmь	-ojǫ
DUAL	NA	MF -i, N -ě	-y	-i	M -a/FN -ě$_2$	-ě$_2$
	GL	-u	-ovu	-ě̂ju	-u	-u
	DI	-ьma	-ъma	-ьma	-oma	-ama
PLURAL	NOM.	M -e/F -i/N -a	-ove	M -ě̂je/F -i	-i$_2$	-y$_2$
	ACC.	MF -i/N -a	-y	-i	-y$_2$	-y$_2$
	GEN.	-ъ	-ovъ	-ě̂jь	-ъ	-ъ
	LOC.	-ьxъ	-ъxъ	-ьxъ	-ě$_2$xъ	-axъ
	DAT.	-ьmъ	-ъmъ	-ьmъ	-omъ	-amъ
	INST.	MF -ьmi/N -y	-ъmi	-ьmi	-y	-ami

yielded North Slavic *mǫž-ě, kož-ě* but South Slavic *mǫž-ę, kož-ę*. The accusative plural ending of the *-ā-/-i̯-ā-* stems spread analogically to the genitive singular and nominative plural on the model of the *-ĭ-* stems. The hard ~ soft alternation *-y* ~ *-ě/-ę* is symbolized by *-y*$_2$.[163]

The alternation *-y* ~ *-ě/-ę* may have another explanation. The normal phonetic development of Nom. Sg. *-ā* and Nom. Pl. *-ās* of the *-ā-* stems would in both cases lead to an *-ā*. To avoid this coincidence and retain the distinction between numbers, Nom. Pl. *-ās* may have been replaced by Acc. Pl. *-āns* > LPSl. *-y*. The resulting syncretism (Nom. Pl. = Acc. Pl.) could then spread from the *-ā-* stems to the *-i̯-ā-* stems, but in a dialectally differentiated way. In North Slavic, Acc. Pl. *-i̯-āns* was replaced by Nom. Pl. *-i̯-ās* > EPSl. *-ē* > LPSl. *-ě*$_3$, while in South Slavic Nom. Pl. *i̯-ās* was replaced by Acc. Pl. *-i̯-āns* > LPSl. *-ę*. Further analogical action led to the spread of the *-y* ~ *-ě/-ę* alternation to the genitive singular of the *-ā-/-i̯-ā-* stems and the accusative plural of the *-ŏ-/-i̯-ŏ-* stems (Moszyński 1984:286).

(b) Long vowels combined with word-final *m* to form nasal vowels, e.g. *g*^{w}*ĕn-ā-m* 'woman' (Acc. Sg.) > *žen-ǫ*. Short vowels in that position, however, showed no nasalization, and *ŏ* was raised to *ŭ*, e.g. *sūn-ŭ-m* 'son' > *syn-ъ, kŏst-ĭ-m* 'bone' > *kost-ь, ŏrbh-ŏ-m* 'slave' > *ŏrb-ŭ-m* > *orb-ъ* (Acc. Sg.). Slavic is alone among the Indo-European languages to derive the genitive plural of the consonantal stems from *-ŏm* rather than *-ōm;* e.g. *sēmĕn-ŏm* 'seed' > *sěmen-ъ*. The genitive plural ending *-ъ* of the consonantal stems was analogically extended to the *-ŏ-* and *-ā-* stems.

(4) All neuter stems syncretized the nominative and accusative. In the consonantal stems the nominative/accusative singular was generalized from the nominative singular (*nĕbh-ŏs-Ø* 'sky' > *neb-o, sē-mēn-Ø* 'seed' > *sěmę*), while in the *-ŏ-* stems the nominative/accusative singular ending *-o* was extended analogically from the pronoun *to* 'that' (< *tŏd*), replacing the expected *-ъ* (< PIE *-ŏ-m*), e.g. *zr̥'n-o* 'grain'. In the nominative/accusative plural all neuter stems had *-a* (< PIE *-ā*), e.g. *nebes-a, sěmen-a, zr̥'n-a.*

(5) The nominative singular ending *-ъ* of the *-ŏ-* stems and the vocative ending *-u* of the *-i̯-ŏ-* stems were taken over from the *-ŭ-* stem declension. In the post-Proto-Slavic period the *-ŭ-* stem declension, though unproductive as a whole, provided several individual case endings of the *-ŏ-* stems. The most ancient instance of these analogical developments is the practically general North Slavic replacement of the instrumental plural ending *-omь* of the *-ŏ-* stems by the ending *-ъmь* of the *-ŭ-* stems.

(6) The masculine and feminine consonantal and *-ĭ-* stem endings influenced each other. The *-ĭ-* stem endings *-ьmь* and *-ь̂jǫ* (Inst. Sg.), *-i* (Nom./Acc. Du.), *-ьma* (Dat./Inst. Du.), *-ьxъ* (Loc. Pl.), *-ьmъ* (Dat. Pl.), and *-ьmi* (Inst. Pl.) spread to the consonantal stems. By contrast, the ending *-i* (Dat. Sg.) of the consonantal stems was taken over by the *-ĭ-* stems.

(7) The ending *-i*$_2$ (Nom. Pl.) of the *-ŏ-* stems was derived from the pronominal ending *-ŏi̯* which replaced the substantival ending *-ŏs*. The expected *-ě*$_2$ was probably analogically displaced by *-i*$_2$ (< *-ĕi̯*) of the *-i̯-ŏ-* stems. The nominative plural of all the feminine nouns was analogical to the accusative plural.

(8) The ending *-ojǫ/-ejǫ* (Inst. Sg.) of the *-ā-/-i̯-ā-* stems is pronominal in origin. The ending *-ь̂jǫ* arose analogically in the feminine consonantal and *-ĭ-* stem declensions.

(9) Also pronominal is the ending *-ě*$_2$*xъ* < *-ŏi̯-sŭ* (Loc. Pl.) of the *-ŏ-* stems. The ending *-axъ* of the *-ā-* stems for the expected *-asъ* was analogically extended from the phonetically regular endings of the locative plural in other vocalic declensions (**2.14**).

163. This is an adaptation of the device used by Whitfield (1962) in his descriptive rules for Old Church Slavonic morphophonemics.

(10) Lacking a satisfactory explanation are the endings *-e* (Loc. Sg.) of the consonantal stems, *-u* (Dat. Sg.) and *-y-* (Inst. Pl.) of the *-ŏ-* stems.

2.48.2. Pronominal declension. In accordance with their ability to distinguish gender, Proto-Slavic pronouns may be classified as gendered and nongendered. Gendered pronouns were vocalic (thematic). They included two *-ĭ-* stems, the demonstrative *sь, si, se* 'this here' (< *k'*-) and the anaphoric *jь* 'that which is known' and a number of *-ŏ-/-ŏi̯-* and *-ā-/-āi̯-* stems, such as the demonstratives *t-* 'this', *ov-* 'that', *on-* 'that yonder'; the interrogatives *kѣ̂j-* 'which' (< PIE *kʷŭ-i̯-*), *kotor-* 'which (of a number)'; the possessives *moj-* 'my', *tvoj-* 'thy', *svoj-* 'one's own', *čѣ̂j-* 'whose' (< PIE *kʷī-i̯-*), *naš-* 'our' (< PIE *nās-i̯-*), *vaš-* 'your' (< PIE *u̯ās-i̯-*); the qualitative *sic-* 'like this (nearby)' (< PIE *k'ī-k-*), *jak-* 'like that (anaphoric)', *tak-* 'like this', *kak-* 'like what' (< PIE *kʷ-āk-*); the quantitative *mъnog-* 'many', *vьs'-/vьš-* 'all'(< *u̯ĭs'-/u̯ĭš-* < PIE *u̯ĭs-*), *selik-* 'to this degree', *tolik-* 'to that degree', *jelik-* 'to the degree (anaphoric)', *kolik-* 'to what degree'. The third-person pronoun was expressed by the anaphoric *j-*. When functioning as a relative pronoun (with the particle *že*), the stem *j-* was used in all cases. As a personal pronoun (without *že*) it had a suppletive paradigm, with *j-* in the oblique cases and, depending on the dialect, the demonstrative *t-* or *on-* in the nominative case. In the genitive and dative singular nonfeminine, the allegro forms *(jь)go, (jь)mu* also occurred.

The nongendered pronouns included the *-ŏ-* stem interrogative *kъ-(to)* 'who' (< PIE *kʷ-ŏ-*), the *-ĭ-* stem interrogative *čь-(to)* 'what' (< PIE *kʷ-ĭ-*), as well as several consonantal (athematic) pronouns, the reflexive *s-*, and the first- and second-person pronouns, which had suppletive stems:

<table>
<tr><th></th><th>SINGULAR</th><th>DUAL</th><th>PLURAL</th></tr>
<tr><td>FIRST PERSON</td><td>(j)azъ/m- (< ēg' -/m-)</td><td>vě/n-</td><td>my/n-</td></tr>
<tr><td>SECOND PERSON</td><td>t-</td><td colspan="2">v-</td></tr>
</table>

Inflectional endings of the gendered pronouns and of the interrogative nongendered pronouns are given in Table 8, while the paradigms of the demonstrative pronoun *t-*, the anaphoric *j-*, the personal pronouns of the first and second person, and the reflexive are given in Tables 9, 10, and 11:

Table 8: Pronominal endings of Late Proto-Slavic

<table>
<tr><th></th><th colspan="3">SINGULAR</th><th colspan="3">DUAL</th><th colspan="3">PLURAL</th></tr>
<tr><th></th><th>M</th><th>N</th><th>F</th><th>M</th><th>N</th><th>F</th><th>M</th><th>N</th><th>F</th></tr>
<tr><td>NOM.</td><td rowspan="2">-ъ</td><td rowspan="2">-o</td><td>-a</td><td rowspan="2">-a</td><td colspan="2" rowspan="2">-ě$_2$</td><td>-i$_2$</td><td rowspan="2">-a</td><td rowspan="2">-y$_2$</td></tr>
<tr><td>ACC.</td><td>-ǫ</td><td>-y$_2$</td></tr>
<tr><td>GEN.</td><td colspan="2">-o-go</td><td>-oj-y$_2$</td><td colspan="3" rowspan="2">-oj-u</td><td colspan="3" rowspan="2">-ě$_2$-xъ</td></tr>
<tr><td>LOC.</td><td colspan="2">-o-mь</td><td rowspan="2">-oj-i</td></tr>
<tr><td>DAT.</td><td colspan="2">-o-mu</td><td colspan="3" rowspan="2">-ě$_2$-ma</td><td colspan="3">-ě$_2$-mъ</td></tr>
<tr><td>INST.</td><td colspan="2">-ě$_2$-mь</td><td>-oj-ǫ</td><td colspan="3">-ě$_2$-mi</td></tr>
</table>

Table 9: Paradigm of the demonstrative pronoun *t-*

<table>
<tr><th rowspan="2"></th><th colspan="3">SINGULAR</th><th colspan="3">DUAL</th><th colspan="3">PLURAL</th></tr>
<tr><th>M</th><th>N</th><th>F</th><th>M</th><th>N</th><th>F</th><th>M</th><th>N</th><th>F</th></tr>
<tr><td>NOM.</td><td rowspan="2">tъ</td><td rowspan="2">to</td><td>ta</td><td rowspan="2">ta</td><td colspan="2" rowspan="2">tě</td><td>ti</td><td rowspan="2">ta</td><td rowspan="2">ty</td></tr>
<tr><td>ACC.</td><td>tǫ</td><td>ty</td></tr>
<tr><td>GEN.</td><td colspan="2">togo</td><td>tojě/toję</td><td colspan="3" rowspan="2">toju</td><td colspan="3" rowspan="2">těxъ</td></tr>
<tr><td>LOC.</td><td colspan="2">tomь</td><td rowspan="2">toji</td></tr>
<tr><td>DAT.</td><td colspan="2">tomu</td><td colspan="3" rowspan="2">těma</td><td colspan="3">těmъ</td></tr>
<tr><td>INST.</td><td colspan="2">tomь</td><td>tojǫ</td><td colspan="3">těmi</td></tr>
</table>

Table 10: Paradigm of the anaphoric pronoun *j-*

<table>
<tr><th rowspan="2"></th><th colspan="3">SINGULAR</th><th colspan="3">DUAL</th><th colspan="3">PLURAL</th></tr>
<tr><th>M</th><th>N</th><th>F</th><th>M</th><th>N</th><th>F</th><th>M</th><th>N</th><th>F</th></tr>
<tr><td>NOM.</td><td rowspan="2">jь</td><td rowspan="2">je</td><td>ja</td><td rowspan="2">ja</td><td colspan="2" rowspan="2">ji</td><td>ji</td><td rowspan="2">ja</td><td rowspan="2">jě/ję</td></tr>
<tr><td>ACC.</td><td>jǫ</td><td>jě/ję</td></tr>
<tr><td>GEN.</td><td colspan="2">jego/jьgo</td><td>jejě/jeję</td><td colspan="3" rowspan="2">jeju</td><td colspan="3" rowspan="2">jixъ</td></tr>
<tr><td>LOC.</td><td colspan="2">jemь</td><td rowspan="2">jeji</td></tr>
<tr><td>DAT.</td><td colspan="2">jemu/jьmu</td><td colspan="3" rowspan="2">jima</td><td colspan="3">jimъ</td></tr>
<tr><td>INST.</td><td colspan="2">jimь</td><td>jejǫ</td><td colspan="3">jimi</td></tr>
</table>

Table 11: Paradigms of the first and second person and reflexive pronouns

		FIRST PERSON	SECOND PERSON	REFLEXIVE
	NOM.	(j)azъ	ty	—
	ACC.	mę	tę	sę
SG.	GEN.	mene	tebe	sebe
	LOC.	mьně	tebě	sebě
	DAT.[164]	mьně, mi	tebě, ti	sebě, si
	INST.	mъnojǫ	tobojǫ	sobojǫ
	NOM.	vě		
DU.	ACC.	na	va	
	GEN./LOC.	naju	vaju	
	DAT./INST.	nama	vama	
	NOM.	my	vy	
	ACC.	nasъ, ny	vasъ, vy	
PL.	GEN./LOC.	nasъ	vasъ	
	DAT.	namъ, ny	vamъ, vy	
	INST.	nami	vami	

164. The dative singular forms *mi, ti, si* were enclitic and functioned as unmarked indirect objects; the longer forms were emphatic or occurred in prepositional phrases.

Notes:

(1) The pronominal formants *-ŏį-* (M/N) and *-āį-* (F) were monophthongized to *-ě*$_2$ before consonants.

(2) The fronting of back vowels after soft consonants (**2.25**) caused the expected vowel alternations; *-y*$_2$ is written as a shorthand term for the hard ~ soft alternation *y* ~ *ě/ę* (**2.48.1** *note 3a*).

(3) The nongendered pronouns *kъ-to* 'who' and *čь-to* 'what' were inflected according to the masculine singular paradigm. Their nominative was extended by the particle *-to*, derived from the demonstrative pronoun. The genitive of *čь-to* was *čьso/česo*, whose ending reflected PIE *-ĕs(į)ŏ*. The form *čьso* lost ground in the genitive, where it was replaced by the analogical *čego*, but in West Slavic it spread into other cases, replacing the original nominative *čьto* and accusative *čь*. It also provided the stem for the analogical dative in OCS *čьsomu*.

(4) In the genitive masculine/neuter the expected Proto-Indo-European ending is *-ŏs(į)ŏ;* Slavic *-ogo* represents the Proto-Indo-European ablative *-ŏd* extended by the particle *-gă* (Arumaa 1985:175).

(5) The dative/locative singular forms *tebě* and *sebě* are replaced in most North Slavic languages by the forms *tobě* and *sobě*, with *o* extended analogically from the instrumental singular.

2.49. Inflection of adjectives and numerals. The inflection of adjectives and numerals incorporates features of substantival and pronominal declensions.

2.49.1. Adjectives. As compared to other nouns, adjectives displayed a number of grammatical neutralizations. The variety of stem types that characterized the substantives and pronouns, and is still visible in the adjective systems of other Indo-European languages, gave way in Slavic to a unified, gender-based system in which the *-ŏ-/-į-ŏ-* stems became identified with the nonfeminine (masculine and neuter) and the *-ā-/-į-ā-* stems with the feminine. This unification was achieved by transforming the inherited consonantal stems into vocalic ones and extending the old *-ŭ-* and *-ĭ-* stems by a suffix. Thus the PIE *-ŏs-/-ĕs-* stem *uĕt-ŏs-* 'old' (cf. Latin *vetus, -eris* 'old') was extended in Slavic by a stem vowel (cf. OCS *vetъx-* 'old'); the PIE *-ŭ-* stem *săld-ŭ-* 'sweet' (cf. Lith. *saldùs* 'sweet') was extended by the suffix *-k-* (cf. OCS *sladъk-* 'sweet'); the PIE *-ĭ-* stem **ūp-s-ĭ-* 'high' (cf. Greek *húpsi* 'high') was extended by the suffix *-ok-* (cf. OCS *vysok-* 'high').

In addition to their obligatory categories of case, number, and gender, most Proto-Slavic adjectives were either definite or indefinite. The inflection of the indefinite adjectives did not differ from the inflection of the substantives in *-ŏ-/-į-ŏ-* and *-ā-/-į-ā-*. Definite adjectives were formed by combining case forms of the anaphoric pronoun *j-* (**2.48.2,** Table 10) with those of the indefinite adjective. The coalescence of these forms produced the definite inflection of the adjective.[165] It was governed by several principles of composition:

(a) In some instances the anaphoric pronoun was added mechanically:

	M	starъ + jь	PSl. starъ̂jь	OCS staryi/starъi [starъ̂jь]
Nom. Sg.	N	staro + je	staroje	staro[j]e
	F	stara + j	staraja	staraja
Acc. Sg.	F	starǫ + jǫ	starǫjǫ	starǫjǫ
Gen. Sg.	M/N	stara + jego	starajego	stara[j]ego staraago (with assimilation) starago (with contraction)

165. Because of its composite character the definite inflection is also known as *compound* or *pronominal.*

(b) A sequence of two syllables beginning with *j* was reduced by haplology to one syllable:

Loc. Sg. NonF	starě + jeji	PSl. starěji	OCS starě[j]i

The definite instrumental singular feminine *-ǫjǫ* was derived from the original substantival *-ǫ* (< *-ā-m*) rather than from the analogical pronominal ending *-ojǫ* (**2.48.1** *note 8*):

Inst. Sg. F	starǫ + jejǫ	PSl. starǫjǫ	OCS starǫjǫ

(c) Disyllabic substantival endings were replaced by *-y*, extended analogically from the Inst. Pl. M/N *star-y + jimi > staryjimi:*

Inst. Pl. F	star-ami + jimi	PSl. staryjimi	OCS stary[j]imi
Loc. Pl. F	star-axъ + jixъ	staryjixъ	stary[j]ixъ

2.49.2. Numerals. The Proto-Slavic cardinal numbers 'one' to 'ten' may be subdivided into two groups: the gendered 'one' to 'four' were syntactically adjectival and modified the noun counted ('two', 'three', and 'four' distinguished gender in the nominative only); the nongendered 'five' to 'ten' were syntactically substantival and governed the noun counted.

Of the gendered numerals, *jedinъ, -a, -o* 'one' (< *ĕd-īn-*) and *dъva* (M), *dъvě* (F/N) 'two' (< *dŭu̯ō, -ŏi̯*) were of pronominal origin and followed the pronominal inflection (*tъ*). *Jedin-* and *dъv-* formed a kind of suppletive paradigm, with *jedin-* inflected for the singular and plural and *dъv-* for the dual. *Trьje* (M), *tri* (F/N) 'three' (< *tr-ĕi̯-ĕs,* Acc. Pl. *tr-īns*) was inflected like a plural *-ĭ-* stem, while *četyre* (M), *četyri* (F/N) 'four' (< *kʷĕtūr-ĕs,* Acc. Pl. *kʷĕtūr-īns*) was a consonantal stem.

The nongendered numerals *pętь* (< *pĕnkʷ-t-*) 'five', *šestь* (< *ksĕks-t-*) 'six', *sedmь* (< *sĕbdm-*) 'seven', *osmь* (< *ŏk'tm-*) 'eight', *devętь* 'nine' (< *nĕu̯n̥-t-* with the initial *d* by analogy to *desętь* 'ten'), and *desętь* (< *dĕ-k'm̥-t-*) 'ten' were abstract substantival derivatives in *-ĭ-* from the Proto-Indo-European ordinal numerals in *-t-* (Szemerényi 1960:109–113, Stankiewicz 1986:417–418). The numerals 'five' to 'ten' were declined like the *-ĭ-* stems, while *desętь* 'ten', which was originally a consonantal stem, transferred to the *-ĭ-* stem inflection.

The teens were compounds of the base numeral followed by the preposition *na* with the consonantal locative singular of 'ten', e.g. *dъva na desęte* 'twelve'. The tens were formed with the base numeral followed by the appropriate case form of *desętь* 'ten', e.g. *dъva desęti* 'twenty', *trьje desęte* 'thirty', *pętь desętъ* 'fifty'. The root *k'ŏm-/k'm̥-* of the numeral 'ten', extended by the suffix *-t-*, appeared in the numerals *sъto* 'hundred', a neuter *-ŏ-* stem (< *k'm̥-t-ŏ-* with an irregular Slavic reflex ъ for PIE *m̥*) and *tysęt'a/tysǫt'a* 'thousand', a feminine *-i̯-ā-* stem modified by PIE *tū-* 'fat, thick' (< *tū-k'm̥-t-i̯-ā/tū-k'ŏm̥-t-i̯-ā*). The hundreds were formed analogously to the tens, with the appropriate case form of *sъto* 'hundred', e.g. *dъvě sъtě*[166] '200', *tri sъta* '300', *pętь sъtъ* '500'.

2.50. Verbal stems. Since the stems of most Proto-Slavic verbs occurred in two variants, one in the present tense and related forms and one in the infinitive and related forms, it is customary to distinguish between the present-tense and infinitive verbal stems. The

166. Russian *i* in *dvésti* may be explained by the dialectal change *ě > i* (cf. Ukr. *dvísti*) or by dialectal *ikan'e* (unstressed *e > i*) of Moscow and central Russia.

present-tense stems of all but four verbs contained the suffix of the present tense. Such verbs are called *thematic*. The verbs which lacked such a suffix in their present-tense stems are called *athematic*.

2.50.1. Athematic verbs. The four athematic verbs included the following (listed in 3 Sg. Prs.): *dastь* '(s)he will give', *jastь* '(s)he eats', *jestь* '(s)he is', *vĕstь* '(s)he knows'. Except for *jastь* (< *ēd-tĭ*) '(s)he eats', whose infinitive was *jasti* (< *ēd-tēi̯*) 'to eat', the athematic verbs had different present-tense and infinitive stems. The verb *vĕstь* (< *u̯ŏi̯d-tĭ*) '(s)he knows' had the infinitive *vĕdĕti* 'to know', whose stem *vĕd-ĕ-* was derived from 1 Sg. Perf. Middle *vŏi̯d-ăi̯*. The verb *dastь* (< *dād-tĭ*) '(s)he will give' was formed from the reduplicated present-tense stem *dā-d-*, while its infinitive *dati* (< *dā-tēi̯*) 'to give' contained the unreduplicated stem *dā-* (cf. Latin *dare* 'to give'). The verb *jestь* (< *ĕs-tĭ*) '(s)he is' had the infinitive *byti* 'to be' whose suppletive stem *by-* was derived from PIE *bhū-* (cf. Sanskrit *bhavati* 'he is', Latin *fūi* 'I was'); its 3 Pl. Prs. *sǫtь* was formed from the stem *s-* representing the zero grade of *ĕs-* (cf. Latin *sunt* 'they are').

2.50.2. Thematic verbs. Proto-Slavic verbal stems consisted of bare roots or of roots extended by a verb-forming suffix. The absence or presence of a verb-forming suffix allows us to sort all thematic verbs into two classes:

(1) Verbs without the verb-forming suffix in present-tense formations are called *root verbs*. They were unproductive and occurred in three subclasses, consonantic, sonantic and semivocalic.

(a) Bare roots of *consonantic* root verbs ended in stops or sibilants. They had no verb-forming suffix in either the present-tense or infinitive formations:

greb- 'dig'	grebetь	greti (< grĕb-tēi̯)[167]
klad- 'place'	kladetь	klasti (< klăd-tēi̯)
met- 'sweep'	metetь	mesti (< mĕt-tēi̯)
rek- 'say'	rečetь (< rĕk-ĕ-tĭ)	ret'i (< rĕk-tēi̯)
nes- 'carry'	nesetь	nesti (< nĕs-tēi̯)
vez- 'transport'	vezetь	vesti (< u̯ĕz-tēi̯)

The present-tense stems of three consonantic root verbs show the Proto-Indo-European infix *-n-* (cf. Latin *fīgō* 'I fix' vs. *fingō* 'I touch'):

bǫd- 'be' (perfective)	bǫdetь (bū-n-d-ĕ-tĭ)[168]	
lęg-/leg- 'lie'	lęžetь (< lĕ-n-g-ĕ-tĭ)	let'i (< lĕg-tēi̯)
sęd-/sĕd 'sit'	sędetь (< sĕ-n-d-ĕ-tĭ)	sĕsti (< sēd-tēĭ)

(b) Bare roots of *sonantic* root verbs ended in sonants *r n m*. Most of these verbs had no verb-forming suffix in either the present-tense or infinitive formations. Their present-tense and infinitive stems, however, differed because of the Proto-Indo-European ablaut variations: the present-tense stems displayed the zero-grade sequences *ьr ьn ьm* (from the syllabic so-

167. For pertinent consonant alternations, see **2.19, 2.22, 2.36.** Some of the alternations are analogical rather than phonological. Thus the expected reflex of PIE *plĕk-t-ĕ-tĭ* 'he weaves' is **plet'etь* rather than the actually occurring form *pletetь*, which is analogical to forms where the cluster *kt* occurs before a back vowel, e.g. *pletǫ* 'I weave' from *plĕk-t-ō-(m)*; cf. also *plesti* 'to weave' rather than the expected **plet'i*.

168. Compare Latin *-bundus* 'about to be' as in *moribundus* 'about to die'.

nants *r̥ n̥ m̥* before vowels), while the infinitive stems showed the reflexes of the *e*-grade sequences *ĕr ĕn ĕm:*

mьr-/mer- 'die'	mьretь	merti (< mĕr-tēi̯)
pьn-/pen- 'stretch'	pьnetь	pęti (< pĕn-tēi̯)
tьn-/ten- 'cut'	tьnetь	tę-ti (< tĕn-tēi̯)
žьm-/žem- 'squeeze'	žьmetь	žęti (< gĕm-tēi̯)

In several sonantic root verbs the infinitive stem (with zero-grade ablaut) shows the verb-forming suffix *-a-*:

ber-/bьr-a- 'take'	beretь	bьrati
der-/dьr-a- 'tear'	deretь	dьrati
žen-/gъn-a- 'chase'	ženetь	gъnati

(c) In *semivocalic* root verbs the present-tense stems ended in *Vj*. From the Early Proto-Slavic point of view, *j* was either a prothetic semivowel before the syllable-initial *e* (**2.21**) or part of the root (e.g. *pŏi̯-* 'sing'). In Late Proto-Slavic, however, this distinction was obliterated:

bij-/bi- 'beat'	bijetь	biti
čuj-/ču- 'feel'	čujetь	čuti
grěj-/grě- 'warm'	grějetь	grěti
myj-/my- 'wash'	myjetь	myti
poj- 'sing'	pojetь (< pŏi̯-ĕ-tĭ)	pěti (< pŏi̯-tēi̯)
sěj-/sě- 'sow'	sějetь	sěti

Several verbs in *v* (< *u̯*) belonged to this class, e.g. *slov-e-tь* (< *slŏu̯-ĕ-tĭ*) *slu-ti* (< *slŏu̯-tēi̯*) 'be known':

plov- 'swim'	plovetь	pluti
rov- (rev)- 'bellow'	rovetь (revetь)	ruti (r'uti)
trov- 'feed'	trovetь	truti

The verbs *živ-/ži-* 'live' and *pelv-/pel-* 'wood' had *v* in the present-tense stem only: *živetь pelvetь* but *žiti pelti*.

In several semivocalic root verbs the infinitive stem shows the verb-forming suffix *-a-*: *věj-/věj-a-* 'blow', *sěj-/sěj-a-* 'sow', *zov-/zъv-a-* 'call'.

(2) Other thematic verbs contained a verb-forming suffix that occurred in two variants, one in the present-tense stem and one in the infinitive stem. Since the correspondence between the two variants is generally predictable, it is possible to select one of them as basic and use it as a classifying marker. In the six verb classes thus obtained the present-tense variant is shown first (quoted in third-person singular present) and separated by a slash from the infinitive variant. The variant used to label a class is given in boldface:

(a) *-n-/-**nǫ**-* verbs were productive and included two subclsses. In the vocalic *-nǫ-* verbs the verb-forming suffix *-n-/-nǫ-* was preceded by a vowel:

ma-nǫ- 'signal'	manetь	manǫti
mi-nǫ- 'pass'	minetь	minǫti
ply-nǫ- 'flow'	plynetь	plynǫti
sly-nǫ- 'be known'	slynetь	slynǫti
su-nǫ- 'glide'	sunetь	sunǫti

In the consonantic *-nǫ-* verb-forming suffix was preceded by a consonant. Whenever the resultant consonant clusters were simplified in accordance with the law of open syllables (**2.19, 2.44**), the omitted root-final consonant is shown bracketed in the basic stem. The verb-forming suffix was typically omitted in aorist and past participial formations, e.g. *dvignetь dvignǫti* 'move' but *dvigoxъ* (1 Sg. Aorist), *dvigъ* (Nom. Sg. NonF. Past Act. Pple. Indef.), *dviženъ* (Nom. Sg. Masc. Past Pass. Pple. Indef.):

mr̥'z-nǫ- 'freeze'	mr̥'znetь	mr̥'znǫti
sъx-nǫ- 'dry'	sъxnetь	sъxnǫti
to[p]-nǫ- 'drown'	tonetь	tonǫti
vę[d]-nǫ- 'wilt'	vęnetь	vęnǫti
zę[b]-nǫ- 'germinate'	zęnetь	zęnǫti

(b) *-j-* (< *i̯*)/***-a-*** verbs were unproductive. In this large class the verb-forming suffix *-j-* alternated with *-a-* (cf. **c** below). The addition of the suffix *-j-* to the root produced *Cj* (< *Ci̯*) sequences, which were resolved in accordance with the rules of yodization (**2.23**):

kap-a- 'drip'	kapl'etь	kapati
lъg-a- 'lie'	lъžetь	lъgati
plak-a- 'weep'	plačetь	plakati
met-a- 'throw'	met'etь	metati
vęz-a- 'bind'	vęžetь	vęzati

(c) ***-u-j-/-ov-a-*** verbs were productive. This class contained chiefly denominal verbs and differed from the preceding one by the presence of the suffix *-ŏu̯-*, which monophthongized to u_2 in a closed syllable (*-ŏu̯-i̯-* > *-u-j-*, **2.26**) but remained in an open syllable (*-ŏu̯-a-* > *-ov-a-*). After soft consonants *-ov-a-* > *-ev-a-*, in accordance with **2.25.**

cěl-ov-a 'greet'	cělujetь	cělovati
dar-ov-a- 'bestow'	darujetь	darovati
věr-ov-a- 'believe'	věrujetь	věrovati
voj-ev-a- 'make war'	vojujetь	vojevati
vrač-ev-a- 'heal'	vračujetь	vračevati

(d) ***-a-j-*** (< *-ā-i̯-*)/*-a-* and ***-ě-j-*** (< *-ē-i̯-*)/*-ě-* verbs were productive. The *-a-j-* verbs were mostly denominal and derived imperfective, while the *-ě-j-* verbs were mainly deadjectival and intransitive:

děl-a-j- 'do'	dělajetь	dělati
ględ-a-j- 'see'	ględajetь	ględati

gněv-a-j- 'anger'	gněvajetъ	gněvati
u-mir-a-j- 'die'	u-mirajetъ	u-mirati
věnьč-a-j- 'crown'	věnьčajetъ	věnьčati
běl-ě-j- 'appear white'	bělějetъ	běléti
bogat-ě-j- 'grow rich'	bogatějetъ	bogatěti
sъm-ě-j- 'dare'	sъmějetъ	sъměti
um-ě-j- 'know how'	umějetъ	uměti
zъr-ě-j- 'ripen'	zъrějetъ	zъrěti

(e) *-i-* (< *-ěi̯-*)/***-i-*** (< *-ī-*) verbs were productive. This class contained iterative, factitive, and denominal verbs. The verb-forming suffix *-i-* in the present-tense stem of the *-i-* and *-ě-* class verbs (see below) is different in origin from the verb-forming suffix *-i-* in the infinitive stem of the *-i-* class verbs. Since the *-i-* in the infinitive stem was acute and the *-i-* in the present-tense stem was not, one may assume that the former goes back to the long *-ī-*, while the latter is derived from the short diphthong *-ěi̯-* (**2.26**). Hence their dissimilar treatment in those modern Slavic languages which retain reflexes of Proto-Slavic intonational distinctions, e.g. S/Cr. *nȍsi nósiti* and Ru. *nósit nosít'*.

Except in the first-person singular the present-tense suffix of the *-i-* and *-ě-* classes was -*Ø*- (**2.53**). For this reason the presents of these two classes are sometimes referred to as semi-thematic (Kuryłowicz 1964:79–80) or semi-athematic (Vaillant 1966:439):

bud-i- 'awaken'	buditъ	buditi
modl-i- 'ask'	modlitъ	modliti
nos-i- 'carry'	nositъ	nositi
var-i- 'cook'	varitъ	variti
xval-i- 'praise'	xvalitъ	xvaliti

(f) *-i-* (< *-ěi̯*)/***-ě-*** (< *-ē-*) verbs were unproductive. This class contained mostly intransitive stative verbs. As in the *-i-* verbs, the verb-forming suffix in the present tense was *-i-* < *-ěi̯-*, while the present-tense suffix, except in the first-person singular, was -*Ø*-:

gor-ě- 'burn'	goritъ	gorěti
let-ě- 'fly'	letitъ	letěti
mьn-ě- 'think'	mьnitъ	mьněti
tr̥'p-ě- 'suffer'	tr̥'pitъ	tr̥'pěti
vid-ě- 'see'	viditъ	viděti

The *-ě-* verbs included stems in soft consonants after which *ē* was backed to *ā* (**2.27**). Such stems are listed in the nonbacked *-ē-* (*-ě-*) form:

boj-ě- 'be afraid'	bojitъ sę	bojati sę
krič-ě- 'shout'	kričitъ	kričati
lež-ě- 'lie'	ležitъ	ležati
slyš-ě- 'hear'	slyšitъ	slyšati
stoj-ě- 'stand'	stojitъ	stojati

2.51. Verbal aspect. The contrast betweeen completion and noncompletion of action was expressed in Slavic through a system of aspectual distinctions (**2.46**). The overarching aspectual opposition was that between the *perfective* specifying a completed action and the unmarked *imperfective*.[169] In addition, some nonprefixed imperfective verbs (chiefly the verbs of motion) distinguished between two subaspects, the *nondetermined*, indicating a discontinuous (iterative) action, and the unmarked *determined*. Aspectual distinctions were expressed through derivation, yielding pairs of imperfective and perfective verbs.[170] The formal contrast between members of such aspectual pairs was achieved through verbal prefixation and stem derivation. Unprefixed verbs were, as a rule, imperfective, and their prefixed derivatives were perfective. The meaning of the prefixed perfective verb resulted from the fusion of the verbal prefix with the underived verbal stem. It matched the meaning of the corresponding prefixed imperfective verb, whose stem was derived through suffixation. As a result, members of aspectual pairs could contain:

(a) an unprefixed imperfective and a prefixed perfective, e.g. *l'ub-i-* (ipf.) ~ *vъz-l'ub-i-* (pf.) 'love';
(b) an unprefixed perfective and an unprefixed derived imperfective, e.g. *pust-i-* (pf.) ~ *pust'-a-j-* (ipf.) 'release';
(c) a prefixed perfective and a prefixed derived imperfective, e.g. *u-stǫp-i-* (pf.) ~ *u-stǫp-a-j-* (ipf.) 'retreat'.

In addition, derived imperfectives were often characterized by a different ablaut grade (usually lengthened) of the root vowel: *e* ~ *ě*, *o* ~ *a*, *ь* ~ *i*, *ъ* ~ *y* (**2.11**), e.g. *po-rod-i-* (pf.) ~ *po-rad'-a-j-* (ipf.) 'give birth', *pro-zьr-ě-* (pf.) ~ *pro-zir-a-j-* (ipf.) 'regain sight', *po-sъl-a-* (pf.) ~ *po-syl-a-j-* (ipf.) 'send'.

A few aspectual pairs were suppletive, that is, they contained etymologically unrelated stems, e.g. *vъz-jьm-/vъz-jem-* (pf.) ~ *ber-/bьr-a-* (ipf.) 'take'. In addition, the testimony of Old Church Slavonic and other Slavic languages suggests the existence of a small number of biaspectual verbs, e.g. OCS *liš-i-* 'deprive' or Ru. *ran-i-* 'wound'.

2.51.1. Verbal prefixes. Most verbal prefixes, or preverbs, functioned also as prepositions and shared with them their basic meanings:

do- 'up to'	*ot(ъ)-* 'from'
jьz- 'out of'	*podъ-* 'under'
mimo- 'by the side'	*pri-* 'near'
na- 'upon'	*sъ(n)-* 'down from'and 'accompanying'
nadъ- 'over'	*vъ(n)-* 'inside'

The meaning of some preverbs differed from that of homophonous prepositions:

o(b)- 'around' vs. 'against, about'
po- 'after, following' vs. 'after, along'
pro- 'across' vs. 'through'
u- 'away from' vs. 'at'
za- 'beyond' vs. 'after, behind'

169. The perfective aspect has also been viewed as signaling the delimitative, comprehensive (total), or specific function of the verb.

170. Because of the regularity and predictability with which these pairs occur throughout Slavic, aspect, like diminutive nominal suffixation, straddles the line dividing derivation from inflection.

For some preverbs there were no homophonous prepositions:

nizъ- 'down'	*vъz-* 'up(ward)'
orz- 'in different directions'	*vy-* 'out of'
per- 'across'	

2.51.2. Aspectual derivation. The evidence of individual Slavic languages suggests that only two verb classes, *-(v)-a-j-* and *-ov-a-*, were used in Proto-Slavic for the derivation of imperfective stems from underlying perfective stems and of imperfective nondetermined (iterative) stems from underlying imperfective determined stems. The patterns of pairing of derived and underlying stems may generally be established with a great degree of certitude. In some instances, however, dialectal differences make it difficult to decide which of the competing patterns existed in Proto-Slavic. The examples below reflect a wide range of acceptance of a given pattern. They are drawn chiefly from the vocabulary of Old Church Slavonic.

The ***-a-j-* verbs** occurred most commonly as imperfective (nondetermined) counterparts to perfective and imperfective determined verbs belonging to the following verb classes:

(a) Prefixed and unprefixed perfective consonantic root verbs with the same or different root vocalism:

sъ-bl'ud-	sъ-bl'ud-a-j-	'guard'
otъ-sěk-	otъ-sěk-a-j-	'place upon'
o-tręs-	o-tręs-a-j-	'shake off'
pad- (pf.)	pad-a-j-	'fall'
sěd- (pf.)	sěd-a-j-	'sit'
jьz-bod-	jьz-bad-a-j-	'stab'
po-greb-	po-grěb-a-j-	'bury'
sъ-plet-	sъ-plět-a-j-	'intertwine'
per-rek-	per-rěk-a-j-	'contradict'
orz-verz-	orz-vr̥'z-a-j-	'open'

(b) Prefixed perfective sonantic root verbs with a different root vocalism:

pro-kl̥'n-	pro-klin-a-j-	'curse'
na-čьn-	na-čin-a-j-	'begin'
vъz-ьm-	vъz-im-a-j-	'take up'
na-dьm-	na-dym-a-j-	'blow up'
u-mьr-	u-mir-a-j-	'die'

(c) Prefixed perfective and unprefixed perfective and imperfective *-i-* verbs. In these verbs the root-final consonant was yodized, with *i* in prevocalic position yielding *i̯* (**2.23**). Thus, *vъz-bud-i-* (pf.) ~ *vъz-bud'-a-j-* (ipf.) 'awaken':

pri-xod-i-	pri-xad'-a-j-	'arrive'
po-grǫz-i-	po-grǫž-a-j-	'immerse'
u-krěp-i-	u-krěpl'-a-j-	'strengthen'
za-prět-i-	za-prět'-a-j-	'order'
vъ-pros-i-	vъ-praš-a-j-	'ask'

gols-i- (ipf.)	golš-a-j-	'call'
pust-i- (pf.)	pust'-a-j-	'let go'
rod-i- (pf.)	rad'-a-j-	'give birth'
(j)av-i- (pf.)	(j)avl'-a-j-	'manifest'
tvor-i- (ipf.)	tvar'-a-j-	'create'

In a few verbs the root-final consonant was not yodized:

pri-log-i-	pri-lag-a-j-	'attach'
per-lom-i-	per-lam-a-j-	'break'
o-pravьd-i-	o-pravьd-a-j-	'justify'
stǫp-i- (pf.)	stǫp-a-j-	'stride'
vъz-xyt-i-	vъz-xyt-a-j-	'catch'

(d) Prefixed and unprefixed perfective consonantic *-nǫ-* verbs. In these derivatives the suffix *-nǫ-* was omitted:

jьz-čez-nǫ-	jьz-čaz-a-j-	'disappear'
u-gas-nǫ-	u-gas-a-j-	'extinguish'
jьz-ky[d]-nǫ-	jьz-kyd-a-j-	'throw out'
u-to[p]-nǫ-	u-tap-a-j-	'drown'
orz-tr̥g-nǫ	orz-tr̥g-a-j-	'tear up'
dr̥'z-nǫ-	dr̥'z-a-j-	'dare'
dъx-nǫ-	dъx-a-j-	'breathe'
kos-nǫ- sę	kas-a-j- sę	'touch'
klik-nǫ-	klik-a-j-	'call'
tъk-nǫ-	tъk-a-j-	'push'

(e) Prefixed and unprefixed *-a-* verbs:

na-kaz-a-	na-kaz-a-j-	'instruct'
po-maz-a-	po-maz-a-j-	'annoint'
otъ-sъl-a-	otъ-syl-a-j-	'send away'
sъ-zьd-a-	sъ-zid-a-j-	'build'
žęd-a-	žęd-a-j-	'thirst'

(f) Prefixed and unprefixed *-ě-* verbs:

orz-gor-ě-sę-	orz-gar-a-j-	'flame up'
po-mьn-ě-	po-min-a-j-	'remember'
per-pьr-ě-	per-pir-a-j-	'persuade'
vъz-zьr-ě-	vъz-zir-a-j-	'look up'
svьt-ě-	svit-aj-	'grow light'

The ***-v-a-j-* verbs** were a subclass of the *-a-j-* verbs. They formed derived imperfectives from verbs belonging to prefixed semivocalic root verbs. The underlying stem was that of the infinitive:

orz-bi-	orz-bi-v-a-j-	'break up'
sъ-grě-	sъ-grě-v-a-j-	'warm up'
u-my-	u-my-v-a-j-	'wash'
po-zna-	po-zna-v-a-j-	'recognize'
po-ži-	po-ži-v-a-j-	'live'

They were also used with several irregular prefixed and unprefixed verbs:

vъz-sta-n-/-sta-	vъz-sta-v-a-j-[171]	'stand up'
bǫd-/by-	by-v-a-j-	'be'
dad-/da-	da-v-a-j-	'give'

The *-ov-a-* verbs formed derived imperfectives from a small number of *-i-* class verbs:

per-obraz-i-	per-obraz-ov-a-	'transform'
po-sob-i-	po-sob-ov-a	'help'
u-věr-i-	u-věr-ov-a-	'believe'
jьz-věst-i-	jьz-věst-ov-a-	'announce'
po-zor-i-	po-zor-ov-a-	'observe'
dar-i-	dar-ov-a-	'bestow'
gols-i-	gols-ov-a-	'call'
kup-i-	kup-ov-a-	'buy'
liš-i-	lix-ov-a-	'deprive'
pečal-i- sę	pečal-ov-a- sę	'grieve'

The most typical subaspectual opposition was provided by the pairing of the determined *e*-grade root verbs with the nondetermined *o*-grade *-i-* class verbs:

nes-	nos-i-	'carry'
ved-	vod-i-	'lead'
velk-	volč-i-	'drag'
vez-	voz-i-	'transport'
žen-/gъn-a-	gon-i-	'chase'

2.52. Personal endings. The Proto-Indo-European conjugational system distinguished several sets of personal endings. In the indicative the endings characterizing the active voice were opposed to the endings of the middle voice, and the endings of the present tense, or the so-caled primary endings, were opposed to the endings of the preterite tenses, or the secondary endings. Furthermore, some personal endings of the thematic conjugations were different from those of the athematic one. The degree of ending differentiation varied. Thus, in the active voice the first- and second-person singular admitted three distinct endings, the third-person singular and plural distinguished two endings, and other persons and

171. Also *vъz-sta-j-a-j-*. The derived imperfectives of the anomalous verb *děd-j-* (also *dě-j-*, *dě-n-*)/*dě-* 'put' were formed from the stems *-dě-j-a-* or *-dě-v-a-j-*; thus the perfective *o-děd'-* (*o-dě-j-*, *o-dě-n-*)/*o-dě-* 'wrap up, clothe' was matched with the imperfective *o-dě-j-a-* or *o-dě-v-a-j-*.

numbers displayed one ending only. In the list below only the most differentiated forms are shown:

	PRIMARY		SECONDARY
	ATHEMATIC	THEMATIC	
1 SG.	-mĭ	-ō	-m
2 SG.	-sĭ	-ĕi̯ [?]	-s
3 SG.	-tĭ		-t
3 PL.	-ntĭ		-nt

The Proto-Slavic conjugational system, like that of Sanskrit or Ancient Greek, was rich in grammatical oppositions. Verbs were inherently specified for government (that is, they were either transitive or intransitive) and, as obligatory categories, they distinguished aspect and genus (that is, they were either perfective or imperfective and reflexive or nonreflexive). Finite verb forms were inflected for person and number and either tense or mood. Compound finite forms (perfect, pluperfect, conditional) distinguished gender as well. The only form displaying a clearly middle ending was the isolated *vědě* 'I know' found in Old Church Slavonic (*Codex Suprasliensis*), Old East Slavic, Old Slovene (*Freising Fragments*), and Old Czech. The ending goes back to the Proto-Indo-European middle *-ă-i̯* (cf. Greek *loúomai* 'I wash myself'). Since *vědě* is related to the root *vid-* 'see' (< *u̯ĕi̯d-*), its meaning probably developed from 'I have seen for myself' to 'I know'.

2.53. Present tense. Conjugations I and II. Depending on the aspect of the verbal stem, the Proto-Slavic present referred to an action either contemporaneous with the moment of speech (imperfective) or subsequent to it (perfective). Hence it is frequently referred to as the *nonpast* tense. Its person and number endings were derived from Proto-Indo-European primary endings. In the thematic verbs they were added to stems extended by the present-tense suffix. In the root, *-nǫ-*, *-a-*, *-ov-a-*, and *-a-j-/-ě-j-* verb classes the present-tense suffix was *-ŏH_2-* in the first-person singular, *-ŏ-* in the third-person plural, and *-ĕ-* elsewhere. The present-tense forms of these classes are said to belong to Conjugation I. The present-tense forms of the *-i-* and *-ĕ-* verb classes belong to Conjugation II. Their present-tense suffix was *-ŏH_2-* in the first person singular and *-Ø-* elsewhere. Except for the third person plural, the endings were the same in both conjugations, but athematic verbs had special endings in the first and second person singular:

	SINGULAR		DUAL	PLURAL		
	THEMATIC	ATHEMATIC		CONJ. I	CONJ. II	ATHEMATIC
1.	-ǫ	-mь	-vě	-mъ		
2.	-ši	-si	-ta	-te		
3.	-tь		-te	-ǫtь	-ętь	

Table 12 provides examples of the present-tense paradigms of the athematic, root, *-a-*, *-a-j-/-ě-j-*, and *-i-* verb classes.

Table 12: Present-tense paradigms of the verbs *ěd-* 'eat', *vez-* 'transport', *kaz-a-* 'explain', *děl-a-j-* 'do', and *nos-i-* 'carry' in Late Proto-Slavic

		ATHEMATIC	CONJUGATION I			CONJUGATION II
	1	jamь (< ēd-mĭ)	vezǫ	kažǫ	dělajǫ	nošǫ
SG.	2	jasi (< ēd-sēi̯?)	vezeši	kažeši	dělaješi	nosiši
	3	jastь (< ēd-tĭ)	vezetь	kažetь	dělajetь	nositь
	1	javě (< ēd-u̯ē)	vezevě	kaževě	dělajevě	nosivě
DU.	2	jasta (< ēd-tā)	vezeta	kažeta	dělajeta	nosita
	3	jaste (< ēd-tē)	vezete	kažete	dělajete	nosite
	1	jamъ (< ēd-mŏn)	vezemъ	kažemъ	dělajemъ	nosimъ
PL.	2	jaste (< ēd-tē)	vezete	kažete	dělajete	nosite
	3	jadętь (< ēd-n̥tĭ)	vezǫtь	kažǫtь	dělajǫtь	nosętь

Notes: (1) The first person singular *-mь* continues the Proto-Indo-European athematic *-mĭ* (OCS *esmь*, Greek *eími* 'I am'). The thematic *-ǫ* goes back to the Proto-Indo-European thematic *-ŏH_2-* > *ō* (Greek *phérō*, Latin *ferō* 'I carry') extended by the secondary 1 Sg. *-m*. In Conjugation II the sequence *-i-ō-m* yields *-j-ǫ-* without the expected fronting of the vowel (**2.25**) because of the analogical influence of the ending *-ǫ* of Conjugation I.

(2) The second person singular endings were the athematic *-si* and thematic *-ši*, as in OCS *esi* 'you are' or *neseši* 'you carry'. The consonant *š* arose regularly in Conjugation II as a result of the retroflexion of *s* after *i* (see **2.7**) and spread by analogy to Conjugation I. The final *i* (for the expected ь) could have been derived from the Proto-Indo-European second-person singular thematic *-ēi̯*, which some scholars (Meillet 1934:253–254; Szemerényi 1989: 250–251) see also in the Greek 2 Sg. *-eis*, e.g. *phéreis* 'you carry'. In this explanation, the primary thematic ending *-ei̯* was extended in Greek by the secondary ending *-s*, while in Proto-Slavic the ending *-s* was extended by *-ēi̯*.

(3) In the third person singular and plural, Proto-Indo-European *-tĭ* should yield Proto-Slavic *-tь*, and such reflexes do occur in parts of East Slavic. In Old Church Slavonic, however, as well as in some north Russian dialects (including standard Russian), we find *tъ* instead. It is likely that 3 Sg. *-tъ* developed under the influence of the demonstrative pronoun *tъ* 'this', which functioned also as the third person pronoun 'he'. From there *tъ* could have spread analogically to the third person plural. In West Slavic and West South Slavic the ending *-tь/-tъ* has been lost altogether. In other Slavic languages it shows varying degrees of staying power (**2.69**, 27).

(4) The first-person dual *-vě*, instead of the expected *-ve* (< *-u̯ēs*), is probably analogical to the pronoun *vě* 'we two' (< *u̯ēs*).

(5) The first person plural *-mъ* seems to be the reflex of *-mŏn* (cf. Attic Greek *-men*, as in

phéromen 'we carry'). The ending *-mo*, which appears in some Slavic languages (**2.69.28**) is probably derived from *-mŏs*, which is the more common variant of this ending in Proto-Indo-European (cf. Latin *-mus* < *-mŏs* as in *ferimus* 'we carry').

(6) The third person plural ending of the athematic conjugation was *-ętь* (< *-n̥tĭ*). The ending *-ǫtь* (< *-ŏ-ntĭ*) of the root and *-nǫ-* classes spread analogically to the *-a-*, *-ov-a-*, and *-a-j-* classes, replacing the expected *-ętь* (< *-j-ĕ-ntĭ* < *-j-ŏ-ntĭ*). The Conjugation II ending *-ętь* may be due to the influence of the athematic conjugation or may represent the regular phonetic development of *-ĕi̯-ntĭ*.

2.54. Aorist. The aorist designated a completed action without affirming either its duration or resultative value. As such, it served as the narrative preterite tense. Aorist endings were derived from Proto-Indo-European secondary endings and were added to the infinitive stem. Proto-Slavic had three different aorist formations. Two of them, the root (or simple) and sigmatic aorists, were relics inherited from Proto-Indo-European. The third type appeared alongside the two older types and eventually replaced them, thus becoming the only productive aorist formation of Slavic.

The *root aorist* combined the forms of the Proto-Indo-European thematic aorist and imperfect (cf. Vedic Sanskrit *bháram*, Homeric Greek *phéron* 'I carried'). Its endings were preceded by a thematic vowel, which was added directly to the verbal root (the suffix *-nǫ-* in the *-nǫ-* class verbs was omitted). Before *-t* and *-s* the thematic vowel was *-ĕ-*; elsewhere it was *-ŏ-*. The root aorist survived in the consonantic verbs of the root and *-nǫ-* classes. We know, however, from Old Church Slavonic that only in the second and third person singular was it used regularly with all the verbs of these classes. In other persons it was used sporadically with about a dozen stems, such as *jьd-* 'go', *lĕz-* 'climb', *mog-* 'be able'.

Table 13: Root aorist paradigms of *pad-* 'fall' and *dvig-(nǫ-)* 'move'

	1	padъ	dvigъ (< -ŏ-m, see **2.48.1 n3b**)
Sg.	2	pade	dviže (< -ĕ-s)
	3	pade	dviže (< -ĕ-t)
	1	padově	dvigově
Du.	2	padeta	dvižeta
	3	padete	dvižete
	1	padomъ	dvigomъ
Pl.	2	padete	dvižete
	3	padǫ	dvigǫ (< -ŏ-nt)

The *sigmatic aorist* was found with verbs of the *-i-* class and with sonantic and about twenty consonantic verbs of the root class, e.g. *greb-* 'bury', *męt-* 'stir', *tek-* 'run'. The endings of the sigmatic aorist were preceded by the formant *-s-* (hence the name "sigmatic"), followed in the first person of all numbers by the thematic vowel *-ŏ-*. The root vowel of the root verbs was lengthened: *ĭ ĕ ŏ* > *ī ē ō*.

Table 14: Sigmatic aorist paradigms of the verbs *bod-* 'pierce' and *nos-i-* 'carry', and partial paradigms of *čьt-* 'read', *pьn-/pen-*(< *pn̥-/pěn-*) 'stretch', *mьr-/mer-* 'die', *rek-* 'say' in Late Proto-Slavic

	1	basъ (< bōd-s-ŏ-m)	nosixъ (< nŏs-ī-s-ŏ-m)
SG.	2	bode (root aorist)	nosi (< nŏs-ī-s-s)
	3	bode (root aorist)	nosi (< nŏs-ī-s-t)
	1	basově	nosixově
DU.	2	basta (< bōd-s-tā)	nosista (< nŏs-ī-s-tā)
	3	baste	nosiste
	1	basomъ	nosixomъ
PL.	2	baste (< bōd-s-tě)	nosiste
	3	basę (< bōd-s-n̥t)	nosišę (< nŏs-ī-s-n̥t)

SG.	1	čisъ (< kīt-s-ŏ-m)	pęsъ (< pēn-s-ŏ-m)
PL.	2	čiste (< kīt-s-tě)	pęste (< pēn-s-tě)
	3	čisę (< kīt-s-n̥t)	pęsę (< pēn-s-n̥t)

SG.	1	merxъ (< mēr-s-ŏ-m)	rěxъ (< rēk-s-ŏ-m)
PL.	2	merste (< mēr-s-tě)	rěste (< rēk-s-tě)
	3	meršę (< mēr-s-n̥t)	rěšę (< rēk-s-n̥t)

Notes: (1) Forms corresponding to the Proto-Slavic sigmatic aorist occur in some but not all Indo-European languages; cf. the Greek aorist *édeiksa* 'I showed', Latin perfect *dīxī* 'I said'. Of the immediate neighbors of Proto-Slavic, this aorist does not occur in either Baltic or Germanic.

(2) It is often claimed that the lengthening of the root vowel in the root- class verbs was the result of compensatory lengthening following the simplification of consonant clusters. Such a lengthening, however, is not observed in analogous situations elsewhere, e.g. *ŏpsā* > *osa* 'wasp'. It is more probable, therefore, that the lengthening was morphophonemic in nature.

(3) There were no second and third person singular sigmatic aorist forms with the consonantic verbs of the root class; root aorist forms were used instead.

(4) In Old Church Slavonic the second and third person singular of the sonantic verbs were extended by the suffix *-tъ*, e.g. *pę(tъ), mrě(tъ).* This suffix appears to have spread there by analogy from the third person singular present.

The *productive aorist* arose within Proto-Slavic as an analogical extension of the sigmatic aorist of the *-i-* class verbs. In verbs whose infinitive stem ended in a vowel the impulse for this analogical development must have been provided by the forms in which *-s-* was pre-consonantal. In these environments all such verbs developed in a similar fashion. Compare the following forms of *nos-i-* 'carry' and *děl-a-j-* 'do':

Sg. 2	nosi (< nŏs-ī-s-s)	děla (< dēl-ā-s-s)
3	nosi (< nŏs-ī-s-t)	děla (< dēl-ā-s-t)
Pl. 2	nosiste (< nŏs-ī-s-tĕ)	dělaste (< dēl-ā-s-tĕ)

These similarities were analogically extended to forms in which *-s-* was prevocalic, that is, to environments in which the phonological development of the *-i-* class verbs was different from that of other verbs with a vocalic infinitive stem. Thus, such phonologically regular forms as

Sg. 1	nosixъ (< nŏs-ī-s-ŏ-m)
Pl. 1	nosixomъ (< nŏs-ī-s-ŏ-mŏn)
3	nosišę (< nŏs-ī-s-n̥t)

led to the creation of analogical forms in such stems as *kaz-a-* 'explain', *věr-ov-a-* 'believe', *děl-a-j-* (infinitive stem *děl-a-*) 'do', *vid-ě-* 'see', *pьn-* (infinitive stem *pę-*) 'stretch':

Sg. 1	kazaxъ	věrovaxъ	dělaxъ	viděxъ	pęxъ
Pl. 1	kazaxomъ	věrovaxomъ	dělaxomъ	viděxomъ	pęxomъ
3	kazašę	věrovašę	dělašę	viděšę	pęšę

In the consonantic verbs of the root and *-nǫ-* classes, the starting point of the analogy must have been the nonlengthened root aorist forms of the second and third person singular which, like the corresponding sigmatic aorist forms of the *-i-* class verbs, ended in a vowel; cf. the following forms of *ved-* 'lead' and *nos-i-* 'carry':

	Root	Sigmatic
Sg. 2	vede (< vĕd-ĕ-s)	nosi (< nŏs-ī-s-s)
3	vede (< vĕd-ĕ-t)	nosi (< nŏs-ī-s-t)

Such forms led to the creation of productive aorist forms in which the abstracted endings of the *-i-* class verbs were added to the nonlengthened roots of the consonantic verbs. The thematic vowel was *-e-* in West Slavic and *-o-* elsewhere.

	West Slavic	South/East Slavic
Sg. 1	vedexъ	vedoxъ
Pl. 1	vedexomъ	vedoxomъ
3	vedexǫ (*-xǫ*, from the imperfect **2.55**)	vedošę

Except for the stems in *r*, which had sigmatic forms only, all the root verbs had productive aorist forms, competing in some of them with one of the unproductive types (Table 15):

Table 15: Different aorist formations in Old Church Slavonic

	Root		Sigmatic		Productive	
	1 Sg.	3 Pl.	1 Sg.	3 Pl.	1 Sg.	3 Pl.
mьr-/mrě- 'die'			mrěxъ	mrěšę		
[j]i-/[j]ьd- 'go'	idъ	idǫ			idoxъ	idošę
mog- 'be able'	mogъ	mogǫ			mogoxъ	mogošę
dvig-nǫ- 'move'	dvigъ	dvigǫ			dvigoxъ	dvigošę
čьt- 'read'			čisъ	čisę	čьtoxъ	čьtošę
[j]ьm-/[j]ę- 'take'			ęsъ	ęsę	ęxъ	ęšę
rek- 'say'			rěxъ	rěšę	rekoxъ	rekošę

2.55. Imperfect. The imperfect (Table 16) arose as a Slavic innovation following the reinterpretation of the Proto-Indo-European imperfect as the Proto-Slavic root aorist. It indicated noncompletion of a past action and stressed its duration or repetition. Because of such a semantic specification, the imperfect was restricted almost exclusively to imperfective verbs. The formant of the imperfect was complex and consisted of the suffix *-ěa-* or *-aa-* followed by the suffix *-x-*. The endings were those of the root aorist.

Table 16: Paradigms of the imperfect of *nes-* 'carry', *mog-* 'be able', *děl-a-j-* 'do', *vid-ě-* 'see', and *nos-i-* 'carry' in Late Proto-Slavic

	1	nesěaxъ	možaaxъ	dělaaxъ	viděaxъ	nošaaxъ
Sg.	2	nesěaše	možaaše	dělaaše	viděaše	nošaaše
	3	nesěaše	možaaše	dělaaše	viděaše	nošaaše
	1	nesěaxově	možaaxově	dělaaxove	viděaxově	nošaaxově
Du.	2	nesěašeta	možaašeta	dělaašeta	viděašeta	nošaašeta
	3	nesěašete	možaašete	dělaašete	viděašete	nošaašete
	1	nesěaxomъ	možaaxomъ	dělaaxomъ	viděaxomъ	nošaaxomъ
Pl.	2	nesěašete	možaašete	dělaašete	viděašete	nošaašete
	3	nesěaxǫ	možaaxǫ	dělaaxǫ	viděaxǫ	nošaaxǫ

Notes: (1) The *-a-*, *-ov-a-* and *-ě-* verbs formed the imperfect on the infinitive stem, while the *-nǫ-* and some irregular verbs formed it on the present-tense stem. The imperfect of other verb classes could be interpreted as being based on either stem. It appears, however, that the oldest imperfects were built on the present-tense stem. After the loss of the intervocalic yod in the *-a-j-* class verbs (see *note 4*) the present-tense stem was reinterpreted as the infinitive stem, thus providing the model for other classes.

(2) The endings of the imperfect were taken over from the root aorist, which consisted of the Proto-Indo-European secondary endings preceded by a thematic vowel.

(3) The suffix *-x-* appears to have been introduced into the imperfect from the productive aorist.

(4) There is no agreement on the origin of the suffixes *-ěa-* and *-aa-*. It is likely that the suffix was abstracted from the combination of a stem vowel and a Proto-Indo-European stative suffix *-ē-* (LPSl. *-ě-*). This suffix appeared in the stative verbs of the *-ě-* class, e.g. *sěděti* 'to be sitting' (cf. Latin *sedēre* 'to be sitting', *manēre* 'to remain'), in the infinitive *jьměti* 'to have', contrasted with the present *jьmamь* 'I have' (cf. Old High German *habēn* 'to have'), and in *bě-*, the imperfective aorist stem of the verb *byti* 'to be' (see *note 6*). It was also present in the Latin imperfect, e.g. *legēbam* 'I was reading', *agēbam* 'I was acting'.

For the verbs of the *-a-j-* class, the phonetic development could be viewed in two ways. The stative suffix *-ē-* could have been added to the yod of the present-tense stem and changed to *ā* after it (**2.27**). After the intervocalic yod was lost, the present-tense stem was reinterpreted as the infinitive stem, and this formation spread by analogy to the *-a-*, *-ov-a-*, and *-ě-* verb classes. Alternatively, the stative suffix was added to the final vowel of the infinitive stem of the *-a-*, *ov-a-*, *-a-j-*, and *-ě-* classes, and a prothetic yod developed between the two vowels, causing the change *ē* > *ā*. In either case, the loss of the intervocalic yod could lead to the contraction of the two vowels in hiatus. Thus, *āē* > *ājē* > *ājā* > *aa* (with a possible contraction to *a*) and *ēē* > *ējē* > *ējā* > *ěa* (with a possible contraction to *ě* or *ä* [æ]).

With the verbs of the root, *-nǫ-*, and *-i-* classes, the addition of the stative suffix *-ē-* should yield *nesěxъ, možaxъ* (< *mŏg-ē-x-ŏ-m*), *dvigněxъ, nošaxъ* (< *nŏs-i̯-ē-x-ŏ-m*), and such forms do in fact occur. Under the influence of the imperfects of the other verb classes, however, these forms were extended by the vowel *a*, yielding *nesěaxъ, možaaxъ, dvigněaxъ, nošaaxъ*.

(5) Therefore, such imperfect forms as *nesěxъ, možaxъ, nošaxъ, bijaxъ, živěxъ, iděxъ* could represent the older state of the language, before their extension by the vowel *a*. On the other hand, one cannot exclude the possibility that these forms were derived from the younger forms *nesěaxъ, možaaxъ, nošaaxъ, bijaaxъ, živěaxъ, iděaxъ*, with a contraction of the sequences *ěa* or *aa* paralleling the development of such clearly contracted forms as *dělaxъ, dělaše* from *dělaaxъ, dělaaše*.

(6) A special case was that of the verb 'to be' whose forms with the stative suffix *-ē-* took the endings of the productive aorist and were interpreted as the imperfective aorist, while the younger forms, which occurred in the third person only, were interpreted as the imperfect and were so inflected. Here are the third-person forms of the two paradigms:

	Imperfective Aorist	Imperfect
3 Sg.	bě	běaše
3 Du.	běste	běašete
3 Pl.	běšę	běaxǫ

2.56. Imperative. Proto-Slavic was alone among the Indo-European languages to derive its imperative from the Proto-Indo-European optative mood. In the athematic verbs the Proto-Indo-European optative took secondary personal endings preceded by the optative suffix *-i̯ē-* (Sg.)/*-ī-* (Du. and Pl.); in the thematic verbs the optative suffix was *-ŏ-ī-*. This distinction was retained in the Proto-Slavic imperative, but with a number of analogical levelings. In the thematic conjugation the Proto-Indo-European sequence *-ŏ-ī-* yielded the diphthong *-ōi̯-*, whose length may be inferred from its subsequent development into an acute monophthong. After *i̯* (that is, in the *-a-*, *-ov-a*, and *-a-j-* classes) the diphthong *-ōi̯-* was fronted to *-ēi̯-* and monophthongized to *-ī*, e.g. *zna-j-* 'know' formed 2 Sg. Impv. *zna-j-i* (< *znā-i̯-ēi̯-s* < *znā-i̯-ōi̯-s*) and 2 Pl. Impv. *zna-j-i-te* (< *znā-i̯-ēi̯-tē* < *znā-i̯-ōi̯-tē*). In the athematic conjugation the suffix *-i̯-ē-* (Sg.) was replaced by *-i̯ī-* which was either derived from *-i̯-ŏ-ī-*, with the expected fronting of *ŏ*, or was analogical to *-ī-* (Du. and Pl.), e.g. *da-/ dad-* 'give' formed 2 Sg. Impv. *dad'i* < *dād-i̯-ī-s* (OCS *daždi*, shortened eventually to *daždь*), 2 Pl. *dadite* < *dād-ī-tē*.

This development made *-i-* the favorite formant of the imperative, leading to its spread to other imperative formations. Thus, in the singular of the root and *-nǫ-* classes, *-ě₂-*, resulting from the monophthongization of *-ōi̯-*, was analogically replaced by *-i-*, e.g. OCS 2 Sg. Impv. *beri* 'take!', *rьci* 'say!', *dvigni* 'move!' (versus OCS 2 Pl. *berěte, rьcěte, dvigněte*). The Old Church Slavonic forms *rьci* (of *rek-* 'say') or *moʒi* (of *mog-* 'be able') show that the analogical replacement of *-ě₂-* by *-i-* took place after the second palatalization of velars. The suffix *-i-* also occurred with all the imperative forms of Conjugation II verbs, e.g. 2 Sg. *nosi* (< *nŏs-ī-s*), *nosite* 'carry!'; *mьni* (< *mĭn-ī-s*), *mьnite* 'think!'.

2.57. Infinitive and supine. The morphologically least marked verbal forms were the infinitive and the supine. Like all the nonfinite forms, they were not inflected for person, tense, or mood. In fact, they distinguished only aspect and genus, the two obligatory categories of the verb. The infinitive and supine endings, *-ti* and *-tъ* respectively, were originally case forms of Proto-Indo-European deverbal nouns in the suffix *-t-*, inflected as the *-ĭ-* and *-ŭ-* stems respectively. The form of the supine and its function (specification of goal or purpose with verbs of motion) point to the accusative singular in *-ŭm* as its Proto-Indo-European source (Meillet 1934:242). The specific case from which the infinitive was derived is more difficult to establish. Its semantic affinity is with the dative; however, the acute *i* of the infinitive ending (exemplified by the oxytonic stress of such Russian infinitives as *bljustí* 'to guard', *rastí* 'to grow') suggests that it was derived from the long diphthong *ēi̯*, which characterizes the ending of the locative singular (**2.48.1**).[172] The infinitive tended to displace the functionally more restricted supine and, unlike the latter, remained in most Slavic languages. It also influenced the phonetic development of the supine in the velar stems of the root class verbs. Thus, the Old Church Slavonic reflex of the Proto-Slavic supine *pěk-t-ŭ-m* of *pek-* 'bake' was *peštъ* (rather than the expected **petъ*) by analogy to the infinitive *pešti* (< PSl. *pet'i* < *pěk-t-ēi̯*; **2.35**). Because of its semantic and formal simplicity, the infinitive is traditionally used as the citation ("dictionary") form of the Slavic verb.

2.58. Participles. Participles combined the functions of verbs with those of adjectives. They were inflected for the adjectival categories of case, number, gender, and specificity and for the verbal categories of aspect, genus, and tense. Participial tense distinctions, however, were defined in relative rather than absolute terms: actions contemporaneous with the tense of the main verb were expressed by present participles, while actions anterior to it were expressed by past participles. In addition, transitive verbs showed distinctions of voice (active vs. passive), and past active participles were either resultative or nonresultative. These distinctions yielded five participles: present active, present passive, past active nonresultative, past active resultative, and past passive.[173]

172. In favoring the dative Meillet (1934:242) was guided by semantic criteria, while Vaillant (1966:127), opting for the locative, gave precedence to formal considerations.

173. The Church Slavonic form *byšęštee* (< *bhū-s-i̯-n̥t-i̯-*) 'about to be' suggests the existence in Proto-Slavic of a future participle of *byti* 'to be' containing the Proto-Indo-European future-tense suffix *-s-i̯-*. Similar participial forms are

The *present active participle* was marked by the Proto-Indo-European suffix *-nt-* (cf. Latin *amāns, amantis* 'loving') added to the present-tense stem and, except in the nominative singular masculine/neuter, extended by the suffix *-j-*. In verbs of Conjugation I the present-tense suffix was *-ŏ-*, which in the nominative singular masculine/neuter fronted to *-ĕ-* after soft consonants (that is, in the *-a-*, *-ov-a-*, and *-a-j-/-ĕ-j-* verb classes) but was retained by analogy in the other cases (**2.52** *note 6*). In verbs of Conjugation II the present-tense suffix was *-ĕi̯-*. In the athematic verbs the original formant of the present active participle must have been *-ęt-* < *-n̥t-*. Its only trace, however, is the rare OCS *vědę* 'knowing'; more recent forms show an analogical thematic *-ǫt-* < *-ŏ-nt-*.

The declension of the present active participle followed the Proto-Indo-European consonantal (athematic) type in the endings *-s* (Nom. Sg. M), *-Ø* (Nom. Sg. N), *-ī-Ø* (Nom. Sg. F), *-ĕs* (Nom. Pl. M), and the vocalic (thematic) type *-i̯-ŏ-* (M/N) and *-i̯-ā-* (F) in the other cases. The vowel *ŏ* in *-ŏ-nt-s* (Nom. Sg. M) and *-ŏ-nt-Ø* (Nom. Sg. N) is expected to be lengthened and raised ($\bar{u}_{l}$ > *y*, **2.48.1,** *note 3.a*). This is how it develops in South Slavic but not in East Slavic or Czech/Slovak, where instead of *-y* we find *-a*. Since *-a* occurred also sporadically in Old Polish (next to *-ę*), one could posit an Early Proto-Slavic dialect isogloss separating the South Slavic -$\bar{u}_{l}$ (with vowel raising) from the North Slavic *ō* (without vowel raising or nasalization). Alternatively, this discrepancy may be explained as a late East Slavic and Czech/Slovak analogical accommodation to the nominative singular masculine/neuter of other verb classes in which *-ę-* > *-ä* (cf. *nosę* > *nosä* of *nos-i-* 'carry'). Since Polish retains nasal vowels, the Old Polish *-a* forms would have to be considered borrowings from Old Czech.

Table 17: Present active participle indefinite forms of *mog-* 'be able', *děl-a-j-* 'do', *nos-i-* 'carry' in Late Proto-Slavic

Nom. Sg. M/N	mogy/moga	dělaję	nosę
Nom. Sg. F	mogǫt'i	dělajǫt'i	nosęt'i
Nom. Pl. M	mogǫt'e	dělajǫt'e	nosęt'e
Gen. Sg. M/N	mogǫt'a	dělajǫt'a	nosęt'a

The *present passive participle* was formed from the present-tense stem of transitive, mostly imperfective verbs by the addition of the suffix *-m-* to the thematic present-tense suffixes *-ŏ-* (Conjugation I) and *-ĕi̯-* (Conjugation II). The suffix *-ŏ-* fronted to *-ĕ-* after soft consonants (that is, in the *-a-*, *-ov-a-*, and *-a-j-/-ĕ-j-* verb classes); the suffix *-ĕi̯-* was monophthongized to *-i-*. Athematic verbs showed an analogical *-ŏ-*. The declension was that of the *-ŏ-* (M/N) and *-ā-* (F) stems.

Following are several Late Proto-Slavic nominative singular masculine present passive participle indefinite forms: *nes-* 'carry', *nesomъ; děl-a-j-* 'do', *dělajemъ; vid-ě-* 'see', *vidimъ; věd-* 'know', *vědomъ.*

The *past active participle* was derived from the Proto-Indo-European suffix *-ŭs-/-u̯ĕs-/-u̯ŏs-*. In Slavic this suffix was simplified to *-ŭs-/-u̯ŭs-* and extended by *-i̯-* in forms other than the nominative singular masculine/neuter (cf. the present active participle), yielding *-ъš-/-vъš-*. It was added to the infinitive stem. The suffix *-ъš-* occurred with the *-i-*, the consonan-

also found in Old Czech. They allow us to posit a Balto-Slavic future-tense formation **bhū-s-i̯-ōm* yielding Lith. *bū́siu* 'I will be' and a hypothetical Slavic **byšǫ*.

tic and sonantic root, and consonantic *-nǫ-* classes, with *-vъš-* occurring elsewhere. In the *-i-* class verbs the stem final *i* became *i̯* before a vowel, causing the expected yodization changes (**2.23**). As in the present active participle, the declension was consonantal in the nominative singular of all genders and in the nominative plural masculine; in other cases it followed the vocalic *-i̯-ŏ-* (M/N) and *-i̯-ā-* (F) stem declensions.

Table 18: Selected Late Proto-Slavic past active participle indefinite forms of *ved-* 'lead', *pьn-/pen-* 'stretch', *dvig-(nǫ-)* 'move', *pros-i-* 'ask', *děl-a-j-* 'do', *vid-ě-* 'see'

NOM. SG. M/N	vedъ	penъ	dvigъ	prošь	dělavъ	viděvъ
NOM. SG. F	vedъši	penъši	dvigъši	prošьši	dělavъši	viděvъši
NOM. PL. M	vedъše	penъše	dvigъše	prošьše	dělavъše	viděvъše
GEN. SG. M/N	vedъša	penъša	dvigъša	prošьša	dělavъša	viděvъša

The *resultative* or *perfect participle* is the most striking example of the tension between adjectival and verbal functions of participles. Its formant was the suffix *-l-* (**2.47.4.g**), which in Proto-Indo-European was adjectival. Its use in deverbative formations, however, favored the development of the participial function. It is for this reason that Slavic *-l-* forms combine adjectival and verbal meanings. Thus, the Russian phrase *Kak on smel* can mean 'How bold he is!' with the adjective *smel* (plural *smély*) or 'How did he dare!' with the past tense of the verb *smet'* 'to dare' (plural *sméli*). Similarly, the Russian adjective *príšlyj* 'foreign' or Polish adjective *przyszły* 'future' uses the same stem as the past tense of the verb 'to come' (Russian *prijtí*, Polish *przyjść*), which, being derived from the Proto-Slavic perfect tense (**2.58**), contains the suffix *-l-*. The resultative participle was formed on the infinitive stem. Its declension was that of the *-ŏ-* (M/N) and *-ā-* (F) stems. The adjectival meaning develops among intransitive verbs: *vęd-(nǫ-)* 'fade', *vęd-l-* 'faded'; *zьrěj-* 'ripen', *zьrě-l-* 'mature'; *gor-ě-* 'burn', *gorě-l-* 'burned'.

The *past passive participle* was formed with the suffixes *-t-* or *-n-* added to the infinitive stem. The declension was that of the *-ŏ-* (M/N) and *-ā-* (F) stems. The distribution of suffixes was as follows: *-t-* with the sonantic verbs of the root class, *-t-* or *-n-* with the semivocalic verbs of the root class, *-n-* elsewhere. The root diphthong in the sonantic verbs was in the zero ablaut grade. In *-i-*, semivocalic root, and consonantic root and *-nǫ-* verbs the suffix *-n-* was linked to the stem by the thematic vowel *-ě-* preceded in the semivocalic verbs by either *i̯* or *u̯*. The stem-final *-i-* of the *-i-* stems became *-i̯-*, causing yodization changes in the preceding consonant (**2.23**).

Table 19: Selected nominative singular masculine past passive participle indefinite forms in late Proto-Slavic

-t-	*pьn-/pen-* 'stretch', *pętъ* (< *pn̥-*) *pьr-/per-* 'push', *pr̥'tъ* (< *pr̥'-*)	*jьm-/jem-* 'seize', *jętъ* (< *m̥-*) *tьr-/ter-* 'rub', *tr̥'tъ* (< *tr̥'-*)
-t-/-n-	*bij-* 'beat', *bitъ/bijenъ*	*čuj-* 'feel', *čutъ/čuvenъ*
-n-	*pri-ved-* 'lead up', *privedenъ* *dar-ov-a-* 'donate', *darovanъ* *dvig-(nǫ-)* 'move', *dviženъ/dvignovenъ*	*u-kaz-a-* 'indicate', *ukazanъ* *sъ-děl-a-j-* 'make', *sъdělanъ*
	jьz-nos-i- 'carry out', *jьznošenъ*	*rod-i-* 'give birth', *rod'enъ*

2.59. Compound verbal categories. In its verbal function the resultative participle was used in compound verbal categories, expressing relative temporal or situational values. Such compound verbal categories consisted of the participle, which retained its gender distinctions, and an auxiliary, which was a finite form of the verb 'to be'.

The *perfect* indicated a connection between the past and the moment of speech. The verb 'to be' was in the present tense:

3 Sg.	M	neslь jestь	'he has carried'
	F	nesla jestь	'she has carried'
	N	neslo jestь	'it has carried'

The *pluperfect* indicated the earlier of two past actions. The verb 'to be' was in the imperfect or imperfective aorist:

3 Sg.	M	neslъ běaše/bě	'he had carried'
	F	nesla běaše/bě	'she had carried'
	N	neslo běaše/bě	'it had carried'

The *second (exact) future* indicated the earlier of two future actions. The verb 'to be' was used in its future tense formed on the stem *bǫd-* inflected according to the root verb class:

3 Sg.	M	neslъ bǫdetь	'he will have carried'
	F	nesla bǫdetь	'she will have carried'
	N	neslo bǫdetь	'it will have carried'

The *conditional* was used as an optative and in irreal 'if' clauses. The verb 'to be' was in the optative formed on the special stem *bi-* or, in younger texts, in the productive aorist. The optative was inflected according to the athematic conjugation and in Old Church Slavonic had the forms Sg. *bimь, bi, bi* and Pl. *bimъ, biste, bǫ*. The forms of the aorist were Sg. *byxъ, by, by;* Du. *byxově, bysta, byste;* Pl. *byxomъ, byste, byšę*. Thus, the conditional *žilъ* (*žila, žilo*) *bi/by* could be used as an optative 'would that he (she, it) lived!' or as a conditional 'if he (she, it) had lived'.

2.60. Verbal substantive. The verbal substantive was an *-i̯-ŏ-* stem neuter substantive formed by the addition of the suffix *-ь̂j-* (< *-ĭi̯-*)[174] to the stem of the past passive participle.

Table 20: Selected nominative singular forms of verbal substantives in Late Proto-Slavic

jьm-/jem- 'seize'	jętь̂je 'seizure'
bij- 'beat'	bitь̂je/bijenьje 'the beating'
pri-nes- 'bring'	prinesenь̂je 'the bringing'
dvig-(nǫ-) 'move'	dviženь̂je 'movement'
u-kaz-a- 'indicate'	ukazanь̂je 'indication'
děl-a-j- 'do'	dělanь̂je 'the doing'
mьn-ě- 'consider'	mьněnь̂je 'consideration'
nos-i- 'carry'	nošenь̂je 'the carrying'

174. In accordance with the alternation rule of tense jers, the suffix *-ь̂j-* could also appear as *-ij-* (**2.42**).

Unlike the past passive participle, however, which was typically formed from transitive verbs only, the verbal substantive was formed from both transitive and intransitive verbs. Like other substantives, the verbal substantive was inflected for case and number in addition to being marked for aspect and genus, the obligatory categories of the verb.

2.61. Syntactic reconstruction. In reconstructing the phonology or morphology of a language we do not search for absolute values of individual sounds or grammatical categories. Considered in isolation such values are not recoverable. Instead, our goal is to reconstruct phonological or grammatical systems of comparable and interrelated elements. Such systems, or paradigms, allow the linguist to view segments of linguistic structure in the context of a larger whole, to determine the relations among these segments, and to define thereby their place and function in the structure of language. To take an example from the vocalic paradigm of Early Proto-Slavic, the vowel *ă* is considered short, back, and low only in so far as it contrasts with other vowels of the inventory, the long *ā*, the front *ĕ* and the high *ŭ*. It is only through such a relativistic but systemic approach that the linguist may gain verifiable insights into the absolute values of individual sounds or grammatical categories and be reasonably certain that the reconstructed forms did in fact exist.

In contrast to phonology and morphology, the organizing principle of syntax is not paradigmatic. There are, to be sure, areas, such as the grammatical categories, where syntax intersects with morphology and where paradigms do enter into the descriptive process. There also exist stable patterns of relations among words in sentences or in segments of sentences, referred to as syntactic constructions. The fact remains, however, that syntactic constructions are not, for the most part, organized paradigmatically. This deprives the syntactician of the verification mechanism that is so useful in assessing the viability of phonological and morphological reconstructions. It also explains why syntactic reconstruction has occupied such a modest place in historical investigations.

There are other reasons for the diffidence with which historians of language propose and evaluate syntactic reconstructions. In the first place, it is difficult to define with any certainty the upper limit of Late Proto-Slavic. If Slavic linguistic unity ended before the Moravian mission (mid-ninth century), that is, about two or three centuries after the breakup of Slavic tribal unity, then Old Church Slavonic must be viewed as a literary language in its own right, descended from the southeastern dialect of Late Proto-Slavic. In this view, Late Proto-Slavic would be considered a spoken vehicle of pre-literary communication. If, however, Slavic linguistic unity is deemed to have extended into the tenth century and to have encompassed the language of the Cyrillo-Methodian translations, then we would have to include in our view of Late Proto-Slavic the mature and sophisticated literary output characterizing its southeastern dialect.

Such divergent views on the nature of Late Proto-Slavic affect the selection of sources on which a syntactic reconstruction is based. Whichever eventuality one adopts, one has to consider the evidence of Old Church Slavonic, the oldest variety of recorded Slavic, and to come to grips with the fact that all Old Church Slavonic texts are translations, often slavishly literal, from Greek or Latin. In this situation the task of sifting what was natively Slavic from what was transplanted, of separating what was common Slavic from what was regionally circumscribed, is crucial to the success of the reconstructing enterprise. There is also the danger that in the absence of definite criteria for the performance of these tasks, the investigator's initial vision of the nature of Late Proto-Slavic may be allowed to intrude upon the research and color the conclusions.

To illustrate these difficulties, let us turn our attention to the (Old) Church Slavonic participial construction known as the *dative absolute*. This construction formed a dependent clause in which a temporal or causal circumstance was expressed by a noun in the dative case modified by a participle (e.g. OCS *glagol'ǫštju emu* 'when/because he was speaking'). Although we have reliable paradigmatic evidence that participles existed in Proto-Slavic as a category inherited from Proto-Indo-European, can we be certain that the dative absolute construction existed there too? If one assumes that Late Proto-Slavic was an exclusively spoken language, one would have to conclude that a literary construction like the dative absolute is not native and that it was probably borrowed and adapted from the equivalent Greek construction, albeit with the dative instead of the Greek genitive. Its occurrence in medieval East Slavic and medieval Czech would then have to be explained as an instance of Old Church Slavonic influence. This view, adopted by many scholars, is opposed by those who cite the occurrence of absolute constructions in various Indo-European languages (dative absolute in Slavic and Germanic, genitive absolute in Greek, ablative absolute in Latin, locative absolute in Sanskrit). Such a wide compass suggests to them that all the particular instances of absolute constructions are descended from a common Proto-Indo-European ancestor whose obligatory oblique case found different expressions in different languages.

Given the ambiguity of Old Church Slavonic evidence, investigators have turned to other sources. Especially promising are those ancient Slavic texts that were least susceptible to non-Slavic literary influences, for instance, some varieties of Old East Slavic. Another useful source of information may be found in the syntax of modern Slavic dialects that are relatively free of outside interference. Important, too, is comparative evidence from other Indo-European languages, above all from Baltic, which was joined with Slavic in a period of shared development. Here, however, a word of caution is in order: our first records of Baltic are so late (Prussian from the fifteenth century, Lithuanian even later) that they may reflect Slavic syntactic models due to several centuries of political and cultural domination emanating from Rus' and Poland.

Descriptions of syntactic constructions may be couched in semantic, syntactic, or morphosyntactic terms. Such general notions as agent, patient, beneficiary, and duration (of an action) are semantic; elements of sentence structure such as subject, direct or indirect object, predicate, and complement are syntactic; morphosyntactic terms include such grammatical categories as gender, person, and tense (**2.46**). Thus, in the clause *jьzloviti rybǫ* 'to catch a fish' *rybǫ* could be described in semantic terms as the patient, in syntactic terms as the direct object, or in morphosyntactic terms as the accusative singular.

2.62. Syntactic constructions. Some syntactic relations were expressed by a system of rection (government), whereby a verb, noun, or preposition required a particular form of a noun—its case. Features of rection also defined the distinction between *transitive* and *intransitive* verbs, the latter specifying an obligatory absence of the direct object. Distinctions of rection were an inherent feature of the verb.

The opposition between the grammatical notions of subject and direct object was expressed by the distinction between the nominative case of the subject and the accusative or genitive cases of the direct object. By contrast, the semantic notions of agent and patient were not correlated with particular cases. The different parameters used in the definition of the grammatical (morphological and syntactic) and semantic notions determined the different functions of the reflexive and passive constructions. The subject-oriented *reflexive* constructions, in contrast to the *nonreflexive* constructions, indicated the centrality of the subject in the action or state expressed by the verb and neutralized the opposition between the agent and the patient. The patient-oriented *passive* constructions, in contrast to the *active* constructions, contained an obligatory patient expressed by the nominative of the subject and an optional agent expressed by an oblique case or a prepositional phrase. Thus, the subject could designate the agent in active constructions: *žena sъpase otrokъ* 'a woman saved the boy', the patient in passive constructions: *otrokъ bystъ sъpasenъ* 'the boy was saved' or either of these terms in reflective constructions: *otrokъ sę sъpase* 'the boy saved himself' or 'the boy was saved'.

While the opposition between the transitive and intrasitive verbs is one of *rection*, the oppositions between reflexive and nonreflexive verbs and between passive and active constructions are ones of verbal *genus* and *voice* respectively. These oppositions existed in a hierarchical rather than coordinate relationship as represented in the diagram below in which the lower branches are subordinated to the higher ones and the marked members of an opposition are on the left:

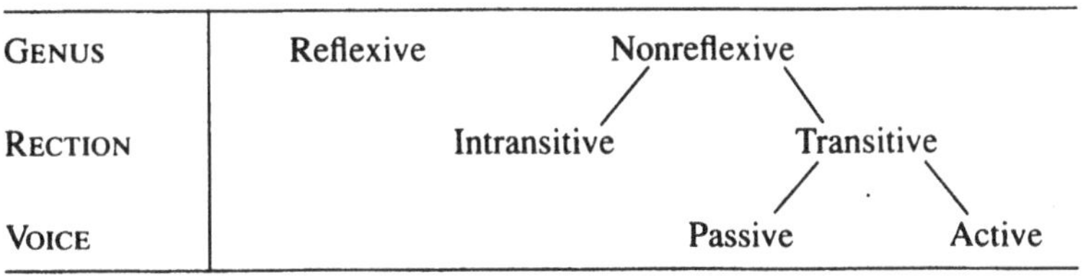

As indicated in the diagram, all verbs distinguished genus, but only nonreflexive verbs distinguished rection and only transitive verbs distinguished voice (**2.46**).

In addition to personal constructions, that is, constructions with a subject expressed by a noun or pronoun or contained in the verbal inflectional ending (see below), Proto-Slavic had *impersonal* (or *subjectless*) constructions which neutralized the categories of person, number, and gender, expressing them by the third-person singular (neuter), the least marked finite form of the verbal paradigm. Impersonal verbs were either intransitive or reflexive. They occurred in predications indicating involuntary or natural phenomena: *ne xъt'etь sę* 'there is no desire', *mьnitь sę* 'it seems', *grьmitь* 'there is thunder', *smr̥'ditь* 'there is a stench'.

The position of subject was typically filled by a nominal phrase in the nominative case, the position of predicate by a finite form of a verb or a nominal clause functioning as a predicative complement. A nominal phrase filling the position of the predicate was joined to the subject by the *copula*, typically the verb 'to be' in the third person. In some instances the copula in the present tense was omissible (Isačenko 1955). In personal constructions, the category of person was expressed by inflectional endings of the first and second person forms allowing for the *omission of the subject pronoun: věmь* 'I know', *věsi* 'thou knowest'. Overt expression of the pronominal subject was reserved for emphasis: *azъ věmь* '*I* know', *ty věsi* '*thou* knowest'.

Nouns (typically substantives) were modified by adjectives, gendered pronouns, numerals from 1 to 4, and participles in *attributive* constructions in which the modifiers agreed with noun heads in case, number, and gender. Attributive adjectives were either *indefinite* (nominal) or *definite* (pronominal), the latter indicating prior knowledge of the head noun. The marked definite adjectives were formed by combining the nominal form of the adjective with the appropriate form of the anaphoric pronoun *j-* (**2.49.1**). Thus, *dobrъ učenikъ/dobra učenica* 'a good pupil' vs. *dobrŝjь učenikъ/dobraja učenica* 'the good pupil (known to the addressee)'.

Verbs were modified by *adverbs*, a large class of uninflected modifiers derived from pronouns, adjectives, or substantives. *Pronominal adverbs* were derived from pronouns, such as the anaphoric *jь* 'that which is known', interrogative *kъ*, quantitative *vьsь/vьšь* 'all', demonstrative *tъ* 'this', *ovъ* 'that', *sь* 'this here', *onъ* 'that yonder' (**2.48.2**), and special pronominal suffixes: *-de* 'place of rest', *-amo* 'motion to', *-ǫdu/-ǫdě* 'motion from', *-gda* 'time when', *-ako* 'manner', *-l-* 'quantity'.[175] These suffixes were added either to the stem of the pronoun (vocalic suffixes) or to the accusative singular masculine or neuter (consonantal suffixes). Thus, *t-/to* 'this' formed the following adverbs: *tamo* 'thither', *tǫdu/tǫdě* 'from there', *togda* 'then', *tako* 'so', *tolь/toli* 'so much'. *Adjectival adverbs* were a productive class formed from the accusative and locative singular neuter of indefinite (nominal) adjectives, e.g. *dobro* and *dobrě* 'well', *soldъko* and *soldъcě* 'sweetly'. The adjectives in *-ьsk-* formed adverbs of manner from the instrumental plural in *-y* (*-ŏ-* stems), e.g. *slověnьsky* 'in Slavic'.[176] *Substantival adverbs* were frozen case forms of substantives denoting time or place. They were typically accusatives or locatives singular, e.g. *dьnь sь* 'today' (accusative), *gorě* 'above' (locative); however, other cases occurred as well, e.g. *domovi* 'homeward' (dative), *not'ьjǫ* 'at night' (instrumental).

According to the testimony of early Slavic literary monuments, *negation* did not have to be doubled, as is the case in modern Slavic languages. Thus, Old Church Slavonic *nikъto že možetъ* 'nobody can' corresponds to modern Russian *niktó ne móžet*. Whether the lack of doubling of negation was a native Slavic construction or was borrowed from Greek remains an open question.

Questions demanding a yes-or-no answer included as their minimum requirement the foregrounding of the word inquired about and a rising phrasal intonation, e.g. *otrokъ jьzlovi rybǫ?* 'did the boy catch a fish?', *jьzlovi otrokъ rybǫ?* 'did the boy *catch* a fish?' For greater emphasis an enclitic interrogative particle (e.g. *li*) followed the first stressed word in the clause, e.g. *vidiši rěkǫ?* 'Do you see the river?' or *vidiši li rěkǫ?* 'Do you *see* the river?' Other questions were introduced by interrogative words containing the Slavic reflexes *k* or *č* of the Proto-Indo-European interrogative root k^{w}- (English *wh-*). They included gendered pronouns, e.g. *čŝj-* 'whose', *kolik-* 'to what degree', *kotor-* 'which (of a number)', *kŝj-* 'which'; nongendered pronouns, e.g. *čьto* 'what', *kъto* 'who' (**2.48.2**); and adverbs, e.g. *kako* 'like what', *kamъ/kamo* 'where to', *kǫdě/kǫdu* 'where from', *kъde* 'where'.

Relative clauses were introduced by the anaphoric pronoun *j-* 'that which is known' and its derivatives, followed by the relativizing particle *že/žь*, e.g. *otrokъ jьže bystь sъpasenъ* 'the boy who was saved', *žena jǫže viděxъ* 'the woman whom I saw', *otrokъ jemuže otьcь jestь umr̥'lъ* 'the boy whose father died', *město jьde jestь umr̥'lъ* 'the place where he died'. In agreement with the law of open syllables, which brought about the shifting of morpheme boundaries (**2.20**), the pronoun *j-* occurring after prepositions was replaced by *n'-* (from *n-j-*), e.g. *pon'eže* (< **po je že*) 'because of that', *don'ьdeže* (< **do jьde že*) 'until when'.[177]

175. Adverbs with *-l-* appeared usually as case forms of the *-ĭ-* stem declension, often extended by the particle *k(o)*.

176. The instrumental plural in *-ьmi* (*-ĭ-* stems) is also found in the adverbial function, e.g. OCS *velьmi* 'much'.

177. This alternation began as an automatic transfer of *n* from the syllable-final position to the syllable-initial position. At first it affected the prepositions *kъn-* 'toward', *sъn-* 'with', and *vъn* 'in' but was later extended by analogy to all prepositions.

Also used in the relativizing function were interrogative words, usually without the particle *že/žь*, e.g. *ne znajǫ česo dati* 'I do not know what to give', *tъ kъto xot'etь* 'he who wishes', *město kъde živetь* 'the place where (s)he lives'.

2.63. Use of cases. Outside of prepositional phrases, cases had the following principal functions:

The *nominative* was the case of the subject and of the predicative complement, e.g. *ta žena bě neplody* 'this woman was barren'.

The *accusative* was a typical case of the direct object, e.g. *orati pol'e* 'to plow a field', *roditi dъt'erь* 'to give birth to a daughter'. It appeared also in predicative apposition to the direct object, e.g. *obrete jь sъdorvъ* '(s)he found him (to be) healthy'. This construction, known as the "double accusative," occurred in Old Church Slavonic and Old East Slavic. The accusative of measure is known chiefly from temporal expressions, e.g. *truditi sę godinǫ* (*dъva dьni, pętь dьnъ, vьsь životъ*) 'to work for an hour (two days, five days, all one's life'). In spatial expressions the accusative was used after verbs of motion: *iti vъnъ* 'to go outside'. The accusative singular neuter of indefinite (nominal) adjectives formed adverbs of manner: *tajьno* 'secretly', *lěpo* 'handsomely', *boso* 'barefoot', *rano* 'early'.

The *genitive* was a quantifying case. In this function it contrasted with the accusative as a direct object of verbs, e.g. *ukrade sěno* (Acc.) '(s)he stole hay' but *ukrade sěna* (Gen.) '(s)he stole some hay'. The genitive functioned also as an object of quantifying words, e.g. *malo sěna* 'a little hay', including numerals (from 'five' up), e.g. *pętь synovъ* 'five sons'. It was also used as the complement of verbs containing an element of quantification, that is, verbs whose domain over their object was not complete. Such were the negated transitive verbs, e.g. *ne dati vody* 'not to give any water'; verbs of durative perception, e.g. *slušati slovesъ* 'to listen to words'; verbs of desire', e.g. *žędati vody* 'to thirst for water'; the supine, e.g. *prijiti lovitъ rybъ* 'to come (in order) to catch fish'; and the verbal substantive, e.g. *lovl'enĭje rybъ* 'the catching of fish'. In possessive and partitive functions the genitive marked the subordinated noun, e.g. *nožь otьca* 'father's knife', *čaša vody* 'a cup of water'.

In certain marked environments, the genitive replaced the accusative as the case of the direct object. One such situation occurred when the falling together of the nominative and accusative singular endings of the masculine *-ŏ-/-i̯-ŏ-* stems (*-ъ/-ь*) and *-ŭ-* stems (*-ъ*) created a potential confusion between the subject and the direct object. To preserve the distinction, the accusative ending was replaced by the genitive ending (*-a*) in nouns denoting male persons, that is, in phrases in which both the subject and the object were equally likely to perform the action. Thus, the genitive ending in *mojь bratrъ sъrěte pǫtьnika* 'my brother met a (male) traveler' contrasted with the regular accusative ending in *mojь bratrъ sъrěte pǫtьnicǫ* 'my brother met a (female) traveler' or *mojь bratrъ ubi vl̥kъ* 'my brother killed a wolf'. The resulting accusative/genitive syncretism led to the creation of the masculine personal or *virile* subgender. This process continued in the histories of individual Slavic languages culminating in the creation of the (masculine) *animate* subgender.

The *dative* was a directional case and, as such, served as the case of the indirect object, e.g. *dad'ь jemu vody* 'give him water!' It also indicated the agent/beneficiary in impersonal constructions, e.g. *jemu sę ne xъt'etь* 'he does not feel like it', and functioned as the head noun in "dative with infinitive" constructions, e.g. *tomu ne byti* 'this will not happen'. The beneficiary aspect of the dative led to its use in the possessive function, e.g. *nožь otьcu* 'father's knife'.

The *locative* singular of nouns denoted localization in time or space, e.g. *utrě* 'on the following day', *zimě* 'in wintertime', *pozdě* 'late', *dolě* 'below'. With indefinite (nominal) adjectives (occasionally also nouns) the locative expressed manner, e.g. *dobrě* 'well', *jarě* 'strongly', *javě* 'openly', *godě* 'agreeably' (from *godъ* 'proper time'), *zadi* 'behind' (from *zadь* 'back'). Eventually such prepositionless locatives were adverbialized and the locative became limited to prepositional phrases, giving rise to its alternative name, the *prepositional* case.

The *instrumental* was a case of an accessory to the performance of an action; it denoted an instrument, e.g. *rězati noženь* 'to cut with a knife', means or manner of performance, e.g. *pomajati rǫkojǫ* 'to wave with one's hand'. In temporal and spatial expressions it became adverbialized, e.g. *jedinojǫ* 'once', *not'ьjǫ* 'at night', *lěsomь* 'through the woods', *dorgojǫ* 'along the way'.

The *vocative* was a form of address which had no syntactic functions and consequently cannot be considered a case. However, it patterned like a case and is therefore conveniently included with case paradigms. It was used with animate, chiefly personal, masculine and feminine singular substantives, and it was only in the singular substantival declension that it had its own distinct forms.[178]

In prepositional phrases all cases except the nominative occurred. Of prepositions governing one case only, the genitive was far and away the most common. It occurred with the simple prepositions *bez* 'without', *do* 'to', *jьz* 'out of', *otь* 'from', and *u* 'near' as well as with derived prepositions such as *blizъ* 'near', *kromě* 'outside', and *vr̥'xu* 'on top', and with compound prepositions such as *jьz-podъ* 'from below' and *jьz-za* 'from behind'. The genitive was also used with the postpositions *děl'a/dьl'a* 'for' and *radi* 'for'. The prepositions *kъ(n)* 'toward' and *protivъ/protivǫ* 'against' took the dative, while *pri* 'next to' and *med'u* 'between' governed the locative and instrumental respectively.

Prepositions governing more than one case had variable meanings or functions. The prepositions *na* 'on', *nadъ* 'above', *o(b)* 'at (against)', *perdъ* 'before', *podъ* 'under', *vъ(n)* 'in', and *za* 'behind, after' with the accusative indicated 'motion toward'. To indicate place of rest or location the prepositions *na* 'on', *o(b)* 'at (about)', and *vъ(n)* 'in' took the locative; *po* 'over, above' took the dative; *perdъ* 'before', *podъ* 'under', and *za* 'behind, after' took the instrumental. The preposition *sъ* meant 'down from' with the genitive but 'accompanied by' with the instrumental. The preposition *po* meant 'for, up to' with the accusative but 'after' with the locative.

2.64. Word order. It may be safely assumed that Late Proto-Slavic syntax did not stray significantly from its Proto-Indo-European base. Both languages had at their disposal extremely rich inflectional systems that allowed for extensive use of morphosyntactic relations, that is, for constructions in which inflectional endings were the chief markers of the function and place of words in their clauses. This freed word order to function as an expressive device. Even so, some constraints on word order should be noted: (a) in phrases consisting of subject, object, and finite verb the subject did not occupy the final position and the object did not occupy the initial position; (b) the indirect object preceded the direct object; (c) the head

178. The special status of the vocative in the declensional system is best illustrated by the fact that it has survived as a grammatical category in modern Bulgarian, where case distinctions have been abolished, but has been eliminated from modern Russian, which not only has preserved Proto-Slavic case distinctions but has added to them.

noun in an attributive construction was typically preceded by the adjective and followed by the genitive of possession; (d) numerals preceded the noun counted; (e) interrogative pronouns and adverbs as well as relative pronouns occupied the initial position in their clauses; (f) enclitics followed the first stressed word in their clause.[179]

2.65. Composition of the word stock. Proto-Slavic lexical stock, as reconstructed through a comparison of vocabularies of all the Slavic languages, belonged to the sphere of man's physical environment and emotional concerns, personal attributes, family and community ties, occupations, basic needs and desires, feelings, and sensations. Many Proto-Slavic words had cognates in other Indo-European languages and may therefore be considered a Proto-Indo-European inheritance. Others were particular to Balto-Slavic or Proto-Slavic, representing local innovations or borrowings from the languages with which the Slavs came into contact.

A sample of Late Proto-Slavic vocabulary is given below. Except in instances of major semantic divergence, roots are typically represented by one lexical item only. Adjectives, pronouns, and verbs are quoted in their basic stems. Except for the numerals, all entries are cited alphabetically.

2.65.1. Substantives.

(a) **Agriculture and crafts:** *borna* 'harrow', *borzda* 'furrow', *br̥tь* 'beehive', *čerda* 'herd', *dolto* 'chisel', *dolъ* 'pit', *gvozdь* 'nail', *jadъ* 'poison', *jarьmo* 'yoke', *jьskra* 'spark', *kalъ* 'dirt', *klinъ* 'wedge', *kolo* 'wheel', *kolъ* 'stake', *koryto* 'trough', *kosa* 'scythe', *krajь* 'edge', *krǫgъ* 'ring', *krupa* 'groats', *lěsъ* 'forest', *lopata* 'spade', *lyko* 'bast', *medъ* 'honey', *med'a* 'boundary line', *melko* 'milk', *merža* 'net', *město* 'place', *měxъ* 'sack', *moltъ* 'hammer', *mostъ* 'bridge', *nitь* 'thread', *nožь* 'knife', *oldь(ji)* 'boat', *ordlo* 'wooden plow', *osь* 'axle', *pila* 'saw', *pivo* 'beer', *plodъ* 'fruit', *plugъ* 'plough', *pojasъ* 'belt', *poltьno* 'cloth', *pol'e* 'field', *pormъ* 'ferry', *pǫto* 'fetter', *remy* 'strap', *rojь* 'swarm', *rovъ* 'hole', *runo* 'fleece', *rъd'a* 'rust', *sedъlo* 'saddle', *sěno* 'hay', *sětь* 'net', *sito* 'sieve', *sokъ* 'juice', *solma* 'straw', *soxa* 'branch', *sr̥'pъ* 'sickle', *stado* 'flock', *stermę* 'stirrup', *stl̥bъ* 'post', *stogъ* 'haystack', *strěla* 'arrow', *syrъ* 'cheese', *těsto* 'dough', *toporъ* 'axe', *trudъ* 'work', *ulêjъ* 'hive', *vědro* 'bucket', *věnьcь* 'wreath', *verteno* 'loom', *vl̥'na* 'wool', *voskъ* 'wax', *xlěbъ* 'bread', *xlěvъ* '(animal) shelter'.

(b) **Animals:** *(j)agnę* 'lamb', *(j)aje* 'egg', *(j)astrębъ* 'hawk', *(j)aščerъ* 'lizard', *blъxa* 'flea', *bobrъ* 'beaver', *bъčela* 'bee', *bykъ* 'bull', *čr̥'vъ* 'worm', *dętelъ* 'woodpecker', *drobь* 'domestic fowl', *drozdъ* 'thrush', *gadъ* 'serpent', *gnida* 'louse', *golǫbь* 'pigeon', *gǫsь* 'goose', *jelenь* 'deer', *ježь* 'hedgehog', *kobyla* 'mare', *komarъ* 'mosquito', *kon'ь* 'horse', *korva* 'cow', *kotъ* 'cat', *koza* 'goat', *kuna* 'marten', *kura* 'hen', *lisъ* 'fox', *lososь* 'salmon', *medvědь* 'bear', *molь* 'moth', *morva* 'ant', *muxa* 'fly', *myšь* 'mouse', *orьlъ* 'eagle', *osa* 'wasp', *osьlъ* 'donkey', *ovьca* 'sheep', *(v)ǫgrь* 'eel', *(v)ǫžь* 'snake', *pa(j)ǫkъ* 'spider', *porsę* 'piglet', *pьsъ* 'dog', *pъta* 'bird', *rakъ* 'crayfish', *ryba* 'fish', *rysь* 'lynx', *skotъ* 'cattle', *sokolъ* 'falcon', *sorka* 'magpie', *sova* 'owl', *sr̥'na* 'doe', *suka* 'bitch', *svinъ* 'pig', *telę* 'calf', *turъ* 'aurochs', *veprь* 'boar', *vl̥'kъ* 'wolf', *volъ* 'ox', *vorna* 'crow', *vornъ* 'raven', *vydra* 'otter', *vъšь* 'louse', *zmêja* 'viper', *zvěrь* 'wild animal', *žaba* 'frog', *žeravъ* 'crane', *žerbę* 'foal', *žl̥'vъ* 'turtle', *žukъ* 'beetle'.

179. Compare Ernst Berneker's (1900 or 1910) analysis and its summary in Birnbaum 1979:195–196.

(c) **Body:** *bedro* 'hip', *bokъ* 'side', *bolь* 'pain', *borda* 'beard', *bry* 'brow', *br'uxo* 'belly', *čelo* 'forehead', *čerpъ* 'skull', *červo* 'womb', *dęsna* 'gum', *dolnь* 'palm', *golěnь* 'shin', *golsъ* 'voice', *golva* 'head', *govьno* 'excrement', *gǫba* 'lip', *griva* 'mane', *grǫdь* 'chest', *gr̥bъ* 'hump', *gr̥dlo* 'throat', *jazva* 'wound', *językъ* 'tongue', *kolěno* 'knee', *kopyto* 'hoof', *kostь* 'bone', *koža* 'skin', *kridlo* 'wing', *kry* 'blood', *likъ* 'face', *lono* 'womb', *lъbъ* 'cranium', *męso* 'meat', *mozgъ* 'brain', *mǫdo* 'testicle', *noga* 'leg, foot', *nogъtь* '(finger)nail', *nosъ* 'nose', *nozdri* 'nostrils', *oko* 'eye', *olkъtь* 'elbow', *ǫsъ* 'moustache', *ǫtroba* 'entrails', *pero* 'feather', *pęstь* 'fist', *pęta* 'heel', *plet'e* 'shoulder', *plěšь* 'baldness', *pl̥tь* 'flesh', *potъ* 'sweat', *pǫpъ* 'navel', *pr̥'sь* 'breast', *pr̥'stъ* 'finger', *ramę* 'arm', *rana* 'wound', *rebro* 'rib', *ręsa* 'eyelash', *rogъ* 'horn', *rǫka* 'hand', *ryjь* 'snout', *sadlo* 'fat', *slina* 'saliva', *slьza* 'tear', *sr̥'dьce* 'heart', *stopa* 'foot', *šȋja* 'neck', *temę* 'cranium', *tělo* 'body', *tukъ* 'fat', *tylъ* 'back', *uxo* 'ear', *usta* 'mouth', *verdъ* 'wart', *věko* 'eyelid', *volsъ* 'hair', *vymę* 'udder', *zadъ* 'behind', *zlьčь* 'bile', *zǫbъ* 'tooth', *žila* 'vein'.

(d) **Household:** *čaša* 'cup', *čel'adь* 'servants', *domъ* 'house', *dъska* 'board', *dvьrь* 'door', *dvorъ* 'courtyard', *dymъ* 'smoke', *gnězdo* 'nest', *gordъ* 'walled place', *gr̥nъ* 'hearth', *gr̥stь* 'handful', *jьstъba* 'hut', *klětь* 'cage', *kl'učь* 'key', *kǫtъ* 'corner', *kotьlъ* 'kettle', *krěslo* 'chair', *lava* 'bench', *lože* 'bed', *měra* 'measure', *okъno* 'window', *ǫglъ* 'corner', *pet'ь* 'oven', *pędь* 'foot (measure of length)', *porgъ* 'threshold', *sad'a* 'soot', *sol'* 'salt', *stěna* 'wall', *stolъ* 'table', *stǫpenь* 'step', *strěxa* 'thatched roof', *svět'a* 'candle', *tьlo* 'floor', *vьsь* 'village', *vorta* 'gate'.

(e) **Landscape and seasons:** *bergъ* 'shore', *blěskъ* 'flash', *bolto* 'bog, marsh', *brodъ* 'ford', *bur'a* 'storm', *dolъ* 'dale', *dorga* 'road', *dьnь* 'day', *dъno* 'bottom', *dъzd'ь* 'rain', *glina* 'clay', *gora* 'mountain', *gradъ* 'hail', *gromъ* 'thunder', *groza* 'storm', *gruda* 'mound', *gvězda/ʒvězda* 'star', *ilъ* 'mud', *jama* 'cave', *jesenь* 'fall', *jezero* 'lake', *(j)utro* 'morning', *jьskra* 'spark', *kamy* 'stone', *kapl'a* 'drop', *kremy* 'flint', *ledъ* 'ice', *lěto* 'summer', *lęda* 'virgin land', *luna* 'moon', *mědь* 'copper', *mělъ* 'chalk', *měsęcь* 'moon', *morkъ* 'darkness', *morzъ* 'frost', *mor'e* 'lake, sea', *mьgla* 'fog', *nebo* 'sky', *not'ь* 'night', *ognь* 'fire', *olovo* 'lead', *ostrovъ* 'island', *ǫglь* 'coal', *pěna* 'foam', *pěsъkъ* 'sand', *popelъ* 'ash', *porxъ* 'dust', *pǫtь* 'way', *rěka* 'river', *rosa* 'dew', *sěra* 'sulfur', *sьrebro* 'silver', *skala* 'rock', *sl̥nce* 'sun', *smola* 'pitch', *sněgъ* 'snow', *solь* 'salt', *struja* 'stream', *světъ* 'light', *tьma* 'darkness', *tǫča* 'cloud', *večerь* 'evening', *vesna* 'spring', *větrъ* 'wind', *vl̥'na* 'wave', *voda* 'water', *vr̥'xъ* 'top', *xl̥mъ* 'hill', *zar'a* 'dawn', *zemь* 'earth', *zima* 'winter', *znojь* '(summer) heat', *zolto* 'gold', *žarъ* 'heat', *želězo* 'iron'.

(f) **People:** *baba* 'grandmother', *brat(r)ъ* 'brother', *čьlověkъ* 'man', *dědъ* 'grandfather, ancestor', *děti* 'children', *děva* 'virgin', *děverь* 'brother-in-law', *dъt'i* 'daughter' *gostь* 'guest', *korl'ь* 'king', *kьmotra* 'godmother', *kъnęʒь* 'prince', *l'udъ* 'people', *mati* 'mother', *mǫžь* 'man, husband', *nevěsta* 'bride', *orbъ* 'slave', *otьcь* 'father', *plemę* 'tribe', *pl̥kъ* 'host', *rodъ* 'family', *sestra* 'sister', *sluga* 'servant', *snъxa* 'daughter-in-law', *strȋjь* 'paternal uncle', *sъlъ* 'envoy', *svatъ* 'matchmaker', *svekry* 'wife's mother-in-law', *synъ* 'son', *tl̥mačь* 'interpreter', *tьstь* 'husband's father-in-law', *vьdova* 'widow', *vod'ь* 'leader', *vojinъ* 'warrior', *vorgъ* 'enemy', *ujь* 'maternal uncle', *zętь* 'male kinsman', *zъly* 'sister-in-law', *žena* 'married woman'.

(g) **Vegetation:** *(j)ablъko* 'apple', *(j)agoda* 'berry', *(j)asenь* 'ash', *berstъ* 'elm', *berza* 'birch', *bobъ* 'bean', *borъ* 'pine (forest)', *bukъ* 'beech', *dervo* 'tree', *dǫbъ* 'oak', *gorxъ* 'pea', *grabъ* 'hornbeam', *gribъ* 'mushroom', *jagoda* 'berry', *jemela* 'holly', *jedla* 'fir', *jęčьmy* 'barley', *jędro* 'kernel', *klenъ* 'maple', *kolsъ* 'ear of corn', *konop'e* 'hemp', *kopriva* 'nettles', *kora* 'bark', *korę* 'root', *kъrь* 'bush', *květъ/cvětъ* 'flower', *lipa* 'linden', *listъ* 'leaf', *lьnъ* 'flax', *malina* 'raspberry', *mъxъ* 'moss', *olьxa* 'alder', *orěxъ* 'nut', *ovьsъ* 'oats', *paportь* 'fern', *plěsnь* 'mold', *proso* 'millet', *pьnь* 'trunk', *pьšenica* 'wheat', *rěpa* 'turnip', *'rъžь* 'rye', *sěmę* 'seed', *sosna* 'pine', *sǫkъ* 'knot', *stьblo* 'blade', *trava* 'grass', *tr̥stь* 'reed', *tr̥'nъ* 'thorn', *versъ* 'heather', *větь* 'branch', *vęzъ* 'elm', *vr̥'ba* 'willow', *zr̥'no* 'grain', *želǫdь* 'acorn'.

(h) **Society:** *beseda* 'conversation', *běda* 'need', *běsъ* 'devil', *bogъ* 'god', *blędь* 'error', *cěna* 'price', *čarъ* 'magic', *časъ* 'time', *čęstь* 'part', *činъ* 'order', *čislo* 'number', *čьstь* 'rank', *čr̥'tъ* 'devil', *čudo* 'wonder', *darъ* 'gift', *dělo* 'work', *divo* 'wonder', *doba* '(propitious) time', *duxъ* 'spirit', *gněvъ* 'anger', *godъ* '(proper) time', *goldъ* 'hunger', *grěxъ* 'sin', *jьgra* 'play, *jьmę* 'name', *krikъ* 'shout', *kъn'iga* 'book', *(pa)mętь* 'memory', *měna* 'exchange', *měra* 'measure', *mirъ* 'peace', *myslь* 'thought', *myto* 'payment', *pelnъ* 'captivity', *plěmę* 'tribe', *rajь* 'paradise', *slovo* 'word', *směxъ* 'laughter', *sǫdъ* 'judgment', *sramъ* 'shame', *svoboda* 'freedom', *terba* 'need', *umъ* 'mind', *věra* 'faith', *vina* 'guilt', *vol'a* 'will', *xvala* 'glory'.

2.65.2. Pronouns. *(j)azъ/m-/v-/n-* '(first person)', *č-* 'what', *čě̂j-* 'whose', *j-* 'that which is known', *jelik-* 'to the known degree', *kak-* 'like what', *kolik-* 'to what degree', *kotor-* 'which (of a number)', *kě̂j-* 'which', *k-* 'who', *moj-* 'my', *mъnog-* 'many', *naš-* 'our', *on-* 'that yonder (third person)', *ov-* 'that', *s-* 'this here', *s-* '(reflexive)', *sam-* 'self', *sic-* 'like this (nearby)', *selikъ* 'to this degree', *svoj-* 'one's own', *t-* 'this (third person)', *t-/v-* '(second person)', *tak-* 'like this', *tolik-* 'to that degree', *tvoj-* 'thy', *vaš-* 'your', *vьs'-/vьš-* 'all'.

2.65.3. Adjectives.

(a) **Animate characteristics:** *bogat-* 'rich', *bolg-* 'good', *bol'ě̂j-* 'better', *br̥z-* 'fast', *buj-* 'violent', *bystr-* 'fast', *čist-* 'clean', *dik-* 'wild', *dobr-* 'timely', *dorg-* 'dear', *drug-* 'other', *glup-* 'foolish', *glux-* 'deaf', *gol-* 'naked', *gotov-* 'ready', *gr̥d-* 'proud', *jar-* 'strong', *krěp-* 'powerful', *lěn-* 'lazy', *lěp-* 'shapely', *mil-* 'likable', *mold-* 'young', *mǫdr-* 'wise', *nag-* 'naked', *něm-* 'dumb', *pěš-* 'pedestrian', *rad-* 'glad', *silьn-* 'strong', *sir-* 'orphaned', *skǫp-* 'avaricious', *slab-* 'weak', *slěp-* 'blind', *star-* 'old', *svěž-* 'fresh', *svęt-* 'holy', *syt-* 'satiated', *sъdorv-* 'healthy', *tix-* 'still', *tęg-* 'heavy', *trězv-* 'sober', *t'ud'-* 'strange', *vesel-* 'merry', *xorbr-* 'brave', *xrom-* 'lame', *xud-* 'bad', *xytr-* 'cunning', *zъl-* 'angry', *živ-* 'alive'.

(b) **Colors:** *běl-* 'white', *blěd-* 'pale', *čr̥'mьn-/čr̥'vl'en-* 'red', *čr̥'n-* 'black', *gněd-* 'chestnut, bay', *jasn-* 'clear', *polv-* 'pale (fallow, blond)', 'gray (blue)', *rud-/rus-/ryd'-* '(brownish) red', *sěr-/šěr-* 'gray', *sin-/sině̂j-* 'livid, dark blue', *siv-* 'silver, gray', *směd-/sněd-* 'swarthy', *vorn-* 'black (of animals)', *zelen-* 'green', *zolt-* 'gold', *žl̥'t-* 'yellow'.

(c) **Sensations:** *bridъk-* 'sharp', *gorьk-* 'bitter', *kysl-* 'sour', *l'ut-* 'harsh', *mękъk-* 'soft', *mokr-* 'wet', *lьgъk-* 'light', *ostr-* 'sharp', *soldъk-* 'sweet', *sux-* 'dry', *syr-* moist', *tepl-* 'warm', *tix-* 'still', *tǫp-* 'blunt', *tvr̥'d-* 'hard', *xold-* 'cold'.

(d) **Time and space:** *blizъk-* 'near', *cěl-* 'whole', *čęst-* 'frequent', *dalek-* 'distant (in space)', *davьn-* 'distant (in time)', *dl̥'g-* 'long', *glǫbok-* 'deep', *kortъk-* 'short', *kriv-* 'crooked', *krǫgl-* 'round', *krǫt-* 'bending', *lěv-* 'left', *lix-* 'extra', *mal-* 'small', *nizъk-* 'low', *nov-* 'new', *orvьn-* 'even', *ǫzъk-* 'narrow', *pl̥'n-* 'full', *prav-* 'right', *prost-* 'straight', *pust-* 'empty', *rědъk-* 'rare', *skor-* 'fast', *širok-* 'wide', *těsn-* 'narrow', *tьnъk-* 'thin', *velik-* 'big', *vysok-* tall'.

2.65.4. Numerals. The basic cardinal numerals were *dъva* '2', *tri* '3', *četyre* '4', *pętь* '5', *šestь* '6', *sedmь* '7', *osmь* '8', *devętь* '9', *desętь* '10', *sъto* '100', *tysęt'ь* '1000'. Of the ordinal numerals, special roots were used by *pr̥'v-* 'first' and *vъtor-* 'second'.

2.65.5. Verbs (see the classification of verbal stems in **2.50**).

(a) **Athematic:** *dad-/da-* 'give', *jad-* 'eat', *jes-/s-* 'be' (present-tense stem), *věd-/věd-ě-* 'know'.

(b) **Consonantic root:** *berg-* 'protect', *běg-* 'run', *blęd-* 'err', *bl'ud-* 'guard', *bod-* 'butt', *cvьt-/cvit-* 'bloom', *čьt-/čit-* 'count, read', *gnet-* 'press', *gǫd-* 'play', *greb-* 'dig', *gręd-* 'go', *gryz-* 'bite', *jeb-* 'copulate', *klad-* 'lay', *krad-* 'steal', *lěz-* 'climb', *lęg-/lěg-* 'lie down', *met-* 'sweep', *męt-* 'stir', *mog-* 'be able', *nes-* 'carry', *orst-* 'grow', *pad-* 'fall', *pas-* 'graze', *pek-* 'bake', *plet-* 'braid', *pręd-* 'weave', *rek-* 'speak', *sěk-* 'cut', *sterg-* 'guard', *strig-* 'shear', *tek-* 'flow', *tep-* 'strike', *tręs-* 'shake', *ved-* 'lead', *velk-* 'drag', *vez-* 'transport', *vold-* 'rule', *žьg-/žeg-* 'burn'.

(c) **Sonantic root:** *čьn-/čen-* 'begin', *klьn-/klen-* 'swear', *mьn-/men-* 'crease', *pьn-/pen-* 'stretch', *dъm-/dom-* 'blow', *jьm-/jem-* 'take', *žьm-/žem-* 'squeeze', *mьr-/mer-* 'die', *pьr-/per-* 'push', *stьr-/ster-* 'stretch', *tьr-/ter-* 'rub'.

(d) **Semivocalic root:** *bij-* 'beat', *brij-* 'cut', *čuj-* 'feel', *gnij-* 'rot', *grěj-* 'warm', *kryj-* 'hide', *kuj-* 'forge', *lij-* 'pour', *myj-* 'wash', *pij-* 'drink', *pl'uj-* 'spit', *poj-* 'sing', *ryj-* 'dig', *spěj-* 'be in time', *šij-* 'sew', *-uj-* 'shoe', *znaj-* 'know', *zьrěj-* 'ripen'; *plov-* 'float'.

(e) **Vocalic *-nǫ-*:** *ma-nǫ-* 'signal', *mi-nǫ-* 'pass', *ply-nǫ-* 'flow', *pl'u-nǫ-* 'spit', *sly-nǫ-* 'be known', *su-nǫ-* 'glide'.

(f) **Consonantic *-nǫ-*** (omitted consonants are bracketed; see **2.50.2 [2a]**): *dъx-nǫ-* 'breathe', *dvig-nǫ-* 'move', *gъ[b]-nǫ-* 'bend', *gy[b]-nǫ-* 'perish', *ka[p]-nǫ-* 'drip', *kos-nǫ-* 'touch', *kys-nǫ-* 'turn sour', *lьg-nǫ-* 'stick', *mr̥'z-nǫ-* 'freeze', *sęg-nǫ-* 'reach', *sty[d]-nǫ-*, 'get cold', *sъx-nǫ-* 'dry', *to[p]-nǫ-* 'drown', *vę[d]-nǫ-* 'wilt', *zę[b]-nǫ-* 'feel cold'.

(g) ***-a-*:** *alk-a-/olk-a-* 'hunger', *baj-a-* 'tell', *čaj-a-* 'expect', *čes-a-* 'comb', *čr̥'p-a-* 'ladle', *isk-a-* 'search', *kap-a-* 'drip', *kǫp-a-* 'bathe', *kaz-a-* 'show', *laj-a-* 'bark', *liz-a-* 'lick', *lъg-a-* 'lie', *maj-a-* 'beckon', *maz-a-* 'spread', *or-a-* 'plough', *plak-a-* 'weep', *plęs-a-* 'dance', *rěz-a-* 'cut', *sěj-a-* 'sow', *sъl-a-* 'send', *sъp-a-* 'sleep', *šьpъt-a-* 'whisper', *taj-a-* 'melt', *tes-a-* 'hew', *tъk-a-* 'prick', *vęz-a-* 'tie', *zьd-a-/zid-a-* 'build'.

(h) ***-ov-a-*:** *cěl-ov-a-* 'greet', *dar-ov-a-* 'donate', *kup-ov-a-* 'buy', *mil-ov-a-* 'love', *věr-ov-a-* 'believe', *voj-ev-a-* 'make war', *vrač-ev-a-* 'heal'.

(i) ***-a-j-*** and ***-ěj-*:** *blisk-a-j-* 'flash', *blьv-a-j-* 'spit', *děl-a-j-* 'do', *ględ-a-j-* 'observe', *gněv-a-j-* 'anger', *jьgr-a-j-* 'play', *kop-a-j-* 'dig', *pl̥z-a-j-* 'crawl', *pyt-a-j-* 'question', *věnьč-a-j-* 'crown', *vit-a-j-* 'inhabit'; *běl-ě-j-* 'appear white', *bogat-ě-j-* 'grow rich', *sъm-ě-j-* 'dare', *um-ě-j-* 'know how,' *zьr-ě-j-* 'ripen'.

(j) ***-i-*:** *(j)av-i-* 'manifest', *blǫd-i-* 'err', *bud-i-* 'awaken', *děl-i-* 'divide', *dl̥b-i-* 'dig out', *doj-i-* 'milk', *drob-i-* 'break down', *glad-i-* 'smooth', *grab-i-* 'rob', *gub-i-* 'destroy', *klon-i-* 'bend', *koj-i-* 'still', *kr̥m-i-* 'feed', *kup-i-* 'buy', *kur-i-* 'smoke', *lěp-i-* 'paste', *lom-i-* 'break', *lov-i-* 'catch', *l'ub-i-* 'like', *měn-i-* 'change', *měs-i-* 'mix', *ml̥v-i-* 'speak', *modl-i-* 'beg', *mǫt-i-* 'muddle', *nos-i-* 'carry', *nud-i-* 'prod', *pal-i-* 'burn', *plat-i-* 'pay', *poj-i-* 'cause to drink', *pros-i-* 'ask', *rod-i-* 'give birth', *skoč-i-* 'jump', *slěd-i-* 'follow', *taj-i-* 'conceal', *top-i-* 'heat', *tvor-i-* 'create', *uč-i-* 'teach', *vab-i-* 'call', *var-i-* 'cook', *vod-i-* 'lead', *xod-i-* 'walk', *xorn-i-* 'protect', *xval-i-* 'praise'.

(k) ***-ě-*** (realized as ***-a-*** after soft consonants; see **2.20**): *boj-ě- sę* 'fear', *bol-ě-* 'be painful', *bъd-ě-* 'be awake', *drъž-ě-* 'hold', *dyš-ě-* 'breathe', *gor-ě-* 'burn', *grьm-ě-* 'thunder', *konьč-ě-* 'end', *krič-ě-* 'shout', *kyp-ě-* 'boil', *let-ě-* 'fly', *lež-ě-* 'lie down', *mьn-ě-* 'think', *ml̥'č-ě-* 'be silent', *pr̥'d-ě-* 'fart', *rъd-ě-* 'redden', *sěd-ě-* 'sit', *slyš-ě-* 'hear', *smr̥'d-ě-* 'reek', *stoj-ě-* 'stand', *šum-ě-* 'ferment', *tresč-ě-* 'creak', *tr̥'p-ě-* 'suffer', *vid-ě-* 'see', *vis-ě-* 'hang', *vr̥č-ě-* 'growl', *vr̥'t-ě-* 'turn', *xъt-ě-* 'want', *zьr-ě-* 'look'.

(l) **Mixed:** *ber-/bьr-a-* 'take', *bor'-/bor-* 'fight', *bǫd-/by-* 'be', *der-/dьr-a-* 'tear', *děd'- (dě-n-)/dě-* 'put', *jad-/ja(xa)-* 'drive', *jьd-/i-/šьd-* 'go', *mel'-/mel-* 'grind', *per-/pьr-a-* 'push', *stan-/sta-* 'become', *ser-/sьr-a-* 'defecate', *stel'-/stьl-a-* 'spread', *zov-/ zъv-a-* 'call', *žen-/gъn-a-* 'drive', *žid-/žьd-a-* 'wait', *živ-/ži-* 'live', *žuj-/žьv-a-* 'chew'.

2.65.6. Prepositions: *bez* 'without', *děl'a/dьl'a* 'for', *do* 'till', *jьz* 'out of', *kъ[n]* 'to', *med'u* 'between', *mimo* 'by', *na* 'on', *nad* 'above', *o* 'against', *ob* 'about', *ot* 'from', *po* 'along, after', *pod* 'under', *perd* 'before', *pri* 'next to,' *pro* 'through', *protivъ* 'against', *radi* 'for the purpose of', *sъ[n]* 'with', *u* 'at', *vъ[n]* 'in', *za* 'after.'

2.66. Lexical borrowing. The lexical stock of Proto-Slavic includes a number of loan words from the languages of various tribes and nations who were neighbors of the Slavs. The earliest lexical or semantic borrowings were from the North Iranian languages of the Scythian, Sarmatian, and Alanic tribes. Many of these borrowings had religious connotations, including such terms as *bogъ* 'god', *divъ* 'demon', *gatati* 'to divine', *rajь* 'paradise', *svętъ* 'holy', as well as the name of the supreme Slavic pagan deity, *Svarogъ*. However, such non-religious terms as *(j)aščerъ* 'serpent', *patriti* 'to look after', *radi* 'for the purpose of', *sobaka* 'dog', *toporъ* 'axe', *xata* 'house', *xvala* 'glory' are also of Iranian origin.

A few words may have originated in Celtic, e.g. *bagno* 'bog', *jama* 'cave', *korsta* 'canker', *sěta* 'grief', *sluga* 'servant', *tragъ* 'foot(step)'.

It is generally acknowledged that of the various languages which left their mark on early Slavic lexical stock, Germanic occupies a position of special importance. Contacts between Slavic and Germanic began when the Gothic migrations to the shores of the Black Sea exposed the Slavs to Proto-Germanic, then eventually East Germanic, and continued when the Slavs, having pushed into Central Europe and the Balkans, encountered West Germanic, especially Old High German and Middle High German dialects. The antiquity and duration of contacts between the Slavic and Germanic tribes have made it singularly difficult to assess the time and source of particular borrowings.[180]

Here are some examples of early Germanic loan words (words in the source language are glossed only when their meaning differs from Slavic): *duma* 'thought' (Goth. *dōms* 'judgment'), *gotoviti* 'to prepare' (Goth. *gataujan*), *kupiti* 'to buy' (Goth. *kaupōn*) *kusiti* 'to try' (Goth. *kausjan*), *kъnęʒь* 'duke' (OHG *kuning*), *lěkъ* 'medication' (PGmc. **lēka-*, cf. Goth. *lēkeis* 'physician'), *lixva* 'usury' (*leihva* 'loan'), *lьstь* 'cunning' (Goth. *lists* 'intrigue'), *měčь* 'sword' (Goth. *mēkeis*), *pl̥kъ* 'host' (PGmc. **fulkaz* 'military detachment'), *stьklo* 'glass' (Goth. *stikls* 'goblet'), *šelmъ* 'helmet' (PGmc. **helmaz*), *t'ud'ь* 'foreign' (Goth. *þiuda* 'people', cf. Eng. *Dutch*), *tynъ* 'fence' (PGmc. **tūnaz*), *xǫdogъ* 'wise' (Goth. **handags* 'agile'), *xlěbъ* 'bread' (Goth. *hlaifs* 'loaf'), *xlěvъ* 'stall' (Goth. *hlaiw* 'dugout'), *xl̥mъ* 'hill' (PGmc. **hulmaz*), *xyzъ* 'house' (PGmc. **hūs*).

Later loans were often restricted to specific Slavic dialects: *bl'udo* 'dish' (Goth. *biuþs, biudis*), *buky* 'script' (Goth. *bōka* 'letter'), *gobьʒiti* 'to be fruitful' (Goth. *gabigs* 'rich'),

180. The most thorough survey of pertinent research may be found in Kiparsky 1934.

gonoziti 'to rescue' (Goth. *ganasjan*), *istъba* 'house' (OHG *stuba* 'bathhouse'), *myto* 'tax' (OHG *mûta*), *smoky* 'fig' (Goth. *smakka* 'fig', lit. 'delicacy'), *useręʒь* 'earring' (Goth. *ausihrings*), *vr̥'togordъ* 'orchard' (Goth. *aúrtigards*), *opica* 'monkey' (OHG *affo*), *penęʒь* 'coin' (OHG *pfenning*), *plugъ* 'plow' (OHG *pfluog*), *stodola* 'barn' (OHG *stadal* 'sty'). Perhaps the most celebrated Germanic loan word was *korl'ь* 'king', derived from the name of Charlemagne (OHG *Kar(a)l*). It was initially borrowed into West Slavic dialects and spread from there throughout the Slavic territory.[181]

Germanic served also as a transmitting channel for many Latin and occasionally Greek borrowings into Slavic: *cěsar'ь* 'emperor' (Lat. *Caesar,* Goth. *Káisar*), *cr̥'ky* 'church' (Gk. *kyrikón,* Gmc. **kirikō*), *čeršn'a* 'cherry' (Popular Lat. *ceresia,* OBa. *chersia*), *dъska* 'board' (Lat. *discus,* OHG *tisc*), *kotъ* 'cat' (Popular Lat. *cattus,* Gmc. **katts*), *kotьlъ* 'kettle' (Popular Lat. *catillus,* Goth. *katils*), *mъša* 'mass' (Lat. *missa,* OHG *missa*), *ocьtъ* 'vinegar' (Lat. *acetum,* Goth. *akeit*), *osьlъ* 'ass' (Lat. *asinus,* Goth. *asilus*), *papežь* 'pope' (Popular Lat. *pāpex,* OBa. *pâpes*), *raky, -ъve* 'casket' (Lat. *arca,* OHG *arkô*), *velьbǫdъ* 'camel' (Gk. *eléphas, -antos* 'elephant', Goth. *ulbandus* 'camel').

Some Greek and especially Latin words seem to have entered Slavic without Germanic mediation; e.g. *kadь* 'pail' (Gk. *kádion*), *korab'ь* 'boat' (Gk. *karábion*), *polata* 'abode' (Byzantine Gk. *palátion* 'palace'); *konop'a* 'flax' (Popular Lat. **canapis*), *lęt'a* 'lentil' (Lat. *lens, -tis*), *lot'ika* 'lettuce' (Lat. *lactūca*), *(na)gorditi* 'to replace' (Popular Lat. *(re)gardare* 'reward, compensate'), *poganъ* 'peasant' (Lat. *pāgānus*), *port'a* 'lot, work' (Lat. *portiō* 'share'), *skǫdělь* 'tile, crockery' (Lat. *scandula* 'lath, shingle'), *vino* 'wine' (Lat. *vīnum*). At the end of Slavic linguistic unity Greek and Latin provided models for the nascent Slavic Christian terminology, the choice of the language reflecting the division of Slavdom into Byzantine and Roman ecclesiastic domains; e.g. *adъ* 'hell' (Gk. *hádēs*), *dijavolъ* 'devil' (Gk. *diábolos*), *idolъ* 'idol' (Gk *eídōlon*), *popъ* 'priest' (Gk. *papâs*), *psalъmъ* 'psalm' (Gk. *psalmós*), *sǫbota* 'Sabbath' (Gk. *sámbaton*), *xrizma* 'consecrated ointment' (Gk. *khrîsma*); *kolęda* 'Christmas eve, winter solstice' (Lat. *calendae*), *komъkati* 'to communicate' (Lat. *commūnicāre*), *križь* 'cross' (Lat. *crux, crucis*), *kъmotra* 'godmother' (Popular Lat. *commāter*), *olъtar'ь* 'altar' (Lat. *altāria*), *židъ* 'Jew' (Balkan Romance *ǯūd-* from Lat. *iudaeus,* cf. It. *giudeo*).

The relations of the Slavs with various Turkic tribes (chiefly Bulgars, Khazars, and Pechenegs) were reflected in such local borrowings as *bagъr-* 'purple', *bisьrъ* 'pearls', *bogatyr'ь* 'hero', *bol'arinъ* 'nobleman', *kar-* 'black', *kolpakъ/klobukъ* 'hat, cowl', *kovъčegъ* 'box', *kъn'iga* (Sg.) 'letter (of the alphabet)', *kъn'igy* (Pl.) 'book', *sanъ* 'dignity', *sapogъ* 'boot', *sokačijь* 'cook, butcher', *suje* 'in vain', *tl̥mačь* 'interpreter', *tьma* 'myriad', *xъmel'ь* 'hops'.[182]

Rapid slavicization of the Viking merchants and settlers in Rus' must be responsible for the small number of Scandinavian borrowings into East Slavic. In addition to such ethnic terms as *Rus',* *varjagъ* 'Varangian', and *kъlbjagъ* 'member of the Novgorod Varangian community of merchants', they include *gridь* 'freeman', *jakorь* 'anchor', *larь* 'box', *pudъ* 'measure of weight', *Sudъ* 'Golden Horn (port of Constantinople)', *ti(v)unъ* 'administrative title in Novgorod', *vitjazь* 'hero', and a few others (Kiparsky 1975:94–98).

181. Words like *korl'ь* 'king', whose incidence in Slavic is due to lexical diffusion during historical times, might be designated as Common Slavic in order to distinguish them from prehistorical Proto-Slavic vocabulary (cf. note 113).

182. On the possible Turkic influence on Slavic phonology, see Galton 1994.

2.67. Grammatical productivity. The mechanism of assignment of borrowings to particular stem types allows us to distinguish between productive and unproductive morphological classes, the former admitting loan words, the latter not. Borrowed substantives are found in the following productive stem types: *-ŏ-/-i̯-ŏ-* (e.g. *plugъ* 'plow', *cěsar'ь* 'emperor'), *-ā-/-i̯-ā-* (e.g. *stodola* 'barn', *konop'a* 'flax'), *-ĭ-* (e.g. *kadь* 'pail'), and *-ū-/-ŭu̯* (e.g. *buky* 'letter, script'). Borrowed verbs made their way into the following productive classes: *-nǫ-* (e.g. *goneznǫti* 'to be rescued'), *-ov-a-* (e.g. *kupovati* 'to buy'), *-a-j-* (e.g. *komъkati* 'to communicate'), and *-i-* (e.g. *kusiti* 'to try').

2.68. Grammatical analogy. The process of the incorporation of borrowings into the Slavic grammatical system illustrates the importance of identifying productive grammatical classes. It also shows the way in which analogy helps to regularize all that is atypical, irregular, and unexpected in the development of language. Examples of such potential irregularities that were leveled out by the power of analogy may be provided by the treatment in Slavic of some borrowed Germanic substantives.

The neuter substantive *stьklo* 'glass' was borrowed from the Gothic masculine *stikls* 'goblet'. The unexpected shift in gender from masculine to neuter was probably caused by the semantic change whereby a word denoting an object came to denote a substance. The model was provided by the Slavic native neuters in *-l-o*, such as *sadlo* 'fat', *jadlo* 'food', *prędlo* 'weft', which denoted substances.

The masculine substantive *korl'ь* 'king' is usually derived from Old High German *Kar(a)l*. However, unlike other Germanic loan words in *l*, it did not become an *-ŏ-* stem (cf. *kъbьlъ* 'pail', *kotьlъ* 'cattle', *osьlъ* 'ass', *stьklo* 'glass'), but rather joined the *-i̯-ŏ-* stems. The reason for this deviation should again be sought in analogy. Since *korl'ь* was the only personal noun in *l* borrowed from Germanic, the linguistic consciousness of the West Slavs, who were the first to receive this loan word, associated it with their many Church Slavonicisms in *-tel-i̯-* (*učitel'ь* 'teacher', *prijatel'ь* 'friend', *roditel'ь* 'parent', *dělatel'ь* 'performer', etc.). In addition, all other Slavic terms denoting rulers belonged to the soft stem declension (cf. OCS. *cěsar'ь, pravitel'ь, vlastel'ь, kъnęʒь*). The pressure of these models led to the replacement of **korlъ* by *korl'ь* (cf. also OCS *Izdrail'ь* 'Israel' and *Kocel'ь* 'Kocel').[183]

A curious combination of factors appears to be responsible for the assignment of an inordinately large number of borrowings to the *-ū-/-ŭu̯-* stems of Slavic. At the dawn of the historical period the *-ū-/-ŭu̯-* stems seem to have lost their derivational productivity within Slavic while assuming the role of the favorite repository of Germanic feminine *-n-* stems (that is, of the so-called weakly inflected nouns) borrowed into Slavic, e.g. Gmc. **bōkō* 'letter' > LPSl. *buky, -ъve*, Gmc. **bardō* 'axe' > LPSl. *bordy, -ъve*, Gmc. **kirikō* 'church' (< Gk. *kyrikón*) > LPSl. *cr̥'ky, -ъve*. Also assigned to the *-ū-/-ŭu̯-* stems were some, chiefly horticultural, Latin nouns in *-a*, e.g. Lat. *brassica* 'cabbage' > LPSl. *brosky, -ъve*, Lat. *mōra* (pl.) 'mulberry' > LPSl. *mory, -ъve*.

183. A notable exception to the rule of Germano-Slavic gender agreement is presented by the neuter nouns, which generally switch over to masculine (*glazъ* 'polished stone', *xlěvъ* 'stable', *xysъ* 'house', *tynъ* 'wall', *pl̥kъ* 'people'). Depending on the antiquity of the loan words, this shift may be attributed either to a regular development of Proto-Germanic Nom./Acc. Sg. *-ŏm* to *-ъ* or, if the borrowing was made from Gothic or Old High German, to an automatic extension of the stem-final consonant by *-ъ*.

It is not easy to understand why the moribund *-ū-/-ŭu̯-* stems should be the choice over the fully productive *-ā-* stems. For the loans from Germanic one could accept Kuryłowicz's (1951) conjecture that the Germanic feminine *-n-* stems, finding no exact counterpart in the Slavic nominal system, were assimilated by the Slavic feminine *-ū-/-ŭu̯-* stems, which in turn had no counterpart in Germanic. In other words, the two stem classes, though different, were matched because their members were of the same gender and had a similar heteroclitic structure. The phonological starting point for such a connection could be the Slavic reception of the final *-ō* in Germanic as $\bar{u}_1$ > *-y*. As for the borrowings from Latin (perhaps also *xorǫgy*, *-ъve* 'banner' from Mongolian), for which no phonological or morphological explanation is available, the preference for the *-ū-/-ŭu̯-* stems may have been dictated by their having assumed the role of a domesticating inflectional class for specialized terminology (cf. Vaillant 1958:285–286).[184]

2.69. Late Proto-Slavic dialect isoglosses. It is highly probable that the process of dialect differentiation marking the end of the Early Proto-Slavic period began soon after the sixth century A.D., when the Slavs scattered throughout central and southeastern Europe. It is more difficult to determine when these dialect distinctions became so pronounced as to justify the assumption of the dissolution of Proto-Slavic linguistic unity and of the rise of separate Slavic languages. The commonly accepted dating of this process into the ninth or tenth century is based primarily on political events of the period, such as the attainment of statehood by Bulgaria, Carantania, Croatia, Serbia, Moravia, Pannonia, Bohemia, Poland, and Kievan Rus'. It seems likely, however, that by the end of the ninth century there emerged at least three distinct dialects, South Slavic, East Slavic, and West Slavic, the latter two combining as North Slavic. As always in dialectology, one also has to posit a number of transitional areas.

In the following list of isoglosses, only those dialect features that have not been discussed in this survey are furnished with examples; the features that were previously mentioned are appropriately cross-referenced.[185]

2.69.1. South Slavic (SSl.) versus North Slavic (NSl.):

(1) PSl. *#ăRC* (**2.35a**) yielded *#RāC* in SSl., *#RăC* in NSl.
(2) PSl. *ę* (**2.40c**) yielded *ę* in SSl., *ę̌* [æ̨] in NSl. (cf. 17).
(3) Acc. Pl. of the *-i̯-ŏ-/-i̯-ā-* stems (**2.48.1** *note 3a*) was *-ę* in SSl., *-ě₃* in NSl.
(4) Instr. Sg. of the *-ŏ-* stems (**2.48.1** *note 5*) was *-omь* in SSl., *-ъmь* in NSl. (except for some peripheral areas), e.g. OCS *godomь* 'year', OESl. *godъmь*.
(5) Nom. Sg. M Pr. Active Pple. Indefinite (**2.51.6**) was *-y* in SSl., *-a* in NSl.
(6) Verb prefix 'out' was *jьz-* in SSl., *vy-* in NSl., e.g. OCS *iz-bьrati* 'to choose', OESl. *vy-bьrati*.

2.69.2. West Slavic (WSl.) versus South/East Slavic (S/ESl.):

(7) Second palatalization of *x ku̯ gu̯ sk* (**2.31**) yielded *š kv gv šč* in WSl., *s' cv ʒv sc* in S/ESl.
(8) Third palatalization of *x* (**2.31**) yielded *š* in WSl., *s'* in S/ESl.
(9) PSl. *tl dl* (**2.33**) yielded *tl dl* in WSl., *l* in S/ESl. *Note: tl dl* occur in some Slovenian dialects of South Slavic; *kl gl* occur in the Pskov and Novgorod dialects of East Slavic and the Kashubian and Mazovian dialects of West Slavic.
(10) 1 Sg. and 3 Pl. of the productive aorist (**2.51.2**) were *-exъ -exǫ* in WSl., *-oxъ -ošę* in S/ESl.

184. The hypothesis that there existed a particular class reserved for the novel, mostly technical concepts borrowed by the early Slavs from their neighbors is strengthened by the evidence from Polabian, where numerous loans from Middle Low German were also assigned to the *-ū-/-ŭu̯-* stems.

185. For a survey of phonological features of the individual Slavic languages, see Carlton (1991:231–333).

Eventually the tripartite division of Slavic gave way to a highly differentiated dialect picture. South Slavic split into a western and an eastern dialect, the former giving rise to preliterary Slovenian and Serbian/Croatian, the latter to Bulgarian and Macedonian. Practically all extant texts of canonical Old Church Slavonic may be considered examples of literary eastern South Slavic. West Slavic distinguished three dialect groups. The largest was Lechitic, the ancestor of Polish, Kashubian, and Polabian and of the extinct Pomeranian Slavic dialects attested to by surviving place names and personal and place names mentioned in medieval chronicles. The two smaller ones were Sorbian, from which modern Lower and Upper Sorbian are derived, and Czech/Slovak, which gave rise to Czech and Slovak. East Slavic split into southwestern and northeastern variants, the former being the forerunner of Ukrainian and Belarussian, the latter of Russian.

2.69.3. Western South Slavic (WSSl.) versus North Slavic and eastern South Slavic (N/ESSl.):

(11) Phonemic pitch was retained in WSSl., lost in N/ESSl., e.g. S/Cr. *rúka rȗku* 'hand', Cz. *ruka ruku.*
(12) PSl. circumflex (**2.39**) yielded vowel length in WSSl., vowel brevity in N/ESSl.
(13) PSl. *C* before a front vowel yielded *C* in WSSl., *C'* in NSl. and partly in ESSl., e.g. S/Cr. *tȋ* 'for you', *dȇset* 'ten'; Po. *ci, dziesięć.*

2.69.4. Some other early isoglosses:

(14) PSl. **ь ъ** (the jers in strong position) merged as *a* in WSSl. and as *e* in WSl.; remained distinct elsewhere (*ь ъ* in OCS, *e o* in East Slavic and Macedonian); e.g. PSl. *dьnь* 'day', *sъnъ* 'sleep': S/Cr. *dân, sȁn,* Cz. *den, sen,* OCS *dьnь sъnъ;* Ru. *den', son.* Exceptions include Bg. *ъ*, Sln. *a* in long syllables and *e* [ə] in short ones; Plb. *å* (*a, ė*), Slk. *e o a* through dialect mixture. In Sorbian *e* > *o/a* in some environments.
(15) PSl. *e* in some environments backed to *o* in East Slavic and eastern Lechitic, e.g. PSl. *žena* (Nom. Sg.) *ženъ* (Gen. Pl.) 'woman': Ukr. *žoná žon,* Ru. *žená žën,* Po. *żona żon.* However, the conditions of this shift were language-specific.
(16) PSl. *ě* (**2.40b**) backed to *a* in Lechitic before hard dentals (cf. 17); tended to merge with *a* in Bulgarian under stress; merged with *e* or *i* elsewhere; e.g. PSl. *bělъ̂jь* 'white', *sněgъ* 'snow': Po. *biały, śnieg,* Bg. *bjal, snjag,* Ru. *bélyj, sneg,* Ukr. *bílyj, snih.*
(17) PSl. *ę ǫ* (**2.34**) retained their nasal resonance in Lechitic and in some Slovenian and Bulgarian dialects; lost it elsewhere; e.g. PSl. *pętь* 'five', *rǫka* 'hand': Po. *pięć, ręka,* Plb. *pąt, rǫkă,* S/Cr. *pêt, rúka,* Ru. *pjat', ruká* . In Lechitic *ę* merged with *ǫ* before hard dentals (cf. 16).
(18) PSl. *ǫ* (**2.40c**) yielded rounded vowels [ų] or [ǫ] in North Slavic and western South Slavic; unrounded vowels [ъ̨] or [ą] in eastern South Slavic.
(19) PSl. *CR̥C* (**2.35b**) yielded *CR̥C* in South Slavic and Czech/Slovak; *CVRC* in Lechitic, Sorbian, and East Slavic. The sequence *CRъC* in OCS reflects the spelling rule requiring open syllables (**2.17**).
(20) PSl. *Cr̥'C* yielded *Cr̥C* in South Slavic and Czech/Slovak in all environments and in Lechitic and Sorbian before hard dentals (cf. 16 and 17); *Cr̥'C* elsewhere; e.g. PSl. *tvr̥'dъ* 'hard', *tvr̥'diti* 'to affirm': S/Cr. *tvȓd, tvȓditi,* Cz. *tvrdý, tvrditi,* Po. *twardy, twierdzić,* Ru. *tvërdyj, tverdít'*.
(21) PSl. *Cl̥'C* (**2.35b**) yielded *Cl̥'C* in Sorbian, Polish, and Czech; *Cl̥C* elsewhere.
(22) PSl. *CĕRC CăRC* (**2.35c**) yielded
CRēC CRāC in South Slavic and Czech/Slovak
CĕRəC CăRəC in East Slavic
CəRĕC CəRăC in Lechitic and Sorbian.
(23) PSl. *CĕlC* (**2.35c**) yielded *Cā̆lC* in western Lechitic and East Slavic.

(24) PSl. *Pl'* < *Pi̯* followed by a morphemic boundary (**2.23c**) yielded *P'* in eastern South Slavic and West Slavic.

(25) PSl. *g* yielded [ɣ] or *h* in southern East Slavic, Czech/Slovak, Upper Sorbian, and western Slovenian, e.g. PSl. *noga* 'leg': Ukr. *nohá*, Cz. *noha*, Ru. *nogá*, S/Cr. *nòga*.

(26) PSl. *t' d'* (**2.35**) yielded
c ʒ in West Slavic and Old Church Slavonic of the Moravian recension
č ǯ in East Slavic and Slovenian (in standard Slovenian *ǯ* > *j*)
ć ʒ́ in Serbian/Croatian
k' g' in Macedonian, *št žd* in Bulgarian
št' žd' in Old Church Slavonic of the Bulgarian/Macedonian recension.

(27) PSl. 3 Sg./3 Pl. Pr. *-tь/-tъ* (**2.53** *note 3*) correspond to
-Ø/-Ø in western South Slavic and West Slavic
-Ø/-t in eastern South Slavic
-t/-t in most northeastern dialects of East Slavic (including standard Russian)
-Ø/-t' (Conjugation I) and *-t'/-t'* (Conjugation II) in the southwestern and some northeastern East Slavic dialects.

(28) PSl. 1 Pl. Pr. *-mъ* (**2.53** *note 5*) corresponds to
-mъ in OCS and northeastern East Slavic
-mo in western South Slavic and southwestern East Slavic
-me in eastern South Slavic and Czech/Slovak
-my in Lechitic and Sorbian.

3. EARLY WRITING

3.1. Paleography. Paleography is the study of ancient writing systems. It deals with the decipherment of texts, graphic conventions, the origins, styles, and dating of graphic symbols, and the materials upon which writings are found, including perishable materials such as papyrus, parchment, paper, wax, or tree bark and more durable surfaces like clay tablets. The branch of paleography that studies inscriptions found on stone, masonry, pottery, wood, or metal is called epigraphy. Paleography is also concerned with such nongraphic aspects of manuscript writing as ornamentation and binding, as well as writing implements and scriptorial practices.

The vast majority of ancient Slavic writings dealt with in this chapter are on parchment. Also surviving are many documents from northern Rus' written on birch bark, as well as various inscriptions and graffiti made on church walls, clay vessels, stone, drinking bowls, crosses, seals, coins, and various wooden objects.

3.2. Slavic alphabets. Of the two major Slavic writing systems in use today, one is based on Greek, the other on Latin. Their domains are delimited by confessional divisions, with the Greek-based Cyrillic alphabet being used in the lands of Orthodox Slavdom and the Latin-based Roman alphabet having been adopted by the Catholics and Protestants, that is, in the lands that submit or submitted until the Reformation to the ecclesiastic authority of Rome.[186]

In addition to these two alphabets the Slavs used the so-called Glagolitic alphabet, designed specifically for the use of the Moravian mission. Glagolitic, widely adopted at the dawn of Slavic letters, has gradually lost its appeal. Its postmedieval flowering was limited to western Croatia, and it is there, in a handful of Catholic parishes in northwestern Dalmatia, chiefly the islands of the Quarner archipelago, that its use in the liturgy survived until the beginning of the twentieth century. One should also mention two short-lived Glagolitic enclaves among the western Slavs. One appeared when Charles IV of Bohemia (r. 1346–1378),

186. This apportionment breaks down in a few minor instances. Thus, the Cyrillic alphabet is being used by the Uniate Catholics of Western Ukraine and Belarus and by the Moslems in Bosnia. It is interesting, however, that in the beginning of the twentieth century the Belarussian Catholics attempted to follow the confessional lines by replacing the Cyrillic script with Roman. One should also note that from the mid-fourteenth century till the mid-eighteenth century Cyrillic was the sole alphabet of the Romance-speaking Orthodox Romanians and Moldovans. They used it throughout that period in Church Slavonic, which was the language of their religious and administrative pursuits, and, from the sixteenth century on, in their Romance vernacular. The Romanian spelling reform of 1860 introduced the Roman alphabet in place of Cyrillic. The formerly Soviet Moslem republics of Central Asia had a double change of alphabets: after the revolution of 1917 their traditional Arabic alphabet was replaced by the Roman alphabet the latter yielding in 1940 to Moscow-favored Cyrillic.

having received the pope's permission to reintroduce the Slavic liturgy, invited a group of Benedictine monks from Glagolitic parishes in Dalmatia to the Emmaus monastery in Prague. This initiative, dictated apparently by political considerations, ended with the destruction of the monastery during the Hussite wars. Equally unsuccessful was the attempt of King Casimir the Great of Poland (r. 1333–1370) to emulate Charles IV by inviting Glagolitic monks to the Benedictine monastery in Kleparz near Cracow.

There were also instances of the use of Arabic and Hebrew alphabets to transcribe Slavic. The former was used by the Moslem population in Bosnia and by the Slavicized Moslem Tartars, who remained on the territory of the Grand Duchy of Lithuania after the defeat of the Golden Horde in the fourteenth century. The latter was employed sporadically by Jewish merchants in Bohemia and Poland to record commercial transactions.[187]

3.3. The genealogy of Glagolitic. Newly devised alphabets have, as a rule, traceable origins. Most of them are derived, ultimately, from the Semitic consonantal script, which has survived in modern Hebrew and Arabic. The Greeks transformed the North Semitic script into a true alphabet in which consonants and vowels have equal stature. The Greek consonantal-vocalic alphabet, being better suited to the structure of Indo-European, served as a model for the Latin alphabet, which incorporated some Etruscan admixtures, and for the Gothic alphabet, which was created in the fourth century by the Visigothic bishop Ulfila and, along with Latin, incorporated Germanic runic elements. The Armenian alphabet, devised in the beginning of the fifth century by St. Mesrop, is a curious restructuring of the Semitic-based Parsi script of Iran on the pattern of Greek.[188]

It would thus seem reasonable to believe that the source of Glagolitic should also be easy to uncover. This expectation, however, has not been fully realized. Glagolitic has yielded some, but far from all, of its secrets. The very fact that there is hardly an ancient alphabet which has not been invoked as a model for Glagolitic letters[189] demonstrates the difficulty of the problem and the confutability of the proposed solutions.

The most widely accepted theory was proposed in 1880 by the British paleographer Isaac Taylor. It attributed the shapes of most Glagolitic letters to Greek cursive writing in a development which, according to Taylor, was analogous to the derivation of the Irish uncial alphabet of the seventh century from the old Roman cursive. Taylor's hypothesis was accepted by such scholars as the German philologist August Leskien (1905), the Croatian Slavist Vatroslav Jagić (1911), and the Czech paleographer Josef Vajs (1932).

Many scholars, however, have denied the plausibility of a single source of Glagolitic and, in particular, the likelihood of a morphological connection between Glagolitic and cursive Greek.[190] They have argued that Constantine had every reason to wish to produce a distinctive writing system, one without clear associations with any of the other known alphabets. Such a goal would have been consistent with Constantine's opposition to the "trilingual heresy" and with his determination to gain for Slavic a position of doctrinal equality and for Moravia the status of political and cultural independence (**1.35, 3.11**).

187. Some Polish coins minted in the twelfth century bear Polish inscriptions transcribed with Hebrew letters (**3.55**).

188. The Greek alphabet was also the base of the Coptic script used by the early Christians in Egypt and surviving to this day in Coptic liturgy.

189. Including Hebrew, Phoenician, Samaritan, Ethiopian, Armenian, Georgian, and Greek. The totally anachronistic attribution of Glagolitic to the authorship of St. Jerome (ca. 347–420!) was widespread in Croatia, due undoubtedly to the saint's Dalmatian origins. For an overview of the problem, see Vaillant 1955.

190. Sir Ellis H. Minns (1925) noted: "The general impression of Glagolitic is singularly unlike any sort of cursive Greek" [Diringer 487].

In support of this view one could cite references to the activities of the Moravian mission which suggest that Glagolitic was not recognized by the contemporaries of Constantine and Methodius as being based on Greek. We learn, for instance, from the *Conversio Bagoariorum et Carantanorum* that "a certain Greek, Methodius by name, has with deceitful sophistry [*philosophice superducens*] degraded the Latin language and the Roman doctrine as well as the authority of Latin books through the use of newly invented Slavic letters" (12). The emphasis on the innovative character of the alphabet devised by Constantine implies, it would seem, that it had not been a mere adaptation of the Greek letters to the needs of Slavic.

3.4. Glagolitic and Cyrillic letters. At the same time one cannot deny that some Glagolitic letters, though dominated by the principle of geometric shapes and symmetry, do betray similarities to several writing systems known to Constantine. Even among the most plausible derivations, however, the stylizations and alterations are so extensive as to make one wary of unqualified attributions.[191]

The tradition of Glagolitic writing, though gradually waning, survived for about one millennium, from the mid-ninth century to the beginning of the twentieth century. During that time both the Glagolitic alphabet and the Glagolitic writing conventions underwent various modifications. Chief among them was the change from the rounded shapes characteristic of the oldest monuments of Bulgarian (Macedonian) provenience to the distinctly angular letters of the later Croatian manuscripts and printed books. In addition, the older texts had few ligatured spellings (letters joined to one another to form a single grapheme), while in the later texts such spellings occurred regularly.

The Cyrillic alphabet arose as a fairly straightforward adaptation of the Byzantine Greek uncial alphabet to the needs of Slavic. Problems arose only in those instances where the differences between the Greek and Slavic phonetic systems forced the adapters to seek non-Greek letters in order to render the Slavic sounds that had no counterparts in Greek. The most important among them were the Slavic hushing consonants (*š ž č*), the jers, jat', and the nasal vowels.

Listed below are the letters of the Glagolitic and Cyrillic alphabets along with their Slavic names and a discussion of their possible sources. The order of letters follows their numerical value (in parentheses) in the Glagolitic alphabet. It agrees, by and large, with the surviving abecedaria and the so-called *Alphabet Prayer,* whose extant Cyrillic codices are probably based on a Glagolitic original. The first part of the alphabet consisted of letters whose sound value could be identified with the Greek alphabet. Those were the letters from Ⰰ (azъ) to Ⱁ (otъ). Their order followed the Greek practice except that Ⰱ (buky) and Ⰲ (vědě) were assigned the second and third place in the alphabet, replacing Greek Β (bêta), whose classical Greek sound value of /b/ was replaced in Byzantine Greek by /v/.[192] Other letters in the first part of the alphabet whose sound values did not occur in Greek were Ⰶ (živěte), which was assigned the place and numerical value of Greek ζ (7), and Ⰸ (zemlja), which had the position and numerical value of Greek θ (9), to which it was similar in design. Letters denoting specifically Slavic sounds were placed in the second part of the alphabet. Greek models for Cyrillic letters are, unless otherwise noted, Byzantine uncials.

191. The only exception is the letter Ⱎ (ša), which was taken over from Semitic with minimal changes.

192. Hence the difference in their numerical values: Greek Α = 1, Β = 2, Γ = 3 etc. but Glagolitic Ⰰ = 1, Ⰱ = 2, Ⰲ = 3, Ⰳ = 4, etc.

Name	Transliteration	Glagolitic	Cyrillic
azъ	a	(1) Ⰰ From Hebrew א *aleph* or the image of the cross	(1) А From Greek α *álpha*; in later texts iotated α was written ІА or Ꙗ
buky	b	(2) Ⰱ Source unknown. Samaritan /m/ is ࠌ, a mirror image of Ⰱ	Б Origin uncertain. Perhaps a variant of Greek Β *bêta*
vědě	v	(3) Ⰲ Perhaps from Latin V	(2) В From Greek Β *bêta*
glagoli	g	(4) Ⰳ Perhaps from cursive Greek γ *gámma*	(3) Г From Greek Γ *gámma*
dobro	d	(5) Ⰴ From Greek Δ *délta*; cf. Ⰲ /v/, i.e., inverted Ⰴ	(4) Д From Greek Δ *délta*
estъ	e	(6) Ⰵ Perhaps from Samaritan ࠄ /he/ or Greek numeral *sampî* ϡ (900)	(5) Є Є Є From Greek Ε *epsilón*; in later texts iotated Є was written Ѥ
živěte	ž	(7) Ⰶ Source unknown	Ж Perhaps from Glagolitic Ⰶ
ʒělo	ʒ	(8) Ⰷ Source unknown	(6) Ѕ Ѕ Ꙃ Ꙁ From Greek ϛ *digámma* or Latin S; for the variant ꙃ from Greek ζ *zêta*, see below
zemlja	z	(9) Ⰸ Possibly a variant of Greek θ *thêta*	(7) Ꙁ З From Greek ζ *zêta*
iže	i		(8) Н И Ch. Sl. *i osmeričьno;* from Greek Η *êta*
	ı ι	(10) Ⰺ Ⰹ Possibly from Greek ι *iôta* with dieresis	(10) І (ı) Ї Ch.Sl. *i desętеričьno;* from Greek ι *iôta*

Name	Transliteration	Glagolitic	Cyrillic
	i	(20) Ⰻ Source unknown; the inclusion in Glagolitic of the letters Ⰹ/Ⰺ and Ⰻ with the same sound value was probably intended to imitate Byzantine Greek orthography where both η *êta* and ι *iôta* were pronounced as /i/; it is possible that in the oldest texts Ⰻ rendered the *i* which alternated with *ĭ* (**2.34**)	
ĝervь *d'ervь*	Ⰼ/ĝ/d'	(30) Ⰼ Source unknown; since the original sound value of Ⰼ/ĝ/d' approximated /ʒ́/, it was used to render the Byzantine Greek pronunciation of palatalized g' in such borrowings as *g'eona* ⰌⰅⰅⰐⰀ 'hell' from Greek γεέννα, as well as the reflexes of PSl. *d'* in Western South Slavic medieval texts (**2.36**)	
kako	k	(40) Ⰽ From Hebrew ק koph	(20) К From Greek Κ *káppa*
ljudie	l	(50) Ⰾ Perhaps from cursive Greek λ *lámbda*	(30) Л From Greek Λ *lámbda*
myslite	m	(60) Ⰿ From cursive Greek μ *mû*	(40) М М From Greek Μ *mû*
našь	n	(70) Ⱀ Source unknown	(50) Н From Greek Ν *nû*
onъ	o	(80) Ⱁ Source unknown	(70) О О From Greek Ο *omikrón*
pokoi	p	(90) Ⱂ Perhaps a variant of early Greek Π *pî*	(80) П From Greek Π *pî*

Name	Transliteration	Glagolitic	Cyrillic
rьci	r	(100) Ⱃ Perhaps related to cursive Greek ρ *rhô*	(100) р From cursive Greek ρ *rhô*
slovo	s	(200) Ⱄ Source unknown; Ⱄ occurs frequently with its inversion (Ⰺ) in the abbreviation of the name of Jesus (Ⰺ̄Ⱄ)	(200) с From Greek C *sîgma*
tvrьdo	t	(300) Ⱅ Perhaps from the crossbar of Greek cursive τ *taû*	(300) т From Greek T *taû*
ukъ	u	(400) Ⱆ A digraph composed of Ⱁ *onъ* and Ⱛ *ižica;* its independent position in the alphabet suggests that it functioned as a single phoneme	(400) ѹ ꙋ ȣ A digraph composed of о and ѵ side-by-side or ѵ on top of о; these Glagolitic and Cyrillic digraphs follow the Greek practice of rendering /u/ with ου
frьtъ	f	(500) Ⱇ Ⱇ A variant of Greek Φ *phî*	(500) ф From cursive Greek φ *phî*
		The letter *f*, which was found originally in borrowings only, was also rendered with Glagolitic and Cyrillic *fita* Ⱚ derived from Greek Θ *thêta*	
xěrъ	x	(600) Ⱈ Source unknown; compare /g/ Ⰳ and Latin *h*	(600) Х х From Greek X *khî*
otъ	ō	(700) Ⱉ A digraph made up of Ⱁ *onъ* and its mirror image	(800) ѡ Ѡ From Greek ω *oméga*
šta	št	(800) Ⱋ A digraph made up of Ⱎ /š/ over Ⱅ /t/; its independent position in the alphabet suggests that it functioned as a single phoneme	щ From Glagolitic Ⱋ
ci	c	(900) Ⱌ From Hebrew צ *tsade*	(900) ц Adapted from Glagolitic Ⱌ

Name	Transliteration	Glagolitic	Cyrillic
čьrvь	č	(1000) Ⱈ Source unknown; cf. Ⱆ /št/	(90) Y Ч (Ҁ) Y adapted from Glagolitic Ⱈ Ч adapted from Cyrillic Ц
ša	š	Ⱉ From Hebrew ש *shin*	Ш From Glagolitic Ⱉ /š/
erъ	ъ	Ⱊ, later Ⱊ Ⱊ Perhaps from Glagolitic Ⰼ /o/	Ъ Perhaps from Glagolitic Ⱊ /ъ/
erь	ь	Ⱋ, later T Perhaps from Glagolitic Ⰼ /o/	Ь Perhaps from Glagolitic Ⱋ /ь/
jatь	ě	Ⱌ Perhaps from epigraphic Greek A *álpha*	Ѣ Perhaps a variant of Cyrillic Ь
ju	ju	Ⱎ Source unknown; its shape suggests that it functioned as a single phoneme /ü/	Ю From an iotated and truncated Ѹ /u/ which suggests a biphonemic status as /ju/
Nasality	N	Ⱏ Front nasal vowel from Greek E *epsilón;* it functioned also as a marker of nasality in nasal vowels Ⱓ /ǫ/, ⰅⰟ /ę/, Ⱔ /ǫ̈/	Ѧ From epigraphic Greek A *álpha*
Nasal *o*	ǫ	Ⱓ Back nasal vowel written as a digraph made up of Ⰼ *onъ* and Ⱏ (nasality)	Ѫ (Ѫ) Variant of epigraphic Greek A *alpha;* it is known in Russian as *jus bol'šój*
Nasal *e*	ę	ⰅⰟ Front nasal vowel written as a digraph made up of Ⰵ *estъ* and Ⱏ (nasality)	Ѧ From epigraphic Greek A *alpha;* it is known in Russian as *jus málуj;* /ę/ iotated was written Ѩ
Nasal *ö*	ǫ̈ or jǫ	Ⱔ A digraph made up of a letter of unknown origin and Ⱏ (nasality); its independent position in the alphabet suggests that it functioned as a single phoneme	Ѭ Iotated /ǫ/ whose shape suggests a biphonemic status as /jǫ/

Name	Transliteration	Glagolitic	Cyrillic
fita	θ	Ⱚ From Greek θ *thêta*	Ѳ From Greek Θ *thêta*
ižica	i (υ)	Ⱛ Source unknown	Ѵ ѵ From Greek uncial Y or cursive υ; *ižica* was the regular second member of the Cyrillic digraph ѹ /u/; When used alone, in borrowings from Greek, its original sound value was probably /u/

In addition to these letters, several special cases have to be mentioned:

(a) The Cyrillic alphabet used the Greek letters ѯ *ksî* and ψ *psî* as the numerals 60 and 700.

(b) The Glagolitic alphabet included a rare spider-shaped letter Ⱒ whose identity is in doubt. It occurred in the Paris and Munich abecedaria and in the *Sinai Psalter* and the *Codex Assemanianus* with the sound value of *x*, as the first letter of the word *xlъmъ* 'hill' (this was also its name in Old Church Slavonic). What was the difference in usage between the exceptional Ⱒ (xlъmъ) and the regular Ⱈ (xěrъ)? Mareš's view, expressed in 1971, that Ⱒ rendered the voiced *h* in words borrowed from Germanic, while Ⱈ was reserved for the native fricative *x* (179–181), is difficult to accept because at the time of the creation of Glagolitic PSl. *xl̥mъ* < PGmc. *hulmaz* must have been totally assimilated in Slavic. Tkadlčik was perhaps closer to the truth when he surmised in 1964 that Ⱒ was written originally before back vowels, while Ⱈ was used before front vowels.

(c) Even less is known about the letter ⰒⰪ (pě) attested from the *Munich Abecedarium* only. Some scholars assign to it the sound value of the more recent letter Ⱋ (šta), which took the position of ⰒⰪ in the alphabet and had the same numerical value, 800. On the other hand, ⰒⰪ might have functioned as a variant of Lat. *P*, corresponding perhaps to Greek ψ (*psî*).

(d) The high back unrounded vowel /y/ *ery* was a digraph composed of a back or front jer and either Ⰺ (ı) or Ⰹ (ι): Glagolitic ⰟⰊ/ⰟⰉ/ⰠⰊ, Cyrillic **ъı/ъι/ы**.

(e) Symbols employed to show punctuation and the palatalization of consonants (velar and labial consonants and the yodized *n' r' l'*) and to mark abbreviations, numerals, and dates are discussed in **3.15–3.18.**[193]

3.5. Slavic writing before the Moravian mission. The ample documentation on the Moravian mission of the mid-ninth century provides us with the first indication of the existence of Slavic writing. We have a fairly good idea what books were brought by the mission from Constantinople and what books were translated later in Moravia. There remains, however, the question whether the books used by the mission represented the very first speci-

193. The various diacritics (macrons, breves, soft and rough breathings) written over vowels in syllable-initial positions reflected mechanically the Byzantine Greek usage rather than any features of the Slavic sound system.

mens of Slavic writing. Did the Slavs have some kind of script predating the Moravian mission? According to the *Vita Constantini*, the Philosopher himself wondered about such a possibility when the Byzantine emperor Michael III asked him to head the projected mission:

> And the Philosopher answered: 'Though I am weary and sick in body, I shall go there gladly if they have a script for their language'. Then the Emperor said to him: 'My grandfather and my father and many others have sought this but did not find it. How then can I find it'? And the Philosopher answered: 'Who can write a language on water and acquire for himself a heretic's name'? And together with his uncle, Bardas, the Emperor answered him again: 'If you wish, God may give you this as He gives to everyone that asks without doubt, and opens to them that knock'. (*Vita Constantini* 14)

Constantine's question was certainly no more than a rhetorical device used by his hagiographer. As an accomplished linguist raised in the Slavic-speaking milieu of Thessalonica, Constantine must have known whether a Slavic script would be available to him. Nor can one take at face value the emperor's categorical denial of the earlier existence of Slavic writing. The intent of the *Vita Constantini*, like that of any hagiography, was to justify the canonization of its protagonist. To this end it was supposed to focus on the miraculous nature of the saint's achievements and not to dwell on any factual evidence that could detract from his accomplishments. An admission of the prior existence of Slavic letters would have gone against the claim made in the vita that Constantine's feat was accomplished with divine assistance and would have diminished Constantine's stature as a scholar. We are justified, therefore, in allowing the possibility of the existence of a pre-Constantinian Slavic script and in subjecting Emperor Michael's disclaimer, apocryphal or not, to careful scrutiny.[194]

3.6. The testimony of the monk Khrabr. One indirect reference to the existence of such a script may be found in the famous treatise *On the Letters (O pismenexъ)* by the monk Khrabr. The treatise, which may have been composed as early as the end of the ninth or beginning of the tenth centuries, contains the following assertion:

> Earlier the Slavs did not have books but by strokes and notches (*črьtami i rězami*) read and divined, being heathen. And when they were baptized, they had to write their Slavic speech with Roman and Greek letters without design (*bezъ ustroenija*). Because how could one adequately write with Greek letters *bogъ* ['God'] or *životъ* ['stomach'] or *ʒělo* ['very much'] or *crьky* ['church'] or *čajanie* ['expectation'] or *širota* ['width'] or *ědь* ['poison'] or *ǫdu* ['where'] or *junostь* ['youth'] or *ęzykъ* ['tongue'] or other similar words? And so it was for many years. (Džambeluka-Kossova 1980)

Khrabr's *črьty i rězy* have long puzzled scholars. Were they merely marks made on wood to be used as an aid in counting or did they represent some sort of systematized adaptation of Germanic or Turkic runes? The runic hypothesis is not totally implausible, for some Germanic runes were employed in the Greek-based Gothic alphabet created by the Visigothic bishop Ulfila of Moesia (ca. 311–383) for his translation of the Bible, and Turkic runes oc-

194. It is important to note, however, that not even the oldest Bulgarian epigraphic monuments predate the mission of Constantine and Methodius.

curred in Proto-Bulgarian epigraphy. Yet despite the proximity of historical and prehistorical Slavs to Germanic and Turkic tribes, authentic Slavic runes have not been discovered, nor can it be shown that Constantine's Glagolitic alphabet contains runic elements. It seems likelier, therefore, that Khrabr's *črъty i rězy* had a numerical or religious value.

Much easier to accept is Khrabr's claim that for some time before the Moravian mission the Slavs used Roman and Greek letters "without design." Settled in the midst or in immediate proximity of Greek and Latin civilizations, the Slavs, whether baptized or not, may well have tried to adapt the Greek and Latin alphabets to their language. As Khrabr tells us, this was not an easy task. The initial letters of the examples cited by him are meant to exemplify the difficulty of bending the Greek alphabet to suit the Slavic sound system. Thus, Slavic *bogъ* could not be rendered adequately with Greek letters because in Byzantine Greek voiced stops had become spirantized, and the Greek letters β and γ were pronounced as labial and velar fricatives. In *živoтъ, ʒělo, crъky, čajanie,* and *širota* the initial consonants were altogether foreign to Greek. Equally foreign to Byzantine Greek were the nasal vowels exemplified by *ǫdu* and *ęzykъ,* as well as the initial syllable of *junostь,* whether it was pronounced as a rising diphthong [ju] or a fronted [ü]. As for Slavic *ě* in *ědь,* it could not be spelled with the Greek η which by that time had acquired the sound value of [i].

3.7. Unsystematic Slavic adaptations of Greek and Latin alphabets. The need to write down Slavic words and texts must have been felt especially acutely by the Balkan Slavs. Living side by side with the Greeks for some three hundred years before the start of the Moravian mission, they took part in the daily affairs of the state, be they administrative, military, commercial, or ecclesiastic in nature. Through such contacts the Slavs must have become familiar with the Greek alphabet and must have tried to adapt it to the needs of Slavic, even though it was not best suited for that purpose.[195] The claim of the monk Khrabr that the first attempts at using the Greek alphabet to record Slavic words were "without design" is borne out by several ancient Bulgarian epigraphic monuments and by the Byzantine renditions of Slavic place and personal names. Illustrative of the difficulty of the task are the following transcriptions of Slavic names included in the survey of the empire undertaken by Emperor Constantine Porphyrogenitus (r. 944–959) and best known by its Latin name, *De administrando imperio:*

Βουσεγραδέ = Vyšegradъ	Κιάβος = Kievъ
Κριβιτζοί = Kriviči	Μιλινίσκα = Smolьnьskъ
Μουντιμήρος = Mǫtimirъ	Πρεσθλάβος = Prěslavъ
Σφενδοπλόκος = Svętoplukъ	Τζερνιγώγα = Černigovъ

Similar needs were experienced by the Slavs living within the cultural radius of Latin. Here, for instance, is an example from a monument known as the *Freising Fragments,* which were recorded in the Latin alphabet in Central Europe at the end of the tenth century. The text, which combines Slovenian and Church Slavonic features, may be considered a specimen of Old Slovenian or the Pannonian recension of Church Slavonic:

195. Of the scholars who argue for the existence of a Greek-based pre-Constantinian alphabet, the Bulgarian Emil Georgiev (1952) is the most confident and insistent. Much more prudent is Lunt's (1964) "agnostic" stance. A survey of literature dealing with this and other issues of Slavic paleography may be found in Eckhardt (1989) with a bibliographic update by Christian Hannick.

Freising Fragments:	*Transcription:*	*Translation:*
Ecce bi deat naſ neze	Ešte bi děd naš ne se	If our ancestor had not
greſil tevuekigemube	grešil, te v veki jemu be	sinned, he would have
ſiti ſtaro ſti neprigem	žiti, starosti ne prijem	lived forever, without old
lióki nikolige ſe pet	l'oči, nikolije že peč	age, not having any sorrow
ſali neimugi niſlzna	ali ne imyji, ni slzna	whatever, nor having
telezeimoki nuúvue	tělese imoči, no v ve	grieving flesh, but he would
kigemubesiti bone	ki emu be žiti. Po ne	have lived forever. Since,
sezavuiztiubui ne	že zavistju by ne	because of diabolical envy,
pri iazninu uvignan	prijazninu vignan	he was expelled

Short as it is, this excerpt shows the difficulties experienced by the scribe. Thus, the letter ſ stands for /s/, /š/ and /ž/, while the letter *z* stands for /z/ and /s/. (A larger excerpt of this text is provided in facsimile and transcription in **4.1.3.**

A much more satisfactory example of such unsystematic writing is represented by the Old Czech sentence inscribed into the foundation charter of the capitular church in Litoměřice (**3.55**):

Litoměřice Charter:	*Transcription:*	*Translation:*
Pauel dal geſt	Pavel dal jest	Paul has given
ploſcouicih zemu.	Ploskovicích zem'u,	land in Ploskovice,
Wlah dalgeſt	Vlach dal jest	Vlach has given
dolaſ zemu bogu	Dolás zem'u Bogu	land in Dolane to God
iſuiatemu ſcepanu	i sv'atému Ščepánu	and to St. Stephen
ſe duema duſnicoma	se dvěma dušníkoma,	with two peasants,
bogucea a ſedlatu.	Bogučeja a Sedlatu.	Bogučej and Sedlata.[196]

It is interesting to compare Greek and Latin renditions of the names of Church Slavonic letters in medieval abecedaria. The Greek illustrations come from a thirteenth-century manuscript discovered by the Benedictine monk Anselmo Banduri (1671–1743) in the Bibliothèque Nationale in Paris and known as the *Anselmus Banduri Abecedarium* (published in 1711 and 1729). The Latin examples are the eleventh- and twelfth-century glosses inscribed in a Latin manuscript of the tenth or eleventh century preserved in the Bibliothèque Nationale and known as the *Paris Abecedarium.*

	ChSl.	*Banduri*	*Paris*
b	buky	μπούκη	bócobi
ž	živěte	ζήβητ	gíuete
i	iže	ἤζε	íſe
r	rьci	ριτζίη	recí
t	tvrьdo	ντβέρδω	tordo
f	frьtъ	φέρωτ	fort
č	čгъvь	τξέρβη	ſaraué

196. That is, to the church of St. Stephen with the farmsteads of Bogučej and Sedlata. The prepositionless locative plural *Dolas* (< **dălān-sŭ*) is one of the few Slavic examples of PIE *-sŭ* before it was replaced by *-хъ* (**2.14**).

3.8. The 'Russian' letters in the *Vita Constantini*. To prove the existence of Slavic letters before the Moravian mission, some scholars cite an event reported to have occurred in the Greek colony of Cherson (Khersones) in the Crimea, where the Byzantine embassy to the Khazars headed by Constantine spent the winter of 860/861. While engaged in various linguistic pursuits in preparation for the forthcoming meeting with the Khazars, Constantine is said to have learned a language whose name in the various codices of the *Vita Constantini* appears as *rušьkъ, rošьkъ, rusьskъ,* or *rosьskъ*. Philologically the most straightforward interpretation of these adjectives is "Russian," so that the translation of the passage in which they are found might read: "And there [in Cherson] Constantine found the Gospels and the Psalter written in Russian letters. And he found a man who spoke that language and, having conversed with him, [Constantine] acquired the force of his speech. Comparing it to his own language, he distinguished the letters, vowels, and consonants. He offered a prayer to God, and soon began to read and speak [it]" (*Vita Constantini* 8).

The question arises, however, what actual language was meant by the hagiographer. To understand "Russian" as Slavic, as V. Istrin, E. Georgiev, and many Russian scholars do, would imply the existence of a Slavic alphabet and of a Slavic translation of the Gospels and the Psalter in the mid-ninth century. Such an inference is not supported by other sources and runs counter to the hagiographic spirit of the vita, for it takes away from Constantine the distinction of being the inventor of the Slavic alphabet and the first translator of the Scriptures into Slavic. The anachronistic and atypical character of this lection has led many scholars to seek alternative interpretations. Some, like Šafařík, Fortunatov, Vondrák, Kul'bakin, Lavrov, Šaxmatov, Vajs, and Lehr-Spławiński have concluded that what was meant was the language of the Varangian Norsemen and that "Russian" stood for "Germanic" in its broadest sense. In this view, the passage in question could refer to Ulfila's Gothic translation of the Bible made in the fourth century. Others, like Vaillant, Grégoire, Jakobson, Unbegaun, and Čyževs'kyj have surmised that the original adjective was *surьskъ* 'Syriac' with transposed letters *s* and *r*, a hypothesis strengthened by several similar instances of inversion of consonants. Should this theory be correct, the passage in question should be translated 'written in Syriac letters'. It is also possible that we are dealing here with a late interpolation introduced in Bulgaria (L'vov 1975) or in Muscovy (Goldblatt 1986).[197]

3.9. The abecedarium from St. Sophia in Kiev. It has also been suggested that the so-called *St. Sophia Abecedarium* (in Russian *Sofijskaja azbuka,* 3.53) demonstrates the existence in Rus' of an ancient system of writing based on the Greek alphabet. The *St. Sophia Abecedarium* is a graffito discovered in 1969 on the wall of the Cathedral of St. Sophia in Kiev. As described by its finder, S. A. Vysockij (1970), the abecedarium consists of twenty-three letters of the Greek alphabet plus four Slavic letters: **Б Ж Ш Щ**. Vysockij thought that this alphabet was used in Rus' in the ninth or tenth century and that it represented a link between the Greek alphabet of twenty-four letters and the later Cyrillic one of thirty-eight. Vysockij went so far as to speculate on the nature of the literary monuments that could have been written in the alphabet reflected by the *St. Sophia Abecedarium*.[198] There is, however,

197. All extant manuscripts of the *Vita Constantini* are East Slavic and late (from the fifteenth century on). For a survey of the "Russian letters" question, see Florja (1981:115–117).

198. The existence of a pre-Cyrillic alphabet in Rus' was first posited by Vsevolod Miller (1884:26–28). Similarly unverifiable is a conjecture made by the Russian scholars Valentin Kiparsky (1979:26) and Lidia Žukovskaja (1981:13–14) that the *Gnezdovo inscription* (**3.53**) is an example of writing in pre-Christian Rus'.

no reason to see in the graffito anything more than an incomplete Cyrillic alphabet, which could not have appeared on the wall of the Kiev St. Sophia before the mid-eleventh century, when the cathedral was built.

3.10. The origin of the terms *Glagolitic* and *Cyrillic*. Since the time when Glagolitic came to the attention of scholars some two centuries ago, its origin, the time of its introduction, and the reasons for its adoption have been the object of detailed scrutiny and have engendered many debates. Some of the problems may be said to have been resolved to everyone's satisfaction. Some, inevitably, are still a matter of scholarly contention. Let us try to summarize here the most salient issues in the discussion.

To begin with, it is not certain when and where the term *Glagolitic* (Slavic *glagolica*) was introduced. Since it was not in use in the Middle Ages, one may asume that it was a late coinage. It is also probable that the term was created in the Catholic milieu of Dalmatia, which was the postmedieval stronghold of the Glagolitic tradition. Before the introduction of the term *Glagolitic*, the alphabet which is known today by this name may have actually been called Cyrillic. This is what many scholars inferred from the postscript to the Book of the Prophets,[199] copied in 1047 by the Novgorod priest Upyrь Lixyi and preserved in several codices dating from the turn of the fifteenth and sixteenth centuries: **Сла́ва тебѣ г҃и ц҃рю нб҃ныи. ꙗко сподоби мѧ||написати книги си. ис кȣ́рилловицѣ кн҃||зю влодимирȣ новѣгородѣ кнѧжащю. ||с҃нви ꙗрослáвлю болшемȣ.** 'Praise be to Thee, O Heavenly King, for letting me write these books *from* Cyrillic for Prince Vladimir ruling in Novgorod, the elder son of Jaroslav' (emphasis added). Since Upyrь Lixyi's text is *in* Cyrillic, it was surmised that its original must have been Glagolitic. The corollary of this hypothesis was that the term *Cyrillic* was at some point transferred from the alphabet designed by Constantine to its Greek-based replacement and that the terminological void created thereby was filled by the new coinage.[200]

The derivational base of *glagolica* is the Old Church Slavonic noun *glagolъ* 'word', which is a reduplicated form of the Proto-Slavic root *gol-* (cf. PSl. *gol-s-* 'voice' yielding OCS *glasъ*, Russian *gólos*). A derivative of this noun is the Old Church Slavonic verb *glagolati* 'to speak' (occurring also with prefixes). It seems that the specifically Church Slavonic associations of the stem *glagol-* were deemed appropriate for the name of an alphabet that was used solely in church services.[201] At some point after the term *glagolica* was introduced, there arose in Dalmatia the term *glagoljaši*, an agent noun referring to the local Catholic priests, who had the dispensation to use Slavic Glagolitic books (in preference to Latin) in church services.

3.11. Why was Glagolitic introduced? The monk Khrabr's complaint that the pre-Constantinian attempts of the Balkan Slavs to adapt the Greek writing system to Slavic suffered from the lack of "design" was certainly justified. Yet aside from the problem presented by the typically Slavic sounds enumerated by Khrabr, the early Greek-based writing could

199. Actually, the Prophets with commentaries.

200. This widely held view was criticized by Andrzej Poppe (1985), who recalled that in one of the codices the phrase **ис коуридовицѣ** read actually **ис коурилоцѣ**. Poppe agreed with Archimandrite Leonid (1883), who took the latter reading to be older and connected it with the noun *kurělъkъ* 'prototype, original'.

201. The stem *glagol-* does not occur in South Slavic outside of (Old) Church Slavonic. As for West and East Slavic, there occur modern Czech expressive *hlahol* 'uproar', *hlaholiti* 'make a racket' and Russian dialectal *gologólit'* 'to chatter'. It is probable that these forms hark back to the unsuccessful attempts to introduce Glagolitic services in Bohemia at the end of the fourteenth century and in Rus' a few centuries earlier.

not have been very different from what we know as the Cyrillic alphabet. Why, then, instead of adjusting the Greek alphabet to the needs of Slavic (as was done later in Bulgaria), did Constantine consider it necessary to design for the mission to Moravia an entirely new alphabet?

A theological answer to this question was provided by Constantine himself during the great debate in Venice. Church scholars who gathered there cast doubts upon the doctrinal legitimacy of the special Slavic letters created by Constantine "which none else have found before." "We know," they continued, "of only three languages worthy of praising God in the Scriptures: Hebrew, Greek, and Latin." Constantine parried these objections by citing historical precedents. He enumerated the various peoples "who possess writing and render glory unto God, each in its own language: . . . Armenians, Persians, Abkhazians, Iberians [i.e. Georgians], Sogdians, Goths, Avars, Turks, Khazars, Arabs, Egyptians, and many others" (*Vita Constantini* 16).[202] In the eyes of Constantine and his contemporaries, the possession of a distinct alphabet bestowed upon Slavic the dignity requisite for undertaking the sacred task of Bible translation and secured for it a place of equality among the major languages of medieval Christendom.

More importantly, however, the creation of a specifically Slavic system of writing, one that had no immediate associations with other well-known alphabets, held several political advantages. By steering clear of recognizable Hebrew, Greek, or Latin models, Constantine challenged the claim, advanced most vocally by the Bavarian clergy, that only those three languages were worthy of transmitting the sanctity of the Scriptures and the liturgy. Secondly, possessing holy books couched in their own distinctive alphabet placed the Slavs on a par with the civilized nations of the time and made them legitimate and equal members of the Christian commonwealth. Finally, a writing system based on Greek or Latin would have inevitably carried with it an implication of political and doctrinal dependence. In particular, the adoption of a Greek-based alphabet could have been interpreted as a sign of Moravia's subservience to Byzantium, thus further complicating the mission's position vis-à-vis the Bavarian clergy.[203]

3.12. The locale of Glagolitic. Since the Glagolitic alphabet was specifically designed for the mission of Constantine and Methodius, we may assume that in the second half of the ninth century Glagolitic writings were in use in Moravia and Pannonia. The Moravian Glagolitic tradition gave us such monuments of Old Church Slavonic as the *Prague Fragments* and the *Kiev Folios*.

Following the death of Methodius and the expulsion of Slavic monks from Moravia, the Glagolitic tradition was continued in western Bulgaria (Macedonia). Particularly important was the Ohrid center of Slavic monastic activity, which was the principal source of Glagolitic monuments belonging to the Old Church Slavonic canon. It is likely that the fourfold Gospels in the codices *Zographensis* and *Marianus*, the evangeliaries in the *Codex Assemanianus* and the *Ohrid Gospel*, the *Psalterium Sinaiticum*, the *Euchologium Sinaiticum*, and the *Glagolita Clozianus* all belong to the Ohrid scriptorial tradition. In addition, the Cyrillic

202. Not all of the peoples mentioned by Constantine are known to have had their own script; see n. 102 in Kantor 1983 (94).

203. This is what actually happened a century later in Bulgaria when the Glagolitic alphabet was replaced by Greek-based Cyrillic. An analogical situation arose in the Moslem republics of the Soviet Union. First, in order to stress the secularization of their societies, the original Arabic script was replaced by the Roman alphabet. Later, the encroaching Russian political and cultural domination forced the replacement of the Roman alphabet by Cyrillic.

evangeliary known as the *Sava Book* has been shown to be a transcription from the original Macedonian Glagolitic (Ščepkin 1901).[204] It is probable that the abecedaria inscribed in two Latin manuscripts, the Glagolitic *Paris Abecedarium* and the Cyrillic/Glagolitic *Munich Abecedarium,* are Macedonian as well.

The influx of the Slavic monks expelled from Moravia may also be responsible for the continuation of the Glagolitic tradition in Croatia. This tradition was especially well established in the Bay of Quarner in the northern part of the Adriatic, where it persisted into the twentieth century. Of several early epigraphic monuments from that region, the long inscription on the *Baška stone* is particularly noteworthy.

The Glagolitic tradition left a few traces in eastern Bulgaria and in Rus'. There are Glagolitic inscriptions in the Round Church in Preslav and in the Cathedral of St. Sophia in Novgorod. In fact, among the earliest monuments of Glagolitic epigraphy is the *Preslav Abecedarium* inscribed on the wall of the baptistry in the Round Church. The Novgorodian priest Upyrь Lixyi is thought to have been responsible for transcribing an eleventh-century Glagolitic manuscript into Cyrillic.

3.13. The precedence of Glagolitic. Which alphabet did Constantine design for Slavic? Ever since Pavel Jozef Šafařík's (1853) study of Glagolitic monuments, there has been a virtual consensus that it was Glagolitic rather than Cyrillic. The arguments in support of this thesis are linguistic, paleographic, and historical:

(a) The Slavic lands using the Latin alphabet took long to adapt it systematically to their local linguistic needs. It was not until the advent of printing that the process of developing a system based on Roman letters enriched by digraphs and diacritics may be said to have been completed. By contrast, the introduction of the Greek alphabet in the lands of the Orthodox Slavdom proceeded relatively quickly and efficiently. The reason for this difference is that while Latin was bent to the requirements of Slavic in an arduous process of trial and error, Greek had the benefit of replacing an alphabet that was specifically designed to fit the sound system of Slavic. This leads us to conclude that the Greek-derived Cyrillic alphabet was but a transliteration of the older Glagolitic alphabet.

(b) The small number of surviving Glagolitic monuments suggests that they belonged to a writing tradition that went out of use and was replaced by a younger and more vigorous Cyrillic tradition.

(c) As a rule, Old Church Slavonic Glagolitic monuments are older than their Cyrillic counterparts.

(d) The most ancient linguistic features (the uncontracted and unassimilated endings *-aego, -aemu;* the productive aorist endings *-šeta, -šete* rather than *-sta, -ste;* root and sigmatic aorists) are more frequent in Old Church Slavonic Glagolitic monuments than in Cyrillic texts.

(e) Surviving (Old) Church Slavonic palimpsests are Glagolitic over Glagolitic, Cyrillic over Glagolitic, Cyrillic over Cyrillic, but never Glagolitic over Cyrillic.

(f) Some Cyrillic manuscripts contain occasional Glagolitic letters, words, or sentences, all written by the same hand. By contrast, Cyrillic letters or words found in Glagolitic manuscripts are later additions.

204. Thus, all the Old Church Slavonic Gospel translations derive ultimately from the Macedonian Glagolitic tradition. It is possible, in fact, that the East Slavic *Ostromir Evangeliary* goes back to an East Bulgarian Cyrillic reworking of a Macedonian Glagolitic original (Ščepkin 1901:VI–VIII).

(g) There are Cyrillic glosses in Glagolitic manuscripts but not the other way around.

(h) The numerical value of Glagolitic letters represents an orderly progression of numbers in strict agreement with the sequence of letters in the Glagolitic alphabet. The Cyrillic alphabet, by contrast, follows the Greek numerical usage and assigns no numerical value to several non-Greek letters. Consequently, most Glagolitic and Cyrillic numbers are represented by different letters (**3.4**). Scribal errors due to this lack of equivalence indicate transpositions from the Glagolitic numerical system to Cyrillic rather than the other way around.

(i) The close relation between the Glagolitic monuments in Moravia and those in the Balkans is best explained by the expansion of the Glagolitic tradition from Moravia. Such an expansion must have taken place before the tenth century, when the Magyar-German wedge separated the western from the southern Slavs.

3.14. Digraphs and ligatures. As we have seen above, some Slavic sounds were graphically represented by digraphs, that is, by combinations of two otherwise independent letters either blending into a new letter or retaining their separate shapes. The former situation may be exemplified by the letter *ukъ* ⱆ, made up of the letters *onъ* ⱁ and *ižica* ⱛ, the latter by the digraphs ⱏⰹ or ⱏⰻ, which represented the phoneme /y/.

Digraphs, trigraphs, and even tetragraphs and pentagraphs whose components blend into new graphic units while retaining their sound values are called *ligatures*. The Slavic practice of using ligatured spellings followed Greek and Latin models, where ligatures arose as a way of expediting the writing process or economizing space on various kinds of writing surfaces, notably on stone in epigraphy. At first, ligatured spellings were used to transcribe frequent consonant clusters, but eventually they spread to consonant-vowel sequences, especially those that shared a graphic feature (stem, bar, circle, etc.). Ligatures may be found in the earliest Old Church Slavonic monuments (*Codex Assemanianus, Euchologium Sinaiticum*) but they gained special popularity in the angular Croatian Glagolitic.

Here are some fourteenth- and fifteenth-century examples of Croatian Glagolitic ligatures with the letter ⰲ /v/:[205]

Other frequently used letter combinations included:

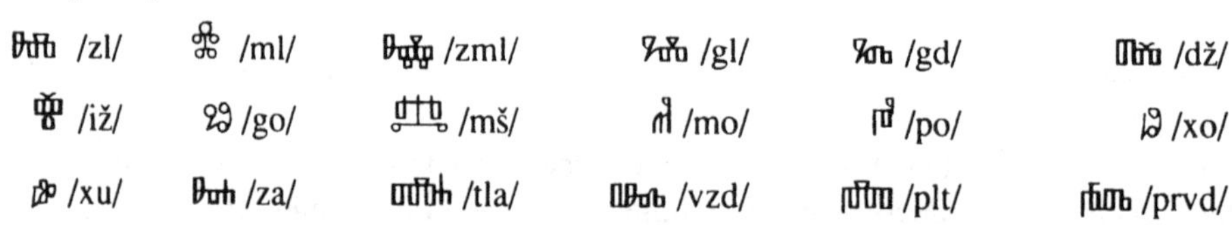

Greek and Cyrillic letters were less suitable for ligatured spellings than the Glagolitic ones. Even though such ligatures as ѡ + т = ѿ and ρ + ѣ = [ligature] occurred in south Slavic manuscripts as early as the thirteenth century, the bulk of Cyrillic ligatures depended on the relatively infrequent occurrence of adjacent and concordant stems of letters (e.g. л + к = [ligature], а + н = [ligature], п + ч = [ligature], ш + ч = [ligature]).[206] Both Byzantine and Cyrillic manuscript writing, however, developed a particular kind of ornamental ligature in which letters were intricately interconnected not only through the device of sharing graphic elements but also through in-

205. For surveys of Glagolitic ligatures, see Jagić (1911:216–226) and Lunt (1957).

206. Compare Latin NB for *nota bene* 'take notice'. Examples of ligatured spellings in a modern Cyrillic alphabet are provided by Serbian њ (н + ь) and љ (л + ь).

scription and subscription. In this kind of calligraphy, known in Russian as *vjaz'*, letters were elongated and their size was adjusted to make them fit so snugly into the adjacent letters as to create the impression of a continuous ornament and to approach, on occasion, the goals of cryptography. *Vjaz'* became especially popular among the eastern Slavs from the fifteenth century on (see Plate 3).

3.15. Abbreviations. Ligatures were a special case of a spelling tendency whereby certain frequently used words or expressions were abbreviated. The original impulse for this practice, observable since classical times, must have been a desire to save space and time. Writing surfaces were expensive and the process of copying texts by hand was laborious. This motivation is behind such commonly used Roman abbreviations as *S.P.Q.R.*, standing for *Senatus populusque Romanus* 'Roman senate and people', and *etc.* = *et cetera* 'and the rest'.

With the advent of Christianity another class of abbreviations gained popularity. Its origin is to be found in ancient Hebrew biblical texts, which reflect the Jewish tenet that God's name is ineffable. Hellenized Jews adapted this Hebrew tradition to Greek translations of the Old Testament (the Septuaginta), whence it spread eventually to Christian texts, affecting other words of sacred content and forming a class of so-called sacred names or *nomina sacra*.[207] Although the original function of the nomina sacra was not to economize but to leave unexpressed, they proliferated and with time reached beyond their original religious function and so are best viewed as abbreviations.

The practice of abbreviating the nomina sacra was also adopted in Slavic texts. Following the rules of Greek orthography, Slavic abbreviations were set off from nonabbreviated words by superimposed lines of different shapes (⁻ ⁻ ‾ ˜), known as *titla* (singular *titlo* < Greek *títlos* 'title, superscription'). Most of the Old Church Slavonic nomina sacra were nouns. They were abbreviated according to the following conventions: word initials (including clusters of consonants) were retained; stem-final letters and monosyllabic inflectional endings also tended to be retained; medial letters, especially vowels, tended to be omitted; first vowels of disyllabic inflectional endings tended to be retained. Thus, for the singular paradigm of *prorokъ* 'prophet' one finds the following abbreviations: Nom. *pr(r)kъ*, Gen./Acc. *pr(r)ka*, Loc. *pr(r)cě*, Dat. *pr(r)ku*, Inst. *pr(r)k(o)mь*. Other frequent abbreviations included:

agglъ	aggelъ 'angel'	i(s)lъ	iz(d)railъ 'Israel'
aplъ	apostolъ 'apostle'	isъ	iisusъ 'Jesus'
b(g)ъ	bogъ 'God'	krstъ	krъstъ 'cross'
crь	cěsar'ь 'emperor'	mti	mati 'Mother'
crky	crъky 'church'	mčkъ	mǫčenikъ 'martyr'
čl(v)kъ	člověkъ 'man'	nbo	nebo 'Heaven'
d(a)dъ	davidъ 'David'	ocь	otьcь 'Father'
dxъ	duxъ 'Spirit'	sr(d)ce	srъdьce 'heart'
ęzkъ	ęzykъ 'tongue, tribe'	sp(s)ъ	spasъ 'Savior'
glъ	glagolъ 'word'	stъ	svętъ 'sacred'
gь	gospodь 'Lord'	xsъ	xristosъ 'Christ'

207. Such Greek abbreviations as κς for κυριος and θς for θεός, which occur in the Septuaginta, are direct calques from Hebrew. Their Latin equivalents are *dns* for *dominus* and *ds* for *deus*. The term *nomina sacra* was introduced by the German paleographer Ludwig Traube (1907). This is how the principle was formulated by an East Slavic bookman: **єже что҃ сто и гдви оугодное то҃ пишетсѧ по҃ титломъ. а еже что҃ бгоу мерзко ѿпшее то пишетсѧ все складомъ ѿню не покрываетсѧ** 'What is holy and pleasing to the Lord is written under the *titlo* but what to God is loathsome, corrupt, is written all in full [and] is not superscribed at all' (Karskij 1928:232 quoting from Jagić 1895:693). For a survey of the *nomina sacra* in Slavic, see Sill (1972).

Instead of being omitted, consonants could also be placed above the abbreviated word, with or without a rounded titlo (in Russian, *vynosnye bukvy*). Here are several examples from the Glagolitic *Codex Assemanianus:* ⰁⰟⰋ (bъi) for *bystъ* 'was', ⰏⱅⰂⰀ (mtvā) for *molitva* 'prayer', ⰏⱌⰠ (mсь) for *měsęcь* 'month', ⰄⰅ (de) for *dьnь* 'day'. Superscript letters were used frequently for word-final letters (other than the jers), as in the following title of a prayer said over a feverish person, found in the Glagolitic *Euchologium Sinaiticum:* ⰏⰑ ⱀⰀ ⰂⰔⰡ ⱅⱃⰝⱄⱁⰏⱁ ⱅⱃⰝⱄⰀⰂⰋⱌⰅ (Mo na vsě trNsomo trNsavicę) for *Molitva nadъ vьsěmь tręsomomь tręsavicejǫ* 'Prayer over all that is shaked by fever'.

Abbreviations of this type were especially common in the rubrics containing instructions on the manner of performance of hymns or poems during the course of the Orthodox service. Consider, for instance, the shorthand notation of the following rubric to the office for Methodius as it appears in the *Dragan menaeum* (Lavrov, ed. 1930:122):

Вє҃ на ги҃ вꙁва҃ ѿ с҃ ѕ. и покⷨ сти҃ ·г҃· по в҃ щи. гла҃ ·д҃· по҃. дасть зна.

With its abbreviations resolved, this line reads:

Вечерниꙗ на господи въꙁвахъ октоихъ стихиръ шесть и покмъ стихиръ три по дъвацни гласъ четврьтъи подобьнъ дасть ꙁнамение[208]

3.16. Numerals. The letters of the Glagolitic and Cyrillic alphabets had numerical values attached to them. The numerical system of Glagolitic was based on a simple system of assigning the value of units, tens, and hundreds to successive letters of the alphabet:

Units		Tens		Hundreds	
1 Ⰰ	6 Ⰵ	10 Ⰺ Ⰹ	60 Ⰿ	100 Ⱃ	600 Ⱈ
2 Ⰱ	7 Ⰶ	20 Ⰻ	70 Ⱀ	200 Ⱄ	700 Ⱉ
3 Ⰲ	8 Ⰷ	30 Ⰼ	80 Ⱁ	300 Ⱅ	800 Ⱋ
4 Ⰳ	9 Ⰸ	40 Ⰽ	90 Ⱂ	400 Ⱆ	900 Ⱌ
5 Ⰴ		50 Ⰾ		500 Ⱇ	

The teens were written so as to reflect the sequence of numbers in the compound. Thus, Ⰰ 1 and Ⰺ 10 rendered 11 *edinъ na desęte* = ⰀⰊ, and Ⰱ 2 and Ⰺ 10 rendered 12 *dъva na desęte* = ⰁⰊ.

The numerical system of Cyrillic followed the Greek system. It did not assign any numerical value to the letters that did not occur in Greek (**б ж ш ъ ь ѣ ю ꙗ** etc.) but retained otherwise unused letters that had a numerical value in Greek (ѯ = 60, ѱ = 700, ѵ = 400).

In both Glagolitic and Cyrillic, letters used as numerals had to be distinguished from letters used in their primary function. This was done by placing a titlo over each letter in a numeral or over the entire numeral. Thousands were marked by placing the sign ͵ or ҂ before the numeral: Ⰰ҃ = 1, Ⰱ҃ = 2, ͵Ⰰ = 1000, ҂Ⰱ = 2000[209]

208. That is, the sticheiron is **на "господи въꙁвахъ"** 'Lord, I cry unto thee' (Ps. 140/141); it is for six verses (which are to be interpolated after verse 3 of Psalm 129/130); in tone IV as in the hymn **дасть ꙁнамение** 'You gave the signs'; **дъвацни** is derived from **дъвашьдн**, cf. modern Russian *dváždy* 'twice'.

209. However, 1000 was also expressed with the letter Ⱍ /č/. Extrapolating from this and from the fact that **Ш** occurred in later texts with the value of 2000, Trubetzkoy (1954:18) surmised that the last nine letters of the Glagolitic alphabet must originally have had the numerical value of thousands.

3.17. Dates. Early Slavic texts recorded dates according to the Byzantine (or Constantinople) era, a method of reckoning the passage of time from the "creation of the world." It consisted in adding 5508 (the presumed date of Jesus' birth) to the date of the recorded event. The conversion from the Byzantine date to the modern one is complicated by the differences in the organization of the calendar, in particular by the three competing dates for the new year: Julian January 1, Paschal March 1, and ecclesiastic September 1.[210] For the calendar whose new year falls on September 1, one deducts 5508 from a Byzantine date between the months of January and August, and 5509 from a date between September and December. Thus, the date of the death of Methodius, reported in *Vita Methodii* 17 as being April 6, 6393, should be understood as April 6, 885 (i.e. 6393 minus 5508). When the month of an event is not known, some scholars take a chance on probability (eight to four) and deduct 5508, while others deduct 5509 and 5508 and record the date with a slash. Thus, the year 6501 in the *Tsar Samuil Inscription,* the oldest dated monument of Old Church Slavonic, may be converted to 993 or 992/993.[211]

An auxiliary unit of measuring time was a fifteen-year cycle called *indiction.* The year of the indiction is the difference between the year of the event and the nearest previous year divisible by fifteen. Thus Methodius' death is said to have occurred in the third indiction because 6393 minus 6390 equals 3.

3.18. Punctuation and diacritics. Punctuation practices were modeled on the Byzantine Greek usage and, like it, were not fully systematized. By and large, the following rules were observed: the basic punctuation mark was a point; a single point raised to the top of the line (˙) was "stronger" than a single point placed at the bottom (.) or in the middle of the line (·); single points were "weaker" than two or more points; multiple points occurred in different arrangements (: ⁖ ⁘ ∷ ⁘ :·:).

Some Old Church Slavonic texts used a raised mark (ˆ) to indicate the palatization of consonants. Thus, the *Codex Zographensis* is noted for its faithful rendition of the PSl. *n' l'* as Ⱀ̂ Ⰾ̂ . The apostrophe (') and the *paerók* (՝) were often used to indicate omitted vowels, usually the jers in weak position.

The supralinear diacritics that are often found in Old Church Slavonic texts over vowels in syllable-initial positions imitated the Greek practice of marking the place of stress and of indicating the so-called rough and soft breathings on initial vowels.[212] The only text where the supravocalic diacritics may have had some independent phonetic value is the Latin-based Glagolitic *Kiev Missal.* In addition to its putative rough and soft breathings, this monument contains such accent markings as ´ ` ˆ ˇ which possibly had something to do with the pronunciation or with the chanting of the text. (For a specimen folio of the *Kiev Missal,* showing all the punctuation and supralinear markings, see App. D, Glag. 1.)

210. March 1, the date of the new year in ancient Rome, was replaced by January 1 in 153 B.C., the latter date adopted also by the Julian calendar of 46 B.C. The ecclesiastic new year celebrated on September 1 was set in 325 A.D. by the First Ecumenical Council in Nicaea. It represented an adaptation of the Jewish new year, whose relevance for Christianity was derived from Jesus' embracement (Luke 4.19) of the prophet Isaiah's reference to the "acceptable year of the Lord" (Isa. 61.2). September 1 was also the date of the conversion of Constantine the Great, the convener of the Council, after he saw a vision of the cross in the sky and the Latin inscription *In hoc signo vinces* 'In this sign thou shalt conquer'.

211. The Paschal new year beginning in March was used in Rus' until the mid-fourteenth century. Its rules of conversion require the subtraction of 5508 from March through December and of 5507 from January through February. Thus, the date 6391, which according to the *Primary Chronicle* was the year when Oleg campaigned against the Derevlians, may be transcribed as 883/884. A synopsis of the Orthodox church calendar is given in appendix C.

212. The symbols for rough and soft breathings (⊢ and ⊣) represented originally the left and right sides of the letter H.

3.19. Styles of handwriting. Shapes of letters depended to a large degree on the function of the text and on the writing surface. The most formal and elegant Cyrillic letters were in the uncial style of writing (Russian *ustáv*). They were derived from the dignified style of stone inscriptions and were characterized by carefully drawn upright letters of equal size (except for initials), without ligatures. There were few abbreviations and no word spacing. Uncial writing was typical of solemn biblical texts such as the *Ostromir Evangeliary* copied in 1056/1057. East Slavic legal and business documents from the fourteenth century on were characterized by a less formal style known as semi-uncial (Russian *poluustáv*). Its letters may be slightly inclined, vertical lines are elongated and often curved, and there are more abbreviations, ligatures, superscribed letters, and stress marks. Semi-uncial eventually gave way to cursive writing (Russian *skóropis'*), which appeared in the Balkans in the thirteenth century and from there spread to Rus'.

This traditional classification of handwriting is applicable to Cyrillic but less so to Glagolitic. The two main styles of Glagolitic are both of the uncial type. They are the round letters of the oldest monuments from Moravia and Pannonia (e.g. the *Kiev Missal*) and from Macedonia (e.g. the codices *Assemanianus, Zographensis,* and *Marianus*) and the angular letters typical of early Croatian liturgical texts. From the fifteenth century on, Croatian angular Glagolitic is characterized by a large number of ligatures. At the same time nonliturgical texts, especially legal monuments, begin to show features combining semi-uncial and cursive styles. A unique example of transition from round to angular styles is represented by the inscription on the *Baška Stone* from the beginning of the twelfth century (App. D, Glag. 4).

3.20. Physical description of manuscripts. The description of early Slavic manuscripts must contain a note about their physical aspect, including the layout of the page, format, writing materials and implements, and binding and decorative elements. All of the oldest Slavic manuscripts were written on parchment and consisted of one or more folios (leafs) with writing on one or both sides (pages). The front (first) side of a folio is called *recto* (*r*), its back side *verso* (*v*). The writing could be right across the page or it could be organized in two columns, for which are used the designations *a* and *b*. Single-folio texts are either documents (charters) or fragments of larger texts. A gathering (or quire) of folios folded and sewn together formed a codex (Slavic *kъn'iga*).[213] A single fold formed a bifolium (two folios, that is, four pages). Two bifolia formed a binion (eight pages), three a ternion (twelve pages), four a quaternion (sixteen pages), etc. The quaternion or, to use its Byzantine name, tetradion (hence Russian *tetrád'* 'notebook') was the basic organizing unit of a manuscript and was subject to consecutive numbering. Pagination in the modern sense of the word did not exist in medieval writing practice, and specific folios were referred to by complex numbers, with the first digit indicating the tetradion and the second the folio. Thus гა meant the first folio of the third tetradion.[214] The tetradia were sewn together with a thread and protected by a binding made of two boards covered with leather and locked with one or two metal clasps.

3.21. Writing materials. The favorite medieval writing surface was parchment.[215] It was produced from the skin of larger domestic animals, such as sheep, goats, calves, and even cows.

213. This term occurred usually in the plural as *kъn'igy*. It was borrowed into Slavic from Turkic, but its ultimate origin seems to have been the ancient Chinese word for 'scroll'. The word *codex* is derived from Latin *caudex* 'tree trunk'; cf. English *book* (< OE *bōk*) and *beech* (< OE *bēk* < Gmc. *bōkjan*).

214. Foliation or numbering by folios was not introduced until the advent of printing, and in many instances considerably later. The process of putting loose *tetradia* in order was facilitated by the catchword at the bottom of each page which anticipated the first word on the following page.

215. So known because of the Anatolian town of Pergamon, which was one of the larger parchment manufacturing centers of antiquity.

The skin was first soaked in caustic calcium lye to loosen the hair and dissolve the fat. Then it was washed, stretched on a frame, and dried. This durable but very expensive material was used in the writing of all early Slavic codices and documents.[216] The surfaces devised for personal correspondence and other kinds of informal writing were cheaper but perishable. Thus, no trace remains of the northern practice of writing on wooden boards (Russian *lub*), and the only reason for the survival of many birchbark documents from Novgorod, Pskov, and Smolensk is that they were trapped between superimposed layers of log pavements, which sank gradually into the practically oxygen-free bogs of northern Russia. Stones and objects made of wood, clay, or metal, such as looms, amphoras, drinking bowls, crosses, seals, and coins, bear various kinds of engraved inscriptions, and church walls had graffiti scratched onto them.

The recipes for black ink (**čr̥'nidlo*) differed from scriptorium to scriptorium. The main ingredients were soot, sulfate of iron, gall nuts, and boiled-down bark of certain trees. The intensity of the original color tends to fade with time, producing the brownish tint that one often sees in surviving manuscripts. Cinnabar (sulfide of mercury) and other red inks were used for page ornaments (Russian *zastávki*) and highlighted portions of the text including titles and large initials. Occasionally other colors are also found, green and yellow in the *Codex Assemanianus*, green, blue, and gold in the *Ostromir Evangeliary*, gold in the charter of the great prince Mstislav to the Monastery of St. George near Novgorod.

The scribe was seated at a small sloping desk on which he had his writing implements. For writing on parchment they included a quill pen, a horn to hold the ink, and a knife or razor for sharpening the quill and for erasing. If the design of the lining system was left to the scribe, he needed a punctorium for marking out the margins (text and column width) and an awl and a ruler for tracing lines. Colored initials, ornaments, and illuminations were executed separately at the end of the copying process by specially trained scribes.[217] For writing on birchbark all that was needed was a sharp tool (stylus) for scratching letters onto the back side of bark.

3.22. Palimpsests. Because of the high price of parchment, unneeded texts were often "recycled" by erasing the original writing and replacing it with another, forming the so-called *palimpsests*.[218] Modern ultraviolet technology allows scholars to partly recover the underlying text. An example is the octoechos from the Saltykov-Ščedrin Public Library in St. Petersburg, whose Glagolitic Old Church Slavonic text was erased to make room for a fourteenth-century Cyrillic manuscript. The largest Slavic palimpsest is the *Bojana Gospel*, an evangeliary of the late twelfth or early thirteenth century written in Cyrillic over an erased Glagolitic text. It was acquired in the village of Bojana, near Sofia, in 1845. Another palimpsest evangeliary is the thirteenth-century *Koxno Gospel*, in which a Cyrillic text was written over Greek. It is named for a captain of the Russian army who bought the manuscript in Bulgaria during the Russo-Turkish war of 1877–1878. Also in Cyrillic written over Greek is the *Slepče Apostol*. An example of a Glagolitic text written over Glagolitic is provided by a seventeen-folio segment (out of 304 folios) of the *Codex Zographensis*.

3.23. The term *Old Church Slavonic*. Contacts between the Slavs and the civilizations of Christian Europe began in the sixth century and culminated three centuries later with the

216. As far as one can tell, all parchment used in early Slavic manuscripts was imported. Paper began to be introduced among the Slavs in the thirteenth and fourteenth centuries but cannot be said to have gained a permanent foothold until the introduction of printing around 1500.

217. Note the derivation of PSl. *pis-/pьs-* 'write' from PIE *pěi̯k'-/pĭk'-* 'adorn' (cf. Latin *pingō, -ere, pictus* 'paint').

218. From Greek *pálin* 'again' and *psḗn* 'to rub away'. For a list of Slavic palimpsests, see Granstrem 1964.

most important event of Slavic cultural history—the creation of a Slavic written language. Its appearance followed an intensive drive emanating from the West to bring the Slavs into the Christian fold. The earliest Western missions to reach the Slavs were the Irish and Scottish Benedictines, whose evangelizing efforts on the European continent began in the eighth century. They were followed by the Bavarian missions from Salzburg, Regensburg, and Passau and by the Italian missions from Aquileia. None of the Western missions, however, was concerned with the development of a Slavic literary idiom, even though some areas of proselityzing activity (such as the homiletics) must have called for the use of Slavic. It fell to the mission from Constantinople, under the leadership of Constantine and Methodius, to engage in a specific program of translations of the Scriptures and the liturgy into Slavic. These goals determined the religious nature of the oldest Slavic literary monuments.[219] They also justify the epithet *church* in the names most commonly used for the language of these monuments: *Old Church Slavonic* or *Old Church Slavic*. Of the other terms that are in use, *Old Slavic* is popular in Russian (*staroslavjánskij jazýk*) and in France (*vieux slave*), and *Old Bulgarian* is favored in Bulgaria (*starobălgarski ezik*). The former appears to be too encompassing for a language whose functional geographic ranges are strictly circumscribed. The latter, on the other hand, is not broad enough for a language whose development is linked not only with the Slavs of the Balkans but also with those inhabiting the lands north of the Danube.[220]

There is no denying that Old Church Slavonic reached its maturity in tenth-century Bulgaria and that it acquired there its distinctive Bulgarian linguistic imprint. It is also true, however, that Old Church Slavonic was created through the efforts of Constantine and Methodius, who hailed from the southernmost Macedonian town of Thessalonica, and that it was the Slavic dialect of their native town which provided the basis for the nascent literary idiom. Nor should we forget that Moravia was the destination and, together with Pannonia, the locus of the brothers' missionary activity, and that it was with the help of their Moravian and Pannonian disciples that many Old Church Slavonic translations were first produced. The *Kiev Missal*, with its many West Slavic features, testifies to the vitality of the Moravian period of Old Church Slavonic.

3.24. Old Church Slavonic and Proto-Slavic. Old Church Slavonic appeared at the time when the rise of independent Slavic states (Carantania, Pannonia, Bulgaria, and Moravia) gave greater weight to Proto-Slavic dialect distinctions and speeded the ultimate breakup of Slavic linguistic unity. By the mid-ninth century, however, this process had not yet gone far enough to obliterate the formal similarity between Old Church Slavonic and other Slavic dialects. There are good reasons, in fact, for maintaining that Old Church Slavonic represents the southeastern dialect of a language that was still common to all the Slavs (Lunt 1984/1985). One could propose, therefore, that the term *Common Slavic* (discussed in **2.5**) be reserved for the earliest period of *written* Slavic, whether it is documented or not. That period would include the Slavic of the lost writings of the Moravian mission, the earliest Old Church Slavonic monuments dated from the end of the tenth century and the turn of the tenth/eleventh centuries, and the bulk of the Old Church Slavonic corpus from the

219. In addition to purely religious texts, the corpus of Old Church Slavonic includes the oldest monuments of lay epigraphy (**3.53**).

220. Its older native appellation was simply *slověnьskyi ęzykъ* 'the Slavic language'. The problem of nomenclature has been aggravated by the different terminological resources of various languages. Thus the possibility of employing the difference between *drevneslavjanskij* and *staroslavjanskij* (Picchio 1963:122–126) may be present in Russian, but it does not exist in many other languages.

eleventh century. We must bear in mind, however, that the line separating the notions of dialect and language is fluid and, more often than not, politically determined, and that the early period of Old Church Slavonic is not documented at all. Thus, the acceptability of the view that Old Church Slavonic was a dialect of Late Proto-Slavic (or Common Slavic) hinges upon its reconstruction which, depending on the scholar's convictions, might stress the features that were common to the two languages or the signs of the incipient dissolution of Late Proto-Slavic. It is nonetheless a fact that "the Slavic language of the first translators in the ninth century, while presenting numerous easily discernible characteristic dialectal particularities, is still sufficiently close to Common Slavic [Proto-Slavic] . . . to serve linguists as a convenient substitute for Common Slavic which was not recorded" (Meillet 1921:8).[221]

3.25. The periodization of Old Church Slavonic. As mentioned above, the period during which canonical Old Church Slavonic texts were copied lasted from the middle of the ninth century till the turn of the twelfth century, about two hundred and fifty years. The corpus of Old Church Slavonic, however, provides us with textual evidence for only the last one hundred years of that stretch of time. Its initial history, for which no written sources have survived, must be reconstructed on the basis of the evidence found in ancillary sources (**1.31**), in particular the vitae of Constantine and Methodius. On the strength of this testimony we can posit four basic periods in the history of Old Church Slavonic.

First and probably shortest was the Constantinopolitan period, during which Constantine and Methodius readied themselves for their mission to the Slavs. This period saw the creation of the Slavic alphabet and the first set of translations of the liturgical texts destined for Moravia.[222] The language of these first translations was based in all likelihood on the Macedonian dialect of Thessalonica, the native city of the brothers.

Second was the Moravo-Pannonian period, which flourished for about twenty five years, from the arrival of the mission of Constantine and Methodius in Moravia in 863 till its expulsion shortly after Methodius' death in 885, but survived for a hundred years or so beyond that time in isolated enclaves like the Sázava monastery in Bohemia. That was the period during which the bulk of the biblical translations was accomplished. The language of these translations was probably lacking in dialectal uniformity. It must have been characterized by varying degrees of amalgamation of the Macedonian dialect of Constantine and Methodius and the Moravo-Pannonian dialect of their local disciples.

Third was the undocumented Bulgarian and Macedonian, perhaps also Croatian, period.[223] It lasted about one hundred years, from the arrival of the Moravian missionaries in Bulgaria at the end of the ninth century to the end of the tenth century, the time from which the first extant Old Church Slavonic texts date. Linguistically, this period was probably marked by an ever-increasing Bulgarization of Moravo-Pannonian texts and the preparation of new translations devoid of any West Slavic characteristics. The *Kiev Missal* is the only canonical Old Church Slavonic monument in which the specifically Moravo-Pannonian regionalisms (cf.

221. The linguistic success of the missionary endeavor of Constantine and Methodius is, of course, a significant indication that the brothers' Macedonian dialect was easily understood and assimilated by the Moravians. One has to remember, however, that even several centuries later (Old) Church Slavonic functioned as the literary *lingua franca* of all the Orthodox Slavs.

222. It is quite possible that some of these texts were originally used or intended to be used in the Christianization of Bulgaria (Fine 1983:113–114).

223. It was, in fact, sparsely documented by a handful of fragments of inscriptions (Krepča of 921, Preslav of 931, and Dobruja of 943 [?], **3.53**).

3.29) are overlaid with Bulgarian linguistic features. It is possible that an analogous process took place in Croatia. The Glagolitic writing, which is documented there from the twelfth century on, may have been started by some of the displaced members of the Moravian mission.

Fourth and last was the fully documented Bulgarian and Macedonian period, also about one hundred years in duration, from the end of the tenth century to the end of the eleventh century. It is from this period that practically all of the Old Church Slavonic monuments date. Its Bulgarian and Macedonian components are identified with the two chief monastic centers of Bulgaria, one in Preslav, Pliska's successor as the Bulgarian capital, the other in Macedonian Ohrid and its environs. In this way, after two and a half centuries of development, Old Church Slavonic returned to its dialectal beginnings in Macedonia.

3.26. The Ohrid and Preslav schools. Linguistically, the Ohrid and Preslav centers or schools, located as they were in the eastern South Slavic dialect area, must have been very close to each other. Yet in actual scriptorial practice they differed considerably. The Ohrid school, founded by Clement, a disciple of Methodius, was marked by linguistic conservatism exemplified by its fidelity to the Glagolitic tradition. The Ohrid translators were also skillful in finding adequate Slavic equivalents to the complex syntactic structures of Greek. The Preslav school, by contrast, founded by Tsar Symeon himself and nurtured by Naum, another of Methodius' disciples, was much more dependent on Greek models. This can be observed in its translating practices and in its readiness to abandon Glagolitic in favor of the Greek-based Cyrillic alphabet.

In phonology the two schools differed in their treatment of PSl. **ъ** and *ja*. In the texts of the Ohrid school these were frequently rendered with *o* and *ě* respectively, while in the texts of the Preslav school they were preserved as ъ and *ja*.[224] It is the lexicon, however, that offers the clearest evidence of the differences between these two schools. Here is a list of some of those differences, as compiled by Mirčev (1963:50):[225]

	Ohrid	*Preslav*
threshing floor	gumьno	tokъ
house	xramina	xlěvina
sacrifice	žrъtva	trěba
life	životъ	žitie
inheritance	dostoěnie	naslědie
grace	blagodětь	blagodatь
stick	drъkolь	žrъdь
bridegroom	ženixъ	zętь
companion	klevrětъ	podrugъ
coin	skъlęзь	cęta
gathering	sъnьmъ	sъborъ
large	velii	velikъ
sorrowful	dręselъ	sětьnъ
near	iskrьnii	bližьnii
only	tъkъmo	tъčiję
for	radi	dělьma
from the beginning	iskoni	isprъva

224. This difference does not contradict the claim of greater linguistic conservatism in Ohrid. It merely reflects an important dialect isogloss separating Macedonian from Bulgarian.

225. For a fuller list of such lexical contrasts, see Slavova 1989.

3.27. The canon of Old Church Slavonic. In addition to dialectal and chronological criteria, the corpus of Old Church Slavonic is defined by an important cultural consideration—evidence that a text does not depart significantly from the original design of Constantine and Methodius, that is, that it belongs to what has come to be known as the Cyrillo-Methodian tradition. A text that does not meet all of these three criteria—linguistic, chronological, and cultural—is barred from inclusion in the canon of Old Church Slavonic. There are, to be sure, instances of disputable assignments. Thus the *Freising Fragments,* dating from the eleventh century and showing some linguistic and cultural traits of Old Church Slavonic,[226] are usually not included in the canon because some features of their phonology appear to be Alpine Slavic in origin. Similarly, the oldest dated Slavic manuscript, the *Ostromir Evangeliary* (1057), shows dialect features that betray its East Slavic rather than South Slavic origin. On the other hand, the *Kiev Missal,* though containing a Western liturgy and several West Slavic linguistic features, is included in the Old Church Slavonic canon because of its Bulgarian linguistic overlay and its probable connection with the activities of the Moravian mission.

Old Church Slavonic monuments may be classified into two groups, Glagolitic and Cyrillic, according to the alphabet in which they were written.[227] Glagolitic texts are all manuscripts on parchment and, unless otherwise indicated, date from the eleventh century. With the possible exception of the *Kiev Missal,* which exhibits West Slavic features, and the *Glagolita Clozianus,* which may be Croatian, all Glagolitic texts are assumed to be of Macedonian provenience. They are:

Kiev Missal (KM), seven folios, late tenth century (**3.41.5**)
Codex Zographensis (Zo.), 288 folios, tenth/eleventh century (**3.42**)
Codex Marianus (Mar.), 173 folios, early eleventh century (**3.42**)
Codex Assemanianus (Ass.), 158 folios, early eleventh century (**3.41.1**)
Psalterium Sinaiticum (Ps.), 177 folios (**3.41.4**)
Euchologium Sinaiticum (Euch.), 109 folios (**3.41.5**)
Glagolita Clozianus (Cloz.), fourteen folios (**3.44**)
Ohrid Folios (Ohr.), two folios (**3.41.1**)
Rila Folios (Ril.), two folios and five folio fragments (**3.44**)

The oldest Cyrillic texts are Bulgarian inscriptions (**3.53**), of which the most important are:

Mostič's Inscription, thirty words on a tombstone, mid-tenth century
Temnič Inscription, fifteen words on stone, mid-tenth century (?)
Paul Khartophylaks' Inscription, six words on plaster, tenth century
Ktētōr's (Founder) Inscription, fourteen words on stone, tenth century
Spinning Wheel Inscription, two words on clay, tenth century (?)
Tsar Samuil's Inscription, thirty-one words on a tombstone, 992/993

Except for the *Zographos Fragments,* which are Macedonian, all Cyrillic parchment manuscripts are of Bulgarian provenience and date from the eleventh century:

Sava's Book (Sav.), 126 folios (**3.41.1**)
Codex Suprasliensis (Supr.), 284 folios (**3.44**)

226. Especially close to the Old Church Slavonic tradition is the homily (known as the *Adhortatio ad poenitentiam* or *Freising* II) with its clear echoes of the *Homily on the Apostle or Martyr* attributed to Clement of Ohrid (possibly as a translation from John Chrysostom). Note that the large *Slovník jazyka staroslověnského* of the Czecho-Slovak Academy of Sciences does include the *Freising Fragments* in the canon of Old Church Slavonic.

227. For the content and other features of the monuments of Old Church Slavonic, see the cross-referenced sections below.

Enina Apostol (En.), thirty-nine folios (**3.41.2**)
Hilandar Folios (Hil.), two folios (**3.44**)
Undol'skij's Fragments (Und.), two folios (**3.41.1**)
Macedonian Folio (Mac.), one folio (**3.31**)
Zographos Fragments (Zogr. Fr.), two folio (**3.48.1**)
Sluck Psalter (Sl.), five folios (**3.41.4**)

3.28. Old Church Slavonic and Church Slavonic. As we have seen, the language we call Old Church Slavonic is represented by a relatively small number of texts. The rest of medieval Slavic writing that belongs to the Cyrillo-Methodian tradition is either too late or too suffused with dialectal features to be included in the canon of Old Church Slavonic. The language of such texts is conventionally referred to as Church Slavonic. The importance of Church Slavonic in the cultural development of Orthodox Slavdom cannot be overstated. It served all the domains of the intellectual life of the Orthodox Slavs from the end of the Old Church Slavonic period until the modern era, when its secular functions began to be taken over by national literary languages. During the period of its preeminence Church Slavonic was the only supranational literary idiom of Orthodox Slavdom, playing a role comparable to that of Latin in the Roman West. Today, Church Slavonic functions as the liturgical language of the Slavic national Orthodox churches in Bulgaria, Macedonia, Serbia, Ukraine, Belarus, and Russia.[228] In this strictly specialized sphere of use it is referred to by some scholars as New Church Slavonic (Mareš 1979:12–13).

Old Church Slavonic, with its restricted functional compass, was a relatively homogeneous language. Its South Slavic and, more narrowly, eastern South Slavic dialect base is shown by such features as South Slavic *s'* from PSl. *x* by the progressive palatalization of velars (**2.31**), South Slavic *l* from PSl. *tl dl* (**2.33**), South Slavic *#RaC* from PSl. *#ăRC* (**2.35**), Bulgarian *št' žd'* from PSl. *t' d'* (**2.36**),[229] and Macedonian *ě* from PSl. *a* after soft consonants (**2.24, 2.27**).

The antiquity of Old Church Slavonic is confirmed by the similarity of its phonological system to that of the reconstructed system of Late Proto-Slavic. In particular, the texts of the Old Church Slavonic canon are characterized by the continued operation of the law of open syllables illustrated by the rendition of late Proto-Slavic vocalic liquids with sequences of a liquid followed by a jer (**2.35.b**), the preservation of Late Proto-Slavic nasal vowels, and the relatively faithful retention of the etymological jers in strong position.[230] At the same time departures from the expected quality of the jers in strong position offer a criterion for dividing Old Church Slavonic into three dialect areas: a conservative area, where **ь ъ** remain (KM, Sav., Supr. II, Sl.), the West Bulgarian or Macedonian area, where **ь** > *e* and **ъ** > *o* (Zo., Mar., Ass., Ps., Euch., Cloz.), and the East Bulgarian area, where **ь** > *e* and **ъ** remains (Ohr., Supr. I, Hil., Und.).

3.29. Local recensions of Church Slavonic. Church Slavonic, which in contrast to Old Church Slavonic was used over a vast territory during a long period of time and in a variety functions, incorporated a number of formal characteristics of the Slavic vernaculars with

228. Until the eighteenth century, Church Slavonic was also the language of the Romanian Orthodox church. It has been in continuous use by the Catholic *glagoljaši* of the West Dalmatian littoral and by the Uniate Church of Western Ukraine and Western Belarus. For a survey of Church Slavonic (including Old Church Slavonic), see Picchio 1980.

229. But West Slavic *c z* in the *Kiev Missal*. However, the West Slavic features of the *Kiev Missal* are overlaid with such South Slavic features as *l* < PSl. *tl dl* (rather than *tl dl*); *s'* < PSl. *x* by the progressive palatalization of velars (rather than *š*); *#RaC* < PSl. *#ăRC* (rather than *#RoC*).

230. The jers are particularly faithfully rendered in the *Kiev Missal*.

which it coexisted. The identification of these characteristics allows us to classify Church Slavonic into several local varieties, known as *recensions*.[231]

3.29.1. The Bulgarian and Macedonian recensions (also referred to as Middle Bulgarian) exhibit most of the characteristics of Old Church Slavonic. They are distinguished from it by several phonological features, of which the most important is the treatment of the reflexes of Proto-Slavic nasal vowels (*ę ǫ*), which in most Bulgarian and Macedonian dialects became denasalized. The traditional Cyrillic representation of these vowels was retained (ѧ = ę, ѫ = ǫ), but these spellings were not always used in accordance with etymology. They depended instead on more or less consistently applied distributional criteria reflecting the characteristics of the local dialect or on an artificially selected morphological principle. The former may be illustrated by the usage of manuscripts originating in the Ohrid region:

(a) PSl. *ę* was replaced by *ǫ* after Proto-Slavic soft consonants, e.g. *čǫstь* 'part', *šǫtati* 'walk', *štǫděti* 'save', *žǫtva* 'harvest,' *jǫzykъ* 'tongue' (OCS *ę: čęstь, šętati, štęděti, žętva ęzykъ*).
(b) PSl. *ǫ* was replaced by *ę* after PSl. *n' r' l'* and after soft labials (following the loss of the epenthetic *l*), e.g. *xranję* 'I guard', *tvorję* 'I do', *volję* 'I prefer', *sъp'ę* 'I sleep' (OCS *ǫ: xranjǫ, tvorjǫ, voljǫ, sъpljǫ*).

Another phonological feature distinguishing the manuscripts of the Bulgarian recension is provided by the treatment of the Proto-Slavic jers. In most manuscripts the spellings reflected the merger of the jers in the local dialects (a tendency noticeable also in Old Church Slavonic texts). Some manuscripts retained the two jers but used them either indiscriminately or according to some nonetymological principle (e.g. *ъ* word-internally and *ь* word-finally). The majority of manuscripts, however, used only one jer, with *ъ* predominating in the texts from the southern scriptoria (Ohrid) and *ь* characterizing the texts copied in the areas adjacent to Serbia (the single *ь* orthography is in fact a feature of the Serbian recension of Church Slavonic).[232]

3.29.2. The Serbian and Croatian recensions are characterized by the following phonological features:

(a) PSl. *ę ǫ* > *e u*, e.g. *ime* 'name', *sutь* 'they are' (OCS *ę ǫ: imę, sǫtъ*).
(b) PSl. *y* > *i*, e.g. *ti* 'thou', *posilaetь* 'sends' (OCS *y: ty, posylaetъ*).
(c) PSl. *ь ъ* (jers in weak position) merged, and only one of them tended to be used. In Serbian texts it was mostly *ь*, while in Croatian Glagolitic texts it was mostly *ъ*. In Old Church Slavonic the distinction between *ь* and *ъ* was generally preserved.
(d) PSl. **ь ъ** (jers in strong position) > *a*, e.g. *mastь* 'revenge', *krepak* 'strong' (OCS **ь ъ**: *mьstь, krěpъkъ*).
(e) PSl. *CR̥'C CR̥C* > *CRC*, e.g. *krstъ* 'cross', *trgъ* 'market' (OCS *CRьC CRъC: krьstъ, trъgъ*).
(f) PSl. *ě* > *e*, e.g. *svetlostь* 'light' (OCS *ě: světьlostь*).
(g) PSl. *#vьC #vъC* > *#uC*, e.g. *udovica* 'widow', *u věki* 'forever', *usta* < **vъz-sta* '(s)he stood up' (OCS *#vьC #vъC: vьdovica, vъ věky, vъsta*).

3.29.3. The Czech (West Slavic) recension is exemplified by the *Prague Fragments*. It showed the following features:

231. The emphasis here is on the phonological characteristics, even though morphology, syntax, and lexicon provide equally valid criteria; witness the distribution of the instrumental singular ending of the *-ŏ-* stems, which in North Slavic is generally replaced by the *-ŭ*-stem ending-*ъmь*, e.g. ESl. **отрокъмь** vs. OCS *otrokomь* 'servant'.

232. Interestingly, in the *Codex Assemanianus* a predilection for *ь* is clearly discernible. Single *ь* spellings also characterize Croatian Glagolitic texts.

(a) PSl. *ę* > *a*, e.g. *postaviša* 'they placed' (OCS *ę: postavišę*).
(b) PSl. *ǫ* > *u*, e.g. Acc. Sg. *obidu* 'offense' (OCS *ǫ: obidǫ*). There were also instances of hypercorrect forms in which *u* < PSl. *u* was spelled *ǫ*, e.g. *pomilǫi* 'have mercy'! (OCS *pomilui*).
(c) PSl. *tį dį* > *c z*, e.g. Dat. Pl. Def. *xvalęcimъ* 'praising', *utvrъzenie* 'confirmation' (OCS *št žd: xvalęštimъ, utvrъždenie*).
(d) PSl. *sk* + FV > *šč*, e.g. Loc. Sg. *sudišči* 'judgment' (OCS *št: sǫdišti*).
(e) PSl. *dl* > *dl*, e.g. Acc. Sg. *modlitvu* 'prayer' (OCS *l: molitvǫ*).
(f) PSl. *x* > *š* by progressive palatalization of velars, e.g. Nom. Pl. M *v(ь)ši* 'all' (OCS *s': vьsi*).
(g) PSl. *Pį* > *P'*, e.g. *prěstavenie* 'Assumption', Gen. Sg. *zemę* 'earth' (OCS *Pl': prěstavl'enie, zeml'ę*).

The *Kiev Missal* is considered part of the canon of Old Church Slavonic despite some West Slavic features:

c < PSl. *tį* and *kt* + FV, e.g. Nom. Pl. M *prosęce* (< **tį*) 'asking', *pomocь* (< **kt* + FV) 'help' (Blg./Mac. OCS *št: prosęšte, pomoštь*).

cě < PSl. *tįa*, e.g. *oběcěnie* 'promise' (Blg./Mac *oběštanie/oběštěnie*).

šč < PSl. *stį* and *sk* + FV, e.g. *očiščenię* 'purification' (Gen. Sg.), *zaščiti* 'defend'! (Blg./Mac. OCS *št: očištenię, zaštiti*).

z < PSl. *dį*, e.g. *dazь* 'give'! (Blg./Mac. OCS *žd: daždь*).

The *Kiev Missal* also contains several lexical West Slavicisms: *mьšě* 'Mass' (Blg./Mac. OCS *službba*), *oplatъ* 'oblation', *papežь* 'pope', *poganьskъ* 'pagan', *prěfacię* 'Preface'.

3.29.4. The Russian recension is known from a very large number of manuscripts and inscriptions. It represents a mix of East Slavic and Church Slavonic (South Slavic) features:

(a) PSl. *ę ǫ* were denasalized in East Slavic, yielding *ä u*. For these vowels two sets of letter symbols were used, the phonetic **ꙗ ѹ** (**ю**) and the traditional **ѧ ѫ** (**ѭ**) taken over from the earliest Cyrillic alphabet (OCS *ę ǫ jǫ*), e.g. **ꙗзыкъ** 'tongue', **пѧть** 'five', Dat. Sg. **мѹжѹ мѫжѫ мѹжю мѫжѭ** 'man' (OCS *ęzykъ, pętь, mǫžju*).[233]
(b) PSl. *#ju* > East Slavic *#u*, which was used alongside Bulgarian Church Slavonic *#ju* (**ю**), e.g. **югъ, ѹгъ** 'south' (OCS *jugъ*).[234]
(c) PSl. *#je* > East Slavic *#o*, which was used alongside Bulgarian Church Slavonic *je* (**ѥ**), e.g. **ѥдинъ, одинъ** 'one' (OCS *edinъ*).
(d) PSl. *#ăRC* > East Slavic *#RoC*; however, South Slavic *#RaC* was also used, e.g. **рабъ, робъ** 'servant' (OCS *rabъ*).
(e) PSl. *CR̥'C CR̥C* > East Slavic *CьRC CъRC*, which was used alongside Bulgarian Church Slavonic *CRьC CRъC* or rare *CьRъC CъRъC* (second polnoglasie), e.g. **търгъ, тръгъ, търъг** 'market' (OCS *trъgъ*). Note that PSl. *Cl̥'C* > East Slavic *Cl̥C*, e.g. LPSl. *vl̥'kъ* > East Slavic **вълкъ** [vl̥kъ] 'wolf'.
(f) PSl. *CerC* > East Slavic *CereC*; however, South Slavic *CrěC* or its East Slavic substitute *CreC* were also used, e.g. **дрѣво, древо, дерево** 'tree' (OCS *drěvo*).
(g) PSl. *CorC* > East Slavic *CoroC;* however, South Slavic *CraC* was also used, e.g. **градъ, городъ** 'town' (OCS *gradъ*).
(h) PSl. *CelC* > East Slavic *ColoC;* however, South Slavic *ClěC* or its East Slavic substitute *CleC* were also used, e.g. **млѣко, млеко, молоко** 'milk' (OCS *mlěko*).
(i) PSl. *ColC* > East Slavic *ColoC;* however, South Slavic *ClaC* was also used, e.g. **глава, голова** 'head' (OCS *glava*).
(j) PSl. *tį* > East Slavic *č* (**ч**), which was used alongside Bulgarian Church Slavonic **щ** (pronounced *št'* in Old Church Slavonic but *šč* in East Slavic), e.g. **свѣча** or **свѣща** 'candle' (OCS *svěšta*).

233. Spellings such as -**ѫ** (-**ѭ**) for the Dat. Sg. *-u* (*-ju*) are due to the East Slavic denasalization of PSl. *ǫ* and its merger with *u;* cf. also **кѫ** 'to him', **ѫтѣха** 'consolation' (OCS *emu, utěxa*), etc.

234. This is responsible for such Modern Russian doublets as *užin* (with *ž* < *g*) 'supper' vs. *jug* 'south'.

(k) PSl *di̯* > East Slavic *ž* (ж), which was used alongside Bulgarian Church Slavonic *žd* (жд), e.g. **прѣже, прежде** 'before' (OCS *prěžde*).[235]

(l) PSl. -*ę*/*ě*$_3$ > East Slavic -*ě* (ѣ); however, South Slavic *ę* (written -ѧ or ꙗ) was also used, e.g. Gen. Sg. or Nom./Acc. Pl. **ꙃемлѧ, ꙃемлꙗ, ꙃемлѣ** 'earth', Acc. Pl. **конѧ, конꙗ, конѣ** 'horse' (OCS *zemlję, kon'ę*) (**2.48.1** *note 3a*).

3.30. (Old) Church Slavonic literary community. It is important to remember that Church Slavonic was not the only Slavic medium of literary expression. Before the schism that split Christianity into Eastern and Western churches, the separation between the Byzantine and Roman worlds, particularly in the areas exposed to both traditions, was not rigid. In such regions as Carantania, Moravia, Bohemia, and even southern Poland, allegiances could change and borders shift. These lands, before submitting to the domination of Latin, produced a small but significant flow of Slavic texts which, along with the powerful stream of Slavic originating in the Balkans and Rus', constitute the corpus of medieval Slavic literature.

During the early period, however, the overwhelming majority of Slavic literary monuments arose within the radius of the cultural influence of Byzantium. Of all the Slavic texts produced through the end of the eleventh century, only the *Kiev Missal* and the *Freising Fragments* were inspired by Western models. The rest of Slavic writing belongs to the Byzantine tradition, according to which the task of the writer was to edify rather than entertain. Hence belles lettres, in the modern sense of the word, did not exist. There were, of course, some secular texts, such as the codes of law, charters, correspondence, or inscriptions. But the bulk of literary output was either strictly religious in nature or, as in the case of chronicles or miscellanies, contained various blends of sacred, piously didactic, and profane topics.

The religious nature of early Slavic literature entailed doctrinal concerns which in turn determined its derivative character. In order not to be branded heretical, the books used by the Greek missionaries and their Slavic disciples had to be faithful translations of authoritative Christian sources. Gradually, however, Slavic medieval literature began a life of its own, venturing into original and, eventually, secular compositions. The vehicle for this literary production was Church Slavonic, which in the guise of various local recensions became the supraethnic literary medium serving all of Orthodox Slavdom and functioning in a symbiotic relationship with the nascent Slavic national languages (Picchio 1980:21–23).

The supraethnic character of Church Slavonic was a reflection of the borderless compass of early Slavic literature, especially of early literature of Orthodox Slavdom. It was a literature in which all was shared, from language and monuments to style and traditions. In the words of Lixačev (1987:263–264):

> The eastern Slavs (Russians, Ukrainians, Belarussians), the Bulgarians, the Serbs, the Romanians possessed a single literature, a single written tradition, and a single literary (Church Slavonic) language. The main treasure-house of Church Slavonic monuments was held in common. Liturgical, homiletic, ecclesiastic and didactic, hagiographic, and, to an extent, historical (chronographic) and narrative writings were common to all of the Orthodox of southern and eastern Europe. . . . Moreover, a literary community existed not only for eastern and southern Slavs but in the oldest period it included also the western Slavs. . . . In the literatures of Orthodox Slavdom one may observe common changes in style, common intellectual trends, a constant exchange of literary works and manuscripts. Literary monuments were under-

235. Church Slavonic *žd'* is pronounced (*ž*)*ž'* in Modern Russian of Moscow, e.g. *prěžde* /pr'éžž'i/ 'before', *dožd'* /doš'/ 'rain', Gen. Sg. *doždjá* /dažž'á/.

standable without translations and there is no reason to doubt that Church Slavonic was the common language of all the Orthodox Slavs.

The existence of a Church Slavonic linguistic and literary community allows us to forgo the narrowly national criteria in the classification of medieval Slavic texts and to adopt instead a comprehensive and unitary approach based on the premise that "one can readily create a single history of literature of southern and eastern Slavs up to the sixteenth century. And this single history of literature will not be a mechanical, chronologically ordered gathering of diverse materials assembled from various national literatures, but can be construed and written as a single whole" (Lixačev 1987:264).

3.31. Translations versus original works. The task undertaken by Constantine and Methodius, a task of transforming the language of a primitive Slavic civilization into an effective vehicle of European civilization, was so ambitious that its successful accomplishment appeared miraculous to the contemporaries. Even today the earliest Slavic translations strike the reader as surprisingly skillful. They captured and rendered faithfully, often elegantly, the grammatical and stylistic complexities of the original Greek, with its rich abstract vocabulary, involved syntactic constructions, and refined rhetorical devices. Early Slavic translators used and developed such complex syntactic structures as the dative absolute and the relative and conditional clauses, and displayed an understanding of the stylistic potential of choosing among related constructions, such as the active, passive, and reflexive, or between clauses with or without the copula. Above all, they displayed themselves inventive in domesticating foreign concepts either through outright borrowing or through loan translations. The former was especially common in religious and technical terms, the latter in abstract vocabulary. The following are some examples of the two kinds of borrowing into Old Church Slavonic from Greek:

Loan words:

Gk.	diábolos	OCS	dijavolъ	'devil'
	hiereýs		ierei	'priest'
	kapiklários		kapiklarii	'jailer'
	patriárkhēs		patriarxъ	'patriarch'
	pistikḗ		pistik'i(i)	'pistachio'
	prosphorá		prosvora	'Host'
	rhētorikós		ritorьskъ	'rhetorical'
	Sábbaton		sǫbota (sobota)	'Sabbath'
	tálanton		talantъ	'talent'
	týmpanon		tumьpanъ	'kettledrum'

Loan translations (calques):

Gk.	dipsykhía	OCS	dъvodušie	'doubt'
	eukharistêin		blagodariti	'be grateful'
	megalýnein		veličiti	'praise'
	pantokrátōr		vьsedrъžitelь	'allmighty'
	philadelphía		bratroljubie	'brotherly love'
	pseudómartys		lъžesъvědětelь	'false witness'
	sarkophágos		plъtojadivъ	'carnivorous'
	sýmphonos		sъglasьnъ	'agreeing'
	kheiropoíētos		rǫkotvorjenъ	'handmade'
	khrysóstomos		zlatoustъ	'gold-mouthed'

The stylistic potential of Slavic comes to the fore in those instances where it possesses the means to vary its loan translations from Greek in order to transmit a particular shade of meaning. Such is the case of the Old Church Slavonic words that translate the Greek prefix *a-* either with the negative prefix *ne-* or with the privative prefix *bez-*:

akakía	nezlobie 'kindliness'	bezlobie 'lack of anger'
apistía	nevěrie 'nonbelieving'	bezvěrie 'lack of belief'
athánatos	nesъmrъtьnъ 'immortal'	besъmrъtьnъ 'deathless'
atimía	nečьstie 'disgrace'	bečьstie 'lack of honor'

To some extent, of course, the soil on which the early translators labored had been prepared by preceding generations. One must not forget that the Moravian mission was the culmination of three centuries of Greek acculturation of the Slavs. During those centuries the Slavs dwelled side by side with the Greeks, either in Slavic villages (*sklavinias*) in the Byzantine empire or just across the border in Bulgaria. The daily life of the empire must have provided the Slavs with countless opportunities to express in their native language some of the foreign concepts with which they came into contact.

Such historical perspective should not diminish in any way one's admiration for the skill and sophistication of the first Slavic translators. Their remarkable understanding of the goals of translation may be gleaned from a single-folio document called the *Macedonian Folio,* which some scholars have assigned to the heritage of the Moravian mission (**3.49**). Should this be so, the extant eleventh-century monument would have to be a version of an even older text. As one can see from the selection below, the author approached the art of biblical translation with a well-designed working plan:

> We have attempted to use precise terms, fearful of adding to the Gospel. And if something, however slight, is found added anywhere, let the reader understand that this was done out of necessity and not out of arrogance or daring. For nobody is so bold and forgetful of himself as to dare add or take away a word. . . . [It is not out of] laziness that words were rendered by exactly the same expression. For we do not need words and expressions but the meaning. And this is why, wherever there was agreement between Greek and Slavic, we translated by the same word. But where an expression was longer [or] was losing its meaning, then, not forsaking the meaning, we rendered it with [another] word. Because the Greek language, translated into another one, cannot always be rendered in the same way. And this is how it is with every language that is being translated. And often a word which is beautiful in one language, in another one is [not]. What in one language is insolent, in [another one is not]. What in one is important, in another one [is not. And the noun which in one language is] masculine, in another language is feminine. As in Greek, the noun[s] *potamós, astḗr* [are] masculine, and in Slavic *rěka, ʒvězda* [are] feminine. . . . For it [is impossible to retain everywhere] a Greek word, but it is necessary to preserve the meaning. (Vaillant 1948:7–10)

Original works were primarily of historical, legal, didactic, or epigraphic nature. Some religious genres, however, also lent themselves to original literary expression. This was especially true of sermons and various compositions such as canons, offices, hymns, eulogies, and vitae devoted to the cult of Slavic saints. There were also original polemical writings composed in connection with some topical issue of the day (Bogomilism, the schism, the alphabet) and some apocryphal compositions (**3.40**).

3.32. Authors and authorship. Given the fairly large number of early Slavic writings, it may appear surprising that we know so little about their authors. This anonymity, far from being an accident of history, is consonant with the prevailing attitudes of the time. The Byzantine artist was a preserver of values, not their creator. He willingly submitted to the received order of things, leashed in his own creative urges, and reproduced the inherited wisdom without changing its sacred code. This attitude was especially true of the visual arts, but it applied to literary pursuits as well. The writer who saw himself as a link in a continuous chain of transmission had little incentive to reveal his identity. It is symptomatic that when we attribute a text to a specific writer, we do so not so much on the strength of his own claim to authorship but usually on the authority of tradition verified by modern scholarship.

Occasionally, however, the writer's desire to partake of the sanctity of the text prompted him to overcome the authorial reticence and include his name in the composition. Copyists of major texts might do so in a marginal note or in a formulaic addendum to the main text. Such, for instance, is the often quoted postscript to the *Ostromir Evangeliary,* in which the monk Gregory expressed his hope that a better copyist "would not scorn him" and begged the reader "not to curse [his mistakes] but to correct them."

Authors of hymnographic compositions might reveal their names through the artful device of acrostics. A good example of this is provided by the case of Naum, a disciple of Constantine and Methodius. After the death of Methodius and the scattering of the Moravian mission, Naum fled to Bulgaria. We know from his Slavic and Greek vitae that he dedicated himself there to continuing the evangelizing and didactic work of his teachers. In fact, Naum is credited with the flourishing of the Preslav school of Slavic letters (**3.26**). Yet Naum's literary activity would have been totally unknown had it not been for an acrostic containing his name, which the Bulgarian medievalist Stefan Kožuxarov discovered in 1978 in a canon for the apostle Andrew.[236]

Medieval writers often are known to us solely as names attached to their compositions. This is true of several writers of the golden age of Slavic letters, the era ushered in by the rule of the highly cultivated Bulgarian tsar Symeon (893–927). In the case of the monk Khrabr ('Brave'), we do not even know the name concealed by this epithet. His famous treatise *On the Letters* (*O pismenexъ*) is a polemical comparison of the Slavic and Greek alphabets. In the case of presbyter Gregory, we know the writer's name and the extent of his literary activity but not the works themselves. According to a table of contents preserved in an East Slavic fifteenth-century manuscript, Gregory translated all or large portions of the octateuch.

The identity of the presbyter Cosmas is also one about which next to nothing is known, even though his treatise, *Against the Bogomils,* has come down to us in its entirety. All that can be ascertained with certainty about its author are his name and his sacerdotal calling. A few guesses, though, might be ventured on the basis of the internal evidence of the treatise, Cosmas' only known work. The author was most probably a Bulgarian who was connected with the Preslav school. He must have written his treatise soon after the priest Bogomil began to preach his heretical doctrine (**3.49**) but before Svyatoslav's campaign against Byzantium (969–971 or 972), which was fought mainly on the territory of Bulgaria. Hence Cosmas must have been active in the early part of the second half of the tenth century.

The writer's backing away from exposure went hand in hand with a lessened sense of re-

236. The acrostic reads: *Prvoago Xrstova sla xvali niščii Naum* 'Lowly Naum praised the first apostle of Christ' (Kožuxarov 1984).

sponsibility for the facts reported. The notions of true and false were applicable to the interpretation of sacred doctrine but not to the description of purportedly historical events. This applied not only to artistic works but also to chronicles whose accounts of "bygone years" were a melange of fact and legend. Nor did the notion of plagiarism come into play. A writer was free, even expected, to borrow from his predecessors without any compulsion to acknowledge his sources.[237] Attribution was used for the solely practical purpose of affirming the doctrinal legitimacy of one's text. This is true, above all, of religious texts, which had to rely on the authority of their sacred antecedents in order to gain the requisite measure of prestige and acceptance.

Still, despite the tendency for anonymity, the names of some of the most important Slavic medieval translators and authors have been preserved, and some episodes from their lives have come to light. This is especially likely to be the case with writers who eventually were canonized, for the conferral of sainthood was predicated on the knowledge of the saint's biography. In fact, the saints' vitae are usually our only sources of biographical information. Since there often exist more than one version of a saint's vita, the modern investigator may be in a position to compare them and select the more plausible bits of information.

3.33. Constantine and Methodius. As creators and pioneers of Slavic letters and accomplished translators from Greek into Slavic, the brothers Constantine and Methodius are deservedly the most celebrated Slavic literary personalities. It is a pity, therefore, that their vitae, generous as they are on biographical detail, are less informative on the extent of the brothers' literary production. As for translations, we may infer from the *Vita Constantini* that Constantine was responsible for translating the evangeliary and the main liturgical books, while the *Vita Methodii* gives credit to both brothers for the translation of the psalter, the Gospels, the Acts of the Apostles, and selected liturgies. In addition, according to his vita, Methodius and his disciples translated all the books of the Bible, except the Maccabees, as well as the nomocanon and the *otьčьskyę kъnigy*. The exact content of the latter text is not known, but it probably was a *paterik* (**3.48.3**), a collection of edifying tales from the life of monks and hermits.

Much less is known about the brothers' original writings. The papal librarian Anastasius wrote a letter to Bishop Gauderich informing him that Constantine was the author of three Greek texts dealing with St. Clement: the *Storiola* (*Short History*), which gave an account of the discovery of the saint's relics in 861; a sermon celebrating the bringing of the relics to Rome; and a canon of such beauty that Anastasius refrained from translating it into Latin for fear of not doing justice to its poetic qualities. Anastasius did translate the first two compositions of Constantine. Their fragments have been preserved in a late Church Slavonic version called the *Discourse on the Discovery and Translation of the Relics of St. Clement* (also known as the *Cherson Legend*). As for Slavic compositions, it is possible that it was Constantine the Philosopher rather than Constantine of Preslav who composed the *Alphabet Prayer*, and that it was he rather than John the Exarch who wrote the so-called *Macedonian Folio*. Methodius has been mentioned as a possible author or co-author of the *Vita Constantini* and the probable author of a canon honoring Demetrius, the patron saint of Thessalonica, and of a homily addressed to the "princes and judges" preserved in a fourteen-folio fragment known as the *Glagolita Clozianus*.

237. This contributed to the so-called open tradition characterizing most of medieval Slavic writing (Picchio 1987).

3.34. Clement of Ohrid. Clement of Ohrid was a disciple and close collaborator of both Constantine and Methodius, and a member of the Moravian mission. After the expulsion of the mission Clement found refuge in Bulgaria, where his qualifications were viewed as a boon to the Bulgarian rulers' efforts to install and spread vernacular Christian worship. With Boris/Michael's (r. 852–889) support, Clement started a theological seminary in Macedonia, in which he trained Slavic-speaking clerics and organized scriptoria. In this way he laid the foundation for a center of medieval Slavic culture, which is often referred to as the Ohrid school. The texts translated and copied there bear the features of the southwest Bulgarian (Macedonian) stage in the development of Old Church Slavonic. Since many of the Macedonian texts, such as the *Codex Assemanianus,* were transcribed in Glagolitic, it is assumed that Glagolitic was the preferred alphabet in Ohrid. In 893 Clement was appointed by Tsar Symeon (r. 893–927) to the bishopric of Velica near Ohrid, which he headed until his death in 916. Clement's biography is known chiefly from his Greek vita, written in the beginning of the twelfth century by the archbishop of Ohrid, Theophylact.[238]

Unfortunately, the vita does not tell us much about Clement's considerable literary activity. We know that his writings included simple and unassuming homilies as well as lofty and solemn compositions known as encomia or panegyrics (*poxvaly* or *poxvalьnaja slovesa*). Some of the homilies were sermons composed for specific feast days; others were short instructions (*poučenja*) dealing with more general subjects. Among the encomia one may mention those dedicated to Constantine/Cyril and Methodius, Pope Clement I, and Demetrius of Thessalonica. Clement of Ohrid is also credited by some scholars with the authorship of the *Vita Methodii.* It must be stressed, however, that Clement's authorship of specific works is very difficult to establish. Therefore, the three-volume edition of Clement's writings published in Bulgaria in the 1970s cannot be considered definitive.[239]

3.35. Constantine of Preslav. Although Constantine of Preslav was a disciple of Methodius, his whereabouts at the time of the liquidation of the mission are not known. Eventually he also ended up in Bulgaria, where he became a close collaborator of Clement of Ohrid and particularly of Naum, with whom he seems to have been connected by family ties or friendship. It is quite possible that Constantine reached Bulgaria via Constantinople. He could have been among the missionaries who, according to the vita of Naum, were sold into slavery after the dissolution of the Moravian mission. The missionaries surfaced at a slave market in Venice, where they were redeemed by the Byzantines and taken to Constantinople.

Beginning as a priest in Pliska and Preslav, the two successive capitals of Bulgaria, Constantine was elevated to the rank of bishop of Preslav. There he continued the pastoral work of Naum and by his own literary activity contributed to the formation of the Preslav school of Slavic letters, which, unlike the Ohrid school, was predominantly Cyrillic. He is best known for his skillful adaptations from Greek, especially for the so-called *Homiliary Gospel* and the *Ecclesiastic Discourse* by the Ecumenical Patriarch Germanus (715–730). He also translated four homilies against the Arians by Athanasius of Alexandria. Constantine's original writings are more difficult to identify because of the confusion of his name with that of Constantine the Philosopher. Thus, the famous *Preface to the Gospel* and the *Alphabet Prayer* have been alternately ascribed to the two writers, with authorship by Constantine of Preslav

238. Its English translation is included in Dujčev, ed., 1985.

239. Angelov, Bonju St. et al., eds. 1970–1977. See also an account of Clement's life and works in Stančev and Popov 1988. Popov discovered several hymnographic compositions with Clement's name concealed in acrostics.

gaining greater acceptance. Clearly original are his introduction to the *Homiliary Gospel* and the forty-second homily in it. There are also hymnographic compositions with Constantine's name spelled out in acrostics, such as a long office in honor of Methodius (Kostić 1937–1938), the canon for archangel Michael (Kožuxarov 1983), or a hymn in the Lent triodion (Popov 1978).[240]

3.36. John the Exarch. John the Exarch shares with Constantine of Preslav the distinction of being one of the founders of the Preslav school of Slavic letters. Since neither was honored with canonization, we do not possess their vitae and our knowledge about them is sparse. In the case of John, we are not even sure of the exact significance of the rank *exarch.* It must have referred to a high ecclesiastic office, perhaps the hegumenship of a monastery. Indirect evidence tells us something about John's age, origin, and education. He was probably born around the middle of the ninth century in Bulgaria, to which he referred with familiarity and pride. The erudition displayed in his writings points to an excellent education, obtained probably in Constantinople. His closeness to the court of Tsar Symeon suggests that he came from the ranks of Bulgarian nobility.

John the Exarch belongs to the second generation of Slavic literary personalities, a generation that developed outside the immediate circle of Constantine and Methodius. In this sense he may be said to represent the beginnings of the Cyrillo-Methodian tradition. John's literary reputation rests on two major works of translation and adaptation, *Heavens* (*Nebesa*) and the *Hexaemeron* (*Šestodьnevъ*). The former is a translation of a large fragment of *On the Orthodox Faith,* which formed a part of the theological treatise *The Fount of Knowledge* by John of Damascus. The latter is a compilation modeled on similar Greek works in which John the Exarch blended the biblical account of the six days of Creation with excerpts from scientific and philosophical treatises and with his own observations on the world around him. Often quoted is his anatomy of the human body based on Aristotle's *History of the Animals.* He was also the author of several encomia and homilies and is presumed to be the author of a programmatic statement on the art of translation (partly quoted in **3.31**).

3.37. Textual criticism. While the problems of medieval Slavic alphabets and writing conventions belong to the discipline of paleography, the study of connected texts is the domain of two kindred but autonomous disciplines, literary criticism and textual criticism (also known as textology). The former concentrates on the intellectual and aesthetic qualities of a text, while the latter deals solely with the mechanisms of textual transmission. In its methodology, textual criticism is at once descriptive and comparative. It aims to describe the text at hand, confront it with related texts, evaluate their similarities and differences and determine the nature of the relations among them. The ultimate goal of textual criticism is to re-create the path traveled by a text through time and space and to establish its earliest form. In some cases, however, the investigator may wish to come as close as possible to what he believes was the original shape of the text—in other words, to reconstruct it. This is especially tempting in poetic compositions, where the availability of many formal devices, such as meter and rhyme, facilitate the reconstructive effort.[241] One must remember, however, that reconstructions, despite the insights they bring, are hypothetical abstractions that go beyond the tes-

240. For an informative introduction to Constantine of Preslav, see Emil Georgiev's contribution to Dujčev, ed. 1985:161–180.

241. The *Preface to the Gospel* (**3.47**) was the object of several such attempts (Sobolevskij 1910, Georgiev 1956:165–201, Nahtigal 1943:76–122, Vaillant 1956, Jakobson 1963).

timony of the extant texts without acquiring the value of documentary evidence (Picchio 1988:3.14).

For the sake of clarity and precision it may be useful at this point to review the definitions of some of the terms used in textual criticism. A *text* is any written sequence, and its history is its *tradition*. A handwritten text is a *manuscript*. A text transcribed from another text is a *copy*. The text from which a copy was made is called the *exemplar*. An *autograph* is a text in the author's hand (there are no extant medieval Slavic autographs). A *variant reading* is a text or its segment differing from the exemplar. The *stemma* is a diagram (usually in the form of a downward-branching tree) of a chronological and typological collation of related texts. The *archetype* is the exemplar for more than one text, that is, the node dominating two or more texts in a stemma. The ultimate archetype is sometimes referred to as the *protograph*. Related texts dominated by one archetype represent the *closed tradition* of textual transmission, while related texts without an archetype belong to the *open tradition*. The genealogical (stemmatic) method yields best results in texts of closed tradition, which are, as a rule, few in number and in which faithfulness of textual transmission is better controlled. It is of more limited use in the study of texts of open tradition, which, hailing as they often do from different locales, periods, and historical settings, show a greater tolerance for textual emendation. The genealogical method may, however, be applied to subsets of texts of open tradition where it may yield a number of related but free-standing stemmata.[242]

Texts sharing features introduced spontaneously and unconsciously (for instance, dialectal characteristics) represent a particular *recension* (Russian *izvod*). Texts sharing features introduced intentionally and consciously (for instance, ideological tendencies) constitute a *redaction* (Russian *redakcija*). In other words, a recension refers specifically to the linguistic properties of a text, while a redaction is defined primarily by its cultural context.[243] A text used as historical evidence is a *monument*. An assemblage of thematically related texts (especially chronicles) is a *compilation* (Russian *svod*).

3.38. Early Slavic texts.[244] Since survival of manuscripts is largely fortuitous, the antiquity of a text cannot be determined by the age of its oldest manuscript, nor can extant manuscripts be regarded as more than mere links in a chain of other manuscripts lost to us through the vicissitudes of history.[245] This consideration has important consequences in Slavic, for despite the ninth-century origin of Slavic letters, our first extant Slavic texts come from the end of the tenth century at the earliest, and the main stream of Slavic manuscripts begins in the eleventh and twelfth centuries. In fact, in some instances the time differential between a text at hand and its presumed origin may amount to several centuries. As an example, the *Vita Constantini*, composed most probably during or soon after the Moravian mission, has come

242. Translated texts present an additional problem for it is usually impossible to tell whether variant readings are due to textual emendations or to multiple translations. An account of the genealogical method may be found in Maas 1950. On closed and open traditions, see Picchio 1987.

243. It must be noted, however, that these two terms are not always so strictly defined or even discriminated. In some treatments the term redaction functions generically in reference to both the linguistic and cultural aspects of textual variation; in others the two terms are used interchangeably (cf. Picchio 1967 and Bogdanov 1978:141, n18).

244. References to texts mentioned in **3.38–3.55** are given in parentheses. They refer to editions, translations, and vocabularies for which a full bibliographic entry may be found in the Bibliography. For secondary literature, the reader is advised to turn to several encyclopedic and bibliographic guides to which references are provided according to the following code: Dinekov, ed. 1985 as *D* (by page), Kowalenko, ed. 1961– as *Ko* (by volume and page), Kuev 1979 as *Ku* (by page), Lixačev, ed. 1987, 1988, 1989 as $L_{(1,2,3)}$ (by page), and Šmidt, ed. 1984 as *Š* (by entry number).

245. For the histories of some Slavic manuscripts, see Kuev 1979.

down to us in about fifty manuscripts of which none dates from before the fifteenth century. In this case, the earliest exemplar or protograph must be some six centuries older than the extant copies.

Larger manuscripts, whether consisting of a single text or of multiple texts, have come down in codices, medieval counterparts of modern books. Unlike books, however, codices were unique creations, shaped by the design of their compilers, accident of history, or the linguistic and paleographic individualities of their texts. Consequently, some codices contain texts that are thematically disparate and chronologically heterogeneous. Generally speaking, the higher the dignity of a text, whether because of its sacred status, the weight of tradition, or the prestige of the author, the greater the likelihood that the codices containing it are relatively stable. The very nature of a Gospel, a psalter, or a euchologium precluded modifiability, both in the text itself and in the structure of the codex. Also stable in content, though with a greater degree of compositional freedom, were such liturgical texts as the menaea and the prologues. Secular texts or texts with a lower rank of sanctity, such as the apocrypha, homilies, exegeses, vitae of saints, or private prayers, were not so restricted. They were regularly included in collections of texts known as miscellanies or florilegia, which showed varying degrees of latitude with respect to content.

Complete lists of medieval Slavic texts, regardless of the date of their transmission, cannot be given here. They belong in the histories of individual Slavic literatures or literary languages. Yet the origin and the characteristics of the oldest Slavic texts must be considered, and to this end the turn of the thirteenth century has been established as an arbitrary cutoff point for all extant manuscripts. Later manuscripts will be discussed only if their lost protographs are known to have originated during the earliest period of Slavic letters.[246]

3.39. Biblical texts. As Constantine and Methodius set out to bring the Slavs into the Christian fold, a great variety of texts had to be translated. The most immediate need was for the New Testament, the liturgy, and the Psalter—books without which religious instruction and church services could not be conducted.[247] Also translated but with a lesser degree of urgency were other books of the Old Testament as well as the apocrypha and patristic writings. Beyond the Psalter, Old Testament translations used by the Moravian mission have not survived (except in quotations), probably because they were not copied frequently enough to assure their perpetuation.[248]

Difficult to substantiate is the contention that the East Slavic translation of the book of Esther, extant since the fourteenth century, was executed in the twelfth century directly from Hebrew (Meščerskij 1956). Similar claims have been made for the Song of Songs (Alekseev 1986), the pseudepigraphic book of the Secrets of Enoch, and some other texts that did not enter the canon of the Old Testament (Meščerskij 1978:30–31).

3.40. Apocrypha and pseudepigrapha (*D* 85–93). The semantic scope of the term *apocrypha* (derived from the Greek *apókryphos* 'hidden') has varied in different religious

246. For a selection of thirteenth-century Bulgarian texts translated into modern Bulgarian, see Božilov and Kožuxarov (1987).

247. This order of priorities is confirmed by the *Vita Methodii* (**3.33**). Slavic translations of the Bible are discussed in Lixačev, ed., 1987:68–83.

248. The first complete Slavic translation of all the books of the Old Testament to come down to us is the *Gennady's Bible* from the end of the fifteenth century, so named because of its sponsor, the Novgorod archbishop Gennady. The remarkable thing about this Bible is that its main translator, Dimitry Gerasimov, worked from the Latin Vulgate for books which were not available in Slavic.

traditions and at different times. In the Judaic tradition, which was adapted by the Protestant church, the term is applied to those books which are outside the official canon of Judaism, that is, outside the Old Testament. The most important among them are Esdras I and II, Tobit, Judith, the expanded book of Esther, the Wisdom of Salomon, Ecclesiasticus or the Wisdom of Joshua (Jesus) ben Sirach, Baruch, and Maccabees I and II. By contrast, in the early Christian tradition, preserved in the Orthodox and Catholic churches, these books were not treated as apocryphal but were admitted into the canon as deuterocanonical. Christianity did, however, identify its own set of noncanonical books, the so-called *pseudepigrapha* (lit. 'falsely attributed') or proscribed books (*otrečenьnyę kъnigy*), which have also come to be known as apocryphal. These Christian apocrypha, often identified with particular sects and heresies, included a variety of texts ranging from the Old and New Testament tales, prayers, and lives of saints to astrology, soothsaying, and interpretation of dreams. Such a broad thematic reach placed the apocrypha on the borderline between religious and secular literature, ensuring their popularity with the reader.

Although no Old Church Slavonic apocrypha have survived, Slavic translations of apocryphal texts must have existed at an early date. The *Izbornik of 1073* lists twenty-five titles of apocryphal texts that had been placed on the index.[249] Most of these translations were made in Bulgaria, whence they spread to other lands of the Byzantine commonwealth. Also of Bulgarian origin was a small number of native Slavic apocrypha, such as the compilation of apocryphal stories by the priest Jeremiah, the presumed author of the popular *Tale of the Tree for the Cross*. Some native apocrypha show the influence of the Bogomil heresy, which arose in Bulgaria in the tenth century.

Many Slavic apocrypha and pseudepigrapha were contained in miscellanies (*izborьniki, sъborьniki*).[250] Thus, the *Vision of the Prophet Isaiah*, the *Tale of the Prophet Jeremiah on the Capture of Jerusalem*, the *Sermon of Eusebius of Alexandria on the Descent of John the Baptist into Hell*, the *Sermon of Gregory of Antioch on the Entombment and Resurrection of Jesus Christ*, the *Tale of Agapius*, the *Descent of the Virgin Mary into Hell*, and the *Apocalypse of Baruch* are to be found in several East Slavic miscellanies from the twelfth and thirteenth centuries, among them the *Uspenskij sbornik* and the *Sinai Palimpsest*. The majority of Slavic apocryphal texts, however, are contained in later codices. Of these, the *Book of the Secrets of Enoch* or *Enoch 2* (Vaillant, ed. 1952; L_1 40–41) is particularly important, for it has not survived except in Slavic translation.[251]

3.41. Liturgical and paraliturgical texts. At various points in the history of the church and on different occasions in the church year different liturgies have been used. The first major reform of the liturgy was introduced in the patriarchate of Antioch by Basil the Great of Caesarea (ca. 330–379). It is still celebrated during five days of Lent, on the eves of Christmas and Epiphany, and on the day of the feast of St. Basil (January 1 in the Orthodox church). In use during most of the year is an abbreviated version of the liturgy of Basil the Great introduced by John Chrysostom (ca. 354–407). To these two liturgies was added the liturgy of the Presanctified used on certain days during Lent. Its authorship is attributed to Pope Gregory the Great.

249. To be sure, the inclusion of a text in the index, which was translated from Greek, does not necessarily imply that the text itself was available in Slavic.

250. Slavic specialized terms (but not specific titles) are conventionally cited in their actual or reconstructed Old Church Slavonic form; thus, *izborьnikъ* or *sъborьnikъ* 'miscellany' but *Izbornik of 1073* or *Uspenskij sbornik*.

251. The various classificatory criteria used in the systematization of Slavic apocrypha are discussed by Naumow (1976:58–76).

The Orthodox worship requires the use of a number of liturgical books. The service book with the Byzantine liturgy is the *liturgiarium* (*službьnikъ*). The order and text of daily services is specified by the *horologium* (*časoslovъ*). For the weekly cycle of services there are three different liturgical books. The Lenten Triodion (*postьnaja Triodь*) is used during the ten weeks of the pre-Lenten and Lenten periods, the Festal Triodion or *pentecostarion* (*cvětьnaja triodь*) is used for Easter Sunday and the eight weeks following it, through Pentecost, till the Sunday of All Saints. During the remaining part of the year the *octoechos* (*oktoixъ* or *osmoglasьnikъ*) is used. The offices for the yearly cycle are contained in the service menaeum (*mineja službьnaja*), which provides texts for the offices for each month of the year.[252] The texts of the sacraments (except for the Eucharist) and the prayers for various private occasions (*trěby*) are in the *euchologium* (*trěbьnikъ*). The *prologue* was a liturgical book, corresponding to the Byzantine synaxarion, containing short sermons and short vitae of saints to be read on the days of their feasts (*pamęti*).[253]

In addition, there were service books containing lections from the Old Testament, called in Church Slavonic *parimeiniki* or *paremeiniki*, the Psalter, the evangeliaries or lectionary (Sunday) Gospels, and the Acts and the Epistles of the Apostles, referred to usually as the *apostols*. These lectionary books, because of their function in the divine service, were an essential missionary resource. The high priority that the Moravian mission accorded to them may be inferred from a passage in chapter 14 of the *Vita Constantini*, which tells us that Constantine began his Slavic translation with the first lines of the Gospel of St. John: "In the beginning was the Word, and the Word was with God, and the Word was God." This citation was regularly used as the first lection in Byzantine evangeliaries.

The vitae of Constantine and Methodius credit the brothers with the translation of the matins, the hours, vespers, compline, the Divine Liturgy, the Psalter, the Gospel, the Acts of the Apostles, and some prayers. The selection of these particular texts should not surprise us, for the books listed are all needed for the conduct of daily services. Nor is it surprising that of all the early Slavic texts, liturgical and paraliturgical texts survived the best—being most in use, they were copied the most frequently. In fact, the earliest extant Slavic texts are all liturgical. Chief among them are the Glagolitic texts discovered by Stefan Kožuxarov and Georgij Popov dating from the tenth century and the *Kiev Missal* from the tenth or eleventh centuries.

3.41.1. Evangeliaries (L_l 70–71). An evangeliary (Sunday Gospel) is a book of Gospel readings for particular church services. In the Slavic tradition it is known as an *aprakos* Gospel (from Greek *ápraktos hēméra* 'holy day'), or as *izborьnoe evang'elie* (from *izborъ* 'selection'). It is normally divided into two parts, a *synaxarion* and a *menology*. The synaxarion contains prescribed readings from the four Gospels based on the movable cycle of the ecclesiastic year (that is, the Easter cycle). The menology is arranged according to the fixed yearly cycle (that is, the cycle starting on September 1, the ecclesiastic New Year's Day) and contains offices for feasts (*pamęti*) honoring saints and various important events in the life of the church. There are two types of evangeliaries. Oldest and chiefly South Slavic in origin are short evangeliaries that contain readings for all days of the eight weeks from Palm

252. The term *mineja* is derived from the plural of the Middle Greek term *mēnaîon* 'monthly' which the Slavs reinterpreted as a singular. Service menaea should be distinguished from menologies or lectionary menaea (East Slavic ChSl. *mineja četьja*), which are miscellanies containing saints' lives and special offices for each day of the month (cf. **3.46**).

253. See n.48. For a discussion of prologues, see Lixačev, ed. 1987:376–380.

Sunday to Pentecost, and Saturday and Sunday for the remaining weeks of the year. Full evangeliaries are somewhat younger and chiefly East Slavic. They contain Saturday and Sunday readings for the six weeks of Lent and readings for all days of the week during the rest of the year. Evangeliaries were among the most frequently copied religious books, and several of them belong to the oldest layer of Slavic. It is, in fact, fair to assume that the Gospel translation reported in the *Vita Methodii* was an evangeliary. Two of the most renowned evangeliaries, *Codex Assemanianus* and *Sava's Book,* belong to the canon of Old Church Slavonic.

Codex Assemanianus (Črnčić 1878, Vajs/Kurz 1929/1955, Ivanova-Mavrodinova/Džurova 1981; *Ku* 151–152) is a Glagolitic short evangeliary of 158 handsomely illuminated parchment folios dating from the beginning of the eleventh century. It bears the name of its finder, the Jesuit scholar and Vatican librarian Joseph Assemani, who came upon it in Jerusalem in 1736. It has since been kept in the Vatican library. The 1981 Bulgarian edition of the *Codex Assemanianus* contains facsimile reproductions (App. D, Glag. 3).

Sava's Book (Ščepkin 1901; Ščepkin, ed., 1903; *Ku* 157–158, *Š* #2) is an eleventh-century Cyrillic short evangeliary copied from a lost Glagolitic text. The original 126 parchment folios (ff. 25–151) are of Bulgarian provenience; they were bound into a larger codex with later additions of the Russian recension. The codex owes its appellation to the copyist, the priest Sav(v)a, who inscribed his name on two of the original folios. The early history of *Sava's Book* is not known. What can be ascertained is that the codex was in the Seredkino monastery near Pskov till at least the seventeenth century. It was then moved to the manuscript collection of the Moscow Synodal Printing House, where in 1866 it was found by I. I. Sreznevskij, the well-known compiler of a dictionary of Old Russian. Today it is housed in the Central State Archive of Old Documents (CGADA) in Moscow (App. D, Cyr. 3).

Also belonging to the Old Church Slavonic canon are two short evangeliary fragments. One is the two-folio Macedonian Glagolitic *Ohrid Folios* (Il'inskij, ed., 1915; *Š* #13), discovered in 1845 in Ohrid by Viktor I. Grigorovič. Today it is preserved in the Odessa State Research Library. The other, also in two folios, is the Cyrillic *Undol'skij's Fragments* (Karskij, ed., 1904; *Š* #11), in the manuscript collection of Vukol M. Undol'skij in the Russian State Library in Moscow. Karskij's edition contains facsimile reproductions.

Two short evangeliaries are palimpsests. The *Bojana Evangeliary* (*D* 236, *Ku* 173–174, *Š* #191) was acquired by Grigorovič in 1845 in Bojana, which then was a village near Sofia and now is its suburb. The text of a Cyrillic evangeliary of early thirteenth century is written over an erased text of a Glagolitic evangeliary which appears to be from the end of the eleventh century (Dobrev 1972). Even more ancient is the underlying Cyrillic text in a palimpsest discovered in the early 1980s in the Vatican Library (Džurova et al. 1985). Its Greek overlay of ninety-nine folios is from the twelfth or thirteenth century.

Other evangeliaries belong to various local traditions. The oldest of the short evangeliaries is *Ostromir's Evangeliary* (Vostokov, ed., 1843, *Ostromirovo Evangelie* 1883 and 1988; *Ku* 15, *Š* #3), a Cyrillic manuscript executed in 1056–1057 for Ostromir, the *posadnik* (governor) of Novgorod. As a text of East Slavic recension, it is especially valuable for its faithful rendition of Proto-Slavic jers and vocalic liquids. Since 1896 the manuscript has been in the Russian Public Library in St. Petersburg. In 1988 a full-size facsimile edition of the *Ostromir's Evangeliary* was published in Leningrad (App. D, Cyr. 5). Only slightly younger is another East Slavic short evangeliary, the *Archangel Evangeliary* of 1092 (Georgievskij, ed. 1912; *Ku* 15–16, *Š* #6). It was acquired in 1877 in the district of Archangel and was deposited in the Rumjancev Museum (Moscow State Library). Both evangeliaries appear to have been copied from South Slavic sources. Other early short evangeliaries include the eleventh-century *Turov Evangeliary* (*Ku* 20, *Š* #10), a fragment of an East Slavic codex. It was discovered in the town of Turov (Belorussian Turau̯), in southern Belarus, and is now preserved in the library of the Lithuanian Academy of Sciences in Vilnius.

The sixteen Cyrillic folios of the *Reims Evangeliary* (Bogdanov 1990; Leger 1899; Žukovskaja, ed., 1978) contain Gospel readings from October to March according to the Orthodox calendar. The Old and New Testament readings in the much longer Glagolitic part date from the second half of the fourteenth century and follow the Western calendar. The history of the Cyrillic part of the *Reims Evangeliary* has not been ascertained. A Glagolitic postscript to the codex ascribes it to Procopius, the abbot of the Sázava monastery in Bohemia. This attribution must be apocryphal, for the Cyrillic text dates from the middle of the twelfth century and Procopius died in 1053. Perhaps the Cyrillic text was copied on the occasion of the canonization of Procopius in 1204, or possibly it was a vestige of Slavic worship at Sázava, practiced there until the end of the eleventh century. In 1372 the Cyrillic text was presented by Emperor Charles IV to Emmaus, the newly founded Benedictine monastery in Prague, which obtained the authorization of Pope Clement II to conduct the divine services in Slavic. There the Glagolitic part of the evangeliary was added, most probably by the Croatian *glagoljaši* whom the emperor had invited to Prague to help introduce the Glagolitic liturgy. When the Hussites destroyed the Emmaus monastery in 1419, the Cyrillo-Glagolitic codex fell into their hands. Following the condemnation of Hussitism at the Council of Florence (1439–1442), the moderate Utraquist wing of the movement turned to the patriarch of Constantinople and asked to be received into the fold of the Orthodox church. The petition was accompanied by the gift of the Emmaus evangeliary. Before long, however, Constantinople fell to the Turks, and the codex turned up in private hands. In 1554 Charles de Guise, archbishop of Reims and cardinal of Lorraine, bought the codex during his visit to Constantinople and offered it to the Reims cathedral.[254] There the codex became the *Texte du sacre*, that is, the Bible upon which all the French kings, beginning with François II, took their oath during coronation ceremonies in the cathedral. The text was thought to be Greek until, during the visit of Peter the Great to Reims in 1717, some members of the tsar's entourage identified the Cyrillic section of the codex as Slavic, claiming that it was written in their "natural language." Not surprisingly, however, they could not read the Glagolitic part. In 1782 Catherine the Great asked Louis XVI to make her a copy of the manuscript. That copy was published in 1839 in the journal *Syn otečestva*. In the meantime, during the French Revolution, the original was stolen, and it was not recovered until 1836 with its binding stripped of all the precious stones. It has since been kept in the city library in Reims.

Of the many full evangeliaries preserved, two deserve special mention.[255] *Mstislav's Evangeliary* (Žukovskaja, ed. 1983; *Š* #51) of the early twelfth century ranks next to *Ostromir's Evangeliary* as one of the most important and lavish of East Slavic codices. It was ordered by the Novgorod prince Mstislav, son of Vladimir Monomakh, and copied with utmost care for its lettering and illuminations. Another beautifully ornamented East Slavic monument is the twelfth-century *Yuryev Evangeliary* (*Š* #52) executed for the hegumen of the

254. Legend has it that the evangeliary was brought to Reims by Anna, the youngest daughter of Prince Yaroslav the Wise of Kiev, when she arrived there in 1049 as the bride of Henry I, the widowed king of France.

255. Full evangeliaries are the subject of a well-documented study by Žukovskaja (1976).

monastery of St. George near Novgorod. Other early full evangeliaries include the East Slavic *Dobrilo's Evangeliary* of 1164 (*Š* #55) and the Serbian *Miroslav's Evangeliary* of the end of the twelfth century (Rodić/Jovanović, eds., 1986; Stojanović, ed., 1893–1894; *Š* #56). The latter is especially noteworthy for its exquisite miniatures and initials and an idiosyncratic selection of readings (App. D, Cyr. 6).

3.41.2. Apostols (*D* 93–101, L_l 71–72). New Testament readings from the Acts and Epistles of the Apostles are known as the *apostols* (from the Greek *apóstolos*). The apostols are organized like the evangeliaries into a synaxarion and a menology, and like them occur in two variants, a shorter apostol-aprakos and a longer full apostol. The oldest apostols are of the aprakos variety. Of those which date from the twelfth century, one should mention the *Enina Apostol* (Kodov, ed., 1983; Mirčev/Kodov, eds., 1965), found in the village of Enina near Kazanlăk in Bulgaria in 1960; the *Slepče Apostol* (Il'inskij, ed., 1911; *Ku* 166–170, *Š* ##110–114) from the monastery of St. John the Baptist in Slepče in Western Macedonia; and the *Ohrid Apostol* (Kul'bakin, ed., 1907; *Ku* 170–171, *Š* #109) discovered in 1845 in St. Sophia's Cathedral in Ohrid. The first two are Cyrillic palimpsests over a Glagolitic text, while the third is Cyrillic with Glagolitic insertions.

Two of these apostols offer instructive examples of the kinds of perils that face manuscripts. The *Enina Apostol,* when found in the yard of an old church, presented, in the words of its Bulgarian editors, "a formless mass of parchment folios covered with dirt, lime, and brick dust, and one could hardly hope to be able to extract from it a readable book"—a feat successfully performed by a team of restorers in the Sofia National Library. The *Slepče Apostol* was discovered in the Monastery of John the Baptist in Slepče and was still a single codex in 1845. It has since been broken up into six parts, now located in four cities: Moscow, St. Petersburg (two in the Public Library, one in the Library of the Academy of Sciences), Kiev, and Plovdiv.

3.41.3. Parimeiniki (L_l 72). The *parimeinik* (from Greek *paroimía* 'proverb') was a collection of lessons from the Old Testament read primarily at vespers and in the Liturgy of the Presanctified.[256] It included all of the book of Jonah, large fragments from the books of Genesis, Proverbs, and Isaiah, and shorter selections from other books of the Bible and some apocrypha. The oldest is *Grigorovič's parimeinik* (also known as the *Hilandar parimeinik*), a Bulgarian text of the twelfth or thirteenth century, one of the many manuscripts discovered on Mount Athos by Grigorovič (Brandt, ed. 1894, 1900, 1901; *Ko* 4:35, *Ku* 172–173, *Š* #161). The manuscript is a Cyrillic palimpsest written over an erased Greek short evangeliary of the ninth century. The oldest East Slavic *parimeinik* was copied in 1271 by Zachariah, a priest of the church of St. Demetrius in Novgorod, and by his son Onufrij, for a parish on the Northern Dvina. It is especially notable for including a lesson on Boris and Gleb (**3.46**). In 1822 the manuscript of *Zachariah's parimeinik* was acquired by the Russian Public Library in St. Petersburg (*Š* #181).

3.41.4. Psalters (L_l 72–74). The Psalter was the only book of the Old Testament that was used regularly in church services. This is why it was translated early and copied frequently, thus ensuring its survival as an unbroken and complete entity.[257] The earliest Slavic Psalter,

256. The *parimeinik* is no longer used as a liturgical book in the Orthodox service.

257. The Psalter exists in about four thousand Slavic codices from the eleventh to the seventeenth centuries (Alekseev 1988:128).

the *Psalterium Sinaiticum* (Altbauer, ed., 1971; Arnim, ed., 1930; Severjanov, ed., 1922; *Ko* 4:404–405, *Ku* 154–155) is an eleventh-century Glagolitic manuscript whose linguistic features are sufficiently conservative to qualify it as Old Church Slavonic. The manuscript was found in the monastery of St. Catherine on Mt. Sinai and has remained there to this day. Its major part (177 folios) was discovered in 1850 by the Russian archimandrite Porfirij Uspenskij, and an additional fragment of thirty-two folios turned up in 1968. Both parts were published in a facsimile edition by Moshe Altbauer (1971). A short fragment of an Old Church Slavonic Psalter is the eleventh-century *Sluck Psalter* (*Ku* 20–21), whose five Cyrillic folios, published in 1868 by I. I. Sreznevskij, are now lost. Also Cyrillic is the East Slavic *Byčkov's Psalter* (Altbauer/Lunt, eds., 1978; *Š* #28) from the turn of the eleventh and twelfth centuries, now split between the Saltykov-Ščedrin Public Library in St. Petersburg (part of Psalm 17, Psalms 18–23, beginning of Psalm 24) and the monastery of St. Catherine on Mt. Sinai (from the end of Psalm 24).

In addition to the Psalters used in the divine service, there existed the exegetic or explicatory Psalter (**3.43**). Eventually, the exegetic Psalter came to function as a favorite text for reading and writing instruction in medieval schools.

West Slavic translations of the Psalter are comparatively late. The oldest are the fourteenth-century Czech *Wittenberg Psalter* and Polish *St. Florian Psalter*, adapted from a lost Czech manuscript.

3.41.5. Other service books. The *Euchologium Sinaiticum* (Frček, ed., 1933; Nahtigal, ed., 1941, 1942; Słoński 1934; *Ku* 156–157, *Š* ##34, 35, 36) is a Glagolitic euchologium (also known as the *Sinai trebnik*) of 109 parchment folios containing parts of the liturgy of St. John Chrysostom. As an eleventh-century monument, it belongs to the canon of Old Church Slavonic. Like the *Psalterium Sinaiticum*, the manuscript of *Euchologium Sinaiticum* was discovered in 1850 by Porfirij Uspenskij in the Monastery of St. Catherine on Mount Sinai. It is still there, except for three folios taken by Uspenskij to Russia. Among the Sinai manuscripts discovered in 1975 is a twenty-eight-folio fragment of the *Euchologium Sinaiticum* (Ševčenko 1982, Tarnanidis 1988).

Earlier and linguistically more interesting is a seven-folio fragment of a Glagolitic Roman-rite liturgy contained in a Western-type missal. The missal, acquired by Andrej Kapustin (Archimandrite Antonin) and donated by him in 1872 to the Kiev Theological Academy, has come to be known as the *Kiev Missal* or the *Kiev Folios*. After the revolution the missal was transferred to the library of the Ukrainian Academy of Sciences in Kiev. The *Kiev Missal* (Hamm 1979; Jagić, ed., 1890; Mohlberg, ed., 1928; Nimčuk, ed., 1983; *Š* #1) dates from the tenth or early eleventh century and is thus one of the earliest extant monuments of Old Church Slavonic (App. D, Glag. 1). The clearly West Slavic linguistic features of the missal (**ti̯* > *c*, **di̯* > *ʒ* > *z'*) and Latin religious terminology allow us to assume that it originated in Moravia or Bohemia. This is hardly surprising, for we know from other sources that the proselytizing activity of Frankish and Bavarian missionaries among the western Slavs predated the Moravian mission of Constantine and Methodius.

Although it is clear that the liturgy contained in the *Kiev Missal* was translated from Latin, the question of whether the translation was executed within the compass of the Moravian mission cannot be answered with certainty. It is possible that Constantine and Methodius took the liturgy of John Chrysostom to Moravia and that they had to abandon it in favor of a liturgy that was familiar to the local population. This might have been the Roman rite represented by the *Kiev Missal* or, as some scholars surmise, the liturgy of St. Peter, a Greek adaptation of a Roman missal.

The early date of Bavarian missionary activity, emanating from the archbishopric of Salzburg and the bishoprics of Regensburg and Passau and targeting the neighboring Slavic provinces of Carantania, Pannonia, Moravia, and Bohemia finds other textual confirmations. Chief among them is a five-folio monument known as the *Freising Fragments* (Faganel et al., eds., 1993; Isačenko 1943; Kopitar 1836; Ramovš/Kos 1937), which contains a collection of formulas, following the Roman rite, for confessions and baptisms and an exhortation to penitence (App. D, Rom.). The Slavic text is written in the margins of a Latin manuscript found in the beginning of the nineteenth century in a monastery in the Bavarian town of Freising and transferred later to the Munich State Library. The phonetic interpretation of the monument is problematic because the text is transcribed in the unadapted Roman alphabet. It is partly for this reason that, despite its dating from the end of the tenth century, the text's Old Church Slavonic credentials have been questioned (cf. fn. 226). It is not even clear whether it should be viewed as the only example of the Slovene recension of Church Slavonic or as Old Slovene. At any rate, it appears to be a copy of an even earlier text translated from Old High German.

The earliest surviving horologium (*časoslovъ*), a thirteenth-century parchment manuscript from the Monastery of St. Catherine at Mount Sinai, was brought to Russia by Porfirij Uspenskij. It is now in the Russian Public Library in St. Petersburg (*Š* ##321, 322). The same library holds an eight-folio fragment of a poorly legible Glagolitic palimpsest which Horace G. Lunt identified as an Old Church Slavonic octoechos dating from the eleventh century (Lunt 1958; *Š* #305). The earliest triodion is the so-called *Lazarev Monastery Festal Triodion* (*Š* #49) from the end of the eleventh or beginning of the twelfth century, transferred from the collection of the Synodal Printing House to the Central State Archive of Ancient Documents (CGADA) in Moscow.

Of the liturgical books, the service menaea are among the oldest and most numerous. Especially noteworthy are the eleventh-century *Novgorod Menaea* (*Ku* 21, *Š* ##7, 8, 9) for the months of September, October, and November held in CGADA. They exhibit Novgorod dialect features and contain two important liturgical canons: one honors St. Wenceslas of Bohemia (September 28) and exemplifies early Czech influences upon the lands of Rus'; the other, whose authorship is ascribed to Methodius, honors St. Demetrius of Thessalonica. The Saltykov-Ščedrin Public Library in St. Petersburg owns the *Putjata's Menaeum* (*Ku* 21–22, *Š* #21) for May and *Dubrovskij's Menaeum* (*Š* #22) for June. *Dragan's Menaeum* (*Ku* 178–180, *Š* ##356, 357) for the whole year is a thirteenth-century monument of Bulgarian recension. In addition to the services, it contains a number of short synaxarion-type vitae and offices and an intricate musical notation. The office for Methodius contains a canon whose authorship has been attributed to Constantine of Preslav. The codex has been split into four parts. The Bulgarian monastery of St. Zographos on Mount Athos has 219 folios (also known as the *Zographos Trefologion*), the Russian monastery of St. Panteleimon, also on Mount Athos, has six folios; the Russian State Library in Moscow has two folios (Grigorovič's segment); and the Saltykov-Ščedrin Public Library in St. Petersburg has three folios (Porfirij's segment). The Bulgarian *Dobrian's Menaeum* (*Š* ##358, 359), discovered in the Monastery of St. Zographos by Grigorovič during his travels in the Balkans in 1844–1845, contains among others an office for Constantine/Cyril (February 14) and one for Methodius (April 6) ascribed to Clement of Ohrid. Seventy-six folios of the codex are in the Odessa Research Library, and sixteen folios are in the Library of the Academy of Sciences in St. Petersburg.

The dispensation of 1248 and 1252, whereby Pope Innocent IV allowed Slavic worship to the bishops of Senj and Krk, led to the spread of Glagolitic liturgical books in western Dalmatia. Surviving to this day is a number of fourteenth- and fifteenth-century missals and breviaries that had been copied (later printed) for the benefit of the local clergy, the *glagoljaši* (App. D, Glag. 6). Late as they are, these books hark back to the original corpus of Cyrillo-Methodian translations and may be used in its reconstruction (Weingart 1938). An intermediate link in this chain of transmission is the so-called *Vienna Fragments* (Jagić 1911, Vajs 1948, Weingart 1938), two Croatian Glagolitic folios of the early twelfth century containing a segment of the mass for the feast of One and Two Apostles (*commune apostolorum*).

3.42. Fourfold Gospels. A fourfold Gospel or, in Greek, the *tetraeuangélion* (often abbreviated as *tetra*) contains a full text of the four Gospels in the traditional order of Matthew, Mark, Luke, and John. Its primary function was to provide readings for individual instruction (hence its Church Slavonic name *četie evang'elie*). With appropriate annotations and additions, however, it could also be used in church services. Two of the earliest Old Church Slavonic texts are the Glagolitic fourfold Gospels, the codices *Zographensis* and *Marianus*.

Codex Zographensis (Jagić, ed., 1879; Moszyński 1961 and 1975/1990; *Ku* 146–148, *Š* #15) is a Glagolitic monument of Macedonian origin dating from the tenth or early eleventh century. It consists of 304 parchment folios of which 288 contain the Gospel text, beginning at Matthew 3:11. Of this number, seventeen folios in square Glagolitic are clearly a later addition replacing what must have been lost. The remaining sixteen folios contain a thirteenth-century Cyrillic synaxarion. The length of the manuscript and its conservative phonetic features make it into one of the most valuable sources of documentation for Slavic philology and historical linguistics. The manuscript was discovered in 1834 in the Bulgarian monastery of St. Zographos on Mount Athos by Antun Mihanović, a Croatian collector and amateur scholar who at that time served as the Austrian consul in nearby Thessalonica. In 1860 the monks of St. Zographos presented the manuscript to Tsar Alexander II of Russia, who donated it in turn to the Russian (now Saltykov-Ščedrin) Public Library in St. Petersburg. It was first described in 1877 by Viktor I. Grigorovič, and two years later its Glagolitic part was published in a Cyrillic transliteration by the Croatian Slavist Vatroslav Jagić. Other scholars who worked extensively on the *Codex Zographensis* include the Czech Josef Kurz and the Pole Leszek Moszyński (App. D, Glag. 2).

Codex Marianus (Jagić, ed., 1883; *Ku* 148–151, *Š* #14) is a Glagolitic fourfold Gospel (from Matthew 5:24 to John 21:17) containing 173 parchment folios. It is of Macedonian provenience and dates from the beginning of the eleventh century. The major part of the codex, consisting of 171 folios, was discovered in the mid-nineteenth century by Grigorovič in a hermitage belonging to the Monastery of the Holy Mother of God on Mount Athos. Grigorovič took the manuscript to Kazan', and after his death in 1876 it was deposited in the Rumjancev Museum in Moscow. Even before Grigorovič's discovery, Mihanović acquired a two-folio fragment and gave it to the Viennese Slavist Franz Miklosich, who published it in 1850. Following Miklosich's death, the fragment was deposited in the National Library in Vienna. In 1883 Vatroslav Jagić published the *Codex Marianus* in a Cyrillic transliteration and supplied it with an extensive philological commentary.

The codices *Zographensis* and *Marianus* are the only fourfold Gospels that are traditionally assigned to the canon of Old Church Slavonic. Other codices are predominantly Cyrillic and, being younger, reflect local varieties or recensions of Church Slavonic. Of about 150 extant pre-fifteenth-century fourfold Gospels, only the four oldest will be mentioned here.

Dobromir's Gospel (Altbauer, ed., 1973; Stančev 1981; Velčeva, ed., 1975; *Ku* 164–166, *Š* #71), so known because of the priest Dobromir, who was one of its two copyists, is a Cyrillic codex of 183 parchment folios dating from the beginning of the twelfth century and containing the incomplete Gospels of Mark, Luke, and John. Some linguistic features, such as **ъ** > *o* and **ь** > *e*, betray the monument's Macedonian provenience. The codex was discovered in 1870 in the library of the Monastery of St. Catherine on Mount Sinai by the head of the Russian Church Mission in Jerusalem, Andrej Kapustin. One hundred and sixty folios were acquired in 1897 by Vatroslav Jagić, who published them one year later. In 1899 Jagić sold his part of the codex to the Public Library in St. Petersburg. Seven years later the Russian scholar Vladimir Rozov discovered and identified the remaining twenty-three folios during his visit to the Monastery of St. Catherine. After that, the Sinai folios dropped out of view until their rediscovery by the Israeli Slavist Moshe Altbauer in 1968. In 1981 the Bulgarian textologist Krasimir Stančev identified two folios owned by the Bibliothèque Nationale in Paris as part of the *Dobromir's Gospel* codex.

The *Halyč Gospel* (Le Juge, ed., 1897; *Ku* 23, *Š* #53) belonged originally to the bishopric of Halyč in Galicia. It is a Cyrillic codex of 260 parchment folios displaying features of the dialect of southwestern Rus'. A scribal note on folio 228 fixes the year of its writing as 1144. This makes it the oldest dated East Slavic fourfold Gospel. A synaxarion, menology, and other additions bound with the Gospel are from the fourteenth century. The *Halyč Gospel* was discovered in 1576 by the bishop of Lvov, Hedion Balaban. In the second half of the seventeenth century it was brought to Moscow and, eventually, deposited in the Synod Library. From there it was moved to the State Historical Museum, which after the 1917 revolution took over the Synod collection.

Dobrejšo's Gospel (Conev, ed., 1906; *Ku* 176–178) is a thirteenth-century Cyrillic codex of Macedonian recension containing a fourfold Gospel with lacunae and a synaxarion. The name of the priest Dobrejšo is inscribed on two folios of the manuscript. The linguistic value of the monument is equaled by the artistic qualities of its fine illuminations and miniatures. The codex is broken into two parts. The larger part of 127 parchment folios was acquired in 1899 by the National Library in Sofia. The smaller part of forty-eight folios was in the National Library in Belgrade and was lost when the library burned down during a German air raid in World War II.

3.43. Biblical exegeses. Biblical books or their fragments were often provided with explanatory annotations written by early Church Fathers or later Byzantine or Roman theologians. Such books, which came to be known as exegetic (ChSl. *tlъkovyę kъnigy*), constitute a special genre of Byzantine religious literature. Exegetic books may have a single author, such as the Psalter commentary by Theodoret, bishop of Cyrrhus in Syria (d. ca. 458), or they may be collections of various commentators (*catenae*), such as the exegesis of the books of the Prophets, which was current in Novgorod as early as the eleventh century.

Of the exegetic Gospels, especially important are the commentaries (*besědy*) of Pope Gregory the Great (*Š* #227). Their thirteenth-century East Slavic text is known to be an adaptation of a tenth-century Czech translation from Latin, thus providing an example of the existence of early cultural relations between Bohemia and Rus'. The exegetic *Theophylact's Gospel* (*Š* #259) is interesting because its compiler, the Greek archbishop of Ohrid (ca. 1090–1109), is also the author of the vita of St. Clement of Ohrid, an important source of information on the post-Moravian phase of the Byzantine mission. Its excerpts have been published.

A special case of an exegetic Gospel is the *Homiliary Gospel* (*Ku* 23–24, *Š* #118) composed at the end of the ninth century by Constantine, one of the younger disciples of Methodius and the future bishop of Preslav (**3.35**). The *Homiliary Gospel* (ChSl. *evang'elie učitelьnoe*) is a collection of homilies on Gospel readings for all Sundays of the year except Easter Sunday. All but one of the homilies were translated from the Greek of John Chrysostom and Cyril of Alexandria. However, the introduction to the work and the forty-second homily were written by Constantine himself. The earliest text of the *Homiliary Gospel* is in a twelfth-century codex of East Slavic recension preserved in the State Historical Museum in Moscow.[258] It has been published in excerpts.

Exegetic Psalters include the eleventh-century East Slavic *Evgenij's Psalter* (Kolesov, ed. 1972; *Ku* 18–19, *Š* ##29, 30) and the *Čudovo Psalter* (Pogorelov, ed. 1910_1 and 1910_2; *Ku* 19–20, *Š* #31), which was a translation of the Psalter annotated by Bishop Theodoret. Both were discovered in the first half of the nineteenth century in the vicinity of Novgorod, the former in the Monastery of St. George (Yuryev) by the archbishop of Novgorod Evgenij Bolxovitinov, the latter in the Čudovo monastery. Also exegetic are the thirteenth-century Macedonian *Bologna Psalter* (Dujčev, ed. 1968, Jagić, ed. 1907; *Ko* 4:403–404, *Ku* 174–176), a richly illuminated Cyrillic copy of an older Glagolitic text, and *Pogodin's Psalter* (Jagić, ed. 1907; *Ku* 40; *Š* #385). The former was transferred from the Ohrid region in Macedonia, where it was executed in the first half of the thirteenth century, to the library of the University of Bologna. The latter, a monument of Bulgarian recension of the second half of the thirteenth century, became part of the manuscript collection of the Russian historian Mixail Pogodin (1800–1875) and is housed with it in the Saltykov-Ščedrin Public Library in St. Petersburg.

3.44. Homiletic texts. Homilies or sermons (*slovo*) made up a genre that lent itself well to original literary expression, for they often dealt with issues of local import, be they didactic sermons on topical problems, celebrations of local events and holidays, or encomia dedicated to local saints. No homilies of the Moravian period of Slavic letters have survived, but the Bulgarian period has given us texts by such eminent practitioners of the homiletic art as Methodius's disciples Constantine of Preslav and Clement of Ohrid as well as John the Exarch. After the baptism of Rus' an East Slavic homiletic tradition arose, represented most impressively by the Kiev metropolitan Hilarion in the eleventh century and the bishops Cyril of Turov in the twelfth and Serapion of Vladimir in the thirteenth.

Slavic vernacular homiletic writing found its inspiration in the models provided by patristic literature, above all in the homilies authored by such fourth-century Church Fathers as Athanasius of Alexandria, Gregory of Nazianzus (Gregory the Theologian or Grigorii Bogoslov), and the brothers Basil of Caesarea and Gregory of Nyssa. Particularly popular in the lands of Rus' were the sermons of John Chrysostom of Antioch (ca. 347–407), a forceful and eloquent preacher (hence his Greek name, meaning 'golden-mouthed', ChSl. *Zlatoustъ*) and

258. The *Homiliary Gospel* is preceded in this codex by the famous *Alphabet Prayer* (**3.47**), whose authorship is also frequently attributed to Constantine of Preslav.

from 397 the patriarch of Constantinople. John's sermons, marked by a vivid and elaborate style, religious zeal, and social concern, were frequently anthologized in individual collections called *Zlatostrui* (L_l 187–190). The earliest specimen of the genre is the *Zlatostruj Byčkova* (Il'inskij, ed. 1929; *Ku* 17–18, *Š* #18) from the eleventh century, whose four surviving folios are kept in the Saltykov-Ščedrin Public Library in St. Petersburg.[259] Another favorite Byzantine writer of homilies was the eighth-century philologian and philosopher John of Damascus, otherwise known for his resolute stand against iconoclasm. If the *otьčьskyę kъnigy* mentioned in the *Vita Methodii* were not a *paterik* (**3.48.1**), they may have referred to a collection of Greek patristic writings.

Homiletic texts are subject to some terminological ambiguity. In the first place, the preferred method of bringing homilies to the reader was not in individually authored books, but in miscellanies (**3.45**). Secondly, as we have seen, early Byzantine homilies were also examples of patristic literature. Furthermore, a homily usually provided an interpretation and amplification of a particular biblical passage. Such a homily could, therefore, be classified as an exegetic rather than homiletic text. The *Homiliary Gospel* by Constantine of Preslav is a good example of such a dual association. Another example is provided by the East Slavic *prologues*, which in addition to short lives of saints came to contain various homiletic and didactic texts. The earliest extant examples of this genre include the *Sofijskij Prologue* (*Š* #162) from September to February, whose first part goes back to the twelfth or thirteenth century, and *Lobkov's Prologue* (*Š* #177) from September to January, dating from the second half of the thirteenth century.

The so-called *Glagolita Clozianus* (Dostál 1959, Kopitar 1836, Miklosich 1860, Vondrák 1893; *Ku* 153–154) is an Old Church Slavonic Glagolitic miscellany of the eleventh century. What remains of an originally very large codex are fourteen folios containing two complete homilies, one by John Chrysostom and one by Athanasius of Alexandria, and three fragments of homilies, one by John Chrysostom, one by Epiphanius of Cyprus, and one that Grivec (1943), Vaillant (1947) and Vašica (1956) attributed to Methodius. The codex has been broken up into two parts. Twelve folios are in the City Museum in Trent, donated there in the mid-nineteenth century by Count Paris Cloz. The remaining two folios, discovered by the Slovenian Slavist Franz Miklosich, are in the Ferdinandeum in Innsbruck.

The eleventh-century Cyrillic *Codex Suprasliensis* (Meyer 1935, Sever'janov, ed., 1904, Zaimov/Capaldo 1982, 1983; *Ku* 159–164, *Š* #23) is the largest extant Old Church Slavonic manuscript. It is a lectionary menaeum for the month of March, intersecting with the movable Easter cycle. It contains twenty-four lives of saints and twenty-four homilies, most of them by or attributed to John Chrysostom. The codex was discovered in 1823 by Canon Michał Bobrowski in the Uniate Basilian monastery in Supraśl in northeastern Poland. It was subsequently split into three parts: 118 folios in the University Library in Ljubljana, 150 folios in the National Library in Warsaw, and sixteen folios in the Saltykov-Ščedrin Public Library in St. Petersburg.[260]

The *Hilandar Folios* (Kul'bakin 1900, Minčeva 1978, Vaillant 1932; *Š* #27), another Cyrillic Old Church Slavonic text, is an eleventh-century fragment of two homilies by Cyril

259. The end of John Chrysostom's sermon on the Annunciation from the *Codex Suprasliensis* may be found in App. D., Cyr. 4.

260. The large manuscript collection of the Supraśl monastery was moved to Vilnius and is now housed in the Lithuanian National Library. The peripatetic history of the *Codex Suprasliensis* is described in Kuev 1979: 160–163.

of Jerusalem (ChSl. *poučenija oglasitelьnaja*). Its two folios are in the State Research Library in Odessa. An almost complete collection of homilies by Cyril of Jerusalem is in a late eleventh- or early twelfth-century East Slavic manuscript kept today in the Synodal collection of the Moscow State Historical Museum (*Ku* 22–23, *Š* #45).

The *Paraenesis* ('counsel') of Ephraim the Syrian (*Ku* 191–192, L_l 296–299, *Š* #466) was a popular collection of homilies by a noted Syrian theologian of the fourth century. Its oldest codices are fragmentary, and it is not until the fourteenth century that we find texts with most of the homilies. The earliest fragments of the *Paraenesis* are in the Glagolitic *Rila Folios* (Gošev, ed., 1956, Il'inskij 1909; *Ku* 61–62, *Š* #25), an Old Church Slavonic monument dating from the eleventh century. Two complete and five fragmentary folios are in the Rila Monastery in Bulgaria, where the monument was discovered in 1845 by Grigorovič. One folio that Grigorovič took with him to Kazan' is now in the Library of the Academy of Sciences in St. Petersburg.

An eleventh-century East Slavic codex of 377 parchment folios contains thirteen *Homilies of Gregory of Nazianzus* (Budilovič, ed., 1871/1875; *Ku* 22, *Š* #33). In 1824 the codex was acquired by the Public Library in St. Petersburg.

Native Slavic homiletic writing has come down to us in copies from the twelfth century on. The best-known homilies of Clement of Ohrid are sermons celebrating various Christian holidays. Of Clement's homilies dedicated to the memory of particular saints, the oldest is the commemorative sermon for Cyril (Constantine) and Methodius (Lavrov 1930) included in the *Uspenskij sbornik.* Constantine of Preslav's reputation in the field of homiletics rests upon his *Homiliary Gospel,* a collection of homilies most of which were translated from patristic sources. Constantine's crowning achievement in the art of translation is his rendition of four sermons against the Arians by Athanasius of Alexandria. The most famous homily of John the Exarch, the sermon on the Feast of Assumption, is also to be found in the *Uspenskij sbornik.*

The first examples of East Slavic homiletics are by two church leaders of the eleventh century, Luka Židjata, the bishop of Novgorod, and Hilarion, the metropolitan of Kiev and the first native head of church. The earliest text of Luka's *poučenie* comes from the fourteenth or fifteenth century. Contrasting with its terse style is Hilarion's ornate *Sermon on Law and Grace* (Franklin 1991, Moldovan, ed. 1984; *Š* #388). Its fragment appeared in a thirteenth-century miscellany; the full text of the sermon, however, comes from a sixteenth-century manuscript. The earliest homily of Bishop Cyril of Turov was on the parable of the Samaritan woman. It was included in the *Uspenskij sbornik.*

The earliest extant West Slavic homilies are two Polish collections of sermons from the fourteenth-century, the *Holy Cross Sermons* (*Kazania świętokrzyskie*) and the *Gniezno Sermons* (*Kazania gnieźnieńskie*) published by Łoś/Semkowicz, eds. (1934), and Vrtel-Wierczyński, ed. (1953), respectively.

3.45. Miscellanies and florilegia. Anthological texts known as miscellanies (*izborьnikъ* 'selection' or *sъborьnikъ* 'collection') allowed the greatest degree of freedom for their compilers. In fact, a great variety of Slavic medieval texts, mostly religious but occasionally also secular, have come down to us in miscellanies of one kind or another. The thematic range of miscellanies may be gleaned from a selection of entries (ca. 380 in toto) in the oldest Slavic representative of the genre, the *Izbornik of 1073* (Dinekov, ed., 1991–1993, Žukovskaja, ed., 1983; *Ku* 16–17, L_l 194–196, *Š* #4). The prototype of this miscellany, copied for the Kievan prince Svyatoslav, was a Slavic translation from Greek executed for the Bulgarian tsar Symeon in the early tenth century and subsequently lost. According to its own characterization, it was a "collection from many Fathers—an interpretation of the abstruse utterances in the Gospels, and in the *apostol,* and in other books, concisely assembled for the sake of memory and for ready answer." It included examples of the finest patristic writings, such as the homilies by Justin Martyr, Isidore of Alexandria, Irenaeus of Lyons, Hippolytus of Rome, Eusebius of Caesarea, Basil of Caesarea, Gregory of Nyssa, Gregory of Nazianzus, Cyril of Alexandria, John Chrysostom, Anastasius of Sinai, Andrew of Crete, Maximus the Confessor [Jan. 21], Augustine of Hippo, John of Damascus, and Michael of Jerusalem. It also contained an index of twenty-five apocryphal texts, a translation of an abbreviated version of the treatise *On Tropes and Figures* by the Byzantine rhetorician George Choeroboscus, and the *Concise History* by Patriarch Nicephorus.

Other ancient miscellanies include the *Izbornik of 1076* (Golyšenko et al., eds., 1965, Šimanovskij, V. S. (1887); L_I 196–198, *Š* #5) and three East Slavic miscellanies of the twelfth and thirteenth centuries, the *Vygoleksinskij sbornik* (Dubrovina et al., eds. 1977; *Š* #119),[261] the *Troicko-Sergeevskij sbornik* (*Ku* 24–25, *Š* #163), and the famous *Uspenskij sbornik* (Kotkov, ed. 1971, Šaxmatov/Lavrov, eds. 1899; *Ku* 25, *Š* #165).

A special kind of miscellany was represented by the *pandects.* These were Byzantine encyclopedic digests containing precepts for Christian conduct excerpted from various religious writings. As such, their content was not fixed. The most popular pandects were collected by Antioch of Galatia in the beginning of the seventh century, and it is in fact an eleventh-century East Slavic codex of the *Pandects of Antioch* (Popovski, ed. 1989; L_I 290–292, *Š* #24) that is the earliest Slavic example of the genre. Antioch's follower, the monk Nikon of the Black Mountain monastery in Syria, compiled his pandects in the eleventh century. The earliest Slavic version of the *Pandects of Nikon* is included in the so-called *Sinai palimpsest* (L_I 292–294, *Š* #166), a partly East Slavic, partly Bulgarian miscellany of the thirteenth century.

The Greek *Mélissa* ('Bee'), composed in the eleventh century by the monk Anthony, was a florilegium of short quotes from the Scriptures or from ancient authors on a variety of philosophical and existential problems. Thus the entry on "Laughter" was illustrated by quotes from the Gospels, *Apostol,* Wisdom of Solomon, Ecclesiasticus, Basil of Caesarea, Gregory of Nazianzus, John Chrysostom, Plutarch, John Moschus, Epictetus, and Cato. There are indications that *Mélissa* was known in Rus' in the twelfth century, but its oldest extant East Slavic version, called *Pčela* (derived from **bъčela*), is from the end of the fourteenth century.

3.46. Hagiography. The primary concern of hagiography was to provide models of exemplary Christian behavior through the presentation of the biographies (lives) of saints, monks, and Christian martyrs. The Latin term *vitae* (Church Slavonic *žitija*) has the advantage of referring unambiguously to the hagiographic genre. The term *lives* will be reserved for the beginnings of secular biography and autobiography, a genre that is also dealt with in this section. The edifying and apologetic function of the vitae lent them the aspect of panegyrics in which the known elements of a saint's biography were overlaid with the expected Christian tropes (virtuous life, martyrdom, miracles, fate of the relics) and where realistic passages mingled with rhetorical topoi. This combination of biography and homiletics, of the human and the supernatural, of the terrestrial and the otherworldly, contributed to the development of hagiographic writing into the most popular literary genre of early Christianity.

261. From two neighboring monasteries in northern Russia, a male one on the Vyg and a female one on the Leksa.

The vitae are usually found in miscellanies, their arrangement corresponding to the order of feasts in the church calendar. Depending on their intended purpose, vitae existed in full (extensive) and short (abbreviated) versions. Full vitae (*prostranьnaja žitija*) were normally included in the menologies, while the short ones were typical of the synaxaria, which in the Slavic tradition came to be known as the prologues. Hence, in East Slavic Church Slavonic a synaxarion vita is called *proložьnoe žitie*.

The *Vita of St. Anthony* by Athanasius of Alexandria served as a general model for Byzantine hagiography, whether composed in Greek or in any other language of the commonwealth. Slavic hagiography began, naturally enough, with translations, but a native hagiographic tradition was not long in developing. Thus, the eleventh-century Old Church Slavonic lectionary menaeum, the *Codex Suprasliensis*, contains twenty-four vitae of Byzantine and Roman saints and martyrs (Paul and Juliana, Basiliscus, Konon, the Forty Martyrs of Sebastea, Pope Gregory the Great, Sabinus, Alexander of Sidon, Paul the Simple, John the Silent), while the East Slavic *Uspenskij sbornik* of the twelfth or thirteenth century contains not only a number of translated vitae (Athanasius of Alexandria, Irene, Christopher, Pachomius, Erasmus of Antioch, Vitus of Sicily, Fevronia, Theodosia of Constantinople, Epiphanius of Cyprus) but also several vitae composed in Slavic: Methodius, Boris and Gleb, and Theodosius, hegumen of the Cave Monastery in Kiev.

It must be remembered that the date of the initial composition of a text need not have anything to do with the age of its oldest extant manuscript. Thus, of the vitae of Constantine and Methodius (Duichev 1985: 49–92, Florja 1981:71–101 and 105–172, Kantor 1983:25–138, Lavrov 1930:1–78, Teodorov-Balan, ed. 1920, 1934; *Š* #165), the *Vita Methodii*[262] has come down to us in a text from the twelfth or thirteenth centuries, but it was most probably composed soon after Methodius's death in 885. Even more strikingly, the earliest extant text of the *Vita Constantini* is to be found in a mid-fifteenth-century East Slavic manuscript, even though its earliest version may have been composed before the *Vita Methodii*. Nor do we have a truly ancient text of the *Vita of Naum* (Duichev 1985:139–142, Lavrov 1930:181–192), the only disciple of Constantine and Methodius to have his own Slavic hagiography.[263] In some instances, the existence of a vita may be inferred from other evidence, the vita itself being lost. Such is the case of the *Vita of Antonius*, a monk in the Kiev Caves Monastery and a cellmate of Theodosius, which was used in the composition of the *Primary Chronicle* and of the *Caves Monastery Paterik*.

Most of the original Slavic hagiography deals with the personalities of Rus' (Boris and Gleb, Theodosius of the Caves Monastery, Leontius of Rostov, Barlaam of Xutyn', Euphrosyne of Polock) or has survived in East Slavic versions as did the vitae of the martyred Czech saints, Prince Wenceslas (Kantor 1983:99–138, Mareš 1979:104–130) and his grandmother Ludmila (Mareš 1979:130–133). The life stories of Boris and Gleb, the first East Slavic saints, offer an instructive example of the multiplicity of agencies for hagiographic writings. The most extensive account of the brothers' martyrdom is the *Lesson (Čьtenie) on the Life and Murder of the Blessed Passion-Sufferers Boris and Gleb* found in the fourteenth-century *Sil'vestrovskij sbornik*. An artistically enhanced version entitled *Tale and Passion and Encomium of the Holy Martyrs Boris and Gleb* (*Sъkazanie i strastь i poxvala*) is included in the *Uspenskij sbornik* and followed there by the *Tale of the Miracles* wrought by the saintly

262. Following a frequent practice, the vitae of Constantine and Methodius are referred to in Latin as *Vita Constantini* and *Vita Methodii*.

263. Clement of Ohrid, another member of the Moravian mission, is the subject of a Greek vita by Theophilact of Ohrid.

brothers. Another account of the martyrdom of Boris and Gleb is in an eight-folio insert into the *Primary Chronicle* under the year 1015. Finally, there are lessons on Boris and Gleb in the *parimeiniki*, the oldest of them being a nine-folio lesson in *Zachariah's Parimeinik* of 1271, and various short *proložьnaja žitija*, memorial offices dedicated to the brothers, and a menological encomium (Abramovič, ed. 1916, Hollingsworth 1992, Kantor 1983:165–253, Lenhoff 1989; *Š* #165).[264]

Of the important South Slavic subjects of vitae, one should mention Ivan of Rila (ca. 876–946), the founder of Bulgarian eremitism, and Sava or Sabbas (1175–1235), the organizer of the Serbian national church. The prologue-type vita of Ivan of Rila is included in the *Dragan Menaeum*. Of the two vitae of Sava, one was written by Domentian, the other by Theodosius (Daničić 1860), two thirteenth-century monks at the Hilandar Monastery on Mount Athos.[265] Short episodes from the *vitae* of monks may also be found in the *pateriks*, or histories of particular monastic communities.

Sava's father, Stefan Nemanja (ca. 1132–1200), the first ruler of the independent Serbian state and the founder of the Nemanjić dynasty, received two vitae, both written by his sons and both having some of the earmarks of biographies. Sava gave a very intimate account of the years he spent with his father in the Hilandar Monastery, where Stefan retired after his abdication. The account by Stefan Nemanjić (1165–1228), Stefan Nemanja's elder son and successor to the throne of Serbia, is less personal in tone and more concerned with his father's political career (Kantor 1983:257–304, Šafařík 1873).[266]

Autobiography as a genre does not appear before the seventeenth century, its first East Slavic representative being the *Life of the Archpriest Avvakum*. There existed, to be sure, earlier writings that offered outlets for autobiographic disclosures, such as travel accounts (ChSl. *xoždenija*) by pilgrims and merchants. The most celebrated example is the description of a pilgrimage to the Holy Land by Daniel, hegumen of a monastery in Chernigov, composed in 1106–1108. Daniel's travelogue, containing vivid scenes of Palestine, is extant in many manuscripts from the fifteenth century on.[267] The *Instruction* of Vladimir Monomakh (1053–1125), in which the Kievan prince prepares his children for their future responsibilities, is not a reliable example of the autobiographic genre, even though it is sometimes so considered. In the first place, Vladimir's authorship of the text cannot be ascertained since the *Instruction* survives in a late and unique version (in the Laurentian codex of 1377). Secondly, the *Instruction* follows the well-known topos of an ideological testament made by an aging ruler on his deathbed.

3.47. Hymnography and other poetic works. Slavic poetry found its first written expression in translations of some of the poetic books of the Old Testament (Psalter, Song of Songs) and of Byzantine liturgical hymnody. The latter turned out to be especially important for the development of native Slavic poetic tradition by offering ready models for original

264. English translations of these texts may be found in a study by Hollingsworth (1992) on East Slavic hagiography, including translations of the vitae of Theodosius of the Caves Monastery and Avraamij of Smolensk, and of an encomium for Prince Vladimir.

265. Since Domentian's vita was composed before that by Theodosius and became its main source, there is confusion about the authorship of the latter; cf. the title of Daničić's edition of the vita by Theodosius: *Život svetoga Save napisao Domentijan*.

266. The vitae of Constantine the Philosopher, Methodius, Wenceslas, Boris and Gleb, and Stefan Nemanja (by Sava) are available in an English translation by Kantor (1983).

267. An account of a commercial trip to India, made in 1466–1472 by Afanasij Nikitin, is also partly autobiographical.

Slavic compositions. In fact, acrostics in various hymnographic compositions show that in the ninth and tenth centuries this genre vied in popularity with homiletic literature.

The solemn mode of the divine office (*služьba*), in particular the canon with which the faithful honored their saints and commemorated special church occasions, offers the earliest examples of such poetic compositions. It is possible that the first canon composed in Slavic was one honoring Demetrius, the patron saint of Thessalonica. There is even some basis for speculation that the canon was written by Methodius himself: Thessalonica was Methodius's native town, and Methodius is reported to have celebrated an office for St. Demetrius (*Vita Methodii* 15). This surmise is strengthened by a reference in the canon to the work of the Moravian mission. The earliest text of the canon for St. Demetrius comes from the eleventh century. Another famous canon, one that honored Constantine/Cyril and Methodius, may have been composed soon after the latter's death. It is known from a twelfth-century East Slavic service menaeum for the month of April (Lavrov, ed. 1930:111–115; *Š* #87).

An anonymous office for Constantine is in a twelfth-century East Slavic service menaeum for the month of February (*Š* #85), while an office for Methodius, attributed to Constantine of Preslav (Kostić 1937–1938), is known from the Bulgarian *Dragan Menaeum* (Duichev, ed. 1985:153–156, Lavrov, ed. 1930:116–127, *Ku* 178–180, *Š* ##356, 357) of the thirteenth century. A joint office for the two brothers, composed probably in the eleventh century in Bohemia, has survived in Croatian Glagolitic breviaries of the fourteenth century. An office in honor of the Czech prince Wenceslas is preserved in an eleventh-century Novgorod menaeum for the month of September (*Š* #7).

Authors of some hymnographic works can be identified thanks to the Byzantine device of "signing" compositions by including the poet's name in an acrostic woven into the text. This is the way in which some of the writings of Clement of Ohrid, Naum of Ohrid, and Constantine of Preslav have come to light (Kostić 1937–1938), Kožuxarov 1984, 1988, Popov 1978, 1982, 1985, 1988, Stančev/Popov 1988.[268] The most frequent vehicle for acrostics was the canon (Gk. *kanō̃n* 'rule'), which from the seventh century, when it was first introduced, became the favorite form of Byzantine hymnography. The canon consists of nine odes (*pěsni*) of several stanzas each corresponding and referring to the biblical canticles of Moses (Ex. 15.1–19, Dt. 32.1–43),[269] Hannah (1 Sa. 2.1–10), Habbakuk (3.1–19), Isaiah (26.9–20), Jonah (2.2–9), Azariah (Dn. 3.26–47, 52–57), the Virgin Mary (Lk. 1.46–55), and Zachariah (Lk. 1.68–79). Each ode is introduced by an *heirmos* (from Gk. *héirō* 'I join'; ChSl. *irmos*), which addresses the theme of the canticle and serves as a formal model for the following *troparia* (Gk. *tropárion* from *trópos* 'musical mode'), usually three or four. The *troparia* are the truly original stanzas of the canon and, as such, they become available for the composition of acrostics. The final stanza of each ode is a *theotokion* (*Bogorodičьnъ*) that glorifies the Mother of God (Gk. *theós* 'god' and *tekeĩn* 'to give birth'). Inserted after the third ode is the *kathisma* (ChSl. *kafizma* or *sědalьnъ*), a stanza that may be recited in a sitting position (Gk. *kathístēmi* 'I am set'), while the sixth ode is followed by two stanzas, a *kontakion* (ChSl. *kondakь*) and an *oikos* (ChSl. *ikos*), which echo the theme of the canon.

The canon for Methodius from the *Dragan Menaeum* has yielded the following acrostic:

268. To be sure, an acrostic may reveal the name of the author but cannot identify him as a particular person. Thus, however well founded is Kostić's (1937–1938) surmise that the name Constantine stands for Constantine of Preslav, it must remain a surmise.

269. The second ode is usually omitted because of the mournful mood of the second canticle of Moses.

DOBRO METODI TĘ POJǪ KONSTANTIN 'Well, Methodius, do I praise you. Constantine'. To show how Kostić (1937–1938:201–203) arrived at this reading, here is a sample of the reconstruction of the initial words of each stanza, with the letters used for the acrostic transcribed in boldface:

Ode 1	Heirmos	Grędete . . .
	Troparion	**D**aždь . . .
	Troparion	**O**stavivъ . . .
	Troparion	**Br**anь . . .
	Theotokos	Kъto . . .
Ode 3	Heirmos	Outvrъdi . . .
	Troparion	**O** prěslavьne . . .
	Troparion	**M**efodie . . .
	Troparion	**E**že . . .
	Theotokos	Marie . . .
	Kathisma	Jako . . .
Ode 4	Heirmos	Ouslyšaxъ . . .
	Troparion	**T**ę . . .
	Troparion	**O** desnǫjǫ . . .
	Troparion	**D**oušǫ . . .
	Theotokos	Molę . . .
Ode 5	Heirmos	Světa . . .
	Troparion	**I**styi . . . etc.

Besides the canons and offices, the poetic legacy left by the Moravian mission includes two dodecasyllabic poems, the *Preface to the Gospel* and the *Alphabet Prayer.* The *Preface* (*Proglasъ*) celebrates the creation of Slavic letters and of Slavic religious books with a ringing hymn glorifying them and the Scriptures and extolling their importance for the Slavs (Butler 1980:5–15, Duichev, ed. 1985:147–150, Jakobson 1963, Lavrov, ed. 1930:196–198, Nahtigal 1943, Vaillant 1956). Its oldest text is in a thirteenth-century codex of a fourfold Gospel from the Hilandar Monastery at Mt. Athos. However, a sixteenth-century Russian text of the first forty-four lines is in many respects more conservative. Here is a reconstruction of the opening lines of the poem, with the caesura typically after the fifth syllable (passages from the Scriptures are in quotation marks):

Jako proroci | prorekli sǫtь prěžde,	As the prophets prophesied of old,
Xristosъ grędetъ | sъbьratъ ęzyky,	"Christ comes to gather the nations,"
Světъ bo estъ | vьsemu miru semu.	For he is "the light of this whole world,"
Se sъbystъ sę | vъ sedmyi věkъ sь.	It has come to pass in this seventh age.
Rěšę bo oni | slěpii prozьrętъ,	For they have said, "The blind will see,
Glusi slyšętъ | slovo bukъvьnoe,	The deaf will hear the word of the Book."
Boga že ubo | poznati dostoitъ.	For it is proper that God be known.
Těmь že uslyšite | slověne vьsi!	Therefore harken, all ye Slavs!
Darъ bo estъ | otъ boga sь danъ,	For this gift is given by God,
Darъ božii | estъ desnyę čęsti,	A divine gift from [God's] right hand,
Darъ dušamъ | nikoliže tьlěę,	A gift to men which never perishes,

The *Alphabet Prayer* (Duichev 1985:143–146, Lavrov 1930:199–200, Stančev 1981, Vajs/Kurz 1929, 1955; L_I 32–34, *Š* #118) is an alphabetic acrostic, that is, a poem whose lines begin with consecutively arranged letters of the alphabet. It forms the introduction to the *Homiliary Gospel* by Constantine of Preslav (first codex from the twelfth century), who may well be the author. Its message is similar to that of the *Preface*. Here are the poem's opening fifteen lines in their East Slavic version and in translation (the letters of the alphabet are given in boldface):

Azъ slovomь simь molju sja bogu,	I pray to God with these words:
Bоže vseja tvari i zižditelju,	O, God of all creation and maker
Vidimyimъ i nevidimyimъ.	Of what is visible and what is invisible,
Gospodi, duxa posъli živuščaago,	O, Lord, send the living Spirit,
Da vъdъxnetь vъ srьdьce mi slovo,	Let it breathe the Word into my heart,
Ježe budetь na uspěxь vьsěmъ,	With which will prosper all
Živuščiimъ vъ zapovědьxъ ti.	Who live by your commandments.
Ʒělo bo jestь světilьnikъ žizni	Because your law is the light of life
Zakonъ tvoi i světъ stьzamъ	And the illumination of the paths of him
Iže iščetь evangelьska slova	Who seeks the words of the Gospel
I prositь dary tvoja prijati.[270]	And asks to receive your benefactions.
Letitь[271] bo nyně i slověnьsko plemę.	And now the Slavic people take wing.
Kъ krьščeniju obratišasę vьsi	All those turned towards baptism
Ljudije tvoi nareščisę xotęšče.	Who wish to be called your people.
Milosti tvojeja, bože, prosętь zělo.	They fervently pray for your mercy.

East Slavic codices preserved two other ancient alphabet acrostic poems. One, beginning with *Azъ tebě pripadaju milostive,* is in the thirteenth-century *Jaroslavl' Euchologium* (Sobolevskij 1910: 29, 33–34; *Š* #387); the other, transcribed on the last two folios of the *Pandects of Antioch,* is a Slavic translation of the alphabet poem (*alphabetarium*) composed by Pope Gregory the Great (Karinskij 1930; *Ku* 18). It is remarkable for having every line of the acrostic begin not just with a letter of the alphabet but with the letter's name (the first line reads *Azъ jesmь vьsemu miru světъ*).

There are also numerous examples of highly organized rhetorical and hieratic prose whose rhythmic and rhyming devices come close to the structure of the poetic line. The degree to which such devices are used may vary in one and the same composition depending on the need to highlight a portion of the text. Segments characterized by a high density of poetic devices may in fact qualify as poems in their own right. Such are the versified encomium to Tsar Symeon (readdressed to Prince Svyatoslav), found at the end of the *Izbornik of 1073,* the prayers in the compositions of Cyril of Turov or the inserts in some of the vitae. Examples of such inserts are provided by the inscription on Solomon's goblet (*Vita Constantini* 13) as reconstructed by Jakobson (1957:115–116) or the deathbed instruction given by Constantine/Cyril to Methodius in the *Vita Methodii* 7 (Tschižewskij 1976:18). A striking example of rhythmic prose is provided by the coda of the encomium to Constantine/Cyril and Metho-

270. The two I's represent different letters of the Cyrillic alphabet, і with the numerical value of 10 and и with the numerical value of 8.

271. The fact that this line does not conform to the alphabetical principle of the poem suggests that it may be a later insertion.

dius whose composition is attributed to Clement of Ohrid (**1.35**). In the following excerpt the continuous text found in the *Uspenskij sbornik* is broken down into short segments united by various formal devices (syntactic constructions, syllable count, stress, rhyme, and alliteration):[272]

B(og)odъxnovenyi darъ o(tъ) B(og)a priimъša,
mrakъ nevěděnija vьsjudu progъnasta,
soboju obrazъ vьsěmъ prědlagajušča,
o(tъ) ustьnu d(u)xovьnuju sladostь istačajušča,
poganьstvu že vьsękomu razdrušьnika javista sę,
jeretikomъ supostata, běsomъ progonьnika,
světъ omračenyimъ, učitelę mladenьcemъ,
istačajušča d(u)xovьnuju sladostь,
alъčjuščiimъ neskudьnaja pišča,
žadьnyimъ neprěstajai istočьnikъ,
nagyimъ obilьnoje oděnije podajušča,
siryimъ pomoščьnika,
stranьnyimъ priimьnika,
bolьnyimъ posětitelja,
pečalьnyimъ utešitelja,
napastьnyimъ zaščitьnika,
vьdovamъ i sirotamъ pomoščьnika . . .

Having accepted the gift of divine inspiration,
You (two) have dispelled the darkness of ignorance everywhere.
Setting yourselves as an example for everyone,
Exuding spiritual sweetness from your mouths,
You became destroyers of all paganism,

272. This is reminiscent of artistic devices found in medieval Latin prose, where the "art of dictation" (*ars dictaminis*) called for pauses in delivery and a rhythmic cadence. The rhythmic segments, or cola, produced in this process could also be rhymed. Two cola having the same number of syllables were called a sequence. As a sample of Latin rhythmic and rhymed prose, consider the Latin text of the second paragraph of the passage from the chronicle of *Anonymous Gallus* that was cited in English in **1.44.** The excerpt is broken down into cola:

Que regio quamvis multum sit nemorosa,
auro tamen et argento, pane et carne,
pisce et melle satis est copiosa.
Et in hoc plurimum aliis preferenda
quod cum a tot supradictis gentibus
et christianis et gentilibus sit vallata
et a cunctis insimul et a singulis
multociens inpugnata,
nunquam tamen ab ullo
fuit penitus subiugata.
Patria ubi aër salubris, ager fertilis,
silva melliflua, aqua piscosa,
milites bellicosi, rustici laboriosi,
equi durabiles, boves arabiles,
vacce lactose, oves lanose.

Purely syllabic segmentation should not be confused with the "isocolic principle," which defines rhythmic structures in medieval Slavic prose by the number of stresses (Picchio 1973, 1980).

Enemies of heretics, harriers of devils,
Light to those in darkness, teachers of the young,
Exuding spiritual sweetness,
Copious food for the hungry,
An ever plentiful source for the thirsty,
Offering abundant clothing for the naked,
Helpers of the bereft,
Protectors of the wayfarers,
Visitors of the sick,
Comforters of the sad,
Defenders of the attacked,
Helpers of widows and orphans . . .

A special case is presented by the *Igor Tale* (*Slóvo o polkú Ígoreve*), hailed as the greatest work of medieval East Slavic literature (Adrianova-Peretc, ed. 1950, Grégoire/Jakobson/Szeftel, eds. 1948, Nabokov 1960). This epic poem of about 2,750 words describes the unsuccessful campaign of 1185 by Prince Igor Svyatoslavich of Novgorod-Seversk against the Polovtsi, a Turkic tribe that followed the Pechenegs as the occupiers of the steppe corridor. The only manuscript of the *Igor Tale,* dating from the sixteenth century, was discovered at the end of the eighteenth century in the town of Yaroslavl, northeast of Moscow. In 1795–1796 a copy of the manuscript was made for Catherine the Great, and in 1800 the manuscript itself was published. This was fortunate, for soon the original manuscript was to perish in the fires that engulfed Moscow after it had been occupied by Napoleon. Since the original text contained a number of hapax legomena and its handwritten and printed versions cannot be fully trusted, a number of scholars have impugned the authenticity of the *Igor Tale* and pronounced it an eighteenth-century forgery based on a description of the 1185 campaign as found in the Hypatian codex of the chronicle. This view, which in the West was represented most tenaciously by the French scholar André Mazon, has been challenged in many studies of the *Igor Tale,* notably in its 1948 critical edition by Henri Grégoire, Roman Jakobson, and Marc Szeftel. They and most Russian Slavists have argued that philological evidence points to the end of the twelfth century as the date of the original composition of the epic.[273]

Two West Slavic religious hymns, the Czech *Hospodine, pomiluj ny* (Mareš 1979:104–130) and the Polish *Bogurodzica* (Woroñczak 1962), appear to belong to the Cyrillo-Methodian tradition, even though their oldest texts are fairly late (fourteenth and fifteenth centuries, respectively). The language of the Czech poem contains Church Slavonic hallmarks and has even been reconstructed as Church Slavonic of the Czech recension (Jakobson 1950), while the text of the oldest part of the Polish hymn has been shown to parallel the model of the Byzantine icon of the *deesis,* in which Jesus is flanked by the Virgin Mary and John the Baptist in supplicating poses (Birkenmajer 1937).

The *Prague Fragments* (Mareš 1979:41–45) contain two Glagolitic folios of the eleventh century, with several versified *světi(d)lьny* (that is, hymns sung at the morning service) and a segment of the liturgy for Good Friday. They are Church Slavonic of the Czech recension and are preserved in the Metropolitan Capitular Library in Prague.

273. In an ironic twist, the events described in the *Igor Tale* demand that, if it is deemed authentic, it has to be dated with precision to the year 1187.

3.48. Monasticism. Medieval learning was closely connected with the establishment of monastic communities, in which those who strove for a closer union with God could devote themselves to prayer and meditation free from worldly concerns. It was in the contemplative atmosphere of the monasteries that the cult of the written word and learning flourished. Texts were translated, assembled, and sometimes composed anew; they were copied in monastic scriptoria and taught in monastic schools. It was only in the Byzantine part of Slavdom and on the Dalmatian coast, however, that Slavic texts were regularly produced. In the West, the supreme rule of Latin was rarely challenged. The work of the Moravian mission was the most signal instance of Slavic incursion into the dominion of Latin, but it took place, before the fissure between the Byzantine and Roman approaches to Christianity had a chance to deepen into the chasm that it was soon to become. To be sure, even after the liquidation of the mission at the end of the ninth century, the practice of celebrating the divine liturgy in the vernacular survived or resurfaced here and there in the West Slavic lands, most notably in the Sázava monastery in Bohemia, where Slavic worship continued throughout most of the eleventh century.

Although the first Slavic monasteries arose in Bulgaria (Ohrid and Preslav), spreading later into Serbia and Rus', it was a monastic colony at Mount Athos, outside Slavic territory, that turned out to be crucial for the preservation of the earliest Slavic texts. Mount Athos is the synecdochic name applied to the easternmost of the three narrow promontories extending south from Macedonia into the Aegean Sea. Its remoteness and inaccessibility made it a favorite retreat for hermits and eventually for larger cenobitic communities. By the eleventh century it was a flourishing monastic community and one of the holiest shrines of the Orthodox church, its "Holy Mountain" (*hágion óros*). As such, it attracted monastic settlements from all of Eastern Christianity, including three monasteries from the Slavic countries—Zographos, tied with Bulgaria; St. Panteleimon, with Rus'; and Hilandar, with Serbia.[274] Sheltered from external strife and self-ruled by a council of hegumens of its twenty monasteries whose only authority was the ecumenical patriarch in Constantinople, the monastic "republic" of Mount Athos became the center of Orthodox learning. Monks traveled to it to obtain training as bookmen, to translate and to copy, and to commune with their brethren hailing from the remotest corners of the Byzantine commonwealth. Back in their native countries they spread the seeds of Athonite monasticism, becoming its local envoys and champions. It is to the monastic libraries on Mount Athos that we owe the survival of such literary treasures as the two earliest Slavic translations of the fourfold Gospel, the codices *Zographensis* and *Marianus*.

Another important center of Slavic monasticism and, what goes with it, medieval Slavic writing was the monastery of St. Catherine on Mount Sinai. Protected by Byzantine emperors, it attracted monks from all over the Byzantine commonwealth. It was smaller than the Mount Athos community and therefore even more successful in propagating a uniform vision of Orthodox spirituality.[275] The early discoveries of Sinai Slavic texts made by the Russian scholars Uspenskij (*Psalterium Sinaiticum* and *Euchologium Sinaiticum*) and Kapustin

274. For more details, see Vlasto 1970:296–307 and Obolensky 1974:387–397.

275. In fact, Slavic monks regardless of their national origin had at their disposal a common dormitory on Mount Sinai. This may be inferred from a note found in a fourteenth-century manuscript: "Let it be known to every monk who comes to Sinai, be he Serb, Bulgar, or Russian, concerning this cell that by the grace of the Very Reverend Bishop Lord German, I found it and left it; let no one harm it" (Tarnanidis 1988:51).

and Rozov (*Dobromir Gospel*)[276] have been complemented by the finds made by Altbauer (**3.42**) and Tarnanidis (**3.41.5**). Among the manuscripts reported on by Tarnanidis (1988) are twenty-eight missing folios of the *Euchologium Sinaiticum,* thirty-two folios of the *Psalterium Sinaiticum,* nine folios of the *Dobromir Gospel,* seventeen folios of an eleventh or twelfth century East Slavic Cyrillic Psalter, 145 folios of a twelfth-century South Slavic Glagolitic Psalter with an inserted medical text, eighty folios of an early Glagolitic missal using Roman terminology (*mьša, prefaciě,* etc.) reminiscent of the *Kiev Missal,* and two folios of an early Glagolitic menaeum with Cyrillic additions.

3.48.1. Monastic rules. Monastic life was regulated by a set of rules, known by its Greek name as *týpikon* or in Slavic as *ustavъ.*[277] Ultimately these regulations derived from the rule formulated by Basil the Great of Caesarea (ca. 330–379). The earliest Slavic record of that rule is in the Old Church Slavonic *Zographos Fragments* (Lavrov 1926, Lavrov/Vaillant 1930), two Cyrillic folios found in 1906 by Petr Alekseevič Lavrov in the Zographos monastery on Mount Athos. Since eastern monasteries submitted to the authority of local patriarchs or metropolitans, they could modify some aspects of the basic rule, molding it to fit their particular needs and circumstances. Thus, under the hegumenship of Theodore (759–826), the monastery of Studios in Constantinople evolved its own rule, which incorporated some of the special customs observed in Palestinian monasteries. The Studios (or Studite) Rule was adopted by the newly founded Slavic monasteries in the Balkans and Rus', including the famous Caves Monastery in Kiev.[278] The oldest extant text of the Studite Rule is the East Slavic *Ustavъ studiiskii* of the end of the twelfth century, now in the State Historical Museum in Moscow (*Š* #138).

3.48.2. The *Ladder of Divine Ascent* (L_3 9–17, *Š* ##62, 206) was a basic manual of monastic comportment written in mid-sixth century. Its author, John Climacus, so named after the Greek title of his work, *Klìmaks* 'ladder', was the hegumen of the Monastery of St. Catherine on Mt. Sinai. He used the iconographic image of a ladder with thirty rungs to symbolize the degrees in a monk's ascent to spiritual perfection. Of the many translations of the work, the Spanish one, made from the Latin *Scala paradisi,* came out in Mexico in 1532, the first book to be printed in the Western Hemisphere. The Slavic translation of the *Ladder* (*Lěstvica*) was probably executed in Bulgaria in the tenth century. Chapter 28 of *Lěstvica* is included in the *Izbornik of 1076,* but full Slavic translations are not older than the twelfth or thirteenth century and come from Rus'. It is there that the great majority of the extant manuscripts of the *Ladder* were copied in the fourteenth through sixteenth centuries, particularly during the ascendance of the Hesychasts.

3.48.3. *Pateriks.* The monastic experience produced collections of tales from the lives of monks and hermits, the so-called *pateriks* (from Greek *biblíon paterikón* 'the Book of Fathers'). Blending hagiographic and belletristic elements, the pateriks became one of the most popular genres of medieval literature. From Palestine and Egypt, where the earliest her-

276. It is also likely that A. I. Kapustin (1817–1894), who as Archimandrite Antonin headed the Russian church mission in Jerusalem, obtained the manuscript of the *Kiev Missal* during his stay in the monastery of St. Catherine on Mount Sinai in 1870.

277. The Slavic term *ustav* also designates one of the main liturgical books used in the Orthodox worship, a guide to the order of the divine service and a comportment manual for the worshipers within and without the church.

278. In the fifteenth century, Russian monasteries switched to the Jerusalem Rule, which was commonly used in Palestine. It was formulated by Sabas of Cappadocia (d. 532), hegumen of the Euthymian Monastery near Jerusalem.

mitages and monastic communities were founded, they spread to other Christian lands, either in the form of translations or as original compositions patterned after older models.

A favorite source of the paterik stories was a Greek miscellany called *Apophthégmata tōn patérōn* (Sayings of the Fathers). It forms the main part of two pateriks, the *Azbučьno-Ierusalimьskii* (Capaldo 1981; L_I 299–302), which was probably translated in Bulgaria in the tenth century but whose oldest manuscript is a Serbian one from the fourteenth century and the *Skitьskii* (from Greek *skêtis* 'hermitage'), whose earliest fragments, also of Serbian recension, come from the mid-thirteenth century (Veder 1974; L_I 321–325, *Š* #217). The former is organized alphabetically, the latter topically. Another source of edifying tales from the lives of saintly men was the *Spiritual Meadow* of John Moschus (ca. 538–619). It entered into the *Sinai Paterik*, which survives in an eleventh-century copy of East Slavic recension (Golyšenko/Dubrovina 1967; *Š* #26). While the *Sinai Paterik* contains tales from various monastic retreats, including some in the Sinai, the *Egyptian* and *Roman* pateriks have Egypt and Italy, respectively, as their specific locales. The earliest text of the *Egyptian Paterik* (L_I 302–308) is of Bulgarian recension and dates from the first half of the fourteenth century. The *Roman Paterik* (Birkfellner 1979; L_I 313–316) was originally composed in Latin by Pope Gregory I (ca. 540–604) and was subsequently translated into Greek. It is from the Greek version that the Slavic translation was prepared. There is a plausible theory that the *otьčьskyę kъnigy*, translated by Methodius and his disciples during the last years of their mission in Moravia (*Vita Methodii* 15), referred to the *Roman Paterik* (Sobolevskij 1904, Mareš 1972).[279] Whether this claim is correct or not, the *Roman Paterik* must have been translated very early, if not in Moravia at the end of the ninth century, then soon thereafter in Bulgaria. Also in Bulgaria were translated the *Sinai* and *Egyptian* pateriks, the former in the tenth and the latter in the eleventh century. Much work on the connections among various paterik traditions was done by the Dutch Slavists Nicolaas van Wijk and William R. Veder, the Italian Mario Capaldo, and the Bulgarian Svetlina Nikolova.

Of the original Slavic pateriks, the best known is connected with a specific monastic community, the Caves Monastery in Kiev. The core of the *Kievan Caves Monastery Paterik* (Abramovič 1911, Heppel 1989; L_I 308–313, *Ko* 4:41–42) consists of two long epistles written in the first half of the thirteenth century. One is from Simon, a former monk in the Cave Monastery and later bishop of Vladimir and Suzdal, to his friend and disciple, the monk Polycarp; the other is from Polycarp to Akindin, hegumen of the Caves Monastery. The epistles recount various feats of ascetism performed by the monks of the monastery and recall the miraculous events accompanying the construction of the monastery's cathedral. The *Caves Monastery Paterik* was an open-ended monument, and in its subsequent redactions it was expanded by related writings.[280] There are about two hundred extant codices of the *Caves Monastery Paterik*, the earliest, compiled by Arsenii, bishop of Tver, dates from 1406. It is preserved in the Saltykov-Ščedrin Public Library in St. Petersburg.

3.49. Learning. This very broad category comprises what one would refer to nowadays as theology, philosophy (including ethics and aesthetics), and science. Although today these branches of learning are distinct, in the Middle Ages they were linked by the all-encompass-

279. There must have been a need for a paterik in the Moravian mission, which formed a monastic community. In another view, the *otьčьskyę kъnigy* referred to collections of homilies by the Church Fathers (Grivec 1960:136).

280. In fact, it was not until 1462 that it became known as the *Caves Monastery Paterik*. Two notable additions were Nestor's tale of the founding of the monastery in the mid-eleventh century and his *Life of Theodosius*, the second hegumen of the monastery (**3.46**).

ing canopy of Christianity. Whether in its Roman or its Byzantine guise, Christianity was the spiritual cornerstone of medieval culture and permeated all of its manifestations. It defined both the outer limits and the core of the intellectual universe of a medieval bookman, allowing little room for analytical fragmentization and categorization. The goal of learning, whatever its ultimate emphasis, was to comprehend God's design as set forth in the Scriptures and in the teachings of the Church Fathers, and to transmit to others the knowledge of its immutable laws.

The first Slavic work of theology was a tenth-century composition which in the Slavic tradition has come to be known as *Heavens* (*Nebesa*) or as *Theology* (*Bogoslovie*). Its compiler, the Bulgarian writer of the Preslav school John the Exarch, selected and translated *Heavens* from the theological treatise *The Fount of Knowledge* by John of Damascus. The earliest copy of *Heavens* is in a miscellany of East Slavic recension from the twelfth or thirteenth century. It is kept today in the State Historical Museum in Moscow (Bodjanskij 1877; *Š* #141).

The physical world of the Middle Ages was interpreted in two kinds of compendia, the *hexaemeron* (*šestodьnevъ*) and the *physiologue* (*fiziologъ*). The hexaemeron was a blend of biblical and mythological stories and of direct observations of nature. Its name refers to the biblical story of the six days of Creation, with each day offering the context for a discussion of various natural phenomena. The oldest Slavic hexaemeron was compiled by John the Exarch. It is a selection of texts translated from Byzantine hexaemera of Basil of Caesarea, Severianus of Gabala, Theodoret of Cyrrhus, Gregory of Nazianzus, and Gregory of Nyssa, and expanded by John's own observations from his native Bulgaria. The oldest extant copy of the hexaemeron of John the Exarch dates from 1263 and is of Serbian recension. It is preserved in the State Historical Museum in Moscow (Bodjanskij, ed. 1879; Aitzetmüller, ed. 1958–1975; *Ku* 39–40, *Š* #178). A survey of Byzantine and Slavic hexaemera may be found in L_I 478–483.

Here, in Aitzetmüller's reconstruction, are two passages from the hexaemeron of John the Exarch, the first taken from the section dealing with the habits of sea creatures in Chapter Five (*Slovo pętoje*), the second from the preface to Chapter Six (*Slovo šestaago dьne*):

(1)	. . . karkinъ jestъ, da	There is the crab, and
	tъ želajetъ zělo ja	he wants very much
	sti plъti ostreje	to eat the meat of the oyster;
	vy; nъ bědьno jemu	but it is difficult for him
	jestъ uloviti je, i	to catch it,
	mьže odežda jemu je	for [the oyster's] garment
	stъ aky črěpina	is like a hard
	žestoka. . . . da	shell. . . . And
	jegda je ubljudetъ	when he espies it
	vъ zavětrъně mě	in a windless place
	stě zělo sladъcě sę	very comfortably
	grějǫšte i protivǫ	warming itself and in
	slъnьcju svoi luscě	the sunshine opening up
	razvrъzъše, tъgda	its two shells, then
	že otai priděbъ	the crab steals up quietly
	karkinъ i kamy	and taking a small
	čьcь vъzьmъ vъ sko	stone [and]
	lьcě vъvrъgъ ne da	throwing [it] inside the two shells
	stъ sъstęgnǫti je	does not let them contract
	ju ni zatvoriti.	or close up. (1968:59–62)

(2) Jakože smrъdъ i ni	Like a humble and
štь člověkъ i stra	poor man and a stranger,
nьnъ prišьdъ iz	having come from
daleče kъ prěvo	afar to the portals
ramъ kъnęžju dvoru	of a prince's court
i videvъ ję divitъ	and having seen them is amazed;
sę; i pristǫpivъ	and having come close
kъ vratomъ čjudi	to the gates marvels
tъ sę vъprašaję; i	asking [to be let in]; and
ǫtrь vъšьdъ vidi	having come inside sees
tъ na obě straně	on both sides
xramy stojęštę, u	houses standing,
krašeny kameni	embellished with stone
emь i drěvomь,	and wood,
ispьsany; i proče	painted all over; and further,
je vъ dvorьcь vъšь	[when] having entered the courtyard
dъ i uzьrěvъ po	and seeing tall
laty vysoky i	palaces and
crъkъvi izdobreny	churches decorated
bez goda kamenije	richly with stone
mь i drěvomь i	and wood and
šaromь, izǫtri	paint, and on the inside
že mramoromь i	with marble and
mědijǫ, sьrebromь	copper, silver
i zlatomь; tače	and gold, then
ne vědy česomь pri	he does not know with what
ložiti ixъ ne	to compare them
bo jestъ vidělъ	because he had not seen
na svojei zemli	in his own land
togo, razvě xyzъ	such [things], only a poor hut
slamnъ i ubogъ;	covered with straw.
ti aky pogubi	And, as if he had lost
vъ si umъ čjudi	his mind, he marvels
tъ sę imъ tu.	at them there. (1971:1–3)[281]

The *physiologues* were Byzantine bestiaries and lapidaries in which the characteristics, real or imaginary, of various animals and minerals (and some trees) were endowed with Christian symbolism (L_l 461–462). Surviving Slavic physiologues are all of East Slavic recension translated from Greek. The earliest one dates from the fifteenth century.[282]

281. It is often claimed that this passage presents a realistic depiction of Preslav and of Symeon's palace (just as the description of the prince in a later passage is said to refer to Symeon himself; see Obolensky 1966:502). This, however, does not have to be the case. The humble man's reaction to the glamour of the princely residence and to the prince's imposing appearance may be an instance of the "topos of modesty" and correspond to the expressions of awe before the wonders of human anatomy with which this section of the *Hexaemeron* is concerned.

282. There is a reference to the *Hexaemeron* of John the Exarch in the *Instruction* of Prince Vladimir Monomakh (1053–1125), and some of Monomakh's imagery may be derived from a *physiologue*. Whether this suggests an early availability of these texts in Rus' hinges on the evidential worth of Monomakh's writings.

The earliest Slavic text dealing with the arts of healing is a Glagolitic collection of remedies for various ills, called *Cosmas's Healer (Vračьba Kozminaja)*. Its three-folio text was inserted into a twelfth-century Glagolitic Psalter found in 1975 in the monastery of St. Catherine on Mr. Sinai. The monument was transcribed into Cyrillic by Tarnanides (1988:99). Here is an example of its prescriptions:

> If a person has a sick stomach or a tumor or constipation, then [medicinal] roots are to be boiled in wine and a glass of this is to be drunk. And one should know that if constipation persists, then healing salts are to be boiled with honey and used as an enema. And if a wound starts burning, then ground leaves or roots of nettles are to be sprinkled on the wound.

Slavic philology is the beneficiary of the treatise *On the Letters* (*O pismenexъ*), a work dealing with the origin of Slavic letters, whose author is known merely as the monk Khrabr ('Brave'). Offering a spirited argument, Khrabr extols the virtues of the Slavic alphabet and pronounces it superior to Greek. He did not, however, specify which Slavic alphabet he had in mind, Glagolitic or Cyrillic. Since textual evidence indicates that the protograph of the treatise was Glagolitic, one may surmise that the treatise aligned itself with the Glagolitic cause and that its polemical edge was turned against Cyrillic under the guise of Greek. Such an inference, if correct, would lead to the conclusion that the treatise was composed at the turn of the tenth century and that its anonymous author was someone connected with the Ohrid school, perhaps Clement of Ohrid or Naum or one of their disciples.[283]

There are about eighty extant Cyrillic codices of the treatise. The oldest of them is in a Bulgarian miscellany compiled in 1348 and known by one of the three names connected with its history—its scribe Lavrentii, its commissioner the Bulgarian tsar John Alexander (1331–1371), and the Synodal Library in Moscow, its resting place between the mid-seventeenth and mid-nineteenth centuries. Transcribed in Tărnovo, the miscellany was first moved north to Wallachia or Moldavia and then south to Mt. Athos. In 1655 it was taken to Russia by a monk of the Holy Trinity–St. Sergius monastery, Arsenii Suxanov. After two hundred years in Moscow, the miscellany was deposited in the Public Library in St. Petersburg (Duichev 1985:157–160, Džambeluka-Kossova, ed. 1980, Florja 1981:102–104, 174–189, Kuev 1967, Lavrov 1930:162–164; *Ko* 1:43, *Ku* 74–75).

Also philological in content is a brief text known as the *Macedonian Folio* (Dobrev 1981, Il'inskij 1906, Minčeva 1981, Vaillant 1948; *Ku* 79–80, *Š* #46), which outlines the rewards and the pitfalls awaiting translators from Greek into Slavic (**3.31**). The text used to be considered a version of John the Exarch's preface to his translation of John of Damascus. André Vaillant (1948), however, argued that it is a preface to an evangeliary, and he ascribed its authorship to Constantine the Philosopher himself. According to Vaillant, Constantine's text served John the Exarch as a model for his preface. The folio is in a very poor state of preservation, and it is only thanks to the reconstructive effort of Vaillant and his followers, Dobrev and Minčeva, that we can treat it as an integral text.[284]

The treatise *Against the Bogomils* by the presbyter Cosmas (**3.32**) deals with the Bogomil heresy as practiced in Bulgaria (Begunov, ed. 1973, Davidov 1976, Popruženko 1936,

283. Such dating of the treatise is buttressed by a claim made in several codices that some of Khrabr's contemporaries remembered Constantine and Methodius.

284. The Slavic text of the selections from the *Macedonian Folio* quoted in **3.31** either is legible or, when not, is taken from the text of John the Exarch.

Puech/Vaillant, eds. 1945). Cosmas's work, while combatting Bogomilism as a dangerous heresy, offers an excellent account of its tenets. The Bogomils claimed that the world is rooted in two beginnings, the divine and the satanic, locked in a relentless and unresolvable conflict. All that is ethereal and spiritual derives from God, all that is material and palpable proceeds from the devil. In this inherently dualistic universe, man is the battlefield on which the body combats the soul. Since there is no divine redemption, man's only path to God is in forswearing all material ends and embracing total spirituality. Hence, the often-mentioned "puritanism" of the Bogomils. Bogomilism was one in a chain of dualistic doctrines that spread in the postclassical and medieval periods from the Near East to Bulgaria, Rus', Serbia, Bosnia, Italy, and Provence.[285] *Against the Bogomils* is known in about twenty-five copies, all of East Slavic recension and all fairly late. The earliest of them is in the so-called *Volokolamsk Miscellany* of 1494, preserved today in the Russian State Library in Moscow. It was published in Sofia by Popruženko.

3.50. Historiography. Like religious and quasi-religious genres, Slavic historiography took its initial impetus from Byzantium. The first Slavic translations of Byzantine chronicles were executed as early as the tenth century, during the reign of Tsar Symeon of Bulgaria. These translations, which spread throughout Orthodox Slavdom, brought with them the riches of classical civilization and provided models for native chronicle-writing (Meščerskij 1978, Weingart 1923).

3.50.1. Translated chronicles. The Byzantine chronicles that the Slavs selected for translation were by and large religious works. They were compiled by churchmen who viewed history in a holistic and teleological way as it unfolded from its biblical beginnings to the Christian era. Events, whatever their historical status, were presented in their chronological rather than causal relation, and no attempt was made to interpret them in terms other than Christian. Lay Byzantine historians, such as Procopius or Constantine Porphyrogenitus, heirs to classical Greek historiography, were not translated by the Slavs. The only exception to this preference for history interpreted through divine intervention was the anonymous East Slavic translation of the *Jewish War* by Josephus Flavius.[286]

The earliest Byzantine chronicler to be translated into Slavic was John Malalas. He was born in Antioch at the end of the fifth century and spent the first half of his life there. About 540 he moved to Constantinople, where he compiled an eighteen-book chronicle, titled *Khronographía*. It begins with the mythical tales of ancient Egypt, Greece, and Rome and goes up to the rule of Emperor Justinian. Because of its simple but entertaining narrative the *Chronicle of John Malalas* merited a Slavic translation as early as the tenth century (Istrin 1897, 1902, 1905, 1910, 1912, 1914, 1915; L_I 471–474, Š #74). It was executed in Bulgaria and spread from there to Serbia and Rus'. Since a complete text of the Slavic translation has not survived, it has to be reconstructed from fragments included in various historical compilations, known as *chronographs*, such as the East Slavic *Chronograph "po velikomu izloženiju"* (L_I 476–477) compiled at the end of the eleventh century. The first extant fragment of the *Chronicle* comes from an East Slavic *Zlatostrui* of the twelfth century (L_I 471–474, Š #74).[287]

285. Including the Gnostic, Manichean, Paulician, Patarene, and Cathar religious movements. For an account of the Bogomil heresy, see Obolensky 1948.

286. Slavic translations of chronicles are discussed in Meščerskij 1978:68–108.

287. Although the very beginning of the *Chronicle of John Malalas* is missing, one may surmise that it dealt with the Creation. Of interest to Slavic historians is a brief mention of the Avars and Slavs raiding Thrace and breaching the outer walls of Constantinople in 558.

In the beginning of the tenth century, George Syncellus, secretary of the Ecumenical Patriarch Tarasius (784–806), compiled a chronicle that extends from the Creation to the rule of the Roman emperor Diocletian (beginning of the fourth century). A short version of the *Chronicle of George Syncellus* was translated into Slavic and is extant in four East Slavic codices dating from the fifteenth century (Istrin 1903; L_1 470–471). It is assumed, however, that the translation was executed at least a century earlier, most probably in Rus'.

The Concise History (*Khronographía sýntomos*), compiled by Tarasius' successor, Patriarch Nicephorus (806–815), was a chronological table listing the main personalities of ancient history, from the biblical patriarchs to the Roman and Byzantine emperors, supplied with brief annotations. It was translated in the tenth century in Bulgaria as *Lětopisьcь vъskorě* (or *vъkratcě*) and became a popular aid in the composition of native Slavic chronicles (Stepanov, ed. 1912, L_1 231–234). It was included in the *Izbornik of 1073* and in the *Novgorod kormčaja* of 1280.

Of all the Byzantine chronicles, the best known among the Slavs was the *Concise Chronicle* (*Khronikón sýntomon*) by George the Monk (also known as George Hamartolus (from Greek *hamartōlós* 'sinner'), who lived during the times of Emperor Michael III (842–867).[288] The chronicle was given two Slavic translations, both of them originating in Bulgaria. Its tenth-century rendition (*Vrěmenьnikъ*) became common in Rus', while the fourteenth-century one (*Lětovьnikъ*) became popular in Serbia.[289] The earliest extant text of the chronicle is East Slavic, from the fourteenth century. It is known as *Xronika Georgija Amartola* and is kept in the Russian State Library in Moscow (Istrin, ed. 1920, 1922, 1930; L_1 467–470).

Belying its name, the *Historical Compendium* (*Epitomē historíōn*) by John Zonaras was an eighteen-book composition chronicling world events from the Creation to the year 1118 (Jacobs, ed. 1970; L_3 492–494). It was written around the middle of the twelfth century by a learned monk who had access to sources that have since perished. The *Chronicle of John Zonaras* was translated into Slavic in the fourteenth century and became popular in Serbia before making its way to Rus'. It is assumed, in fact, that the translation was executed either in Serbia or in Bulgaria. The oldest Slavic manuscript of the chronicle, a fifteenth-century Serbian text, was destroyed in 1941 when the Belgrade National Library was hit by a bomb during a German air raid.

A contemporary of John Zonaras was Constantine Manasses, author of the *Historical Survey* (*Sýnopsis historikē*), which is remarkable for its being couched in Greek iambic decameter. Its Slavic translation (Dujčev, ed. 1963, *Ku* 193–196) was in prose and was made in Bulgaria during the rule of Tsar John Alexander (1331–1371).[290] This information is provided in a note found in the so-called *Moscow Codex* of 1345, which was also prepared under the patronage of John Alexander. In its Slavic version the *Chronicle of Constantine Manasses* was extended by a number of additions dealing with events of Bulgarian history. The Turkish occupation of the Balkans subjected the two oldest texts of the chronicle to an extended migration from their original home in Tărnovo, John Alexander's capital. Sharing the fates of an early text of the treatise by the monk Khrabr (**3.49**), the *Moscow Codex* was first taken

288. For the years 842–848 the *Concise Chronicle* was extended by the work of the tenth-century chronicler Symeon the Logothete.

289. The popularity of these translations in Rus' and Serbia has prompted some scholars to claim that they were also executed there (Meščerskij 1978:70–79).

290. As such, it is beyond the chronological confines of this survey. Its popularity in Byzantine Slavdom, however, argues for its inclusion.

north across the Danube and then south to the Hilandar monastery on Mount Athos, where in 1665 Arsenii Suxanov, an envoy of Patriarch Nikon, located it and brought it to Moscow. Today it is kept in the State Historical Museum. The beautifully illuminated *Vatican Codex* was first moved to Dalmatia and at the end of the fifteenth century to the Vatican Library.

Parts of chronicles and chronographs provided enough thematic unity to be excerpted. Such, for instance, was Book V of the *Chronicle of John Malalas*. It contained the history of the Trojan War (*O trojanьskyixъ vrěmenaxъ* or *Trojanьskaja dějanija*) based on a semi-legendary tale ascribed to Dictys of Crete, who claimed to have accompanied the Cretan king Idomeneus to Troy. Similarly, a fictionalized history of Alexander the Great was excerpted from chronographs and is in fact referred to as the *Chronograph Alexandreis* to distinguish it from other and later biographies of Alexander. It is based on the Greek *Romance of Alexander the Great*, whose anonymous author was thought to have been the historian Callisthenes (hence its ascription to "Pseudo-Callisthenes"). As a tale straddling the genres of historical biography and adventure novel, it was very popular in the Middle Ages and was translated into many languages. A West European version of the story was the basis for a versified Czech *Alexandreis* whose earliest manuscript comes from the 1330s.

It is also to a chronograph that we owe the preservation of a remarkable Slavic monument of pre-Slavic history, the *List of Proto-Bulgarian Khans*, containing the names of twelve Turkic rulers of Bulgaria from legendary times to 766. The *List* has survived in three sixteenth-century East Slavic codices of a chronograph compilation known as the *Lětopisьcь ellinьskyi i rimьskyi* (L_3 18–20).[291] The Slavic text of the *List* is either an eighth-century translation from Greek or an original composition of the ninth or tenth century. In either case, the original seems to have been compiled in Bulgaria. The *List* uses the original Turkic calendar, which, like the Chinese calendar, was based on the duodecimal cycle, with every year identified by an animal designation (the year of the bear, the ox, the wolf, the rabbit, etc.).

3.50.2. *On the Jewish War* by Josephus Flavius. Perhaps the most interesting of Slavic historical translations is the treatise *On the Jewish War* (*Perì toû Ioudaikoû pólemou*) by Josephus Flavius (37/38–ca. 100). As a member of a priestly Jewish family, Josephus was well versed in Jewish lore and law. When the insurrection against the Roman rule of Judea broke out in 66 Josephus joined it, but upon being captured he sided with the victorious Romans and moved permanently to Rome, where he devoted himself to writing. His treatise, despite its pro-Roman slant, provides a reliable account of the conduct of the Roman campaign against the Jewish insurgents. Josephus' treatise was translated in Rus' from its Greek version not later than the twelfth century. The translation, known as *O Ijudeiskoi voině* or *O razorenii Ierusalima* (Istrin, ed. 1934, Meščerskij, ed. 1958; L_1 214–215), is remarkable for its literary qualities and for the skill with which the anonymous translator adapted Josephus' matter-of-fact account to the literary sensibilities of the East Slavic reader. It has been noted, in fact, that the translation shows many stylistic affinities to several medieval East Slavic, monuments including the *Igor Tale*. The popularity of the Slavic version of the treatise is reflected in its thirty-five extant codices, unfortunately none of them earlier than the fifteenth century.

3.50.3. Native chronicles. Habits of chronicle writing were not uniform across Slavdom. The West Slavs joined the mainstream of medieval Western literature and produced works in Latin, such as the twelfth-century Czech *Chronicle of Cosmas* or Polish *Chronicle*

291. The adjectives *ellinьskyi* and *rimьskyi* refer here to Ancient Greece and Byzantium respectively.

of Anonymous Gallus. The earliest South Slavic historical work was *Istorikii*, a brief chronology of world events by Constantine of Preslav found in the twelfth-century East Slavic copy of his *Homiliary Gospel* (*Š* #118). The South Slavs, however, did not develop a native annalistic tradition. Among the East Slavs, by contrast, chronicle writing became one of the most popular literary genres. In fact, the skein of medieval East Slavic chronicles is composed of so many intricately interwoven strands that the task of disentangling them has proven to be inordinately complex.

The main difficulty lies in the open-endedness of these texts, their characteristic heterogeneity. Typically, a chronicle combined sections composed anew with sections compiled from other chronicles. Hence the composite nature of annalistic texts, which gave rise to the notion of a *svod* (or compilation) of a particular chronicle. The *svody* differed from one another because their compilers, undeterred by their monastic calling, were sensitive to local ideological and political issues and were eager to respond to them. A similar motivation was responsible for the frequent editing and altering of annalistic texts, a practice that yielded different redactions (*redakcii*) of the same *svod*. In addition, chronicles could be classified into different recensions (*izvody*)[292] according to the different dialect features displayed by them. These complexities are compounded by the difficulty of establishing the chronological sequence of texts emanating from many centers of annalistic writing, the habitual anonymity of the chroniclers, and the relative lateness of most extant codices. Little wonder that the problem of re-creating and classifying the genealogy of East Slavic chronicles has not been conclusively resolved.

Still, some facts have been established and plausible hypotheses made to explain them. It was observed, for instance, that the oldest extant annalistic text, the *Primary Chronicle* (*Načalьnaja lětopisь*), also known as the *Tale of Bygone Years* (*Pověstь vrěmenьnyxъ lětъ*), is actually a compilation of two thematically distinct textual components brought together in the beginning of the twelfth century. In their attempts to identify and date these components, the Russian scholars Aleksej A. Šaxmatov and Dmitrij S. Lixačev determined that the segment consisting of tales dealing with the introduction of Christianity in Rus' goes back to the time of Yaroslav the Wise (1019–1054), while the segment concerned with the genesis of Rus' statehood may be dated from the second half of the eleventh century. From these components Šaxmatov reconstructed the primary *svod* compiled, according to him, toward the end of the eleventh century. In his view, the two oldest extant East Slavic annalistic *svody*, the *Primary Chronicle* and the *First Novgorod Chronicle*, compiled in the first half of the twelfth century, were based on different redactions of the primary *svod*.

The *Primary Chronicle* (Adrianova-Peretc, ed. 1950, Cross/Sherbowitz-Wetzor, eds. 1953, Šaxmatov 1916; L_I 337–343), compiled as it was by the monk Nestor of the Kiev Caves Monastery, was executed according to the grand design consistent with the locally perceived role of Kiev as the cradle of Rus' statehood, the "mother of all Rus' cities." The chronicle was extended by the biblical story of the initial distribution of races, as told by George the Monk (Hamartolus), and by Nestor's own account of the initial settlement of Slavic tribes, including his "Danubian" theory of the original homeland of the Slavs (**1.8**). The chronicle reaffirmed the Scandinavian origins of the Rjurikoviči, the first ruling dynasty of Rus', and extolled their virtues and power. As to its narrative style, much of the chronicle was couched in stately and formal Church Slavonic.

292. In the Russian practice, the terms *redakcija* and *izvod* are often used interchangeably.

Novgorodian chronicle writing responded to an entirely different political agenda. Its concern was above all with the prosperity of Novgorod brought about by a vast network of the city's commercial ties with both the West and the East and by its republican system of self-rule. Lacking the sweep and Byzantine grandiloquence of Kievan chronicle writing, the Novgorod annals were down-to-earth and matter-of-fact narratives. While reporting on the most important political events of the day, they also functioned as a kind of community gazette, with entries on the weather, the crops, disease, high prices, and tribute collection. The mundane interests of the Novgorod chronicles were reflected in their language, which was replete with regional dialect features.

The earliest surviving East Slavic chronicle is the Synodal codex or the *First Novgorod Chronicle* of the thirteenth and fourteenth centuries, kept in the State Historical Museum in Moscow (Michell/Forbes, ed. 1914; Nasonov, ed. 1950, L_l 245–247). The oldest extant text of the *Primary Chronicle* is in the Laurentian codex of 1377, copied by the monk Lavrentii for Grand Duke Dmitrii Konstantinovič of Suzdal (L_l 241–245). About fifty years younger is the text of the *Primary Chronicle* in the Hypatian codex, a monument of Ruthenian redaction which belonged to the Hypatian Monastery in Kostroma (L_l 235–241). The Laurentian codex is kept in the Saltykov-Ščedrin Public Library in St. Petersburg, while the Hypatian codex is in the Academy of Sciences Library also in St. Petersburg.[293]

3.51. Legal texts. The formation of independent Slavic states was accompanied by a greater formalization of internal governance and international obligations. These included, first of all, the adoption of formal legal codes, the drafting of international treaties, and the promulgation of charters.

3.51.1. Codes of laws. The work of the Byzantine mission in Moravia shows that the empire attached great importance, not only to the spread of Christianity, but also to the propagation of the Byzantine legal system. Thus, for Methodius, the translation of the Byzantine code of laws, the *Nomocanon,* merited the same degree of urgency as the translation of the basic religious texts.[294] In the *Vita Methodii* 15, the *Nomocanon* is glossed as *Zakonu pravilo* ('the rule of law'); in later Slavic translations and adaptations of Byzantine legal codes, however, the Church Slavonic term *krъmčaja kъniga* ('helmsman's book') was used. The earliest Byzantine *Nomocanon,* the so-called *Gathering of Fifty Articles* (*Synagogḗ*), goes back to the legal reforms of Emperor Justinian I (527–565) and was compiled by John Scholasticus, the future ecumenical patriarch (565–577). It is conjectured that a Slavic translation of a ninth-century revision of the *Nomocanon,* attributed to Patriarch Photius, was executed in Preslav during the rule of Tsar Symeon and that it spread from Bulgaria to Rus'. It is reflected in the East Slavic *Efremovskaja kormčaja* of the twelfth century (Beneševič, ed. 1906, Undol'skij, ed. 1867; *Ku* 25–26, *Š* #75).

Another Slavic code of laws, the *Zakonъ sǫdьnyi ljudemъ* (*Commoners' Code of Law*), was a translation of the Byzantine *Ecloga,* compiled under Emperor Leo III (r. 717–740).

293. For concise accounts of East Slavic chronicle writing, see Lixačev 1947, Lixačev, ed. 1989:69–109, Goldblatt 1985; for particular chronicles, see Lixačev, ed., 1987:235–251 and 1989:26–69 and the Bibliography. The Novgorod chronicles were translated into English and provided with historical and textological introductions by Michell and Forbes (1914). An English translation of the *Primary Chronicle* as it appears in the Laurentian codex was prepared in 1930 by S. H. Cross and revised in 1953 by O. P. Sherbowitz-Wetzor.

294. The *Nomocanon* was a Byzantine code of canonical laws (Greek *kanónes*) and of imperial edicts relating to church matters (Greek *nómoi* 'civil [originally, Solon's] laws).

This code dealt primarily with matters of family and criminal law. Its oldest extant text is in the *Ustjug kormčaja* from the end of the thirteenth century, preserved today in the State Public Library in Moscow (Dewey/Kleimola, eds. 1977; Š #476). It was assumed at first that the *Zakonъ* was translated in Bulgaria, but more recent investigations (especially by Josef Vašica) have suggested the possibility that the translation was executed in Moravia and that this code was in fact included in the *Nomocanon* mentioned in the *Vita Methodii*. At any rate, the *Zakonъ* incorporates Western legal concepts, and its text exhibits some West Slavic linguistic features. On the other hand, one cannot exclude the possibility that the Methodian text was a translation of the *Synagogē̄* as it appears in two East Slavic legal monuments, one of them being the *Ustjug kormčaja*.

The last Slavic revision of the *Nomocanon* was made in the beginning of the thirteenth century by St. Sava of Serbia. It included a translation of the *Prókheiron*, a Byzantine civil code compiled in the late ninth century, along with the commentaries by John Zonaras. The oldest extant text of this code is the *Nomocanon* of 1262 copied in Bulgaria on the order of Despot Jakov Svetoslav for Cyril, the metropolitan of Kiev (1242–1282). Other thirteenth-century texts are in the East Slavic *Novgorod kormčaja* of 1280, kept in the State Historical Museum in Moscow (Š #183), and the *Rjazanskaja kormčaja* of 1284, preserved in the Saltykov-Ščedrin Public Library in St. Petersburg (Š #186).

Specifically East Slavic was the Rus' code of laws *Pravьda rusьskaja* (Grekov, ed. 1940, 1947), which is a compilation of native and Germanic legal customs. The code's independence of Byzantine legal models is reflected in its terminology, which is virtually free of Church Slavonicisms. The *Pravьda rusьskaja* was first compiled during the rule of Prince Jaroslav the Wise (1016–1054). It has come down to us in two redactions, short and extensive. The extensive redaction, which is younger, exists in more than a hundred codices, the oldest of them being in the *Novgorod kormčaja* of 1280.

An important native collection of laws was the Čakavian *Vinodol Law Code* of 1288, known from its only fifteenth-century manuscript. It dealt primarily with criminal offenses. An English translation of excerpts of the code is given in Butler 1980.

3.51.2. Treaties. The oldest recorded Slavic international treaties were concluded between Rus' and Byzantium. The Greek originals have not survived, but full texts of their Slavic translations are known from entries in the *Primary Chronicle*. The peace treaties of 911 and 944 were signed in Constantinople, the former by the envoys of Oleg on the Rus' side and of Emperor Leo VI, his brother Alexander, and his son Constantine Porphyrogenitus on the Byzantine side, the latter by the envoys of Igor and of Emperor Romanus Lecapenus, his son Stephen, and Constantine Porphyrogenitus. It is remarkable that all of the Rus' signatories of these treaties bore purely Scandinavian names. The peace treaty of 971 was signed in Silistria on the Danube by Svyatoslav and Emperor John Tzimiskes.

Also preserved are texts of two East Slavic commercial treaties with Hanseatic ports, one of 1229 and one of 1262. The treaty of 1229 was concluded by the Smolensk prince Mstislav Davidovič with the city of Riga and the island of Gotland (Avanesov, ed. 1963:18–62, Obnorskij/Barxudarov 1952:44–50). The text of the treaty is remarkable for its Smolensk dialectalisms and Germanisms. Especially striking is its inconsistent spelling of the vowels. The second treaty was concluded in 1262–1263 by Alexander Nevsky and the citizens of Novgorod with the city of Lübeck and the island of Gotland (Obnorskij/Barxudarov 1952:51–52). The treaty of 1229 has been preserved in seven copies, of which two are contemporary with the original. The best of them (Copy A), along with the original of the treaty of 1262, are in the Central State Archive in Riga.

3.51.3. Donation charters. The earliest mention of a donation charter is in the *Primary Chronicle* under the years 994–996, when Prince Vladimir bestowed a tithe of his property to the freshly built Kiev church, known since that time as the Tithe Church (*Desjatinьnaja*).

The two earliest original charters to have survived are from Novgorod. The older is a grant of land and silver made around 1130 by the Kiev great prince Mstislav and his son Vsevolod to the Monastery of St. George (Yuryev) near Novgorod. It is written on parchment with gold lettering. The other charter is a grant of land, serfs, and cattle offered by a certain Varlaam to the Monastery of the Savior in Khutyn near Novgorod. The charter could date from 1192 (the commonly accepted date), when, according to the Novgorod chronicle, a Varlaam built a church in Khutyn, or from 1211, when he died. Both charters are free of Church Slavonicisms. The earlier one is almost faultless in its rendition of the weak jers and of the vowel *jat'*, while the later one is not. It also displays some Novgorod dialect features. Both charters are kept in the Novgorod Museum (Marks 1914, Obnorskij/Barxudarov 1952:32–36).

Several Bulgarian charters of the thirteenth century have also been preserved. The oldest is the donation charter of 1220 by Despot Alexis Slavus granting the village of Katunica to the Monastery of the Holy Mother of God Spileotisa in Melnik (Papadopoulos/Vatopèdinos 1933:1–6). The Bulgarian tsar John Asen II (r. 1218–1241) issued two charters soon after his victory over Epirus in the battle of Klokotnica (1230). One gave the village of Semalto to the Vatoped Monastery of the Holy Mother of God on Mount Athos, the other allowed the Dubrovnik merchants to trade freely in the Bulgarian lands (Ivanov 1930:578).

3.52. Epistolary literature and correspondence. Citations of letters served a dual purpose in Slavic medieval monuments. They could be used as a literary device intended to reinforce the immediacy and believability of the narrative or they could be a record of authentic historical documents. The former may be exemplified by the letter in which Prince Rostislav asked Emperor Michael III to send Byzantine missionaries to Moravia (*Vita Constantini* 14). An illustration of the latter is the bull from Pope Hadrian II recommending Methodius to Prince Kocel of Pannonia (*Vita Methodii* 8).[295] Clearly fictional is the letter from Prince Vladimir Monomakh to Oleg Svyatoslavich, quoted along with Monomakh's *Instruction* in the Laurentian codex of 1377. It portrays Monomakh as a zealously Christian and patriotic ruler who in the name of higher values is willing to forgive the death of his son Izyaslav on the battlefield. Equally belletristic appears to be the exchange of letters between Simon and Polycarp reported in the Kievan *Caves Monastery Paterik*.

The only authentic example of early correspondence is provided by the remarkable discovery, primarily in Novgorod but also in Pskov and Smolensk, of the so-called *birchbark gramoty*. These strips of birchbark, with short texts scratched upon them with a stylus, have been coming to light since 1951 and now number in the thousands. They deal primarily with commercial and legal matters but on occasion contain personal messages. The oldest date from the eleventh century and thus constitute one of the earliest documentations of connected Slavic texts (Arcixovskij/Borkovskij, eds. 1958, Arcixovskij/Tixomirov 1953).

295. A variant of the text of Pope Hadrian's bull may be found in the encomium of Constantine and Methodius (Florja 1981:149).

been coming to light since 1951 and now number in the thousands. They deal primarily with commercial and legal matters but on occasion contain personal messages. The oldest date from the eleventh century and thus constitute one of the earliest documentations of connected Slavic texts (Arcixovskij/Borkovskij, eds. 1958, Arcixovskij/Tixomirov 1953).

An example of this genre is the Novgorod birchbark gramota #109, from the turn of the twelfth century (App. D, Cyr. 7). According to its discoverer, Artemij V. Arcixovskij (1958:38–41), this gramota should be interpreted in the light of one of the laws of *Pravьda rusьskaja*, whereby the original owner of a stolen and resold serf has the right to claim the serf and demand that the new owner indicate in a judicial confrontation (*sъvody*) from whom the stolen property was bought and provide a temporary replacement. Linguistically, gramota #109 is remarkably archaic. Except for the merger of *ě* with *e* and the one-jer (ъ) orthography, all the expected East Slavic features are retained, notably the weak jers and *č* where it is etymologically expected. Denasalized vowels are spelled as expected, with *ę* (ѧ) and *u* (оу), except in *vъzalъ*, where instead of *ę* we find *a* (а).

3.53. Epigraphic texts. Inscriptions and graffiti provide an important source of philological and historical information. As expected, the most ancient among them are from the Balkans (Dobrev/Popkonstantinov 1985, Gošev 1961).

An important source of Glagolitic inscriptions is the Round Church in Preslav (Medynceva/Popkonstantinov 1985, Popkonstantinov 1980), built during the reign of Tsar Symeon and excavated methodically since 1927, when it was discovered. Especially interesting is the *Preslav Abecedarium*, consisting of the first thirteen letters of the Glagolitic alphabet (through *k*). There are also fragments of Glagolitic inscriptions in the Monastery of St. Naum on Lake Ohrid.

A number of later Glagolitic inscriptions come from the Quarner region of Dalmatia (Fučić, ed. 1971, 1982). The longest among them was discovered in the middle of the nineteenth century in the Benedictine monastery of St. Lucia near the village of Baška on the North Adriatic island of Krk and is therefore known as the *Baška stone* (Mohorovičić/Strčić 1988; App. D, Glag. 4). The inscription, made in the beginning of the twelfth century, tells of a land grant by the Croatian king Zvonimir to the Church of St. Lucia. The thirteen lines of text represent a transitional style between rounded Glagolitic of the older Macedonian manuscripts and the newer angular writing typical of Croatia. The Baška stone is kept in the Croatian Academy of Sciences in Zagreb. Other Glagolitic inscriptions from northern Dalmatia come from the eleventh century. The oldest is the Slavo-Latin *Valun inscription* from the island of Cres. One should also mention two Istrian inscriptions, the incomplete *Plomin inscription* from the Church of St. George in Plomin and the *Hum graffito* from the Church of St. Jerome in Hum (App. D, Glag. 5).

Balkan Cyrillic inscriptions are more numerous. Several short inscriptions of the ninth or tenth century are to be found alongside the Glagolitic ones in the Round Church in Preslav. In one of them, *Paul Xartofylaks* (Greek *khartophýlaks* 'librarian') takes credit for building the Church of St. John. Also from Preslav is *Mostič's inscription* (App. D, Cyr. 1) found in 1952 on the tombstone of one Mostič, identified as a *črgubylja* under the kings Symeon and his son Peter (r. 927–969). The inscription is thus one of the oldest monuments of Cyrillic

296. Besides the *Mostič inscription*, the Turkic title *boila* or *buila* 'noble' appears in Slavic as *bylja* 'dignitary' in the *Codex Suprasliensis* and in the *Igor Tale* in the phrase *sъ černigovьskimi byljami* 'with the boyars of Černigov' (Malov 1946, Ivanova 1955:62–63).

dated Old Church Slavonic text (its date of 6501 corresponds to our 992/993). Both the *Mostič's* and *Samuel's inscriptions* are now preserved in the National History Museum in Sofia. The *Bitola inscription* was made during the rule of Samuel's nephew, Tsar John Vladislav (r. 1015–1018), and commemorated the reconstruction of the Bitola castle and the Bulgarian military campaigns against Emperor Basil II. The stone onto which it was carved is badly damaged, for it was used for many centuries as a threshold in a mosque in the Macedonian town of Bitola (Serbian Bitolj). The inscription was discovered in 1956 and is kept today in the National Museum of Bitola. The *Temnić inscription* is not dated, but its paleographic features are similar to those of *Mostič's inscription* and it may therefore come from the tenth or eleventh century at the latest (Stojanović 1913). The inscription was found at the end of the nineteenth century in the village of Temnić, north of Kruševac in eastern Serbia, and is preserved in the National Museum in Belgrade. Several Cyrillic inscriptions were discovered in northern Dobruja, which used to belong to Greater Bulgaria. In 1950 an inscription containing the name *Župan Dimitrii* was found. Although it is dated, the date is poorly legible and could be read as 6451 (942/943) or 6651 (1142/1143). Some scholars think that the later dating is more consistent with the graphic characteristics of the inscription. Other Dobruja inscriptions come from the environs of Constanza.

Cyrillic inscriptions from Rus' are more variegated than the ones from the Balkans (Karskij 1928:61–62, Kiparsky 1971:32–33, 38–39, Obnorskij/Barxudarov 1952:16, 35, Orlov 1952). The *Gnezdovo inscription* on an amphora (East Slavic *kъrčaga*) is dated from the first quarter of the tenth century (Avdusin/Tixomirov 1950, Jakobson 1985, Schenker 1989). It was found in 1949 in a burial mound of a large necropolis near the village of Gnezdovo, west of Smolensk. The inscription consists of a sequence of seven or eight Cyrillic or Greek letters (the number depending on the reading) scratched on the surface of the vessel after it had been fired. Of the several readings offered, the one that appears most likely is *gorunja* or the feminine form of a possessive adjective derived from a personal name. An inscription whose authenticity has been questioned by some scholars is the *Tmutorokan' inscription*, which contains one sentence saying that in 1068 Prince Gleb Svyatoslavich of Novgorod measured the distance across the frozen straits of Kerch. It is carved on a slab of marble and is kept in the Hermitage Museum in St. Petersburg. Testifying to the importance of Rus' waterways is the *Sterzh cross inscription*, carved on a large stone cross found near the place where the upper Volga empties into Lake Sterzh. According to the inscription, the cross was set up by one Ivanko Pavlovič, who began to "dig up the river" on July 15, 1133. It is kept in the City Museum in Tver. The *Drinking bowl inscription* announces that the silver bowl on which it was made belonged to Prince Volodimir Davydovič. It also expressed the hope that anyone drinking from the bowl would do so in "good health." Since Prince Vladimir of Chernigov died in 1151, the inscription had to be made before that date. The bowl with the inscription is kept in the Hermitage Museum. *Efrosinija's cross inscription* was made in 1161 on a wooden cross decorated with gold, silver, and pearls. The votive inscription on the cross says that Princess Efrosinija of Polock donated it to the Church of the Holy Savior in Polock.

Brief Cyrillic inscriptions from Rus' may be found on such objects as stone markers, walls, looms, vessels, articles of clothing, bindings, icons, knives, and coins. Some of them recorded the name of the maker of the object, preceded by the formulaic *Gospodi pomoʒi rabu tvoemu . . .* 'Lord, help your servant . . .' Many wall inscriptions, especially in stone churches, are of the graffito type. The earliest are from the cathedrals of St. Sophia in Kiev (built in 1036) and in Novgorod. Especially interesting is an abecedarium, the so-called *Sofijskaja azbuka,* whose discovery in 1969 on the wall of the Kiev cathedral led some scholars to speculations on the existence in Rus' of a Greek-based Slavic alphabet before the introduction of either Glagolitic or Cyrillic (**3.9**). Occasionally an inscription may be dated by reference to another monument. Thus, the approximate date of the inscription in the Cathedral of St. Sophia in Kiev marking the death of Bishop Luka Belogorodskij may be inferred from a note in the chronicles that mentions the bishop under the year 1089 (Vysockij 1966). Exceptional in Rus' are the Glagolitic graffiti from the eleventh and twelfth centuries found on the walls of the Church of St. Sophia in Novgorod.

3.54. Glosses. Glosses are marginal or interlinear notes or comments added to the main text of a monument, often non-Slavic, by scribes or readers. Of South Slavic glosses the greatest interest is evoked by those in two abecedaria. The *Paris (Bulgarian) Abecedarium* (Kopitar 1836) contains the Glagolitic alphabet inscribed in the eleventh or twelfth century into a Latin manuscript that is approximately a hundred years older. The manuscript used to be kept in the Bibliothèque Nationale in Paris but is now lost. Each letter of the alphabet is identified by its Slavic name written in Latin. The *Munich Abecedarium* (Trubetzkoy 1930) is also to be found in a Latin manuscript from about the tenth century. Its Cyrillic and Glagolitic alphabets each containing thirty-eight letters date from the twelfth century. Both abecedaria are reproduced and discussed in Mareš 1971:154–159; see also Vajs 1932:134.[297]

Some texts have marginal notes made by users, such as the touching addition to folio 19 v of the *Codex Suprasliensis* containing a fragment of John Chrysostom's homily on the raising of Lazarus:

г҃и помо	g(ospod)i pomo	Lord, help
ӡи рабꙋ	zi rabu	[your] servant,
амосꙋоꙋо	amosuo uo[298]	Amos. I am
чю сѧ писа	čju sę pisa	learning how to
ти	ti	write.

An East Slavic manuscript of the Bulgarian translation of the *Chronicle of George the Monk* (**3.50.1**) was glossed, not only to explain Greek words—for instance, *dokitь rekše jako kopije* '*dokítēs,* that is, a javelin'—but also to interpret the Bulgarianisms that were not readily understandable to East Slavic readers, such as *sedmicь rekše neděli našьsky* 'a week, that is *nedělja* in our language'. East Slavic glosses often contained penitent scribal remarks of the type *Gospodi pomoӡi nedostoinumu rabu svoemu* . . . 'O Lord, help your unworthy servant [name]' or *Gospodi prosti grěšьnago i ubogago raba svoego* . . . 'Forgive, o Lord, your sinful and wretched servant [name]'. Such, for instance, are the glosses in the *Novgorod Menaea* of 1095–1097 (**3.41.5**).

The oldest West Slavic glosses are found in medieval Hebrew texts from northern France and the Rhineland (Kupfer/Lewicki 1956:21–31, 87–95, 101–123, 176–195). From the eleventh century come Slavic glosses in the Mainz commentary to the Talmud by Rabbi

297. For a survey of early Slavic abecedaria (with an extensive bibliography), see B. Velčeva's entry in Dinekov, ed. 1985:20–26.

298. With a reversal of *o* and *u* in the spelling for /u/.

Solomon ben Isaac (Rashi) of Troyes. There are more Slavic glosses in the writings of the twelfth-century rabbi Joseph Kara from northern France and the thirteenth-century scholar Abraham ben Asriel from Bohemia. They testify to the knowledge of Slavic (in medieval Hebrew referred to as Canaanitic) among the Jewish merchants operating between Western Europe and such Slavic trading centers as Prague, Cracow, or Kiev.[299]

Other important West Slavic glosses occur in Latin documents. One hundred twenty-two glosses from the eleventh century are found in a Latin Bible from northern France. They exhibit Church Slavonic and Czech linguistic features, which point to their Bohemian origin. Since this Bible is preserved in the Austrian State Library in Vienna, the glosses are known in scholarship as the *Vienna glosses* (Jagić 1903). Also from the eleventh-century are the Czech *Gregorian glosses* (Mareš, ed. 1979:213–216) in the text of the dialogues (*besědy*) of Pope Gregory the Great. Some of these glosses show traces of having been lifted from a Church Slavonic translation of the dialogues; for example, Latin *mactaverunt* is glossed with Church Slavonic *izbišę* instead of the expected Old Czech *zbichú*, Latin *subsistit* is glossed with Church Slavonic *stojal by* rather than Old Czech *stál by*. Among the Gregorian glosses there is the oldest recorded Czech clause, *[mysl] l'uta ote vznesenia nadutia otdu*, translating Latin *mens effera ab elationis fastu detumuit* 'wild thought swelled from arrogance of haughtiness' (Flajšhans 1924:129–130). There are also numerous Czech glosses in the Prague copy of the *Mater Verborum* (or *Glossae Salomonis*). The manuscript, preserved in the National Museum in Prague, is a twelfth- or thirteenth-century copy of an encyclopedic dictionary compiled at the end of the ninth century by Salomon, the abbot of the Swiss monastery of St. Gallen.

The best-known Old Polish glosses are to the 103 Latin sermons contained in a codex that includes the ten Polish *Gniezno sermons* (**3.44**). Most of the Latin sermons are supplied with Polish glosses translating individual Latin expressions and sentences, and even entire texts (as is the case with the sermon on St. Paul).

3.55. Place and personal names. Slavic place and personal names mentioned in various medieval non-Slavic documents, such as Latin or German chronicles, royal or princely charters, and papal bulls, offer valuable linguistic information, especially in the areas of phonology and word formation.

The most important Greek source of Slavic place and personal names is in the writings of Emperor Constantine Porphyrogenitus (944–959), especially his *De administrando imperio*. Particularly valuable for linguistic history is his bilingual Scandinavian-Slavic list of names of the Dnieper rapids (Shevelov 1955, Tolkačev 1962) and his transcription of the name of the Serbian prince *Mǫtimirъ* as *Mountimēros*, showing that in this dialect PSl. *ǫ* was still nasalized but already raised to *ų*.

Among glossed Latin monuments one should cite the so-called *Gospel of Cividale* (*Codex Aquileiensis*), a sixth-century evangeliary originally kept in one of the Aquileian monasteries. On its margins there are more than 350 Slavic signatures entered during the ninth century by distinguished visitors to the monastery, either in person or by proxy. Though difficult to interpret linguistically, some of these signatures display Central and South Slavic dialect features (Cronia 1952).

299. The term *Canaanitic* appears to be a loan translation of medieval Latin *sclavus* 'slave' derived from the Slavic ethnic self-designation. Medieval Hebrew *ʿebed Kanaʿan* (*Kenaʿan*) 'non-Jewish slave' referred to the indigenous inhabitants of Canaan (the Biblical 'Promised Land') conquered by Israelite colonizers (Kupfer/Lewicki, eds. 1956:28–30).

Although technically not Slavic, the Cyrillic *Signature of Anna*, daughter of Great Prince Yaroslav the Wise of Kiev and widow of the French king Henri I, is of interest as a linguistic curiosity (Obnorskij/Barxudarov 1952:16). In 1063, acting on behalf of her eleven-year-old son Philippe I, Anna placed her signature under a Latin charter for the monastery in Soissons, rèndering Old French *Anna reina* 'Queen Anna' with Cyrillic ана ръина.

Onomastic data are especially important for the countries of Roman Slavdom, which because of their cultural Latinization did not produce early texts in the vernacular. Their primary source is various Latin chronicles, mainly of German provenience. The *Annals of Fulda* record historical events from 830 to 901 in the eastern part of the Carolingian state and contain onomastic data from all of Slavdom but particularly from the Moravian state. Many names of West Slavic tribes are contained in the anonymous *Bavarian Geographer*, an East Frankish description of the territories north of the Danube, compiled in the ninth century. The *Thietmar Chronicle* of the Saxon kings, written by Bishop Thietmar of Merseburg between 1012 and 1018, provides especially valuable information on the phonologies of the Sorbian dialects spoken on German territory (Stieber 1979:50). Even more linguistic data are to be found in the *Helmold Chronicle* of the twelfth century, which is concerned mainly with the Lechitic Slavs settled in the lower basins of the Elbe and Oder rivers. Specifically Czech names occur in the oldest Latin legends of the Czech saints Václav, Vojtěch (Adalbert), Ludmila, and Prokop. Thus, in the legend of the martyred and sainted Czech prince Václav written in the second half of the tenth century by Gumpold, the form *Venceslaus* is still uncontracted and the nasal *ę* is still perceived (< **Vęt'eslavъ*, cf. German *Wenzel*.) Some four hundred Czech names occur in the Latin *Chronicle of Cosmas* of the mid-twelfth century.

Rich Old Czech and Old Slovak materials may be found in Latin charters. The foundation charter for the Cathedral of St. Stephen in the northern Bohemian town of Litoměřice, while not the oldest (ca. 1055–60), is the best known, for in addition to a large number of place and personal names it contains the oldest (thirteenth-century) full Czech sentence (Porák 1979:31).[300] Slovak donation charters, cited and discussed by Jan Stanislav (1957:93–118), include a charter for the Veszprém Vōlgy convent issued by the Hungarian king Stephen I and ratified by Coloman in 1109, two charters for the Zobor abbey from 1111 and 1113, one for the Bakonybéla abbey of 1131, one for the parish of Dōmōs of 1138, and one for the Cathedral of Esztergom of 1156.

From approximately the same time comes the most important monument of Old Polish, the *Papal Bull of 1136* (Taszycki 1975:3–36), issued by Pope Innocent II to the archbishopric of Gniezno. The bull contains more than four hundred place and personal names which, despite their awkward Latin spelling, provide invaluable information on Old Polish phonology and derivational morphology. Several geographic names were mentioned in the oldest Polish document, the so-called *Dagome iudex*, sent by Prince Mieszko I (d. 992) to the papal see. The document itself is lost, but copies of its twelfth-century summaries have survived. An intriguing testimony to the knowledge of Slavic among Jewish mint masters employed at Polish princely courts in the twelfth century is provided by several Hebrew inscriptions on Polish bracteates. One of them bears the words *Mško krl plsk [Mieszko król Polski]* 'Mieszko king of Poland' (Balaban 1925, 2:329).[301]

300. The sentence as well as its transcription and translation are given in **3.7**.

301. This is a reference to Prince Mieszko III Stary (1127–1202), who, without actually being crowned king of Poland, used the title *dux totius Poloniae*. The royal aspirations of Mieszko III are corroborated by the Jewish merchant Yitshak ben Dorbalo, who referred to Mieszko's Poland by the Hebrew term *malkut* 'kingdom' (Kupfer/Lewicki 1956:155).

APPENDIX A: THE RISE OF SLAVIC PHILOLOGY

Philology is a study of language in the broadest sense of the word. It encompasses the structure and history of language, the relations of languages to each other, and the study of texts, that is, of language as it manifests itself in writing.[302] Thus defined, philology is a creature of the modern era. It is in fact barely three centuries old, begotten by the Enlightenment, with its belief in reason and interest in causality, and by Romanticism, with its fascination with history folklore, and national identity.

Linguistic investigations. This is not to say that languages were not studied before the eighteenth century. Grammars were written in ancient India, Greece, and Rome, philological investigations were undertaken in medieval Araby, and classical languages were the object of scholarly study during the Renaissance. Some of these works achieved such a degree of sophistication that their formulations are still of interest to modern scholarship—for instance, the Sanskrit grammar by Pāṇini, an Indian grammarian who lived in the fourth century B.C., or the concise grammar of Greek by Dionysius Thrax, a Greek grammarian of the second century B.C. Unlike their modern counterparts, however, most pre-Enlightenment linguistic investigations did not approach the description of language as an aim in itself. Some of them were undertaken in order to safeguard the purity of the ritualistically sanctified language against the encroachment of lay vernaculars. Some had specifically philosophical concerns and examined the essence of the relation between a word and its referent and delved into the nature of the universals. Some took upon themselves the didactic aim of presenting the classical languages as examples of logic and models of precision. Their aims were descriptive rather than historical, and their treatment of the subject was atomistic rather than systemic. It was not until the advent of the modern period that language became the object of investigation for its own sake and linguistics became legitimized as an independent branch of learning. Only then did serious attention begin to be paid to the internal mechanics of language, its systemic nature as well as its external connections, either on the vertical axis of change and development, which gave rise to historical linguistics, or on the horizontal plane of relations among languages, which led to the formulation of the comparative method and to the fusion of the two axes in comparative-historical grammar.

302. This sketch is limited thematically and chronologically. It does not deal with the formation and development of individual standard languages, nor does it extend beyond the formative years of Slavic philology, that is, beyond the beginning of the twentieth century. For the more recent periods, see the histories of Slavic philology listed in the Bibliography, especially Suprun and Kaljuta 1981.

The difference in kind between the descriptive pursuits of old and the realization that languages had a temporal dimension and spatial connections may account for the fact that neither of the two precursors of the new field of scholarly inquiry was a grammarian.[303] One was Gottfried von Leibniz (1646–1716), a German mathematician with broad ethnological interests which led him to the examination of a number of languages of Europe and Asia.[304] Noting various similarities among these languages, Leibniz surmised that they were indicative of genetic affinity. The other was Sir William Jones (1746–1794), a British jurist who managed to combine his official duties as a judge in Calcutta with serious study of Sanskrit. Jones was struck by the similarity of Sanskrit to Greek and Latin and concluded that "no philologer could examine them all three without believing them to have sprung from some common source which perhaps no longer exists." Jones made this pronouncement in a lecture delivered in 1786 before the Asiatic Society in London as part of a broader hypothesis in which Sanskrit, Greek, Latin, Old Persian, Gothic, and Celtic were all deemed to have been descended from a common ancestor. This insight became the cornerstone of Indo-European historical linguistics, a field that was to come into full bloom in the nineteenth century in the works of the Danish scholar Rasmus Kristian Rask (1787–1832) and two German scholars, Jacob Grimm (1785–1863)[305] and Franz Bopp (1791–1867). It was also in the nineteenth century that Slavic philology, along with other Indo-European philologies, came into being.[306]

The formative period of Slavic philology bore the imprint of Romanticism, in particular of its philosophy of language as expounded in the writings of the German philosophers Johann Gottfried Herder (1744–1803) and Wilhelm von Humboldt (1767–1835). They found in language the essence of the national psyche and ascribed to it the mystique and the powers of a spiritual fetish. Language was equated with national identity, and its study became a tool in the search for national consciousness and, ultimately, national autonomy. The first Slavic philologists had access to a very limited corpus of data as compared with our present knowledge of Slavic antiquities. The great majority of ancient Slavic texts had not yet been discovered,[307] the confines of Old Church Slavonic had not yet been determined, and the

303. One should remember, however, the achievements of the Age of Reason in the realm of "pure" grammar. Among the most important was the Port Royal grammar of French, so known because of the abbey of Port-Royal-des-Champs, near Versailles, where it was developed and published in 1660. Though firmly rooted in the classical heritage and schematic in its descriptive techniques, the Port Royal grammar aimed to live up to the program announced in its title: "*General and reasoned grammar containing the foundations of the art of speaking explained in a clear and natural manner. Reasons for what is common to all languages and main differences among them: many new observations on the French language*." The Port Royal grammar, with its concern for "what is common to all languages," is sometimes credited with laying the philosophical foundation for the "deep structure" dimension of the generative grammar.

304. Leibniz contributed directly to Slavic linguistics by publishing two Polabian texts, an anonymous glossary of 137 words and several short religious passages, including the Lord's Prayer.

305. Otherwise known for the collection of fairy tales that he and his brother Wilhelm compiled.

306. A curious chapter in the history of Slavic "philology" was written in the seventeenth century by the linguistically gifted Croatian priest Juraj Križanić (1617–1683), whose Pan-Slavist ideas prompted him to travel throughout the Slavic lands and learn a number of Slavic languages. While visiting Russia, he was accused of spreading Papist propaganda and deported to Siberia, where he remained for fifteen years (1661–1675). During that time Križanić wrote a grammar of "Russian," which was in fact an idiosyncratic mixture of East Slavic and Croatian in a stillborn attempt to introduce an artificial Slavic lingua franca. Despite its unrealistic goals Križanić's grammar contains perceptive observations on a variety of Slavic linguistic topics. Križanić died while serving in the armies of the Polish king Jan III Sobieski during the 1683 defense of Vienna against the Ottoman Turks.

307. The most productive period in this respect was the mid-nineteenth century, when a number of Old Church Slavonic codices came to light (*Zographensis* in 1843, *Marianus* in 1845, *Psalterium Sinaiticum* and *Euchologium Sinaiticum* in 1850, and the *Prague Fragments* in 1855).

Glagolitic alphabet was known chiefly from late Croatian texts. This makes the achievements of early Slavic philology appear all the more admirable.[308]

It is a remarkable happenstance that the first three major Slavists hailed from three different Slavic nations representing the three principal linguistic branches of Slavic—the south, the west, and the east. The most versatile among them was the Czech Josef Dobrovský (1753–1829) whose interests included practically every branch of the humanities. In his early work on the history of Czech, *Geschichte der böhmischen Sprache und Literatur* (1792), and especially in his later compendium of Church Slavonic bearing the awe-inspiring title *Institutiones linguae slavicae dialecti veteris, quae quum apud Russos, Serbos, aliosque ritus graeci, tum apud Dalmatas glagolitas ritus latini Slavos in libris sacris obtinet* (1822), Dobrovský established a number of fundamental facts of Slavic comparative phonology and morphology, including such phenomena as the prothesis of vowels, the metathesis of vowels and liquid sonants, and the palatalization of consonants. Dobrovský's broad scholarly interests provided Slavic philology with a research agenda for years to come. His linguistic investigations were accompanied by studies in Slavic history and prehistory (including the problem of the primordial habitat of the Slavs), the activities of Constantine and Methodius, the early Slavic alphabets and texts, and the spread of Slavic church services to such Latin-dominated lands as Bohemia. Dobrovský's follower and collaborator was the Slovene Jernej Bartolomej Kopitar (1780–1844). Kopitar wrote the first grammar of his native Slovenian (1808–1809) and in 1836 edited and published in Vienna the Trent portion of the *Glagolita Clozianus* with discussions of other Old Church Slavonic texts and a sketch of Old Church Slavonic grammar. Kopitar's work on the *Freising Fragments* gave rise to his theory of the Pannonian origins of Old Church Slavonic. The third of the "founding fathers" of Slavic philology was the Russian Aleksandr X. Vostokov (1781–1864), author of *Rassuždenie o slavjanskom jazyke* (1820), in which he used phonetic correspondences to determine affinities among the Slavic languages.[309] He lay the groundwork for Slavic textual investigations with an exemplary edition of *Ostromir's Evangeliary* (1843), a work that has retained its scholarly value to this day. Also of lasting importance is Vostokov's description of the collections of Russian and Slavic manuscripts in the Rumjancev Museum (the Russian State Library) in Moscow (1842).

The activities of Dobrovský and Kopitar established the universities of Prague and Vienna as the principal centers of Slavic philology and as the natural breeding grounds for the next generation of Slavists. With Austria-Hungary incorporating Croatia, Slovenia, Slovakia, Moravia, and Bohemia, as well as Polish and Ukrainian Galicia, Vienna, which was the empire's capital, and Prague, which was its major Slavic city, became virtual laboratories for the nascent Slavic studies. Prague, with its desire for Czech national rebirth and dreams of pan-Slavic cultural cooperation,[310] held a particular attraction for the Slavs coming from var-

308. The thematic confines of this book dictate the exclusion of treatments of individual Slavic languages, such as those of Czech by Jan Hus (1371–1415), Polish by Jakub Parkoszowic (first half of the fifteenth century), and Russian by Heinrich Wilhelm Ludolf (1655–1712) and Mixail V. Lomonosov (1711–1765). Similarly excluded are discussions of Church Slavonic grammars and dictionaries such as those by the Ukrainian Meletij Smotryc'kyj (ca. 1578–1633) or the Swede Joannes Sparwenfelt (1655–1727), as well as collections of folkloristic texts such as those by the Serb Vuk Karadžić (1787–1864) or the Russian Aleksandr F. Gil'ferding (1832–1872).

309. Among his phonological contributions is the determination that Old Church Slavonic ѧ and ѫ were nasal vowels.

310. Czech *vzájemnost* 'reciprocity', a term devised by the Slovak writer and literary historian Ján Kollár (1793–1852).

ious parts of the empire. It was at the University of Prague that the Slovak Pavel Josef Šafařík (1795–1861) worked first as the librarian and later as professor of Slavic studies. His variegated scholarly interests included early Slavic history (*Slovanské starožitnosti*, 1836–1837), folklore (*Slavische Volkskunde*, 1842), and language (*Geschichte der slawischen Sprache und Literatur nach allen Mundarten*, 1826). Upon the 1855 discovery of the Glagolitic *Prague Fragments*, Šafařík, in his "Über den Ursprung und die Heimat des Glagolismus" (1857), became the first scholar to come out decisively in favor of Glagolitic over Cyrillic in the spirited debate over the primacy of the two early Slavic alphabets.

Another illustrious scholar whose career was for a time connected with the University of Prague was the German linguist August Schleicher (1821–1868). Schleicher's name is associated primarily with the first clear and consistent formulation of the comparative method in linguistic investigations. A convinced Darwinian, he is credited in particular with the introduction of the biological "family tree" approach to the description of the evolution of related languages. He applied that model in his *Compendium der vergleichenden Grammatik der Indo-Germanischen Sprachen* (1861–1862), an overview of the development of the Indo-European family of languages and a reconstruction of its ultimate Proto-Indo-European source. Schleicher contributed significantly to Slavic historical linguistics by noting the close kinship of Slavic with Baltic and of Balto-Slavic with Germanic. His most important publications dealing with Baltic and Slavic include *Handbuch der litauischen Sprache* (1856–1857), *Formenlehre der kircheslavischen Sprache* (1852), and *Laut- und Formenlehre der polabischen Sprache* (1871).

The University of Vienna was especially fortunate in its selection of incumbents for the chair in Slavic philology. Kopitar's tenure there was followed by that of another Slovene, Franz Miklosich (1813–1891), who emerged as the leading Slavist of the nineteenth century, author of several fundamental linguistic works, including the four-volume *Vergleichende Grammatik der slavischen Sprachen* (1852–1875), *Etymologisches Wörterbuch der slavischen Sprachen* (1886), *Formenlehre der altslovenischen Sprache* (1850),[311] and the rich *Lexicon palaeoslovenico-graeco-latinum* (1862–1865). He also dealt in his writings with a number of lexical topics, such as loan words and specialized terminology. Miklosich's most successful student was the Croat Vatroslav Jagić (1838–1923), who occupied chairs in Slavic philology in Berlin and St. Petersburg (1880–1886)[312] and who eventually succeeded his mentor in Vienna. Jagić was not only an astonishingly versatile and productive scholar but also an energetic teacher and organizer of research. He founded and edited the first international journal devoted to Slavic philology (*Archiv für slavische Philologie*, Berlin) and organized in St. Peterburg an ambitious series of monographic philological studies under the title *Enciklopedija slavjanskoj filologii*.

It would seem natural for Russia to show an early interest in Slavic philology. It was, after all, the only powerful independent Slavic country.[313] In addition to ethnically Russian lands, it included Ukrainian and Belorussian territories and showed a lively political, cultural, and religious interest in the Slavic lands of the Ottoman-held regions of the Balkans, principally Orthodox Serbia and Bulgaria but also Bosnia and Hercegovina, which had a

311. Miklosich followed his teacher Kopitar in considering Old Church Slavonic to be of Pannonian (Slovenian) origin.

312. Vatroslav Jagić worked and published in Russia using the first name Ignatij. In adopting this name he played on the semantic correspondence between Slavic *vatra* 'fire' and Latin *īgnis* 'fire' (hence Latin *Ignatius*).

313. The only other independent Slavic country at that time was Montenegro.

mixed Moslem and Orthodox population.[314] Yet in the first half of the nineteenth century Russian universities lagged behind their Western counterparts in the promotion of Slavic studies.[315] In fact, with the exception of Vladimir I. Lamanskij (1833–1914), who pioneered Slavic historical and ethnographic investigations in Russia, it was not until the last quarter of the nineteenth century that Russian Slavic studies joined the mainstream of Western scholarship, marked at that time by the advent of the neogrammarian school in historical linguistics.

The neogrammarians were a group of predominantly German Indo-Europeanists who were active in the 1870s in the universities of Leipzig and Jena. Confident that their discoveries in the reconstruction of Proto-Indo-European heralded the transformation of the comparative-historical method into an exact science, the neogrammarians proclaimed the principle of regularity of phonetic change. They assumed that phonetic laws have no exceptions and that apparent counterexamples are due either to faulty formulation of the law or to linguistic analogy.[316] The most prominent neogrammarians were Karl Brugmann (1849–1919) and Bertold Delbrück (1842–1922), co-authors of the five-volume *Grundriss der vergleichenden Grammatik der indogermanischen Sprachen;* the Slavist August Leskien (1840–1916), whose grammar of Old Church Slavonic, *Handbuch der altbulgarischen Sprache* (1871), is still in use; and Hermann Paul (1846–1921), who laid the theoretical foundations of the neogrammarian school in his *Prinzipien der Sprachgeshichte* (1880). Belonging to this group of German scholars were the American Sanskritist William Dwight Whitney (1827–1894) and the Danish Germanist Karl Werner (1846–1896), who showed that the apparent exceptions to Grimm's Law may be explained by the place of word stress (ictus) in Proto-Indo-European.

Some of the most important discoveries in the reconstruction of Proto-Indo-European as well as of Proto-Slavic were made by linguists who adopted the basic tenets of the neogrammarian school. Among the Indo-Europeanists whose work dealt extensively with Slavic, four names stand out: Ferdinand de Saussure (1857–1913), a Swiss linguist, author of the pioneering *Mémoires sur le système primitif des voyelles dans les langues indo-européennes* (1878), a work whose very title portends the development of Saussure's later views on language as a structured system; the Frenchman Antoine Meillet (1866–1936), author of *Introduction à l'étude comparative des langues indo-europeénnes* (1903) and of *Le slave commun* (1924), which in its version revised by André Vaillant (1934) is still one of the main handbooks of Proto-Slavic; the Russian Filipp F. Fortunatov (1848–1914), founder of the Moscow school of linguistics, whose name is linked with that of Saussure in a phonetic law explain-

314. Serbia won its independence from the Ottoman empire in 1830 as did Bulgaria in 1878. Also in 1878 Bosnia and Hercegovina passed under the administrative control of Austria-Hungary.

315. These strictures do not apply to specifically Russian studies, which developed well since the days of M. V. Lomonosov (1711–1765). Among the more interesting Russianists of the mid-nineteenth century were G. P. Pavskij (1787–1863), I. I. Sreznevskij (1812–1880), K. S. Aksakov (1817–1860), F. I. Buslaev (1818–1897), and N. P. Nekrasov (1828–1908). Methodologically interesting are the works of the Ukrainian Oleksandr Potebnja (1835–1891), who wrote on topics in general linguistics and literary theory. Earlier on, the activities of Admiral Alexander S. Šiškov (1754–1841) provided a distinctive chapter in the history of Slavic studies in Russia. An accomplished writer of Slavophile persuasion, Šiškov served in various government capacities under the tsars Alexander I and Nicholas I, including a brief stint as minister of education (1824–1828) and a longer tenure as president of the Russian Academy (1813–1841). His conservative views prompted him to consider Church Slavonic the only proper lexical base of literary Russian and to oppose the importation of Western Slavists to Russian university posts.

316. Thus, the Proto-Slavic second palatalization of velars (**2.24**) would demand that the dative singular of Russian *ruká* 'hand' be **rucé*. The form *ruké*, which we find there instead, is to be explained by analogical pressure exerted by the other case forms in the paradigm of *ruká*.

ing stress alternation between the root and the desinence in Lithuanian and Slavic; the Pole Jan Rozwadowski (1867–1935), a general linguist who specialized in morphological derivation and semantics but also contributed significantly to Slavic accentology[317] and onomastics.

By the beginning of the twentieth century, the neogrammarian model became the norm in historical lingustics. In addition to Meillet, for whom it was always a vital resource, there were many other Slavists whose work betrayed a greater or lesser degree of reliance on the neogrammarian approach to the history of language. Best known among them were the Czech Václav Vondrák (1859–1925), whose two-volume *Vergleichende slavische Grammatik* (1906–1908) is especially valued for its detailed syntactic component; the Finn Josef Mikkola (1866–1946), author of the important, though unfinished, *Urslavische Grammatik* (1913, 1942, 1950); the Serb Aleksandar Belić (1876–1960), whose main contributions to Proto-Slavic were in the area of accentology and morphology; the Slovene Rajko Nahtigal (1877–1958), whose clear and concise *Slovanski jeziki* (2nd ed. 1952) merited translations into Russian and German; the Dutchman Nicolaas van Wijk (1880–1941), who in 1937 published a series of five articles on the history and typology of Slavic (reissued in 1956 as *Les langues slaves: de l'unité à la pluralité*); and the Russian Afanasij M. Seliščev (1886–1942), author of *Vvedenie v sravnitel'nuju grammatiku slavjanskix jazykov* (1914).

The neogrammarians scored their greatest successes in historical linguistics. Indeed, the comparative method which they introduced is, in a modified form, still fruitfully employed in historical research. Yet, for all the meticulous investigations of data culled from a variety of related languages, the neogrammarians failed to realize that language is not a sum of loosely connected parts but a system of structurally and functionally linked elements. To be sure, they had to operate with some elements of the systemic view of language. These were present, for instance, in the formulation of Grimm's Law, which describes the development of stops, that is, of a formally defined subset of Proto-Indo-European sounds. Likewise, the operation of grammatical analogy presupposes the recognition of systemic structures (paradigms) because the form affected by analogy must be functionally similar to its model. It was not until the end of the nineteenth century, however, that there developed the view that language is a coherent system of elements which, though endowed with their own forms and their own functions, are so closely interconnected and interdependent that a change in the status of any of them entails a change in the system itself. This insight made scholars realize the importance of discovering and describing linguistic structures, an approach that has characterized linguistic research during the better part of the twentieth century. It has come to be known as *structuralism*.

Structuralist principles were first formulated in 1916 in the posthumously published *Cours de linguistique générale* by Ferdinand de Saussure. Of all the distinctions introduced by Saussure, the dichotomy of synchrony versus diachrony is of particular interest for historical investigations. Synchrony is concerned with the state of language at a particular moment; it provides a "horizontal" dissection of language, a single stage frozen in time. Diachrony, by contrast, deals with the evolution of language in time; it produces a "vertical" dissection, which reveals two or more stages in the development of language. The coexistence of the synchronic and diachronic axes lends language its dynamic aspect.

Saussure's views on the development of Indo-European have a direct bearing on the phonological structure of Early Proto-Slavic. Especially important was his novel approach

317. The term *neoacute* for the new rising pitch is of his coinage (**2.31**).

to the system of Proto-Indo-European vowels (the laryngeal hypothesis) and his demonstration of the connection between the onset of stress and the rising intonation in Lithuanian. When the Russian linguist Fortunatov ascertained, independently of Saussure, that an analogous connection existed in Slavic, the phonetic law formulated by these two scholars became known as the law of Saussure/Fortunatov.[318]

Another pioneer of structuralism was Saussure's contemporary, the Polish linguist Jan Baudouin de Courtenay (1845–1929), whose scholarly career is linked primarily with the Russian universities of Kazan and St. Petersburg. Baudouin's main interest lay in the area of phonology, and he contributed to it the notions of distinctive features and morphophonemic alternations. As far as Proto-Slavic is concerned, Baudouin's most important contribution was the identification of the so-called progressive or third palatalization of velars (1894), which is referred to sometimes as the Baudouin palatalization.

The most outstanding practitioners and promoters of the ideas of Saussure and Baudouin in Slavic scholarship were the Pole Jerzy Kuryłowicz (1895–1978) and the Russian Roman Jakobson (1896–1982). Although both scholars made important contributions to general and historical linguistics,[319] it was Kuryłowicz who was especially active in the area of Indo-European and Proto-Slavic phonology. Jakobson, in addition to his scholarly activities, was a brilliant teacher and organizer of research, first in Prague and, after World War II, at Columbia and Harvard. His stay in Prague coincided with the formation of a linguistic circle that drew together a group of structuralist-minded Czech and emigré Russian scholars. The new movement came to be known as the Prague school of linguistics, with the journal *Travaux du Cercle Linguistique de Prague* as its mouthpiece. Among the linguists of the Prague school who dealt with problems of Proto-Slavic, Old Church Slavonic, and early Slavic texts was the Russian Nikolaj S. Trubeckoj (1890–1938) of the University of Vienna, author of a well-known introduction to structuralist phonology, *Grundzüge der Phonologie* (1939), and of a number of contributions to Russian, Polabian, and Old Church Slavonic scholarship. Also active in the Prague group was the Czech Bohuslav Havránek (1893–1978), whose *Genera verbi v slovanských jazycích* (1927) deals with diathesis in Slavic.

At the same time the traditional model retained its popularity in historical investigations. Two grammars of Proto-Slavic deserve special mention, the five-volume *Grammaire comparé des langues slaves* (1950–1977) by the Frenchman André Vaillant (1898–1977) and the *Urslavische Grammatik* (1964, 1976, 1985) by the Estonian Peeter Arumaa (1900–1982). The former is our most reliable and complete guide to the subject; the latter provides a clear and well-argued treatment but is, unfortunately, unfinished.[320] Another historian of Proto-Slavic who remained faithful to the traditional approach was the Pole Tadeusz Lehr-Spławiński (1891–1965), whose main research interests were in phonology, the history of West Slavic, and the location of the ancestral homeland of the Slavs.

Old Church Slavonic particularly received many traditional treatments. The list is headed by the grammar of August Leskien (1871) and includes the grammars of Ljubomir G. Miletič (1888), Václav Vondrák (1900), Mykola K. Hruns'kyj (1906), Stepan M. Kul'bakin

318. Or simply as the law of Fortunatov (Shevelov 1965:46).

319. The languages of their research interests were varied. Kuryłowicz worked primarily on Indo-European, Semitic, and Polish materials; Jakobson was chiefly interested in Russian and Czech but drew upon data from a number of other languages.

320. Steering a middle course between traditionalism and structuralism are *A Prehistory of Slavic: The Historical Phonology of Common Slavic* by the Ukrainian George Y. Shevelov (1965) and *Zarys gramatyki porównawczej języków słowiańskich* by the Pole Zdzisław Stieber (1979).

(1911/1912), Jan Łoś (1922), Tadeusz Lehr-Spławiński (1923), Nicolaas van Wijk (1931), Paul Diels (1932/1934), Miloš Weingart (1937/1938), and Afanasij M. Seliščev (published posthumously in 1951/1952). Some of the more important treatments of selected aspects of Old Church Slavonic grammar include the phonology by Aleksej I. Sobolevskij (1891), noun declension by Boris M. Ljapunov (1905), and morphology by František Pastrnek (1909). The first structuralist grammar of Old Church Slavonic is the *Altkirchenslavische Grammatik* by Nikolaj S. Trubeckoj (published posthumously in 1954).[321]

One should also mention here some of the etymological and comparative Slavic dictionaries: *Etymologisches Wörterbuch der slavischen Sprachen* (1886) by Franz Miklosich (1813–1891), *Slavisches etymologisches Wörterbuch* (1908–1913) by Erich Berneker (1874–1937), and *Baltisch-slavisches Wörterbuch* (1923) by Reinhold Trautmann (1883–1951). Except for the etymological dictionaries of Russian by A. G. Preobraženskij, published in 1910–1914 (a new, enlarged edition appeared in 1958) and of Polish by Aleksander Brückner, published in 1927, all etymological dictionaries of individual Slavic languages appeared after World War II.[322]

Textual investigations. Kopitar's publication of the *Glagolita Clozianus* and the *Freising Fragments* (1836) and Vostokov's edition of *Ostromir's Evangeliary* (1843) began an era of heightened interest in collecting and editing early Slavic texts. Especially active in this enterprise were scholars who had behind them the bountiful resources of the Russian government, whose imperial Slavophile interests meshed with the academic concerns of those Slavists eager to travel to Central Europe and the Balkans in order to establish contacts with the leading philologists of the time and to search for Slavic antiquities.[323] State funds made available for such purposes were supplemented by private donors. Among the most zealous promoters of Slavic philological studies was Count Nikolaj P. Rumjancev (1754–1826), who amassed an enormous collection of ancient Slavic manuscripts and financed many of their finest editions.[324] One of the beneficiaries of Rumjancev's love for early Slavic texts was

321. After World II many more traditional grammars of Old Church Slavonic appeared, among them Josip Hamm (1947), André Vaillant (1948), Stanisław Słoński (1950), Bernhard Rosenkranz (1955), Grigore Nandriş (1959), Hans Holm Bielfeldt (1961), Rudolf Aitzetmüller (1978), Ján Stanislav (1978, 1987), and others, particularly in Russia. Structuralist in design is *Old Church Slavonic Grammar* by Horace G. Lunt (1959), whose sixth edition (1974) has an added section on Old Church Slavonic phonology presented in generative terms.

322. Among the general Slavic etymological dictionaries published since World War II are the *Etymologický slovník slovanských jazyků* (1966–) by E. Havlová, ed.; *Etimologičeskij slovar' slavjanskix jazykov* (1974) by Oleg N. Trubačev (b. 1930); and *Słownik prasłowiański* (1974–) by Franciszek Sławski (b. 1916). For individual Slavic languages see, for Old Church Slavonic, Linda Sadnik and Rudolf Aitzetmüller (1955); Bulgarian, Stefan Mladenov (1941) and Vladimir I. Georgiev et al. (1971–); Serbian/Croatian, Petar Skok (1971–1974); Slovenian, Frane Bezlaj (1976–); Czech, Josef Holub and František Kopečny (3d ed., 1952); Czech and Slovak, Václav Machek (1957), Sorbian, Heinz Schuster-Šewc (1978–); Polish, Franciszek Sławski (1954–); Kashubian, Wiesław Boryś and Hanna Popowska-Taborska (1994–); Polabian, Kazimierz Polański (1962–1994); Russian, Max Vasmer (1953–1958) and Nikolaj M. Šanskij et al. (1972); Ukrainian, Jaroslav B. Rudnyc'kyj (1962–); and Belarussian, Viktar V. Martynaŭ et al. (1978–). The largest dictionary of Old Church Slavonic was undertaken under the direction of Josef Kurz in Prague in 1958.

323. Russia's interest in acquiring Slavic manuscripts goes back to the period of Patriarch Nikon's reforms, when in 1651 Arsenij Suxanov, a monk in the Holy Trinity–St. Sergius Monastery, was sent to the Balkans and Asia Minor in search of authoritative Greek church books. Suxanov returned in 1653 bringing a vast collection of Greek and Slavic manuscripts, which he deposited in the Synodal Printing Office Library. The size of the collection may be gauged by the fact that from the monasteries on Mount Athos alone Suxanov took close to five hundred manuscripts including the oldest extant copy of the *Hexaemeron* by John the Exarch (Serbian recension of 1263). On Suxanov's mission, see S. A. Belokurov, *ČOIDR* (1891, vols. 1–2, and 1894, v. 2).

324. Rumjancev served for years in various government posts as ambassador in Frankfurt, minister of trade, and minister of foreign affairs. He left government service in 1814 and devoted himself to the promotion of the arts and sciences.

Konstantin F. Kalajdovič (1792–1832), also a passionate collector of old manuscripts. Two of Kalajdovič's most important contributions to Slavic philology were financed by Rumjancev, his discovery in 1817 of *Svyatoslav's Izbornik of 1073* and his discovery and edition (1818–1824) of the writings of John the Exarch. Also active at that time was Canon Michał Bobrowski (1785–1848) who taught theology at the Stefan Batory University in Vilnius but whose scholarly interests were philological. Bobrowski's most important contribution to the development of Slavic studies was his discovery in 1823 of the Cyrillic *Codex Suprasliensis.*

Another patron of Slavic philological ventures was the Moscow historian and editor Mixail P. Pogodin (1800–1875), whose correspondence with some of the most prominent Slavists provides a wealth of information on the formative period of Slavic philology. Equally informative is the correspondence left behind by the scholars whom the Russian government sent to the West to study and to meet with other Slavists. They included Osip M. Bodjanskij (1803–1877), who was to occupy the Slavic chair at the University of Moscow; Izmail I. Sreznevskij (1812–1880), who taught at the universities of Kharkov and St. Petersburg and published a description of the East Slavic texts from the tenth through the sixteenth centuries (1863–1866);[325] Petr I. Prejs (1810–1846), who taught at the University of St. Petersburg; and Viktor I. Grigorovič (1815–1876), who held Slavic chairs at the universities of Kazan and Odessa. During his visits to the monasteries on Mount Athos and in Ohrid, Rila, and Bojana, Grigorovič discovered a number of our most valuable early Slavic texts, which he then brought to Russia, among them the *Codex Marianus,* the *Rila Folios,* the *Ohrid Folios, Grigorovič's (Hilandar) Parimeinik,* the *Dobrian Menaeum,* and the *Bojana Evangeliary.*

Grigorovič offered his manuscripts to two libraries, the State Library of Odessa and the Russian State Library in Moscow. In each of them they are known as the Grigorovič collection.[326] Similarly, other Russian collections of manuscripts bear the names of their acquirers. The Norov collection in the Russian State Library in Moscow contains a number of Slavic manuscripts which the Russian writer and statesman Avraam S. Norov (1795–1869) brought to Russia from his trip to Jerusalem in 1834–1835. The Uspenskij collection was presented to the Public Library in St. Petersburg by Porfirij Uspenskij (1804–1885), a churchman and a Byzantinist who served as the head of the Russian church mission in Jerusalem and acquired Slavic manuscripts in St. Catherine's Monastery on Mount Sinai and in the Zographos and Hilandar monasteries on Mount Athos. In contrast to the collections of Grigorovič, Norov, and Uspenskij, the Undol'skij collection (1,350 manuscripts) was gathered almost entirely in Russia by the Russian bibliophile Vukol M. Undol'skij (1816–1864). After Un-

---

Rumjancev's collections formed the core of the Rumjancev Museum in Moscow, founded in 1862. During the early years of the Soviet period the museum was transformed into a library and was named after Lenin. Today it is known as the Russian State Library.

325. Sreznevskij's lexical excerpts from these texts were published as a three-volume dictionary titled *Materialy dlja slovarja drevnerusskogo jazyka po pis'mennym pamjatnikam* (1893, 1895, 1903). Despite its modest title, it remains the only completed dictionary of Old East Slavic. Of the two Moscow dictionaries that have started coming out, *Slovar' russkogo jazyka XI–XVII vv.* (1975–), begun under the editorship of Stepan G. Barxudarov and Fedot P. Filin, appears to be well on its way to completion. It will take longer to complete the publication of *Slovar' drevnerusskogo jazyka (XI–XIV v.),* edited originally by Ruben I. Avanesov, which has not progressed much beyond the first letters of the alphabet since it started coming out in 1988. A convenient extract of Sreznevskij's dictionary is Horace G. Lunt's *Concise Dictionary of Old Russian (11th–17th Centuries)* with glosses in Russian (Munich, 1970).

326. For a description of major collections of Church Slavonic manuscripts of Bulgarian recension, see Kuev 1979. A list of Russian archives and manuscript collections may be found in Šmidt, ed. 1884:16–18.

dol'skij's death the collection was sold to the Rumjancev Museum. Its oldest manuscript is the Old Church Slavonic *Undol'skij's Fragments*.[327]

Two other collections that ended up in Russian libraries ought to be mentioned. The Gil'ferding collection in the Public Library in St. Petersburg was deposited there by Aleksandr F. Gil'ferding (1831–1872), a versatile scholar with interests in the Slavs of the Danubian lands and in the Slavic languages of Germany. Most of the manuscripts in the collection were acquired in Serbia, Bosnia and Hercegovina, and Macedonia, the oldest among them being the *Macedonian Folio*. Another scholar collecting in the Balkans was Polixronij A. Syrku (1855–1905), a Russian-trained Moldovan Slavist. The oldest manuscript of the Syrku collection is a fragment (thirty-four folios) of an evangeliary of the twelfth century, now in the Odessa Archaeological Museum (Šmidt, ed. 1984, #115). The collection of the Moscow Synodal Library was described in detail by Aleksandr V. Gorskij (1812–1875) and Kapiton I. Nevostruev (1815–1872).

The most successful non-Russian collector of ancient Slavic manuscripts was the Croat Antun Mihanović (1796–1861) who discovered in 1843 in the library of the Bulgarian monastery of St. Zographos on Mount Athos the celebrated *Codex Zographensis*. One year later the manuscript was seen by Grigorovič, who recognized its importance and became the first scholar to describe it. Except for the *Codex Zographensis*, which is kept in the Public Library in St. Petersburg, all other manuscripts acquired by Mihanović (mostly on Mount Athos) are preserved today in the library of the Croatian Academy in Zagreb. Foremost among them is another *tetra*, the *Tărnovo Gospel*, a Cyrillic codex of Bulgarian recension containing 247 folios, half of them parchment and half paper (*xartija*)—the first Bulgarian manuscript in which paper was used. It was copied in 1273 in Tărnovo, the ancient capital of Bulgaria, and was the object of several investigations, the earliest by M. Valjavec (1888, 1889).

The efforts of the nineteenth-century collectors brought to light many ancient manuscripts whose description and publication presented a challenge to a new generation of scholars interested in paleography, textual studies, and editorial work. Among them Vatroslav Jagić stands as a towering figure. His publications deal mainly with Old Church Slavonic, in particular with its Glagolitic monuments, and include editions of the codices *Zographensis* (1879) and *Marianus* (1883), some newly discovered Glagolitic fragments (*Glagolitica* 1890), and the *Bologna Psalter* (1907), which is a Cyrillic copy of a Glagolitic text. His magisterial (and very readable) history of Slavic philology appeared as the first volume of the *Enciklopedija slavjanskoj filologii* (1910). Of special interest is Jagić's fundamental study *Entstehungsgeschichte der kirchenslavischen Sprache* (1900, 1913_2) in which he promoted the now commonly accepted view of the Macedonian origins of Old Church Slavonic. Jagić's two paleographic studies, a detailed history of the Glagolitic alphabet and an article on the purported existence of Slavic runes, appeared in the third volume of the *Enciklopedija* (1911).

Most textologists and paleographers active at the end of the nineteenth and the beginning of the twentieth centuries came from the Slavic lands of the Russian empire. Aleksej I. Sobolevskij (1856–1929) was a versatile scholar who combined his primary interest in Russian historical grammar with valuable textual work. Of lasting significance is his *Cerkovnoslavjanskie teksty moravskogo proisxoždenija* (1900), in which he investigated Church Slavonic texts displaying West Slavic linguistic features. Petr A. Lavrov (1856–1929) was a special-

327. Undol'skij was the fortunate discoverer of the *Homiliary Gospel* by Constantine of Preslav, three homilies by Clement of Ohrid in a *sbornik* from the turn of the thirteenth century (Šmidt, ed. 1984, #163), and the *Uspenskij sbornik*.

ist in texts belonging to the Cyrillo-Methodian tradition. A very useful selection of these texts was published in 1930. Evfimij F. Karskij (1860–1931) edited several short Old Church Slavonic texts and wrote on the place of his native Belarussian within East Slavic. Vjačeslav N. Ščepkin (1863–1920) edited *Sava's Book* and studied its language. These last three scholars were also authors of excellent introductions to Cyrillic paleography: Lavrov's *Paleografičeskoe obozrenie kirillovskogo pis'ma* (1914), Karskij's *Slavjanskaja kirillovskaja paleografija* (1928), and Ščepkin's *Učebnik russkoj paleografii* (1918). Mixail N. Speranskij (1863–1938) investigated and edited East Slavic *sborniki* of translated apothegmata and described Slavic manuscripts in Palestine, in the Monastery of St. Catherine on Mount Sinai and in the Uspensky Cathedral in the Kremlin, including the *Uspenskij sbornik*. Aleksej A. Šaxmatov (1864–1920) was an extremely productive scholar who concentrated on Russian, its history, syntax, and earliest monuments, in particular East Slavic chronicles. Vasilij M. Istrin (1865–1937) worked in the area of translated texts, especially Byzantine chronicles. Vladimir N. Peretc (1870–1935) catalogued and described the Slavic manuscripts in the libraries of the universities of Moscow, Samara, and Minsk.

This impressive list (and it could be extended) testifies to the extraordinary vitality of Slavic textual studies in the lands of the Russian empire around the turn of the twentieth century. Other Slavic countries had neither the resources nor the archival holdings to match those of Russia and, in the period surveyed, could not vie for leadership in philological investigations of (Old) Church Slavonic texts.[328] Despite this handicap, a number of scholars hailing from the hands of the southern and western Slavs contributed significantly to our understanding of the Cyrillo-Methodian period and tradition.

Among the southern Slavs, the Bulgarians Aleksandăr S. Teodorov-Balan (1859–1959) prepared an edition of the vitae of Constantine and Methodius (1920); Ben'o S. Conev (1863–1926) edited the *Dobrejšo Gospel* and described the Zagreb and Sofia National Library manuscript collections; Vasil N. Zlatarski (1866–1935) was a medievalist whose major work, a three-volume history of the medieval Bulgarian state, interprets the activities of Constantine and Methodius and of their disciples, Clement and Naum (vol. 1, 1918). The Serb Djura Daničić (1825–1882) published the *Vita Constantini* (1869) and edited several Church Slavonic texts of Serbian recension, including the vita of St. Sava. The Croatian Slavist German Barac (1835–1922) drew parallels between Cyrillo-Methodian literature and Jewish religious traditions. The Slovene Matija Murko (1861–1952) wrote the *Geschichte der älteren südslavischen Literaturen* (1908), while his compatriot Fran Grivec (1878–1963) focused his attention on the vitae of Constantine and Methodius and on the history of the Moravian mission and its legacy in Bulgaria.

Among the western Slavs, the Cyrillo-Methodian tradition found its greatest resonance in Czech and Slovak scholarship, which focused, naturally enough, on texts pertaining to the activities of the Moravian mission and its legacy in Bohemia. Josef Vajs (1865–1959) is best known for his study of Church Slavonic texts of the Moravian recension dealing with the Czech saints Ludmila and Václav (1929), a handbook of Glagolitic paleography (1932), and his reconstruction of the texts of the Old Church Slavonic Gospels (1935–1936). The cult of the early Czech saints figured prominently in the early writings of Josef Vašica (1884–1968), who later turned to such Cyrillo-Methodian topics as the problem of Slavic liturgy, the *Kherson Legend*, the *Zakonъ sudnyi ljudemъ*, the canon for St. Demetrius, and Methodius' pre-

328. This situation changed dramatically after World War II, when Bulgaria became preeminent in Slavic textology.

sumed authorship of the anonymous homily in the *Glagolita Clozianus*. Miloš Weingart (1890–1939) studied the Czech/Slovak recension of Church Slavonic (1949).

Latin was the major vehicle of Polish medieval culture, and it remained an important element of Polish literary expression during the Renaissance alongside the gradually expanding Polish vernacular idiom. It is not surprising, therefore, that Polish philologists showed their greatest concern for the classical languages and Polish. Some of them, however, also turned their attention to the vestiges of the Moravian mission in southern Poland, mindful of the passage in the *Vita Methodii* according to which the lands of the Polish Vistulans were converted to Christianity through the efforts of Methodius.[329] Of these, the most important contributions were made by Aleksander Brückner (1856–1939), who stressed the religious aspects of the Moravian mission, and Tadeusz Lehr-Spławiński (1891–1965), who studied the problem of the existence of the Cyrillo-Methodian tradition on the territory of Poland and published a reconstruction of the vitae of Constantine and Methodius. He also wrote on the development of Slavic studies in Polish universities.

329. The Vistulans occupied the lands along the Upper Vistula, including the towns of Cracow and Wiślica. Methodius' call, which is cited in 1.44, appears to have been motivated by religious as well as political aims.

APPENDIX B: CHRONOLOGICAL TABLE

Listed below are the most important dates of events and personalities mentioned in Chapter 1:

1st-c. B.C.–2nd-c. A.D.	The Veneti appear in the writings of the Roman historians (Cornelius Nepos, Pomponius Mela, Caesar, Pliny the Elder, Tacitus).
306–337	Rule of Constantine the Great, Roman (Byzantine) emperor and founder of Constantinople.
311–383	Ulfila (Wulfila), Arian bishop of the Visigoths. Inventor of the Gothic alphabet and translator of the Bible into Gothic (341–347).
325	Nicaean council of the Christian churches.
370	The Ostrogoths defeated by the Huns. Start of the Great Migrations.
379–395	Reign of Theodosius I the Great, Roman (Byzantine) emperor. Proclaimed Christianity the state religion.
ca. 385–460	Patrick, bishop and patron saint of Ireland.
434–453	Conquest of Central Europe by Attila's Huns.
448	The term *médos* 'mead' recorded in Pannonia by the Byzantine historian Priscus.
482–511	Reign of Clovis, Merovingian king of the Franks. Converted to Christianity ca. 500.
521–597	Columba, Irish missionary in Scotland.
538–594	Gregory of Tours, chronicler of the Merovingian Franks. Mentioned the Avar raids of 562 and 566 in Central Europe.
mid-6th c.	Jordanes, historian of the Goths. First to mention the Slavs (Sclaveni) in his *History of the Goths* and to identify the Veneti and the Antes as Slavic-speaking.
ca. 562	Death of Procopius of Caesarea, Byzantine historian. Described Slavic customs in the treatise *De bellis*.
568	Invasion of Italy by the Lombards and occupation of Pannonia by the Avars end the Great Migrations.

582–602	Reign of Maurice, Roman (Byzantine) emperor. Described Slavic war tactics in the *Strategikon*.
ca. 585	Death of John of Ephesus, Syriac historian. Described Slavic raids into Thrace, Macedonia, and Greece in *Ecclesiastical History*.
590–604	Pontificate of Gregory the Great. Mentioned the presence of the Slavs in Istria and Dalmatia in his correspondence.
610–641	Reign of Heraclius I, Roman (Byzantine) emperor. Involved in frequent conflicts with the Slavs. Settles the Croats and the Serbs in the Balkans.
624–659	Samo's Slavic state in Central Europe.
626	Constantinople besieged by the Avars and the Slavs.
673–754	Boniface (Winfrid), bishop and archbishop of the Carolingians. Organizer of the church in Franconia, Thuringia, and Bavaria (Salzburg, Freising, Regensburg, Passau). Some contacts with the northwestern Slavs.
679–681	Turkic-speaking Bulgars under Asparukh cross the Danube and settle in Thrace (modern Bulgaria).
ca. 720–ca. 790	Paul the Deacon, Lombard historian. Described a Slav raid into Benevento in his *History of the Lombards*.
ca. 743–748	Rule of Boruta, duke of Carantania.
746–784	Episcopate of Virgil in Salzburg.
751–768	Reign of Pepin the Short, king of the Franks.
ca. 751–769	Rule of Hotimir, duke of Carantania.
ca. 752–818	Theophanes the Confessor, Byzantine historian. Described the Bulgarian conquest of Dobrudja and the military encounters between the Slavs and the Byzantines in his *Chronographia*.
771–814	Reign of Charlemagne, king of the Franks. Crowned emperor of the Romans in 800.
777–802	Patriarchate of Paulinus II in Aquileia.
785–821	Episcopate (from 798 archiepiscopate) of Arno in Salzburg.
789	Charlemagne in alliance with the Obodrites and the Sorbs defeats the Veleti.
791–803	Charlemagne wages war on the Avars culminating in total annihilation of the Avar state.
811	Charlemagne decrees the border between the dioceses of Salzburg and Aquileia to be on the Drava.
814–840	Reign of Louis the Pious, Roman (Western) emperor.
ca. 816–885	Methodius, Byzantine churchman and missionary (from 873 archbishop) to the Slavs of Pannonia and Moravia.
ca. 825–846	Reign of Mojmir 1, duke of Moravia.
826–869	Constantine (Cyril) the Philosopher, Byzantine scholar and churchman. Together with his brother Methodius led the mission to the Slavs of Pannonia and Moravia.
829–836	Einhard composes the *Life of Charlemagne*.

842–867	Reign of Michael III, Roman (Byzantine) emperor.
843	Treaty of Verdun divides the Carolingian empire into western, middle, and eastern states, precursors of modern France, Italy, and Germany.
843–876	Reign of Louis I the German, king of the eastern Frankish state (825–843 duke of Bavaria).
846–870	Rule of Rostislav, duke of Moravia.
ca. 850	The *Bavarian Geographer* enumerates the Slavic tribes dwelling north of the Danube.
858–867	Pontificate of Nicholas I.
858–867, 878–886	Patriarchate of Photius in Constantinople.
859–873	Archiepiscopate of Adalwin in Salzburg.
860	Constantine and Methodius undertake their mission to the Khazars and find relics of Pope Clement I off the Crimean coast.
862	The legendary calling of the Varangians by the eastern Slavs.
863	Start of the mission of Constantine and Methodius to the Slavs of Moravia and Pannonia.
865	Khan Boris of Bulgaria (r. 852–889) adopts Christianity and assumes the Christian name of Michael.
867–872	Pontificate of Hadrian II.
868–869	Constantine and Methodius in Rome where Constantine dies.
870	Pope Hadrian II's bull *Gloria in excelsis* (preserved in Church Slavonic) to the dukes Rostislav, Svatopluk and Kocel.
871	Treatise *Conversio Bagoariorum et Carantanorum* affirming Salzburg's diocesan rights in Carantania.
871–894	Reign of Svatopluk, duke of Moravia.
872–882	Pontificate of John VIII.
876–880	Rule of Carlomann, duke of Bavaria.
876–882	Reign of Louis the Younger, king of the eastern Frankish state (Franconia and Saxony).
879	John VIII's bull *Predicationis tuae* to Methodius.
880	John VIII's bull *Industriae tuae* to Svatopluk.
880–893	Episcopate of Wiching in Nitra.
883	Christianity adopted in Bohemia under Bořivoj.
885–891	Pontificate of Stephen V.
885	Stephen V's bull *Quia te zelo* to Svatopluk. Methodius dies. Soon thereafter Methodius' mission expelled from Moravia.
889–893	Constantine of Preslav translates the *Homiliary Gospel.*
891–905	Rule of Spytihněv, duke of Bohemia.
893–927	Reign of Symeon I the Great, tsar of Bulgaria.
894–906	Rule of Mojmir II, duke of Moravia.
ca. 895	King Alfred (r. 872–899) translates the *A History concerning the Pagans* by Orosius, adding to it a list of West Slavic tribes.

896–909	Moravia defeated by the Magyars who settle in Pannonia.
899–911	Reign of Louis the Child. Division of East Frankish kingdom into Saxony, Franconia, Bavaria, Swabia, and Lorraine.
905–916	Rule of Vratislav, duke of Bohemia.
910	Death of Naum in Ohrid.
912	First treaty between Rus' and Byzantium.
916	Death of Clement of Ohrid.
916–ca. 929	Rule of Venceslas, duke of Bohemia (Drahomira acts as his regent till 922). Murdered by his brother Boleslav I.
919–936	Reign of Henry I the Fowler, king of Germany. Wars with the western Slavs.
920–972	Liudprand of Cremona, author of several historical works dealing with the times of Otto I.
ca. 929–967	Rule of Boleslav I, duke of Bohemia.
936–973	Reign of Otto I the Great, king (from 962 emperor) of Germany.
944–959	Reign of Constantine VII Porphyrogenitus, Roman (Byzantine) emperor. Described the route taken by the Varangians to Byzantium in *De administrando imperio.* Of special interest to Slavic philology is his reference to the names of the cataracts on the Dnieper.
945	Second treaty between Rus' and Byzantium.
957	Conversion of Olga, regent (945–964) for her son Svyatoslav I of Kiev.
ca. 960	Widukind of Corbea compiles his *History of the Saxons* dealing with the reigns of Henry I and Otto I and containing numerous references to the western Slavs.
ca. 960–992	Rule of Mieszko I, Polish duke. Adopts Christianity in 966.
964–972	Rule of Svyatoslav I of Kiev. Bulgaria occupied in 969–970.
965	Ibrāhīm ibn Ja'qūb's travels in Slavic lands.
968	Foundation of the archbishopric in Magdeburg. Missions to the western Slavs.
973–983	Reign of Otto II, emperor of Germany.
976–1014	Reign of Samuel, tsar of the West Bulgarian state.
983–1002	Reign of Otto III, emperor of Germany.
992–1025	Reign of Bolesław I the Brave, duke of Poland. Crowned king in 1025.
975–1018	Episcopate of Thietmar in Merseburg. West Slavs described in his *Chronicle* (1013–1018).
989	Christianity adopted by Vladimir I, duke of Kiev (r. 978–1015).
1018	Defeat and occupation of the first Bulgarian empire by the Byzantines.
1054	The Great Schism splits the Christian church into Western (Roman) and Eastern (Byzantine) branches.

1072–1076	Adam of Bremen compiles his *History of the Archbishops of Hamburg* with references to the Baltic and Polabian Slavs.
1110–1117	Anonymous Gallus compiles his *Polish Chronicle.*
ca. 1110	The *Primary Chronicle* compiled in Kiev.
ca. 1110–1125	Cosmas of Prague compiles his *Chronicle of the Czechs.*
1167–1172	Helmold compiles his *Chronicle of the Slavs.*

APPENDIX C: THE ORTHODOX CHURCH CALENDAR

The Orthodox church year is divided into two cycles: The movable (lunar) cycle is determined by Easter, which falls on the first Sunday after the first vernal (post-equinox) full moon (but not before Passover). The movable cycle begins seventy days before Easter Sunday, on the Sunday of the Publican and the Pharisee, and ends fifty-seven days after Easter Sunday, on the Sunday of All Saints (that is, one week after Pentecost or the Sunday of the Trinity, which follows Easter Sunday by fifty days). Easter Sunday divides the movable cycle into two periods, during which different liturgical books are in use. In the ten weeks preceding Easter Sunday the Lenten Triodion (*postьnaja triodь*) is used, while on Easter Sunday and in the following eight weeks it is replaced by the Festal Triodion (*cvětьnaja triodь*)[330] or *Pentecostarion*. During the Lenten Triodion period Sundays are the last days in the week, while during the Festal Triodion period Sundays begin the week.

The fixed (solar) cycle fills the remaining portion of the year. It is based on the Julian (old style) calendar, which lags thirteen days behind the Gregorian (new style) calendar adopted in the West and in some Orthodox churches. In the Julian calendar New Year's Day falls on September 1, while in the Gregorian calendar it falls on January 1.[331] The liturgical book used during the fixed cycle is the *octoechos* (*oktoixъ*).

Easter is the holiest feast of the Orthodox church. Next to it in importance are twelve major feasts (Russian *dvanadesjatye prazdniki*), of which three belong to the movable cycle:

(1) The Entry of Our Lord into Jerusalem or Palm Sunday (*Vъxodъ Gospodьnъ vъ Ierusalimъ*), one week before Easter
(2) The Ascension of Our Lord (*Vъznesenie Gospodьne*), forty days after Easter
(3) Pentecost or Trinity Sunday (*Pętidesętьnica* or *Troica*), fifty days after Easter

Nine major feasts belong to the fixed cycle:

(4) The Nativity of the Mother of God (*Roždьstvo Prěsvętoę Bogorodicę*), September 8
(5) The Exaltation of the Cross of Our Lord (*Vъzdviženie Krьsta Gospodьnja*), September 14
(6) The Presentation of the Mother of God in the Temple (*Vъvedenie vъ xramъ Prěsvętoę Bogorodicę*), November 21
(7) The Nativity of Christ (*Roždьstvo Xristovo*), December 25

330. In some traditions the Festal Triodion includes the prayers for the Holy Week beginning with Palm Sunday. This practice is perhaps reflected in the name *cvětьnaja triodь*.

331. In Rus', up to the mid-fourteenth century, the ancient Roman year beginning on March 1 was used; it was dubbed the "Paschal" year.

(8) The Baptism of Our Lord or Epiphany (*Krьščenie Gospodьne*), January 6
(9) The Presentation of Our Lord (*Sъrětenie Gospodьne*), February 2
(10) The Annunciation of the Mother of God (*Blagověščenie Prěsvętoę Bogorodicę*), March 25
(11) The Transfiguration of Our Lord (*Prěobraženie Gospodьne*), August 6
(12) The Dormition (or Assumption) of the Mother of God (*Usъpenie Prěsvętoę Bogorodicę*), August 15

Sundays and some of the weeks during the movable cycle have their own names (Flier 1984):

	SUNDAY	WEEK	SUNDAY
PRE-LENT			Publican and Pharisee
		Fast-free	Prodigal Son
		Meatfast	Meatfast
		Cheesefast (*Maslenica*)	Cheesefast
LENT		1. Theodore (Synod)	Triumph of Orthodoxy
		2.	Gregory Palamas
		3.	Adoration of the Cross
		4. Adoration of the Cross	John Climacus
		5. Laudation	Mary of Egypt
		6. Palm (Willow)	Palm (Willow)
		7. Holy	
EASTERTIDE	Easter	Bright (Easter)	
	Thomas		
	Myrrhophores		
	Paralytic		
	Samaritan Woman		
	Blind Man		
	Nicaean Fathers		
	Pentecost (Trinity)		
	All Saints[332]		

332. The Sunday following All Saints is dedicated to the celebration of the local saints.

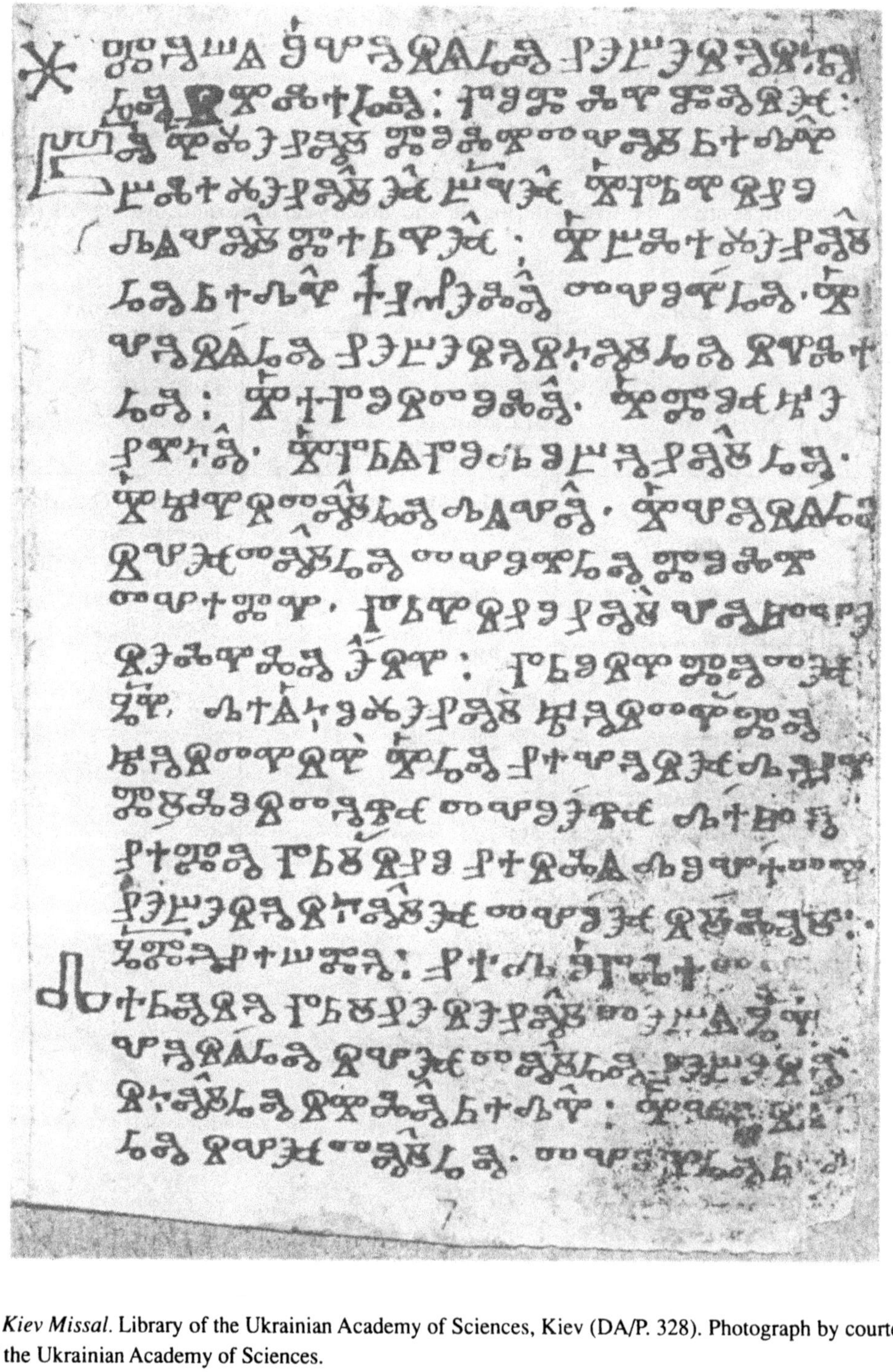

1. *Kiev Missal.* Library of the Ukrainian Academy of Sciences, Kiev (DA/P. 328). Photograph by courtesy of the Ukrainian Academy of Sciences.

APPENDIX D: SAMPLES OF EARLY SLAVIC WRITING

Specimens of several early Slavic texts, in Glagolitic, Cyrillic, and Roman alphabets are provided below in facsimile, transliteration or modified transcription, and translation. Resolved abbreviations and superposed letters are transcribed in parentheses; added or reconstructed segments are bracketed.

Glagolitic

1. The *Kiev Missal* (**3.41.5**), also known as the *Kiev Fragments* or *Kiev Folios,* is a seven-folio fragment of a Western-rite sacramentary from the end of the tenth or beginning of the eleventh century. The missal represents the oldest extant type of half-rounded Glagolitic writing. Reproduced here is folio 7r with the text of the Mass for All the Celestial Virtues:[333]

[Transliteration]	[Translation]
*MЬŠĚ Ȯ VЬŠĚ́XЪ NEBESЬSKЪI	MASS FOR ALL THE CELESTIAL
XЪ SILAXЪ : Pom(o)limъ sę :˙	VIRTUES. Let us pray.
B(og)ъ ỉže nъì molitvъi radî	God, who because of the prayer
blaženъ̂ię̂ b(ogorodi)cę̂ ỉ prisno	of the blessed Mother of God and ever
děvъ̂i marię̂ : ỉ blaženъ̂i	virgin Mary, and because of
xъ radî ȃng'elъ̂ tvoíxъ ·ỉ	your blessed angels and
vьsě́xъ nebesьskъixъ sila	of all the celestial virtues,
xъ : ỉ apostolъ̂ · ỉ mǫče	and of the apostles and martyrs,
nikъ̂ · ỉ prěpodobьnъ̂ixъ ·	and of the holy
i čistъ̂ixъ děvъ̂ · ỉ vъsě́xъ	and pure virgins, and with the
svętъ̂ixъ tvoixъ moli	prayers of all your saints,
tvami · prisno nъì vъzve	have caused us ever to
selilъ ě̂si : prosimъ tę	rejoice, we ask you
g(ospod)i · da ě̂kože nъì čьstĭmъ	o, Lord, that we may celebrate
čьsti sỉixъ na vъsę dьni	their festivals on all days.
milostьjǫ tvoéjǫ dázь	With your grace let
námъ prĭsno naslědováti ·	us ever follow
nebesьskъ̂ię tvóę sílъi :	your celestial virtues.
g(ospodь)mъ naš(i)mь : NAD	By our Lord. OVER THE
ȮPLAT(O)MЬ :	OBLATION.

333. The supralinear marks of the *Kiev Folios* have not yet received a satisfactory interpretation. The nominal phrase in line 7 should be genitive rather than locative.

Darъ sь prinesenѣ̂i tebě g(ospod)i	This gift brought to you o, Lord,
vьsě́xъ svętѣ̂ixъ nebesь	because of all the holy
skѣ̂ixъ sılѣ̂ radî: ſvъsě	celestial virtues and of all
xъ svętѣ̂ixъ · tvoıxъ radı	your saints

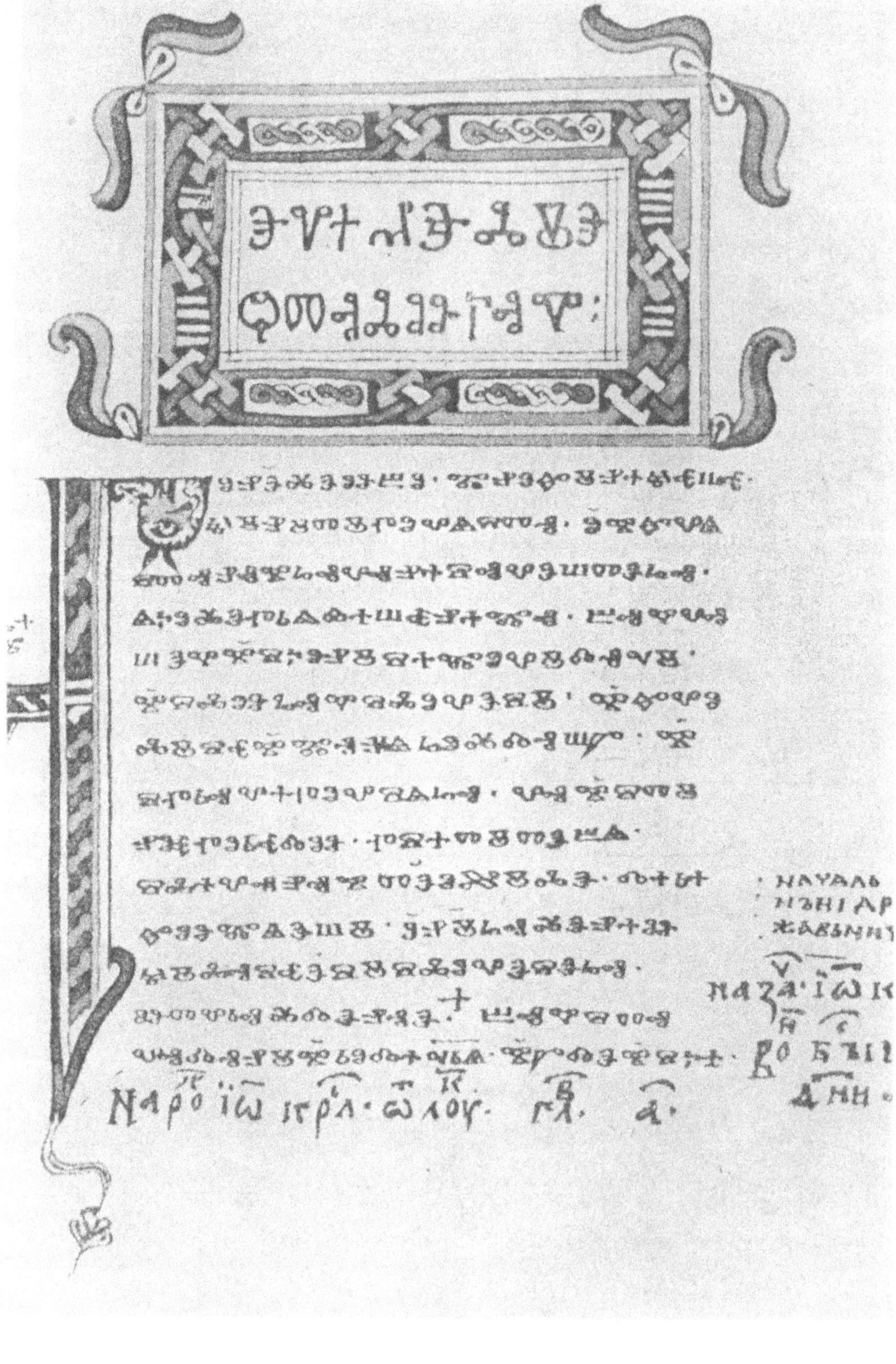

2. *Codex Zographensis*. National Library of Russia, Saint Petersburg (Glag. 1). Photograph by Sean Kernan from Vajs 1932.

2. The *Codex Zographensis* (**3.42**) is a Macedonian fourfold Gospel from the end of the tenth or beginning of the eleventh century. Folio 131r contains the beginning of the Gospel of Luke (1.1–5).[334] The recognized antiquity of the phonetic features of the *Zographensis* includes consistent marking of the softness of *n'* (*pon'eže, o n'ixъže*). On the other hand, note the omission of the jers within roots (*mnozi, vsěxъ, psati*) and the replacement of *ь* by *ъ* in the adjectival suffix *-ьn-* (*izvěstъnъıxъ, slavъnъı*). On the right margin of the folio there is a Cyrillic notation which appears to be as old as the codex itself consisting of a two-word vocative expression, *načNlьnъıı dr[ь]žavьnič[e]* 'O, supreme Master!'. Below it and at the bottom of the page there is a later addition in red ink identifying the day on which the church calendar prescribes the reading of this portion of the Gospel, which shows that the tetra was also used as a full lectionary Gospel (evangeliary). A cross is inscribed slightly above the line at the beginning of verse 5 (line 15).

[Transliteration]	[Translation]
EVAG'ELIE	GOSPEL
ŎT LOUKЪI:	OF LUKE:
[1] Pon'eže ubo · mnozi načNšN ·	[1] Forasmuch as many have begun
činiti pověstь · ŏ ızvě	to compose a tale about
stъnъıxъ vъ nasъ veštexъ ·	things well known among us,
[2] ěkože prědašN namъ · bъıvъ	[2] Even as they delivered them unto
šeı ĭskoni samovidьci ·	us, who from the beginning were eye
ĭ slugъı slovesi · [3] ĭzvo	witnesses and ministers of the word;
li sN ĭ mьně xoždьšü · ĭ	[3] It also seemed good to me, having
sprъva po vsěxъ vъ ĭsti	had firsthand knowledge of all this,
nǫ po rędu psati tebe ·	to write to you in order,
slavъnъı ĭeofile · [4] da ra	most excellent Theophilus, [4] so that
zuměeši · ŏ n'ixъže nau	you will understand the certainty
čilъ sN ěsi slovesexъ ·	about the words about which you
utvrъždenьe · + [5] bъıstъ	have learned. [5] There was
vъ dьni ĭroda c(ěsa)rě · ĭüdeĭska ·	in the days of Herod, the king of Judea,

334. Here and in other examples, the text of the Gospels is segmented and numbered according to the system devised by the deacon Ammonius of Alexandria (second–third centuries). Ammonius' system was used in Slavic manuscripts up to the seventeenth century, when it was replaced by the now familiar segmentation into chapters as proposed in 1205 by Stephen Langton, archbishop of Canterbury (1207–1228). The segmentation into verses was introduced in 1551 by the Parisian printer Robert Stephane.

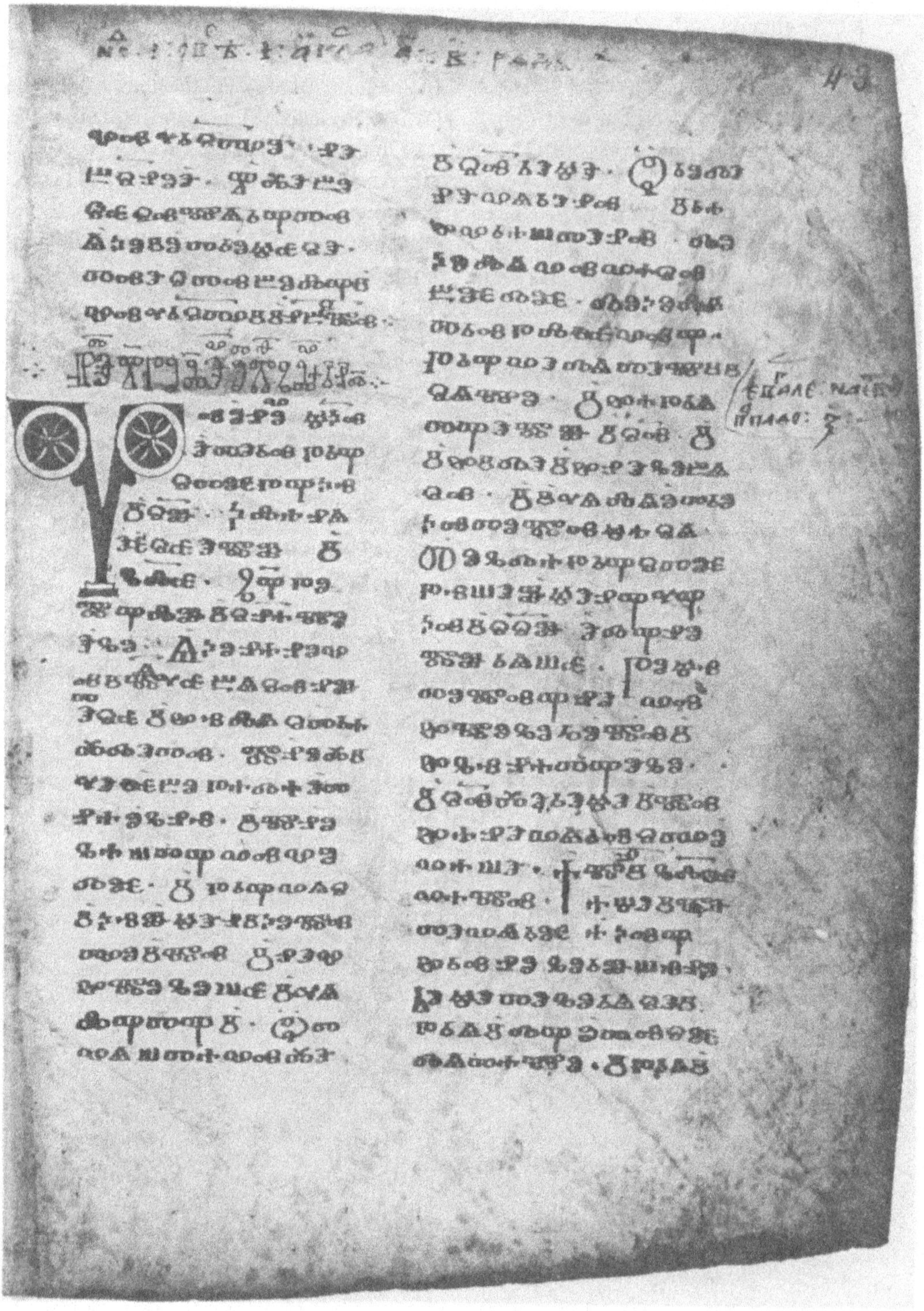

3. *Codex Assemanianus*. Vatican Library (Cod. Vat. Slav. 3). Photograph by courtesy of Aksinia Džurova.

3. The *Codex Assemanianus* (**3.41.1**) is a Macedonian evangeliary of the eleventh century written in classical rounded Glagolitic letters. Folio 43r contains portions of readings for the tenth Saturday and Sunday after Pentecost (the end of a reading from Matthew 18 and the first part of a reading from Matthew 17). Among the spelling peculiarities of the monument, note especially the non-etymological use of the jers: *ь* written after *k* and g, *ъ* written for *ь* after *r*, omission of weak jers in line-final position, random confusion of the jers (*zьlě*). At the top of the folio there is a Cyrillic note specifying the day of the week and the tone: *ne(dělja)* · ı : *svě(s)*[335] · ı : *a gla(s) a* : : *v̈* : *rędь* : - 'the tenth week, the tenth *světilьnъ*, and the first tone of the second row [i.e., the fifth tone]'. Another Cyrillic note was added in the right margin: *eva(nge)le* : *na ev(t)ap(a)pado* : *z̄* : - 'Gospel for *heptapápadon* 7'. The Greek term *heptapápadon* 'that which is consecrated by seven priests' refers to holy oil used in the administration of extreme unction.[336]

[Transliteration]	[Translation]
a	**a**
[**Matt. 18.3**] vъ c(ěsarъ)stvo ne	[**Matt. 18.3**] "into the Heavenly
b(e)snoe · [**4**] ıže bo	Kingdom. [**4**] But he who
sN sъměrıtъ	will humble himself
ěko ī otročN se ·	like this child,
tъ ēstъ bolıi	he is the greatest
vъ c(ěsa)rstvii n(e)b(esьněe)mъ	in the Heavenly Kingdom."
NE(DĚLJA Ī PO L̂ E(VANG'ELIE)	10th SUNDAY AFTER 50 [PENTECOST]
O(T) M(ATΘEJA) GL(AV)A R̂N̂D̂ · : -	GOSPEL ACCORDING TO MATTHEW
	CHAPTER 175
Vъ ōno (vrěmę) [**Matt. 17.14**] č(lově)kъ	At that time [**Matt. 17.14**] a
ēterъ prı	man came
stǫpı kь	up to
is(us)u · Klaně	Jesus bowing
ę̄ sN emu ī	to Him and
gl(agol)N · [**15**] G(ospod)ı po	saying, [**15**] "Lord,
mıluī s(y)na mo	have mercy on my
ego · Ěko na nov	son, for he is
ъi m(ěsę)cN běsъnu	moonstruck[337]
e(tъ) sN ī zьlě str̄a	and suffers
ždetъ · mn̄oži	greatly, For he
cejǭ bo padaēt	often falls
na ógnь · ī mn̄o	into fire and
gaštı vъ vo	often into
dǫ · [**16**] Ī pr ıvěs	water. [**16**] And I brought
ī kь učenikomъ	him to your
tvoīmъ Ī ne v	disciples and they

335. For expected *svět*, which stands for *světilьnъ*, that is, a troparion asking for light and enlightenment, chanted during the morning service after the last (ninth) canticle of the canon.

336. The note marks the verse of the Gospel that is recited by the priest administering the sacrament. Such Cyrillic notes, occurring throughout the monument, suggest that for a time Glagolitic and Cyrillic were used concurrently in the liturgy.

337. Literally, 'on new moons he is possessed'.

zmogošN īcě
lıtı ī · [**17**]ŏt
věštavъ že

b

ī(su)sъ reče · Ȏ rode
nevěrenъ ī ra
zvraštenъ · do
kolě vъ vasъ
bǫdǫ · do kolě
trъpljǫ vъı ·
prıveděte mi ī
sěmo · [**18**] Ī zaprě
tı ēmu ī[su]sъ · Ī
īzide ȉz nego bě
sъ · Ī īcělě otro
kъ tomъ časě ·
[**19**] T̃ogda prıstǫ
pьše ūčenıcı
kь is(u)su édıno
mu rěšN · Po čь
to mъı ne vъ
zmogoxomъ ī
zgьnatı ēgo ·
[**20**] I(su)sъ že reče īmъ
za nevěrьstvo
vaše · Āmi(n) g(lago)ljǫ
vamъ · āšte ima
te věrǫ ākъı
zrъno gorušьno ·
Rečete gorě seī ·
preīdı ótъ sǫ
dě tamo · i prěī
[detъ]

could not
cure him."
[**17**] And answering

b

Jesus said, "O faithless
and perverse
generation! How
long shall I be
among you? How long
shall I suffer you?
Bring him to me
hither." [**18**] And Jesus
rebuked him [the devil]. And
the devil departed out of
him. And the child
was cured that very hour.
[**19**] Then the disciples
having come up
to Jesus [when he was] alone,
said, "Why
[is it that] we
could not
cast him out?"
[**20**] And Jesus said to them,
"Because of your unbelief.
Verily I say
to you, if you have
[as little] faith as
a grain of mustard seed,
you will say to this mountain,
'Move from here
to there,' and it will
[move]."

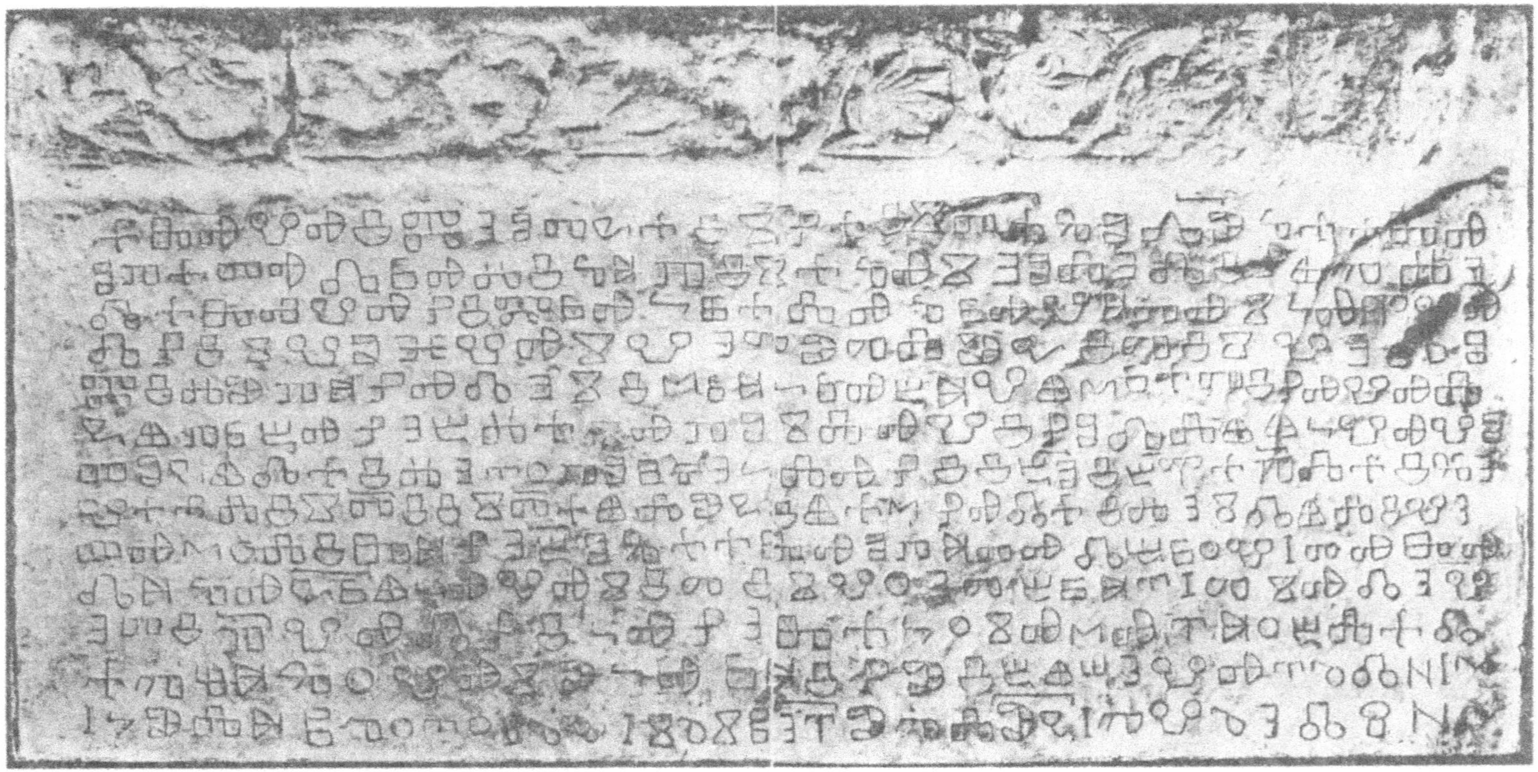

4. *Baška Stone*. Croatian Academy of Sciences, Zagreb. Photograph by Sean Kernan from a reconstruction in Katičić/Novak 1988.

4. The *Baška Stone* contains an inscription from about 1100 affirming a land donation made by the Croatian king Zvonimir to the parish of St. Lucia on the island of Krk. The Baška inscription exhibits features of Church Slavonic of Croatian recension, writing *(j)u* for *(j)ǫ*, *e* for *ę*, *i* for y, and using one jer only (ъ). It provides the only example of transition from Glagolitic of the rounded Macedonian type to the angular Croatian alphabet.[338]

[Transliteration]

✢ . . . [vъ ime ot]ca i sina [i sve]tago duxa azъ
opat[ъ] drъžixa pisaxъ se o ledině juže
da zvъnъmirъ kralъ xrъvatъskъ[i vъ]
dni svoę vъ svet[uju] luciju i s[vedo]
mi županъ desimra krъbavě mra[tin]ъ vъ l[i]
cě pr(ez)b(itr)ъ neb(o)gъ a . . . ъ posl . . . vin . . . lě . . . vъ . . . v o
tocě da iže to por(e)če klъni i bo(gъ) i 12 a(posto)la i 4 e
va(n)g'(e)listi i s(ve)taě luciě am(e)nъ da iže sdě žive
tъ moli za ne boga azъ opatъ d(o)brovitъ zъ
daxъ crěkъvъ siju i svoeju bratiju sъ dev
etiju vъ dni kъneza kosъmъta oblad
ajucágo vъsu kъrainu i běše vъ tъ dnim
ikula vъ octočъci sъ svetuju luciju vъ edino

[Translation]

✢ . . . In the name of the Father and the Son and the Holy Ghost, I,
abbott Drъžixa, wrote this concerning the land which
Zvonimir, the Croatian king, gave in
his days to St. Lucia. And the witnesses [were]
župan Desimir in Krbava, Martin in Lika,
the unworthy priest . . . [?] in
Otok. Whoever denies this, let him be cursed by God and the twelve apostles and the four
evangelists and Saint Lucia. Amen. And whoever lives here
let him pray for it to God. I, abbot Dobrovit,
built this church with nine of my brethren
in the days of prince Cosmas ruling
over the entire province. And in those days [the parish of St.]
Nicholas in Otočac was joined with [the parish of] St. Lucia.

338. The inscription is generally well preserved. There are, however, several places where individual letters and even words cannot be made out with certainty, leading to variant readings. I have adopted here some of the reconstructions proposed by Hamm 1952 and Fučić 1971. In line 1 the letter ✢, symbolizing the cross, appears to be followed by a numeral (date?). The second half of line 6 is too damaged to allow verifiable interpretations.

5. *Hum Graffito*. Church of Saint Jerome, Hum, Istria. Photograph by Sean Kernan from Katičić/Novak 1988. Tracing from Fučić 1971.

5. The *Hum Graffito* was discovered in 1949 by Branko Fučić among the frescoes of the Church of St. Jerome in the village of Hum in Istria and may be dated from the end of the twelfth or beginning of the thirteenth century. It represents an attempt by the church priest to keep count of the masses said for the eternal rest of one of his parishioners, a certain Martin the smith. The priest marked the number of masses by making notches on the wall next to the altar and added the following reminder to himself (Fučić 1971:252–254, Katičić and Novak, eds. 1988:35):

[Transliteration]	[Translation]
Kovača Marъtine e svě g' e vzeta ino oš̑te edna	For Martin the smith 30 [masses] altogether. [An obligation to say] one more has been taken.

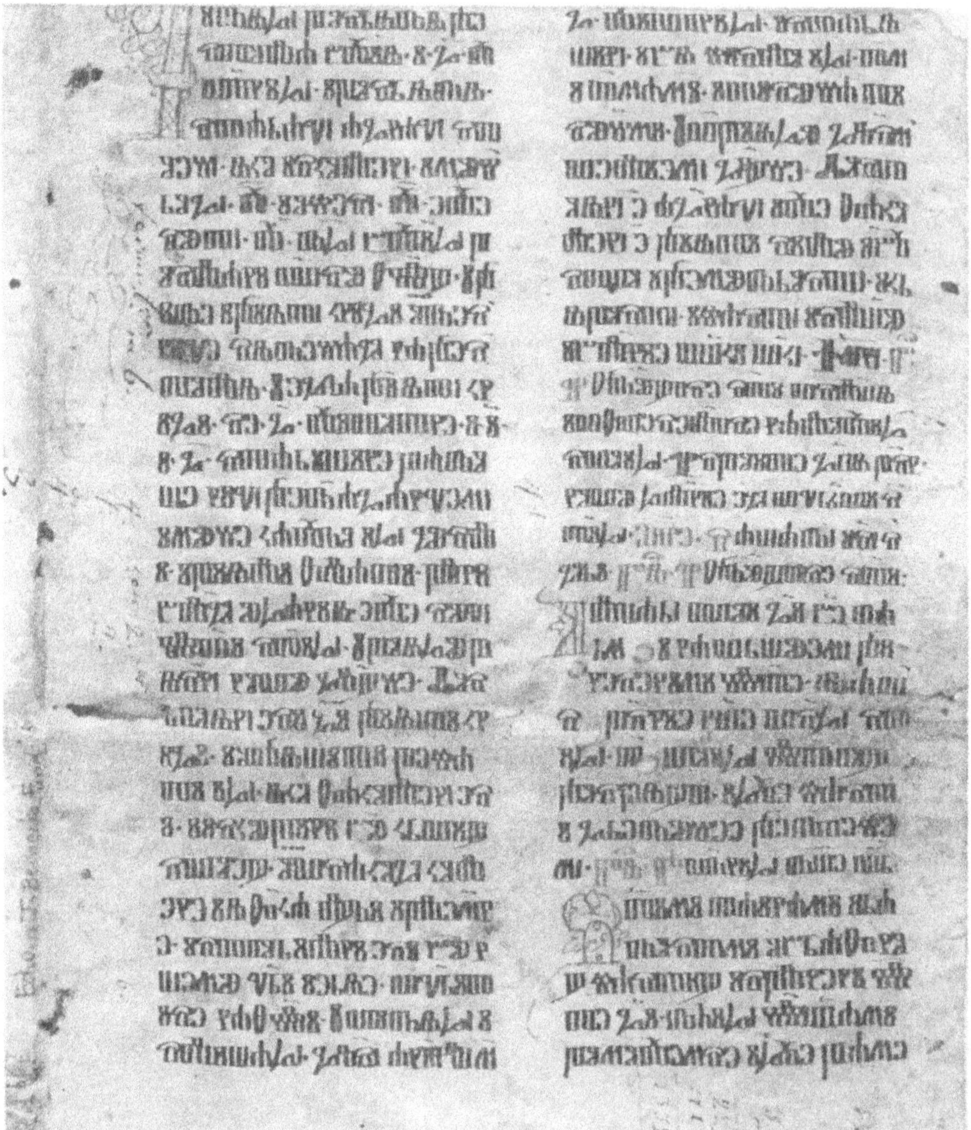

6. *Beinecke Glagolitic Fragment*. Beinecke Library, Yale University, New Haven, Conn. Photograph by Sean Kernan.

6. The *Beinecke Glagolitic Fragment* is a bifolium containing a fragment of a Croatian missal of the late fourteenth or early fifteenth century housed in the Beinecke Rare Book and Manuscript Library at Yale University. Note the features of the Croatian recension of Church Slavonic: *i* for y , *e* for *ę*, *u* for *ǫ*, *ć* for LPSl. *t'*, one-jer (ь) orthography, *a* for the jers in strong position. The writing is angular Glagolitic with many ligatures, typical of Croatia from the fourteenth century on. Folio 1, columns a and part of b, contain the reading for the Vigil of All Saints (Revelation 5.6–12):

[Transliteration]	[Translation]
a	
[**6** Se azь v]	[**6** and I]
iděxь po srědě pre	beheld in the midst of the
stola b(o)žiě · i · g̑ ž	divine throne and of the four
iv(o)tnixь · i po srědě ·	beasts, and in the midst
starась agnacь st	of the elders, a Lamb standing,
oečь · ěkȯ iskolenь · imuć'	as [it had been] slaughtered, having
rogь · ž̑ · i očesь · ž̑ · eže	seven horns and seven eyes which
sutь · ž̑ · d(u)xь b(o)žixь po	are the seven Spirits of God sent
slani v(ь) vsu z(e)mlju · [**7**] I pr	forth into all the earth. [**7**] And he
ide i priětь knigi o(t) des	came and took the book from the right
nice sědėćago na pres	hand of him sitting upon the throne.
tolě · [**8**] I egda prietь kn	[**8**] And when he had taken the
igi · se · g̑ · životne · i · ȋ ·	book, lo, the four beasts and twenty
i · g̑ · starišine pado	and four elders fell
še nicь pred(ь) agancemь	down before the Lamb,
imuće každo ixь gusl	each having a harp
i · i piěli zlati · plni	and golden vials full of
bl(a)gouxaniě eže sutь	aroma which are the
m(o)l(it)vi s(ve)tixь ·[**9**] i poěxu p	prayers of saints. [**9**] And they sang
ěsnь novu gl(agol)juće · Dos	a new song saying, "You are
toěnь esi g(ospod)i priěti kn	worthy, o Lord, to take the
igi · i otrěšiti peča	book and to open
ti ixь · ěko zakolenь es	its seals; for you were slaughtered and
i · i iskupi ni b(og)u krviju	with your blood redeemed us for God,
svoeju · o(t) vsakogo kol	[men] from every tribe
ene i ěz(i)ka ljudi i plem(e)n	and tongue, people and nation."
e · [**10**] i stvoril ni esi b(og)u n(a)	[**10**] and have made us unto our God
šemu c(ěsa)ri i erěe · vc(ěsa)rit	emperors and priests to reign
i se na z(e)mli · [**11**] I viděxь i	on the earth. [**11**] And I beheld and
slišaxь · gl(a)sь ang'(e)lь m[nozixь]	heard the voice of many angels
b	
[okolo prěstola i]	[around the throne and of]
g̑ · živ(o)tnixь · i starě	the four beasts and the elders.
šinь · i bě čislo ixь · t'm	And the number of them was multitudes
i t'mami · i tisuća ti	of multitudes and a thousand of
suć(a)mi ·[**12**] I v'piěxu gl(a)s(o)m'	thousands. [**12**] And they cried with a

veliemь g(lago)ljuće · Dost
oěnь e(stь) ag(a)nacь iže zako
lenь e(stь) priěti silu i b(o)ž
stvo i premudrostь i kr
epostь · i častь i sl(a)vu
i bl(agoslove)nie v v(ě)ki v(ě)kь ·

loud voice saying, "Worthy
is the Lamb that was slaughtered
to receive power, and Godliness,
and wisdom, and strength
and honor, and glory,
and blessing for ever and ever.

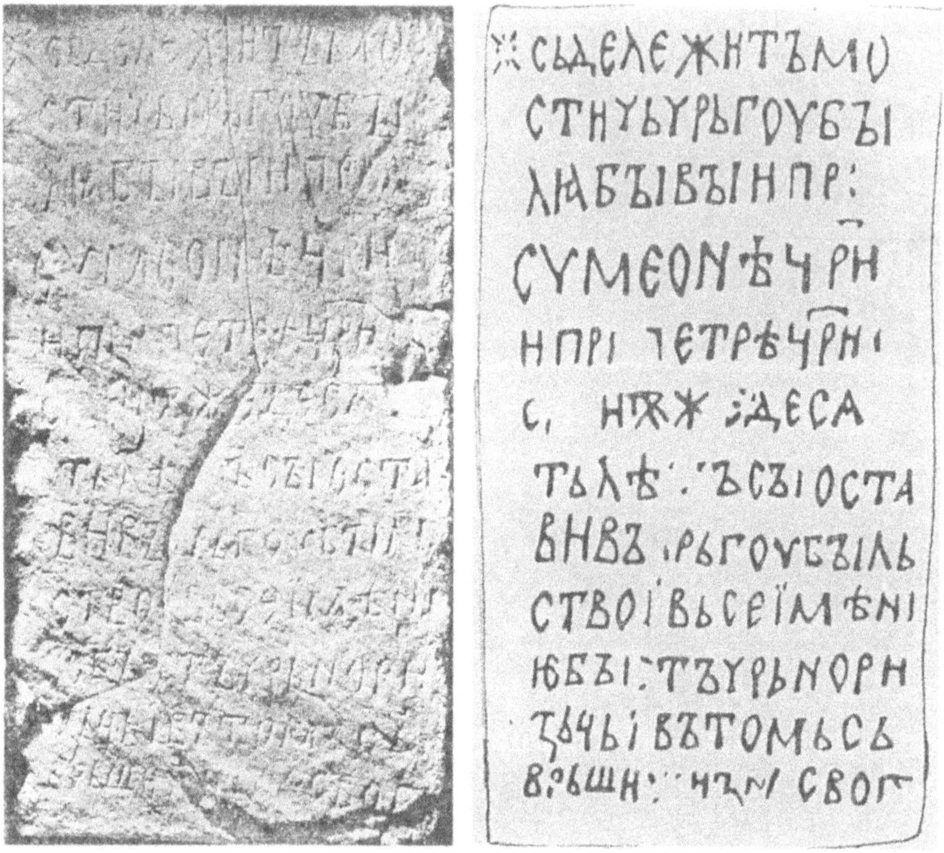

7. *Mostič's Inscription*. National History Museum, Sofia. Photographs by Sean Kernan from Ivanova 1955. Tracing from Stojanov/Janakiev 1960.

Cyrillic

1. *Mostič's Inscription* (**3.53**) is inscribed on the slab covering the tomb of a certain Mostič, who was a *črgubylja*[339] during the reign of the Bulgarian kings Symeon (893–927) and Peter (927–969). It was found in 1952 in Preslav, the ancient capital of Bulgaria.

[Transliteration]	[Translation]
sьde ležitъ mo	Here lies
stičь črъgoubъı	Mostič, who was
lja bъıvъıi pr(i)	črgubylja at [the time of]
sümeonĕ c(ĕsa)ri	King Symeon
i pri petrĕ c(ĕsa)ri o	and King Peter.
s(m)njǫ že desę	Being eighty years
tь lĕtъ sъı osta	old, having given
vivъ črъgoubъılь	up the [rank of] črgubylja
stvo ï vьse ımĕni	and all possesions,
je bъıstъ črъnori	he became a monk
zьcь ı vъ tomь sь	and thus
vrъši žiznь svojǫ	ended his life.

339. Apparently a Proto-Bulgarian official rank, but the exact meaning of this term is not known.

8. *Samuel's Inscription*. National History Museum, Sofia. Photographs by Sean Kernan from Ivanova 1955. Tracing from Karskij 1928.

2. *Samuel's Inscription* (**3.53**) is inscribed on the tombstone that Tsar Samuel (976–1014) placed over the grave of his parents and brother in 6501 (992/993). It is thus the only dated Old Church Slavonic text. It was found in 1898 on Lake Prespa in northern Greece and is now preserved in the National History Museum in Sofia. The names of Samuel's family are confirmed or reconstructed on the basis of information provided by the eleventh-century Byzantine chronicler John Scylitzes. Samuel was the youngest son of Nicholas and Ripsimia; his three brothers were David, Moses, and Aaron.[340]

[Transliteration]	[Translation]
+ Vъ imę ōtьca i sъ	In the name of the Father and
ina i s(vę)tago douxa a	the Son and the Holy Ghost, I
zъ Samoipь[341] rabъ b(o)ž[ii]	Samuil, God's servant,
polagaǫ pamętь [otьc]	place the memorial to my
u i materi i brat[u n]	father and mother and brother.
a krъstěxъ si[xъ že]	And at baptism
imena ousъpъš[ixъ ni]	the names of the deceased
kola rabъ boži[i ripsimi]	Nicholas, God's servant, Ripsimia,
ě davdъ napisa[xъ se vъ]	David. I wrote this in the
lěto otъ sъtvo[reniě miro]	year from the creation of the
u ҂ꙃ͡· : f͡a · inъdi[kta . . .]	world 6501, indiction . . .

340. It was Tsar Samuel who built up the Western Bulgarian kingdom (modern Macedonia). His defeat at the hands of the Byzantines in 1014 in the mountain pass of Kleidion in the Belašica range culminated in one of the most gruesome episodes in all history: Emperor Basil II had the Bulgarian captives (some fourteen thousand) blinded, except that one man in every hundred was left with one eye in order to be able to lead the rest back to Samuel.

341. Over *p*, which was incised by mistake, there is a faint image of a correction to *l*.

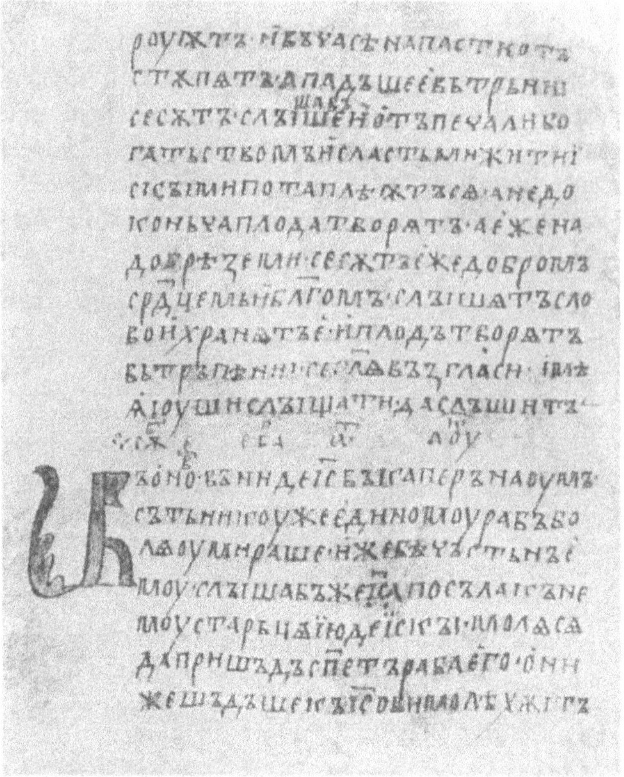

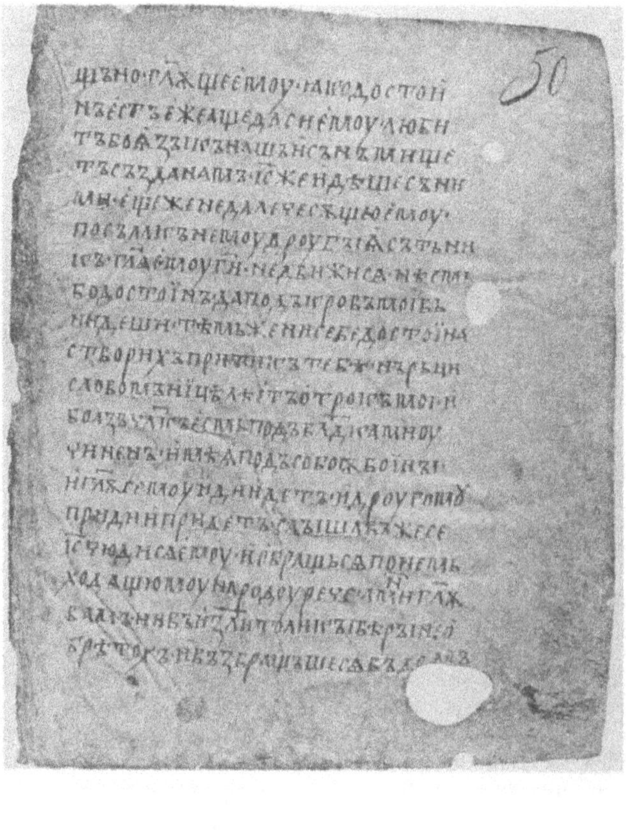

9. *Sava's Book*. Central State Archive of Ancient Documents (CGADA), Moscow (*Fond* 381, No. 14). Photographs by Sean Kernan from Karskij 1928 and Ščepkin 1901.

3. *Sava's Book* is a short evangeliary of the eleventh century transcribed from a lost Glagolitic text. Folios 49v lower half and 50r contain the parable of the healing of the centurion's ailing servant (Luke 7.1–10), which is the reading for the fifth Saturday of the new year:[342]

[Transliteration]

49v

Vъ ono (vrěmę) · [**1**] vъnide ı(su)s(ъ) vъ kaperъnaoumъ ·
[**2**] sъtьnikou že edinomou rabъ bo
lę oumiraše · iže bě čъstьnъ e
mou · [**3**] slъıšavъ že ı(su)sa posъla kъ ne
mou starъcę ïjudeïskъı · molę sę
da prišъdъ sp(as)etъ raba ego · [**4**] oni
že šъdъše kъ ı(su)sovi molěxǫ ı tъ

50r

š͡tъno · g(lago)lǫ͡šte emou · jako dostoi
nъ estъ eže a͡šte dasi emou · [**5**] ljubi
tъ bo ęzъıkъ našъ i sъnъmište
tъ sъzda namъ · [**6**] ı[su]s[ъ] že iděše sъ ni
mi · e͡šte že ne daleče sǫ͡štju emou ·
posъla kъ nemou drugъıę sъtni
kь · g(lago)lę emu g(ospod)i · ne dviži sę · něsmь
bo dostoïnь · da podъ krovъ moı vь
nideši · [**7**] těmь že ni sebě dostoïna
stvorixъ priti kъ tebě · nъ rъci
slovomъ i ïcělěetъ otrokъ moı [**8**] i
bo azъ čl(ově)kъ esmь podъ vl(a)d(ъı)kami ou
činenъ · iměę podъ sobojǫ voïnъı ·
i g(lago)lǫ semou idi idetъ · i drougomou
pridi i pridetъ · [**9**] slъıšavъ že se
ı(su)s(ъ) čjudi sę emou · i obra͡štь sę po nemь
xodę͡štjumou narodou reče · ami(nъ) g(lago)lǫ
vamъ · ni vъ iz(drai)li tolikъı věrъı ne o
brětoxъ · [**10**] i vъzvra͡štъše sę vъ domъ
[poslanıı · obrětǫ bolę͡štago raba · icělěvъša :]

[Translation]

49v

At that time [**1**] Jesus entered Capernaum.
[**2**] And a certain centurion's servant,
who was dear to him, was sick and dying.
[**3**] And hearing of Jesus, he sent to him

342. Line 12 of folio 49v is in faded red. The letter *s* in *semu* (folio 50r, line 14) was corrected from ı. This and other such corrections suggest that *Sava's Book* was transcribed from Glagolitic, with the scribe confusing Glagolitic Ⰼ (s) with Glagolitic Ⰻ (ı); see Ščepkin 190 1:III–VI.

the elders of the Jews, beseeching [him] to come and save his servant. [**4**] And they, having come to Jesus, asked him

50r

earnestly, saying to him that he to whom you might grant [this] was worthy. [**5**] "For he loves our nation and he has built a synagogue for us." [**6**] And Jesus went with them. And when he was not too far, the centurion sent friends to him saying to him, "Lord, do not trouble yourself, for I am not worthy that you should enter under my roof. [**7**] And this is why I did not deem myself worthy of coming to you. But say in a word, and my servant will be healed. [**8**] For I am a man placed under commanders, having soldiers under me. And I say to one, 'Go!' [and] he goes, and to another, 'Come!' and he comes." [**9**] And hearing this, Jesus marveled at him and turning toward the people following him, said, "Amen, I say to you, not even in Israel have I found so much faith." [**10**] And returning to the house, [the messengers found the ailing servant healed.]

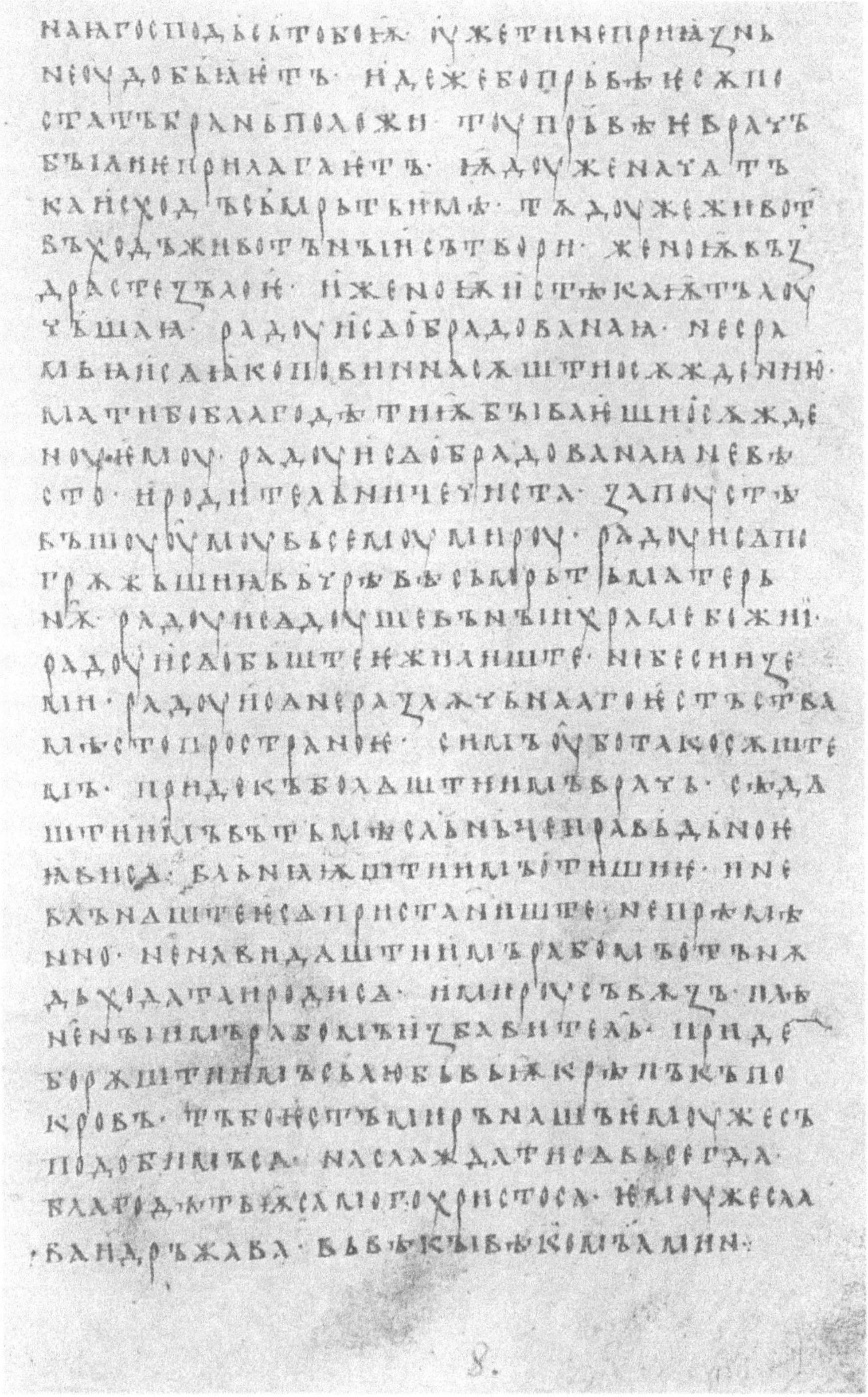

10. *Codex Suprasliensis*. National Library of Russia, Saint Petersburg (Q.p.I. 72). Photograph by courtesy of Aksinia Džurova.

4. The *Codex Suprasliensis* (**3.44**) is an East Bulgarian menaeum of the eleventh century for the month of March. Chapter 21 contains a homily for the feast of the Annunciation attributed to John Chrysostom. The Slavic translation departs here and there from the Greek text as given in Migne 60, pp. 791–796. Reproduced here is the final part of the homily (folio 8r of the seventeenth *tetradion*):

[Transliteration]

[Radouí sN óbradova]
naja gospodь sь tobojǫ̂ · ouže ti neprijâznь
ne oudobьjájétъ · íde že bo prьvěje sǫpo
statъ branь položi · tou prьvěje vračъ
bъılije prilagajétъ · jǫ̂dou že načNtъ
ka isxodъ sьmrъtь imě · tǫdou že život'
vъxodъ životъnъıi sъtvori · ženojǫ̂ vъz'
draste zъlojé · i ženojǫ̂ ístěkajǫ̂tъ lou
čьšaja · radouí sN óbradovanaja · ne sra
mьjaí sN jáko povinna sǫšti ósǫždenijû ·
mati bo blagodětijǫ̂ bъıvajéši ósǫžde
noujému · radouí sN óbradovanajá nevě
sto · í roditelьnice čista · zapoustě
vъšouoûmu vьsemou mirou · radouí sN po
grǫžьšija vь črěvě sьmьrtь materь
nǫ̂ · radouí sN douševъnъıì xrame božiï ·
radouí sN óbьšteje žilište · nebesi í ze
mi · radouí sN nerazlǫčьnaago jéstъstva
města prostranojé · simъ ôubo tako sǫšte
mъ · pride kъ bolęštiímъ vračь · sědN
štiímъ vь tьmě slьnьce pravьdьnojė
jávi sN · vlъnjajǫ̂štiímъ ótišije · i ne
vlъnNštejé sN pristanište · neprěmě
nno · nenavidNštiímъ rabomъ ótъnǫ
dь xodatai rodi sN · í mirou sъvǫzъ · plě
nênъıímъ rabomъ izbavitelь · pride
borǫštiimъ sь ljubьvьjǫ̂ krěpъkъ po
krovъ · tъ bo jéstъ mirъ našъ jémouže sъ
podobimъ sN · naslaždati sN vьsegda ·
blagodětьjǫ̂ samogo xristosa · jémouže sla
va í drъžava · vъ věkъı věkomъ áminъ ·:·

[Translation]

[Hail, favored woman!]
Lord be with you! Disfavor is no longer
over you. For wherever the enemy [devil]
first placed his curse, there the physician first
applies the remedy. For whence
from the beginning death issued, there life
created a vital entrance. Through woman

evil grew, and through woman the better things
gush forth. Hail, favored woman! Do not be
ashamed as if deserving of condemnation!
For through grace you are becoming mother of the
condemned. Hail, favored bride
and pure progenitrix of all the
blighted world! Hail, you
who have buried in your womb mother's death!
Hail, spiritual temple of God!
Hail, common dwelling-place of heaven
and earth! Hail, limitless space of indivisible
being! For because of this
the physician has come to the sick;
to those sitting in darkness the sun of righteousness
has appeared; to those tossed by waves—a shelter
and becalmed harbor; to the ever-
hating[343] slaves from now on
a defender and a bond of peace is born;
to the enslaved the Redeemer has come;
to those who struggle—a fortress.
For He is our peace, and may we
be like Him to take delight always
by grace of Christ Himself! To whom
be glory and power for ever and ever! Amen.

343. In Greek *misouménois* 'to the hated'.

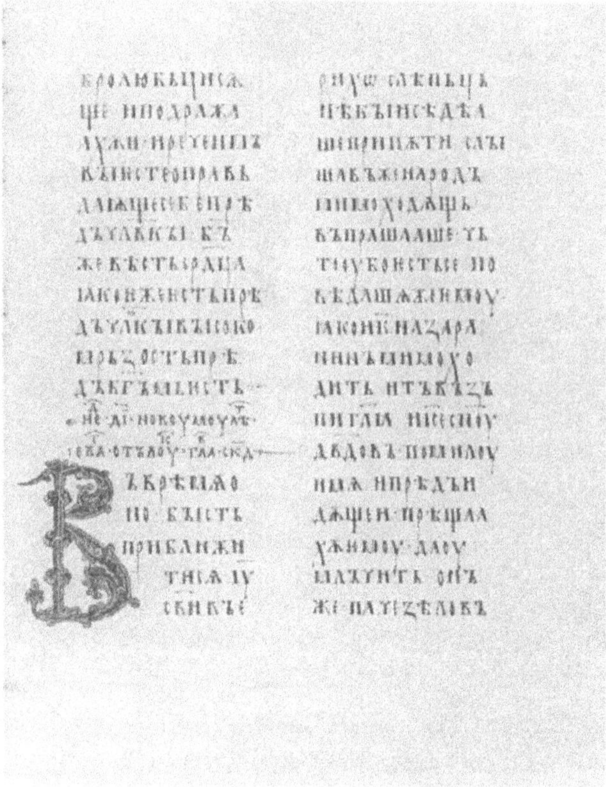

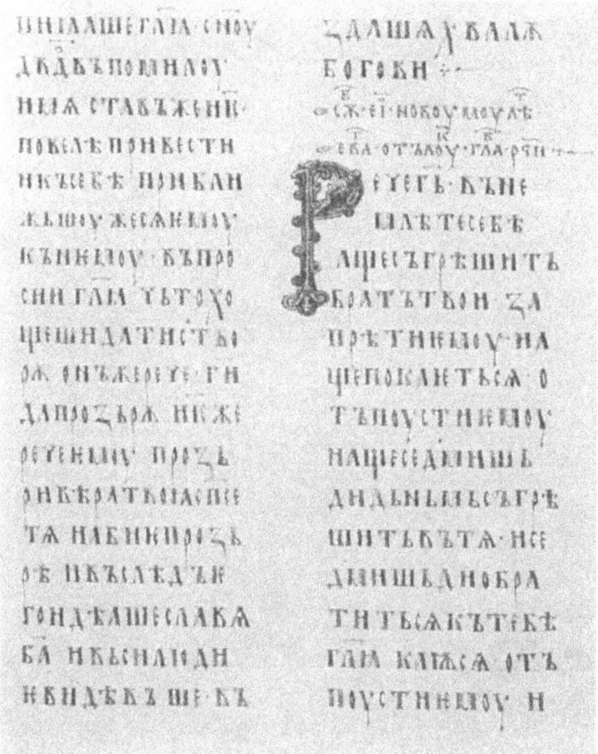

11. *Ostromir's Evangeliary.* National Library of Russia, Saint Petersburg (F.p.I. 5). Photographs by Sean Kernan from the facsimile edition *Ostromirovo evangelie* 1988.

5. *Ostromir's Evangeliary* (**3.41.1**) is an example of the most festive and elegant Cyrillic uncial writing. It is also the earliest dated Slavic manuscript. It was copied in 1056/1057, most probably in Kiev, for the Novgorod *posadnik* (governor) Ostromir. Folio 112r and v contains the parable of Christ restoring the blind man to his sight (Luke 18.35–43):[344]

[Transliteration]	[Translation]
112r	
a	
ne(dělja) · d͡ï · novoumou l(ět)ě	14th Sunday of the new year[345]
: eva(ngelie) otъ lou(ky) gla(va) s͡kd	Gospel according to Luke, chapter 224
Vъ vrěmę o	At that time
no · [**35**] bъıstь	[**35**] it happened
približi	that as Jesus
ti sę · ı(s)u	approached
s(o)vi vъ e	Jericho,
b	
rixo̎ · slěpьcь	a certain blind man
někъıi sěděa	was sitting
še pri pǫti [**36**] slъı	by the road.
šavъ že narodъ	[**36**] And hearing people
mimoxodę̑štь ·	passing by,
vъprašaaše · čь	he asked
to oubo jestь se [**37**] po	what this was [about].
vědašę že jemou ·	[**37**] And they told him
jako iı(su)s(ъ) nazara	that Jesus of Nazareth
ninъ mimoxo	was passing by.
ditь [**38**] i tъ vъzъ	[**38**] And he cried
pi g(lago)lja iı(su)se s(y)nou	saying, "Jesus, Son
d(a)v(i)dovъ · pomilou	of David, have mercy
i mę [**39**] i prědъı	on me!" And those
dǫ̑štei · prěštaa	[**39**] who went in front forbade
xǫ jemou · da ou	him [saying] that he should be
mlъčitь onъ	silent, but he
že · pače zělo vъ	cried much more
112v	
a	
pijaaše g(lago)lja · s(ъı) nou	saying, "Son
d(a)v(i)d(o)vъ pomilou	of David, have mercy on me!"
i mę [**40**] stavъ že iı(su)s(ъ) ·	[**40**] And Jesus, having stopped,
povelě privesti	commanded that he
i kъ sebě pribli	be brought to him.
žьšou že sę jemou	When he approached

344. The letters are brown, the initials are red, green, and gold, and the headings of particular readings are gold.
345. That is, the New Year of the September cycle.

kъ njemou · vъpro	him, he asked him
si i [**41**] g(lago)lja čьto xo	[**41**] saying, "What do you
šteši da ti s'tvo	want that I do for you?"
rǫ onъ že reče · g(ospod)i ·	And he said, "Lord,
da prozьrǫ [**42**] ii(su)s(ъ) že	that I may see." [**42**] And Jesus
reče jemou prozь	said to him, "Become sighted!
ri věra tvoja s(ъ)p(a)se	Your faith has saved you."
tę [**43**] i abije prozь	[**43**] And immediately
rě i vъslědъ je	he became sighted and went
go iděaše slavę	after him, glorifying
b(og)a i vьsi ljudi	God and all the people
je viděvъše · vъ	who had seen [it]

b

zdašę xvalǫ	gave praise
bogovi ⁘ -	to God.

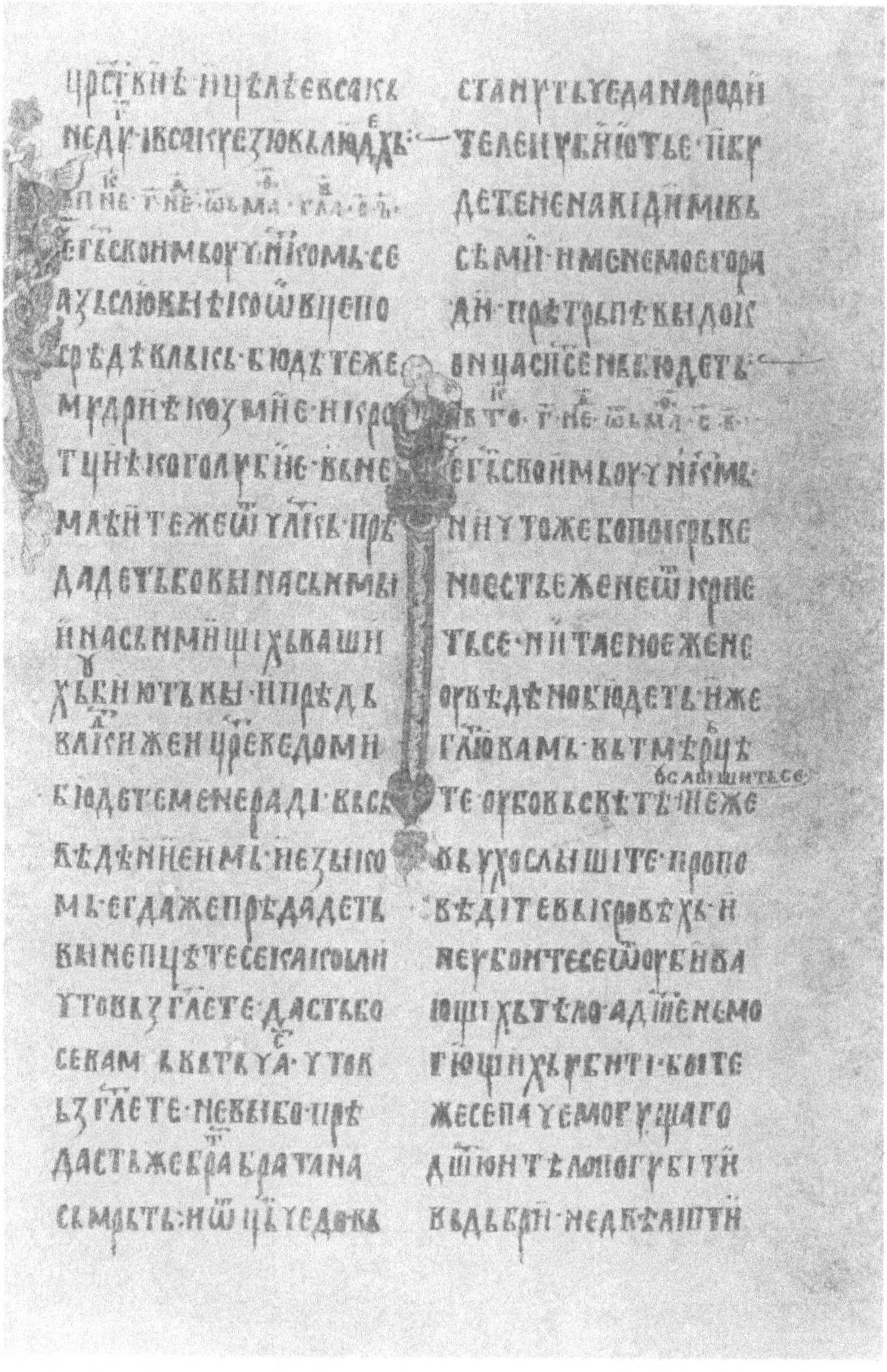

12. *Miroslav's Evangeliary.* National Museum, Belgrade (SFRJ, No. 1536). Photograph from Stojanović, ed., 1893–1894, by the Hilandar Research Library, Ohio State University, Columbus, courtesy of Predrag Matejic.

6. *Miroslav's Evangeliary* (**3.41.1**) is a richly illuminated manuscript transcribed in the province of Hum (modern Hercegovina) in the late twelfth century. It exhibits characteristic features of the Serbian recension of Church Slavonic (*ь* for *ъ*, *(j)u* for *(j)ǫ*, *e* for *ę*, occasionally *i* and *ju* for *y* and *u*). Folio 70 a–b contains the end of Matthew 4.23 and Matthew 10:16–22, 10:26–28:

[Transliteration]

a

[**4.23**] . . . c(ěsa)rstvïě · ïcělěe vsakь
nedu(g) · ı vsaku ezjü vь ljüdexь: -

v p(o)ne(dělьnik) · g̑ · ne(dělja) · ō(t)ь ma(tθěja) · gl(av)a · ȏ : ʒ̑ ·

R(eč)e g(ospod)ь svoïmь ouč(e)nikomь · [**10.16**] se
azь sljü vы ěko ȍvce po
srědě vlьkь · bjuděte že
mudrï ěko zmïe · i kro
tcï ěko golubïe · [**17**] vьne
mlěïte že ō(t) č(e)l(ově)kь · prě
dadetь bo vы na sьnmы
i na sьnmiš̑tıxь vaši
xь (ou)bijutь vы · [**18**] i prědь
vl(ady)ki že i c(ěsa)re vedomi
bjudete mene radı · vь sь
věděnïe ïmь · i ezыko
mь. [**19**] egda že prědadetь
vы ne pcěte se[346] kako ıli
čto vьzg(lago)lete · dastь bo
se vamь vь tѣ̑ ča(s) · čto v
ьzg(lago)lete · [**20**] ne vы bo ·[347] [**21**] prě
dastь že bra(t) brata na
sьmrъtь: i ō(tь)cь čedo · vь

b

stanutь čeda na rodi
tele i ubijütь e · [**22**] i budete nenavıdimı vь
sěmï · imene moego ra
dï · prětrъpěvы do k
onca sp(a)senь bjïdetь: -

v vto(rъk) · g̑ · ne(dělja) · ō(t)ь ma(tθěja) · s̑ · v̑ · :

R(eč)e g(ospod)ь svoïmь ouč(e)n(i)k(o)mь ·
[**26**] nïčtože bo pokrъve
no estь eže ne ō(t)krie
tь se · nï taeno eže ne
ouvěděno bjüdetь · [**27**] iže

346. *pьcěte sę* is 2 Sg. Impv. of *pešti sę* 'to concern oneself', cf. *pešti, pekǫ* 'cook'.
347. Most of verse 20 is missing.

g(lago)ljü vamь · vь tmě rьcě te · oubo vь světě (ou)slьišitь se · i eže vь uxo slьišite · propo vědite vь krověxь · [**28**] i ne uboite se ō(t) oubïva jüŝtixь tělo · a d(u)še ne mo gjüŝtixъ ubiti · boite že se pače moguŝtago d(u)šju i tělo pogubitï vь dьbrï · [**29**] ne dvě li ptï[ci]

[Translation]

[**4.23**] . . . kingdom and healing all manner of sickness and all manner of disease among the people.

On Monday, third week, according to Matthew, chapter 76

The Lord said to His disciples, [**10.16**] "Behold, I send you forth as sheep in the midst of wolves. Be, therefore, wise like serpents and gentle like doves. [**17**] But beware of men, for they will deliver you to the assemblies and in your synagogues will kill you. [**18**] And you will be led before governors and kings for my sake to offer testimony for them and for the heathens. [**19**] But when they deliver you up do not concern yourselves how or what you will say, for it will be given to you at that hour what you will say. [**20**] For it is not you . . . [**21**] And the brother will deliver the brother to death, and the father the child.

b

The children will rise up against their parents and will kill them. [**22**] And you will be hated by all for the sake of my name. He who endures to the end will be saved."

On Tuesday, third week, according to Matthew, chapter 202

The Lord said to His disciples, [**10.26**] "There is nothing covered which will not be revealed,

nor hidden which
will not be known. [**27**] What
I tell you in darkness,
say so that it will be heard, and what
you hear in the ear,
preach from the rooftops. [**28**] And
do not fear those who kill
the body but are unable
to kill the soul, but fear
rather him who is able
to destroy the soul and the body
in the abyss. [**29**] Are not two [birds]

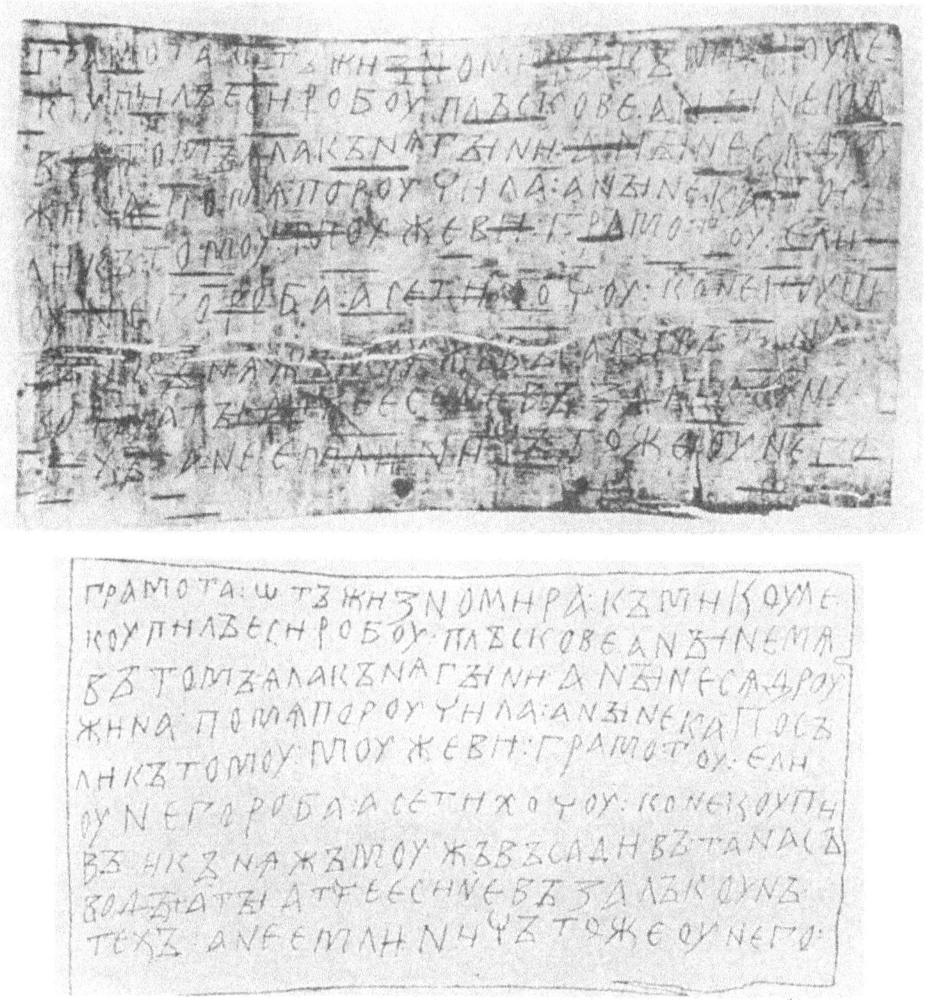

13. ***Birchbark gramota***, no. 109. Novgorod archaeological excavations. Photographs by Sean Kernan from Arcixovskij/Borkovskij 1958.

7. The *birchbark gramoty* of northwestern Rus' are short texts (usually letters) scratched on birchbark with a stylus. They provide valuable documentation of informal Cyrillic writing practices. Reproduced here is the Novgorod *birchbark gramota* #109 from the turn of the twelfth century, published and interpreted by its discoverer, Artemij V. Arcixovskij (1958:38–41). It concerns a legal problem faced by Žiznomir, the sender of the gramota. Žiznomir is being accused by the princess because a certain Mikula had purchased in Pskov a female serf or servant. (One imagines that Mikula was Žiznomir's associate or relative and that the slave had been stolen.) The retinue has pledged for Žiznomir (so that he would not be arrested for buying stolen property). Žiznomir instructs Mikula to find out whether the seller has a female slave (probably as a temporary replacement for the stolen one) and wants Mikula to buy a horse so that an investigator may be sent to the judicial confrontation (*sъvody*). He also instructs Mikula not to accept any money if he has not done so already (presumably as a refund from the seller to the buyer). A brief linguistic commentary on this gramota is provided in **3.52:**

[Transcription]

gramota: ōtъ žiznomira: kъ mikoule:
koupilъ esi: robou: plъskove: a nъıne mę:
vъ tomъ: ęla kъnęgyni: a nъıne sę drou
žina: po mę poroučila: a nъıne ka: posъ
li kъ tomou: mouževi: gramotou: e li
ou nego roba: a se ti xoču: kone koupi
vъ: i kъnęžъ moužъ vъsadivъ: ta na sъ
vodъı: a ty atče esi ne vъzalъ kunъ:
texъ: a ne emli: ničъtože u nego:

[Translation]

Gramota from Žiznomir to Mikula.
You have bought a female serf in Pskov. And now
the princess has accused me. And now the
retinue has pledged for me. And now send
a gramota to that man, whether he has a
female serf. And this is what I want you to do: having bought a horse
and having given it to [lit. having put on it] the prince's officer, [let him]
go to the *sъvody*. And you, if you have not taken that
money, do not take anything from him.

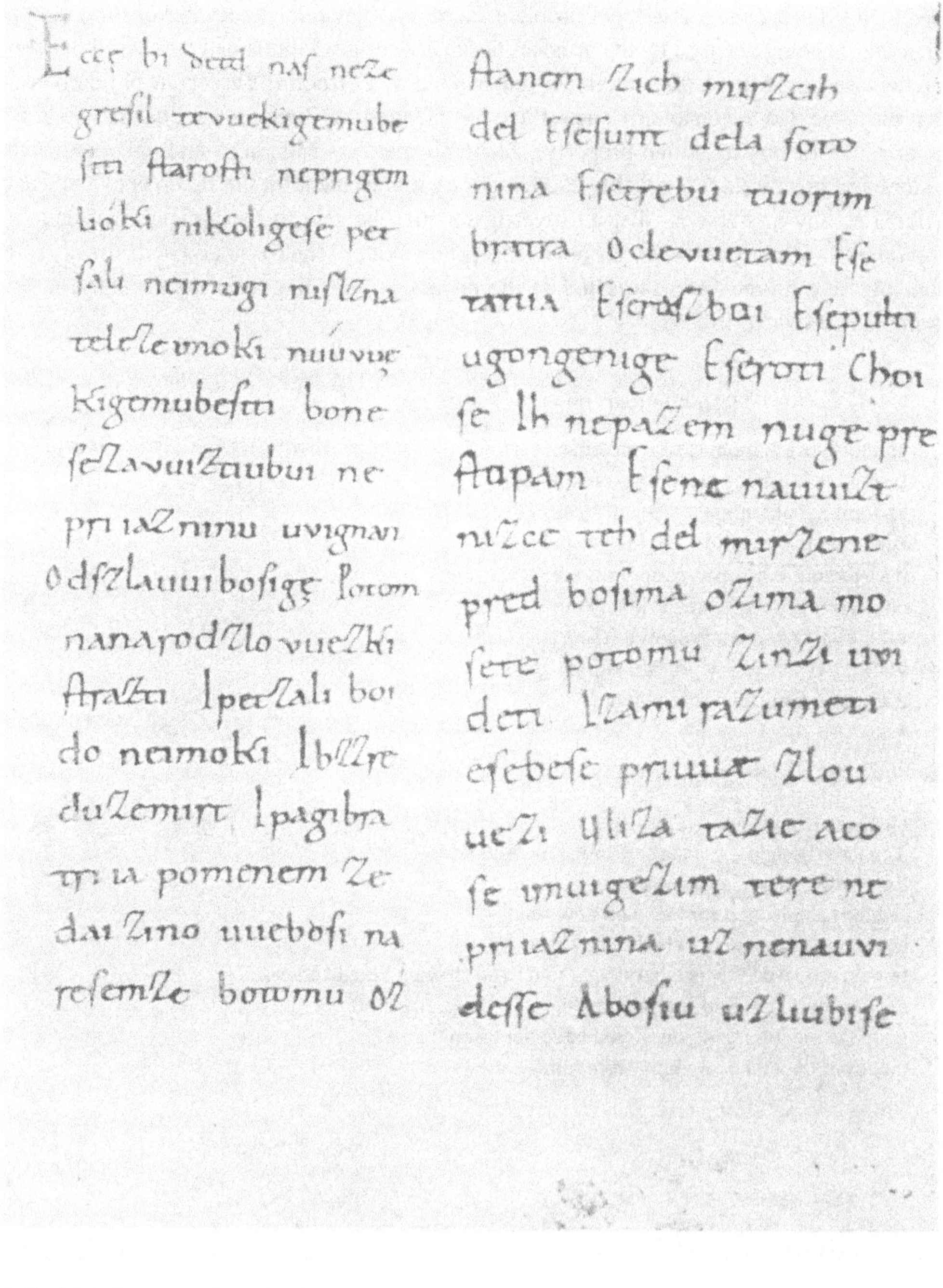
Ecce bi detd nas neze
grefil tevuekigemube
siti starosti neprigem
lioki nikoligese per
sali nemogi nislena
telese unoki nuuvue
kigemubesiti bone
sezavuizaubui ne
priiazninu uvignan
odszlauuibosige potom
nanarodzlo vuezki
stradati Ipet zali boi
do nemoki Ibeze pre
duzemirt Ipagibra
tri ia pomenem ze
dai zino uuebosi na
resemze bovomu oz
stanem zich mirzcih
del Esesum dela soto
nina Esetrebu tuorim
bratra Oclevuetam Ese
tatua Esera zboi Eseputi
ugongenige Eserotti Choi
se Ih nepazem nuge pre
stopam Esene nauuizt
nizce teh del mirzene
pred bosima ozima mo
sete potomu zinzi uvi
deti Iizami pazumeti
esebese priuuae zlou
vezi ulize tazie aco
se unuigezlim tere ne
priiaznina uz nenauvi
desse Abosiu uzliubise

14. *Freising Fragments.* Bavarian State Library, Munich (Clm 6426). Photograph by Sean Kernan from Isačenko 1943.

Roman

The *Freising Fragments* represent the oldest extant attempt to use the Latin alphabet (Carolingian miniscule) to record a Slavic text (**3.41.5**). They contain two confessional formulas (*Freising* I and III) and a homily on penitence or the *Adhortatio ad pœnitentiam* (*Freising* II). Following is the normalized transcription of the first folio of *Freising* II, in which the spirants (*s, z, š, ž*) and affricates (*c, č*) have been reconstructed. The vowels, except for several instances where *ǫ, ě,* and *y* are written eytmologically in the text (*ǫ* as *un* in b2, *ě* as *æ* in b13, *y* as *ui* in a5, a8, a10, b15), are transcribed as found (assuming loss of jers in the weak position). Here are a few examples from the beginning and the end of the passage: *ded* is written for etymological *děd* (a1), *v veki* for *v věky* (a2), *be* for *bě* (a2), *prijeml'oči* for *prijeml'ǫči* (a4), *jesim* for *jes[e]m* (b15), *vznenavideše* for *vznenaviděšę* (b16–17), *vzljubiše* for *vzljubišę* (b17).

[Transcription]	[Translation]
a	
Ešte bi ded naš ne se	If our ancestor had not
grešil, te v veki jemu be	sinned, he would have lived
žiti, starosti ne prijem	forever, without experiencing
l'oči, nikolije že peč	old age, not having any sorrow
ali ne imuji [imy?], ni slzna	whatever, nor having a grieving
telese imoči, no v veki	flesh, but he would have
jemu be žiti. Pone	lived forever. Since
že zavistju by ne	he was expelled by
prijazninu vignan	diabolical envy
od slavy božije, potom	from God's glory, from then on
na narod človecki	sufferings and sorrows descended
strasti i ipečali poj	upon humankind,
do, nemoči i bzz[348] re	diseases and random [?]
du semirt. I paki, bra	death. And yet, brothers,
trija, pomenem se,	let us remember that we too
da i sinove boži na	are called the sons of God.
rečem se. Potomu os	Therefore, let us

b	
tanem six mirzkix [mirskix?]	relinquish those vile [worldly?] deeds
del eže sǫt dela soto	which are the deeds of Satan.
nina. Eže trebu tvorim,	Whether we offer sacrifices, slander
bratra okleveta[e]m, eže	[our] brother, whether [for] thievery,
tatva, eže razboj, eže pulti	whether [for] murder, whether [for]
ugojenije, eže roti koi[x]	gratification of the flesh, whether [for]
že ne pasem [pazim?], no je pre	oaths which we do not keep but
stopa[e]m, eže nenavist,	break them, whether [for] hate,
nic že tex del mirže ne	there is nothing more odious before

348. The interpretation of this segment is difficult. Textologically simplest would be the reading *bez redu* (LPSl. *bez rędu*) translated as 'without order', that is, 'random'.

pred božima očima. mo
žete potomu, sinci, vi
deti I sami razumeti
eže beše prvæ člo
věci V lica tacie ako
že i my jesim tere ne
prijaznina vznenavi
deše A božiju[349] vzljubiše

God's eyes than these deeds. You
can, therefore, see, my sons,
and understand yourselves
that people were formerly
in appearance the same as
we are. They also
hated diabolical [deeds]
and loved divine

349. The feminine form of the adjective presupposes a feminine head noun which is not given in the text.

BIBLIOGRAPHY

This bibliography does not pretend to do more than skim the surface of the vast reservoir of scholarly literature dealing with the subjects touched upon in this survey. Its primary aim is to provide full references for the studies mentioned in the text. Beyond that it offers a selection of other pertinent titles, unfortunately severely limited by space considerations. For additional references the reader is advised to turn to standard bibliographies, encyclopedic guides, major surveys (e.g. Birnbaum 1979, Horálek 1962, Hussey, ed. 1966–1967, Jagič 1910, Petkanova, ed. 1992), as well as to bibliographies appended to individual studies.

1. Abbreviations

Academies and Institutes

AAAS	American Academy of Arts and Sciences, Cambridge, Mass.
AN	Akademija Nauk [SSSR = USSR, Moscow; BSSR = Belarussian SSR, Minsk; UkrSSR = Ukrainian SSR, Kiev]
BAN	Bălgarska akademija na naukite, Sofia
ČSAV	Československá Akademie věd, Prague
HURI	Harvard Ukrainian Research Institute, Cambridge, Mass.
IAN	Imperatorskaja Akademija Nauk, St. Petersburg
IES	Institut d'études slaves, Paris
JAZU	Jugoslavenska Akademija Znanosti i Umjetnosti, Zagreb
KAW	Kaiserliche Akademie der Wissenschaften, Vienna
MAA	The Medieval Academy of America, Cambridge, Mass.
MAI	Moskovskij Arxeologičeskij Institut, Moscow
MANU	Makedonska Akademija na naukite i umetnostite, Skopje
ÖAW	Österreichische Akademie der Wissenschaften, Vienna
PAN	Polska Akademia Nauk, Warsaw
[P]AU	[Polska] Akademia Umiejętności, Cracow
RAN	Rossijskaja Akademija Nauk, St. Petersburg
SAN	Srpska Akademija Nauka, Belgrade
SAV	Slovenska [Slovak] Akademia vied, Bratislava

SAZU Slovenska [Slovenian] Akademija Znanosti in Umetnosti, Ljubljana [formerly, Akademija Znanosti in Umetnosti v Ljubljani]

Periodicals and Serials

AAV *Acta Academiae Velehradensis*, Olomouc

ACICS *American Contributions to the International Congresses of Slavists*

ALH *Acta Linguistica Hafnensia*, Copenhagen

APARA *Atti della Pontificia Academia Romana di archeologia*, Rome

AQdGM *Ausgewählte Quellen zur deutschen Geschichte des Mittelalters*, Darmstadt: Wissenschaftliche Buchgesellschaft

AsPh *Archiv für slavische Philologie*, Berlin

AUSzDSl *Acta Universitatis Szegediensis de Atila Jószef nominatae. Dissertationes slavicae*, Szeged

BB *Byzantino-Bulgarica*, Sofia

BE *Bălgarski ezik*, Sofia

BPTJ *Biuletyn Polskiego Towarzystwa Językoznawczego*, Cracow

ByzSl *Byzantinoslavica*, Prague

CIBAL *Centre International d'information sur les sources de l'histoire balkanique et mediterranéenne*, Sofia

ČMF *Časopsis pro moderní filologii*, Prague

ČOIDR *Čtenija v obščestve istorii i drevnostej rossijskix*, Moscow

CyrMeth *Cyrillomethodianum*, Thessalonica

EMSVD *Editiones monumentorum slavicorum veteris dialecti*, Graz: Seminar für slavische Philologie der Universität Graz

Fil *Filologija*, Zagreb

FS *Folia Slavica*, Columbus, Ohio

HUS *Harvard Ukrainian Studies*, Cambridge, Mass.

IF *Indogermanische Forschungen*, Berlin, New York

IJSLP *The International Journal of Slavic Linguistics and Poetics*, 's-Gravenhage, The Hague, Lisse, Columbus, Ohio

IRJa *Issledovanija po russkomu jazyku*, St. Petersburg: IAN

IZfaSw *Internationale Zeitschrift für allgemeine Sprachwissenschaft*, Leipzig

IzvOLJa *Izvestija Otdelenija literatury i jazyka AN SSSR*, Moscow

IzvORJas *Izvestija Otdelenija russkogo jazyka i slovesnosti Akademii Nauk*, St. Petersburg, Petrograd, Leningrad

IzvRJaSl *Izvestija AN SSSR po russkomu jazyku i slovesnosti*, Leningrad

JF *Južnoslovenski Filolog*, Belgrade

JSL *Journal of Slavic Linguistics*, Bloomington, Ind.

KMS *Kirilo-Metodievski studii*, Sofia

Krat *Kratylos*, Wiesbaden

KZ *Zeitschrift für vergleichende Sprachforschung* (*Kunz Zeitschrift*)

Lg	*Language*, Baltimore
LitIst	*Literaturna istorija*, Sofia
LitM	*Literaturna misăl*, Sofia
PB	*Palaeobulgarica*, Sofia
PDRL	*Pamjatniki drevnerusskoj literatury*, St. Petersburg/Petrograd
PF	*Prace filologiczne*, Warsaw
PK	*Polata kъnigopisьnaja*, Nijmegen, Amsterdam
PKJ	*Prace Komisji Językowej* PAU, Cracow
PSSlJa	*Pamjatniki staroslavjanskogo jazyka*, St. Petersburg/Petrograd
PZ	*Przegląd Zachodni*, Poznań
RES	*Revue des études slaves*, Paris
RicSl	*Ricerche slavistiche*, Rome
RL	*Russian Linguistics*, Amsterdam
RO	*Rocznik orientalistyczny*, Cracow, Lwów, Warsaw
RS	*Rocznik slawistyczny*, Cracow
RStSlI	*Radovi Staroslavenskog instituta*, Zagreb
SEEJ	*Slavic and East European Journal*
SEER	*Slavonic and East European Review*, London
SF	*Slavjanskaja filologija*, Moscow
Slavia	*Slavia: Časopis pro slovanskou filologii*, Prague
Slovo	*Slovo: Časopis Staroslavenskog instituta*, Zagreb
SlRev	*Slavistična revija*, Ljubljana
SLS	*Studies in the Linguistic Sciences*, Urbana, Ill.
SORJaS	*Sbornik Otdelenija Russkogo Jazyka i Slovesnosti IAN*, St. Petersburg
SovArx	*Sovetskaja arxeologija*, Moscow
SR	*Slavic Review*, New York
StBLit	*Starobălgarska literatura*, Sofia
SWord	*Slavic Word*. See *Word*
TLP	*Travaux linguistiques de Prague*, Prague
TMAO	*Trudy Moskovskogo Arxeologičeskogo Obščestva*, Moscow
TODL	*Trudy Otdela drevnerusskoj literatury RAN*, St. Petersburg
UZKFP	*Učenye zapiski Karelo-finskogo pedinstituta*, Petrozavodsk
VestAN	*Vestnik AN SSSR*, Moscow
VJa	*Voprosy jazykoznanija*, Moscow
VSJa	*Voprosy slavjanskogo jazykoznanija*, L'vov
Word	*Word*, New York (nos. 4 in vols. 8–11 = *Slavic Word* 1–4)
WSJ	*Wiener slavistisches Jahrbuch*, Vienna
ZFL	*Zbornik Matice Srpske za filologiju i lingvistiku*, Novi Sad
ZfsPh	*Zeitschrift für slavische Philologie*, Leipzig

ZIFFPU *Zapiski Istoriko-filologičeskogo fakul'teta Imperatorskogo St-Peterburgskogo universiteta*

ŽMNP *Žurnal Ministerstva Narodnogo Prosveščenija*, St. Petersburg

ZORGB *Zapiski Otdela rukopisej Gosudarstvennoj Biblioteki SSSR imeni V. I. Lenina*, Moscow

ZPSSl *Z polskich studiów slawistycznych: Językoznawstwo*, Warsaw

2. Bibliographies and Guides to Archives

Abramovič, Dmitrij I. (1905–1910), *Opisanie rukopisej St.-Peterburgskoj duxovnoj akademii*, St. Petersburg: IAN.

Birkfellner, Gerhard (1975), *Glagolitische und kyrillische Handschriften in Österreich*, Vienna: ÖAW.

Bogdanović, Dimitrije (1978), *Katalog ćirilskix rukopisa manastira Xilandara*, 2 vols., Belgrade: SAN.

Byčkov, Afanasij F. (1882), *Opisanie cerkovno-slavjanskix i russkix rukopisej imper. Publičnoj Biblioteki*, St. Petersburg: Byčkov.

Conev, Benjo (1910, 1923), *Opis na răkopisite i staropečeatnite knigi na Narodna biblioteka v Sofia*, vols. 1 and 2, Sofia: Dăržavna Pečatnica. [Continued by Stojanov/Kodov.]

Djaparidze, David (1957), *Mediaeval Slavic Manuscripts: A Bibliography of Printed Catalogues*, Cambridge, Mass.: MAA.

Dujčev, Ivan, et al. (1983), *Kirilometodievska bibliografija, 1940–1980*, Sofia: Sofijski universitet "Kliment Oxridski."

Džurova, Aksinija, et al. (1985), *Opis na slavjanskite răkopisi văv Vatikanskata Biblioteka*, Sofia: Svjat.

Gorskij, A. V., and K. I. Nevostruev (1855, 1859, 1862, 1869, 1917), *Opisanie slavjanskix rukopisej Moskovskoj Sinodal'noj Biblioteki*, 5 vols., Moscow: Sinodal'naja Tipografija. [Reprint (1964) in *Monumenta Linguae slavicae dialecti veteris*, vol. 2, Wiesbaden: Otto Harrassowitz.]

Granstrem, E. E. (1953), *Opisanie russkix i slavjanskix pergamennyx rukopisej*, Leningrad: Biblioteka.

Grimsted, Patricia Kennedy (1972), *Archives and Manuscript Repositories in the USSR: Moscow and Leningrad*, Princeton, N.J.: Princeton University Press.

——— (1976), *Archives and Manuscript Repositories in the USSR: Moscow and Leningrad; Supplement 1: Bibliographical Addenda*, Inter Documentation Company AG, Zug, Switzerland.

Hille, A. (1959), *Bibliographische Einführung in das Studium der slawischen Philologie*, Halle (Saale): Max Niemeyer.

Il'inskij, G. A. (1934), *Opyt sistematičeskoj kirilo-mefod'evskoj bibliografii pod redakciej i s dopolnenijami M. G. Popruženka i St. M. Romanskogo*, Sofia: Pečatnica P. Gluškov. [Reprint (1967), Inter Documentation Company A. G., Zug, Switzerland.]

Kirmagova, A., and A. Paunova (1971), *Bibliografija na bălgarskite publikacii, izlezli okolo čestvuvaneto na 1100-godišnata ot smărtta na Konstantin-Kiril Filosof*, in *Konstantin-Kiril Filosof: Dokladi ot simpoziuma, posveten na 1100- godišnata ot smărtta mu*, Sofia: BAN, pp. 373–417.

Kodov, Xristo (1969), *Opis na slavjanskite răkopisi v Biblioteka na Bălgarskata Akademija na naukite*, Sofia: BAN.

Matejić, Mateja (1989), *Slavic Codices of the Great Lavra Monastery [at Mount Athos]: A Description*, Sofia: CIBAL.

Matejic, Predrag, and Hannah Thomas (1992), *Catalog: Manuscripts on Microform of the Hilandar Research Library (The Ohio State University)*, 2 vols., Columbus, Ohio: Resource Center for Medieval Slavic Studies of the Ohio State University.

Matejka, Ladislav (1965), *Introductory Bibliography of Slavic Philology*, Ann Arbor, Mich.: Dept. of Slavic Languages and Literatures, University of Michigan.

Mathiesen, Robert (1983), "Handlist of manuscripts containing Church Slavonic translations from the Old Testament," *PK* 7:3–48.

Mošin, Vladimir (1955, 1952), *Čirilski rukopisi Jugoslavenske akademije*, 2 vols., Zagreb: JAZU.

——— (1971), *Slovenski rakopisi vo Makedonija*, 2 vols., Skopje: Arxiv na Makedonija.

Možaeva, I. E. (1980), *Bibliografija po kirillo-mefodievskoj problematike, 1945–1974 gg.*, Moscow: Nauka.

Orlov, A. S. (1952), *Bibliografija russkix nadpisej XI–XV vv.*, Moscow: Akademija Nauk SSSR.

Pokrovskaja, V. F. (1976), *Pergamennye rukopisi Biblioteki Akademii nauk SSSR: Opisanie russkix i slavjanskix rukopisej XI–XVI vekov*, Leningrad: Nauka.

Popov, Andrej N. (1872), *Opisanie rukopisej i katalog knig cerkovnoj pečati biblioteki A. I. Xludova*, Moscow: Sinodal'naja tipografija.

Popruženko, M., and St. Romanski (1942), *Kirilometodievska bibliografija za 1934–1940 god*, Sofija: Dăržavna pečatnica.

Šmidt, Sigurd O., et al. (1984), *Svodnyj katalog slavjano-russkix rukopisnyx knig, xranjaščixja v SSSR, XI–XIII vv.*, Moscow: Nauka.

Stankiewicz, Edward, and Dean S. Worth (1966, 1970), *A Selected Bibliography of Slavic Linguistics*, 2 vols., The Hague: Mouton.

Stojanov, Man'o, and Xristo Kodov (1964, 1971), *Opis na slavjanskite răkopisi v Sofijskata Narodna Biblioteka*, vols. 3 and 4, Sofia: Nauka i izkustvo. [Continuation of Conev.]

Tarnanidis, Ioannis, C. (1988), *The Slavonic Manuscripts Discovered in 1975 at St. Catherine's Monastery on Mount Sinai*, Thessalonica: Hellenic Association of Slavic Studies.

Tixomirov, N. B. (1962–1972), *Katalog russkix i slavjanskix pergamennyx rukopisej XI–XII vekov. xranjaščixsja v Otdele rukopisej Gos. b-ki SSSR im. V. I. Lenina*, in *ZORGB* (1962) 25:143–183; (1965) 27:93–148; (1968) 30:87–156; (1972) 33:213–220.

Xristova, Borjana, et al. (1982), *Bălgarski răkopisi ot XI do XVIII vek zapazeni v Bălgarija: Svoden katalog*, vol. 1, Sofia: Narodna Biblioteka "Kiril i Metodij."

3. Historical Setting

Primary sources are shown in small capitals. Full references to Slavic texts (along with the Byzantine chronicles which were translated into Slavic and gained popularity throughout Orthodox Slavdom), whether cited as primary sources for historical or linguistic investigations or as monuments of early Slavic writing, are given in section 5. Whenever possible, existing English translations were used (occasionally with minor adjustments). When such translations could not be located, citations were translated anew. See also the list of sources for early Slavic history compiled by Peisker (1913:770–773) and a selection of the earliest sources in Plezia (1952).

Adam of Bremen = Tschan 1959.

Alcuin = Allott 1974.

Alfred = Bosworth 1859.

Al-Istarkhī, in Dunlop 1967.

Allott, Stephen (1974), *Alcuin of York: His Life and Letters*, York, Eng.: William Sessions.

Anastasius to Gauderich, in Grivec/Tomšič, eds, pp. 64–66 [Latin text]; in Havlík, ed. (1969), 134:176–181 [Latin text and Czech translation].

Angelov, Dimităr (1980), *Bogomilstvoto v Bălgarija*, Sofia: Nauka i izkustvo.

Annals of Fulda = Reuter 1982.

Annals of St. Bertin = Nelson 1991.

Anonymous Gallus = Plezia 1982.

Bavarian Geographer = Nazarenko, ed., 1993, pp. 7–58.

Birkenmajer, Józef (1937), *Bogarodzica dziewica: Analiza tekstu, treści i formy*, Lwów.

Birnbaum, Henrik (1993), "On the ethnogenesis and protohome of the Slavs: The linguistic evidence," *JSL* 1/2:352–374.

Bosworth, Joseph, ed. and trans. (1859), *King Alfred's Anglo-Saxon Version of the Compendious History of the World by Orosius*, London: Longman, Brown, Green, and Longmans.

Bretholz, Bertold, ed. (1923), *Die Chronik der Böhmen des Cosmas von Prag* [= *Monumenta Germaniae Historica, Scriptores rerum Germanicarum*, Nova series, vol. 2, Berlin: Weidmannsche Buchhandlung].

Constantine Porphyrogenitus = Moravcsik, ed., 1967.

Conversio = Wolfram, ed., 1979.

Cosmas of Prague = Bretholz, ed., 1923.

Cross, Samuel H. (1948), *Slavic Civilization through the Ages*, Cambridge: Harvard University Press.

Czekanowski, Jan (1957), *Wstęp do historii Słowian*, 2nd ed., Poznań: Instytut Zachodni.

Dalton, O. M., trans. (1927), *The History of the Franks*, vol. 2, Oxford: Clarendon Press.

Dennis, George T., trans. (1984), *Maurice's Strategikon: Handbook of Byzantine Military Strategy*, Philadelphia: University of Pennsylvania Press.

Devos, Paul, and Paul Meyvaert (1955), "Trois énigmes Cyrillo-Méthodiennes de la Legende Italique résolues grâce à un document inédit," *Annalecta Bollandiana* 73:375–461.

Dewing, H. B., trans. (1962), *History of the Wars*, vol. 4, Cambridge, Mass.: Harvard University Press.

Dindorf, Ludwig, ed. (1870), *Historici Græci minores*, vol. 1, 275–352, Leipzig: B. G. Teubner.

Duichev [= Dujčev], Ivan, ed. (1985), *Kiril and Methodius: Founders of Slavonic Writing; A Collection of Sources and Critical Studies*, English translation by Spass Nikolov, Boulder, Colo.: East European Monographs, Distributed by Columbia University Press.

Dujčev, Ivan (1970), *Slavia Orthodoxa: Collected Studies in the History of the Slavic Middle Ages*, London: Variorum Reprints.

——— (1983), *Proučvanija vărxu srednevekovnata bălgarska istorija i kultura*, Sofia: Nauka i izkustvo.

Dunlop, D. M. (1967), *The History of the Jewish Khazars*, New York: Schocken Books.

Dvornik, Francis (1949), *The Making of Central and Eastern Europe*, London: The Polish Research Centre.

——— (1956), *The Slavs: Their Early History and Civilization*, Boston: AAAS.

——— (1964), "Byzantium, Rome, the Franks, and the Christianization of the Southern Slavs," in Hellmann et al., eds., pp. 85–125.

——— (1970), *Byzantine Missions Among the Slavs: SS. Constantine-Cyril and Methodius*, New Brunswick, NJ: Rutgers University Press.

EINHARD = Thorpe, ed., 1969.

Every, George (1962), *The Byzantine Patriarchate*, 451–1204, 2nd ed., London: S.P.C.K.

Falk, Knut-Olof (1951), *Dneprforsarnas namn i Kejsar Konstantin VII Porfyrogennetos' De administrando imperio*, Lund [= Lunds Universitets Årsskrift, N.F., vol. 46, no. 4].

Fine, John V. A., Jr. (1983), *The Early Medieval Balkans*, Ann Arbor: University of Michigan Press.

Filin, Fedot P. (1962), *Obrazovanie jazyka vostočnyx slavjan*, Moscow: Akademija Nauk SSSR.

FREDEGAR = Wallace-Hadrill 1960.

Gieysztor, Aleksander (1982), *Mitologia Słowian*, Warsaw: Wydawnictwa artystyczne i filmowe.

Gil'ferding, Aleksandr (1868), "Drevnejšij period istorii slavjan," *Vestnik Evropy* 4:256–285.

Gimbutas, Marija (1971), *The Slavs*, New York: Praeger.

Godłowski, Kazimierz (1979), *Z badań nad zagadnieniem rozprzestrzenienia Słowian w V–VII w. n.e.*, Kraków: Akademia Górniczo-Hutnicza.

——— (1985), *Przemiany kulturowe i osadnicze w południowej i środkowej Polsce w młodszym okresie przedrzymskim i w okresie rzymskim*, Wrocław, Cracow: Ossolineum.

Gołąb, Zbigniew (1983), "The ethnogenesis of the Slavs in the light of linguistics," in Michael S. Flier, ed., *ACICS*$_9$, 1:131–146, Columbus, Ohio: Slavica.

——— (1992), *The Origins of the Slavs: A Linguist's View*, Columbus, Ohio: Slavica.

GREGORY OF TOURS = Dalton 1927.

Grivec, Fran, and Fran Tomšič, eds. (1960), *Constantinus et Methodius Thessalonicenses: Fontes*, Zagreb: *RStSlI* 4:67–77.

Grivec, Franz (1960), *Konstantin und Method: Lehrer der Slaven*, Wiesbaden: Otto Harrasowitz.

Gwatkin, H. M., and J. P. Whitney, eds. (1913), *The Rise of the Saracens and the Foundation of the Western Empire*, Cambridge: At the University Press [= *Cambridge Medieval History*, vol. 2].

Havlík, Lubomír E., ed. (1966, 1967, 1969, 1971, 1977), *Magnae Moraviae Fontes Historici*, 5 vols., Brno: Universita J. E. Purkyně [= *Spisy University J. E. Purkyně v Brně*, Filosofická Fakulta, nos. 104, 118, 134, 156, 206].

HEBREW SOURCES = Kupfer/Lewicki, eds., 1956.

Hellmann, M., et al., eds. (1985), *Cyrillo-Methodiana: Zur Frühgeschichte des Christentums bei den Slaven, 863–1963*, Cologne, Graz: Böhlau Verlag.

HELMOLD = Tschan, ed., 1935.

Hensel, Witold (1980), *Polska starożytna*, 2d ed., Wrocław: Ossolineum.

Herrmann, Joachim, ed. (1986), *Welt der Slaven: Geschichte, Gesellschaft, Kultur*, Munich: C. H. Beck.

Hirt, Heinrich (1907), *Die Indogermanen*, vol. 2, Strasbourg: K. J. Trübner.

Holtzmann, R., ed. and trans. (1974), *Thietmar von Merseburg, Chronik*, 5th ed. [Latin text and annotated German translation], revised by Werner Trillmich [= *AQdGM* 9].

Hussey, J. M., ed. (1966, 1967), *The Cambridge Medieval History*, vol. 4, parts 1 and 2, Cambridge: At the University Press.

IBN FADLAN, AHMAD = Kmietowicz et al., eds., 1985 [Arabic text and Polish translation]; Smyser 1965 [English translation].

IBN HURDADBEH, ʿABD ALLAH = Lewicki, ed., 1956 [Arabic text and Polish translation].

IBN JAʿQUB, IBRAHIM, in Havlík, ed., 1969, 134:410–420 [Arabic text and Czech translation].

IBN RUSTAH = Lewicki, ed., 1977 [Arabic text and Polish translation].

ITALIAN LEGEND, [in Grivec/Tomšič, eds., 1960:59–64 [Latin text]; Havlík, ed. (1967) 118:120–133 [Latin text and Czech translation]; Duichev, ed. (1985), 131–137 [English translation].

Ivanov, Jordan (1925), *Bogomilski knigi i legendi*, 3d ed., Sofia: BAN.

Jagić, Vatroslav (1927), "The conversion of the Slavs," *Cambridge Medieval History*, vol. 4, pp. 215–229.

Jażdżewski, Konrad (1947), *Gdzie była prakolebka Słowian?* Łódź: Łódzkie Towarzystwo Naukowe.

Jenkins, R. J. H., et al., eds. (1962), Commentary to *De administrando imperio*, vol. 2, London: Athlone Press.

Jeżowa, Maria (1961–1962) *Dawne słowiańskie dialekty Meklemburgii w świetle nazw miejscowych i osobowych*, Wrocław: Ossolineum.

JOHN OF EPHESUS = Smith 1860.

JORDANES = Mierow, ed. 1960.

Kazhdan, Alexander P., et al., eds. (1991), *The Oxford Dictionary of Byzantium*, 3 vols., New York: Oxford University Press.

King, P. D., ed. and trans. (1987), *Charlemagne: Translated sources*, Lambrigg Kendal: King.

Kmietowicz, Anna, et al., eds. (1985), *Źródła arabskie do dziejów Słowiańszczyzny*, vol. 3, Wrocław, Warsaw, Cracow, Gdansk, Lodz: PAN.

Kos, Franc, ed. (1902–1928), *Gradivo za zgodovino Slovencev ve srednjem veku*, 5 vols., Ljubljana: Leonova Družba.

Kostrzewski, Józef (1961), *Kultura prapolska*, 3d ed., Warsaw: PWN.

Kowalenko, Władysław, et al., eds. (1961–), *Słownik starożytności słowiańskich*, 8 vols., Wrocław: Ossolineum.

Kuhar, Aloysius L. (1962), *Slovene Medieval History: Selected Studies*, New York, Washington: Studia Slovenica.

Kupfer, Franciszek, and Tadeusz Lewicki, eds. (1956), *Źródła hebrajskie do dziejów Słowian i niektórych innych ludów środkowej i wschodniej Europy*, Wrocław: Ossolineum [Hebrew text and Polish translation].

Lehr-Spławiński, Tadeusz (1946), *O pochodzeniu i praojczyźnie Słowian*, Poznań: Instytut Zachodni.

Lewicki, Tadeusz, ed. (1956), *Źródła arabskie do dziejów Słowiańszczyzny*, vol. 1, pp. 43–157, Wrocław and Cracow: PAN.

——— (1977), *Źródła arabskie do dziejów Słowiańszczyzny*, vol. 2, part 2, Wrocław, Warsaw, Cracow, Gdansk: PAN.

LIUDPRAND = Wright, ed., 1930.

Lohmann, H. E., et al., eds. and trans. (1971), *Quellen zur Geschichte der sächsischen Kaiserzeit: Sachsengeschichte* [Latin text and annotated German translation], revised by Albert Bauer and Reinhold Rau [= *AQdGM* 8].

Łowmiański, Henryk (1957), *Zagadnienie roli Normanów w genezie państw słowiańskich*, Warsaw: PWN.

——— (1963, 1967, 1970, 1973), *Początki Polski: Z dziejów Słowian w I tysiącleciu n. e.*, vols. 2, 3, 4, 5, Warsaw: PWN.

——— (1967), "Neurowie," in Kowalenko, et al., eds. 3:367–369.

——— (1986), *Religia Słowian i jej upadek (w. VI–XII)*, 2nd ed., Warsaw: PWN.

Magoulias, Harry J. (1970), *Byzantine Christianity: Emperor, Church and the West*, Chicago: Rand McNally.

Mańczak, Witold (1992), *De la préhistoire des peuples indo-européens*, Cracow: Uniwersytet Jagielloński.

MAURICE = Dennis 1984.

Meillet, Antoine (1927), "De quelques mots relatifs à la navigation," *RES* 7:1–8.

Menges, Karl H. (1953), *An Outline of the Early History and Migrations of the Slavs*, New York: Department of Slavic Languages, Columbia University.

Meyendorf, John (1983), *Byzantine Theology: Historical Trends and Doctrinal Themes*, 2nd revised ed., New York: Fordham University Press.

Mierow, Charles Christopher, ed. and trans. (1960), *The Gothic History of Jordanes*, Cambridge: Speculum Historiale, New York: Barnes & Noble.

Migne, J.-P., ed. (1860), *Paskhalion seu Chronicon Paschale*, in Migne, J.-P. *Patrologiae Graecae cursus completus . . .*, vol. 92, Paris: J.-P. Migne.

Miodowicz, Konstanty (1984), "Współczesne koncepcje lokalizacji pierwotnych siedzib Słowian: Dane językoznawcze," *Prace etnograficzne* 19:7–49, Cracow: Uniwersytet Jagielloński [= *Zeszyty Naukowe Uniwersytetu Jagiellońskiego*, no. 722].

Mirčeva, Bojka, and Slavija Bărlieva, eds. (1987), "Predvaritelen spisăk na Kirilo-Metodievskite izvori" [latinski, grăcki, romano-germanski], *KMS* 4:499–514.

Moravcsik, Gyula, ed. (1967), *De administrando imperio*, translated by R. J. H. Jenkins, Washington, D.C.: Dumbarton Oaks Center for Byzantine Studies.

MORAVIAN LEGEND, in Havlík, ed. (1967) 118:255–268 [Latin text and Czech translation].

Mošin, Vladimir A. (1930), "Varjago-russkij vopros," *Slavia* 10:109–136, 343–379, 501–537.

Moszyński, Kazimierz (1957), *Pierwotny zasiąg języka prasłowiańskiego*, Wroclaw: Ossolineum.

Moszyński, Leszek $(1992)_1$, "Zagadnienie wpływów celtyckich na starosłowiańską teonimię," *ZPSSl* Warsaw: Energeia, 171–176.

——— $(1992)_2$, *Die vorchristlische Religion der Slaven im Lichte der slavischen Sprachwissenschaft*, Cologne, Weimar, Vienna: Böhlau Verlag.

Nalepa, Jerzy (1968), *Słowiańszczyzna północno-zachodnia: Podstawy jedności i jej rozpad*, Poznań: PWN.

Nazarenko, Aleksandr V., ed. (1993), *Nemeckie latinojazyčnye istočniki IX–XI vekov: Teksty, perevod, kommentarij*, Moscow: Nauka. [*Drevnejšie istočniki po istorii vostočnoj Evropy.*]

Nelson, Janet L., ed. and trans. (1991), *The Annals of St-Bertin*, Manchester and New York: Manchester University Press.

Niederle, Lubor (1923), *Manuel de l'antiquité slave*, vol. 1, Paris: Édouard Champion.

——— (1925), *Slovanské starožitnosti*, 2nd ed., vol. 1, Prague: Bursík & Kohout.

Obolensky, Dimitri (1948), *The Bogomils: A Study in Balkan Neo-Manichaeism*, Cambridge: At the University Press.

——— (1974), *The Byzantine Commonwealth: Eastern Europe, 500–1453*, London: Sphere Books. [Reprint (1982), Crestwood, N.Y.: St. Vladimir's Seminary Press.]

Ochmański, Jerzy (1982), *Historia Litwy*, 2d ed., Wrocław: Ossolineum.

Ohienko, Ivan (1927, 1928), *Kostjantyn i Mefodij: Jix žyttja ta dijal'nist'*, parts 1 and 2, Warsaw: Druk. E. i Dra K. Koziańskich. [Reprint (1970), Winnipeg: Volyn'.]

PAPAL CORRESPONDENCE, in Grivec/Tomšič, eds. 1960:67–77 [Latin text]; Havlík, ed. (1969), 134:67–77 [Latin text and Czech translation].

Paschal Chronicle = Migne, ed., 1860.

Pastrnek, František (1902), *Dějiny slovanských apoštolů Cyrilla a Methoda, s otiskem hlavních pramenů*, Prague: Česká společnost nauk.

Paszkiewicz, Henryk (1954), *The Origin of Russia*, New York: Philosophical Library.

Paul the Deacon = Peters, ed., 1974.

Peisker, J. (1913), "The Expansion of the Slavs," in Gwatkin/Whitney 1913, pp. 418–459, 770–773.

Peters, Edward, ed. (1974), *History of the Lombards/Paul the Deacon*, translated by William Dudley Foulke, Philadelphia: University of Pennsylvania Press.

Plezia, Marian, ed. (1952), *Greckie i łacińskie źródła do najstarszych dziejów Słowian*, part 1, Poznań, Cracow: Polskie Towarzystwo Ludoznawcze.

——— (1982), *Anonim tzw. Gall, Kronika polska*, 5th ed., Polish translation by Roman Grodecki, Wrocław: Ossolineum.

Pogodin, A. L. (1901), *Iz istorii slavjanskix peredviženij*, St. Petersburg: Arxeologičeskij Institut.

Popowska-Taborska, Hanna (1991), *Wczesne dzieje Słowian w świetle ich języka*, Wrocław: Ossolineum.

Presbyter of Duklja [excerpt], in Havlík, ed., (1966), 104:238–245 [Latin text and Czech translation].

Primary Chronicle = Cross/Sherbowitz-Wetzor, eds., 1953.

Priscus of Pania = Dindorf, ed., 1870.

Pritsak, Omeljan (1981), *The Origin of Rus'*, vol. 1: *Old Scandinavian Sources Other than the Sagas*, Cambridge, Mass.: HURI.

Procopius = Dewing 1962.

Reuter, Timothy, ed. and trans. (1982), *The Annals of Fulda*, Manchester and New York: Manchester University Press.

Rostafiński, Józef (1908), "O pierwotnych siedzibach i gospodarstwie Słowian w przedhistorycznych czasach," *Sprawozdania z czynności i posiedzeń AU w Krakowie*, vol. 13, no. 3:6–25.

Royal Frankish Annals = King, ed., 1987.

Rozwadowski, Jan (1913), "Kilka uwag do przedhistorycznych stosunków wschodniej Europy i praojczyzny indoeuropejskiej na podstawie nazw wód," *RSl* 6:39–58.

Runciman, Steven (1930), *A History of the First Bulgarian Empire*, London: G. Bell.

Šafařík, Pavel J. (1862), *Slovanské starožitnosti*, vol. 1, Prague: Bedřich Tempský.

Schenker, Alexander M. (1985), "Were there Slavs in Central Europe before the Great Migrations?" *IJSLP* 31–32:359–373.

Sedov, V. V. (1982), *Vostočnye slavjane v VI–XIII vv.*, Moscow: Nauka.

Ševčenko, Ihor (1988/1989), "Religious missions seen from Byzantium," *HUS* 12/13:7–27.

Shevelov, George Y. (1955), "On the Slavic names for the falls of the Dnepr in the 'De administrando imperio' of Constantine Porphyrogenitus," *Word* 11 [= *SW* 4]: 503–530.

Smith, R. Payne, trans. (1860), *The Third Part of the Ecclesiastical History of John, Bishop of Ephesus*, Oxford: University Press.

Smyser, H. M. (1965), "Ibn Faḍlān's account of the Rūs with some commentary and some allusions to *Beowulf*," in Jess B. Bessinger, Jr. and Robert P. Creed, eds., *Franciplegius: Medieval and Linguistic Studies in Honor of Francis Peabody Magoun, Jr.*, New York: New York University Press, pp. 92–119.

Stender-Petersen, Ad. (1953), *Varangica*, Aarhus: Bianco Lunos Bogtrykkeri.

Sulimirski, Tadeusz (1956), "Czasy prehistoryczne," in *Polska i jej dorobek dziejowy w ciągu tysiąca lat istnienia*, ed. Henryk Paszkiewicz, 1:80–85.

THEOPHANES THE CONFESSOR = Turtledove, ed., 1982.

THEOPHYLACT OF OHRID, in Duichev, ed. 1985:93–126 [English translation of *Vita of St. Clement of Ohrid*, also known as the *Bulgarian Legend*].

THEOPHYLACT SIMOCATTA = Whitby/Whitby, eds., 1986.

THIETMAR = Holtzmann, ed., 1974.

Thorpe, Lewis, ed. and trans. (1969), Einhard and Notker the Stammerer, *Two Lives of Charlemagne*, Harmondsworth and New York: Penguin Books.

Tixomirov, Mixail N., ed. (1940), *Istočnikovedenie istorii SSR s drevnejšix vremen do konca XVIII v.*, vol. 1, Moscow: OGIZ.

Tolkačev, A. I. (1962), "O nazvanii dneprovskix porogov v sočinenii Konstantina Bagrjanorodnogo 'De administrando imperio,'" in Avanesov, ed., pp. 29–60.

Tret'jakov, P. N. (1953), *Vostočnoslavjanskie plemena*, 2d ed., Moscow: Akademija Nauk SSSR.

Trubačev, Oleg N. (1982), "Jazykoznanie i ètnogenez slavjan: Drevnie slavjane po dannym ètimologii i onomastiki," *VJa* 4:10–26 and 5:3–17.

——— (1991), *Etnogenez i kul'tura drevnejšix slavjan: Lingvističeskie issledovanija*, Moscow: Nauka.

Tschan, Francis J., ed. and trans. (1935), *The Chronicle of the Slavs by Helmold, Priest of Bosau*, New York: Columbia University Press.

——— (1959), *History of the Archbishops of Hamburg-Bremen*, New York: Columbia University Press.

Turtledove, Harry, ed. and trans. (1982), *The Chronicle of Theophanes: An English Translation of* Anni mundi *6095–6305 (A.D. 602–813)*, Philadelphia: University of Pennsylvania Press.

Udolph, Jürgen (1979), *Studien zu den slavischen Gewässernamen: Ein Beitrag zur Frage nach der Urheimat der Slaven*, Heidelberg: Carl Winter.

——— (1988), "Kamen die Slaven aus Pannonien?" in Gerard Labuda and S. Tabaczyński, *Studia nad etnogenezą Słowian i kulturą Europy wczesnośredniowiecznej*, Wrocław: Ossolineum, pp. 167–173.

Urbańczyk, Stanisław (1991), *Dawni Słowianie: Wiara i kult*, Wrocław, Warsaw, Cracow: Ossolineum.

Vasmer, Max (1926), "Die Urheimat der Slaven," *Der ostdeutsche Volksboden*, 118–144.

——— (1974), "The ancient population situation of Russia in the light of linguistic research," New York: Institute on East Central Europe, Columbia University [= Occasional Papers 1].

VITA CONSTANTINI, in Lavrov 1930:1–66; Teodorov-Balan, ed. 1920, 1934; Duichev, ed. 1985:49–80 [English translation]; Kantor 1983:25–96 [English translation]; Florja 1981:71–92, 105–142 [Russian translation with commentary].

VITA METHODII, in Lavrov 1930:67–78; Teodorov-Balan, ed. 1920, 1934; Duichev, ed. 1985:81–92 [English translation]; Kantor 1983:99–138 [English translation]; Florja 1981:93–101, 143–172 [Russian translation with commentary].

Vlasto, A. P. (1970), *The Entry of the Slavs into Christendom*, Cambridge: Cambridge University Press.

Vzdornov, G. I. (1980), *Iskusstvo knigi v Drevnej Rusi: Rukopisnaja kniga Severo-Vostočnoj Rusi XII–načala XV vekov*, Moscow: Iskusstvo.

Wallace-Hadrill, J. M., trans. (1960), *The Fourth Book of the Chronicle of Fredegar with Its Continuations*, London: Thomas Nelson.

Ware, Timothy (1984), *The Orthodox Church*, rev. ed., Harmondsworth: Penguin Books.

Whitby, Michael, and Mary Whitby, eds. and trans. (1986), *The History of Theophylact Simocatta*, Oxford: Clarendon Press.

WIDUKIND = Lohmann et al., eds. 1971.

Wolfram, Herwig, ed. and trans. (1979), Conversio Bagoariorum et Carantanorum: *Das Weissbuch der salzburger Kirche über die erfolgreiche Mission in Karantanien und Pannonien*, Vienna, Cologne, Graz: Hermann Böhlau.

Wright, F. A., ed. and trans. (1930), *The Works of Liudprand of Cremona*, London: George Routledge.

Zagiba, Franz (1971), *Das Geistesleben der Slaven im frühen Mittelalter: Die Anfänge des slavischen Schrifttums auf dem Gebiete des östlichen Mitteleuropa vom 8. bis 10. Jahrhundert*, Vienna, Cologne, Graz: Böhlau [Series Instituti Slavici Salisburgo-Ratisbonensis].

Zlatarski, Vasil N. (1970–1972), *Istorija na bălgarskata dăržava prez srednite vekove*, 3 vols., 2nd ed., Sofia: BAN.

4. Language

Included in this section are etymological dictionaries of individual Baltic and Slavic languages. For a fuller coverage, see the richly annotated bibliographic surveys in Birnbaum 1979 and Birnbaum/Merrill 1983.

Andersen, Hennig (1968), "IE *s after *i, u, r, k* in Baltic and Slavic," *ALH* 11/2: 171–190.

——— (1969), "Lenition in Common Slavic," *Lg* 45:553–574.

——— (1985), "Protoslavic and Common Slavic—Questions of periodization and terminology," in Flier/Worth, eds., pp. 67–82.

Arntz, Helmut (1933), *Sprachliche Beziehungen zwischen Arisch und Balto-slawisch*, Heidelberg: Carl Winters Universitätsbuchhandlung.

Arumaa, Peeter (1964, 1976, 1985), *Urslavische Grammatik: Einführung in das vergleichende Studium der slavischen Sprachen*, vols. 1–3, Heidelberg: Carl Winter.

Auty, Robert (1969), "The western lexical elements in the *Kiev Missal*," in W. Krauss et al., eds., *Slawisch-deutsche Wechselbeziehungen in Sprache, Literatur und Kultur*, pp. 3–6.

Avanesov, Ruben I., ed. (1962), *Istoričeskaja grammatika i leksikologija russkogo jazyka: Materialy i issledovanija*, Moscow: Akademija Nauk SSSR.

Baudouin de Courtenay, Jan (1894), "Einiges über Palatalisierung (Palatalisation) und Entpalatalisierung (Dispalatalisation)," *IF* 4:45–57.

Benni, Tytus, et al. (1915), *Język polski i jego historia z uwzględnieniem innych języków na ziemiach polskich*, 2 vols., part 3 of *Encyklopedia polska PAU*, Cracow: PAU. [Revised edition (1923) *Gramatyka języka polskiego*, Cracow: PAU.]

Benveniste, Émile (1967), "Les relations lexicales slavo-iraniennes," *To Honor Roman Jakobson*, 1:197–202.

Berneker, Erich (1900), *Die Wortfolge in den slavischen Sprachen*, Berlin: B. Behr.

——— (1908–1913), *Slavisches etymologisches Wörterbuch [A-mor]*, Heidelberg: Carl Winter.

Bernštejn, Samuil B. (1958), "Balto-slavjanskaja jazykovaja soobščnost'," *SF* 1:45–67.

——— (1961, 1974), *Očerk sravnitel'noj grammatiki slavjanskix jazykov*, vol. 1, Moscow: Akademija Nauk SSSR; vol. 2 (Čeredovanija), Moscow: Nauka.

Bezlaj, France (1976–), *Etimološki slovar slovenskega jezija*, Ljubljana: Mladinska knjiga.

Bidwell, Charles E. (1961), "The chronology of certain sound changes in Common Slavic as evidenced by loans from Vulgar Latin," *Word* 13:105–127.

Birnbaum, Henrik (1963), "Reinterpretacje fonologiczne nosówek słowiańskich (na podstawie materiału prastowiańskiego, starosłowiańskiego i polskiego)," in $ACICS_5$, 1:27–48, The Hague: Mouton.

——— (1966), "The dialects of Common Slavic," in Birnbaum/Puhvel, eds., pp. 153–197.

——— (1979), *Common Slavic: Progress and Problems in Its Reconstruction*, Columbus, Ohio: Slavica. [Russian translation in V. A. Dybo and V. K. Žuravleva, eds. (1987), *Praslavjanskij jazyk: Dostiženija i problemy v ego rekonstrukcii*, translated by V. A. Dybo, Moscow: Progress.]

Birnbaum, Henrik, and Peter T. Merrill (1983), *Recent Advances in the Reconstruction of Common Slavic (1971–1982)*, Columbus, Ohio: Slavica. [Russian translation in Birnbaum (1979).]

Birnbaum, Henrik, and Jaan Phuvel, eds. (1966), *Ancient Indo-European Dialects: Proceedings of the Conference on Indo-European Linguistics Held at UCLA on April 25–27, 1963*, Berkeley and Los Angeles: University of California Press.

Boryś, Wiesław, and Hanna Popowska-Taborska (1994–), Słownik etymologiczny kaszubszczyzny, Warsaw: Sławistyczny Ośrodek Wydawniczy, PAN.

Bräuer, Herbert (1961, 1969), *Slavische Sprachwissenschaft*, vols. 1–2, Berlin: de Gruyter.

Brückner, Aleksander (1914), "Die lituslav. Spracheinheit," *KZ* 46:217–239.

——— (1927), *Słownik etymologiczny języka polskiego*, Cracow: Krakowska Spółka Wydawnicza. [Reprint (1957) Warsaw: Wiedza Powszechna.]

Brugmann, Karl (1884), "Zur Frage den Verwandschaftverhältnissen der indogermanischen Sprachen," *IZfaSw* 1:226–256.

Bulaxovs'kyj, Leonid A. (1975, 1976, 1977, 1980, 1983), *Vybrani praci v p'jati tomax*, 5 vols., Kiev: Naukova Dumka.

Carlton, Terence R. (1991), *Introduction to the Phonological History of the Slavic Languages*, Columbus, Ohio: Slavica.

Čekman, V. N. (1979), *Issledovanija po istoričeskoj fonetike praslavjanskogo jazyka: Tipologija i rekonstrukcija*, Minsk: Nauka i Texnika.

Channon, Robert (1972), *On the Place of the Progressive Palatalization of Velars in the Relative Chronology of Slavic*, The Hague: Mouton.

Comrie, Bernard, and Greville Corbett, eds. (1993), *The Slavonic Languages*, London: Routledge.

Dybo, Vladimir A. (1981), *Slavjanskaja akcentologija: Opyt rekonstrukcii sistemy akcentnyx paradigm v praslavjanskom*, Moscow: Nauka.

Entwistle, W. J., and W. A. Morison (1964), *Russian and the Slavonic Languages*, London: Faber and Faber.

Ferrell, James O. (1963), "Some notes on Slavic gendered pronominal inflection," in $ACICS_5$ 1:59–112, The Hague: Mouton.

——— (1967), "On the prehistory of the locative singular of the Common Slavic consonant stems," in *To Honor Roman Jakobson*, 1:654–661.

Filin, Fedot P. (1972), *Proisxoždenie russkogo, ukrainskogo i belorusskogo jazykov*, Leningrad: Nauka.

Flier, Michael S., and Dean S. Worth, eds. (1985), *Slavic Linguistics, Poetics, Cultural History: In Honor of Henrik Birnbaum on His Sixtieth Birthday, 13 December 1985*, Columbus, Ohio: Slavica [= *IJSLP* 31–32].

Flier, Michael S., ed. (1983), *$ACICS_9$: Linguistics*, Columbus, Ohio: Slavica.

Fraenkel, Ernst (1950), *Die baltischen Sprachen: Ihre Beziehungen zu einander und zu den indogermanischen Schwesteridiomen als Einführung in die baltische Sprachwissenschaft*, Heidelberg: Carl Winter.

——— (1962, 1965), *Litauisches etymologisches Wörterbuch*, 2 vols., Heidelberg: Carl Winter; Göttingen: Vandenhoeck & Ruprecht.

Furdal, Antoni (1961), *Rozpad języka prasłowiańskiego w świetle rozwoju głosowego*, Wrocław: Ossolineum.

Galton, Herbert (1962), *Aorist und Aspekt im Slavischen: Eine Studie zur funktionellen und historischen Syntax*, Wiesbaden: Harrassowitz.

——— (1994), "The phonological influence of Altaic on Slavic," *JSL* 2/1:77–91.

Gamkrelidze, Tomas V., and Vjačeslav Vs. Ivanov (1973), "Sprachtypologie und die Rekonstruktion der gemeinindogermanischen Verschlüsse," *Phonetica* 27:150–156.

——— (1984), *Indoevropejskij jazyk i indoevropejcy: Rekonstrukcija i istoriko-tipologičeskij analiz prajazyka i protokul'tury*, vol. 1, Tbilisi: University of Tbilisi. [English translation (1988), *Indo-European and the Indo-Europeans*, Berlin: Mouton de Gruyter.]

Garde, Paul (1976), *Histoire de l'accentuation slave*, 2 vols., Paris: IES.

Georgiev, Vladimir I. (1964), *Vokalnata sistema v razvoja na slavjanskite ezici*, Sofia: BAN.

——— (1969), *Osnovni problemi na slavjanskata diaxronna morfologija*, Sofia: BAN.

Georgiev, Vladimir I., et al. (1962–), *Bălgarski etimologičen rečnik*, Sofia: BAN.

Holub, Josef, and František Kopečný (1952), *Etymologický slovník jazyka českého*, 3d ed., Prague: Statní nakladatelství učebnic.

Hopper, Paul J. (1973), "Glottalized and murmured occlusives in Indo-European," *Glossa* 7:141–166.

Horálek, Karel (1962), *Úvod do studia slovanských jazyků*, 2nd ed., Prague: ČSAV. [English translation (1992), *An Introduction to the Study of the Slavonic Languages*, 2 vols., translated by Peter Herrity, Nottingham: Astra Press.]

Illič-Svityč, Vladislav M. (1963), *Imennaja akcentuacija v baltijskom i slavjanskom*, Moscow: Akademija Nauk SSSR.

Isačenko, Aleksandr V. (1955), "O vozniknovenii i razvitii 'kategorii sostojanija' v slavjanskix jazykax," *VJa* 6/48–65.

Ivšić, Stjepan (1970), *Slavenska poredbena gramatika*, Zagreb: Školska knjiga.

Jakobson, Roman (1950), "Slavic mythology," *Funk and Wagnall's Standard Dictionary of Folklore, Mythology and Legend*, New York: Funk and Wagnall.

——— (1952), "On Slavic diphthongs ending in a liquid," *Word* 8:306–310 [Reprint (1962) 443–448.]

——— (1955), *Slavic Languages: A Condensed Survey*, 2nd ed., New York: King's Crown Press.

——— (1957), "Typological studies and their contribution to historical comparative linguistics," *Proceedings of the Eighth International Congress of Linguists (Oslo)*," pp. 17–25. [Reprint (1962) 523–532.]

——— (1962), *Selected Writings*, vol. 1, The Hague: Mouton.

——— (1963), "Opyt fonologičeskogo podxoda k istoričeskim voprosam slavjanskoj akcentologii: Pozdnij period slavjanskoj jazykovoj praistorii," in *$ACICS_5$* 1:153–178, The Hague: Mouton.

Jakobson, Roman, and Morris Halle (1956), *Fundamentals of Language*, 's-Gravenhage: Mouton.

Kiparsky, Valentin (1934), *Die gemeinslavische Lehnwörter aus dem Germanischen* [= Annales Academiae Fennicae, B XXXII.2]. Helsinki: Finnische Literaturgesellschaft.

——— (1963–1975), *Russische historische Grammatik*, 3 vols., Heidelberg: Carl Winter Universitätsverlag. [English translation (1979) *Russian Historical Grammar*, translated by J. I. Press, vol. 1, Ann Arbor, Mich.: Ardis.]

Knutsson, Knut (1929), *Die germanische Lehnwörter in Slavischen vom typus buky* [= Lunds Universitets Årsskrift. Ny Följd, Avd. 1. Vol. 24. Nr. 9]. Lund: C. W. K. Gleerup.

Kopečný, František (1973, 1980), *Etymologický slovník slovanských jazyků: Slova gramatická a zájmena*, vol. 1: *Předložky, koncové partikuly*, vol. 2: *Spojky, částice, zájmena a zájmenná adverbia*, Prague: Academia.

Kortlandt, Frederik H. H. (1975), *Slavic Accentuation: A Study in Relative Chronology*, Lisse: Peter de Ridder Press.

Kurkina, L. V. (1992), *Dialektnaja struktura praslavjanskogo jazyka po dannym južnoslavjanskoj leksiki*, Ljubljana: SAZU.

Kuryłowicz, Jerzy (1951), "Związki językowe słowiańsko-germańskie." *PZ* 7/2, 191–206.

——— (1952), *L'accentuation des langues indo-européennes*, 2nd ed., Wrocław: Ossolineum.

——— (1956), *L'apophonie en indo-européen*, Wrocław: Ossolineum.

——— $(1958)_1$, "Na marginesie ostatniej syntezy akcentuacji słowiańskiej," *RS* 20:40–53.

——— $(1958)_2$, "O baltoslavjanskom jazykovom edinstve," *VSJa* 3:15–49.

——— (1964), *The Inflectional Categories of Indo-European*, Heidelberg: Carl Winter.

——— (1977), *Problèmes de linguistique indo-européenne*, Wrocław: Ossolineum [= Komitet Językoznawstwa PAN *Prace Językoznawcze* 90].

Kurz, Josef, ed. (1963), *Issledovanija po sintaksisu staroslavjanskogo jazyka/Contributions to Old Church Slavonic Syntax*, Prague: ČSAV.

Kuznecov, Petr S. (1961), *Očerki po morfologii praslavjanskogo jazyka*, Moscow: Akademija Nauk SSSR.

Lamprecht, Arnošt (1987), *Praslovanština*, Brno: Univerzita J. E. Purkyně.

Lehmann, Winfred P. (1952), *Proto-Indo-European Phonology*, Austin: University of Texas Press.

Lehr-Spławiński, Tadeusz (1918), "O prasłowiańskiej metatonii," *PKJ* 3 [Reprinted in Lehr-Spławiński 1957:52–92].

——— (1957), *Studia i szkice wybrane z językoznawstwa słowiańskiego*, Warsaw: PWN.

Lekov, Ivan (1960), *Nasoki v razvoja na fonologičnite sistemi na slavjanskite ezici*, Sofia: BAN.

——— (1968), *Kratka sravnitelno-istoričeska i tipologičeska gramatika na slavjanskite ezici*, Sofia: BAN.

Liewehr, Ferdinand (1955), *Slawische Sprachwissenschaft in Einzeldarstellungen*, Vienna: Rudolf M. Rohrer.

Lindeman, Fredrik Otto (1987), *Introduction to the "Laryngeal Theory,"* Oslo: Norwegian University Press.

Lunt, Horace G. (1981), *The Progressive Palatalization of Common Slavic*, Skopje: MANI.

——— (1984/1985), "On Common Slavic," *ZFL* 27/28:417–422.

——— (1985), "On the progressive palatalization of Early Slavic: Synchrony versus history," *SLS* 15/2:149–169.

Machek, Václav (1957), *Etymologický slovník jazyka českého a slovenského*, Prague: ČSAV.

Mareš, František V. (1956), "Vznik slovanského fonologického systému a jeho vývoj do konce období slovanské jednoty," *Slavia* 25:443–495. [English translation (1965), *The Origin of the Slavic phonological System and Its Development up to the End of Slavic Language Unity*, translated by J. F. Snopek and A. Vitek, Ann Arbor: Dept. of Slavic Languages and Literatures, University of Michigan.] [German translation (1965), *Die Entstehung des slavischen phonologischen Systems und seine Entwicklung bis zum Ende der Periode der slavischen Spracheinheit*, Munich: Sagner.]

——— (1962), "Rannij period morfologičeskogo razvitija slavjanskogo sklonenija," *VJa* 6:13–21.

——— (1964), "The Proto-Slavic and Early Slavic declension system," *TLP* 1:163–172.

Markov, Vladimir, and Dean S. Worth, eds. (1983), *From Los Angeles to Kiev*, Columbus, Ohio: Slavica [= *UCLA Slavic Studies* 7].

Martinet, André (1970), *Economie des changements phonétiques*, 3d ed., Bern, Francke Verlag.

Martynaŭ, Viktar U., et al. (1978–), *Etymalahičny sloŭnik belaruskaj movy*, Minsk: Navuka i tèxnika.

Martynov [= Martynaŭ], Viktor V. (1963), *Slavjano-germanskoe leksičeskoe vzaimodejstvie drevnejšej pory*. Minsk: AN BSSR.

Meillet, Antoine (1902, 1905), *Etudes sur l'étymologie et le vocabulaire du vieux slave*, 2 vols., Paris: E. Bouillon.

——— (1925), "Les origines du vocabulaire slave I: Le problème de l'unité balto-slave," *RES* 5:5–13.

——— (1926), "Le vocabulaire slave et le vocabulaire indo-iranien," *RES* 6:165–174.

——— (1934), *Le slave commun*, 2nd ed., revised by André Vaillant, Paris: Librairie Champion. [Russian translation (1951), *Obščeslavjanskij jazyk*, translated by P. S. Kuznecov, Moscow: Izdatel'stvo inostrannoj literatury.]

Mikkola, Josef J. (1913, 1942, 1950), *Urslavische Grammatik: Einführung in das vergleichende Studium der slavischen Sprachen*, 3 vols., Heidelberg: Carl Winter.

Miklosich, Franz (1875–1883), *Vergleichende Grammatik der slavischen Sprachen*, 4 vols., 2nd ed., Vienna: Wilhelm Braumüller, Heidelberg: Carl Winter.

——— (1886), *Etymologisches Wörterbuch der slavischen Sprachen*, Vienna: Wilhelm Braumüller. [Reprint (1970), Amsterdam: Philo Press.]

Mladenov, Stefan (1941), *Etimologičeski i pravopisen rečnik na bălgarskija knižoven ezik*, Sofia: X. G. Danov.

Moszyński, Leszek (1984), *Wstęp do filologii słowiańskiej*, Warsaw: PWN.

Nahtigal, Rajko (1952), *Slovanski jeziki*, 2nd ed., Ljubljana: Jože Moškrič. [German translation (1961), *Die slavische Sprachen: Abriss der vergleichenden Grammatik*, translated by Joseph Schütz, Wiesbaden: Harrassowitz.] [Russian translation (1963), *Slavjanskie jazyki*, translated by N. M. Elkina, Moscow: Izdatel'stvo inostrannoj literatury.]

Němec, Igor (1958), *Genese slovanského systému vidového*, Prague: ČSAV.

Polański, Kazimierz (1962–1994), *Słownik etymologiczny języka Drzewian połabskich*, Wrocław, Warsaw, Cracow, Gdansk: Ossolineum [first fascicle with Tadeusz Lehr-Spławiński, fifth and sixth fascicles published by Energeia].

Preobraženskij, Aleksandr G. (1910, 1914; 1949), *Etimologičeskij slovar' russkogo jazyka*, 3 vols., Moscow: Tipografija G. Lisskera in D. Sovko; Akademija Nauk SSSR. [Reprints (1951), New York: Columbia University Press, in one volume; (1958) Moscow: Gos. Izd-vo inostrannyx i nacional'nyx slovarej.]

Prokosch, Eduard (1939), *A Comparative Germanic Grammar*, Philadelphia and Baltimore: Linguistic Society of America and University of Pennsylvania.

Rozwadowski, Jan (1912), "O pierwotnym stosunku wzajemnym języków bałtyckich i słowiańskich," *RS* 5:1–36 [Reprinted in Rozwadowski 1961:96–113.]

——— (1914–1915), "Stosunki leksykalne między językami słowiańskimi i irańskimi," *RO* 1:95–110 [Reprinted in Rozwadowski 1961:114–125].

——— (1915), "Historyczna fonetyka czyli głosownia," in Benni et al. 1915, vol. 2:319–331. [Revised edition in Benni et al. 1923:57–206, reprinted in Rozwadowski 1959:29–224].

——— (1959, 1961, 1960), *Wybór pism*, 3 vols., Warsaw: PWN.

Rudnicki, Mikołaj (1959, 1961), *Prasłowiańszczyzna-Lechia-Polska*, vol. 1: *Wyłonienie się Słowian spośród ludów indoeuropejskich i ich pierwotne siedziby*, vol. 2: *Wspólnota słowiańska-wspólnota lechicka-Polska*, Poznań: PWN.

Rudnyc'kyj, Jaroslav B. (1962–), *An Etymological Dictionary of the Ukrainian Language*, Winnipeg: Ukrainian Free Academy of Sciences.

Sadnik, Linda, and Rudolf Aitzetmüller, eds. (1963–), *Vergleichendes Wörterbuch der slavischen Sprachen*, Wiesbaden: Otto Harrassowitz.

Šanskij, Nikolaj M., et al. (1975), *Kratkij ètimologičeskij slovar' russkogo jazyka*, 3rd ed., Moscow: Prosveščenie.

Savčenko, Aleksej N. (1974), *Sravnitel'naja grammatika indo-evropejskix jazykov*, Moscow: Vysšaja škola.

Schelesniker, Herbert (1964), *Beiträge zur historischen Kasusentwicklung des Slavischen*, Graz-Cologne: Hermann Böhlaus Nachf. (= *WSJ*, vol. 5).

Schenker, Alexander M. (1993), "Proto-Slavonic," in Comrie/Corbett, eds., 1993:60–121.

Schenker, Alexander M., ed. (1988), *$ACICS_{10}$: Linguistics*, Columbus, Ohio: Slavica.

Schleicher, August (1861–1862), *Compendium der vergleichenden Grammatik der indogermanischen Sprachen: Kurzer Abriss einer Laut- und Formenlehre der indogermanischen Ursprache*, Weimar: Böhlau. [English translation (1874–1877), *A Compendium of the Comparative Grammar of the Indo-European, Sanskrit, Greek and Latin Languages*, translated by Herbert Bendall, London: Trübner.]

Schuster-Šewc, Heinz (1978–), *Historisch-etymologisches Wörterbuch der ober- und niedersorbischen Sprache*, Bauzen: Domowina-Verlag.

Senn, Aflred (1966), "The relationships of Baltic and Slavic," in Birnbaum/Puhvel, eds. (1966), pp. 139–151.

Shevelov, George Y. (1965), *A Prehistory of Slavic: The Historical Phonology of Common Slavic*, New York: Columbia University Press.

Skok, Petar (1971–1974), *Etimologijski rječnik hrvatskogo ili srpskogo jezika*, 4 vols., Zagreb: JAZU.

Sławski, Franciszek (1954–), *Słownik etymologiczny języka polskiego*, Cracow: Towarzystwo Miłośników Języka Polskiego.

——— (1974–), *Słownik prasłowiański*, Wrocław: Ossolineum.

Sobolevskij, A. I. (1910), *Materialy i issledovanija v oblasti slavjanskoj filologii i arxeologii* [= *SORJaS* 88:1–287]. [Reprint (1966), Nendeln, Liechtenstein: Kraus Reprints.]

Stang, Christian S. (1942), *Das slavische und baltische Verbum*, Oslo: Jacob Dybwad.

——— (1957), *Slavonic Accentuation*, Oslo: Aschehoug W. Nygaard.

——— (1972), *Lexikalische Sonderübereinstimmungen zwischen dem Slavischen, Baltischen und Germanischen*, Oslo: Universitetsforlaget.

Stankiewicz, Edward (1966), "The Common Slavic prosodic pattern and its evolution in Slovenian," *IJSLP* 10:29–38 [Reprinted in Stankiewicz 1979:32–41, 1986:35–43].

——— (1973), "The historical phonology of Common Slavic (review article)," *IJSLP* 16:178–192 [Reprinted in Stankiewicz 1986:21–34].

——— (1979), *Studies in Slavic Morphophonemics and Accentology*, Ann Arbor: Michigan Slavic Publications.

——— (1986), *The Slavic Languages: Unity in Diversity*, Berlin, New York, Amsterdam: Mouton de Gruyter.

——— (1988), "The nominal accentuation of Common Slavic and Lithuanian," in Schenker, ed. (1988), 1:293–319, Columbus, Ohio: Slavica.

——— (1993), *The Accentual Patterns of the Slavic Languages*, Stanford, Calif.: Stanford University Press.

Stender-Petersen, Adolf (1925), *Slavisch-germanische Lehnwortkunde: Eine Studie über die ältesten germanischen Lehnwörter im Slavischen in sprach- und kulturgeschichtlichen Beleuchtung*. Gothenburg: Wettergren & Kerber.

Stieber, Zdzisław (1979), *Zarys gramatyki porównawczej języków słowiańskich*, Warsaw: PWN.

Szemerényi, Oswald $(1957)_1$, "The problem of Balto-Slav Unity: A critical survey," *Krat* 2:97–123.

——— $(1957)_2$, *Studies in the Indo-European System of Numerals*, Heidelberg: Carl Winter.

——— (1990), *Einführung in die vergleichende Sprachwissenschaft*, 4th ed., Darmstadt: Wissenschaftliche Buchgesellschaft. [Russian translation of 2nd ed. (1980), *Vvedenie v sravnitel'noe jazykoznanie*, translated by B. A. Abramov, Moscow: Progress.]

Tedesco, Paul (1948), "Slavic *ne*-presents from older *je*-presents," *Lg* 24:346–387.

Timberlake, Alan $(1983)_1$, "Compensatory lengthening in Slavic 1: Conditions and dialect geography," in Vladimir Markov and Dean S. Worth, eds. *From Los Angeles to Kiev*, Columbus, Ohio: Slavica, pp. 206–235.

——— $(1983)_2$, "Compensatory lengthening in Slavic 2: Phonetic reconstruction," in Flier, ed. (1983), 1:293–319, Columbus, Ohio: Slavica.

To Honor Roman Jakobson (1967), *Essays on the Occasion of His Seventieth Birthday, 11 October 1966*, 3 vols., The Hague, Paris: Mouton [= *Janua Linguarum*, Series Major 31–33].

Toporov, Vladimir N. (1961), *Lokativ v slavjanskix jazykax*, Moscow: Akademija Nauk SSSR.

Trautmann, Reinhold (1923), *Baltisch-slavisches Wörterbuch*, Göttingen: Vandenhoeck & Ruprecht.

——— (1947), *Die slavischen Völker und Sprachen: Eine Einführung in die Slavistik*, Göttingen: Vandenhoeck & Ruprecht.

Trubačev, Oleg N., ed. (1974–), *Etimologičeskij slovar' slavjanskix jazykov: Praslavjanskij leksičeskij fond*, Moscow: Nauka.

Trubeckoj, Nikolaj S. [= N. S. Trubetzkoy, Troubetzkoy] (1925), "Les voyelles nasales des langues léchites," *RES* 5:24–37.

——— (1928), "Ob otraženijax obščeslavjanskogo ę v češskom," *Slavia* 6:661–684.

Vaillant, André (1950, 1958, 1966, 1974, 1977), *Grammaire comparée des langues slaves*, vols. 1–2, Lyon, Paris: IAC; vols. 3–5, Paris: Klincksieck.

——— (1957), "L'unité linguistique balto-slave," *Fil* 1:23–35.

Vasmer, Max (1953–1958), *Russisches etymologisches Wörterbuch*, 3 vols., Heidelberg: Carl Winter Universitätsverlag. [Russian translation (1964–1973), *Etimologičeskij slovar' russkogo jazyka*, 4 vols., translated and expanded by O. N. Trubačev, Moscow: Progress.

Velčeva, Borjana [= Boryana Velcheva] (1980), *Praslavjanski i starobălgarski fonologičeski izmenenija*, Sofia: BAN. [English translation (1988), *Proto-Slavic and Old Bulgarian Sound Changes*, translated and edited by Ernest A. Scatton, Columbus, Ohio: Slavica.]

Vondrák, Wenzel (1924, 1928), *Vergleichende slavische Grammatik*, vols. 1–2, Göttingen: Vandenhoeck & Ruprecht.

Watkins, Calvert (1969), *Geschichte der indogermanischen Verbalflexion*, Heidelberg: Carl Winter [= Jerzy Kuryłowicz, ed., *Indogermanische Grammatik*, vol. 3, part 1].

Wijk, Nicolaas van (1956), *Les langues slaves: De l'unité à la pluralité*, The Hague: Mouton.

5. Early Writing

Included in this section are Old Church Slavonic grammars and dictionaries but not grammars and dictionaries of local recensions of Church Slavonic (see notes 308 and 321). References to the monuments discussed in **3.38–3.55** cover major editions, translations, and vocabularies but do not, as a rule, include secondary literature (see note 244).

Abramovič, Dmitrij I., ed. (1916), *Žitija svjatyx mučenikov Borisa i Gleba i služby im*, Petrograd [= *PDRL*, no. 2]. [Reprint, L. Müller, ed. (1967), Munich: Eidos Verlag (= *Slavische Propyläen*, vol. 14).]

——— (1930), *Kyevo-Pečers'kyj pateryk*, Kiev: Vseukraïns'kaja Akademija nauk. [Reprint, Dmitrij Čiževskij, ed. (1964), *Das Paterikon des Kiever Höhlenklosters*, nach der Ausgabe von D. Abramovič, Munich: Eidos Verlag (= *Slavische Propyläen*, vol. 2).]

Adrianova-Peretc, Varvara P., ed. $(1950)_1$, *Povest' vremennyx let*, 2 vols., Moscow, Leningrad: Akademija Nauk SSSR.

——— $(1950)_2$, *Slovo o polku Igoreve*, Moscow, Leningrad: Akademija Nauk SSSR.

Aitzetmüller, Rudolf (1978), *Altbulgarische Grammatik als Einführung in die slavische Sprachwissenschaft*, Freiburg im Breisgau: U. W. Weiher.

Aitzetmüller, Rudolf, ed. (1958–1975), *Das Hexaemeron des Exarchen Johannes*, 7 vols., Graz: Akademische Druck- u. Verlagsanstalt.

Alekseev, Aleksej A. (1985), "Filologičeskie kriterii vyjavlenija biblejskix perevodov sv. Mefodija," *PK* 14–15:8–14.

——— (1986), "Citaty iz Pesni pesnej v slavjanskoj pis'mennosti (citaty i tekstologija)," *StBLit* 18:74–92.

Altbauer, Moshe, ed. (1971), *Psalterium Sinaiticum: An 11th century Glagolitic Manuscript from St. Catherine's Monastery, Mt. Sinai*, Skopje: MANU.

——— (1973), *Dobromirovo evangelie: Kirilski spomenik od XII vek*, facsimile ed., Skopje: MANU.

Altbauer, Moshe, and Horace G. Lunt, eds. (1978), *An Early Slavonic Psalter from Rus'*, vol. 1, Cambridge, Mass: HURI.

Angelov, Bonju St., ed. (1958, 1967, 1978), *Iz starata bălgarska, ruska i srăbska literatura*, 3 vols., Sofia: BAN.

Angelov, Bonju St., et al., eds. (1970, 1977, 1973), *Kliment Oxridski: Săbrani săčinenija*, 3 vols., Sofia: BAN.

Angelov, Dimităr, ed. (1968), *Kliment Oxridski: Materiali za negovoto čestvuvane po slučaj 1050 godini ot smărtta mu*, Sofia: BAN.

Arcixovskij, Artemij V., and Viktor I. Borkovskij, eds. (1958), *Novgorodskie gramoty na bereste (iz raskopok 1953–1954 gg.)*, Moscow: Akademija Nauk SSSR.

Arcixovskij, Artemij V., and Mixail N. Tixomirov, eds. (1953), *Novgorodskie gramoty na bereste*, Moscow: Akademija Nauk SSSR.

Arnim, B. von, ed. (1930), *Studien zum altbulgarischen Psalterium Sinaiticum*, Leipzig: Slavisches Institut an der Friedrich-Wilhelms-Universität Berlin.

Auty, Robert (1960), *Handbook of Old Church Slavonic*, vol. 2: *Texts and Glossary*, London: Athlone Press [see Nandriş 1959].

Avanesov, Ruben I., ed. (1963), *Smolenskie gramoty XIII–XIV vekov*, Moscow: Akademija Nauk SSSR.

Avdusin, D. A. and M. N. Tixomirov (1950), "Drevnejšaja russkaja nadpis'," *VestAN*, vol. 20, fasc. 4, pp. 71–79.

Begunov, Ju. K. (1973), *Kozma Presviter v slavjanskix literaturax*, Sofia: BAN.

Beneševič, V. N., ed. (1906), *Syntagma XIV Titulorum sine scholiis secundum versionem Palaeo-Slovenicam*, vol. 1, St. Petersburg: IAN. [Reprint (1974) *Drevne-slavjanskaja Kormčaja XIV titulov bez tolkovanij* in *Subsidia byzantina lucis ope iterata*, Leipzig, vol. 2b.]

Beneševič, V. N., and Ja. N. Ščapov, eds. (1974), *Drevne-slavjanskaja kormčaja XIV titulov bez tolkovanij*, vol. 2, Sofia: BAN.

Bielfeldt, Hans Holm (1961), *Altslawische Grammatik*, Halle (Saale): Max Niemeyer.

Birkfellner, Gerhard (1979), *Das Römische Paterikon: Studien zur serbischen, bulgarischen und russischen Überlieferung der Dialoge Gregors des Grossen mit einer Textedition*, 2 vols., Vienna: ÖAW.

Birnbaum, Henrik (1974), *On Medieval and Renaissance Slavic Writing: Selected Essays*, The Hague: Mouton.

——— (1981), *Essays in Early Slavic Civilization*, Munich: Wilhelm Fink.

Birnbaum, Henrik, and Michael Flier, eds. (1984), *Medieval Russian Culture*, Berkeley and Los Angeles: University of California Press [= California Slavic Studies, vol. 12].

Bláhová Emilie (1989–), *Etymologický slovník jazyka staroslověnského*, Prague: Academia.

Bodjanskij, Osip M., ed. (1877), *Bogoslovie svjatogo Ioanna Damaskina v perevode Ioanna eksarxa bolgarskogo* (edition corrected by Andrej N. Popov), *ČOIDR*, vol. 1.

——— (1879), *Šestodnev sostavlennyj Ioannom eksarxom bolgarskim: Po xaratejnomu spisku moskovskoj sinodal'noj biblioteki 1263 goda* (edition corrected by Andrej N. Popov), *ČOIDR*, vol. 3.

Bogdanov, Ivan (1978), *Bălgarskata kniga prez vekovete*, Sofia: Narodna prosveta.

——— (1990), "Rejmsko evangelie," *LitM* 5:156–165.

Bodganović, Dimitrije (1980), *Istorija stare srpske knijiževnosti*, Belgrade: Srpska književna zadruga.

Božilov, Ivan, and Stefan Kožuxarov, eds. (1987), *Bălgarskata literatura i knižnina prez XIII vek*, Sofia: Bălgarski pisatel.

Brandt, Roman F. (1909), *Lekcii po slavjano-russkoj paleografii*, Moscow: MAI.

Brandt, Roman F., ed. (1894, 1900, 1901), *Grigorovičev parimejnik*, in *ČOIDR*, vols. 1, 3 (1894); vol. 2 (1900); vol. 2 (1901).

Budilovič, Anton S., ed. (1875), *XIII Slov Grigorija Bogoslova v drevneslavjanskom perevode XI v. po ruk[opisi] P[ubličnoj] B[iblioteki]*, St. Petersburg: Izdanie Otdelenija russkogo jazyka i slovesnosti IAN.

Butler, Thomas, ed. (1980), *Monumenta Serbocroatica: A Bilingual Anthology of Serbian and Croatian Texts from the 12th to the 19th Century*, Ann Arbor: Michigan Slavic Publications.

Čaev, Nikolaj S., and Lev V. Čerepnin (1946), *Russkaja paleografija*, Moscow: Glavnoe arxivnoe upravlenie MVD SSSR.

Capaldo, Mario (1981), "L'Azbučno-Ierusalimskij paterik," *PK* 4:26–49.

Čerepnin, Lev V. (1956), *Russkaja paleografija*, Moscow: Gos. Izd. Polit. Lit.

Christopher, Henry G. T. (1938), *Palaeography and Archives: A Manual for the Librarian, Archivist and Student*, London: Grafton.

Čiževskij [= Tschižewskij, Čyževs'kyj, Čiževsky], Dmitrij (1960), *History of Russian Literature: From the Eleventh Century to the End of the Baroque*, 's-Gravenhage: Mouton.

Colucci, Michele, et al., eds. (1986), *Studia Slavica Mediaevalia et Humanistica Riccardo Picchio Dicata*, Rome: Edizioni dell'Ateneo.

Conev, Ben'o, ed. (1906), *Dobrejšovo četveroevangelie: Srednobălgarski pametnik ot XIII v.*, Sofia: Dăržavna pečatnica.

Črnčić, Ivan, ed. (1878), *Assemanovo izborno evangjelje*, Rome: Published privately.

Cronia, E. (1956), *Storia della letteratura serbo-croata*, Milan: Nuova accademia editrice.

Cross, Samuel H., and Olgerd P. Sherbowitz-Wetzor, eds. (1953), *The Russian Primary Chronicle: Laurentian Text*, Cambridge, Mass.: MAA.

Daničić, Djuro, ed. (1860), *Život svetoga Save napisao Domentijan*, Belgrade: U Državnoj štampariji. [Reprint (1973) by Djordje Trifunović as Teodosije Hilandarac, *Život svetoga Save*, Belgrade.]

Davidov, Angel A. (1976), *Rečnik-indeks na Prezviter Kozma*, Sofia: BAN.

Dewey, Horace W., and Ann M. Kleimola, trans. (1977), *Zakon sudnyi ljudem Court Law for the People*, Ann Arbor: Dept. of Slavic Languages and Literatures, University of Michigan [= *Michigan Slavic Materials*, no. 14].

Diels, Paul (1932, 1934), *Altkirchenslavische Grammatik*, 2 parts, Heidelberg: Carl Winter.

Dinekov, Petăr, ed. (1991, 1993), *Simeonov sbornik (po Svetoslavovija prepis ot 1073 g.)*, 2 vols., Sofia: BAN.

Dinekov, Petăr, et al. eds. (1962), *Starobălgarska literatura*, in *Istorija na bălgarskata literatura*, vol. 1, Sofia: Ban.

——— (1985–), *Kirilo-Metodievska enciklopedija*, Sofia: BAN.

Diringer, David (1968), *The Alphabet: A Key to the History of Mankind*, 3d ed., New York: Funk & Wagnalls.

D'jačenko, Grigorij (1899), *Polnyj cerkovno-slavjanskij slovar'*, 2 vols., Moscow: Tipografija Vil'de. [Reprint (1993), Moscow: Izdatel'skij Otdel Moskovskogo Patriarxata.]

Dobrev, Ivan (1972), *Glagoličeskijat tekst na Bojanskija palimpsest: Starobălgarski pametnik ot kraja na XI vek*, Sofia: BAN.

——— (1981), "Sădărža li makedonskijat kirilski list otkăs ot proizvedenie na Konstantin Filosof-Kiril prevodačesko izkustvo?" in *StBLit* 9:20–32.

Dobrev, Ivan, and Kazimir Popkonstantinov (1985), "Epigrafika starobălgarska," in Dinekov et al., eds. 1985–, vol. 1, pp. 662–677.

Dostál, Antonín, ed. (1959), *Clozianus: Staroslověnský hlaholský sborník tridentský a innsbrucký*, Prague: ČSAV.

Dubrovina, V. F., et al., eds. (1977), *Vygoleksinskij sbornik*, Moscow: Nauka.

Duichev [= Dujčev], Ivan (1985), "A nationality-building factor: The role of the Slavic script for the Bulgarians," in Duichev, ed., 1985:37–47 [full bibliographic entry on p. 308].

Dujčev, Ivan, ed. (1963), *Letopista na Konstantin Manasi*, Sofia: BAN.

——— (1968), *Bolonski psaltir: Bălgarski knižoven pametnik ot XIII vek*, Sofia: BAN [facsimile edition].

Durnovo, Nikolaj (1929), "Mysli i predpoloženija o proisxoždenii staroslavjanskogo jazyka i slavjanskix alfavitov, *ByzSl* 1:48–85.

Džambeluka-Kossova, Alda, ed. (1980), *Černorizec Xrabăr: O pismenex*, Sofia: BAN.

Eckhardt, Thorvi (1989), *Azbuka: Versuch einer Einführung in das Studium der slavischen Paläographie*, Vienna, Cologne: Böhlau Verlag.

Faganel, Jože, et al., eds. (1993), *Brižinski spomeniki: Znanstvenokritična izdaja*, Ljubljana: SAZU [= SAZU, Razred za filološke in literarne vede, Dela No. 39].

Flier, Michael S. (1984), "Sunday in medieval Russian culture: *nedelja* versus *voskresenie*," in Birnbaum/Flier, eds., pp. 107–149.

Florja, B. N., ed. (1981), *Skazanija o načale slavjanskoj pis'mennosti*, Moscow: Nauka.

Franklin, Simon (1991), *Sermons and Rhetoric of Kievan Rus'*, Cambridge, Mass.: HURI.

Frček, Jan (1933), *Euchologium Sinaiticum: Texte slave avec sources grecques et traduction française*, 2 vols., Paris [= R. Graffin, *Patrologia orientalis*, vol. 24, fasc. 5 and vol. 25, fasc. 3].

Fučić, Branko (1971), "Najstariji hrvatski glagolski natpisi," *Slovo* 21:227–254.

——— (1982), *Glagolski natpisi*, Zagreb: JAZU.

Gardner, Johann von (1980), *Russian Church Singing*, vol. 1, *Orthodox Worship and Hymnography*, trans. Vladimir Morosan, St. Vladimir's Seminary Press: Crestwood, N.Y.

Gellrich, Jesse M. (1988), *The Idea of Book in the Middle Ages*, Ithaca, N.Y.: Cornell University Press.

Georgiev, Emil (1952), *Slavjanskaja pis'mennost' do Kirilla i Mefodija*, Sofia: BAN.

——— (1956), *Kiril i Metodij, osnovopoložnici na slavjanskite literaturi*, Sofia: BAN.

——— (1966), *Literatura na izostreni borbi v srednevekovna Bălgarija*, Sofia: BAN.

——— (1985), "Konstantin Preslavski," in Duichev, ed., 1985:161–180 [see p. 308].

Georgievski, Mixajlo, ed. (1979), *Makedonskoto književno nasledstvo od XI do XVIII vek: Pregled*, Skopje: Prosveten rabotnik.

Georgievskij, G. P., ed. (1912), *Arxangel'skoe Evangelie 1092 g.* [description and facsimile], Moscow: Rumjancevskij muzej.

Goldblatt, Harvey (1985), "*Létopisi* (Annals)," in Terras, ed., pp. 252–254.

——— (1986), "On *rusьskymi pismeny* in the *Vita Constantini* and Rus'ian religious patriotism," in Colucci et al., eds., 311–328.

Golyšenko, V. S., and V. F. Dubrovina (1967), *Sinajskij paterik*, Moscow: Nauka.

Golyšenko, V. S., et al., eds. (1965), *Izbornik 1076 goda*, Moscow: Nauka.

Gošev, Ivan (1961), *Starobălgarski glagoličeski i kirilski nadpisi ot IX i X v.*, Sofia: BAN.

Gošev, Ivan, ed. (1956), *Rilski glagoličeski listove*, Sofia: BAN.

Granstrem, E. (1964), "Slavjano-russkie palimpsesty," *Arxeografičeskij ežegodnik za 1963 g.*, Moscow, pp. 218–222.

Grégoire, Henri, et al., eds. (1948), *La geste du Prince Igor': Epopée russe du douxième siècle*, New York: Rausen Brothers, Printers.

Grekov, B. D., ed. (1940, 1947), *Pravьda rusьskaja*, 2 vols., Moscow, Leningrad: Akademija Nauk SSSR.

Grivec, Fran (1943), "Clozov-Kopitarjev glagolit v slovenski književnosti in zgodovini," *Razprave SAZU* 1.5:343–408.

Gudzij, N. K. (1966), *Istorija drevnej russkoj literatury*, 7th ed., Moscow: Prosveščenie.

Hamm, Josip (1947), *Pregled gramatike starocrkvenoslavenskog jezika s hrestomatijom i rječnikom*, 2 vols., Zagreb: Nakladni zavod Hrvatske.

——— (1958), *Staroslavenska gramatika*, Zagreb: Školska knjiga.

——— (1964), "Serbskaja i xorvatskaja redakcija obščeslavjanskogo literaturnogo jazyka," *VJa* 3, 84–87.

——— (1979), *Das Glagolitische Missale von Kiev*, Vienna: ÖAW.

Heppel, Muriel (1989), *The Paterik of the Kievan Caves Monastery*, Cambridge, Mass.: HURI [English translation with commentary].

Hercigonja, Eduard (1975), *Srednjovjekovna književnost*, in Hercigonja et al., eds.

Hercigonja, Eduard, et al., eds. (1975–), *Povijest hrvatske književnosti u sedam knjiga*, Zagreb: Liber Mladost.

Hollingsworth, Paul (1992), *The Hagiography of Kievan Rus'*, Cambridge, Mass.: HURI [English translation with commentary].

Hruns'kyj, Mykola K. (1906), *Lekcii po drevne-cerkovno-slavjanskomu jazyku*, Dorpat (Juriev): Tip K. Mattisena.

Huntley, David (1993), "Old Church Slavonic," in Comrie/Corbett, eds., pp. 125–187.

Il'inskij, Grigorij A. (1906), "Makedonskij listok: Otryvok neizvestnogo pamjatnika kirillovskoj pis'mennosti XI–XII v." in *PSSlJa*, vol. 1, fasc. 3.

——— (1909), "Makedonskij glagoličeskij listok," in *PSSlJa*, vol. 1, fasc. 6.

Il'inskij, Grigorij A., ed. (1911), *Slepčenskij apostol XII v.*, Moscow: Tipografija G. Lissnera i D. Sobko.

——— (1915), *Oxridskie glagoličeskie listki: Otryvok drevne-cerkovno-slavjanskogo evangelija XI v.*, in *PSSlJa*, vol. 3, no. 2.

——— (1929), "Zlatostruj A. F. Byčkova XI veka," in *Bălgarski starini*, vol. 10, Sofia: BAN.

Isačenko, Aleksandr V. (1943), *Jazyk a pôvod Frizinských pamiatok*, Bratislava: SAVU.

Istrin, Vasilij M. (1903), "I z oblasti drevne-russkoj literatury. I. Xronika Georgija Sinkella," *ŽMNP* 348:381–414. [Also (1906), in *Issledovanija v oblasti drevnerusskoj literatury*, pp. 2–34, St. Petersburg: Senatskaja tipografija.]

——— (1922), *Očerk istorii drevnerusskoj literatury domoskovskogo perioda (11–13 vv.)*, Petrograd: Nauka i škola.

Istrin, Vasilij M., ed. (1897, 1902, 1905, 1910, 1912, 1914, 1915), *Xronika Ioanna Malaly* (bibliographic details in Lixačev, ed. 1987:473–474).

——— (1920, 1922, 1930), *Knigy vrěmenьnyę i obrazьnyę Georgija Mnixa: Xronika Georgija Amartola v drevnem slavjano-russkom perevode*, 3 vols., Petrograd/Leningrad: RAN/AN SSSR. [Reprint (1972), *Die Chronik des Georgios Hamartolos in altslavischer Übersetzung*, Munich (= Slavische Propyläen, vol. 135).]

——— (1934), *La prise de Jérusalem de Joseph le Juif*, edition prepared by André Vaillant, French translation by Pierre Pascal, Paris: IES.

Istrin, Viktor A. (1963), *1100 let slavjanskoj azbuki*, Moscow: Akademija Nauk SSSR.

Ivanov, J., ed. (1931), *Bălgarski starini iz Makedonija*, 2nd ed., Sofia: BAN, Dăržavna pečatnica. [Reprint (1970).]

Ivanova, Vera (1955), "Nadpisăt na Mostič i preslavskijat epigrafski material," in Stančev et al. 1955:43–144.

Ivanova-Mavrodinova, Vera, and Aksinia Džurova (1981), *Asemanievo evangelie*, Sofia: Nauka i izkustvo.

Ivanova-Mirčeva, Dora (1984), *Starobălgarski rečnik*, Sofia: BAN [introductory volume].

Jacobs, A., ed. (1970), *ZŌNARAS-Zonara: Die byzantinische Geschichte bei Joannes Zonaras in slavischer Übersetzung*, Munich: Wilhelm Fink Verlag [= Slavische Propyläen, vol. 98].

Jagić, Vatroslav [= Ignatij V. Jagič] (1895), "Rassuždenija južnoslavjanskoj i russkoj stariny o cerkovno-slavjanskom jazyke," in *IRJa*, vol. 1.

——— (1903), "Kirchenslavisch-böhmische Glossen saec. XI.–XII.," *Denkschriften der ÖAW, Philosophisch-historische Klasse*, vol. 50, part 2.

——— (1911), "Glagoličeskoe pis'mo," in Jagić, ed. (1910–1929), vol. 3:53–262, I–XXXVI.

——— (1913), *Entstehungsgeschichte der kirchenslavischen Sprache*, 2nd rev. ed., Berlin: Weidmannsche Buchhandlung.

Jagić, Vatroslav [= Ignatij V. Jagič], ed. (1879), *Quattuor evangeliorum codex glagoliticus olim Zographensis nunc Petropolitanus*, Berlin: Weidmann. [Reprint (1954), in *EMSVD*.]

——— (1883), *Mariinskoe četveroevangelie s primečanijami i priloženijami*, St. Petersburg: IAN, Otdelenie russkogo jazyka i slovesnosti. [Reprint (1960), in *EMSVD*.]

——— (1890), "Glagolitica. Würdigung neuentdeckter Fragmente," *Denkschriften der KAW*, vol. 38, fasc. 2, pp. 1–62.

——— (1907), *Slovenskaja psaltyr': Psalterium Bonionense*, Vienna: Gerold; Berlin: Weidmann; St. Petersburg: C. Ricker.

——— (1910–1929), *Enciklopedija slavjanskoj filologii*, vols. 1–5, 10–12, St. Petersburg: IAN; Akademija Nauk SSSR.

Jakobson, Roman (1950), "O stixotvornyx reliktax rannego srednevekov'ja v češskoj literaturnoj tradicii," *SlRev* 3:267–273. Also in *Selected Writings* (The Hague: Mouton, 1985), 6/1:381–388.

——— (1957), "Stixotvornye citaty v velikomoravskoj agiografii," *SlRev* 10:111–118. Also in *Selected Writings* (The Hague: Mouton, 1985), 6/1:277–285.

——— (1963), "St. Constantine's Prologue to the Gospels," *St. Vladimir's Seminary Quarterly* 7/1:14–19. Also in *Selected Writings* (The Hague: Mouton, 1985), 6/1:191–206.

——— (1985), "Goroun's urn," in *Selected Writings* (The Hague: Mouton, 1985), 7:332–335.

Jončev, Vasil, and Olga Jončeva (1982), *Dreven i săvremenen bălgarski šrift*, Sofia: Bălgarski xudožnik.

Kalajdžieva, Konstantinka, ed. (1976), *Bălgarska răkopisna kniga X–XVIII v.*, Sofia: Izložba.

Kantor, Marvin, ed. (1983), *Medieval Slavic Lives of Saints and Princes*, Ann Arbor: Michigan Slavic Publications.

——— (1990), *The Origins of Christianity in Bohemia: Sources and Commentary*, Evanston, Ill.: Northwestern University Press.

Karinskij N. (1930), "Vizantijskoe stixotvorenie *Alfavitarь* v russkom spiske XI v.," *IzvRJaSl* 3:259–268.

Karskij, Evfimij F. (1902), *Obrazcy slavjanskogo, kirillovskogo pis'ma s X–XVIII vek*, Warsaw: Tip. Varšavskogo učebnogo okruga.

——— (1928), *Slavjanskaja kirillovskaja paleografija*, Leningrad: Akademija Nauk SSSR. [Reprint (1979), Moscow: Nauka.]

Karskij, Evfimij F., ed. (1904), *Listki Undol'skogo*, in *PSSlJa*, vol. 1, no. 3.

Katičić, Radoslav, and Slobodan P. Novak, eds. (1987), *Two Thousand Years of Writing in Croatia*, Zagreb: Sveučilišna naklada Liber.

Kiparskij, Valentin (1968), "O proisxoždenii glagolicy," in Angelov, ed. pp. 91–97.

Kodov, Xristo N., ed. (1983), *Eninski apostol: Faksimilno izdanie*, Sofia: Nauka i izkustvo.

Kolesov, Vladimir V., ed. (1972), *Evgenievskaja psaltyr'*, in *AUSzDSl*, vol. 8, pp. 57–69.

Kopitar, Jernej (1836), *Glagolita Clozianus id est Codicis Glagolitici inter Suos Facile Antiqissimi . . . Comidis Paridis Cloz Tridentini* [including an edition of the *Freising Fragments*], Vienna: apud Carolum Gerold.

Kostić, Dragutin (1937–1938), "Bugarski episkop Konstantin—pisac službe sv. Metodiju," *ByzSl* 7:189–211.

Kotkov, S. I., ed. (1971), *Uspenskij sbornik XII–XIII vv.*, Moscow: Nauka.

Kožuxarov, Stefan (1984), "Pesennoto tvorčestvo na starobălgarskija knižovnik Naum Oxridski," *LitIst* 12:3–19.

Kuev, Kujo M. (1967), *Černorizec Xrabăr*, Sofia: BAN.

——— (1979), *Sădbata na starobălgarskite răkopisi prez vekovete*, Sofia: Nauka i izkustvo.

Kul'bakin, Stepan M. (1900), *Xilandarskie listki: Otryvok kirillovskoj pis'mennosti XI v. s četyr'mja fototipičeskimi snimkami*, in *PSSlJa*, vol. 1.

——— (1907), *Oxridskaja rukopis' Apostola konca XII veka*, in *Bălgarski starini*, vol. 3, Sofia: Dăržavna pečatnica.

——— (1911/1912), *Drevnecerkovno-slavjanskij jazyk*, 3 vols., Kharkov: M. Zil'berberg.

——— (1915), *Grammatika cerkovno-slavjanskogo jazyka po drevnejšim pamjatnikam*, Petrograd: IAN.

——— (1922), "Du classement des textes vieux-slaves," *RES* 2:175–205.

——— (1929), *Le vieux slave*, Paris: Librairie Ancienne Honoré Champion.

Kurz, Josef, et al., eds. (1958–), *Slovník jazyka staroslověnského. Lexicon linguae paleoslovenicae*, Prague: ČSAV.

Lavrov, Petr A. (1914), *Paleografičeskoe obozrenie kirillovskogo pis'ma*, in Jagič, ed. (1910–1929), vol. 4/1.

——— (1926), "Les Feuillets du Zograph," *RES* 6:5–23.

Lavrov, Petr A., ed. (1930), *Materialy po istorii vozniknovenija drevnejšej slavjanskoj pis'mennosti*, Leningrad [= Trudy slavjanskoj komissii, Akademija Nauk SSSR, vol. 1]. [Reprint (1966), The Hague, Paris: Mouton.]

Lavrov, Petr A., and André Vaillant (1930), "Les règles de Saint Basile en vieux slave: Les Feuillets du Zograph," *RES* 10:5–35.

Leger, Louis Paul Marie, ed. (1899), *L'Évangéliaire slavon de Reims, dit: Texte du sacre* [facsimile edition], Reims: F. Michaud; Prague: F. Řivnáč.

Lehr-Spławiński, Tadeusz (1949), *Zarys gramatyki języka staro-cerkiewno-słowiańskiego na tle porównawczym (głosownia–fleksja)*, 3rd ed., Kraków: Studium słowiańskie Uniwersytetu Jagiellońskiego.

Lehr-Spławiński, Tadeusz, and Czesław Bartula (1959), *Zarys gramatyki języka staro-cerkiewno-słowiańskiego na tle porównawczym*, 4th ed., Wrocław-Cracow: Ossolineum.

Le Juge, Vasil von, ed. (1897), *Das galizische Tetroevangelium von J. 1144: Eine kritische-palaeographische Studie auf dem Gebiete des Altrussischen*, Leipzig [Inaug. Diss., Breslau].

Lenhoff, Gail (1989), *The Martyred Princes Boris and Gleb: A Social-Cultural Study of the Cult and the Texts*, Columbus, Ohio: Slavica [= *UCLA Slavic Studies*, vol. 19].

Leskien, August (1905), *Handbuch der altbulgarischen (altkirchenslavischen) Sprache: Grammatik, Texte, Glossar*, 4th ed., Heidelberg: Carl Winter [9th ed., 1969].

——— (1909), *Grammatik der altbulgarischen (altikirchenslavischen) Sprache*, Heidelberg: Carl Winter.

Lixačev, Dmitrij S. (1947), *Russkie letopisi i ix kul'turno-istoričeskoe značenie*, Moscow/Leningrad: Akademija Nauk SSSR.

——— (1983), *Tekstologija: Na materiale russkoj literatury X–XVII vv.*, 2nd ed., Moscow and Leningrad: Akademija Nauk SSSR.

——— (1987), *Poètika drevnerusskoj literatury*, in *Izbrannye raboty v trex tomax*, vol. 1, pp. 261–654, Leningrad: Xudožestvennaja literatura.

Lixačev [= Likhachev], Dmitrij S., ed. (1985), *Istorija russkoj literatury XI–XVII vv.*, 2nd ed., Moscow: Prosveščenie. [English translation, Dmitry Likhachev, ed. (1989), *A History of Russian Literature: 11th–17th Centuries*, Moscow: Raduga Publishers.]

——— (1987, 1988, 1989), *Slovar' knižnikov i knižnosti Drevnej Rusi*, 3 vols., Leningrad: Nauka.

Ljapunov, Boris M. (1905), *Formy sklonenija v staroslavjanskom jazyke*, Odessa: Ekonomičeskaja tipografija.

Łoś, Jan (1922), *Gramatyka starosłowiańska*, Lwów, Warsaw, Cracow: Ossolineum.

Łoś, Jan, and Władysław Semkowicz, eds. (1934), *Kazania t. zw. świętokrzyskie*, Cracow: PAU.

Lunt, Horace G. (1957), "Ligatures in Old Church Slavonic Glagolitic manuscripts," *SlRev* 10:253–267.

——— (1958), "On Slavonic palimpsests," in *ACICS*$_4$, pp. 191–209, 's-Gravenhage: Mouton [= *Slavistic Printings and Reprintings*, vol. 21].

——— (1959), *Old Church Slavonic Glossary*, Cambridge, Mass.: Dept. of Slavic Languages and Literatures, Harvard University [mimeographed edition].

——— (1964), "The beginnings of written Slavic," *SR* 23:212–219.

——— (1974), *Old Church Slavonic Grammar*, 6th ed., The Hague: Mouton.

——— (1988/89), "The language of Rus' in the eleventh century: Some observations about facts and theories," *HUS* 12/13:276–313.

L'vov, A. S. (1975), "K istokam staroslavjanskoj pis'mennosti," *Slavia* 44:274–283.

Lysaght, T. A. (1983), *Old Church Slavonic (Old Bulgarian)–Middle Greek–Modern English Dictionary*, Vienna: Verlag Brüder Hollinek.

Maas, Paul (1950), *Textkritik*, 2nd ed., Leipzig: B. G. Teubner.

Malov, S. E. (1946), "Tjurkizmy v jazyke 'Slova o polku Igoreve'," *IzvOLJa* 5/2:129–139.

Mareš, František V. (1971), "Hlaholice na Moravě a v Čechách," *Slovo* 21:133–199.

Mareš, František V., ed. (1979), *An Anthology of Church Slavonic Texts of Western (Czech) Origin*, Munich: Wilhelm Fink Verlag [= *Slavische Propyläen*, 127].

Marks, A. (1914), "Dve starejšix russkix gramoty v došedšix do nas podlinnikax," *Drevnosti, TMAO*, vol. 24.

Matejić, Mateja, and Dragan Milivojević, eds. (1978), *An Anthology of Medieval Serbian Literature in English*, Columbus, Ohio: Slavica Publishers.

Mathiesen, Robert (1987), "Some methodological problems in describing Old East Slavic Cyrillic manuscripts and printed books," *PK* 17–18:130–143.

Medynceva, A. A. (1984), "Novgorodskie naxodki i doxristianskaja pis'mennost' na Rusi," *SovArx* 4:49–61.

Medynceva, A. A., and Kazimir Popkonstantinov (1985), *Nadpisi iz krugloj cerkvi v Preslave*, Sofia: BAN.

Meščerskij, Nikita A. (1956), "K voprosu ob izučenii perevodnoj pis'mennosti Kievskogo perioda," *UZKFP*, vol. 2, fasc. 1, pp. 196–219.

——— (1978), *Istočniki i sostav drevnej slavjano-russkoj perevodnoj pis'mennosti IX–XV vekov*, Leningrad: Leningradskij Universitet.

Meščerskij, Nikita A., ed. (1958), *Istorija iudejskoj vojny Iosifa Flavija v drevnerusskom perevode*, Moscow and Leningrad: Akademija Nauk SSSR.

Meyer, Karl H. (1935), *Altkirchenslavisch-griechisches Wörterbuch des Codex Suprasliensis*, Glückstadt and Hamburg: Verlag J. J. Augustin.

Michell, Robert, and Nevill Forbes (1914), *The Chronicle of Novgorod, 1016–1471*, London: Camden Society [= Camden Third Series, vol. 25].

Miklosich, Franz (1860), "Zur Glagolita Clozianus," Vienna: KAW *Denkschriften*, phil.-hist. Cl. X, pp. 195–214.

——— (1862–1865), *Lexicon palaeoslovenico-graeco-latinum*, Vienna: Wilhelm Braumüller.

Miletič, Ljubomir G. (1923), *Starobălgarska gramatika*, 9th ed., Sofia: Dăržavna pečatnica. [Italian translation (1951), *Grammatica paleoslava*, Naples: R. Pironti.]

Miller, Vsevolod (1884), "K voprosu o slavjanskoj azbuke," *ŽMNP* 232, Otdel nauk, 1–35.

Minčeva, Angelina (1978), *Starobălgarski kirilski otkăsleci*, Sofia: BAN.

——— (1981), "Za teksta na Makedonskija kirilski list i negovija avtor," in *StBLit*, vol. 9, pp. 3–19.

Minev, Dimităr (1985), "Asemanievo evangelie," in Dinekov et al., eds, pp. 124–134.

Mirčev, Kiril (1963), *Istoričeska gramatika na bălgarskija ezik*, Sofia: Nauka i Izkustvo.

Mirčev, Kiril, and Xristo N. Kodov, eds. (1965), *Eninski apostol: Starobălgarski pametnik ot XI v.*, Sofia: BAN.

Mirčeva, Bojka, and Slavija Bărlieva, eds. (1987), "Predvaritelen spisăk na Kirilo-Metodievskite izvori" [slavjanski izvori], *KMS* 4:487–499.

Mohlberg, C., ed. (1928), *Il messale glagolitico di Kiew (secolo IX) e il suo prototypo romano del secolo IV–VII*, in *APARA*, ser. 3, Memorie, vol. 2.

Mohorovičić, Andre, and Petar Strčić, eds. (1988), *Baščanska ploča*, 2 vols., Zagreb: JAZU.

Moldovan, A. M., ed. (1984), *"Slovo o zakone i blagodati" Ilariona*, Kiev: Naukova dumka.

Morfill, W. R., and R. H. Charles (1896), *The Book of Secrets of Enoch*, Oxford: Oxford University Press.

Moser, Charles A. (1972), *A History of Bulgarian Literature, 865–1944*, The Hague, Paris: Mouton.

Moszyński, Leszek (1961), *Ze studiów nad rękopisem Kodeksu Zografskiego*, Wrocław: Ossolineum.

——— (1975, 1990), *Język Kodeksu Zografskiego*, 2 parts, Wrocław: Ossolineum [= Monografie slawistyczne Komitetu Słowianoznawstwa PAN Nos. 31 and 52].

Myšanyč, O. V., ed. (1981), *Literaturna spadščyna Kyjivs'koji Rusi i ukrajins'ka literatura XVI–XVIII st.*, Kiev: Naukova Dumka.

Nabokov, Vladimir (1960), *The Song of Igor's Campaign: An Epic of the Twelfth Century*, New York: Vintage Books [English translation].

Nahtigal, Rajko (1943), "Rekonstrukcija treh starocerkvenoslovanskih izvirnih pesnitev," *Razprave I Filozofsko-filološko-hististorični razreda SAZU*, fascicle 2.

——— (1949), *Uvod v slovansko filologijo*, Ljubljana: University of Ljubljana.

Nahtigal, Rajko, ed. (1941, 1942), *Euchologium Sinaiticum*, 2 vols., Ljubljana: SAZU.

Nandriş, Grigore (1959), *Old Church Slavonic Grammar*, vol. 1, London: Athlone Press.

Nasonov, A. N., ed. (1950), *Novgorodskaja pervaja letopis' staršego i mladšego izvodov*, Moscow: Leningrad: Akademija Nauk SSSR.

Naumow, Aleksander E. (1976), *Apokryfy w systemie literatury cerkiewno-słowiańskiej*, Wrocław: Ossolineum [= Prace Komisji Słowianoznawstwa PAN, Nr. 36].

Nikolaeva, A. T. (1956), *Russkaja paleografija: Konspekt kursa*, Moscow: Moskovskij Gosurdarstvennyj istoriko-arxivnyj institut Ministerstva vysšego obrazovanija SSSR, Kafedra vspomogatel'nyx istoričeskix disciplin.

Nimčuk, Vasyl V., ed. (1983), *Kyjivs'ki hlaholyčni lystky*, Kiev: Naukova dumka.

Obnorskij, Sergej, P. and Stepan G. Barxudarov, eds. (1952), *Xrestomatija po istorii russkogo jazyka*, vol. 1, 2nd ed., Moscow: Gos. uč.-ped. izd. Ministerstva prosveščenija RSFSR.

Ostromirovo evangelie (1883), *Ostromirovo evangelie 1056–57 goda, xranjaščeesja v Imperatorskoj Publičnoj biblioteke*, St. Petersburg: Iždiveniem S.-Petersburgskogo kupca Il'i Savinkova [facsimile ed.].

——— (1988), *Ostromirovo evangelie 1056–57 goda, faksimil'noe vosproizvedenie pamjatnika, xranjaščegosja v Gosudarstevennoj Publičnoj biblioteke, im. Saltykova-Ščedrina*, Leningrad: Avrora.

Papadopoulos, J. B., and Arcadios Vatopèdinos (1933), "Un acte officiel du despote Alexis Stlavos au sujet du couvent de Spèléotissa prés de Melenicon," *Spisanie na BAN*, vol. 45 (22), pp. 1–6, Sofia: BAN.

Pastrnek, František (1909), *Tvarosloví jazyka staroslověnského s úvodem a ukázkami*, Prague: A. Wiesner.

Petkanova, Donka (1986/1987), *Starobălgarska literatura*, 2 vols., Sofia: Nauka i izkustvo.

Petkanova, Donka, ed. (1992), *Starobălgarska literatura: Enciklopedičen rečnik*, Sofia: Izdatelstvo Petăr Beron.

Picchio, Riccardo (1963), "A proposito della Slavia ortodossa e della communità slava ecclesiastica," *RicSl* 11:105–127.

——— (1967), "Slave ecclésiastique, slavons et rédactions," in *To Honor Roman Jakobson* 3: 1527–1544.

——— (1972), "Questione della lingua e Slavia Cirillometodiana," in Picchio, ed. 1972, 7–120.

——— $(1980)_1$, "Church Slavonic," in Schenker/Stankiewicz, eds., pp. 1–33.

——— $(1980)_2$, "Vărxu izokolnite strukturi v srednovekovnata slavjanska proza," *LitM* 3:75–107.

——— (1987), *Starobălgarskata tradicija i pravoslavnoto slavjanstvo*, Sofia: Nauka i izkustvo.

——— (1988), "Quelques remarques sur l'interprétation du *Proglas*," *RES* 60:313–324.

Picchio, Riccardo, ed. (1972), *Studi sulla questione della lingua presso gli Slavi*, Rome: Edizioni dell'Ateneo.

Podskalsky, Gerhard, ed. (1982), *Christentum und theologische Literatur in der Kiever Rus' (988–1237)*, Munich: Beck.

Pogorelov, V. A., ed. $(1910)_1$, *Čudovskaja psaltyr' XI v.: Otryvok tolkovanija Feodorita Kirrskogo na psaltyr' v drevnebolgarskom perevode*, in *PSSlJa*, vol. 3, fasc. 1.

——— $(1910)_2$, *Slovar' k tolkovanijam Feodorita Kirrskogo na Psaltyr' v drevnebolgarskom perevode*, Warsaw: Tip. Varšavskogo učebnogo okruga.

Popkonstantinov, Kazimir (1980), "Novootkriti starobălgarski nadpisi ot 10 vek v Severoiztočna Bălgarija," in Velčeva et al., eds., pp. 288–309.

Popov, Georgi (1978), "Novootkrita orginalna starobălgarska čast v teksta na trioda," *BE* 28:497–507.

——— (1982), "Novootkriti ximnografski proizvedenija na Kliment Oxridski," *BE* 31:3–26.

——— (1985), *Triodni proizvedenija na Konstantin Preslavski* [= *KMS* 2].

Popovski, Josif, ed. (1989), *Die Pandekten des Antiochus Monachus*, microfiche edition, 4 vols., Leiden: Inter Documentation Company BV [= Early Slavic Texts on Microfiche, Part 5].

——— (1989), *PK* 23–24 [transcribed Slavic text of *Die Pandekten des Antiochus Monachus*].

Popruženko, Mixail G. (1936), *Kozma Presviter, bolgarskij pisatel' X veka*, Sofia: BAN.

Porák, Jaroslav (1979), *Chrestomatie k vývoji českého jazyka (13.–18. století)*, Prague: Statní Pedagogické Nakladatelství.

Priselkov, M. D. (1938), *Kurs russkoj paleografii*, Leningrad: Leningradskij Gosudarstvennyj Universitet.

Puech, H.-C., and André Vaillant, eds. (1945), *Le traité contre les Bogomiles de Cosmas le Prêtre*, Paris: IES.

Ramovš, Fran, and Milko Kos, eds. (1937), *Brižinski spomeniki*, Ljubljana: Akademska založba.

Rodić, Nikola, and Gordana Jovanović, eds. (1936), *Miroslavljevo jevandjelje*, Belgrade: SANU.

Rosenkranz, Bernhard (1955), *Historische Laut- und Formenlehre des Altbulgarischen (Altkirchenslavischen)*, 's-Gravenhage: Mouton; Heidelberg: Carl Winter.

Sadnik, Linda and Rudolf Aitzetmüller (1955), *Handwörterbuch zu den altkirchenslavischen Texten*, 's-Gravenhage: Mouton.

Šafařík, Pavel (1851), *Památky dřevního písemnictví Jihoslovanů*, Prague: B. Haase.

Šaxmatov, Aleksej A. (1916), *Povest' vremennyx let*, vol. 1: Vvodnaja čast' (all published), Petrograd: Izd. Imp. Arxeografičeskoj komissii.

Šaxmatov, Aleksej A., and Petr A. Lavrov, eds. (1899), *Sbornik XII v. Moskovskogo Uspenskogo Sobora*, *ČOIDR*, vol. 2. [Reprint (1957), The Hague: Mouton.]

Ščepkin, Vjačeslav N. (1901), *Rassuždenie o jazyke Savvinoj knigi*, in *SORJaS*, vol. 67, No. 9.

——— (1903), *Savvina kniga*, in *PSSlJa*, vol. 1, no. 2.

——— (1906), *Bolonskaja psaltyr'*, St. Petersburg: IAN.

——— (1920), *Russkaja paleografija*, Moscow: Gosurdarstvennoe izdatel'stvo. [Reprint (1967), Moscow: Nauka.]

Schenker, Alexander M. (1989), "The Gnezdovo inscription in its historical and linguistic setting," *RL* 13:207–220.

Schenker, Alexander M., and Edward Stankiewicz, eds. (1980), *The Slavic Literary Languages*, New Haven: Yale Concilium on International and Area Studies.

Schmalstieg, William R. (1983), *An Introduction to Old Church Slavic*, 2nd ed., Columbus, Ohio: Slavica.

Seliščev, A. M. (1951, 1952), *Staroslavjanskij jazyk*, 2 vols., Moscow: Učpedgiz.

Ševčenko, Ihor (1982), "Report on the Glagolitic fragments (of the *Euchologium Sinaiticum?*) discovered on Sinai in 1975 and some thoughts on the models for the make-up of the earliest Glagolitic manuscripts," *HUS* 6:119–151.

Sever'janov, S. N., ed. (1904), *Suprasl'skaja rukopis'*, in *PSSlJa*, vol. 2, fasc. 1. [Reprint (1956), in *EMSVD*.]

——— (1922), *Sinajskaja psaltyr': Glagoličeskij pamjatnik XI veka*, in *PSSlJa*, vol. 4. [Reprint (1954), in *EMSVD*.]

Sill, Ute (1972), *"Nomina sacra" im Altkirchenslavischen, bis zum 11. Jahrhundert*, Munich: Wilhelm Fink.

Šimanovskij, V. S. (1888), *K istorii drevnerusskix govorov: Issledovanie s priloženiem polnogo teksta Sbornika Svjatoslava 1076 g.*, Warsaw: Tip . K. Kovalevskogo.

Slavova, Tatjana (1989), "Preslavska redakcija na Kirilo-Metodievija starobălgarski evangelski prevod," *KMS* 6:15–129.

Słoński, Stanisław (1934), *Index verborum do Euchologium Sinaiticum*, Warsaw: Kasa im. J. Mianowskiego.

——— (1950), *Gramatyka języka starosłowiańskiego (starobułgarskiego)*, Warsaw: Państwowe Zakłady Wydawnictw Szkolnych.

Sobolevskij, Aleksej I. (1891), *Drevnij cerkovnoslavjanskij jazyk: Fonetika (iz lekcij)*, Moscow: Universitetskaja tipografija.

——— (1908), *Slavjano-russkaja paleografija*, 2nd ed., St. Petersburg: Sinodal'naja tipografija.

——— (1910), "Drevnie cerkovno-slavjanskie stixotvorenija IX–X vekov," *SORJaS* 88, no. 3.

Sreznevskij, Izmail I. (1893, 1895, 1903), *Materialy dlja slovarja drevnerusskogo jazyka*, 3 vols., St. Petersburg: IAN Otdelenie russkogo jazyka i slovesnosti. [Reprint (1958), Moscow: Gos. izd-vo inostrannyx i nacional'nyx slovarej.]

Stančev, Krasimir (1981), "Neizvestnye i maloizvestnye bolgarskie rukopisi v Pariže," *PB* 5/3:85–91.

Stančev, Krasimir, and Georgi Popov (1988), *Kliment Oxridski*, Sofia: Universitetsko Izdatelstvo "Kliment Oxridski."

Stančev, St., et al. (1955), *Nadpisăt na čărgubilja Mostič*, Sofia: BAN.

Stanislav, Ján (1957), *Dejiny slovenského jazyka*, vol. 3, Bratislava: Vydavatel'stvo SAV.

——— (1978, 1987), *Starosloviensky jazyk*, 2 vols., Bratislava: Slovenské Pedagogické Nakladatel'stvo.

Stepanov, N. V., ed. (1912), "Letopisec vskore patriarxa Nikifora v Novgorodskoj Kormčej, *IzvORJaS* 17/3:295–320 (additional bibliography in Lixačev, ed. 1987:234).

Stojanović, Ljubomir, ed. (1893–1894), *Miroslavljevo jevandjelje: Évangéliaire ancien serbe du Prince Miroslav*, facsimile ed., Belgrade: King Alexander I.

——— (1913), "Temnićki natpis X–XI veka," *JF* 1:4–20.

Taszycki, Witold (1975), *Najdawniejsze zabytki języka polskiego*, 5th ed., Wrocław, Warsaw, Cracow, Gdansk: Ossolineum [= Biblioteka Narodowa, series 1, no. 104].

Taylor, Isaac (1881), "Über den Ursprung des glagolitischen Alphabets," *AsPh* 5:191–192.

Teodorov-Balan, Aleksandăr S., ed. (1920, 1934), *Kiril i Metodi*, 2 vols., Sofia: Dăržavna/Pridvorna pečatnica.

Terras, Victor, ed., (1985), *Handbook of Russian Literature*, New Haven: Yale University Press.

Tixomirov, Mixail N., and Anatolij V. Murav'ev (1966), *Russkaja paleografija*, Moscow: Vysšaja škola.

Tkadlčík, V. (1964), "Dvojí *ch* v hlaholici," *Slavia* 32:182–193.

——— (1971), "Systém hlaholské abecedy," in Marta Bauerová and Markéta Sterbová, eds. *Studia palaeoslovenica*, Prague: Academia, pp. 357–377.

Traube, Ludwig (1907), *Nomina sacra: Versuch einer Geschichte der christlichen Kürzung*, Quellen und Untersuchungen zur lateinischen Philologie des Mittelalters, Munich.

Trost, Klaus, et al., eds. (1988), *Symposium Methodianum: Beiträge der Internationalen Tagung in Regensburg (17. bis 24. April 1985) zum Gedenken an den 1100 Todes Tag des hl. Method*, Neuried: Hieronymus [= *Selecta Slavica* 13].

Trubeckoj [= Trubetzkoy, Troubetzkoy], Nikolaj S. (1930), "Das 'Münchener slavische Abecedarium'," *ByzSl* 2:29–31.

——— (1954), *Altkirchenslavische Grammatik: Schrift-, Laut- und Formensystem*, Vienna: Rudolf M. Rohrer [= Sitzungs-berichte 228, Band 4, ÖAW, Philosophisch-historische Klasse].

Tschižewskij [= Čiževskij], Dmitrij (1976), "Der hl. Method—Organisator, Missionar, Politiker und Dichter," in Zagiba, ed., 7–21.

Undol'skij, Vukol M. (1867), *Opisanie slavjanskix rukopisej Moskovskoj patriaršej biblioteki, ČOIDR*, vol. 2., part 3.

Vaillant, André (1932), "La traduction vieux-slave des Catéchèses de Cyrille de Jérusalem," *ByzSl* 4:253–302.

——— (1947), "Une homélie de Méthode," *RES* 23:34–47.

——— $(1948)_1$, "La préface de l'Évangéliaire vieux-slave," *RES* 24:5–20.

——— $(1948)_2$, *Manuel du vieux slave*, 2 vols., Paris: IES. [Russian translation (1952), *Rukovodstvo po staroslavjanskomu jazyku*, translated by V. V. Borodič, Moscow: Izdatel'stvo inostrannoj literatury.]

——— (1955), "L'alphabet vieux-slave," *RES* 32:7–31.

——— (1956), "Une poésie vieux-slave: La *Préface de l'Évangile*," *RES* 33:7–25.

Vaillant, André, ed. (1952), *Le Livre des secrets d'Hénoch: Texte slave et traduction française*, Paris: Institut d'études slaves.

Vajs, Josef (1932), *Rukověť hlaholské paleografie*, Prague: Slovanský Ustav.

——— (1948), *Najstariji hrvatskoglagoljski misal s bibliografskim opisima svih hrvatskoglagoljskih misala*, Zagreb: JAZU.

Vajs, Josef, and Josef Kurz (1929, 1955), *Evangeliář Assemanův, Kodex Vatikánský 3. slovanský*, 2 vols., Prague: ČSAV.

Valjavec, Matija (1888, 1889), *Trnovsko tetrajevandelije XIII vjeka*, in *Starine* 20:157–241, 21:1–68.

Vašica, Josef (1948), "Slovo na prenesenie moštem preslavnago Klimenta neboli legenda Chersonská," *AAV* 19:38–80.

——— (1951), "Origine cyrillo-méthodienne du plus ancien code slave dit 'Zakon sudnyj ljudem,'" *ByzSl.* 12:154–174.

——— (1956), "Anonymní homilie v rukopise Clozově," *Slavia* 25:221–233.

——— (1966), *Literární památky epochy velkomoravské, 863–885*, Prague: Lidová Demokracie.

Veder, W. R. (1974), "La tradition slave des Apophthegmata patrum," *Slovo* 24:59–94.

Velčeva, Borjana, ed. (1975), *Dobromirovo evangelie: Bălgarski pametnik ot načaloto na XII vek*, Sofia: BAN.

Velčeva, Borjana, et al., eds. (1980), *Paleógraphie et diplomatique slaves: Rapports et communications du Seminaire de paléographie et diplomatique slaves, Septembre 1979, Sofia*, Sofia: CIBAL.

Vinogradova, V. L., ed. (1965–1984), *Slovar'-spravočnik "Slova o polku Igoreve,"* Leningrad: Nauka.

Vondrák, Václav [= Wenzel] (1893), *Glagolita Clozův*, Prague: Česká Akademie Cisaře Františka Josefa.

——— (1912), *Altkirchenslavische Grammatik*, 2nd ed., Berlin: Weidmannsche Buchhandlung.

Vostokov, Aleksandr X. (1858–1861), *Slovar' cerkovno-slavjanskogo jazyka*, 2 vols., St. Petersburg: IAN.

Vostokov, Aleksandr X., ed. (1843), *Ostromirovo evangelie 1056–57 goda*, St. Petersburg: IAN. [Reprint (1964), Wiesbaden: Harrassowitz.]

Vrtel-Wierczyński, Stefan (1953), *Kazania gnieźnieńskie*, Poznań: Poznańskie Towarzystwo Przyjaciół Nauk [= *Zabytki języka i literatury polskiej*, no. 2].

Vysockij, S. A. (1970), "Drevnerusskaja azbuka iz Sofii Kievskoj," *SovArx* 4:128–140.

Vysockij, S. A., ed. (1966), *Drevne-russkie nadpisi Sofii Kievskoj XI–XIV vv.*, no. 1, Kiev: Naukova Dumka.

Weingart, Miloš (1922–1923), *Byzantské kroniky v literatuře církevněslovanské*, 2 vols., Bratislava [= *Spisy Filosofické Fakulty University Komenského v Bratislavě*, vols. 2 (1922) and 4 (1923)].

——— (1937, 1938), *Rukověť jazyka staroslověnského*, 2 vols., Prague: Didaktický kruh Klubu moderních filologů. [Reprint, Ann Arbor: University Microfilms.]

——— (1938), "Hlaholské listy Videňské: K dějinám staroslověnského misálu," *ČMF* 24/2: 105–129.

——— (1949), *Československý typ cirkevnej slovančiny: Jeho pamiatky a význam*, Bratislava: SAV.

Whitfield, Francis J., ed. (1962), *Old Church Slavic Reader*, Berkeley: Dept. of Slavic Languages and Literatures, University of California [mimeograph].

Wijk, Nicolaas van (1931), *Geschichte der altkirchenslavischen Sprache*, vol. 1, Berlin and Leipzig: Walter de Gruyter. [Russian translation (1957), *Istorija staroslavjanskogo jazyka*, translated by V. V. Borodič, Moscow: Izdatel'stvo inostrannoj literatury.]

Woronczak, Jerzy (1962), *Bogurodzica*, Wrocław: Ossolineum.

Xaburgaev, Georgij A. (1974), *Staroslavjanskij jazyk*, Moscow: Prosveščenie.

Zagiba, Franz, ed. (1976), *Methodiana*, Vienna, Cologne, Graz: Hermann Böhlaus Nachf. [= *Annales Instituti Slavici Salisburgo-Ratisbonensis*, no. 9].

Zaimov, Jordan, and Mario Capaldo (1982, 1983), *Suprasălski ili Retkov sbornik*, Sofia: BAN.

Zenkovsky, Serge A., ed. (1974), *Medieval Russia's Epics, Chronicles and Tales*, 2nd ed., New York: Dutton.

Žukovs'ka [= Žukovskaja], Lidia P. (1981), "Hipotezy j fakty pro davn'orus'ku pysemnist' do XII st.," in Myšanyč, ed., 13–14.

Žukovskaja, Lidia P. (1976), *Tekstologija i jazyk drevnejšix slavjanskix pamjatnikov*, Moscow: Nauka.

Žukovskaja, Lidia P., ed. (1978), *Rejmsskoe evangelie: Istorija ego izučenija i tekst*, Moscow: Institut russkogo jazyka AN SSSR.

——— $(1983)_1$, *Aprakos Mstislava Velikogo*, Moscow: Nauka.

——— $(1983)_2$, *Izbornik Svjatoslava 1073 goda: Faksimil'noe izdanie*, Moscow: Kniga.

6. Rise of Slavic Philology

Berezin, Fedor M. (1968), *Očerki po istorii jazykoznanija v Rossii (konec XIX–načalo XX v.)*, Moscow: Nauka.

Bulič, Sergej K. (1904), *Očerk istorii jazykoznanija v Rossii*, vol. 1, St. Petersburg: M. Merkushev [= *ZIFFPU*, vol. 75].

Filin, Fedot P., ed. (1973), *Xrestomatija po istorii russkogo jazykoznanija*, Moscow: Vysšaja škola.

Jagič, Ignatij V. [= Vatroslav Jagić] (1910), *Istorija slavjanskoj filologii*, St. Petersburg: IAN [= *Enciklopedija slavjanskoj filologii*, vol. 1].

Nahtigal, Rajko (1949), *Uvod v slovansko filologijo*, Ljubljana: Univerza v Ljublani.

Părvev, Xristo (1987), *Săzdateli i tvorci na bălgarskoto ezikoznanie*, Sofia: Narodna prosveta.

Rösel, Hubert (1957), *Dokumente zur Geschichte der Slawistik in Deutschland*, Berlin: Akademie-Verlag [= *Veröffentlichungen des Instituts für Slawistik*, no. 12].

Schmid, Heinrich Felix, and Reinhold Trautmann (1927), *Wesen und Aufgaben der deutschen Slawistik*, Leipzig: H. Hässel [= *Slavisch-baltische Quellen und Forschungen*, no. 1].

Stankiewicz, Edward, ed. (1984), *Grammars and Dictionaries of the Slavic Languages from the Middle Ages up to 1850: An Annotated Bibliography*, Berlin, New York: Mouton.

Strakhovsky, Leonid, ed. (1949), *A Handbook of Slavic Studies*, Cambridge, Mass.: Harvard University Press.

Suprun, Adam E., and Aleksandr M. Kaljuta (1981), *Vvedenie v slavjanskuju filologiju*, Minsk: Vyšèjšaja škola.

INDEX

Included are names of places, persons, tribes, and manuscripts, as well as selected linguistic terms.

CPSIA information can be obtained
at www.ICGtesting.com
Printed in the USA
BVHW081521190720
584046BV00006BA/88

9 780300 212402